Instructor's Solutions Manual
to accompany

BUSINESS MATHEMATICS
IN CANADA

Second Edition

F. Ernest Jerome
Malaspina University College

McGraw-Hill
Ryerson

Toronto Montreal New York Auckland Bogotá Caracas Lisbon London
Madrid Mexico Milan New Delhi San Juan Singapore Sydney Tokyo

McGraw-Hill
Ryerson Limited
A Subsidiary of The McGraw·Hill Companies

Instructor's Solutions Manual to accompany
BUSINESS MATHEMATICS IN CANADA
Second Edition

JEROME

ISBN: 0-256-21322-4

TABLE OF CONTENTS

To the Instructor:

Through surveys conducted by IRWIN, feedback from reviewers of both the first edition and the manuscript for the second edition, and the author's contacts with colleagues, we have produced an instructional package which we hope will meet the needs of most instructors and students of business mathematics in Canadian colleges.

While there is a consensus on a number of core topics that should be included in a text for introductory business mathematics courses in business diploma programs, there are diverse opinions on which additional topics ought to be included. Our surveys indicate that basic linear programming, bonds, sinking funds, introduction to probability and statistics, business investment decisions (capital budgeting), and depreciation fall in the group of topics that are covered in only 10% to 30% of introductory business math courses across the country. To avoid ending up with a 1000-page text, we have not included those topics that fall near the 10% end of the range. For the same reason, we are unable to accommodate requests for coverage of more rarely taught topics such as the calculation of excise taxes and customs' duties, and inventory management.

A significant number of reviewers and survey respondents have recommended (sometimes vehemently) that the algebraic approach to the solution of compound interest problems be given reduced coverage (or even be omitted). However, our research shows that at least one-third of business math instructors either emphasize the algebraic approach or give similar weightings to the algebraic and financial calculator methods. Therefore, most example problems on compound interest in the text present parallel solutions employing both approaches. In this manual and in the Student's Solutions Manual, only the algebraic method is presented. It is felt that students can readily infer the financial calculator solution from the algebraic solution.

The sleeve on the jacket of this manual holds a diskette containing spreadsheet templates for developing solutions to problems flagged by a spreadsheet icon in the textbook's margin next to the problem. Completed spreadsheet solutions for these problems are found in a separate directory on the diskette. The directory containing blank templates may be copied for use by students who are familiar with spreadsheet software.

The solutions to the problems in each chapter of this manual are preceded by a brief description of changes made to the first edition. The rationale for the changes is usually given.

Looking ahead to the third edition, the author invites comments and suggestions from users. You are encouraged to comment on changes appearing in the second edition, to point out any errors in the text or in this manual, and to make suggests for further changes for the next edition, by contacting the author at the email address: JEROME @ MALA.BC.CA.

1 Review and Applications of Basic Mathematics

Changes in the Second Edition:

1. The application of basic mathematics to **Taxes** has been moved to an appendix because:

    (i) At the time of writing, the Goods and Services Tax and Provincial Sales Taxes were in the process of being replaced by a "harmonized" sales tax in some provinces, and the federal government was continuing to try to persuade other provinces to do the same.

    (ii) A majority of users of the first edition did not include the former Section 1.3 (Application: Taxes) in the curriculum.

2. The **Basic Percentage Problem** has been moved (from Chapter 3) to Chapter 1 because:

    (i) It is essentially an arithmetic rather than an algebraic calculation.

    (ii) It is used in the topics of Payroll (Commissions) and Taxes which follow in Chapter 1.

3. The topics **Percent Change** and **Rate of Return on Investment** have been moved to Chapter 2 for reasons given in the Chapter 2 preamble.

4. The average-number-of-pay-periods-in-a-year approach to the calculation of weekly or biweekly salary has been dropped from the **Salaries** subsection of **Payroll**. Some users expressed the view that it was an undue complication to an already peripheral topic.

Exercise 1.1

1. $20 - 4 \times 2 - 8 = 20 - 8 - 8 = \underline{\underline{4}}$

2. $18 \div 3 + 6 \times 2 = 6 + 12 = \underline{\underline{18}}$

3. $(20 - 4) \times 2 - 8 = 16 \times 2 - 8 = 32 - 8 = \underline{\underline{24}}$

4. $18 \div (3 + 6) \times 2 = 18 \div 9 \times 2 = 2 \times 2 = \underline{\underline{4}}$

5. $20 - (4 \times 2 - 8) = 20 - (8 - 8) = \underline{\underline{20}}$

6. $(18 \div 3 + 6) \times 2 = (6 + 6) \times 2 = \underline{\underline{24}}$

7. $54 - 36 \div 4 + 2^2 = 54 - 9 + 4 = \underline{\underline{49}}$

8. $(5 + 3)^2 - 3^2 \div 9 + 3 = 8^2 - 9 \div 9 + 3 = 64 - 1 + 3 = \underline{\underline{66}}$

9. $(54 - 36) \div (4 + 2)^2 = 18 \div 6^2 = 18 \div 36 = \underline{\underline{0.5}}$

10. $5 + (3^2 - 3)^2 \div (9 + 3) = 5 + (9 - 3)^2 \div 12$
$\qquad\qquad\qquad\qquad = 5 + 36 \div 12$
$\qquad\qquad\qquad\qquad = 5 + 3$
$\qquad\qquad\qquad\qquad = \underline{\underline{8}}$

11. $\dfrac{8^2 - 4^2}{(4 - 2)^3} = \dfrac{64 - 16}{2^3} = \dfrac{48}{8} = \underline{\underline{6}}$

12. $\dfrac{(8 - 4)^2}{4 - 2^3} = \dfrac{4^2}{4 - 8} = \dfrac{16}{-4} = \underline{\underline{-4}}$

13. $3 (6 + 4)^2 - 5 (17 - 20)^2 = 3 \times 10^2 - 5 (-3)^2$
$\qquad\qquad\qquad\qquad\qquad = 3 \times 100 - 5 \times 9$
$\qquad\qquad\qquad\qquad\qquad = 300 - 45$
$\qquad\qquad\qquad\qquad\qquad = \underline{\underline{255}}$

14. $(4 \times 3 - 2)^2 \div (4 - 3 \times 2^2) = (12 - 2)^2 \div (4 - 3 \times 4)$
$\qquad\qquad\qquad\qquad\qquad\qquad = 10^2 \div (4 - 12)$
$\qquad\qquad\qquad\qquad\qquad\qquad = 100 \div (-8)$
$\qquad\qquad\qquad\qquad\qquad\qquad = \underline{\underline{-12.5}}$

15. $[(20 + 8 \times 5) - 7 \times (-3)] + 9 = (20 + 40 + 21) + 9$
$\qquad\qquad\qquad\qquad\qquad\qquad\quad = 81 + 9$
$\qquad\qquad\qquad\qquad\qquad\qquad\quad = \underline{\underline{9}}$

16. $5[19 + (5^2 - 16)^2]^2 = 5[19 + (25 - 16)^2]^2$
$\qquad\qquad\qquad\qquad = 5(19 + 81)^2$
$\qquad\qquad\qquad\qquad = 5 \times 100^2$
$\qquad\qquad\qquad\qquad = \underline{\underline{50,000}}$

Exercise 1.2

1. $\dfrac{7}{8} = \underline{\underline{0.875}} = \underline{\underline{87.5\%}}$

2. $\dfrac{65}{104} = \underline{\underline{0.625}} = \underline{\underline{62.5\%}}$

3. $\dfrac{47}{20} = \underline{\underline{2.35}} = \underline{\underline{235\%}}$

Exercise 1.2 *(continued)*

4. $-\dfrac{9}{16} = \underline{\underline{-0.5625}} = \underline{\underline{-56.25\%}}$

5. $-\dfrac{35}{25} = \underline{\underline{-1.4}} = \underline{\underline{-140\%}}$

6. $1\dfrac{7}{25} = \underline{\underline{1.28}} = \underline{\underline{128\%}}$

7. $\dfrac{25}{1000} = \underline{\underline{0.025}} = \underline{\underline{2.5\%}}$

8. $\dfrac{1000}{25} = \underline{\underline{40}} = \underline{\underline{4000\%}}$

9. $2\dfrac{2}{100} = \underline{\underline{2.02}} = \underline{\underline{202\%}}$

10. $-1\dfrac{11}{32} = \underline{\underline{-1.34375}} = \underline{\underline{134.375\%}}$

11. $\dfrac{37.5}{50} = \underline{\underline{0.75}} = \underline{\underline{75\%}}$

12. $\dfrac{22.5}{-12} = \underline{\underline{-1.875}} = \underline{\underline{-187.5\%}}$

13. $\dfrac{5}{6} = \underline{\underline{0.8\overline{3}}} = \underline{\underline{83.\overline{3}\%}}$

14. $-\dfrac{8}{3} = \underline{\underline{-2.\overline{6}}} = \underline{\underline{-266.\overline{6}\%}}$

15. $7\dfrac{7}{9} = \underline{\underline{7.\overline{7}}} = \underline{\underline{777.\overline{7}\%}}$

16. $1\dfrac{1}{11} = \underline{\underline{1.\overline{09}}} = \underline{\underline{109.\overline{09}\%}}$

17. $\dfrac{10}{9} = \underline{\underline{1.\overline{1}}} = \underline{\underline{111.\overline{1}\%}}$

18. $\dfrac{-4}{900} = \underline{\underline{-0.00\overline{4}}} = \underline{\underline{-0.\overline{4}\%}}$

19. $-\dfrac{7}{270} = \underline{\underline{-0.0\overline{259}}} = \underline{\underline{-2.\overline{592}\%}}$

20. $\dfrac{37}{27} = \underline{\underline{1.\overline{370}}} = \underline{\underline{137.\overline{037}\%}}$

21. $11.3845 \approx \underline{\underline{11.38}}$

22. $9.6455 \approx \underline{\underline{9.646}}$

23. $0.5545454 \approx \underline{\underline{0.5545}}$

Exercise 1.2 *(continued)*

24. $1000.49 \approx \underline{\underline{1000}}$

25. $1.0023456 \approx \underline{\underline{1.002}}$

26. $0.030405 \approx \underline{\underline{0.03041}}$

27. $40.09515 \approx \underline{\underline{40.10}}$

28. $0.0090909 \approx \underline{\underline{0.009091}}$

29. $\dfrac{1}{6} = \underline{\underline{0.16667}} = \underline{\underline{16.667\%}}$

30. $\dfrac{7}{6} = \underline{\underline{1.1667}} = \underline{\underline{116.67\%}}$

31. $\dfrac{1}{60} = \underline{\underline{0.016667}} = \underline{\underline{1.6667\%}}$

32. $2\dfrac{5}{9} = \underline{\underline{2.5556}} = \underline{\underline{255.56\%}}$

33. $\dfrac{250}{365} = \underline{\underline{0.68493}} = \underline{\underline{68.493\%}}$

34. $\dfrac{15}{365} = \underline{\underline{0.041096}} = \underline{\underline{4.1096\%}}$

35. $\dfrac{0.11}{12} = \underline{\underline{0.0091667}} = \underline{\underline{0.91667\%}}$

36. $\dfrac{0.095}{12} = \underline{\underline{0.0079167}} = \underline{\underline{0.79167\%}}$

37. $\$92\left(1 + 0.095 \times \dfrac{112}{365}\right) = \$92 \times 1.02915 = \underline{\underline{\$94.68}}$

38. $\$100\left(1 + 0.11 \times \dfrac{5}{12}\right) = \$100 \times 1.04583 = \underline{\underline{\$104.58}}$

39. $\$454.76\left(1 - 0.105 \times \dfrac{11}{12}\right) = \$454.76 \times 0.903750 = \underline{\underline{\$410.99}}$

40. $\dfrac{\$790.84}{1 + 0.13 \times \dfrac{311}{365}} = \dfrac{\$790.84}{1.110767} = \underline{\underline{\$711.98}}$

41. $\dfrac{\$3490}{1 + 0.125 \times \dfrac{91}{365}} = \dfrac{\$3490}{1.031164} = \underline{\underline{\$3384.52}}$

42. $\dfrac{\$10,000}{1 - 0.10 \times \dfrac{182}{365}} = \dfrac{\$10,000}{0.95013699} = \underline{\underline{\$10,524.80}}$

43. $\$650\left(1 + \dfrac{0.105}{2}\right)^2 = \$650\,(1.0525)^2 = \underline{\underline{\$720.04}}$

Exercise 1.2 *(continued)*

44. $\$950.75 \left(1 + \dfrac{0.095}{4}\right)^2 = \$950.75 \ (1.02375)^2 = \underline{\underline{\$996.45}}$

45. $\dfrac{\$15,400}{\left(1 + \dfrac{0.13}{12}\right)^6} = \dfrac{\$15,400}{1.0108333^6} = \underline{\underline{\$14,435.88}}$

46. $\dfrac{\$550}{\left(1 + \dfrac{0.115}{2}\right)^4} = \dfrac{\$550}{1.05750^4} = \underline{\underline{\$439.79}}$

47. $\dfrac{\$6600 \left(1 + 0.085 \times \dfrac{153}{365}\right)}{1 + 0.125 \times \dfrac{82}{365}} = \dfrac{\$6600 \ (1.035630)}{1.028082} = \underline{\underline{\$6648.46}}$

48. $\dfrac{\$780 \left(1 + \dfrac{0.0825}{2}\right)^5}{\left(1 + \dfrac{0.10}{12}\right)^8} = \dfrac{\$780 \ (1.22398)}{1.06864} = \underline{\underline{\$893.38}}$

49. $\$1000 \left[\dfrac{\left(1 + \dfrac{0.09}{12}\right)^7 - 1}{\dfrac{0.09}{12}}\right] = \$1000 \left(\dfrac{0.05369613}{0.0075}\right) = \underline{\underline{\$7159.48}}$

50. $\dfrac{\$350}{\dfrac{0.0975}{12}} \left[1 - \dfrac{1}{\left(1 + \dfrac{0.0975}{12}\right)^5}\right] = \dfrac{\$350}{0.008125} \ (0.0396532) = \underline{\underline{\$1708.14}}$

51. $\dfrac{\$9500}{\dfrac{\left(1 + \dfrac{0.075}{4}\right)^5 - 1}{\dfrac{0.075}{4}}} = \dfrac{\$9500}{\dfrac{0.09733216}{0.01875}} - \underline{\underline{\$1830.07}}$

Exercise 1.2 (concluded)

52. $\$45 \dfrac{\left[1 - \dfrac{1}{\left(1 + \dfrac{0.0837}{2}\right)^4}\right]}{\dfrac{0.0837}{2}} + \dfrac{\$1000}{\left(1 + \dfrac{0.0837}{2}\right)^4}$

$= \$45 \dfrac{1 - \dfrac{1}{1.178205}}{0.04185} + \dfrac{\$1000}{1.178205}$

$= \$45\left(\dfrac{0.151251}{0.04185}\right) + \$848.75$

$= \$162.64 + \$848.75$

$= \underline{\underline{\$1011.38}}$

Exercise 1.3

1. Portion $= \dfrac{\% \text{ Rate}}{100\%} \times \text{Base} = \dfrac{1.75\%}{100\%} \times \$350 = \underline{\underline{\$6.13}}$

2. Portion $= \dfrac{6.\overline{6}\%}{100\%} \times \$666.66 = \underline{\underline{\$44.44}}$

3. $\%$ Rate $= \dfrac{\text{Portion}}{\text{Base}} \times 100\% = \dfrac{\$1.50}{\$11.50} \times 100\% = \underline{\underline{13.0\%}}$

4. $\%$ Rate $= \dfrac{\$0.88}{\$44.00} \times 100\% = \underline{\underline{2.00\%}}$

5. Base $= \dfrac{100\%}{\% \text{ Rate}} \times \text{Portion} = \dfrac{100\%}{60\%} \times \$45 = \underline{\underline{\$75.00}}$

6. Base $= \dfrac{100\%}{30\%} \times \$69 = \underline{\underline{\$230.00}}$

7. Portion $= \dfrac{233.3\%}{100\%} \times \$75 = \underline{\underline{\$174.98}}$

8. Portion $= \dfrac{0.075\%}{100\%} \times \$1650 = \underline{\underline{\$1.24}}$

9. $\%$ Rate $= \dfrac{\$134}{\$67} \times 100\% = \underline{\underline{200\%}}$

10. $\%$ Rate $= \dfrac{\$1.34}{\$655} \times 100\% = \underline{\underline{2.05\%}}$

Exercise 1.3 *(continued)*

11. Portion = $\dfrac{150\%}{100\%} \times \$60 = \underline{\underline{\$90.00}}$

12. Portion = $\dfrac{0.58\overline{3}\%}{100\%} \times \$1500 = \underline{\underline{\$8.75}}$

13. Base = $\dfrac{100\%}{7.5\%} \times \$1.46 = \underline{\underline{\$19.47}}$

14. Base = $\dfrac{100\%}{12.75\%} \times \$27.50 = \underline{\underline{\$215.69}}$

15. % Rate = $\dfrac{\$590}{\$950} \times 100\% = \underline{\underline{62.1\%}}$

16. % Rate = $\dfrac{\$950}{\$590} \times 100\% = \underline{\underline{161\%}}$

17. Base = $\dfrac{100\%}{95\%} \times \$100 = \underline{\underline{\$105.26}}$

18. Base = $\dfrac{100\%}{8.\overline{3}\%} \times 10 = \underline{\underline{\$120.00}}$

19. % Rate = $\dfrac{30 \text{ metres}}{3000 \text{ metres}} \times 100\% = \underline{\underline{1.00\%}}$

20. % Rate = $\dfrac{500 \text{ grams}}{2800 \text{ grams}} \times 100\% = \underline{\underline{17.9\%}}$

21. Portion = $\dfrac{0.5\%}{100\%} \times \$10.00 = \underline{\underline{\$0.05}}$

22. Portion = $\dfrac{0.75\%}{100\%} \times \$100 = \underline{\underline{\$0.75}}$

23. Base = $\dfrac{100\%}{120\%} \times \$180 = \underline{\underline{\$150.00}}$

24. Base = $\dfrac{100\%}{113\%} \times \$559.35 = \underline{\underline{\$495.00}}$

25. Portion = $\dfrac{130.5\%}{100\%} \times \$455 = \underline{\underline{\$593.78}}$

26. Portion = $\dfrac{0.0505\%}{100\%} \times \$50,000 = \underline{\underline{\$25.25}}$

Exercise 1.3 *(continued)*

27. Base = $\dfrac{100\%}{225\%}$ × $281.25 = $125.00

28. Base = $\dfrac{100\%}{350\%}$ × $1000 = $285.71

29. Base = $\dfrac{100\%}{0.5\%}$ × $10 = $2000.00

30. Base = $\dfrac{100\%}{0.75\%}$ × $1.25 = $166.67

31. Bonus as percent of sales = $\dfrac{\$7980}{\$532{,}000}$ × 100% = 1.50%

    Bonus as percent of salary = $\dfrac{\$7980}{\$45{,}000}$ × 100% = 17.7%

32. Total number of employees = 113 + 31 = 144

    Percent of employees in the union = $\dfrac{\text{Portion}}{\text{Base}}$ × 100%

    $= \dfrac{113}{144}$ × 100%

    = 78.5%

33. Shots scored from 2-point zone = Rate × Base
    = 0.545454 × 33
    = 18
    Shots scored from 3-point distance = 0.46667 × 15 = 7
    Foul shots scored = 0.793 × 29 = 23
    Total points scored = 18(2) + 7(3) + 23(1) = 80

34. The gross salary is the "base" amount.

    Gross salary = $\dfrac{\text{Portion}}{\text{Rate}} = \dfrac{\$2000}{0.65}$ = $3076.92

35. The budgeted (forecast) expenses are the "base" while the actual expenses are the "portion."

    Forecast expenses = $\dfrac{\text{Portion}}{\text{Rate}} = \dfrac{\$169{,}400}{1.10}$ = $154,000

36. The commission is the "portion" and the selling price is the "base."

    Selling price = $\dfrac{\text{Portion}}{\text{Rate}} = \dfrac{\$13{,}975}{0.065}$ = $215,000

Exercise 1.3 (continued)

37. The selling price is being compared to the original price. Hence, the original price is the "base" and the selling price is the "portion."

$$\text{Original price} = \frac{\text{Portion}}{\text{Rate}} = \frac{\$210,000}{2.50} = \underline{\underline{\$84,000}}$$

38. The dividend (portion) is 8% of the par value (base).

$$\text{Par value} = \frac{\text{Portion}}{\text{Rate}} = \frac{\$3.50}{0.08} = \underline{\underline{\$43.75}}$$

39. The maximum contribution is the "portion" and the desired earned income is the "base."

$$\text{Earned income} = \frac{\text{Portion}}{\text{Rate}} = \frac{\$13,500}{0.15} = \underline{\underline{\$75,000}}$$

40. Portion of commission retained = Rate × Base
    = 0.60 × 6%
    = 3.6%

    The $75,000 income (portion) is 3.6% of sales (base).

$$\text{Sales volume} = \frac{\text{Portion}}{\text{Rate}} = \frac{\$75,000}{0.036} = \underline{\underline{\$2,083,333}}$$

41. The retained commission is

$$\frac{\$134.55}{\$11,500} \times 100\% = 1.17\%$$

of the amount of the transaction. This 1.17% (portion) is 45% of the total commission rate (base) charged to clients. Hence,

$$\text{Rate of total commission} = \frac{\text{Portion}}{\text{Rate}} = \frac{1.17\%}{0.45} = \underline{\underline{2.60\%}}$$

42. The expected number of deaths (portion) among 50,000 males (base) is

$$\frac{\% \text{ Rate}}{100\%} \times \text{Base} = \frac{0.34\%}{100\%} \times 50,000 = \underline{\underline{170}}$$

The number of 35-year-old males in the city of 1.45 million is

$$\frac{0.83\%}{100\%} \times 1,450,000 = 12,035$$

The expected number of deaths in this group in a year is

$$\frac{0.34\%}{100\%} \times 12,035 = \underline{\underline{41}}$$

Exercise 1.4

1.

	a.	*b.*
Gross weekly earnings	$\dfrac{\$29,400}{52} = \$565.38$	$\dfrac{\$29,400}{53} = \$554.72$
Equivalent hourly rate	$\dfrac{\$565.38}{35} = \$16.154$	$\dfrac{\$554.72}{35} = \$15.849$
Overtime rate	$1.5(\$16.154) = \underline{\$24.231}$	$1.5(\$15.849) = \underline{\$23.774}$

2. a. Gross biweekly earnings $= \dfrac{\$37,500}{26} = \$1442.31$

   Equivalent hourly rate $= \dfrac{\$1442.31}{2 \times 37.5} = \underline{\$19.231}$

   b. Gross earnings $= \$1442.31 + 1.5(9)\ \$19.231 = \underline{\$1701.93}$

3. a. Gross biweekly earnings $= \dfrac{\$38,600}{27} = \$1429.63$

   Equivalent hourly wage $= \dfrac{\$1429.63}{2 \times 35} = \underline{\$20.423}$

   b. Total remuneration $= \$1429.63 + 1.5(10.5)\ \$20.423 = \underline{\$1751.29}$

4. Annual earnings $= 52(40)\ \$15.75 = \$32,760$

   Equivalent semimonthly earnings $= \dfrac{\$32,760}{24} = \underline{\$1365.00}$

5. Regular hours worked $= 7.5 + 7.5 + 6 + 6 + 7.5 = 34.5$
   Overtime hours worked $= 4.5 + 1 + 1.5 = 7$
   Gross earnings $= 34.5(\$17.70) + 7(1.5)(\$17.70) = \underline{\$796.50}$

6. Regular hours worked $= 5(8) = 40$
   Overtime hours worked $= 1.5 + 2 + 8$ (for Friday) $= 11.5$
   "Stat" holiday hours worked $= 8$
   Gross earnings $= 40(\$24.50) + 11.5(1.5)\ \$24.50 + 8(2)\ \$24.50$
   $\qquad = \$980.00 + \$422.63 + \$392.00$
   $\qquad = \underline{\$1794.63}$

7. Output in excess of quota $= 4 + 6 + 7 + 8 + 10 = 35$
   Total pay $= 40(\$6.25) + 35(\$2.25) = \underline{\$328.75}$

8. Weight packed per day $= 7.5(250)(0.500 \text{ kg}) = 937.5 \text{ kg}$
   Earnings per day $= 7.5(\$8.25) + (937.5 - 500)(\$0.18) = \underline{\$140.63}$

Exercise 1.4 *(continued)*

9. a. Earnings will be the greater of $450 or

$$0.11(\text{Sales}) = 0.11(\$4236) = \underline{\$465.96}$$

    b. The salesman will earn the $450 from sales if

$$0.11(\text{Sales}) = \$450$$

That is, if

$$\text{Sales} = \frac{\$450}{0.11} = \underline{\$4090.91} \text{ per week}$$

10. a. Earnings = $2000 + 0.022($227,000 − $150,000) = \underline{\$3694.00}$

    b. Average earnings = $2000 + 0.022($235,000 − $150,000)

$$= \$3870.00$$

For a straight commission rate to generate the same monthly earnings,

$$\text{Commission rate} = \frac{\$3870}{\$235,000} \times 100\% = \underline{1.6468\%}$$

11. a. Earnings = 0.05($20,000) + 0.075($20,000) + 0.10($14,880)

$$= \underline{\$3988.00}$$

    b. For the same earnings from a single straight commission rate,

$$\text{Commission rate} \times \$54,880 = \$3988.00$$

$$\text{Commission rate} = \frac{\$3988}{\$54,880} \times 100\% = \underline{7.2668\%}$$

12. Commission earned = $630.38 − $300 = $330.38

Hence,

$$0.03 \text{ (Sales subject to commission)} = \$330.38$$

$$\text{Sales subject to commission} = \frac{\$330.38}{0.03} = \$11,012.67$$

Total sales = $11,012.67 + $20,000 = \underline{\$31,012.67}$

13. Commission earned in August = $3296.97 − $1500.00 = $1796.97

Hence,

$$\text{Commission rate } (\$151,342 - \$100,000) = \$1796.97$$

$$\text{Commission rate} = \frac{\$1796.97}{\$51,342} \times 100\% = \underline{3.50\%}$$

14. Gross earnings = 0.033($50,000) + 0.044 ($50,000) + 0.055 ($40,000)

$$= \underline{\$6050.00}$$

Exercise 1.4 (concluded)

15. Commission earned on first $90,000 of sales was 0.04 ($40,000) + 0.05 ($50,000) = $4100

    Commission earned on sales in excess of $90,000 was $5350 − $4100 = $1250

    That is,

    $$0.06(\text{Sales exceeding } \$90,000) = \$1250$$

    $$\text{Sales exceeding } \$90,000 = \frac{\$1250}{0.06} = \$20,833.33$$

    Total sales for the month = $90,000 + $20,833.33 = $110,833.33

16. Required monthly commission = $4000 − $2000 = $2000

    Commission income on first $50,000 of monthly sales is

    $$0.03(\$50,000 - \$25,000) = \$750$$

    The combined commission and bonus rate on sales exceeding $50,000 is 3% + 3% = 6%.

    Hence,

    $$0.06(\text{Sales exceeding } \$50,000) = \$2000 - \$750$$

    $$\text{Sales exceeding } \$50,000 = \frac{\$1250}{0.06} = \$20,833.33$$

    Required monthly sales = $70,833.33

Exercise 1.5

1. Each number of TV sets per household should be weighted by the number of homes having that number of TVs. The weighted average number of TVs per household in the survey sample is

    $$\frac{(4 \times 4) + (22 \times 3) + (83 \times 2) + (140 \times 1) + (5 + 0)}{254} = 1.53$$

    Based on the survey, we would estimate an average of 1.53 TVs per household.

2. The weighted average cost per share is

    $$\frac{1000(\$15.63) + 500(\$19.00) + 300(\$21.75)}{1800} = \$17.586$$

3. We should weight each "goals against" figure by the number of games in which that number of goals were scored.

    $$\text{GAA} = \frac{1(0) + 2(1) + 3(2) + 4(3) + 7(4) + 2(6) + 1(10)}{20} = 3.50$$

4. The amount of sales subject to each commission rate should be used as the weighting factor.

    a. The average commission rate will be:

    $$\frac{\$30,000(3\%) + \$20,000(4\%) + \$10,000(6\%)}{\$60,000} = 3.8\overline{3}\%$$

    b. The average commission rate will be:

    $$\frac{\$30,000(3\%) + \$20,000(4\%) + \$50,000(6\%)}{\$100,000} = 4.70\%$$

Exercise 1.5 *(continued)*

5. The weighted average interest rate that will be charged on the new $57,500 balance is

$$\frac{\$37,500(9\ 1/2\%) + \$20,000(8\%)}{\$57,500} = \underline{\underline{8.9783\%}}$$

6. The weighted grade point average is

$$GPA = \frac{5(2.3) + 3(2.7) + 4(3.3) + 2(1.7) + 3(3.0) + 4(2.0)}{5 + 3 + 4 + 2 + 3 + 4}$$

$$= \frac{53.2}{21}$$

$$= \underline{\underline{2.53}}$$

7. Each score should be weighted by the number of students who obtained that score. The weighted average score is

$$\frac{2(10) + 6(9) + 9(8) + 7(7) + 3(6) + 2(5) + 1(3)}{30} = \underline{\underline{7.53}}$$

8. Each semester's GPA should be weighted by the number of credits on which the respective GPA was obtained. The cumulative GPA is

$$\frac{6(3.5) + 9(3.0) + 12(2.75) + 7.5(3.2)}{6 + 9 + 12 + 7.5} = \frac{105.0}{34.5} = \underline{\underline{3.04}}$$

9. Note that the age of receivables (rather than the dollar amount of receivables) is to be averaged. The relative importance of each of the three age classifications is determined by the dollar amount in each category. Hence, the weighting factors are the respective dollar amounts of receivables. The (weighted) average age of accounts receivable is

$$\frac{\$12,570(30) + \$6850(60) + \$1325(90)}{\$12,570 + \$6850 + \$1325} = \frac{907,350}{20,745}$$

$$= \underline{\underline{43.74\ days}}$$

10. The rate of return for the entire portfolio is the weighted average return on the five securities in the portfolio. Each rate of return should be weighted by the fraction of the portfolio invested in the respective security. The rate of return on the portfolio is

$$\frac{0.15(14\%) + 0.20(10\%) + 0.10(-13\%) + 0.35(12\%) + 0.20(27\%)}{1.00} = \underline{\underline{12.40\%}}$$

11. a. The weighted average cost of units purchased during the year is

$$\frac{300(\$10.86) + 1000(\$10.47) + 500(\$10.97)}{1800} = \underline{\underline{\$10.674}}$$

b. The weighted average cost of beginning inventory and units purchased is

$$\frac{156(\$10.55) + 1800(\$10.674)}{1956} = \underline{\underline{\$10.664}}$$

c. Value of ending inventory = 239 × Weighted average cost
$$= 239(\$10.664)$$
$$= \underline{\underline{\$2548.70}}$$

Exercise 1.5 (concluded)

12. The weighted average price increase was

$$\frac{0.30(10\%) + 0.20(-5\%) + 0.50(15\%)}{1.00} = \underline{9.50\%}$$

13. Each gross profit margin should be weighted by the fraction of revenue obtained from the respective food category. The weighted average gross profit margin is

$$\frac{0.10(67\%) + 0.50(45\%) + 0.25(50\%) + 0.15(70\%)}{0.10 + 0.50 + 0.25 + 0.15} = \underline{52.2\%}$$

14.

Period	Balance	No. of days
1st to 7th	$35,000	7
8th to 24th	$35,000 + $10,000 = $45,000	17
25th to 31st	$45,000 − $20,000 = $25,000	7

The weighted average balance on the loan was

$$\frac{7(\$35,000) + 17(\$45,000) + 7(\$25,000)}{7 + 17 + 7} = \underline{\$38,225.81}$$

15. We want the average number of people working over the course of the year. The given figures for the number of employees added or laid off at various times are used to determine the cumulative number of people employed.

Period	No. of months	Number of employees
Jan. 1 to Mar. 31	3	14
Apr. 1 to Apr. 30	1	14 + 7 = 21
May 1 to May 31	1	21 + 8 = 29
Jun. 1 to Aug. 31	3	29 + 11 = 40
Sept. 1 to Sept. 30	1	40 − 6 = 34
Oct. 1 to Dec. 31	3	34 − 14 = 20

Each number of employees in the third column must be weighted by the number of months to which it applies. The average number employed was

$$\frac{3(14) + 1(21) + 1(29) + 3(40) + 1(34) + 3(20)}{12} = \underline{25.50}$$

16.

Period	No. of months	Cumulative investment
Sept. 1 to Sept. 30	1	$57,000
Oct. 1 to Oct. 31	1	72,000
Nov. 1 to Jan. 31	3	99,000
Feb. 1 to Feb. 28	1	76,000
Mar. 1 to Apr. 30	2	63,000
May 1 to Aug. 31	4	57,000

The (weighted) average investment was

$$\frac{[1(57) + 1(72) + 3(99) + 1(76) + 2(63) + 4(57)] \times \$1000}{12} = \underline{\$71,333.33}$$

Exercise 1A

1.

Quarter	Sales – Purchases	GST Remittance (Refund)
1	$155,365	$10,875.55
2	(340,305)	(23,821.35)
3	408,648	28,605.36
4	164,818	11,537.26

2.

Month	Sales – Purchases	GST Remittance (Refund)
March	$(77,760)	$(5443.20)
April	(8,255)	(577.85)
May	136,515	9556.05
June	114,875	8041.25

3. The GST charged in each case will be

$$0.07(\$21,900) = \$1533$$

   a. With no PST in Alberta, the total price will be

   $$\$21,900 + \$1533 = \underline{\$23,433}$$

   b. PST in Ontario = 0.08($21,900) = $1752
   Total price = $21,900 + $1533 + $1752 = $\underline{\$25,185}$

   c. PST in Quebec = 0.08($21,900 + $1533) = $1874.64
   Total price = $21,900 + $1533 + $1874.64 = $\underline{\$25,307.64}$

4. PST in British Columbia = 0.07($1000) = $70.00
   PST in Quebec = 0.08($1000 + GST) = 0.08($1070) = $85.60
   The consumer will pay $85.60 – $70.00 = $\underline{\$15.60}$ more in Quebec.

5. a. PST (Saskatchewan) = 0.09($87,940 – $28,637) = $\underline{\$5337.27}$

   b. In Prince Edward Island, consumers pay PST on the post-GST price. The GST paid on the amount subject to PST was

   $$0.07(\$87,940 - \$28,637) = \$4151.21$$

   The PST that must be remitted is

   $$0.10(\$87,940 - \$28,637 + \$4151.21) = \underline{\$6345.42}$$

6.

Province	PST on a $100 item	Total GST + PST	Equivalent Total Tax Rate
Alberta	$ 0	$ 7	7%
British Columbia	7	14	14%
Manitoba	7	14	14%
Ontario	8	15	15%
Prince Edward Island	10.70 [1]	17.70	17.7%
Quebec	8.56	15.56	15.56%
Saskatchewan	9	16	16%

[1] 0.10($100 + $7) = $10.70

7. Property tax $= \dfrac{\text{Mill rate}}{1000} \times$ Assessed value

$$= \dfrac{16.8629}{1000} \times \$227{,}000$$

$$= \underline{\$3827.88}$$

8. a. 0.1 mill $= \dfrac{0.1}{1000} = 0.0001 = \underline{0.01\%}$

   b. Property tax increase $= \dfrac{0.1}{1000} \times \$200{,}000 = \$20.00$

9. Total taxes $= \dfrac{15.0294}{1000} \times \$143{,}000 + \dfrac{4.6423}{1000} \times \$467{,}000$

   $$= \$2149.20 + \$2167.95$$

   $$= \underline{\$4317.15}$$

10. a. Current year's taxes $= \dfrac{15.2193}{1000} \times \$198{,}000 = \$3013.42$

    Previous year's taxes $= \dfrac{15.6324}{1000} \times \$185{,}000 = \underline{\$2891.99}$

    Increase in property taxes $= \underline{\$\ 121.43}$

    b. For the current year's taxes to remain at $2891.99,

    $$\dfrac{\text{New mill rate}}{1000} \times \$198{,}000 = \$2891.99$$

    New mill rate $= \dfrac{\$2891.99}{\$198{,}000} \times 1000 = \underline{14.6060}$

11. a. Tax increase $= \dfrac{\text{Mill rate increase}}{1000} \times$ Assessed value

    $$\$2{,}430{,}000 = \dfrac{\text{Mill rate increase}}{1000} \times \$6{,}780{,}000{,}000$$

    Mill rate increase $= \dfrac{\$2430}{\$6{,}780{,}000} \times 1000 = 0.3584$

    Next year's mill rate $= 7.1253 + 0.3584 = \underline{7.4837}$

    b. Next year's assessment $= 1.05(\$6.78 \text{ billion}) = \$7.119$ billion

    Next year's budget $=$ Current year's taxes $+ \$2{,}430{,}000$

    $$= \dfrac{7.1253}{1000} \times \$6.78 \text{ billion} + \$2{,}430{,}900$$

    $$= \$50{,}739{,}500$$

    Next year's school mill rate applied to next year's assessment must generate enough tax revenue to meet next year's budget.

Exercise 1A *(concluded)*

$$\$50,739,500 = \frac{\text{New mill rate}}{1000} \times \$7.119 \text{ billion}$$

$$\text{New mill rate} = \frac{\$50,739,500}{\$7,119,000} = \underline{7.1273}$$

12. Current budget = Last year's budget + $750,000

$$= \frac{9.4181}{1000} \times \$1.563 \text{ billion} + \$750,000$$

$$= \$14,720,490 + \$750,000$$

$$= \$15,470,490$$

Current assessment = $1563 million + $97 million = $1660 million

Hence,

$$\$15,470,490 = \frac{\text{New mill rate}}{1000} \times \$1660 \text{ million}$$

$$\text{New mill rate} = \frac{\$15,470,490}{\$1,660,000} = \underline{9.3196}$$

Review Problems

1. a. $(2^3 - 3)^2 - 20 \div (2 + 2^3) = (8 - 3)^2 - 20 + (2 + 8)$
   $$= 25 - 20 \div 10$$
   $$= 25 - 2$$
   $$= \underline{\underline{23}}$$

   b. $4(2 \times 3^2 - 2^3)^2 \div (10 - 4 \times 5) = 4(2 \times 9 - 8)^2 \div (10 - 20)$
   $$= 4 \times 10^2 \div (-10)$$
   $$= \underline{\underline{-40}}$$

   c. $\$213.85 \left(1 - 0.095 \times \dfrac{5}{12}\right) = \$213.85(1 - 0.039583) = \underline{\underline{\$205.39}}$

   d. $\dfrac{\$2315}{1 + 0.0825 \times \dfrac{77}{365}} = \dfrac{\$2315}{1.0174041} = \underline{\underline{\$2275.40}}$

   e. $\$325.75 \left(1 + \dfrac{0.105}{4}\right)^2 = \$325.75(1.053189) = \underline{\underline{\$343.08}}$

   f. $\dfrac{\$710}{\left(1 + \dfrac{0.0925}{2}\right)^3} = \dfrac{\$710}{1.145266} = \underline{\underline{\$619.94}}$

Review Problems (continued)

g. $$\$885.75\left(1 + 0.0775 \times \frac{231}{365}\right) - \frac{\$476.50}{1 + 0.0775 \times \frac{49}{365}}$$

$$= \$885.75(1.049048) - \frac{\$476.50}{1.010404}$$

$$= \$929.194 - \$471.593$$

$$= \underline{\underline{\$457.60}}$$

h. $$\$859\left(1 + \frac{0.0825}{12}\right)^3 + \frac{\$682}{\left(1 + \frac{0.0825}{12}\right)^{12}}$$

$$= \$859(1.020767) + \frac{\$682}{1.013797}$$

$$= \$876.839 + \$672.718$$

$$= \underline{\underline{\$1549.56}}$$

2. $\% \text{ Rate} = \dfrac{\$16.39}{\$6.39} \times 100\% = \underline{\underline{256.5\%}}$

3. $\text{Base} = \dfrac{100\%}{80\%} \times \$100 = \underline{\underline{\$125.00}}$

4. $\text{Base} = \dfrac{100\%}{0.75\%} \times \$1.00 = \underline{\underline{\$133.33}}$

5. $\% \text{ Rate} = \dfrac{0.5 \text{ feet}}{2 \times 3 \text{ feet}} \times 100\% = \underline{\underline{8.\overline{3}\%}}$

6. $\text{Forecast profit (Base)} = \dfrac{100\%}{90\%} \times \$23{,}400 = \underline{\underline{\$26{,}000.00}}$

7. a. $\text{Gross biweekly earnings} = \dfrac{\$56{,}600}{26} = \$2176.92$

   $\text{Equivalent hourly wage} = \dfrac{\$2176.92}{2 \times 37.5} = \underline{\underline{\$29.026}}$

   b. $\text{Total remuneration} = \$2176.92 + 4.5(1.5)\ \$29.026 = \underline{\$2372.85}$

8. Regular hours worked = 5(7.5) = 37.5
   Overtime hours = 6 + 1.5 + 0.5 = 8
   "Stat" holiday hours worked = 3
   Gross earnings = 37.5 ($32.50) + 8(1.5) $32.50 + 3(2) $32.50
   $$= \$1218.75 + \$390.00 + \$195.00$$
   $$= \underline{\underline{\$1803.75}}$$

Review Problems *(concluded)*

9. Commission earnings = Commission rate (Sales – $40,000)

   $3188.35 – $1000 = Commission rate ($88,630 – $40,000)

   Commission rate $= \dfrac{\$2188.35}{\$48,630} \times 100\% = \underline{4.50\%}$

10. Rate of return on entire portfolio

    = Weighted average rate of return

    $= \dfrac{\$5000(30\%) + \$20,000(-3\%) + \$8000(-15\%) + \$25,000(13\%) + \$4500(45\%)}{\$5000 + \$20,000 + \$8000 + \$25,000 + \$4500}$

    $= \underline{7.96\%}$

11.

Period	No. of months	Number of employees
July 1 to Aug. 31	2	7
Sept. 1 to Oct. 31	2	7 + 6 = 13
Nov. 1 to Nov. 30	1	13 + 18 = 31
Dec. 1 to Feb. 28	3	31 + 23 = 54
Mar. 1 to Mar. 31	1	54 – 11 = 43
Apr. 1 to Apr. 30	1	43 – 20 = 23
May 1 to June 30	2	23 – 16 = 7

The (weighted) average number of employees was

$$\dfrac{4(7) + 2(13) + 1(31) + 3(54) + 1(43) + 1(23)}{12} = \underline{26.1}$$

Self-Test Exercise

1. a. $96 - (6 - 4^2) \times 7 - 2 = 96 - (-10)\,7 - 2 = \underline{164}$

   b. $81 \div (5^2 - 16) - 4\,(2^3 - 13) = 81 \div 9 - 4(-5) = \underline{29}$

   c. $\dfrac{\$827.69}{1 + 0.125 \times \dfrac{273}{365}} + \$531.49 \left(1 + 0.125 \times \dfrac{41}{365}\right)$

   $= \dfrac{\$827.69}{1.093493} + \$531.49(1.014041)$

   $= \$756.923 + \$538.953$

   $= \underline{\$1295.88}$

   d. $\$550.45 \left(1 + 0.0875 \times \dfrac{195}{365}\right) - \dfrac{\$376.29}{1 + 0.0875 \times \dfrac{99}{365}}$

   $= \$550.45\,(1.046747) - \dfrac{\$376.29}{1.023733}$

   $= \underline{\$208.62}$

Self-Test Exercise *(concluded)*

e. $\$1137\left(1+\dfrac{0.0975}{12}\right)^2 + \dfrac{\$2643}{\left(1+\dfrac{0.0975}{12}\right)^3}$

$= \$1137(1.016316) + \dfrac{\$2643}{1.024574}$

$= \underline{\underline{\$3735.16}}$

2. Base $= \dfrac{100\%}{167.5\%} \times \$100 = \underline{\underline{\$59.70}}$

3. 0.15(Income exceeding \$54,000) = \$4500

   Income exceeding \$54,000 $= \dfrac{\$4500}{0.15} = \$30,000$

   Total net income = \$54,000 + \$30,000 = $\underline{\underline{\$84,000}}$

4. Gross biweekly earnings $= \dfrac{\$61,000}{26} = \underline{\underline{\$2346.15}}$

   Equivalent hourly rate $= \dfrac{\$2346.15}{75} = \underline{\underline{\$31.282}}$

   Gross pay = \$2346.15 + 33(1.5) \$31.282 = $\underline{\underline{\$3894.61}}$

5. Gross earnings = \$1000 + 0.08(\$10,000) + 0.10(\$38,670 − \$30,000)
   $= \underline{\underline{\$2667}}$

6. Rate of return on the portfolio
   = Weighted average rate of return
   $= \dfrac{\$16,800(-4.3\%) + \$25,600(-1.1\%) + \$31,000(8.2\%)}{\$16,800 + \$25,600 + \$31,000}$

   $= \underline{\underline{2.10\%}}$

7.

Period	No. of months	Cumulative investment
Jan. 1 to Feb. 28	2	\$96,400
Mar. 1 to Mar. 31	1	\$96,400 − \$14,200 = \$82,200
Apr. 1 to July 31	4	\$82,200 − \$21,800 = \$60,400
Aug. 1 to Oct. 31	3	\$60,400 + \$23,700 = \$84,100
Nov. 1 to Dec. 31	2	\$84,100 + \$19,300 = \$103,400

Average investment during the year

$= \dfrac{2(\$96,400) + 1(\$82,200) + 4(\$60,400) + 3(\$84,100) + 2(\$103,400)}{12}$

$= \underline{\underline{\$81,308.33}}$

2   Review of Algebra

Changes in the Second Edition:

1. The justifications for the interpretations of **Zero, Negative, and Fractional Exponents** have been moved to an appendix since most instructors do not have the class time to do a rigorous review in this area.

2. The topic **Logarithms** have been moved to a Chapter 9 appendix. Many instructors, particularly those emphasizing the financial calculator approach, do not cover logarithms. For those who do review logarithms, the text's coverage is now in the chapter where logarithms are first employed in the mathematics of finance.

3. Again at the suggestion of reviewers, **Solving Nonlinear Equations in One Variable** has been deleted as a "stand-alone" topic. Solving for an unknown exponent is integrated with coverage of logarithms in a Chapter 9 appendix. Solving for an annuity's interest rate per payment interval by the **Trial-and-Error Method** is presented in an appendix to Chapter 12.

4. **Percent Change** has been substantially revised and moved from Chapter 1 to Chapter 2. An algebraic formulation is more concise, and is more readily manipulated to solve for the initial value or the final value when the percent change is known.

5. **Rate of Return on Investment** has also been moved from Chapter 1 to Chapter 2 because:

    (i)   It is essentially an application of Percent Change.
    (ii) Algebraic formulas for income yield, percent capital gain, and rate of return on investment are less cumbersome than the former "word formulas."
    (iii) It prepares the student for the subsequent topic: **Compounding Percent Changes and Rates of Return.**

6. **Compounding Percent Changes and Rates of Return** is a new section introduced as a natural extension of the two preceding topics, Percent Change and Rate of Return on Investment. As well as being useful in its own right, this section prepares a foundation for later topics such as series discounts and compound interest.

Exercise 2.1

1. $(-p) + (-3p) + 4p = -p - 3p + 4p = \underline{\underline{0}}$

2. $(5s - 2t) - (2s - 4t) = 5s - 2t - 2s + 4t = \underline{\underline{3s + 2t}}$

3. $4x^2y + (-3x^2y) - (-5x^2y) = 4x^2y - 3x^2y + 5x^2y = \underline{\underline{6x^2y}}$

4. $1 - (7e^2 - 5 + 3e - e^3) = 1 - 7e^2 + 5 - 3e + e^3 = \underline{\underline{e^3 - 7e^2 - 3e + 6}}$

5. $(6x^2 - 3xy + 4y^2) - (8y^2 - 10xy - x^2) = 6x^2 - 3xy + 4y^2 - 8y^2 + 10xy + x^2$
$$= \underline{\underline{7x^2 + 7xy - 4y^2}}$$

6. $(7m^3 - m - 6m^2 + 10) - (5m^3 - 9 + 3m - 2m^2) = 7m^3 - m - 6m^2 + 10 - 5m^3 + 9 - 3m + 2m^2$
$$= \underline{\underline{2m^3 - 4m^2 - 4m + 19}}$$

7. $2(7x - 3y) - 3(2x - 3y) = 14x - 6y - 6x + 9y = \underline{\underline{8x + 3y}}$

8. $4(a^2 - 3a - 4) - 2(5a^2 - a - 6) = 4a^2 - 12a - 16 - 10a^2 + 2a + 12$
$$= \underline{\underline{-6a^2 - 10a - 4}}$$

9. $15x - [4 - 2(5x - 6)] = 15x - 4 + 10x - 12 = \underline{\underline{25x - 16}}$

10. $6a - [3a - 2(2b - a)] = 6a - 3a + 4b - 2a = \underline{\underline{a + 4b}}$

11. $\dfrac{2x + 9}{4} - 1.2(x - 1) = 0.5x + 2.25 - 1.2x + 1.2 = \underline{\underline{-0.7x + 3.45}}$

12. $\dfrac{x}{2} - x^2 + \dfrac{4}{5} - 0.2x^2 - \dfrac{4}{5}x + \dfrac{1}{2} = 0.5x - x^2 + 0.8 - 0.2x^2 - 0.8x + 0.5$
$$= \underline{\underline{-1.2x^2 - 0.3x + 1.3}}$$

13. $\dfrac{8x}{0.5} + \dfrac{5.5x}{11} + 0.5(4.6x - 17) = 16x + 0.5x + 2.3x - 8.5 = \underline{\underline{18.8x - 8.5}}$

14. $\dfrac{2x}{1.045} - \dfrac{2.016x}{3} + \dfrac{x}{2} = 1.9139x - 0.6720x + 0.5x = \underline{\underline{1.7419x}}$

15. $\dfrac{P}{1 + 0.095 \times \dfrac{5}{12}} + 2P\left(1 + 0.095 \times \dfrac{171}{365}\right) = 0.96192P + 2.08901P = \underline{\underline{3.0509P}}$

16. $y\left(1 - 0.125 \times \dfrac{213}{365}\right) + \dfrac{2y}{1 + 0.125 \times \dfrac{88}{365}} = 0.92706y + 1.94149y = \underline{\underline{2.8685y}}$

17. $k(1 + 0.04)^2 + \dfrac{2k}{(1 + 0.04)^2} = 1.08160k + 1.84911k = \underline{\underline{2.9307k}}$

18. $\dfrac{h}{(1 + 0.055)^2} - 3h(1 + 0.055)^3 = 0.89845h - 3.52272h = \underline{\underline{-2.6243h}}$

Exercise 2.1 *(continued)*

19. $4a(3ab - 5a + 6b) = \underline{12a^2b - 20a^2 + 24ab}$

20. $9k(4 - 8k + 7k^2) = \underline{36k - 72k^2 + 63k^3}$

21. $-5xy(2x^2 - xy - 3y^2) = \underline{-10x^3y + 5x^2y^2 + 15xy^3}$

22. $-(p^2 - 4pq - 5p)\left(\dfrac{2q}{p}\right) = \underline{-2pq + 8q^2 + 10q}$

23. $(4r - 3t)(2t + 5r) = 8rt + 20r^2 - 6t^2 - 15rt = \underline{20r^2 - 7rt - 6t^2}$

24. $(3p^2 - 5p)(-4p + 2) = -12p^3 + 6p^2 + 20p^2 - 10p = \underline{-12p^3 + 26p^2 - 10p}$

25. $3(a - 2)(4a + 1) - 5(2a + 3)(a - 7) = 3(4a^2 + a - 8a - 2) - 5(2a^2 - 14a + 3a - 21)$
$$= 12a^2 - 21a - 6 - 10a^2 + 55a + 105$$
$$= \underline{2a^2 + 34a + 99}$$

26. $5(2x - y)(y + 3x) - 6x(x - 5y) = 5(2xy + 6x^2 - y^2 - 3xy) - 6x^2 + 30xy$
$$= -5xy + 30x^2 - 5y^2 - 6x^2 + 30xy$$
$$= \underline{24x^2 + 25xy - 5y^2}$$

27. $\dfrac{18x^2}{3x} = \underline{\underline{6x}}$

28. $\dfrac{6a^2b}{-2ab^2} = \underline{\underline{-3\dfrac{a}{b}}}$

29. $\dfrac{x^2y - xy^2}{xy} = \underline{\underline{x - y}}$

30. $\dfrac{-4x + 10x^2 - 6x^3}{-0.5x} = \underline{\underline{8 - 20x + 12x^2}}$

31. $\dfrac{12x^3 - 24x^2 + 36x}{48x} = \underline{\underline{\dfrac{x^2 - 2x + 3}{4}}}$

32. $\dfrac{32a^2b - 8ab + 14ab^2}{2ab} = \underline{\underline{16a - 4 + 7b}}$

33. $\dfrac{4a^2b^3 - 6a^3b^2}{2ab^2} = \underline{\underline{2ab - 3a^2}}$

34. $\dfrac{120(1 + i)^2 + 180(1 + i)^3}{360(1 + i)} = \underline{\underline{\dfrac{2(1 + i) + 3(1 + i)^2}{6}}}$

Exercise 2.1 *(continued)*

35. $3d^2 - 4d + 15 = 3(2.5)^2 - 4(2.5) + 15$
$$= 18.75 - 10 + 15$$
$$= \underline{\underline{23.75}}$$

36. $15g - 9h + 3 = 15(14) - 9(15) + 3 = \underline{\underline{78}}$

37. $7x(4y - 8) = 7(3.2)(4 \times 1.5 - 8) = 22.4(6 - 8) = \underline{\underline{-44.8}}$

38. $I + Pr = \dfrac{\$13.75}{\$500 \times 0.11} = \underline{\underline{0.25}}$

39. $\dfrac{I}{rt} = \dfrac{\$23.21}{0.095 \times \dfrac{283}{365}} = \dfrac{\$23.21}{0.073658} = \underline{\underline{\$315.11}}$

40. $\dfrac{N}{1 - d} = \dfrac{\$89.10}{1 - 0.10} = \underline{\underline{\$99.00}}$

41. $L(1 - d_1)(1 - d_2)(1 - d_3) = \$490(1 - 0.125)(1 - 0.15)(1 - 0.05) = \underline{\underline{\$346.22}}$

42. $P(1 + rt) = \$770\left(1 + 0.13 \times \dfrac{223}{365}\right) = \$770\,(1.079425) = \underline{\underline{\$831.16}}$

43. $\dfrac{S}{1 + rt} = \dfrac{\$2500}{1 + 0.085 \times \dfrac{123}{365}} = \dfrac{\$2500}{1.028644} = \underline{\underline{\$2430.38}}$

44. $(1 + i)^m - 1 = (1 + 0.0225)^4 - 1 = \underline{\underline{0.09308}}$

45. $P(1 + i)^n = \$1280(1 + 0.025)^3 = \underline{\underline{\$1378.42}}$

46. $\dfrac{S}{(1 + i)^n} = \dfrac{\$850}{(1 + 0.0075)^6} = \dfrac{\$850}{1.045852} = \underline{\underline{\$812.73}}$

47. $R\left[\dfrac{(1 + i)^n - 1}{i}\right] = \$550\left(\dfrac{1.085^3 - 1}{0.085}\right) = \$550\left(\dfrac{0.2772891}{0.085}\right) = \underline{\underline{\$1794.22}}$

48. $R\left[\dfrac{(1 + f)^n - 1}{f}\right](1 + f) = \$910\left(\dfrac{1.1038129^4 - 1}{0.1038129}\right)(1.1038129)$

$$= \$910\left(\dfrac{0.4845057}{0.1038129}\right)(1.1038129)$$

$$= \underline{\underline{\$4687.97}}$$

49. $\dfrac{R}{i}\left[1 - \dfrac{1}{(1 + i)^n}\right] = \dfrac{\$630}{0.115}\left(1 - \dfrac{1}{1.115^2}\right) = \underline{\underline{\$1071.77}}$

Exercise 2.1 *(concluded)*

50. $P(1 + rt_1) + \dfrac{S}{1 + rt_2} = \$470\left(1 + 0.075 \times \dfrac{104}{365}\right) + \dfrac{\$390}{1 + 0.075 \times \dfrac{73}{365}}$

$$= \$470\,(1.021370) + \dfrac{\$390}{1.01500}$$

$$= \$480.044 + \$384.236$$

$$= \underline{\underline{\$864.28}}$$

Exercise 2.2

1. $a^2 \times a^3 = \underline{\underline{a^5}}$

2. $(x^6)(x^{-4}) = \underline{\underline{x^2}}$

3. $b^{10} + b^6 = b^{10-6} = \underline{\underline{b^4}}$

4. $h^7 + h^{-4} = h^{7-(-4)} = \underline{\underline{h^{11}}}$

5. $(1 + i)^4 \times (1 + i)^9 = \underline{\underline{(1 + i)^{13}}}$

6. $(1 + i) \times (1 + i)^n = \underline{\underline{(1 + i)^{n+1}}}$

7. $(x^4)^7 = x^{4 \times 7} = \underline{\underline{x^{28}}}$

8. $(y^3)^3 = \underline{\underline{y^9}}$

9. $(t^6)^{\frac{1}{3}} = \underline{\underline{t^2}}$

10. $(n^{0.5})^8 = \underline{\underline{n^4}}$

11. $\dfrac{(x^5)(x^6)}{x^9} = x^{5+6-9} = \underline{\underline{x^2}}$

12. $\dfrac{(x^5)^6}{x^9} = x^{5 \times 6-9} = \underline{\underline{x^{21}}}$

13. $[2(1 + i)]^2 = \underline{\underline{4(1 + i)^2}}$

14. $\left(\dfrac{1 + i}{3i}\right)^3 = \underline{\underline{\dfrac{(1 + i)^3}{27i^3}}}$

15. $\dfrac{4r^5t^6}{(2r^2t)^3} = \dfrac{4r^5t^6}{8r^6t^3} = \dfrac{r^{5-6}\,t^{6-3}}{2} = \underline{\underline{\dfrac{t^3}{2r}}}$

16. $\dfrac{(-r^3)(2r)^4}{(2r^{-2})^2} = \dfrac{-r^3(16r^4)}{4r^{-4}} = -4r^{3+4-(-4)} = \underline{\underline{-4r^{11}}}$

17. $\left(\dfrac{3a^3b^2}{a - b}\right)^4 = \underline{\underline{\dfrac{81a^{12}b^8}{(a - b)^4}}}$

Exercise 2.2 *(continued)*

18. $\left(\dfrac{3}{2x^2}\right)^2 \left(\dfrac{6x^3}{5^2}\right) \left(-\dfrac{x}{5}\right)^{-1} = \left(\dfrac{9}{4x^4}\right) \left(\dfrac{6x^3}{25}\right) \left(-\dfrac{5}{x}\right) = -\underline{\underline{\dfrac{27}{10x^2}}}$

19. $\dfrac{(-2y)^3(x^4)^{-2}}{(x^{-2})^2(4y)^2} = \dfrac{-8y^3(x^{-8})}{x^{-4}(16y^2)} = -\dfrac{yx^{-8-(-4)}}{2} = -\underline{\underline{\dfrac{y}{2x^4}}}$

20. $\dfrac{\left[(x^{\frac{1}{3}})(x^{\frac{2}{3}})x\right]^{\frac{3}{2}}}{(8x^3)^{\frac{2}{3}}} = \dfrac{(x^{\frac{1}{3}+\frac{2}{3}+1})^{\frac{3}{2}}}{4x^2} = \dfrac{(x^2)^{\frac{3}{2}}}{4x^2} = \dfrac{x^3}{4x^2} = \underline{\underline{\dfrac{x}{4}}}$

21. $8^{\frac{4}{3}} = (8^{\frac{1}{3}})^4 = 2^4 = \underline{\underline{16}}$

22. $-27^{\frac{2}{3}} = -(27^{\frac{1}{3}})^2 = \underline{\underline{-9}}$

23. $7^{\frac{3}{2}} = 7^{1.5} = \underline{\underline{18.5203}}$

24. $5^{-\frac{3}{4}} = 5^{-0.75} = \underline{\underline{0.299070}}$

25. $(0.001)^{-2} = \underline{\underline{1,000,000}}$

26. $0.893^{-\frac{1}{2}} = 0.893^{-0.5} = \underline{\underline{1.05822}}$

27. $(1.0085)^5(1.0085)^3 = (1.0085)^8 = \underline{\underline{1.07006}}$

28. $(1.005)^3(1.005)^{-6} = 1.005^{-3} = \underline{\underline{0.985149}}$

29. $\sqrt[3]{1.03} = 1.03^{0.\overline{3}} = \underline{\underline{1.00990}}$

30. $\sqrt[6]{1.05} = \underline{\underline{1.00816}}$

31. $(4^4)(3^{-3})\left(-\dfrac{3}{4}\right)^3 = \dfrac{4^4}{3^3}\left(-\dfrac{3^3}{4^3}\right) = \underline{\underline{-4}}$

32. $\left[\left(-\dfrac{3}{4}\right)^2\right]^{-2} = \left(-\dfrac{3}{4}\right)^{-4} = \left(-\dfrac{4}{3}\right)^4 = \dfrac{256}{81} = \underline{\underline{3.16049}}$

33. $\left(\dfrac{2}{3}\right)^3\left(-\dfrac{3}{2}\right)^2\left(-\dfrac{3}{2}\right)^{-3} = \dfrac{2}{3}\left(-\dfrac{2}{3}\right)^3 = -\dfrac{16}{81} = \underline{\underline{-0.197531}}$

34. $\left(-\dfrac{2}{3}\right)^3 \div \left(\dfrac{3}{2}\right)^{-2} = \dfrac{\left(-\dfrac{2}{3}\right)^3}{\left(\dfrac{2}{3}\right)^2} = -\dfrac{2}{3} = \underline{\underline{-0.666667}}$

35. $\dfrac{1.03^{16} - 1}{0.03} = \underline{\underline{20.1569}}$

36. $\dfrac{(1.008\overline{3})^{30} - 1}{0.008\overline{3}} = \dfrac{0.2826960}{0.008333333} = \underline{\underline{33.9235}}$

Exercise 2.2 *(concluded)*

37. $\dfrac{1 - 1.0225^{-20}}{0.0225} = \dfrac{0.3591835}{0.0225} = \underline{\underline{15.9637}}$

38. $\dfrac{1 - (1.00\overline{6})^{-32}}{0.00\overline{6}} = \dfrac{0.1915410}{0.00\overline{6}} = \underline{\underline{28.7312}}$

39. $(1 + 0.0275)^{\frac{1}{3}} = \underline{\underline{1.00908}}$

40. $(1 + 0.055)^{\frac{1}{6}} - 1 = \underline{\underline{0.00896339}}$

Exercise 2.3

1. $10a + 10 = 12 + 9a$
   $10a - 9a = 12 - 10$
   $a = \underline{\underline{2}}$

2. $29 - 4y = 2y - 7$
   $36 = 6y$
   $y = \underline{\underline{6}}$

3. $0.5\,(x - 3) = 20$
   $x - 3 = 40$
   $x = \underline{\underline{43}}$

4. $\dfrac{1}{3}\,(x - 2) = 4$
   $x - 2 = 12$
   $x = \underline{\underline{14}}$

5. $\quad y = 192 + 0.04y$
   $0.96y = 192$
   $y = \dfrac{192}{0.96} = \underline{\underline{200}}$

6. $x - 0.025x = 341.25$
   $0.975x = 341.25$
   $x = \dfrac{341.25}{0.975} = \underline{\underline{350}}$

7. $12x - 4(2x - 1) = 6(x + 1) - 3$
   $12x - 8x + 4 = 6x + 6 - 3$
   $-2x = -1$
   $x = \underline{\underline{0.5}}$

8. $3y - 4 = 3(y + 6) - 2(y + 3)$
   $\qquad = 3y + 18 - 2y - 6$
   $2y = 16$
   $y = \underline{\underline{8}}$

9. $8 - 0.5(x + 3) = 0.25(x - 1)$
    $8 - 0.5x - 1.5 = 0.25x - 0.25$
    $-0.75x = -6.75$
    $x = \underline{\underline{9}}$

10. $5(2 - c) = 10(2c - 4) - 6(3c + 1)$
    $10 - 5c = 20c - 40 - 18c - 6$
    $-7c = -56$
    $c = \underline{\underline{8}}$

11. $3.1t + 145 = 10 + 7.6t$
    $-4.5t = -135$
    $t = \underline{\underline{30}}$

12. $1.25y - 20.5 = 0.5y - 11.5$
    $0.75y = 9$
    $y = \underline{\underline{12}}$

13. $\dfrac{x}{1.1^2} + 2x(1.1)^3 = \$1000$

    $0.8264463x + 2.622x = \$1000$
    $3.488446x = \$1000$
    $x = \underline{\underline{\$286.661}}$

14. $\dfrac{3x}{1.025^6} + x(1.025)^8 = \$2641.35$

    $2.586891x + 1.218403x = \$2641.35$
    $x = \underline{\underline{\$694.125}}$

15. $\dfrac{2x}{1.03^7} + x + x\,(1.03^{10}) = \$1000 + \dfrac{\$2000}{1.03^4}$

    $1.626183x + x + 1.343916x = \$1000 + \$1776.974$
    $3.970099x = \$2776.974$
    $x = \underline{\underline{\$699.472}}$

16. $x(1.05)^3 + \$1000 + \dfrac{x}{1.05^7} = \dfrac{\$5000}{1.05^2}$

    $1.157625x + 0.7106813x = \$4535.147 - \$1000$
    $x = \underline{\underline{\$1892.17}}$

17. $x\left(1 + 0.095 \times \dfrac{84}{365}\right) + \dfrac{2x}{1 + 0.095 \times \dfrac{108}{365}} = \$1160.20$

    $1.021863x + 1.945318x = \$1160.20$
    $2.967181x = \$1160.20$
    $x = \underline{\underline{\$391.011}}$

Exercise 2.3 *(concluded)*

18. $$\frac{x}{1 + 0.115 \times \frac{78}{365}} + 3x\left(1 + 0.115 \times \frac{121}{365}\right) = \$1000\left(1 + 0.115 \times \frac{43}{365}\right)$$

$$0.9760141x + 3.114370x = \$1013.548$$
$$x = \underline{\$247.788}$$

Exercise 2.4

1. Step 2: Current CPI = 134.4 $\left(\text{after an increase of } \frac{1}{14}\right)$. Let last year's CPI be I.

   Step 3: Current CPI = Previous CPI + $\frac{1}{14}$ (Previous CPI)

   Step 4: $134.4 = I + \frac{1}{14} \cdot I = \frac{15}{14} I$

   Step 5: Multiply both sides by $\frac{14}{15}$. $I = 134.4 \times \frac{14}{15} = \underline{125.44}$

   The index one year ago was 125.44.

2. Step 2: Retail price = \$295.20. Markup = $\frac{4}{5}$ of cost. Let the wholesale cost be C.

   Step 3: Retail price = Cost + $\frac{4}{5}$ (Cost)

   Step 4: $\$295.20 = C + 0.8\ C$

   Step 5: $\$295.20 = 1.8\ C$

   $C = \frac{\$295.20}{1.8} = \underline{\$164.00}$. The wholesale cost is \$164.00.

3. Step 2: Tag price = \$39.95 (including 7% GST). Let the plant's pretax price be P.

   Step 3: Tag price = Pretax price + GST

   Step 4: $\$39.95 = P + 0.07\ P$

   Step 5: $\$39.95 = 1.07\ P$

   $P = \frac{\$39.95}{1.07} = \$37.34$. The amount of GST is $\$39.95 - \$37.34 = \underline{\$2.61}$

4. Step 2: Commission rate = 2.5% on first \$5000 and 1.5% on remainder
   Commission amount = \$227. Let the transaction amount be x

   Step 3: Commission amount = 0.025 (\$5000) + 0.015 (Remainder)

   Step 4: $\$227 = \$125.00 + 0.015\ (x - \$5000)$

   Step 5: $\$102 = 0.015x - \$75.00$
   $\$102 + \$75 = 0.015x$

   $x = \frac{\$177}{0.015} = \underline{\$11,800}$. The amount of the transaction was \$11,800.

Exercise 2.4 *(continued)*

5. **Step 2:** Let the basic price be P. First 20 meals at P.
   Next 20 meals at P − $2. Additional meals at P − $3.

   Step 3: Total price for 73 meals = $810.

   Step 4: $20P + 20 (P - \$2) + (73 - 40) (P - 3) = \$810$.

   Step 5: $20P + 20P - \$40 + 33P - \$99 = \$810$.
   $73P = \$810 + \$99 + \$40$

   $P = \dfrac{\$949}{73} = \underline{\$13.00}$ The basic price per meal is $13.00.

6. **Step 2:** Total bill = $1655. Total hours = 41.
   Hourly rate = $60 for CGA
   $= \$25$ for technician Let x represent the CGA's hours.

   Step 3: Total bill = (CGA hours × CGA rate)
   $+ \text{(Technician hours} \times \text{Technician rate)}$

   Step 4: $\$1655 = x(\$60) + (41 - x)\$25$

   Step 5: $1655 = 60x + 1025 - 25x$
   $630 = 35x$
   $x = \underline{\underline{18}}$

   The CGA performed 18 hours and the technician $41 - 18 = \underline{\underline{23}}$ hours of work.

7. **Step 2:** 24-roll charge = $9.50
   36-roll charge = $1.5(\$9.50) - \$2.00 = \$12.25$
   Number of rolls = 36. Total charges = $288.50
   Let n represent the number of 24-exposure rolls.

   Step 3: Total charges = (Number of 24 exposure rolls × 24-roll charge)
   $+ \text{(Number of 36 exposure rolls} \times \text{36-roll charge)}$

   Step 4: $\$288.50 = n(\$9.50) + (24-n)(\$12.25)$

   Step 5: $\$288.50 = 9.5n + 294 - 12.25n$
   $-5.50 = -2.75n$
   $n = \underline{\underline{2}}$

   There were two 24-exposure rolls and $24 - 2 = \underline{\underline{22}}$ 36-exposure rolls.

8. **Step 2:** Total bonus = $12,000
   A's bonus = 2 (B's bonus) − $1500. Let B represent B manager's bonus

   Step 3: Total bonus = A's bonus + B's bonus

   Step 4: $\$12,000 = 2B - \$1500 + B$

   Step 5: $\$13,500 = 3B$
   $B = \underline{\underline{\$4500}}$

   B's manager should receive $4500 and A's manager should receive
   $\$12,000 - \$4500 = \underline{\underline{\$7500}}$.

Exercise 2.4 *(continued)*

9. Step 2: Total investment = $34,000

Sue's investment = $\frac{3}{5}$ (Joan's investment) + $2000. Let J represent Joan's invesment.

Step 3: Total investment = Sue's investment + Joan's investment

Step 4: $34,000 = $\frac{3}{5}$J + $2000 + J

Step 5: $32,000 = 1.6J
J = $20,000

Joan will invest $20,000 and Sue will invest $34,000 – $20,000 = $14,000.

10. Step 2: Sven's share = 1.4(Robert's share) – $10,000
Net income = $88,880
Let R represent Robert's share

Step 3: Total distributed = Robert's share + Sven's share

Step 4: $88,880 = R + 1.4R – $10,000

Step 5: $98,880 = 2.4R
R = $41,200

Robert should have received $41,200 and Sven the remaining $88,880 – $41,200 = $47,680.

11. Step 2: Time to make X = 20 minutes
Time to make Y = 30 minutes
Total time = 47 hours. Total units = 120. Let Y represent the number of units of Y.

Step 3: Total time = (Number of X × Time for X) + (Number of Y × Time for Y)

Step 4: 47 × 60 = (120 – Y)20 + Y(30)

Step 5: 2820 = 2400 – 20Y + 30Y
420 = 10Y
Y = 42

Forty-two units of product Y were manufactured.

12. Step 2: Price of red ticket = $9.50. Price of blue ticket = $12.75.
Total tickets = 4460. Total revenue = $46,725.
Let the number of tickets in the red section be R.

Step 3: Total revenue = (Number of red × Price of red) + (Number of blue × Price of blue)

Step 4: $46,725 = R($9.50) + (4460 – R)$12.75

Step 5: 46,725 = 9.5R + 56,865 – 12.75R
3.25R = 10,140
R = 3120

3120 seats were sold in the red and 4460 – 3120 = 1340 seats were sold in the blue.

13. Step 2: Each of 4 children receive 0.5 (Wife's share).
    Each of 13 grandchildren receive $0.\overline{3}$ (Child's share)
    Total distribution = $759,000. Let w represent the wife's share.

    Step 3: Total amount = Wife's share + 4(Child's share) + 13(Grandchild's share)

    Step 4: $759,000 = w + 4(0.5w) + 13(0.\overline{3})(0.5w)$

    Step 5: $759,000 = w + 2w + 2.1\overline{6}w$
    $$= 5.1\overline{6}w$$
    $$w = \$146,903.23$$

    Each child will receive 0.5($146,903.23) = $73,451.62

    and each grandchild will receive $0.\overline{3}$($73,451.62) = $24,483.87.

14. Step 2: Stage B workers = 1.6(Stage A workers)
    Stage C workers = 0.75(Stage B workers)
    Total workers = 114. Let A represent the number of Stage A workers.

    Step 3: Total workers = A workers + B workers + C workers

    Step 4: $114 = A + 1.6A + 0.75(1.6A)$

    Step 5: $114 = 3.8A$
    $$A = 30$$

    30 workers should be allocated to Stage A, 1.6(30) = 48 workers to Stage B, and 114 − 30 − 48 = 36 workers to Stage C.

15. Step 2: Hillside charge = 2(Barnett charge) − $1000
    Westside charge = Hillside charge + $2000
    Total charges = $27,600. Let B represent the Barnett charge.

    Step 3: Total charges = Barnett + Hillside + Westside

    Step 4: $27,600 = B + 2B − $1000 + 2B − $1000 + $2000

    Step 5: $= 5B$
    $$B = \$5520$$
    Hence, the Westside charge is 2($5520) − $1000 + $2000 = $12,040.

16. Step 2: Number of dimes = 2(Number of quarters) − 36
    Number of loonies = 0.5 (Number of dimes) + 17
    Total value = $123. Let Q represent the number of quarters.

    Step 3: Total value = $0.10 (Number of dimes) + $0.25(Number of quarters)
    $$+ \$1.00(\text{Number of loonies})$$
    $123 = \$0.10(2Q − 36) + \$0.25Q + \$1.00[0.5(2Q − 36) + 17]$
    $$= 0.2Q − 3.6 + 0.25Q + Q − 18 + 17$$
    $$= 1.45Q − 4.6$$
    $127.6 = 1.45Q$
    $$Q = 88$$
    Number of dimes = 2(88) − 36 = 140
    Number of loonies = 0.5(140) + 17 = 87
    Total number of coins = 88 + 140 + 87 = 315

Exercise 2.4 (concluded)

17. **Step 2:** Assembly time = 0.5(cutting time) + 2 minutes
    Painting time = 0.5(assembly time) + 0.5 minutes
    Total units = 72. Total time = 42 hours. Let C represent the cutting time.

    Step 3: Time to produce one toy = Cutting time + Assembly time + Painting time.

    Step 4: $\dfrac{42 \times 60}{72}$ = C + 0.5C + 2 + 0.5(0.5C + 2) + 0.5

    Step 5: 35 = 1.75C + 3.5
    C = <u>18 minutes</u>

    Cutting requires 18 minutes (per unit), assembly requires 0.5(18) + 2 = <u>11 minutes</u>, and painting requires 0.5(11) + 0.5 = <u>6 minutes</u>.

Exercise 2.5

1. $\%c = \dfrac{V_f - V_i}{V_i} \times 100\% = \dfrac{\$100 - \$95}{\$95} \times 100\% = \underline{\underline{5.26\%}}$

2. $\%c = \dfrac{\$95 - \$100}{\$100} \times 100\% = \underline{\underline{-5.00\%}}$

3. $\%c = \dfrac{135 \text{ kg} - 35 \text{ kg}}{35 \text{ kg}} \times 100\% = \underline{\underline{286\%}}$

4. $\%c = \dfrac{35 \text{ kg} - 135 \text{ kg}}{135 \text{ kg}} \times 100\% = \underline{\underline{-74.1\%}}$

5. $\%c = \dfrac{0.13 - 0.11}{0.11} \times 100\% = \underline{\underline{18.2\%}}$

6. $\%c = \dfrac{0.085 - 0.095}{0.095} \times 100\% = \underline{\underline{-10.5\%}}$

7. $V_f = V_i(1 + c) = \$134.39[1 + (-0.12)] = \$134.39(0.88) = \underline{\underline{\$118.26}}$

8. $V_f = 112g(1 + 1.12) = \underline{\underline{237.44g}}$

9. $V_f = 26.3cm(1 + 3.00) = \underline{\underline{105.2cm}}$

10. $V_f = 0.043[1 + (-0.30)] = \underline{\underline{0.0301}}$

11. $V_i = \dfrac{V_f}{1 + c} = \dfrac{\$75}{1 + 2.00} = \underline{\underline{\$25.00}}$

12. $V_i = \dfrac{\$75}{1+(-0.50)} = \underline{\underline{\$150.00}}$

13. Given: $V_i = \$90$, $V_f = \$100$

    $\%c = \dfrac{\$100 - \$90}{\$90} \times 100\% = \underline{\underline{11.1\%}}$

    $100 is 11.1% more than $90.

Exercise 2.5 *(continued)*

14. $\% \, c = \dfrac{V_f - V_i}{V_i} \times 100\% = \dfrac{\$100 - \$110}{\$110} \times 100\% = \underline{\underline{-9.09\%}}$

    $100 is 9.09% less than $110.

15. Given: $\%c = 25\%$, $V_f = \$100$

    $V_i = \dfrac{V_f}{1 + c} = \dfrac{\$100}{1 + 0.25} = \underline{\underline{\$80.00}}$

    $80.00 increased by 25% equals $100.00.

16. Given: $\%c = 7\%$, $V_f = \$52.43$

    $V_i = \dfrac{V_f}{1 + c} = \dfrac{\$52.43}{1 + 0.07} = \underline{\underline{\$49.00}}$

    $49.00 increased by 7% equals $52.43.

17. Given: $V_f = \$75$, $\%c = 75\%$

    $V_i = \dfrac{V_f}{1 + c} = \dfrac{\$75}{1 + 0.75} = \underline{\underline{\$42.86}}$

    $75 is 75% more than $42.86.

18. Given: $V_i = \$56$, $\%c = 65\%$

    $V_f = V_i(1 + c) = \$56(1.65) = \underline{\underline{\$92.40}}$

    $56 increased by 65% is $92.40.

19. Given: $V_i = \$759.00$, $V_f = \$754.30$

    $\%c = \dfrac{V_f - V_i}{V_i} \times 100\% = \dfrac{\$754.30 - \$759.00}{\$759.00} \times 100\% = \underline{\underline{-0.619\%}}$

    $754.30 is $\underline{0.619\%}$ less than $759.00.

20. Given: $V_i = 77{,}400$, $V_f = 77{,}787$

    $\%c = \dfrac{77{,}787 - 77{,}400}{77{,}400} \times 100\% = \underline{\underline{0.500\%}}$

    77,787 is 0.5% more than 77,400.

21. Given: $V_i = \$75$, $\%c = 75\%$

    $V_f = V_i(1 + c) = \$75(1 + 0.75) = \underline{\underline{\$131.25}}$

    $75.00 becomes $131.25 after an increase of 75%.

22. Given: $V_f = \$100$, $\%c = -10\%$

    $V_i = \dfrac{V_f}{1 + c} = \dfrac{\$100}{1 + (-0.10)} = \underline{\underline{\$111.11}}$

    $100.00 is 10% less than $111.11.

Exercise 2.5 *(continued)*

23. Given: $V_f = \$100$, $\%c = -20\%$

$$V_i = \frac{V_f}{1 + c} = \frac{\$100}{1 + (-0.20)} = \underline{\underline{\$125.00}}$$

$125 when reduced by 20% equals $100.

24. Given: $V_f = \$50$, $\%c = -25\%$

$$V_i = \frac{V_f}{1 + c} = \frac{\$50}{1 + (-0.25)} = \underline{\underline{\$66.67}}$$

$66.67 when reduced by 25% equals $50.

25. Given: $V_f = \$549$, $\%c = -16.\overline{6}\%$

$$V_i = \frac{V_f}{1 + c} = \frac{\$549}{1 + (-0.1\overline{6})} = \underline{\underline{\$658.80}}$$

$658.80 after a reduction of $16\frac{2}{3}\%$ equals $549.

26. Given: $V_i = \$900$, $\%c = -90\%$

$V_f = V_i(1 + c) = \$900[1 + (-0.9)] = \underline{\underline{\$90.00}}$

$900 decreased by 90% is $90.00.

27. Given: $V_i = \$102$, $\%c = -2\%$

$V_f = V_i(1 + c) = \$102(1 - 0.02) = \underline{\underline{\$99.96}}$

$102 decreased by 2% is $99.96.

28. Given: $V_i = \$102$, $\%c = -100\%$

$V_f = V_i(1 + c) = \$102[1 + (-1.00)] = \$102(0) = \underline{\underline{\$0.00}}$

Any positive amount decreased by 100% is zero.

29. Given: $V_i = \$250$, $V_f = \$750$

$$\%c = \frac{V_f - V_i}{V_i} \times 100\% = \frac{\$750 - \$250}{\$250} \times 100\% = \underline{\underline{200\%}}$$

$750 is 200% more than $250.

30. Given: $V_i = \$750$, $V_f = \$250$

$$\%c = \frac{\$250 - \$750}{\$750} \times 100\% = \underline{\underline{-66.7\%}}$$

$250 is 66.7% less than $750.

31. Given: $\%c = 0.75\%$, $V_i = \$10,000$

$V_f = V_i(1 + c) = \$10,000(1 + 0.0075) = \underline{\underline{\$10,075}}$

$10,000 increased by $\frac{3}{4}\%$ is $10,075.

Exercise 2.5 *(continued)*

32. Given: $V_i = \$1045$, $\%c = -0.5\%$

    $V_f = V_i(1 + c) = \$1045[1 + (-0.005)] = \underline{\$1039.78}$

    $1045 decreased by 0.5% is $1039.78.

33. Given: $\%c = 150\%$, $V_f = \$575$

    $$V_i = \frac{V_f}{1 + c} = \frac{\$575}{1 + 1.5} = \underline{\$230.00}$$

    $230 increased by 150% equals $575.

34. Given: $\%c = 210\%$, $V_f = \$465$

    $$V_i = \frac{V_f}{1 + c} = \frac{\$465}{1 + 2.1} = \underline{\$150.00}$$

    $150 increased by 210% equals $465.

35. Given: $V_i = \$150$, $\%c = 150\%$

    $V_f = V_i(1 + c) = \$150(1 + 1.5) = \underline{\$375.00}$

    $150 increased by 150% is $375.

36. Given: $V_i = \$10$, $\%c = 900\%$

    $V_f = V_i(1 + c) = \$10(1 + 9.00) = \underline{\$100.00}$

    $10 increased by 900% is $100.

37. Given: $V_f = \$148.35$, $\%c = 15\%$

    $$V_i = \frac{V_f}{1 + c} = \frac{\$148.35}{1.15} = \underline{\$129.00}$$

    The coat's ticket price was $129.00.

38. Given: $\%c = 24\%$, $V_f = 109,500$

    $$V_i = \frac{V_f}{1 + c} = \frac{109,500}{1.24} = \underline{88,306}$$

    The population 5 years ago was 88,306.

39. a. Given: $V_i = 32,400$, $V_f = 27,450$

    $$\%c = \frac{V_f - V_i}{V_i} \times 100\% = \frac{27,450 - 32,400}{32,400} \times 100\% = \underline{-15.3\%}$$

    The number of hammers sold declined by 15.3%.

    b. Given: $V_i = \$7.55$, $V_f = \$7.75$

    $$\%c = \frac{\$7.75 - \$7.55}{\$7.55} \times 100\% = \underline{2.65\%}$$

    The average selling price increased by 2.65%.

Exercise 2.5 *(continued)*

c. 1996 revenue = 32,400 ($7.55) = $244,620
1997 revenue = 27,450 ($7.75) = $212,737.50

$$\%c = \frac{\$212{,}737.50 - \$244{,}620}{\$244{,}620} \times 100\% = \underline{\underline{-13.0\%}}$$

The revenue decreased by 13.0%.

40. a. Given: V_i = $0.55, V_f = $1.55

$$\%c = \frac{V_f - V_i}{V_i} \times 100\% = \frac{\$1.55 - \$0.55}{\$0.55} \times 100\% = \underline{\underline{182\%}}$$

The share price rose by 182% in the first year.

b. Given: V_i = $1.55, V_f = $0.75

$$\%c = \frac{\$0.75 - \$1.55}{\$1.55} \times 100\% = \underline{\underline{-51.6\%}}$$

The share price declined by 51.6% in the second year.

c. Given: V_i = $0.55, V_f = $0.75

$$\%c = \frac{\$0.75 - \$0.55}{\$0.55} \times 100\% = \underline{\underline{36.4\%}}$$

The share price rose by 36.4% over two years.

41. Given: V_f = 599, %c = 6%

$$V_i = \frac{V_f}{1 + c} = \frac{599}{1.06} = \underline{\underline{565}}$$

565 units were sold in the previous quarter.

42. Given: V_f = $122.85, %c = −35%

$$V_i = \frac{V_f}{1 + c} = \frac{\$122.85}{1 + (-0.35)} = \underline{\underline{\$189.00}}$$

The regular price was $189.00.

43. Given: For 1995, $V_f - V_i$ = −$1.00, V_f = $4.00
For 1996, $V_f - V_i$ = −$1.00, V_i = $4.00

$$\%c(1995) = \frac{V_f - V_i}{V_i} \times 100\% = \frac{-\$1.00}{\$5.00} \times 100\% = \underline{\underline{-20\%}}$$

$$\%c(1996) = \frac{-\$1.00}{\$4.00} \times 100\% = \underline{\underline{-25\%}}$$

The share price fell by 20% in 1995 and 25% in 1996.

44. Given: V_f = $100, %c = −27%

$$V_i = \frac{V_f}{1 + c} = \frac{\$100}{1 - 0.27} = \underline{\underline{\$136.99}}$$

The suggested retail price is $136.99.

Exercise 2.5 *(continued)*

45. Given: $V_f = \$4.360$ million, $\%c = 18\%$

$$V_i = \frac{V_f}{1 + c} = \frac{\$4.360 \text{ million}}{1 + 0.18} = \$3.695 \text{ million}$$

The dollar amount of the revenue increase is $V_f - V_i = (\$4.360 - \$3.695)$ million $= \underline{\$665,000}$.

46. Given: $V_i = 7\%$, $V_f = 8\%$

$$\%c = \frac{V_f - V_i}{V_i} \times 100\% = \frac{8\% - 7\%}{7\%} \times 100\% = \underline{14.3\%}$$

Commission income will increase by 14.3%.

47. Given: $V_i = 10.5\%$, $V_f = 9.75\%$

$$\%c = \frac{V_f - V_i}{V_i} \times 100\% = \frac{9.75 - 10.5}{10.5} \times 100\% = \underline{-7.14\%}$$

The amount of interest is reduced by 7.14%.

48. Given: $V_f = \$1.30$, $\%c = 280\%$

$$V_i = \frac{V_f}{1 + c} = \frac{\$1.30}{1 + 2.8} = \$0.34$$

The price increase is $V_f - V_i = \$1.30 - \$0.34 = \underline{\$0.96}$ per litre.

49. Given: $V_f = \$0.45$, $\%c = 76\%$

$$V_i = \frac{V_f}{1 + c} = \frac{\$0.45}{1 + (-0.76)} = \$1.88$$

Price decline $= V_i - V_f = \$1.88 - \$0.45 = \underline{\$1.43}$. The share price dropped by \$1.43.

50. Given: $V_f = \$24,300$, $\%c = -55\%$

$$V_i = \frac{V_f}{1 + c} = \frac{\$24,300}{1 + (-0.55)} = \$54,000$$

The amount of depreciation is $\$54,000 - \$24,300 = \underline{\$29,700}$.

51. Given: For appreciation, V_i = Purchase price, $\%c = 140\%$, V_f = List price
    For price reduction, V_i = List price, $\%c = -10\%$, $V_f = \$172,800$

$$\text{List price} = \frac{V_f}{1 + c} = \frac{\$172,800}{1 + (-0.1)} = \$192,000$$

$$\text{Original purchase price} = \frac{V_f}{1 + c} = \frac{\$192,000}{1 + 1.4} = \underline{\underline{\$80,000}}$$

The owner originally paid \$80,000 for the property.

Exercise 2.5 *(concluded)*

52. Given: For markup, $V_i = $ Cost, $\%c = 22\%$, $V_f = $ List price

    For markdown, $V_i = $ List price, $\%c = -10\%$, $V_f = \$17{,}568$

$$\text{List price} = \frac{V_f}{1 + c} = \frac{\$17{,}568}{1 + (-0.10)} = \$19{,}520$$

$$\text{Cost (to dealer)} = \frac{V_f}{1 + c} = \frac{\$19{,}520}{1 + 0.22} = \underline{\$16{,}000}$$

The dealer paid $16,000 for the car.

Exercise 2.6

Problem	$\%Y$ $\dfrac{Y}{V_i} \times 100\%$	$\%G$ $\dfrac{V_f - V_i}{V_i} \times 100\%$	$\%ROI$ $\%Y + \%G$
1.	$\dfrac{\$10}{\$100} \times 100\% = \underline{10\%}$	$\dfrac{\$110 - \$100}{\$100} \times 100\% = \underline{10\%}$	$10\% + 10\% = \underline{20\%}$
2.	$\dfrac{\$10}{\$100} \times 100\% = \underline{10\%}$	$\dfrac{\$90 - \$100}{\$100} \times 100\% = \underline{-10\%}$	$10\% - 10\% = \underline{0\%}$
3.	$\dfrac{\$10}{\$90} \times 100\% = \underline{11.11\%}$	$\dfrac{\$86 - \$90}{\$90} \times 100\% = \underline{-4.44\%}$	$\underline{6.67\%}$
4.	0%	$\dfrac{\$151 - \$135}{\$135} \times 100\% = \underline{11.85\%}$	$\underline{11.85\%}$
5.	$\dfrac{\$141}{\$1367} \times 100\% = \underline{10.31\%}$	$\dfrac{\$1141 - \$1367}{\$1367} \times 100\% = \underline{-16.53\%}$	$\underline{-6.22\%}$
6.	$\dfrac{\$280}{\$879} \times 100\% = \underline{31.85\%}$	$\dfrac{\$1539 - \$879}{\$879} \times 100\% = \underline{75.09\%}$	$\underline{106.94\%}$
7.	$\dfrac{\$200}{\$2500} \times 100\% = \underline{8.00\%}$	$\dfrac{\$0 - \$2500}{\$2500} \times 100\% = \underline{-100\%}$	$\underline{-92.00\%}$
8.	$\dfrac{\$250}{\$1380} \times 100\% = \underline{18.12\%}$	$\dfrac{\$2875 - \$1380}{\$1380} \times 100\% = \underline{108.33\%}$	$\underline{126.45\%}$

9. Given: $V_i = \$2000$, $V_f = \$2200$, $\%Y = 5\%$

   To obtain Y, rearrange $\%Y = \dfrac{Y}{V_i} \times 100\%$ to isolate Y

$$Y = \frac{\%Y}{100\%} \times V_i = \frac{5\%}{100\%} \times \$2000 = \underline{\$100.00}$$

$$\%G = \frac{V_f - V_i}{V_i} \times 100\% = \frac{\$2200 - \$2000}{\$2000} \times 100\% = \underline{10.00\%}$$

$$\%ROI = \%Y + \%G = 5\% + 10\% = \underline{15.00\%}$$

Exercise 2.6 *(continued)*

10. Given: $V_i = \$4300$, $V_f = \$3950$, %ROI $= -5\%$

$$\%G = \frac{\$3950 - \$4300}{\$4300} \times 100\% = -8.1395\% = \underline{-8.14\%}$$

$$\%Y = \%ROI - \%G = -5\% - (-8.1395\%) = 3.1395\% = \underline{3.14\%}$$

$$Y = \frac{\%Y}{100\%} \times V_i = 0.031395 \times \$4300 = \underline{\$135.00}$$

11. Given: $V_i = \$3730$, $Y = \$250$, %ROI $= 5\%$

$$\%Y = \frac{Y}{V_i} \times 100\% = \frac{\$250}{\$3730} \times 100\% = 6.7024\% = \underline{6.70\%}$$

$$\%G = \%ROI - \%Y = 5\% - 6.7024\% = -1.7024\% = \underline{-1.70\%}$$

$$G = \frac{\%G}{100\%} \times V_i = -0.017024 \times \$3730 = -\$63.50$$

$$V_f = V_i + G = \$3730 + (-\$63.50) = \underline{\$3666.50}$$

12. Given: $V_i = \$1800$, $Y = \$50$, %G $= 150\%$

$$G = \frac{\%G}{100\%} \times V_i = 1.5 \times \$1800 = \$2700$$

$$V_f = V_i + G = \$1800 + \$2700 = \underline{\$4500.00}$$

$$\%Y = \frac{Y}{V_i} \times 100\% = \frac{\$50}{\$1800} \times 100\% = \underline{2.78\%}$$

$$\%ROI = \%Y + \%G = 2.78\% + 150\% = \underline{152.78\%}$$

13. Given: $V_f = \$1800$, %G $= -40\%$, %ROI $= -30\%$

$$\%Y = \%ROI - \%G = -30\% - (-40\%) = \underline{10.00\%}$$

$$V_i = \frac{V_f}{1 + c} = \frac{\$1800}{1 + (-0.4)} = \underline{\$3000.00}$$

$$Y = \frac{\%Y}{100\%} \times V_i = 0.10 \times \$3000 = \underline{\$300.00}$$

14. Given: $Y = \$100$, %Y $= 5\%$, %G $= 15\%$

$$V_i = \frac{100\%}{\%Y} \times Y = \frac{100\%}{5\%} \times \$100 = \underline{\$2000.00}$$

$$G = \frac{\%G}{100\%} \times V_i = \frac{15\%}{100\%} \times \$2000 = \underline{\$300.00}$$

$$V_f = V_i + G = \$2000 + \$300 = \underline{\$2300.00}$$

$$\%ROI = \%Y + \%G = 5\% + 15\% = \underline{20.00\%}$$

Exercise 2.6 *(continued)*

15. Given: $V_i = \$1600$, $\%Y = 8\%$, $\%ROI = 0\%$

$$Y = \frac{\%Y}{100\%} \times V_i = 0.08 \times \$1600 = \underline{\$128.00}$$

Since $\%ROI = 0\%$, then $G = -Y$ and $\%G = -\%Y$.
Hence, $G = -\$128.00$, $\underline{\%G = -8.00\%}$, and $\underline{V_f} = V_i + G = \underline{\$1472.00}$

16. Given: $Y = \$150$, $V_f = \$2700$, $\%ROI = 80\%$

$$\%ROI = \frac{Y + G}{V_i} \times 100\%$$

$$80\% = \frac{\$150 + (V_f - V_i)}{V_i} \times 100\%$$

$$0.80V_i = \$150 + (\$2700 - V_i)$$
$$1.80V_i = \$2850$$

$$V_i = \frac{\$2850}{1.80} = \underline{\$1583.33}$$

$$\%Y = \frac{Y}{V_i} \times 100\% = \frac{\$150}{\$1583.33} \times 100\% = \underline{9.47\%}$$

$$\%G = \%ROI - \%Y = \underline{70.53\%}$$

17. a. $\%Y = \dfrac{Y}{V_i} \times 100\% = \dfrac{2(\$47.50)}{\$1000} \times 100\% = \underline{9.50\%}$

   b. $\%G = \dfrac{G}{V_i} \times 100\% = \dfrac{\$1034 - \$1000}{\$1000} \times 100\% = \underline{3.40\%}$

   c. $ROI = 10(Y + G) = 10(\$95 + \$34) = \underline{\$1290.00}$

   d. $\%ROI = \%Y + \%G = 9.50\% + 3.40\% = \underline{12.90\%}$

18. For the 18-month holding period, $Y = 3(\$42.50) = \$127.50$ per bond and
    $G = V_f - V_i = \$980 - \$1025 = -\$45$ per bond.

   a. $\%G = \dfrac{-\$45}{\$1025} \times 100\% = \underline{-4.39\%}$

   b. $ROI = 15(Y + G) = 15(\$127.50 - \$45) = \underline{\$1237.50}$

   c. $\%ROI = \dfrac{ROI}{V_i} \times 100\% = \dfrac{\$127.50 - \$45}{\$1025} \times 100\% = \underline{8.05\%}$

19. For the 9-month holding period, $Y = 3(\$0.50) = \$1.50$ and
    $G = \$15.25 - \$13.50 = \$1.75$ per share.

   $$\%ROI = \frac{Y + G}{V_i} \times 100\% = \frac{\$1.50 + \$1.75}{\$13.50} \times 100\% = \underline{24.07\%}$$

Exercise 2.6 *(continued)*

20. Given: $V_i = \$29.37$, $Y = \$0.60$, $V_f = \$24.50$ per share after 3 months.

    a. $\%G = \dfrac{V_f - V_i}{V_i} \times 100\% = \dfrac{\$24.50 - \$29.37}{\$29.37} \times 100\% = \underline{\underline{-16.58\%}}$

    b. $\%ROI = \%G + \%Y = -16.58\% + \dfrac{\$0.60}{\$29.37} \times 100\% = \underline{\underline{-14.54\%}}$

21. Given: $V_i = \$75,000 + \$15,000 = \$90,000$
    $Y = 10(\$700) - \$1550 = \$5450$ for the year.

    a. If $V_f = \$110,000$, then $G = \$110,000 - \$90,000 = \$20,000$ and

    $\%ROI = \dfrac{Y + G}{V_i} \times 100\% = \dfrac{\$5450 + \$20,000}{\$90,000} \times 100\% = \underline{\underline{28.28\%}}$

    b. The selling commission is $0.06 \times \$110,000 = \$6600$.
    Net of the commission, $G = \$20,000 - \$6600 = \$13,400$

    $\%ROI = \dfrac{\$5450 + \$13,400}{\$90,000} \times 100\% = \underline{\underline{20.94\%}}$

22. Net income, $Y = 12(\$575 + \$550) - \$2173 - \$10,127 = \$1200$
    Capital gain, $G = \$170,000 - \$160,000 = \$10,000$
    Initial personal investment, $V_i = \$40,000$

    $\%ROI = \dfrac{G + Y}{V_i} \times 100\% = \dfrac{\$10,000 + \$1200}{\$40,000} \times 100\% = \underline{\underline{28.00\%}}$

23. Given: $V_i = \$5000 + 400 = \$12.50$ per unit. $\%ROI = 22\%$, $V_f = \$13.75$.

    $Y + G = \dfrac{\%ROI}{100\%} \times V_i = 0.22 \times \$12.50 = \$2.75$

    Since $G = V_f - V_i = \$13.75 - \$12.50 = \$1.25$,
    then $Y = \$2.75 - \$1.25 = \underline{\$1.50 \text{ per unit}}$.

    The fund distributed $1.50 per unit during the year.

24. Given: $V_i = \$1090$, $Y = 2(\$50) = \$100$, $\%ROI = 12\%$

    $Y + G = \dfrac{\%ROI}{100\%} \times V_i = 0.12 \times \$1090 = \$130.80$

    Hence, $G = \$130.80 - Y = \$130.80 - \$100 = \$30.80$ and
    $V_f = V_i + G = \$1090 + \$30.80 = \underline{\$1120.80}$.

    A price of $1120.80 in one year would make $\%ROI = 12\%$.

Exercise 2.6 *(concluded)*

25. Given: $\%G = -8\%$, $\%ROI = 1\%$, $Y = 2(\$52.50) = \$105.00$

    $\%Y = \%ROI - \%G = 1\% - (-8\%) = 9\%$

    $$V_i = \frac{100\%}{\%Y} \times Y = \frac{100\%}{9\%} \times \$105 = \$1166.67$$

    $$G = \frac{\%G}{100\%} \, V_i = -0.08 \times \$1166.67 = -\$93.33$$

    Current price, $V_f = V_i + G = \$1166.67 - \$93.33 = \underline{\$1073.34}$

26. Given: $\%ROI = 55\%$, $Y = \$0.72$, $V_f = \$37.50$

    $$\%ROI = \frac{Y + G}{V_i} \times 100\% = \frac{Y + (V_f - V_i)}{V_i} \times 100\%$$

    $$55\% = \frac{\$0.72 + (\$37.50 - V_i)}{V_i} \times 100\%$$

    $$0.55 \, V_i = \$38.22 - V_i$$

    $$V_i = \frac{\$38.22}{1.55} = \underline{\$24.66}$$

    The share price one year ago was $24.66.

27. Given: $G = 0.06 \times \$230,000 = \$13,800$

    $\quad\quad\quad$ $Y = 12(\text{Monthly rental}) - \$12,400 - 12(\$300) - \$2400$

    $\quad\quad\quad$ Required $\%ROI = 15\%$

    $\quad\quad\quad$ Ed's investment, $V_i = 40\%$ of $\$230,000 = \$92,000$

    $$\%G = \frac{G}{V_i} \times 100\% = \frac{\$13,800}{\$92,000} \times 100\% = 15.0\%$$

    Required $\%Y = $ Required $\%ROI - \%G = 15\% - 15\% = 0\%$

    Hence $Y = 0$ and

    $\quad\quad$ $12(\text{Monthly rental}) = \$12,400 + \$3600 + \$2400$

    $$\text{Monthly rental} = \frac{\$18,400}{12} = \underline{\$1533.33}$$

    The monthly rental income would have to be $1533.33 for Ed's rate of return on equity to be 15%.

Exercise 2.7

1. Given: $c_1 = 0.05$, $c_2 = 0.03$, $c_3 = 0.01$, $V_i = \$15.00$

   The hourly wage after the three increases will be

   $$V_{f3} = V_i(1 + c_1)(1 + c_2)(1 + c_3) = \$15.00(1.05)(1.03)(1.01) = \underline{\$16.385/\text{hour}}$$

2. Given: $c_1,...,c_5 = 0.048, 0.056, 0.015, 0.018, 0.003$, $V_i = \$1000$

   The basket of goods costs

   $$V_{f5} = \$1000 \,(1.048)(1.056)(1.015)(1.018)(1.003) = \underline{\$1146.94} \text{ at the end of 1994.}$$

Exercise 2.7 *(continued)*

3. Given: $c_1,...,c_5 = 0.102, 0.124, 0.109, 0.057, 0.044$, $V_i = \$10.00/\text{hour}$

    To keep pace with the rising CPI, the hourly wage at the end of 1984 had to be

    $V_{f5} = \$10.00\ (1.102)(1.124)(1.109)(1.057)(1.044) = \underline{\underline{\$15.158/\text{hour}}}$

4. Given: $c_1,...,c_5 = 0.062, 1.003, 0.348, 0.704, 0.111$

    a. $V_{f5} = V_i(1.062)(2.003)(1.348)(1.704)(1.111) = 5.428\,V_i$

    $$\%c = \frac{V_{f5} - V_i}{V_i} \times 100\% = \frac{5.428\,V_i - V_i}{V_i} \times 100\% = \underline{\underline{442.8\%}}$$

    b. $V_{1994} = V_{1992}(1 + c_{1993})(1 + c_{1994})$
    $= \$67.3\ \text{billion}\,(1.704)(1.111)$
    $= \underline{\underline{\$127.4\ \text{billion}}}$

5. Given: $c_1 = c_2 = 0.25$

    $V_{f2} = V_i(1 + c_1)(1 + c_2) = V_i(1.25)^2 = 1.5625\,V_i$

    The percent increase over the entire two years was $\underline{\underline{56.25\%}}$

6. Given: $c_1 = c_2 = -0.25$

    $V_{f2} = V_i(1 - 0.25)^2 = 0.5625\,V_i$

    $$\%c = \frac{V_{f2} - V_i}{V_i} \times 100\% = \frac{0.5625\,V_i - V_i}{V_i} \times 100\% = \underline{\underline{-43.75\%}}$$

7. Given: $c_1 = 0.50, V_{f2} = V_i$

    Substitute in $V_{f2} = V_i(1 + c_1)(1 + c_2)$
    $$V_i = V_i(1.50)(1 + c_2)$$
    $$1 = 1.50(1 + c_2)$$

    $$c_2 = \frac{1}{1.5} - 1 = -0.3\bar{3} = \underline{\underline{-33.33\%}}$$

    A 33.33% decline in the second year will wipe out a 50% gain in the first year.

8. Given: $c_1 = 0.25, V_{f2} = V_i$
    Then $V_i = V_i(1.25)(1 + c_2)$

    $$c_2 = \frac{1}{1.25} - 1 = -0.20$$

    A $\underline{-20\%}$ return in the second year will nullify a 25% return in the first year.

9. Given: $c_1 = -0.50, V_{f2} = V_i$
    Substitute in $V_{f2} = V_i(1 + c_1)(1 + c_2)$
    $$V_i = V_i(1 - 0.5)(1 + c_2)$$

    $$c_2 = \frac{1}{0.5} - 1 = 1.00$$

    A $\underline{100\%}$ return in the second year is required to break even.

Exercise 2.7 (continued)

10. Given: $c_1 = -0.20$, $V_{f2} = V_i$

    Then $V_i = V_i(1 - 0.20)(1 + c_2)$

    $$c_2 = \frac{1}{0.8} - 1 = 0.25$$

    A **25%** return in the second year is required to break even.

11. Given: $c_1 = c_2 = 0.10$, $V_{f3} = 1.30V_i$

    Substitute in $V_{f3} = V_i(1 + c_1)(1 + c_2)(1 + c_3)$

    $$1.30V_i = V_i(1.10)(1.10)(1 + c_3)$$
    $$1.30 = 1.21(1 + c_3)$$
    $$c_3 = \frac{1.30}{1.21} - 1 = 0.0744$$

    A return of **7.44%** in the third year will produce a cumulative gain of 30%.

12. Given: $c_1 = c_2 = -0.10$, $V_{f3} = 0.70V_i$

    Then $0.70V_i = V_i(1 - 0.10)^2(1 + c_3)$

    $$0.70 = 0.81(1 + c_3)$$
    $$c_3 = \frac{0.70}{0.81} - 1 = -0.1358$$

    A return of **−13.58%** in the third year will produce a cumulative loss of 30%.

13. Given: $c_1 = 0.35$, $c_2 = 0.40$, $c_3 = 0.30$, $c_4 = 0.25$

    Then $V_{f4} = V_i(1.35)(1.40)(1.30)(1.25) = 3.07125V_i$

    $$\%c = \frac{V_{f4} - V_i}{V_i} \times 100\% = \frac{3.07125V_i - V_i}{V_i} \times 100\% = \underline{207.13\%}$$

    The cumulative percent increase was 207.13%.

14. Given: $c_1 = -0.10$, $c_2 = -0.06$, $c_3 = -0.05$, $V_i = 6750$

    Then $V_{3f} = 6750(1 - 0.10)(1 - 0.06)(1 - 0.05) = 5425$

    Hence $6750 - 5425 = \underline{1325}$ positions will be eliminated over the next three years.

15. Given: $c_1 = -0.20$, $c_2 = -0.40$, $c_3 = -0.60$, $V_i = \$1$ billion.

    a. Substitute in $V_{f3} = V_i(1 + c_1)(1 + c_2)(1 + c_3)$

    $$= \$1000 \text{ million}(1 - 0.20)(1 - 0.40)(1 - 0.60)$$
    $$= \underline{\$192 \text{ million}}$$

    The deficit will be $192 million after the third year.

    b. $V_{f2} = \$1000 \text{ million}(1 - 0.20)(1 - 0.40) = \$480$ million

    The projected decrease in the third year is $480 million − $192 million = $\underline{\$288 \text{ million}}$

Exercise 2.7 *(continued)*

16. Given: $V_i = \$400$, $c_1 = 0.10$, $c_2 = 0.22$, $c_3 = 0.18$, $V_{f4} = \$740$

    a. Solve for c_4 in

    $\$740 = \$400(1.10)(1.22)(1.18)(1 + c_4)$

    $\$740 = \$633.424(1 + c_4)$

    $c_4 = \dfrac{\$740}{\$633.424} - 1 = 0.1683$

    The fourth increase was 16.83%.

    b. The fourth increase was $\$740 - \$633.42 = \$106.58$.

17. After 10 years of 10% annual increases, $V_{f10} = V_i(1.10)^{10} = 2.5937 V_i$

    After 5 years of 20% increases and 5 years of 0% increases, $V_{f10} = V_i(1.20)^5 = 2.4883 V_i$

    The cumulative percent increase is 159.37% in the first case and 148.83% in the second.

    The constant 10% increases produce a 10.54% higher cumulative increase.

18. Given: $V_{f4} = \$47,567$, $c_1 = 0.154$, $c_2 = 0.243$, $c_3 = 0.321$, $c_4 = -0.033$

    a. $V_i = \dfrac{\$47,567}{(1.154)(1.243)(1.321)(1 - 0.033)} = \dfrac{\$47,567}{1.8323407} = \$25,959.69$

    Victor's original investment was $\$25,959.69$.

    b. The dollar amount of the increase in the third year was

    $c_3 V_{f2} = c_3 V_i(1 + c_1)(1 + c_2) = 0.321(\$25,959.69)(1.154)(1.243) = \$11,953.13$

    The value of the fund increased by $\$11,953.13$ in year 3.

19. Given: $c_1 = -0.09$, $c_2 = -0.07$, $c_3 = -0.05$, $V_i = 18,750$

    a. Substitute in $V_{f3} = V_i(1 + c_1)(1 + c_2)(1 + c_3) = 18,750(0.91)(0.93)(0.95) = 15,075$

    The company will have 15,075 employees after the third year.

    b. The number of employees cut in the second year will be 7% of the employees remaining after the first year.

    Number cut $= 0.07 V_{f1} = 0.07(V_i)(1 + c_1) = 0.07(18,750)(0.91) = 1194$.

20. Given: $c_1 = -0.045$, $c_2 = -0.067$, $c_3 = -0.105$, $V_{f3} = 7450$

    a. The number of people in the town at the beginning of 1979 was

    $V_i = \dfrac{7450}{(1 - 0.045)(1 - 0.067)(1 - 0.105)} = 9342$

    b. $V_{f1} = 9342(1 - 0.045) = 8922$

    $V_{f2} = V_{f1}(1 - 0.067) = 8922(0.933) = 8324$

Period	Population loss
1979-1983	$9342 - 8922 = 420$
1984-1988	$8922 - 8324 = 598$
1989-1993	$8324 - 7450 = 874$

Exercise 2.7 *(continued)*

21. Given: $c_1 = -0.053$, $c_2 = -0.104$, three-year change $= -0.22$

$$V_{f3} = V_i(1 - 0.22)$$
$$= V_i(1 - 0.053)(1 - 0.104)(1 + c_3)$$

Hence, $0.78\,V_i = V_i(0.947)(0.896)(1 + c_3)$

$$1 + c_3 = \frac{0.78}{(0.947)(0.896)}$$

$$c_3 = 0.9193 - 1 = -0.0807$$

The decrease in 1992 was <u>8.07%</u>

22. Given: $c_1 = -0.0164$, $c_2 = -0.0395$, $c_3 = -0.0159$, $V_{f3} = 18{,}286$

a. $V_i = \dfrac{18{,}286}{(1 - 0.0164)(1 - 0.0395)(1 - 0.0159)} = \underline{\underline{19{,}668}}$

The Nikkei Average stood at 19,668 at the opening of the market on March 31.

b. The loss on April 1 was 3.95% of the closing average on March 31.

That is $0.0395\,V_{f1} = 0.0395(19{,}668)(1 - 0.0164) = \underline{764\ \text{points}}$

The Nikkei Average fell 764 points on April 1, 1992.

23. Given: $c_1 = -0.35$, $c_2 = -0.55$, $c_3 = -0.80$, $V_{f3} = \$0.75$

a. The share price at the beginning of the three years was

$$V_i = \frac{V_{f3}}{(1 + c_1)(1 + c_2)(1 + c_3)} = \frac{\$0.75}{(1 - 0.35)(1 - 0.55)(1 - 0.80)} = \underline{\underline{\$12.82}}$$

b. The drop in the share price in the third year was 80% of the price at the end of the second year.

Hence, Price drop $= 0.80\,V_{f2} = 0.80(\$12.82)(1 - 0.35)(1 - 0.55) = \underline{\underline{\$3.00}}$

NOTE: Problems 24 to 28 all require the calculation of the five-year percent increase in the TSE 300 Total Return Index. An investment of V_i in the TSE 300 portfolio at the beginning of 1990 would have grown to

$$V_{f5} = V_i(1 + c_1)(1 + c_2)(1 + c_3)(1 + c_4)(1 + c_5)$$
$$= V_i(1 - 0.148)(1 + 0.12)(1 - 0.014)(1 + 0.326)(1 - 0.002)$$
$$= 1.2451\,V_i$$

by the end of 1994. Therefore, its value increased by 24.51%.

24. The value at the end of 1994 of an initial investment of V_i in the Altamira Equity fund was

$V_{f5} = V_i(1 - 0.018)(1 + 0.345)(1 + 0.302)(1 + 0.466)(1 + 0.017) = 2.5639\,V_i$. Therefore, the increase in value was <u>156.39%</u> which was $156.39\% - 24.51\%^* = \underline{131.88\%\ \text{better}}$ than the TSE 300 Total Return Index.

*See the preceding note.

Exercise 2.7 *(concluded)*

25. The value at the end of 1994 of an initial investment of V_i in the AGF Canadian Equity fund was
$V_{f5} = V_i(1 - 0.20)(1 + 0.092)(1 + 0.026)(1 + 0.304)(1 - 0.084) = 1.0706V_i$. Therefore, the increase in value was <u>7.06%</u> which was 24.51%* − 7.06% = <u>17.45% worse</u> than the TSE 300 Total Return Index.
*See the note following problem 23.

26. The value at the end of 1994 of an initial investment of V_i in the Industrial Growth fund was
$V_{f5} = V_i(1 - 0.15)(1 + 0.023)(1 - 0.048)(1 + 0.469)(1 - 0.014) = 1.1990V_i$. Therefore, the increase in value was <u>19.90%</u> which was 24.51%* − 19.90% = <u>4.61% worse</u> than the TSE 300 Total Return Index.
*See the note following problem 23.

27. The value at the end of 1994 of an initial investment of V_i in the Royfund Equity fund was
$V_{f5} = V_i(1 - 0.147)(1 + 0.017)(1 + 0.028)(1 + 0.318)(1 - 0.004) = 1.1707V_i$. Therefore, the increase in value was <u>17.07%</u> which was 24.51%* − 17.07% = <u>7.44% worse</u> than the TSE 300 Total Return Index.
*See the note following problem 23.

28. The value at the end of 1994 of an initial investment of V_i in the Trimark Canadian fund was
$V_{f5} = V_i(1 - 0.121)(1 + 0.202)(1 + 0.066)(1 + 0.378)(1 + 0.025) = 1.5908V_i$. Therefore, the increase in value was <u>59.08%</u> which was 59.08% − 24.51%* = <u>34.57% better</u> than the TSE 300 Total Return Index.
*See the note following problem 23.

29. The value of the investment at any year's end is found by applying that year's return (percent change) to the value of the investment at the end of the preceding year.

Value of original $100 investment at the end of:	Campbell Resources Inc.	TSE 300 Total Return Index
1990	$100 (1 − 0.522) = <u>$47.80</u>	$100 (1 − 0.148) = <u>$85.20</u>
1991	$47.80 (1 + 0.082) = <u>$51.72</u>	$85.20 (1 + 0.12) = <u>$95.42</u>
1992	$51.72 (1 − 0.205) = <u>$41.12</u>	$95.42 (1 − 0.014) = <u>$94.08</u>
1993	$41.12 (1 + 2.231) = <u>$132.86</u>	$94.08 (1 + 0.326) = <u>$124.75</u>
1994	$132.86 (1 − 0.118) = <u>$117.18</u>	$124.75 (1 − 0.002) = <u>$124.50</u>

Review Problems

1. a. $\dfrac{9y - 7}{3} - 2.3(y - 2) = 3y - 2.\overline{3} - 2.3y + 4.6 = \underline{0.7y + 2.2\overline{6}}$

    b. $P\left(1 + 0.095 \times \dfrac{135}{365}\right) + \dfrac{2P}{1 + 0.095 \times \dfrac{75}{365}} = P(1.035137) + 1.961706P = \underline{\underline{2.996843P}}$

2. $4(3a + 2b)(2b - a) - 5a(2a - b) = 4(6ab - 3a^2 + 4b^2 - 2ab) - 10a^2 + 5ab$
    $= \underline{-22a^2 + 21ab + 16b^2}$

3. a. $L(1 - d_1)(1 - d_2)(1 - d_3) = \$340(1 - 0.15)(1 - 0.08)(1 - 0.05) = \underline{\$252.59}$

  b. $\dfrac{R}{i}\left[1 - \dfrac{1}{(1 + i)^n}\right] = \dfrac{\$575}{0.085}\left[1 - \dfrac{1}{(1 + 0.085)^3}\right] = \$6764.706(1 - 0.7829081) = \underline{\$1468.56}$

4. $\left(-\dfrac{2x^2}{3}\right)^{-2}\left(\dfrac{5^2}{6x^3}\right)\left(-\dfrac{15}{x^5}\right)^{-1} = \left(\dfrac{3}{2x^2}\right)^2\left(\dfrac{25}{6x^3}\right)\left(-\dfrac{x^5}{15}\right) = \dfrac{5}{8x^2}$

5. a. $\dfrac{(1.00\overline{6})^{240} - 1}{0.00\overline{6}} = \dfrac{4.926802 - 1}{0.00\overline{6}} = \underline{589.020}$

  b. $(1 + 0.025)^{\frac{1}{3}} - 1 = \underline{0.00826484}$

6. a. $\dfrac{x}{1.08^3} + \dfrac{x}{2}(1.08)^4 = \$850$

   $0.793832x + 0.680245x = \$850$

   $x = \underline{\$576.63}$

  Check:

   $\dfrac{\$576.63}{1.08^3} + \dfrac{\$576.63}{2}(1.08)^4 = \$457.749 + \$392.250 = \$850.00$

  b. $2x\left(1 + 0.085 \times \dfrac{77}{365}\right) + \dfrac{x}{1 + 0.085 \times \dfrac{132}{365}} = \$1565.70$

   $2.03586x + 0.97018x = \$1565.70$

   $x = \underline{\$520.85}$

  Check:

   $2(\$520.85)\left(1 + 0.085 \times \dfrac{77}{365}\right) + \dfrac{\$520.85}{1 + 0.085 \times \dfrac{132}{365}} = \$1060.38 + \$505.32 = \$1565.70$

7. a. Given: $\%c = 17.5\%$, $V_i = \$29.43$

   $V_f = V_i(1 + c) = \$29.43(1.175) = \underline{\$34.58}$

   $\$34.58$ is 17.5% more than $\$29.43$.

  b. Given: $V_f = \$100$, $\%c = -80\%$

   $V_i = \dfrac{V_f}{1 + c} = \dfrac{\$100}{1 - 0.80} = \underline{\$500.00}$

   80% off $\$500$ leaves $\$100$.

  c. Given: $V_f = \$100$, $\%c = -15\%$

   $V_i = \dfrac{V_f}{1 + c} = \dfrac{\$100}{1 - 0.15} = \underline{\$117.65}$

   $\$117.65$ reduced by 15% equals $\$100$.

Review Problems *(continued)*

d. Given: $V_i = \$47.50$, $\%c = 320\%$

$$V_f = V_i(1 + c) = \$47.50(1 + 3.2) = \underline{\$199.50}$$

$47.50 increased by 320% is $199.50.

e. Given: $\%c = -62\%$, $V_f = \$213.56$

$$V_i = \frac{V_f}{1 + c} = \frac{\$213.56}{1 - 0.62} = \underline{\$562.00}$$

$562 decreased by 62% equals $213.56.

f. Given: $\%c = 125\%$, $V_f = \$787.50$

$$V_i = \frac{V_f}{1 + c} = \frac{\$787.50}{1 + 1.25} = \underline{\$350.00}$$

$350 increased by 125% equals $787.50.

g. Given: $\%c = -30\%$, $V_i = \$300$

$$V_f = V_i(1 + c) = \$300(1 - 0.30) = \underline{\$210.00}$$

$210 is 30% less than $300.

8. Given:

	1992 value (V_i)	1993 value (V_f)
Gold produced:	34,300 oz.	23,750 oz.
Average price:	$320	$360

a. % change in gold production $= \dfrac{23,750 - 34,300}{34,300} \times 100\% = \underline{-30.76\%}$

b. % change in price $= \dfrac{\$360 - \$320}{\$320} \times 100\% = \underline{12.5\%}$

c. 1992 revenue, $V_i = 34,200(\$320) = \$10.976$ million

1993 revenue, $V_f = 23,750(\$360) = \$8.550$ million

% change in revenue $= \dfrac{\$8.550 - \$10.976}{\$10.976} \times 100\% = \underline{-22.10\%}$

9. Given: For the first year, $V_i = \$3.40$, $V_f = \$11.50$.
For the second year, $V_i = \$11.50$, $\%c = -35\%$.

a. $\%c = \dfrac{V_f - V_i}{V_i} \times 100\% = \dfrac{\$11.50 - \$3.40}{\$3.40} \times 100\% = \underline{238.24\%}$

The share price increased by 238.24% in the first year.

b. Current share price, $V_f = V_i(1 + c) = \$11.50(1 - 0.35) = \underline{\$7.48}$.

Review Problems (continued)

10. Given: For the first year, $\%c = 150\%$

   For the second year, $\%c = -40\%$, $V_f = \$24$

   The price at the beginning of the second year was

   $$V_i = \frac{V_f}{1 + c} = \frac{\$24}{1 - 0.40} = \$40.00 = V_f \text{ for the first year}$$

   The price at the beginning of the first year was

   $$V_i = \frac{\$40.00}{1 + 1.50} = \underline{\underline{\$16.00}}$$

   Barry bought the stock for $16.00 per share.

11. Given: For each of the 15 bonds, $V_i = \$1000$, $V_f = \$980$, $Y = 2(\$40) = \$80$

   a. $\%Y = \dfrac{Y}{V_i} \times 100\% = \dfrac{\$80}{\$1000} \times 100\% = \underline{\underline{8.00\%}}$

   The interest yield was 8.00%.

   b. Percent capital gain, $\%G = \dfrac{V_f - V_i}{V_i} \times 100\% = \dfrac{\$980 - \$1000}{\$1000} \times 100\% = \underline{\underline{-2.00\%}}$

   c. Total return, $ROI = 15(Y + G) = 15(\$80 - \$20) = \underline{\underline{\$900.00}}$

   d. Rate of return on investment, $\%ROI = \%Y + \%G = 8\% - 2\% = \underline{\underline{6.00\%}}$

12. Given: $V_{f5} = 2\,V_i$, $c_1 = 0.18$, $c_2 = 0.17$, $c_3 = 0.14$, $c_4 = 0.13$

   $V_{f5} = V_i(1 + c_1)...(1 + c_5)$

   $\quad = V_i(1.18)(1.17)(1.14)(1.13)(1 + c_5)$

   Equating the two expressions for V_{f5},

   $2V_i = V_i(1.7785)(1 + c_5)$

   $$\frac{2}{1.7785} = 1 + c_5$$

   $$c_5 = \frac{2}{1.7785} - 1 = 0.1246$$

   The number of cell phones increased by $\underline{12.46\%}$ in 1995.

13. Given: $c_1 = 0.23$, $c_2 = 0.10$, $c_3 = -0.15$, $c_4 = 0.05$, $V_{f4} = \$30.50$

   a. Substitute in $V_{f4} = V_i(1 + c_1)...(1 + c_4)$ and solve for V_i

   $\$30.50 = V_i(1.23)(1.10)(0.85)(1.05)$

   $$V_i = \frac{\$30.50}{1.20755} = \underline{\underline{\$25.26}}$$

   A share's initial price was $25.26.

   b. The decline in the third year was 15% of the price at the end of the second year. That is, Price decline $= 0.15V_{f2} = 0.15(\$25.26)(1.23)(1.10) = \underline{\underline{\$5.13}}$

   The share price declined by $5.13 in the third year.

Review Problems (concluded)

14. Given: Grace's share = 1.2(Marie's share)

     Mary Anne's share = $\frac{5}{8}$ (Grace's share)

     Total allocated = $36,000

Let M represent Marie's share.

(Marie's share) + (Grace's share) + (Mary Anne's share) = $36,000

$$M + 1.2M + \frac{5}{8}(1.2M) = \$36,000$$

$$2.95M = \$36,000$$

$$M = \underline{\$12,203.39}$$

Marie should receive $12,203.39.

Grace should receive 1.2M = $\underline{\$14,644.07}$.

Mary Anne should receive $\frac{5}{8}$ ($14,644.07) = $\underline{\$9152.54}$.

15. Given: Total initial investment = $7800
            Value one year later = $9310
            %c in ABC portion = 15%
            %c in XYZ portion = 25%

Let X represent the amount invested in XYZ Inc.

The solution "idea" is:

(Amount invested in ABC)1.15 + (Amount invested in XYZ)1.25 = $9310

Hence, ($7800 − X)1.15 + (X)1.25 = $9310
             $8970 − 1.15X + 1.25X = $9310
                         0.10X = $9310 − $8970
                             X = $\underline{\$3400}$

Rory invested $3400 in XYZ Inc. and $7800 − $3400 = $\underline{\$4400 \text{ in ABC}}$ Ltd.

16. Given: Appliance's costs = 1.5(Upholstered's costs) − $4000
            Wood's costs = 0.75(Appliance's costs) + $5000

Let U represent Upholstered's overhead charge. The total of the three charges is $36,440.

Hence, U + (1.5U − $4000) + [0.75(1.5U − $4000) + $5000] = $36,440
             U + 1.5U − $4000 + 1.125U − $3000 + $5000 = $36,440
                                          3.625U = $36,440 + $2000
                                               U = $\underline{\$10,604.14}$

Thus, Upholstered Furniture is charged $10,604.14,

Appliances is charged 1.5($10,604.14) − $4000 = $\underline{\$11,906.21}$,

and Wood Furniture is charged the remaining $\underline{\$13,929.65}$.

Self-Test Exercises

1. a. $6(4y - 3)(2 - 3y) - 3(5 - y)(1 + 4y) = 6(8y - 12y^2 - 6 + 9y) - 3(5 + 20y - y - 4y^2)$
   $$= \underline{\underline{-60y^2 + 45y - 51}}$$

   b. $\dfrac{5b - 4}{4} - \dfrac{25 - b}{1.25} + \dfrac{7}{8}b = 1.25b - 1 - 20 + 0.8b + 0.875b = \underline{\underline{2.925b - 21}}$

   c. $\dfrac{x}{1 + 0.085 \times \frac{63}{365}} + 2x\left(1 + 0.085 \times \dfrac{151}{365}\right) = 0.985541x + 2.070329x = \underline{\underline{3.05587x}}$

   d. $\dfrac{96nm^2 - 72n^2m^2}{48n^2m} = \underline{\underline{\dfrac{4m - 3nm}{2n}}}$

2. $P(1 + i)^n + \dfrac{S}{1 + rt} = \$2500(1.1025)^2 + \dfrac{\$1500}{1 + 0.09 \times \frac{93}{365}} = \$3038.766 + \$1466.374 = \underline{\underline{\$4505.14}}$

3. a. $\dfrac{(-3x^2)^3(2x^{-2})}{6x^5} = \dfrac{(-27x^6)(2x^{-2})}{6x^5} = \underline{\underline{-\dfrac{9}{x}}}$

   b. $\dfrac{(-2a^3)^{-2}(4b^4)^{\frac{3}{2}}}{(-2b^3)(0.5a)^3} = \dfrac{\left(\frac{1}{4a^6}\right)(8b^6)}{(-2b^3)(0.125a^3)} = \underline{\underline{-\dfrac{8b^3}{a^9}}}$

4. a. $1.0075^{24} = \underline{\underline{1.19641}}$

   b. $(1.05)^{\frac{1}{6}} - 1 = \underline{\underline{0.00816485}}$

   c. $\dfrac{(1 + 0.0075)^{36} - 1}{0.0075} = \underline{\underline{41.1527}}$

   d. $\dfrac{1 - (1 + 0.045)^{-12}}{0.045} = \underline{\underline{9.11858}}$

5. a. $\dfrac{2x}{1 + 0.13 \times \frac{92}{365}} + x\left(1 + 0.13 \times \dfrac{59}{365}\right) = \$831$

   $$1.936545x + 1.021014x = \$831$$
   $$2.957559x = \$831$$
   $$\underline{\underline{x = \$280.97}}$$

   b. $3x(1.03^5) + \dfrac{x}{1.03^3} + x = \dfrac{\$2500}{1.03^2}$

   $$3.47782x + 0.91514x + x = \$2356.49$$
   $$\underline{\underline{x = \$436.96}}$$

6. Given: Last year's revenue = $2,347,000
   Last year's expenses = $2,189,000

   a. Given: %c in revenue = 10%; % change in expenses = 5%

   Anticipated revenues, $V_f = V_i(1 + c)$ = $2,347,000(1.1)$ = $2,581,700
   Anticipated expenses = \qquad\qquad $2,189,000(1.05)$ = $\underline{2,298,450}$
   Anticipated profit = \qquad\qquad\qquad\qquad\qquad\qquad $\quad$ \$ 283,250
   Last year's profit = \qquad $2,347,000 - 2,189,000$ = $ 158,000

   % increase in profit = $\dfrac{\$283,250 - \$158,000}{\$158,000} \times 100\% = \underline{79.27\%}$

   b. Given: %c in revenue = −10%; %c in expenses = −5%

   Anticipated revenues = $2,347,000(1 − 0.10)$ = $2,112,300
   Anticipated expenses = $2,189,000(1 − 0.05)$ = $\underline{\$2,079,550}$
   Anticipated profit = \qquad\qquad\qquad\qquad\qquad\qquad $ \$ \quad 32,750

   % change in profit = $\dfrac{\$32,750 - \$158,000}{\$158,000} \times 100\% = \underline{-79.27\%}$

   The operating profit will decline by 79.27%.

7. Given: Purchase price = $95,000; Amount invested = $45,000

   First year's rental income = 12($500) = $6000
   Second year's rental income = 10($525) = $5250
   Property taxes = $1456 and $1515 in years 1 and 2
   Interest expense = $5453 and $5387 in years 1 and 2
   Selling price = $112,000 less 5.5% commission

   Net rental income, Y = $6000 + $5250 − $1456 − $1515 − $5453 − $5387 = −$2561
   Capital gain, G = $V_f − V_i$ = $112,000(1 − 0.055) − $95,000 = $10,840

   $\%ROI = \dfrac{Y + G}{\text{Initial investment}} \times 100\% = \dfrac{-\$2561 + \$10,840}{\$45,000} \times 100\% = \underline{18.40\%}$

   For the two-year holding period, the rate of return on investment was 18.40%.

8. Given: $V_{f4} = 3V_i$, $c_1 = 0.25$, $c_2 = 0.30$, $c_3 = 0.35$
   $V_{f4} = V_i(1 + 0.25)(1 + 0.30)(1 + 0.35)(1 + c_4) = 3V_i$
   Hence, $2.19375(1 + c_4) = 3$

   $c_4 = \dfrac{3}{2.19375} - 1 = 0.3675$

   To reach the targeted level, R & D spending in the fourth year must be increased by $\underline{36.75\%}$.

9. Given: $V_i = \$6.50$, $c_1 = 1.10$, $c_2 = -0.55$, $c_3 = -0.55$

   a. The price at the end of the third year was
   $V_{f3} = \$6.50(1 + 1.10)(1 − 0.55)(1 − 0.55) = \$2.76$

   Overall $\%c = \dfrac{V_{f3} - V_i}{V_i} \times 100\% = \dfrac{\$2.76 - \$6.50}{\$6.50} \times 100\% = \underline{-57.54\%}$

   The share price declined by 57.54% during the three-year period.

Self-Test Exercises *(concluded)*

b. In the second year, the share price dropped by 55% of the price at the end of the first year.

That is, Price drop $= 0.55V_{f1} = 0.55(\$6.50)(1 + 1.1) = \underline{7.51}$

The share price dropped by $7.51 in the second year.

10. Given: Ken's share $= 0.80$ (Hugh's share) $+ \$15,000$

Total distribution $= \$98,430$

Let H represent Hugh's share. Since

Hugh's share + Ken's share = Total distribution

$$H + 0.8H + \$15,000 = \$98,430$$
$$1.8H = \$83,430$$
$$H = \underline{\$46,350}$$

Hugh should receive $46,350 and Ken should receive $98,430 − $46,350 = $\underline{\$52,080}$.

3 Ratios and Proportions

Changes in the Second Edition:

1. As mentioned in the Chapter 1 preamble, the **Basic Percentage Problem** has been moved from Chapter 3 to Chapter 1.

2. Discussion of **Currency Appreciation and Depreciation** has been added to Section 3.5 while **Linkages among Exchange Rates** has been moved to an appendix. The latter topic is conceptually difficult for students and is not covered by a majority of instructors.

3. The discussion of **Index Numbers** has been somewhat simplified.

1. $12:64 = \underline{\underline{3:16}}$ (each term divided by 4)

2. $56:21 = \underline{\underline{8:3}}$ (each term divided by 7)

3. $45:15:30 = 9:3:6$ (each term divided by 5)
   $= \underline{\underline{3:1:2}}$ (each term divided by 3)

4. $26:130:65 = \underline{\underline{2:10:5}}$ (each term divided by 13)

5. $0.08:0.12 = 8:12$ (each term multiplied by 100)
   $= \underline{\underline{2:3}}$ (each term divided by 4)

6. $2.5:3.5:3 = \underline{\underline{5:7:6}}$ (each term multiplied by 2)

7. $0.84:1.4:1.96 = 84:140:196$ (each term multiplied by 100)
   $= 21:35:49$ (each term divided by 4)
   $= \underline{\underline{3:5:7}}$ (each term divided by 7)

8. $11.7:7.8:3.9 = 117:78:39$
   $= 39:26:13$ (each term divided by 3)
   $= \underline{\underline{3:2:1}}$ (each term divided by 13)

9. $0.24:0.39:0.15 = 24:39:15$
   $= \underline{\underline{8:13:5}}$ (each term divided by 3)

10. $0.091:0.021:0.042 = 91:21:42$
    $= \underline{\underline{13:3:6}}$ (each term divided by 7)

11. $\dfrac{1}{8}:\dfrac{3}{4} = \left(\dfrac{1}{8} \times 8\right):\left(\dfrac{3}{4} \times 8\right) = \underline{\underline{1:6}}$

12. $\dfrac{4}{3}:\dfrac{3}{2} = \left(\dfrac{4}{3} \times 6\right):\left(\dfrac{3}{2} \times 6\right) = \underline{\underline{8:9}}$

13. $\dfrac{3}{5}:\dfrac{6}{7} = \left(\dfrac{3}{5} \times 5 \times 7\right):\left(\dfrac{6}{7} \times 5 \times 7\right) = 21:30 = \underline{\underline{7:10}}$

14. $\dfrac{11}{3}:\dfrac{11}{7} = \left(\dfrac{11}{3} \times 3 \times 7\right):\left(\dfrac{11}{7} \times 3 \times 7\right) = 77:33 = \underline{\underline{7:3}}$

15. $1\dfrac{1}{4}:1\dfrac{2}{3} = \dfrac{5}{4}:\dfrac{5}{3} = \left(\dfrac{5}{4} \times 4 \times 3\right):\left(\dfrac{5}{3} \times 4 \times 3\right) = 15:20 = \underline{\underline{3:4}}$

16. $2\dfrac{1}{2}:\dfrac{5}{8} = \dfrac{5}{2}:\dfrac{5}{8} = \left(\dfrac{5}{2} \times 8\right):\left(\dfrac{5}{8} \times 8\right) = 20:5 = \underline{\underline{4:1}}$

17. $4\dfrac{1}{8}:2\dfrac{1}{5} = \dfrac{33}{8}:\dfrac{11}{5} = \left(\dfrac{33}{8} \times \dfrac{8 \times 5}{11}\right):\left(\dfrac{11}{5} \times \dfrac{8 \times 5}{11}\right) = \underline{\underline{15:8}}$

18. $\dfrac{2}{3}:\dfrac{3}{4}:\dfrac{5}{6} = \underline{\underline{8:9:10}}$ (each term multiplied by 12)

19. $\dfrac{1}{15}:\dfrac{1}{5}:\dfrac{1}{10} = 1:3:\dfrac{3}{2}$ (each term multiplied by 15)

    $= \underline{\underline{2:6:3}}$ (each term multiplied by 2)

Exercise 3.1 *(concluded)*

20. $10\frac{1}{2}:7:4\frac{1}{5} = \frac{21}{2}:7:\frac{21}{5}$

$\qquad\qquad = 105:70:42$ (each term multiplied by 10)

$\qquad\qquad = \underline{15:10:6}$ (each term divided by 7)

21. $7.6:3 = \underline{2.5\overline{3}:1}$ (each term divided by 3)

22. $1.41:8.22 = \underline{1:5.83}$ (each term divided by 1.41)

23. $0.177:0.81 = \underline{1:4.58}$ (each term divided by 0.177)

24. $0.0131:0.0086 = \underline{1.52:1}$ (each term divided by 0.0086)

25. $\frac{3}{7}:\frac{19}{17} = \left(\frac{3}{7}\times\frac{7}{3}\right):\left(\frac{19}{17}\times\frac{7}{3}\right) = \underline{1:2.61}$

26. $4\frac{3}{13}:\frac{27}{17} = \left(\frac{55}{13}\times\frac{17}{27}\right):\left(\frac{27}{17}\times\frac{17}{27}\right) = \underline{2.66:1}$

27. $77:23:41 = \underline{3.35:1:1.78}$ (each term divided by 23)

28. $11:38:27 = \underline{1:3.45:2.45}$ (each term divided by 11)

29. $3.5:5.4:8 = \underline{1:1.54:2.29}$ (each term divided by 3.5)

30. $0.47:0.15:0.26 = \underline{3.13:1:1.73}$ (each term divided by 0.15)

31. $\frac{5}{8}:\frac{17}{11}:\frac{6}{7} = \left(\frac{5}{8}\times\frac{8}{5}\right):\left(\frac{17}{11}\times\frac{8}{5}\right):\left(\frac{6}{7}\times\frac{8}{5}\right) = \underline{1:2.47:1.37}$

32. $5\frac{1}{2}:3\frac{3}{4}:8\frac{1}{3} = 5.5:3.75:8.\overline{3}$

$\qquad\qquad\qquad = \underline{1.47:1:2.22}$ (each term divided by 3.75)

33. Sales in A:Sales in B:Sales in C $= 25\%:35\%:40\%$
$\qquad\qquad\qquad\qquad\qquad = \underline{5:7:8}$

34. Bob's interest:Ron's interest:Don's interest
$\qquad = \$52,000:\$65,000:\$78,000$
$\qquad = 52:65:78$
$\qquad = \underline{4:5:6}$ (each term divided by 13)

35. Debt:Preferred equity:Common equity
$\qquad = (\$3.6 - \$0.55 - \$1.2):\$0.55:\$1.2$
$\qquad = 1.85:0.55:1.2$
$\qquad = \underline{3.36:1:2.18}$ (each term divided by 0.55)

36. Materials:Labour:Overhead $= \$2240:\$3165:\$1325$
$\qquad\qquad\qquad\qquad\qquad = \underline{1.69:2.39:1}$ (each term divided by \$1325)

37. Education:Health services:Social services
$\qquad = \$1040:\$910:\$650$
$\qquad = 104:91:65$ (each term divided by \$10)
$\qquad = \underline{8:7:5}$ (each term divided by 13)

Exercise 3.2

1. $9:7 = 54:b$

$$\frac{9}{7} = \frac{54}{b}$$

$9b = 7(54)$

$b = \underline{\underline{42}}$

2. $17:q = 119:91$

$$\frac{17}{q} = \frac{119}{91}$$

$17(91) = 119q$

$q = \underline{\underline{13}}$

3. $88:17 = a:45$

$$\frac{88}{17} = \frac{a}{45}$$

$88(45) = 17a$

$a = \underline{\underline{232.9}}$

4. $d:13.2 = 16:31$

$$\frac{d}{13.2} = \frac{16}{31}$$

$31d = 16(13.2)$

$d = \underline{\underline{6.813}}$

5. $1.89:0.31 = 175:k$

$$\frac{1.89}{0.31} = \frac{175}{k}$$

$$k = \frac{0.31(175)}{1.89} = \underline{\underline{28.70}}$$

6. $1.56:h = 56.2:31.7$

$$\frac{1.56}{h} = \frac{56.2}{31.7}$$

$$h = \frac{1.56(31.7)}{56.2} = \underline{\underline{0.880}}$$

7. $0.043:y = 550:198$

$$\frac{0.043}{y} = \frac{550}{198}$$

$$y = \frac{0.043 \times 198}{550} = \underline{\underline{0.0155}}$$

Exercise 3.2 *(continued)*

8. $0.057:0.149 = z:0.05$

$$\frac{0.057}{0.149} = \frac{z}{0.05}$$

$$z = \frac{0.05(0.057)}{0.149} = \underline{\underline{0.0191}}$$

9. $m:\dfrac{3}{4} = \dfrac{1}{2}:\dfrac{9}{8}$

$$\frac{m}{\frac{3}{4}} = \frac{\frac{1}{2}}{\frac{9}{8}}$$

$$m = \frac{3}{4} \times \frac{1}{2} \times \frac{8}{9} = \underline{\underline{\frac{1}{3}}}$$

10. $\dfrac{10}{3}:\dfrac{12}{7} = \dfrac{5}{18}:r$

$$\frac{\frac{10}{3}}{\frac{12}{7}} = \frac{\frac{5}{18}}{r}$$

$$r = \frac{5}{18} \times \frac{12}{7} \times \frac{3}{10} = \underline{\underline{\frac{1}{7}}}$$

11. $6:7:5 = n:105:m$

$$\frac{6}{7} = \frac{n}{105} \qquad \text{and} \qquad \frac{7}{5} = \frac{105}{m}$$

$$n = \frac{6(105)}{7} = \underline{\underline{90}} \qquad m = \frac{5 \times 105}{7} = \underline{\underline{75}}$$

12. $3:4:13 = x:y:6.5$

$$\frac{3}{13} = \frac{x}{6.5} \qquad \text{and} \qquad \frac{4}{13} = \frac{y}{6.5}$$

$$x = \frac{3(6.5)}{13} = \underline{\underline{1.5}} \qquad y = \frac{4(6.5)}{13} = \underline{\underline{2}}$$

13. $625:f:500 = g:3:4$

$$\frac{625}{g} = \frac{500}{4} \qquad \text{and} \qquad \frac{f}{3} = \frac{500}{4}$$

$$g = \frac{4(625)}{500} = \underline{\underline{5}} \qquad f = \frac{3(500)}{4} = \underline{\underline{375}}$$

Exercise 3.2 (continued)

14. $a:58:132 = 38:27:b$

$$\frac{a}{38} = \frac{58}{27} \quad \text{and} \quad \frac{58}{27} = \frac{132}{b}$$

$$a = \frac{38(58)}{27} = \underline{\underline{81.63}} \qquad b = \frac{27(132)}{58} = \underline{\underline{61.45}}$$

15. $0.69:1.17:0.4 = r:s:6.5$

$$\frac{0.69}{r} = \frac{0.4}{6.5} \quad \text{and} \quad \frac{1.17}{s} = \frac{0.4}{6.5}$$

$$r = \frac{6.5(0.69)}{0.4} = \underline{\underline{11.21}} \qquad s = \frac{6.5(1.17)}{0.4} = \underline{\underline{19.01}}$$

16. $8500:x:y = \dfrac{1}{3}:\dfrac{1}{4}:\dfrac{5}{12}$

$$\frac{8500}{\frac{1}{3}} = \frac{x}{\frac{1}{4}} \quad \text{and} \quad \frac{8500}{\frac{1}{3}} = \frac{y}{\frac{5}{12}}$$

$$x = \frac{1}{4}(8500)3 = \underline{\underline{6375}} \qquad y = \frac{5}{12}(8500)3 = \underline{\underline{10,625}}$$

17. Let the neighbour's taxes be T.

$$\frac{T}{\$2376} = \frac{\$235,000}{\$210,000}$$

$$T = \frac{235}{210} \times \$2376 = \underline{\underline{\$2658.86}}$$

The neighbour's taxes are $2658.86.

18. Let the number of teachers next year be n.

$$\frac{n}{348} = \frac{7780}{7412}$$

$$n = \frac{7780}{7412} \times 348 = 365.3$$

The board must fill <u>17</u> additional positions.

19. Let the hours of operation be h.

$$\frac{1\frac{1}{2}}{h} = \frac{4}{29.5}$$

$$h = \frac{29.5(1.5)}{4} = \underline{\underline{11.06}} \text{ hours}$$

The generator has been operated for 11.06 hours since it was last refuelled.

Exercise 3.2 (continued)

20. Let Connie's proportionate price be p.

$$\frac{p}{\$128,000} = \frac{23\frac{1}{4}}{14\frac{1}{2}}$$

$$p = \frac{23.25}{14.5} \times \$128,000 = \underline{\$205,241}$$

Connie would receive $205,241 if she sold her land at a proportionate price.

21. Let the expected hours of direct labour be H.

$$\frac{2.3}{H} = \frac{\$87}{\$39,150}$$

$$H = \frac{2.3(\$39,150)}{\$87} = 1035$$

Total budget for direct labour = 1035($18.25) = $\underline{\$18,888.75}$

22. Let W, N, S represent the wife's, son's, and sister's shares in any allocation. Then W:N:S = 7:5:3.

a. $\dfrac{W}{\$9500} = \dfrac{7}{5}$ and $\dfrac{\$9500}{S} = \dfrac{5}{3}$

Hence, Mrs. Bartlett received $\underline{\$13,300}$ and the sister $\underline{\$5700}$.

b. $\dfrac{S}{\$27,000} = \dfrac{3}{7 + 5 + 3} = \dfrac{3}{15} = \dfrac{1}{5} = 0.2$

The sister received 0.2($27,000) = $\underline{\$5400}$.

23. Let the investment in US, Japanese, and British stocks be I_{US}, I_J, and I_B. Then

$$\frac{I_{US}}{\$238M} = \frac{27}{14}, \quad \frac{I_J}{\$238M} = \frac{19}{14}, \quad \text{and} \quad \frac{I_B}{\$238M} = \frac{11}{14}.$$

$$I_{US} = \frac{27}{14} \times \$238M = \underline{\$459 \text{ million}}$$

$$I_J = \frac{19}{14} \times \$238M = \underline{\$323 \text{ million}}$$

$$I_B = \frac{11}{14} \times \$238M = \underline{\$187 \text{ million}}$$

The fund includes $459 million worth of US stocks, $323 million of Japanese stocks, and $187 million of British stocks.

Exercise 3.2 (continued)

24. Let the first-half sales of Ford be S_F and of Chrysler be S_C. Then

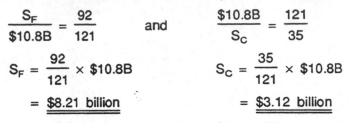

$$\frac{S_F}{\$10.8B} = \frac{92}{121} \quad \text{and} \quad \frac{\$10.8B}{S_C} = \frac{121}{35}$$

$$S_F = \frac{92}{121} \times \$10.8B \qquad S_C = \frac{35}{121} \times \$10.8B$$

$$= \underline{\underline{\$8.21 \text{ billion}}} \qquad = \underline{\underline{\$3.12 \text{ billion}}}$$

The first-half sales of Ford will be $8.21 billion and of Chrysler will be $3.12 billion.

25. Let the volumes of fruit juice and ginger ale be F and G litres respectively.

$$F:G:0.75 = \frac{3}{2}:\frac{3}{5}:\frac{1}{4}$$

$$= 1.5:0.6:0.25$$

$$\frac{F}{0.75} = \frac{1.5}{0.25} \quad \text{and} \quad \frac{G}{0.75} = \frac{0.6}{0.25}$$

$$F = \frac{1.5}{0.25} \times 0.75 \qquad G = \frac{0.6}{0.25} \times 0.75$$

$$= \underline{\underline{4.5 \text{ litres}}} \qquad = \underline{\underline{1.8 \text{ litres}}}$$

4.5 litres of fruit juice and 1.8 litres of ginger ale should be mixed with 0.75 litres of vodka.

26. Let L, C, and M be the investments of Larry, Curley, and Moe, respectively. Let T represent the total investment. We are given:

$$L:C:M:T = 1:1.35:0.85:3.2$$

a. If T = $102,400, then

$$\frac{L}{\$102,400} = \frac{1}{3.2}, \frac{C}{\$102,400} = \frac{1.35}{3.2}, \frac{M}{\$102,400} = \frac{0.85}{3.2}$$

Therefore,

$$L = \frac{\$102,400}{3.2} = \underline{\underline{\$32,000}}$$

$$C = \frac{\$102,400 \times 1.35}{3.2} = \underline{\underline{\$43,200}}$$

$$M = \frac{\$102,400 \times 0.85}{3.2} = \underline{\underline{\$27,200}}$$

Larry contributed $32,000, Curley contributed $43,200, and Moe contributed $27,200.

b. Since C:M = 1.35:0.85,

$$\text{then} \quad \frac{C}{\$6528} = \frac{1.35}{0.85}$$

$$C = \frac{1.35}{0.85} \times \$6528 = \underline{\underline{\$10,368}}$$

Curley's investment was $10,368.

27. Let S, W, and O represent sales, wholesale costs, and overhead expenses, respectively. Then

$$S:W:O = 3.66:2.15:1.13$$

If sales = $5.03 million, then

$$\frac{\$5.03 \text{ million}}{W} = \frac{3.66}{2.15} \text{ and } \frac{\$5.03 \text{ million}}{O} = \frac{3.66}{1.13}$$

$$W = \frac{2.15}{3.66} \times \$5.03 \text{ million} = \underline{\underline{\$2.955 \text{ million}}}$$

$$O = \frac{1.13}{3.66} \times \$5.03 \text{ million} = \underline{\underline{\$1.553 \text{ million}}}$$

Economart's wholesale costs would be $2.955 million and its overhead expenses $1.553 million.

28. Let C, E, and U represent the number of claimants, expenditures, and unemployment rate, respectively. Then C:E:U = 89,300:$53.7 million:11.6%

If the unemployment rate drops to 10.3%, then

$$\frac{E}{10.3\%} = \frac{\$53.7 \text{ million}}{11.6\%} \text{ and } \frac{C}{10.3\%} = \frac{89,300}{11.6\%}$$

$$E = \frac{\$53.7 \text{ million}}{11.6\%} \times 10.3\% = \underline{\underline{\$47.68 \text{ million}}}$$

$$C = \frac{89,300}{11.6\%} \times 10.3\% = \underline{\underline{79,292}}$$

The expected number of claimants next August is 79,292 resulting in expenditures of $47.68 million.

29. Let S, B, and T represent the number of students, the annual budget, and number of teachers. Then

$$S:B:T = 13,450:\$66.3 \text{ million}:635$$

If MSD had the same ratios in relation to its enrolment of 10,320,

$$\frac{10,320}{B} = \frac{13,450}{\$66.3 \text{ million}} \text{ and } \frac{10,320}{T} = \frac{13,450}{635}$$

$$B = \frac{10,320}{13,450} \times \$66.3 \text{ million} = \$50.87 \text{ million}$$

$$T = \frac{10,320}{13,450} \times 635 = 487$$

To bring its budget and staffing in line with the average proportion, MSD would have to <u>reduce</u> its budget by

$$\$52.1 \text{ million} - \$50.87 \text{ million} = \underline{\underline{\$1.23 \text{ million}}}$$

and <u>reduce</u> its staff by

$$498 - 487 = \underline{\underline{11 \text{ teachers}}}.$$

Exercise 3.2 *(continued)*

30.

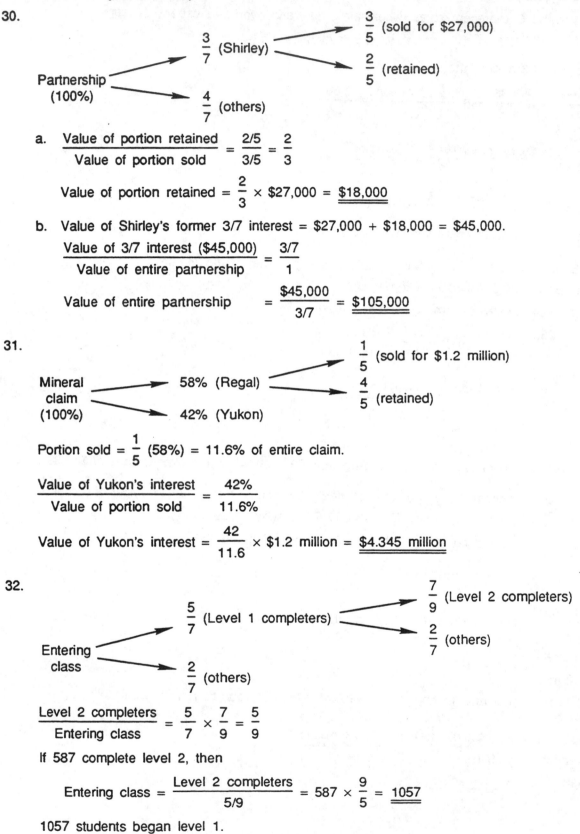

a. $\dfrac{\text{Value of portion retained}}{\text{Value of portion sold}} = \dfrac{2/5}{3/5} = \dfrac{2}{3}$

Value of portion retained $= \dfrac{2}{3} \times \$27{,}000 = \underline{\$18{,}000}$

b. Value of Shirley's former 3/7 interest = \$27,000 + \$18,000 = \$45,000.

$\dfrac{\text{Value of 3/7 interest (\$45,000)}}{\text{Value of entire partnership}} = \dfrac{3/7}{1}$

Value of entire partnership $= \dfrac{\$45{,}000}{3/7} = \underline{\$105{,}000}$

31.

Portion sold $= \dfrac{1}{5}$ (58%) = 11.6% of entire claim.

$\dfrac{\text{Value of Yukon's interest}}{\text{Value of portion sold}} = \dfrac{42\%}{11.6\%}$

Value of Yukon's interest $= \dfrac{42}{11.6} \times \$1.2$ million $= \underline{\$4.345 \text{ million}}$

32.

$\dfrac{\text{Level 2 completers}}{\text{Entering class}} = \dfrac{5}{7} \times \dfrac{7}{9} = \dfrac{5}{9}$

If 587 complete level 2, then

Entering class $= \dfrac{\text{Level 2 completers}}{5/9} = 587 \times \dfrac{9}{5} = \underline{\underline{1057}}$

1057 students began level 1.

Exercise 3.2 (continued)

33.

Inventory

$\dfrac{4}{7}$ (sold at cost in bankruptcy sale)

$\dfrac{3}{7}$ (sold to liquidators for $6700 representing 45% of cost)

a. Let C represent the original cost of the inventory sold to liquidators. Then

$$0.45\ C = \$6700$$
$$C = \underline{\$14,889}$$

The original cost of the inventory sold to liquidators was $14,889.

b. $\dfrac{\text{Proceeds from bankruptcy sale}}{C} = \dfrac{4/7}{3/7} = \dfrac{4}{3}$

Proceeds from bankruptcy sale $= \dfrac{4}{3}\ C = \dfrac{4}{3}\ (\$14,889) = \underline{\$19,852}$

Exercise 3.3

1.

	$	%
Initial value, V_i	$95	100
+ Change	+ 5	%c
= Final value, V_f	$100	

Solve for %c in the proportion

$$\dfrac{\%c}{100} = \dfrac{\$5}{\$95}$$

$$\%c = \dfrac{5}{95} \times 100\% = \underline{5.26\%}$$

2.

	$	%
V_i	$100	100
+ Change	−5	%c
= V_f	$95	

$$\dfrac{\%c}{100\%} = \dfrac{-\$5}{\$100}$$

$$\%c = -\dfrac{5}{100} \times 100\% = -\underline{5.00\%}$$

3.

	kg	%
V_i	35	100
+ Change	+100	%c
= V_f	135	

$$\dfrac{\%c}{100\%} = \dfrac{100}{35}$$

$$\%c = \dfrac{100}{35} \times 100\% = \underline{286\%}$$

4.

	kg	%
V_i	135	100
+ Change	−100	%c
= V_f	35	

$$\dfrac{\%c}{100\%} = \dfrac{-100}{135}$$

$$\%c = -\dfrac{100}{135} \times 100\% = -\underline{74.1\%}$$

5.

		%
V_i	0.11	100
+ Change	+0.02	%c
= V_f	0.13	

$$\dfrac{\%c}{100\%} = \dfrac{0.02}{0.11}$$

$$\%c = \dfrac{2}{11} \times 100\% = \underline{18.2\%}$$

Exercise 3.3 *(continued)*

6.

		%
V_i	0.095	100%
+ Change	− 0.010	% c
= V_f	0.085	

$$\frac{\%c}{100\%} = \frac{-0.010}{0.095}$$

$$\%c = -\frac{10}{95} \times 100\% \; \underline{-10.5\%}$$

7.

	$	%
V_i	$134.39	100
+ Change		−12
= V_f	V_f	88

$$\frac{V_f}{\$134.39} = \frac{88}{100}$$

$$V_f = \frac{88}{100} \times \$134.39 = \underline{\$118.26}$$

8.

	g	%
V_i	112	100
+ Change		+112
= V_f	V_f	212

$$\frac{V_f}{112g} = \frac{212}{100}$$

$$V_f = \frac{212}{100} \times 112g = \underline{237.44g}$$

9.

	cm	%
V_i	26.3	100
+ Change		+300
= V_f	V_f	400

$$\frac{V_f}{26.3 \; cm} = \frac{400}{100}$$

$$V_f = 4 \times 26.3 \; cm = \underline{105.2 \; cm}$$

10.

		%
V_i	0.043	100
+ Change		−30
= V_f	V_f	70

$$\frac{V_f}{0.043} = \frac{70}{100}$$

$$V_f = 0.7 \times 0.043 = \underline{0.0301}$$

11.

	$	%
V_i	V_i	100
+ Change		+200
= V_f	$75	300

$$\frac{V_i}{\$75} = \frac{100}{300}$$

$$V_i = \frac{1}{3} \times \$75 = \underline{\$25.00}$$

12.

	$	%
V_i	V_i	100
+ Change		−50
= V_f	$75	50

$$\frac{V_i}{\$75} = \frac{100}{50}$$

$$V_i = 2 \times \$75 = \underline{\$150.00}$$

13.

	$	%
V_i	$90	100
+ Change	+10	%c
= V_f	100	

$$\frac{\%c}{100\%} = \frac{\$10}{\$90}$$

$$\%c = \frac{1}{9} \times 100\% = \underline{11.1\%}$$

14.

	$	%
V_i	$110	100%
+ Change	− 10	%c
= V_f	$100	

$$\frac{\%c}{100\%} = \frac{-\$10}{\$110}$$

$$\%c = -\frac{1}{11} \times 100\% = \underline{9.09\%}$$

Exercise 3.3 *(continued)*

15.

	$	%
V_i	V_i	100
+ Change		25
= V_f	$100	125

$$\frac{V_i}{\$100} = \frac{100}{125}$$

$$V_i = \frac{100}{125} \times \$100 = \underline{\underline{\$80.00}}$$

16.

	$	%
V_i	V_i	100
+ Change		7
= V_f	$52.43	107

$$\frac{V_i}{\$52.43} = \frac{100}{107}$$

$$V_i = \frac{100}{107} \times \$52.43 = \underline{\underline{\$49.00}}$$

17.

	$	%
V_i	V_i	100
+ Change		75
= V_f	$75	175

$$\frac{V_i}{\$75} = \frac{100}{175}$$

$$V_i = \frac{100}{175} \times \$75 = \underline{\underline{\$42.86}}$$

18.

	$	%
V_i	$56	100
+ Change		65
= V_f	V_f	165

$$\frac{V_f}{\$56} = \frac{165}{100}$$

$$V_f = 1.65 \times \$56 = \underline{\underline{\$92.40}}$$

19.

	$	%
V_i	$759	100
+ Change	−$4.70	%c
= V_f	$754.30	

$$\frac{\%c}{100\%} = \frac{-\$4.70}{\$759}$$

$$\%c = -\frac{\$4.70}{\$759} \times 100\% = \underline{\underline{-0.619\%}}$$

$754.30 is <u>0.619% less</u> than $759

20.

	$	%
V_i	77,400	100
+ Change	387	%c
= V_f	77,787	

$$\frac{\%c}{100\%} = \frac{387}{77,400}$$

$$\%c = \frac{387}{77,400} \times 100\% = \underline{\underline{0.500\%}}$$

21.

	$	%
V_i	$75	100
+ Change		75
= V_f	V_f	175

$$\frac{V_f}{\$75} = \frac{175}{100}$$

$$V_f = 1.75 \times \$75 = \underline{\underline{\$131.25}}$$

22.

	$	%
V_i	V_i	100
+ Change		−10
= V_f	$100	90

$$\frac{V_i}{\$100} = \frac{100}{90}$$

$$V_i = \frac{10}{9} \times \$100 = \underline{\underline{\$111.11}}$$

23.

	$	%
V_i	V_i	100
+ Change		−20
= V_f	$100	80

$$\frac{V_i}{\$100} = \frac{100}{80}$$

$$V_i = \frac{10}{8} \times \$100 = \underline{\underline{\$125.00}}$$

24.

	$	%
V_i	V_i	100
+ Change		−25
= V_f	$50	75

$$\frac{V_i}{\$50} = \frac{100}{75}$$

$$V_i = \frac{100}{75} \times \$50 = \underline{\underline{\$66.67}}$$

25.

	$	%
V_i	V_i	100
+ Change		− 16 2/3
= V_f	$549	83 1/3

$$\frac{V_i}{\$549} = \frac{100}{83.\overline{3}}$$

$$V_i = \frac{100}{83.\overline{3}} \times \$549 = \underline{\underline{\$658.80}}$$

26.

	$	%
V_i	$900	100
+ Change		−90
= V_f	V_f	10

$$\frac{V_f}{\$900} = \frac{10}{100}$$

$$V_f = 0.1 \times \$900 = \underline{\underline{\$90.00}}$$

27.

	$	%
V_i	$102	100
+ Change		−2
= V_f	V_f	98

$$\frac{V_f}{\$102} = \frac{98}{100}$$

$$V_f = 0.98 \times \$102 = \underline{\underline{\$99.96}}$$

28.

	$	%
V_i	$102	100
+ Change		−100
= V_f	V_f	0

$$\frac{V_f}{\$102} = \frac{0}{100}$$

$$V_f = \underline{\underline{\$0.00}}$$

29.

	$	%
V_i	$250	100
+ Change	$500	%c
= V_f	$750	

$$\frac{\%c}{100\%} = \frac{\$500}{\$250}$$

$$\%c = \frac{50}{25} \times 100\% = \underline{\underline{200\%}}$$

30.

	$	%
V_i	$750	100
+ Change	−500	%c
= V_f	$250	

$$\frac{\%c}{100\%} = \frac{-\$500}{\$750}$$

$$\%c = -\frac{50}{75} \times 100\% = \underline{\underline{-66.7\%}}$$

$250 is \underline{66.7\% less} than $750.

31.

	$	%
V_i	$10,000	100
+ Change		0.75
= V_f	V_f	100.75

$$\frac{V_f}{\$10,000} = \frac{100.75}{100}$$

$$V_f = 1.0075 \times \$10,000 = \underline{\underline{\$10,075}}$$

32.

	$	%
V_i	$1045	100
+ Change		−0.5
= V_f	V_f	99.5

$$\frac{V_f}{\$1045} = \frac{99.5}{100}$$

$$V_f = 0.995 \times \$1045 = \underline{\underline{\$1039.78}}$$

33.

	$	%
V_i	V_i	100
+ Change		150
= V_f	$575	250

$$\frac{V_i}{\$575} = \frac{100}{250}$$

$$V_i = \frac{10}{25} \times \$575 = \underline{\underline{\$230.00}}$$

34.

	$	%
V_i	V_i	100
+ Change		210
= V_f	$465	310

$$\frac{V_i}{\$465} = \frac{100}{310}$$

$$V_i = \frac{10}{31} \times \$465 = \underline{\underline{\$150.00}}$$

35.

	$	%
V_i	$150	100
+ Change		150
= V_f	V_f	250

$$\frac{V_f}{\$150} = \frac{250}{100}$$

$$V_f = 2.5 \times \$150 = \underline{\underline{\$375.00}}$$

36.

	$	%
V_i	$10	100
+ Change		900
= V_f	V_f	1000

$$\frac{V_f}{\$10} = \frac{1000}{100}$$

$$V_f = 10 \times \$10 = \underline{\underline{\$100.00}}$$

37.

	$	%
Ticket price	Ticket price	100
+ GST		7
= Total cost	$148.35	107

$$\frac{\text{Ticket price}}{\$148.35} = \frac{100}{107}$$

$$\text{Ticket price} = \frac{100}{107}(\$148.35) = \underline{\underline{\$129.00}}$$

38.

		%
Former pop.	Former pop.	100
+ Change		24
= Current pop.	109,500	124

$$\frac{\text{Former pop.}}{109,500} = \frac{100}{124}$$

$$\text{Former population} = \frac{100}{124} \times 109,500 = \underline{\underline{88,306}}$$

39. a.

	No. hammers	%
V_i	32,400	100
+ Change	−4950	%c
= V_f	27,450	

$$\frac{\%c}{100\%} = \frac{-4950}{32,400}$$

$$\%c = -\frac{495}{3240} \times 100\% = -15.3\%$$

That is, a <u>decline of 15.3%</u>

b.

	$	%
V_i	$7.55	100
+ Change	$0.20	%c
= V_f	$7.75	

$$\frac{\%c}{100\%} = \frac{0.20}{\$7.55}$$

$$\%c = \frac{20}{755} \times 100\% = \underline{\underline{2.65\%}}$$

c.

	Revenue ($)	%
V_i	$244,620	100
+ Change	− 31,882.50	%c
= V_f	$212,737.50	

$$\frac{\%c}{100\%} = \frac{\$31,882.50}{\$244,620.00}$$

$\%c = - 13.0\%$

That is, a <u>decrease of 13.0%</u>

40. a.

	$	%
V_i	$0.55	100
+ Change	+1.00	%c
= V_f	$1.55	

$$\frac{\%c}{100\%} = \frac{\$1.00}{\$0.55}$$

$$\%c = \frac{100}{55} \times 100\% = 182\%$$

b.

	$	%
V_i	$1.55	100
+ Change	−0.80	%c
= V_f	$0.75	

$$\frac{\%c}{100\%} = \frac{-\$0.80}{\$1.55}$$

$$\%c = - \frac{80}{155} \times 100\% = - \underline{51.6\%}$$

That is, a <u>decrease of 51.6%</u>

c.

	$	%
V_i	$0.55	100
+ Change	+0.20	%c
= V_f	$0.75	

$$\frac{\%c}{100\%} = \frac{\$0.20}{\$0.55}$$

$$\%c = \frac{20}{55} \times 100\% = \underline{36.4\%}$$

41.

	Units	%
V_i	V_i	100
+ Change		6
= V_f	599	106

$$\frac{V_i}{599} = \frac{100}{106}$$

$$V_i = \frac{100}{106} \times 599 = \underline{565 \text{ units}}$$

42.

	$	%
V_i	V_i	100
+ Change		−35
= V_f	$122.85	65

$$\frac{V_i}{\$122.85} = \frac{100}{65}$$

$$V_i = \frac{100}{65} \times \$122.85 = \underline{\$189.00}$$

Exercise 3.3 *(continued)*

43.

1995	$	%
V_i	$5	100%
+ Change	– 1	%c
= V_f	$4	

$$\frac{\%c}{100\%} = \frac{-\$1}{\$5}$$

$$\%c = -\frac{1}{5} \times 100\% = -20\%$$

The price <u>decreased 20%</u> in 1995.

1996	$	%
V_i	$4	100%
+ Change	– 1	%c
= V_f	$3	

$$\frac{\%c}{100\%} = \frac{-\$1}{\$4}$$

$$\%c = -\frac{1}{4} \times 100\% = -25\%$$

The price <u>decreased 25%</u> in 1996.

44.

	$	%
V_i	V_i	100
+ Change		–27
= V_f	$100	73

$$\frac{V_i}{\$100} = \frac{100}{73}$$

$$V_i = \frac{100}{73} \times \$100 = \underline{\$136.99}$$

45.

	$	%
V_i		100
+ Change	Change	18
V_f	$4.36 million	118

$$\frac{Change}{\$4.36\ million} = \frac{18}{118}$$

$$Change = \frac{18}{118} \times \$4.36\ million = \underline{\$665,000}$$

46.

	Commission	%
V_i	7%	100%
+ Change	+1%	%c
V_f	8%	

$$\frac{\%c}{100\%} = \frac{1\%}{7\%}$$

$$\%c = \frac{1}{7} \times 100\% = \underline{14.3\%}$$

47.

	Int. rate	%
V_i	10.5%	100%
+ Change	– 0.75%	%c
V_f	9.75%	

$$\frac{\%c}{100\%} = \frac{-0.75\%}{10.5\%}$$

$$\%c = -\frac{0.75}{10.5} \times 100\% = -7.14\%$$

Interest charges were <u>reduced by 7.14%</u>.

48.

	$	%
V_i		100
+ Change	Change	280
= V_f	$1.30	380

$$\frac{Change}{\$1.30} = \frac{280}{380}$$

$$Change = \frac{28}{38} \times \$1.30 = \underline{\$0.96\ per\ litre.}$$

Exercise 3.3 *(concluded)*

49.

	$	%
V_i		100
+ Change	Change	−76
= V_f	$0.45	24

$$\frac{\text{Change}}{\$0.45} = \frac{-76}{24}$$

$$\text{Change} = -\frac{76}{24} \times \$0.45 = -\$1.43$$

The share price dropped by $1.43.

50.

	$	%
V_i		100
+ Change	Change	−55
= V_f	$24,300	45

$$\frac{\text{Change}}{\$24,300} = \frac{-55}{45}$$

$$\text{Change} = -\frac{55}{45} \times \$24,300 = -\$29,700$$

Total depreciation was $29,700.

51.

Sale	$	%
V_i	V_i	100
+ Change		−10
= V_f	$172,800	90

$$\frac{V_i}{\$172,800} = \frac{100}{90}$$

$$V_i = \frac{100}{90} \times \$172,800 = \$192,000$$

Appreciation	$	%
V_i	V_i	100
+ Change		140
= V_f	$192,000	240

$$\frac{V_i}{\$192,000} = \frac{100}{240}$$

$$V_i = \frac{10}{24} \times \$192,000 = \$80,000$$

52.

Markdown	$	%
List price	List price	100
− Reduction		−10
Selling price	$17,568	90

$$\frac{\text{List price}}{\$17,568} = \frac{100}{90}$$

$$\text{List price} = \frac{10}{9} \times \$17,568 = \$19,520$$

Markup	$	%
Cost	Cost	100
+ Markup		22
List price	$19,520	122

$$\frac{\text{Cost}}{\$19,520} = \frac{100}{122}$$

$$\text{Cost} = \frac{100}{122} \times \$19,520 = \$16,000$$

Exercise 3.4

1. Refund : Subscription price = Remaining issues : Total issues

$$\frac{Refund}{\$136} = \frac{2 \times 52 - 17}{3 \times 52}$$

$$Refund = \frac{87}{156} \times \$136 = \underline{\underline{\$75.85}}$$

2. $$\frac{Purchaser's\ share}{Total\ taxes} = \frac{Purchaser's\ days\ of\ possession}{Number\ of\ days\ in\ year}$$

$$\frac{Purchaser's\ share}{\$2849} = \frac{365 - 31 - 30 - 31 - 30 - 24}{365}$$

$$Purchaser's\ share = \frac{219}{365} \times \$2849 = \underline{\underline{\$1709.40}}$$

$$Vendor's\ share = \$2849 - \$1709.40 = \underline{\underline{\$1139.60}}$$

3. Refund : Two-year fee = Remaining days : Total days

$$\frac{Refund}{\$495} = \frac{(2 \times 365) - (29 + 30 + 31 + 31 + 9)}{2 \times 365} = \frac{730 - 130}{730}$$

$$Refund = \$495 \times \frac{600}{730} = \underline{\underline{\$406.85}}$$

4. Deductible expenses : Total expenses = Business km : Total km

$$\frac{Deductible\ expenses}{\$5674} = \frac{14,488}{14,488 + 8329}$$

$$Deductible\ expenses = \frac{14,488}{22,817} \times \$5674 = \underline{\underline{\$3602.79}}$$

5. a. Deductible expenses : Total expenses = Rooms used for business : Total rooms

$$\frac{Deductible\ expenses}{\$8756} = \frac{2}{11}$$

$$Deductible\ expenses = \frac{2}{11} \times \$8756 = \underline{\underline{\$1592.00}}$$

   b. $$\frac{Deductible\ expenses}{\$8756} = \frac{360}{1470 + 360}$$

$$Deductible\ expenses = \frac{360}{1830} \times \$8756 = \underline{\underline{\$1722.49}}$$

Exercise 3.4 *(continued)*

6. Tenant's costs:Total costs = Tenant's leased area:Total area

$$\frac{\text{Tenant's costs}}{\$9872} = \frac{\text{Tenant's leased area}}{172 + 136 + 420}$$

Granny's Chicken's cost $= \dfrac{172}{728} \times \$9872 = \underline{\underline{\$2332.40}}$

Toys 'n Novelties' cost $= \dfrac{136}{728} \times \$9872 = \underline{\underline{\$1844.22}}$

Pine Tree Pharmacy's cost $= \dfrac{420}{728} \times \$9872 = \underline{\underline{\$5695.38}}$

7. A's share:B's share:C's share:Total = 3:8:5:16

   a. A's premium $= \dfrac{3}{16} \times \$900,000 = \underline{\underline{\$168,750}}$

   B's premium $= \dfrac{8}{16} \times \$900,000 = \underline{\underline{\$450,000}}$

   C's premium $= \dfrac{5}{16} \times \$900,000 = \underline{\underline{\$281,250}}$

   b. A's exposure $= \dfrac{3}{16} \times \$38,600,000 = \underline{\underline{\$7,237,500}}$

   B's exposure $= \dfrac{8}{16} \times \$38,600,000 = \underline{\underline{\$19,300,000}}$

   C's exposure $= \dfrac{5}{16} \times \$38,600,000 = \underline{\underline{\$12,062,500}}$

8. The total partners' investment is $122,500 and their total hours worked during the quarter was 1207. Half of the profit is to be allocated on the basis

   Kevin:Lyle:Marnie:$28,115 = $65,000:$43,000:$14,500:$122,500

   and the other half on the basis

   Kevin:Lyle:Marnie:$28,115 = 210:365:632:1207

   Kevin's allocation $= \left(\dfrac{\$65,000}{\$122,500} + \dfrac{210}{1207} \right) \times \$28,115 = \underline{\underline{\$19,810}}$

   Lyle's allocation $= \left(\dfrac{\$43,000}{\$122,500} + \dfrac{365}{1207} \right) \times \$28,115 = \underline{\underline{\$18,371}}$

   Marnie's allocation = $56,230 − $19,809.75 − $18,370.99 = $\underline{\underline{\$18,049}}$

9. Total investment = $25,300,000 + $17,250,000 + $11,900,000 = $54,450,000

   Total sales = $21,200,000 + $8,350,000 + $7,450,000 = $37,000,000

   a. Industrial Products cost:Total costs = $25,300,000:$54,450,000

   $$\text{Industrial Products cost} = \frac{25,300}{54,450} \times \$839,000 = \underline{\underline{\$389,838}}$$

   Similarly,

   $$\text{Fine Paper cost} = \frac{17,250}{54,450} \times \$839,000 = \underline{\underline{\$265,799}}$$

   $$\text{Containers \& Packaging cost} = \frac{11,900}{54,450} \times \$839,000 = \underline{\underline{\$183,363}}$$

   b. $$\text{Industrial Products cost} = \frac{21,200}{37,000} \times \$839,000 = \underline{\underline{\$480,724}}$$

   $$\text{Fine Paper cost} = \frac{8350}{37,000} \times \$839,000 = \underline{\underline{\$189,342}}$$

   $$\text{Containers \& Packaging cost} = \frac{7450}{37,000} \times \$839,000 = \underline{\underline{\$168,934}}$$

10. The sales in excess of quota for Mr. A, Miss B, and Ms. D are $410,000, $255,000, and $115,000 respectively. The total of these excess sales is $780,000.

    Mr. A's bonus:Total bonus = Mr. A's excess sales:Total excess sales

    $$\text{Mr. A's bonus} = \frac{\$410,000}{\$780,000} \times \$10,000 = \underline{\underline{\$5256.41}}$$

    Similarly,

    $$\text{Miss B's bonus} = \frac{\$255,000}{\$780,000} \times \$10,000 = \underline{\underline{\$3269.23}}$$

    $$\text{Ms D's bonus} = \frac{\$115,000}{\$780,000} \times \$10,000 = \underline{\underline{\$1474.36}}$$

11. Total number of outstanding shares = 1550

    a. Value of X's shares:Value of company = Shares owned by X:Total number of shares

    $$\frac{\$175,000}{\text{Value of company}} = \frac{500}{1550}$$

    $$\text{Value of company} = \frac{1550}{500} \times \$175,000 = \underline{\underline{\$542,500}}$$

Exercise 3.4 *(concluded)*

b. Number of shares already owned by W, Y, and Z is 1050. From the 500 shares owned by X,
   W's allocation:500 = W's current shares:Total of W, Y, and Z

   W's allocation = $\dfrac{300}{1050} \times 500 = 142.9$ shares

   Similarly,

   Y's allocation = $\dfrac{350}{1050} \times 500 = 166.7$ shares

   Z's allocation = $\dfrac{400}{1050} \times 500 = 190.47$ shares

   After the buy-out,

   W will own 300 + 143 = 443 shares,

   Y will own 350 + 167 = 517 shares, and

   Z will own 400 + 190 = 590 shares.

c. W's contribution:$175,000 = W's allocation:500

   W's contribution = $\dfrac{143}{500} \times \$175,000 = \$50,050$

   Similarly,

   Y's contribution = $\dfrac{167}{500} \times \$175,000 = \$58,450$

   Z's contribution = $\dfrac{190}{500} \times \$175,000 = \$66,500$

12. Profit to be allocated to employees = $132,500.

   The *total* amount to be allocated to each employee group obeys the proportion:

   Executive group:Supervisor group:Production group:Total

   $= (4 \times 10):(8 \times 7):(45 \times 5):(4 \times 10 + 8 \times 7 + 45 \times 5)$

   $= 40:56:225:321$

   $\dfrac{\text{Executive group}}{\$132,500} = \dfrac{40}{321}$

   Executive group's allocation = $\dfrac{40}{321} \times \$132,500 = \$16,510.90$

   Each executive will receive $\dfrac{\$16,510.90}{4} = \$4127.73$

   Supervisor group's allocation = $\dfrac{56}{321} \times \$132,500 = \$23,115.26$

   Each supervisor will receive $\dfrac{\$23,115.26}{8} = \$2889.41$

   Production group's allocation = $\dfrac{225}{331} \times \$132,500 = \$92,873.83$

   Each production worker will receive $\dfrac{\$92,873.83}{45} = \$2063.86$

Exercise 3.5

1. $US\$1856 = US\$1856 \times 1.35645 \dfrac{C\$}{US\$} = \underline{\underline{C\$2517.57}}$

2. $£123.50 = £123.50 \times 2.27728 \dfrac{DM}{£} = \underline{\underline{DM281.24}}$

3. $C\$14,500 = C\$14,500 \times 80.06 \dfrac{¥}{C\$} = \underline{\underline{¥1,160,870}}$

4. $¥3,225,000 = ¥3,225,000 \times 0.00608 \dfrac{£}{¥} = \underline{\underline{£19,608}}$

5. $DM3251 = DM3251 \times 0.90198 \dfrac{C\$}{DM} = \underline{\underline{C\$2932.34}}$

6. $£56,700 = £56,700 \times 1.51430 \dfrac{US\$}{£} = \underline{\underline{US\$85,860.81}}$

7. $¥756,000 = ¥756,000 \times 0.01249 \dfrac{C\$}{¥} = \underline{\underline{C\$9442.44}}$

8. $DM159,500 = DM159,500 \times 0.66496 \dfrac{US\$}{DM} = \underline{\underline{US\$106,061.12}}$

9. $C\$94,350 = C\$94,350 \times 0.48684 \dfrac{£}{C\$} = \underline{\underline{£45,933.35}}$

10. $DM37,650 = DM37,650 \times 72.21 \dfrac{¥}{DM} = \underline{\underline{¥2,718,707}}$

11. $C\$49,900 = C\$49,900 \times 1.10867 \dfrac{DM}{C\$} = \underline{\underline{DM55,322.63}}$

12. $£8950 = £8950 \times 164.45 \dfrac{¥}{£} = \underline{\underline{¥\ 1,471,828}}$

13. a. $E(C\$:Ffr) = \dfrac{1}{E(Ffr:C\$)} = \dfrac{1}{3.76313} = \underline{\underline{0.26574}}$

    b. $E(A\$:¥) = \dfrac{1}{85.90} = \underline{\underline{0.011641}}$

    c. $E(£:Sfr) = \dfrac{1}{1.85729} = \underline{\underline{0.53842}}$

    d. $E(A\$:C\$) = \dfrac{1}{1.07302} = \underline{\underline{0.93195}}$

Exercise 3.5 *(continued)*

14. $US\$200 = US\$200 \times 1.35645 \dfrac{C\$}{US\$} = C\$271.29$

With an additional 1.5% commission, the cost will be
$V_f = V_i(1 + c) = C\$271.29(1.015) = \underline{C\$275.36}$

15. $US\$48 = US\$48 \times 1.35645 \dfrac{C\$}{US\$} = C\$65.11$

After deduction of the 1.5% commission, Simon will receive
$V_f = V_i(1 + c) = C\$65.11(1 - 0.015) = \underline{C\$64.13}$

16. $£2000 = £2000 \times 2.05407 \dfrac{C\$}{£} = C\$4108.14$

With an additional 0.5% commission, the cost will be
$C\$4108.14(1.005) = \underline{C\$4128.68}$

17. $£350 = £350 \times 2.05407 \dfrac{C\$}{£} = C\$718.92$

After deducting the 0.75% commission, Lois will receive
$C\$718.92(1 - 0.0075) = \underline{C\$713.53}$

18. $US\$23 = US\$23 \times 1.35645 \dfrac{C\$}{US\$} = C\$31.20$

Hence, <u>Canada</u> has a cost of labour advantage of
$C\$31.20 - C\$28.00 = \underline{C\$3.20 \text{ per hour}}$

19. $US\$3.85 = US\$3.85 \times 1.35645 \dfrac{C\$}{US\$} = C\$5.22$

The saving is $C\$5.50 - C\$5.22 = C\$0.28$ per pound
<u>28 C¢ per pound</u>.

20. Initially, $E(£:C\$) = 0.48684$; $E(C\$:£) = 2.05406$
Finally, $E(£:C\$) = 0.54084$; $E(C\$:£) = 1.84898$
Initially £1 would purchase C\$2.05406 but later it would purchase only C\$1.84898. Therefore, the <u>£ has depreciated by</u>

$$\frac{2.05406 - 1.84898}{2.05406} \times 100\% = \underline{9.98\%}$$

21. Initially, $E(C\$:¥) = 0.01249$ and $E(¥:C\$) = 80.064$
Later, $E(C\$:¥) = 0.01249 - 0.00054 = 0.01195$
making $E(¥:C\$) = 83.682$
In other words, C\$1 will now buy ¥83.682 whereas it would previously buy only ¥ 80.064.
Hence, the <u>C\$ has appreciated by</u>

$$\frac{83.682 - 80.064}{80.064} \times 100\% = \underline{4.52\%}$$

Exercise 3.5 *(continued)*

22. If the C$ weakens by 0.5% relative to the DM, C$1 will buy only

$$V_f = V_i(1 + c) = DM\ 1.10867(1 - 0.005) = DM\ 1.103127$$

That is,

$$\underline{E(DM:C\$) = 1.103127} \quad \text{and} \quad \underline{E(C\$:DM)} = \frac{1}{E(DM:C\$)} = \underline{0.90651}$$

23. If the C$ strengthens by 1.2%, a given amount of Canadian currency will purchase 1.2% more US currency. Using $V_f = V_i(1 + c)$ for the appreciation of the C$,

$$\begin{aligned} \text{New } \underline{E(US\$:C\$)} &= \text{Former } E(US\$:C\$)(1 + 0.012) \\ &= 0.73722(1.012) \\ &= \underline{0.746067} \end{aligned}$$

$$\text{and} \quad \underline{E(C\$:US\$)} = \frac{1}{E(US\$:C\$)} = \frac{1}{0.746067} = \underline{1.34036}$$

24. If the C$ appreciates by C¢0.17 = C$0.0017, £1 will purchase C$0.0017 less. That is,

$$E(C\$:£) = 2.05407 - 0.0017 = 2.05237$$

$$\text{and} \quad E(£:C\$) = \frac{1}{E(C\$:£)} = \underline{0.48724}$$

25. If the C$ weakens by C¢0.33 = C$0.0033, US$1 will purchase C$0.0033 more. That is,

$$E(C\$:US\$) = 1.35645 + 0.0033 = 1.35975$$

$$\text{and} \quad E(US\$:C\$) = \frac{1}{E(C\$:US\$)} = \frac{1}{1.35975} = \underline{0.73543}$$

26. If the C$ strengthens by £0.0021, C$1 will purchase £0.0021 more. That is,

$$E(£:C\$) = 0.48684 + 0.0021 = 0.48894$$

$$\text{and} \quad E(C\$:£) = \frac{1}{E(£:C\$)} = \underline{2.04524}$$

27. If the C$ weakens by DM0.021, C$1 will purchase DM0.021 less. That is,

$$E(DM:C\$) = 1.10867 - 0.021 = 1.08767$$

$$\text{and} \quad E(C\$:DM) = \frac{1}{E(DM:C\$)} = \frac{1}{1.08767} = \underline{0.919397}$$

28. $$\text{C\$ Price} = \text{US\$ Price} \times E(C\$:US\$) = \frac{\text{US\$ Price}}{E(US\$:C\$)}$$

$$\text{Former C\$ Price} = \frac{1500}{0.7543} = C\$1988.60$$

$$\text{Current C\$ Price} = \frac{1500}{0.7822} = C\$1917.67$$

$$\text{Price change} = C\$1988.60 - C\$1917.67 = \underline{C\$70.93 \text{ decrease}}.$$

Exercise 3.5 *(continued)*

29. $C\$ \text{ Price} = ¥ \text{ Price} \times E(C\$:¥) = \dfrac{¥ \text{ Price}}{E(¥:C\$)}$

Former C\$ Price $= \dfrac{195{,}000}{71.91} = C\$2711.72$

Current C\$ Price $= \dfrac{195{,}000}{68.33} = C\$2853.80$

Price change $= C\$2853.80 - C\$2711.72 = \underline{C\$142.08 \text{ increase.}}$

30. $C\$ \text{ Revenue} = £ \text{ Revenue} \times E(C\$:£) = \dfrac{£ \text{ Revenue}}{E(£:C\$)}$

Former C\$ Revenue $= \dfrac{23{,}000}{0.5032} = C\$45{,}707.47$

Current C\$ Revenue $= \dfrac{23{,}000}{0.5338} = C\$43{,}087.30$

Revenue change $= \$45{,}707.47 - \$43{,}087.30 = \underline{C\$2620.17 \text{ decrease.}}$

31. $C\$ \text{ Price} = US\$ \text{ Price} \times E(C\$:US\$) = \dfrac{US\$ \text{ Price}}{E(US\$:C\$)}$

Former C\$ Price $= \dfrac{395}{0.7521} = C\$525.20 \text{ per oz.}$

Current C\$ Price $= \dfrac{395}{0.7388} = C\$534.65 \text{ per oz.}$

Price change $= C\$534.65 - C\$525.20 = \underline{C\$9.45 \text{ per oz. increase.}}$

32. For the conversion C\$ → £ → DM,

$C\$1150 = C\$1150 \times E(£:C\$) = C\$1150 \times 0.48684 \dfrac{£}{C\$} = £559.87$

$£559.87 = £559.87 \times E(DM:£) = 559.87(2.27728) = DM1274.98$
For the direct conversion C\$ → DM,
$C\$1150 = C\$1150 \times E(DM:C\$) = 1150 \times 1.10867 = DM1274.97$
Both give the same result $\underline{(DM1274.97)}$ within the five-figure precision of the exchange rates.

33. For the conversion US\$ → yen → pounds,
$US\$2560 = US\$2560 \times E(¥:US\$) = 2560 \times 108.60 = ¥278{,}016$
$¥278{,}016 = ¥278{,}016 \times E(£:¥) = 278{,}016 \times 0.00608 = £1690.34$

For the direct conversion US\$ → pounds,
$US\$2560 = US\$2560 \times E(£:US\$) = 2560 \times 0.66037 = £1690.55$

The results are the same $\underline{(£1690.55)}$ within the three-figure accuracy allowed by $E(£:¥) = 0.00608$.

Exercise 3.5 *(concluded)*

34. Converting the US price per quart to C$ per litre,

$$\text{US\$0.79 per quart} = \text{US\$0.79 per quart} \times \frac{1 \text{ quart}}{0.94635 \text{ litre}}$$

$$= \text{US\$0.8348 per litre} \times E(\text{C\$:US\$})$$
$$= \text{C\$}(0.8348 \times 1.35645) \text{ per litre}$$
$$= \text{C\$1.132 per litre}$$

The percent difference is

$$\frac{\$1.132 - \$1.27}{\$1.27} \times 100\% = -10.9\%$$

That is, the milk is <u>10.9% cheaper in the US.</u>

35. Converting the Canadian price per kg to US$ per pound.

$$\text{C\$8.50 per kg} = \text{C\$8.50 per kg} \times \frac{1 \text{ kg}}{2.2 \text{ pounds}}$$

$$= \text{C\$3.864 per pound} \times E(\text{US\$:C\$})$$
$$= \text{US\$}(3.864 \times 0.73722) \text{ per pound}$$
$$= \text{US\$2.85 per pound}$$

Hence, the pork chops are US$ (3.25 − 2.85) = <u>US$0.40 per pound more expensive in the US.</u>

Exercise 3.6

1. Current index number $= \dfrac{\text{Current value}}{\text{Value on base date}} \times \text{Base value}$

$$= \frac{\$4961}{\$3278} \times 100$$

$$= \underline{\underline{151.3}}$$

2. Current index $= \dfrac{\$4961}{\$3278} \times 1000 = \underline{\underline{1513}}$

3. $\dfrac{\text{Current index}}{\text{Base value}} = \dfrac{\text{Current value}}{\text{Value on base date}}$

$$\frac{119.5}{100} = \frac{\text{Current value}}{\$7532}$$

Current value $= \dfrac{119.5}{100} \times \$7532 = \underline{\underline{\$9000.74}}$

4. $$\frac{\text{Current index}}{\text{Base value}} = \frac{\text{Current value}}{\text{Value on base date}}$$

$$\frac{2278}{\text{Base value}} = \frac{\$431.70}{\$189.50}$$

$$\text{Base value} = \frac{\$189.50}{\$431.70} \times 2278 = \underline{\underline{1000}}$$

5. $$\frac{\text{Current index}}{10} = \frac{\$689}{\$735}$$

$$\text{Current index} = \frac{\$689}{\$735} \cdot \times 10 = \underline{\underline{9.374}}$$

6. $$\frac{89.50}{100} = \frac{\text{Current value}}{\$8950}$$

$$\text{Current value} = \frac{89.50}{100} \times \$8950 = \underline{\underline{\$8010.25}}$$

7. $$\frac{2120}{1000} = \frac{\$7729}{\text{Value on base date}}$$

$$\text{Value on base date} = \frac{1000}{2120} \times \$7729 = \underline{\underline{\$3645.75}}$$

8. $$\frac{441.8}{\text{Base value}} = \frac{\$398.60}{\$451.10}$$

$$\text{Base value} = \frac{\$451.10}{\$398.60} \times 441.8 = \underline{\underline{500}}$$

9. $$\text{CPI} = \frac{\text{Cost of basket in December 1990}}{\text{Cost of basket in the base year}} \times \text{Base value}$$

$$= \frac{\$26,090}{\$21,350} \times 100$$

$$= \underline{\underline{122.2}}$$

10. a. The costs will be in the same ratio as the CPIs.

$$\frac{\text{CPI(July 1995)}}{\text{CPI(July 1985)}} = \frac{\text{Cost in July 1995}}{\text{Cost in July 1985}}$$

$$\frac{133.3}{96.0} = \frac{\$2750}{\text{Cost in July 1985}}$$

$$\text{Cost in July 1985} = \frac{96.0}{133.3} \times \$2750 = \underline{\underline{\$1980.50}}$$

Exercise 3.6 *(continued)*

b. The percent inflation for the entire 10-year period equals the percent increase in the CPI. Since

$$\%c = \frac{CPI(1995) - CPI(1985)}{CPI(1985)} \times 100\% = \frac{133.3 - 96.0}{96.0} \times 100\% = \underline{\underline{38.85\%}}$$

The 10-year percent inflation was 38.85%.

11. Nominal dollar amounts having the same purchasing power will be in the same ratio as the respective CPIs. Hence,

$$\frac{1992 \text{ amount}}{1991 \text{ amount}} = \frac{CPI(1992)}{CPI(1991)}$$

$$\text{Amount required in 1992} = \frac{129.4}{126.7} \times \$1000 = \underline{\underline{\$1021.31}}$$

12. If tuition increased at the same rate as the cost of living, then

$$\frac{\text{Tuition in year 5}}{\text{Tuition in year 1}} = \frac{CPI \text{ in year 5}}{CPI \text{ in year 1}}$$

That is,

$$\text{Tuition in year 5} = \frac{134.0}{119.5} \times \$115 = \underline{\underline{\$128.95}}$$

Current tuition would be only $128.95 if tuition increases kept pace with inflation.

13. a. The costs of the basket of representative goods are in the same ratio as the goods subindex. That is,

$$\frac{\text{Cost in 1995}}{\text{Cost in 1985}} = \frac{\text{Goods subindex in 1995}}{\text{Goods subindex in 1985}}$$

$$\text{Cost in 1995} = \frac{127}{96.8} \times \$1000 = \underline{\underline{\$1311.98}}$$

b. $$\text{Cost in 1995} = \frac{142}{95.2} \times \$1000 = \underline{\underline{\$1491.60}}$$

c. The cost of goods increased by 31.20% while the cost of services increased by 49.16%. As a percentage of 1985 prices, the price of services increased by

$$49.16\% - 31.20\% = \underline{\underline{17.96\%}}$$

more than the price of goods.

14. The aggregate values of the shares at any two dates will be in the same ratio as the TSE 300 index values. That is,

$$\frac{\text{Value of shares (end of 1992)}}{\text{Value of shares (end of 1982)}} = \frac{\text{TSE 300 index (end of 1992)}}{\text{TSE 300 index (end of 1982)}}$$

$$\text{Value of shares (1992)} = \frac{3350}{1958} \times \$50,000 = \underline{\underline{\$85,546}}$$

Exercise 3.6 *(concluded)*

15.   %c (share prices) $= \dfrac{3350 - 1958}{1958} \times 100\% = 71.09\%$

%c (CPI) $= \dfrac{129.4 - 86.1}{86.1} \times 100\% = 50.29\%$

As a percentage of 1982 price levels, share prices rose 71.09% − 50.29% = <u>20.80% more</u> than consumer prices.

16.   The portfolio values will be in the same ratio as the exchange's index. That is,

$$\dfrac{\text{Portfolio value in November 1989}}{\text{Portfolio value in November 1987}} = \dfrac{\text{Index in November 1989}}{\text{Index in November 1987}}$$

Portfolio value (Nov. 1989) $= \dfrac{1999.8}{1464.4} \times \$30{,}000 = \underline{\underline{\$40{,}968}}$

17.   a. $\dfrac{\text{1983 amount}}{\text{1978 amount}} = \dfrac{\text{CPI (1983)}}{\text{CPI (1978)}}$

1983 amount $= \dfrac{114.1}{70.8} \times \$100 = \underline{\underline{\$161.16}}$

b.   Inflation rate = Percent change in the CPI

Inflation rate $= \dfrac{77.1 - 70.8}{70.8} \times 100\% = \underline{\underline{8.90\% \text{ for 1978}}}$

$= \dfrac{84.5 - 77.1}{77.1} \times 100\% = \underline{\underline{9.60\% \text{ for 1979}}}$

$= \dfrac{94.6 - 84.5}{84.5} \times 100\% = \underline{\underline{11.95\% \text{ for 1980}}}$

$= \dfrac{105.4 - 94.6}{94.6} \times 100\% = \underline{\underline{11.42\% \text{ for 1981}}}$

$= \dfrac{114.1 - 105.4}{105.4} \times 100\% = \underline{\underline{8.25\% \text{ for 1982}}}$

Exercise 3A

1.   The general equilibrium condition for the exchange rates among three currencies is

$$E(C_1:C_2) \times E(C_2:C_3) \times E(C_3:C_1) = 1$$

For the A$, Ffr, and £,

$$E(A\$:Ffr) \times E(Ffr:£) \times E(£:A\$) = 1$$

Substituting the given exchange rates,

$$0.2477 \times 7.730 \times E(£:A\$) = 1$$

Solving for $E(£:A\$)$,

$$E(£:A\$) = \dfrac{1}{0.2477 \times 7.730} = \underline{\underline{0.5223}}$$

Exercise 3A *(concluded)*

2. No currency exchange profit can exist when

$$E(C\$:Sfr) \times E(Sfr:DM) \times E(DM:C\$) = 1$$

Isolating and solving for $E(C\$:Sfr)$,

$$E(C\$:Sfr) = \frac{1}{E(Sfr:DM) \times E(DM:C\$)}$$

We are given $E(DM:Sfr) = 1.2261$ and $E(DM:C\$) = 1.1091$. Then

$$E(C\$:Sfr) = \frac{E(DM:Sfr)}{E(DM:C\$)} = \frac{1.2261}{1.1091} = \underline{\underline{1.1055}}$$

Review Problems

1. a. $0.18:0.60:0.45 = 18:60:45 = \underline{6:20:15}$

    b. $\dfrac{9}{8} : \dfrac{3}{4} : \dfrac{3}{2} = 9:6:12$ (each term multiplied by 8)

    $= \underline{3:2:4}$ (each term divided by 3)

    c. $\dfrac{1}{6} : \dfrac{1}{3} : \dfrac{1}{9} = 1:2\dfrac{2}{3}$ (each term multiplied by 6)

    $= \underline{3:6:2}$ (each term multiplied by 3)

    d. $6\dfrac{1}{4} : 5 : 8\dfrac{3}{4} = \dfrac{25}{4} : 5 : \dfrac{35}{4}$

    $= 25:20:35$ (each term multiplied by 4)

    $= \underline{5:4:7}$ (each term divided by 5)

2. a. $t:20:10 = 24:09:s$

    $t:26 = 24:39$ and $26:10 = 39:s$

    $\dfrac{t}{26} = \dfrac{24}{39}$ and $\dfrac{26}{10} = \dfrac{39}{s}$

    $39t = 26(24)$ and $26s = 39(10)$

    $t = \underline{\underline{16}}$ $\qquad s = \underline{\underline{15}}$

    b. $x:3600:y = \dfrac{4}{5} : \dfrac{2}{3} : \dfrac{7}{4}$

    $x:3600 = \dfrac{4}{5} : \dfrac{2}{3} = 12:10$ and $3600:y = \dfrac{2}{3} : \dfrac{7}{4} = 8:21$

    $\dfrac{x}{3600} = \dfrac{12}{10}$ and $\dfrac{3600}{y} = \dfrac{8}{21}$

    $10x = 12(3600)$ and $3600(21) = 8y$

    $x = \underline{4320}$ and $y = \underline{9450}$

Review Problems *(continued)*

3. Mark's holding:Ben's holding:Tanya's holding

$$= 4250:2550:5950$$

$$= 85:51:119 \text{ (each term divided by 50)}$$

$$= \underline{5:3:7} \text{ (each term divided by 17)}$$

4. a.

	$	%
Purchase price		100
+ Commission	Comm.	2
Total paid	$4845	102

$$\frac{\text{Commission}}{\$4845} = \frac{2}{102}$$

$$\text{Commission} = \frac{2}{102} \times \$4845 = \$95.00$$

b. Price (before commission) of 200 shares = $4845 − $95 = $4750

$$\text{Price per share} = \frac{\$4750}{200} = \underline{\$23.75}$$

5. Let B, N, and A represent the number of beds, nurses, and aids, respectively. We are given

$$N:B:A = 4:9:2$$

If B = 436, then

$$\frac{N}{436} = \frac{4}{9} \quad \text{and} \quad \frac{436}{A} = \frac{9}{2}$$

$$9N = 4(436) \quad \text{and} \quad 2(436) = 9A$$

$$N = 193.8 \quad \text{and} \quad A = 96.7$$

$\underline{194 \text{ nurses}}$ and $\underline{97 \text{ aides}}$ need to be hired.

6. D sales:E sales:F sales = 13:17:21

If E sales = $478,000

$$\frac{\text{D sales}}{\$478,000} = \frac{13}{17} \quad \text{and} \quad \frac{\$478,000}{\text{F sales}} = \frac{17}{21}$$

$$17 \text{ (D sales)} = 13(\$478,000) \quad \text{and} \quad 21(\$478,000) = 17 \text{ (F sales)}$$

$$\text{D sales} = \underline{\$365,529} \quad \text{and} \quad \text{F sales} = \underline{\$590,471}$$

The expected sales of department D are $365,529 and of department F are $590,471.

Review Problems (continued)

7.

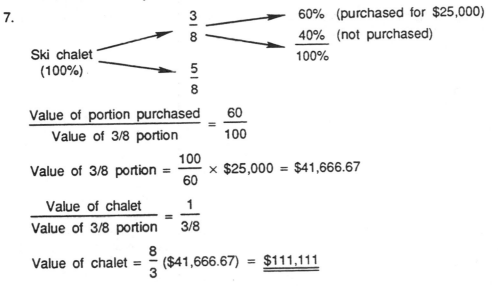

$$\frac{\text{Value of portion purchased}}{\text{Value of 3/8 portion}} = \frac{60}{100}$$

$$\text{Value of 3/8 portion} = \frac{100}{60} \times \$25,000 = \$41,666.67$$

$$\frac{\text{Value of chalet}}{\text{Value of 3/8 portion}} = \frac{1}{3/8}$$

$$\text{Value of chalet} = \frac{8}{3}(\$41,666.67) = \underline{\$111,111}$$

8. Let W, S, and L represent the shares of Wendy, Simone, and Leif. Let T represent the total of the three shares. We are given

$$W:S:L = \frac{3}{2}:\frac{2}{3}:\frac{5}{3} = 9:4:10 \text{ (after multiplying by 6)}$$

Then

$$W:S:L:T = 9:4:10:23$$

If T = $50, then

$$\frac{S}{\$50} = \frac{4}{23} \quad \text{and} \quad \frac{L}{\$50} = \frac{10}{23}$$

$$23S = 4(\$50) \quad \text{and} \quad 23L = 10(\$50)$$

$$S = \underline{\$8.70} \qquad\qquad L = \underline{\$21.74}$$

Wendy, Simone, and Leif should pay $19.56, $8.70, and $21.74, respectively.

9. We are given

A:B:C:D:Total costs = 1260:3800:1550:2930:Total area
where total costs = $28,575 and total area = 9540 square feet.

Then

$$\frac{A}{\$28,575} = \frac{1260}{9540}$$

$$\text{A's share} = \frac{1260}{9540} \times \$28,575 = \underline{\$3774.06}$$

Similar calculations for B's, C's, and D's allocations give $11,382.08, $4642.69, and $8776.18, respectively.

Review Problems (contiued)

10. Let S, Y, and R represent the number of bottles of scotch, rye, and rum. The total number of bottles appropriate for 480 guests is 480 + 10 = 48. Then

$$S:Y:R:48 = 3:5:4:(3 + 5 + 4)$$

$$\frac{S}{48} = \frac{3}{12} \quad \text{and} \quad \frac{Y}{48} = \frac{5}{12}$$

$$12S = 3(48) \quad \text{and} \quad 12Y = 5(48)$$

$$S = \underline{\underline{12}} \quad \text{and} \quad Y = \underline{\underline{20}}$$

$$R = 48 - 12 - 20 = \underline{\underline{16}}$$

12 bottles of scotch, 20 bottles of rye, and 16 bottles of rum should be stocked for the party.

11. 0.5($84,780) = $42,390 should be allocated in proportion to each partner's investment and $42,390 should be allocated in proportion to hours worked. Let H, D, and L represent Huey's, Dewey's, and Louie's shares, respectively. For the allocation in respect of investments,

$$H:D:L:\$42,390 = \$70,000:\$30,000:\$45,000:\$145,000$$

$$= 14:6:9:29$$

$$\text{Then} \quad \frac{H}{\$42,390} = \frac{14}{29}$$

$$29H = 14(\$42,390)$$

To the nearest dollar, Huey's share is $20,464. Similarly, Dewey's share is $8770 and Louie's share is $13,156.

For the allocation in respect of hours worked,

$$H:D:L:\$42,390 = 425:1680:1445:3545$$

$$\text{Then} \quad \frac{H}{\$42,390} = \frac{425}{3545}$$

To the nearest dollar, Huey's share is $5082. Similarly, Dewey's share is $20,089 and Louie's share is $17,219. The combined allocations are:

$$\$20,464 + \$5082 \quad = \underline{\underline{\$25,546 \text{ to Huey}}}$$

$$\$\ \ 8770 + \$20,089 = \underline{\underline{\$28,859 \text{ to Dewey}}}$$

$$\$13,156 + \$17,219 = \underline{\underline{\$30,375 \text{ to Louie}}}$$

12. The C$ needed to purchase £242 was

$$£242 \times E(C\$:£) = £242 \times 2.053 \frac{C\$}{£} = C\$496.83$$

The C$ received from the conversion of £242 was

$$£242 \times E(C\$:£) = £242 \times 2.091 \frac{C\$}{£} = C\$506.02$$

The Percivals gained

$$C\$506.02 - C\$496.83 = \underline{\underline{C\$9.19}} \text{ on the transaction.}$$

Review Problems *(concluded)*

13. Initially, E(C2:C1) = 0.05614

That is, one unit of C1 will purchase 0.05614 units of C2. If C1 weakens by 1.5% relative to C2, then one unit of C1 will purchase 1.5% less of C2. Hence,

New E(C2:C1) = 0.05614(1 − 0.015) = $\underline{0.05530}$

and new E(C1:C2) = $\dfrac{1}{\text{New E(C2:C1)}}$ = $\dfrac{1}{0.05530}$ = $\underline{\underline{18.08}}$

14. C$ cost = US$2000 × E(C$:US$) = $\dfrac{\text{US\$2000}}{\text{E(US\$:C\$)}}$

Former price = C$ $\dfrac{2000}{0.7543}$ = C$2651.46

Current price = C$ $\dfrac{2000}{0.7367}$ = C$2714.81

The importer will pay $\underline{\text{C\$63.35 more}}$ for the item.

15. a. Inflation rate = % change in the CPI

$$= \dfrac{\text{CPI(final)} - \text{CPI(initial)}}{\text{CPI(initial)}} \times 100\%$$

(i) Inflation rate = $\dfrac{\text{CPI(July 1, 1991)} - \text{CPI(July 1, 1990)}}{\text{CPI(July 1, 1990)}} \times 100\%$

$$= \dfrac{126.2 - 119.5}{119.5} \times 100\%$$

$$= \underline{\underline{5.6\%}}$$

(ii) Inflation rate = $\dfrac{128.1 - 126.2}{126.2} \times 100\%$

$$= \underline{\underline{1.5\%}}$$

b. Cumulative % change in prices = $\dfrac{128.1 - 104.4}{104.4} \times 100\% = 22.7\%$

Therefore, $\underline{\$122.70}$ was required on July 1, 1992 to have the same purchasing power as $100 on July 1, 1987.

Self-Test Exercises

1. a. $65:43 = 27.3:x$

$$\frac{65}{43} = \frac{27.3}{x}$$

$$65x = 43(27.3)$$

$$x = \underline{18.06}$$

   b. $1410:2330:870 = a:550:b$

$$\frac{1410}{2330} = \frac{a}{550} \qquad \text{and} \qquad \frac{2330}{870} = \frac{550}{b}$$

$$a = \frac{1410}{2330} \times 550 \qquad \qquad b = \frac{870}{2330} \times 550$$

$$= \underline{332.8} \qquad \qquad \qquad = \underline{205.4}$$

2. Milan:Stephen:Fred:$135,000 = 3:4:2:9$

$$\frac{\text{Milan's investment}}{\$135,000} = \frac{3}{9}$$

Milan's investment $= \dfrac{3}{9} \times \$135,000 = \$45,000$

Similarly,

Stephen's investment = $60,000 and
Fred's investment = $20,000

If each invests an additional $10,000, their total investments will be in the ratio

Milan:Stephen:Fred $= 55,000:70,000:30,000$

$$= \underline{11:14:6}$$

3. $$\frac{\text{Test market sales}}{\text{Test market population}} = \frac{\text{Forecast sales}}{\text{Population}}$$

$$\frac{543}{120,000} = \frac{\text{Forecast sales}}{21,000,000}$$

$$\text{Forecast sales} = \frac{543 \times 21,000,000}{120,000}$$

$$= \underline{95,025 \text{ units}}$$

Self-Test Exercises *(continued)*

4. Education:Health care:Social services = 29:31:21

    $3.17 billion:Health care:Social services = 29:31:21

    $$\frac{\$3.17 \text{ billion}}{\text{Health care}} = \frac{29}{31} \quad \text{and} \quad \frac{\$3.17 \text{ billion}}{\text{Social services}} = \frac{29}{21}$$

    Health care allocation = $\frac{31}{29} \times \$3.17$ billion = $\underline{\underline{\$3.39 \text{ billion}}}$

    Social service allocation = $\frac{21}{29} \times \$3.17$ billion = $\underline{\underline{\$2.30 \text{ billion}}}$

5.

	$	%
Price		100
+ GST	GST	7
Total cost	$23.22	107

    $$\frac{\text{GST}}{\$23.22} = \frac{7}{107}$$

    $$\text{GST} = \frac{7}{107} \times \$23.22 = \underline{\underline{\$1.52}}$$

6. We are given

    L:M:N:P = 1.5:1:0.75:0.5

    If N = $2000, then L:$2000 = 1.5:0.75. Hence,

    $$\frac{L}{\$2000} = \frac{1.5}{0.75} = 2$$

    L = 2($2000) = $4000

    Similarly, M = $2666.67 and P = $1333.33.

    <u>Ms. L received $4000</u>, <u>Mr. M received $2666.67</u>, and <u>Mr. P received $1333.33</u>.

7. Let W, S, and SS represent the wife's, son's and stepson's shares, respectively. We are given

    $$\text{W:S:SS} = \frac{7}{5}:1:\frac{5}{7} = 49:35:25 \text{ (after multiplying by 35)}$$

    For a total distribution of $331,000,

    W:S:SS:$331,000 = 49:35:25:(49 + 35 + 25)

    $$\frac{W}{\$331,000} = \frac{49}{109} \quad \text{and} \quad \frac{S}{\$331,000} = \frac{35}{109}$$

    To the nearest dollar, W = $\underline{\underline{\$148,798}}$, S = $\underline{\underline{\$106,284}}$, and SS = $331,000 − $148,798 − $106,284 = $\underline{\underline{\$75,918}}$.

Self-Test Exercises *(concluded)*

8.
$$C\$1500 = C\$1500 \times E(\text{Lira}:C\$) = \frac{C\$1500}{E(C\$:\text{Lira})} = \frac{1500}{0.0009526} = \underline{\underline{1,574,638 \text{ lira}}}$$

9. For the same purchasing power, the hourly rates should be in the same ratio as the CPI. Hence,

$$\frac{\text{Desired hourly rate}}{\$22.25} = \frac{148.4}{127.6}$$

$$\text{Desired hourly rate} = \frac{148.4}{127.6} \times \$22.25 = \underline{\underline{\$25.88/\text{hour}}}$$

10.
$$C\$ \text{ price} = ¥\,2,965,000 \times E(C\$:¥) = \frac{¥\,2,965,000}{E(¥:C\$)}$$

$$\text{Former } C\$ \text{ price} = C\$\,\frac{2,965,000}{72.11} = C\$41,117.74$$

$$\text{Current } C\$ \text{ price} = C\$\,\frac{2,965,000}{73.89} = C\$40,272.16$$

The price of the car <u>decreased by C\$845.58</u>.

11. Convert the price of Virginia coal to \$C per metric ton.

$$2000 \text{ lb} = \frac{2000}{2.205} \text{kg} = \frac{907.03}{1000} \text{ metric tons} = 0.90703 \text{ metric tons}$$

$$\text{US}\$27.25 \text{ per ton} = \text{US}\$\,\frac{27.25}{0.90703} \text{ per metric ton}$$

$$= \text{US}\$30.043 \text{ per metric ton}$$

$$= \text{US}\$30.043 \times E(C\$:\text{US}\$) \text{ per metric ton}$$

$$= C\$\,\frac{30.043}{0.7528} \text{ per metric ton}$$

$$= C\$39.91 \text{ per metric ton}$$

Therefore, <u>Alberta coal</u> is C\$39.91 − C\$39.50 = <u>C\$0.41 per metric ton cheaper</u>.

4 Mathematics of Merchandising

Changes in the Second Edition:

1. At the "macro" level, the order of the former Chapters 4 and 5 has been reversed. As pointed out by a reviewer, **Trade Discounts, Cash Discounts, Markup,** and **Markdown** provide a more natural progression of topics (in terms of both concept development and degree of difficulty) in going from Percent Change, Ratios, and Proportions (in Chapters 2 and 3) to **Cost-Volume-Profit and Break-Even Analysis** (Chapter 5).

2. The use of the pictorial aid for solving more complex markup and markdown problems (former Section 5.6) had mixed reviews. It has been abandoned in favour of a tabular model (current Sections 4.4, 4.5, and 4.6) whose design impounds the additive relationships among the variables. In addition, the table often helps the user identify a proportion that can be employed to solve for an unknown quantity.

3. To reduce the number of "double-barrelled" symbols, M is now used for markup (instead of MU) and D is used for markdown (instead of MD).

Exercise 4.1

1. Amount of discount $= dL = 0.3\overline{3}$ ($249) = $\underline{\$83.00}$

   Net price $= L - dL = \$249.00 - \$83.00 = \underline{\$166.00}$

2. Amount of discount $= 0.1\overline{6}$ ($995) = $\underline{\$165.83}$

   Net price $= \$995.00 - \$165.83 = \underline{\$829.17}$

3. Amount of discount $= L - N = \$127.98 - \$106.65 = \underline{\$21.33}$

   $\text{Discount rate} = \dfrac{\text{Amount of discount}}{L} \times 100\% = \dfrac{\$21.33}{\$127.98} \times 100\% = \underline{16\tfrac{2}{3}\%}$

4. Amount of discount $= \$49.95 - \$34.97 = \underline{\$14.98}$

   $\text{Discount rate} = \dfrac{\$14.98}{\$49.95} \times 100\% = \underline{30.0\%}$

5. $\text{List price} = \dfrac{dL}{d} = \dfrac{\$612.50}{0.35} = \underline{\$1750.00}$

   Net price $= \text{List price} - \text{discount} = \$1750.00 - \$612.50 = \underline{\$1137.50}$

6. $\text{List price} = \dfrac{dL}{d} = \dfrac{\$7.99}{0.40} = \underline{\$19.98}$

   Net price $= L - \text{discount} = \$19.98 - \$7.99 = \underline{\$11.99}$

7. List price $= N + \text{discount} = \$15.07 + \$12.33 = \underline{\$27.40}$

   $\text{Discount rate} = \dfrac{\text{discount}}{L} \times 100\% = \dfrac{\$12.33}{\$27.40} \times 100\% = \underline{45.0\%}$

8. List price $= N + \text{discount} = \$891.25 + \$258.75 = \underline{\$1150.00}$

   $\text{Discount rate} = \dfrac{\text{discount}}{L} \times 100\% = \dfrac{\$258.75}{\$1150.00} \times 100\% = \underline{22.5\%}$

9. $\text{List price, } L = \dfrac{N}{1 - d} = \dfrac{\$2849.00}{1 - 0.125} = \underline{\$3256.00}$

   Discount $= L - N = \$3256.00 - \$2849.00 = \underline{\$407.00}$

10. $\text{List price, } L = \dfrac{N}{1 - d} = \dfrac{\$413.05}{1 - 0.166667} = \underline{\$495.66}$

    Discount $= L - N = \$495.66 - \$413.05 = \underline{\$82.61}$

11. Net price, $N = L (1 - d) = \$135.00 (1 - 0.38) = \underline{\$83.70}$

12. Net price (Annapolis Gold) = $L(1 - d)$ = $11.50 (1 - 0.30) = $8.05

    Net price (No-Name) = $10.50 (1 - 0.22) = $8.19

    Annapolis Gold's net price is $0.14 per case lower.

13. List price = $\dfrac{dL}{d}$ = $\dfrac{\$111.57}{0.375}$ = $297.52

    Net price = L − discount = $297.52 − $111.57 = $185.95

14. List price = $\dfrac{N}{1 - d}$ = $\dfrac{\$845.75}{1 - 0.15}$ = $995.00

    Discount amount = L − N = $995.00 − $845.75 = $149.25

15. Discount amount = L − N = $369.00 − $287.82 = $81.18

    Discount rate = $\dfrac{dL}{L} \times 100\%$ = $\dfrac{\$81.18}{\$369.00} \times 100\%$ = 22.0%

16. List price = N + Discount amount = $27.06 + $22.14 = $49.20

    Discount rate = $\dfrac{dL}{L} \times 100\%$ = $\dfrac{\$22.14}{\$49.20} \times 100\%$ = 45.0%

17. Net price (Niagara)   = $L(1 - d)$
                                    = $72.00 (1 − 0.24)
                                    = $54.72

    Net price (Silverwood) = $L(1 - d)$
                     $54.72 = $74.50 (1 − d)

    $1 - d = \dfrac{\$54.72}{\$74.50}$ = 0.7345

    d(Silverwood) = 1 − 0.7345 = 0.2655 = 26.55%

18. Reduced (net) price = $L(1 - d)$ = $5.23 (1 − 0.15) = $4.45

19. Selling price, $L = \dfrac{N}{1 - d}$ = $\dfrac{\$160,555.50}{1 - 0.055}$ = $169,900

20. a. Merchant fee = dL = 0.035 ($17,564) = $614.74

    b. Merchant fee, dL = $732.88

    Gross sales, $L = \dfrac{\$732.88}{d}$ = $\dfrac{\$732.88}{0.035}$ = $20,939.43

Exercise 4.1 (concluded)

21. a. Net investment, $N = L (1 - d) = \$5500 (1 - 0.075) = \underline{\$5087.50}$

    b. Total amount placed, $L = \dfrac{N}{1 - d} = \dfrac{\$6105}{1 - 0.075} = \$6600$

    Commission paid $= L - N = \$6600 - \$6105 = \underline{\$495}$

22. a. After-tax increase, $N = L(1 - d) = \$1.25 (1 - 0.42) = \underline{\$0.725 \text{ per hour}}$

    b. Pre-tax earnings, $L = \dfrac{N}{1 - d} = \dfrac{\$1000}{1 - 0.47} = \underline{\$1886.79}$

23. Beginning value, $L = \dfrac{N}{1 - d} = \dfrac{3561}{1 - 0.013} = 3607.9$

    Index decline $= L - N = 3607.9 - 3561 = \underline{46.9 \text{ points}}$

24. Previous price, $L = \dfrac{N}{1 - d} = \dfrac{\$0.80}{1 - 0.73} = \underline{\$2.96}$

25. Hourly rate on overtime $= 1.5 (\$26.50) = \$39.75$

    After-tax hourly rate, $N = L(1 - d) = \$39.75 (1 - 0.415) = \$23.25$

    Time required to earn \$2500 after tax $= \dfrac{\$2500}{\$23.25} = \underline{107.5 \text{ hours}}$

26. a. Amount in prior year's budget, $L = \dfrac{dL}{d} = \dfrac{\$132 \text{ million}}{0.114} = \$1157.9 \text{ million}$

    New budget $= L - \text{reduction} = \$1157.9 \text{ million} - \$132 \text{ million} = \underline{\$1025.9 \text{ million}}$

    b. Current manpower, $L = \dfrac{N}{1 - d} = \dfrac{76,500}{1 - 0.088} = 83,882$

    Proposed cut $= L - N = 83,882 - 76,500 = \underline{7382 \text{ people}}$

Exercise 4.2

1. $d_e = 1 - (1 - d_1)(1 - d_2) = 1 - (1 - 0.30)(1 - 0.16667) = 0.4167 = \underline{41.67\%}$

   $N = L (1 - d_e) = \$99.00 (1 - 0.4167) = \underline{\$57.75}$

2. $d_e = 1 - (1 - 0.20)(1 - 0.125)(1 - 0.08333) = 0.3583 = \underline{35.83\%}$

   $N = \$595.00 (1 - 0.3583) = \underline{\$381.79}$

3. $d_e = 1 - (1 - 0.25)(1 - 0.10)(1 - 0.925) = 0.3756 = \underline{37.56\%}$

   $L = \dfrac{N}{1 - d_e} = \dfrac{\$93.03}{1 - 0.3756} = \underline{\$149.00}$

Exercise 4.2 (continued)

4. $d_e = 1 - (1 - 0.20)(1 - 0.10)(1 - 0.08333) = 0.3400 = \underline{34.00\%}$

$$L = \frac{N}{1 - d_e} = \frac{\$989.00}{1 - 0.34} = \underline{\$1498.48}$$

5. $d_e = 1 - (1 - d_1)(1 - d_2)(1 - d_3)$

$0.4867 = 1 - (1 - d_1)(1 - 0.125)(1 - 0.08333)$

$$1 - d_1 = \frac{1 - 0.48667}{(1 - 0.125)(1 - 0.08333)} = \frac{0.51333}{0.875(0.91667)}$$

$d_1 = 1 - 0.6400 = 0.3600 = \underline{36.00\%}$

$N = L (1 - d_e) = \$366.00 (1 - 0.36) = \underline{\$187.88}$

6. $d_e = 1 - (1 - d_1)(1 - d_2)(1 - d_3)$

$0.334 = 1 - (1 - 0.20)(1 - d_2)(1 - 0.05)$

$$1 - d_2 = \frac{1 - 0.334}{(0.80)(0.95)} = 0.8763$$

$d_2 = 1 - 0.8763 = 0.1237 = \underline{12.37\%}$

$N = L (1 - d_e) = \$39.95 (1 - 0.334) = \underline{\$26.61}$

7. $d_e = 1 - (1 - d_1)(1 - d_2)(1 - d_3)$

$0.4427 = 1 - (1 - 0.3\overline{3})(1 - d_2)(1 - 0.05)$

$$1 - d_2 = \frac{1 - 0.4427}{(0.66667)(0.95)} = 0.8800$$

$d_2 = 1 - 0.8800 = 0.1200 = \underline{12.00\%}$

$$L = \frac{N}{1 - d_e} = \frac{\$769.12}{1 - 0.4427} = \underline{\$1380.08}$$

8. $1 - d_1 = \dfrac{1 - d_e}{(1 - d_2)(1 - d_3)} = \dfrac{1 - 0.38333}{(1 - 0.16667)(1 - 0.075)} = 0.8000$

$d_1 = 1 - 0.8000 = 0.2000 = \underline{20.00\%}$

$$L = \frac{N}{1 - d_e} = \frac{\$122.10}{1 - 0.38333} = \underline{\$198.00}$$

9. Discount amount, $d_e L = L - N = \$49.95 - \$30.57 = \$19.38$

$$d_e = \frac{d_e L}{L} = \frac{\$19.38}{\$49.95} = 0.3880 = \underline{38.80\%}$$

$$1 - d_3 = \frac{1 - d_e}{(1 - d_1)(1 - d_2)} = \frac{1 - 0.3880}{(1 - 0.20)(1 - 0.15)} = 0.9000$$

$d_3 = 1 - 0.9000 = 0.1000 = \underline{10.00\%}$

Exercise 4.2 (continued)

10. Discount amount, $d_e L = L - N = \$1295.00 - \$831.03 = \$463.97$

$$d_e = \frac{d_e L}{L} = \frac{\$463.97}{\$1295.00} = 0.3583 = \underline{\underline{35.83\%}}$$

$$1 - d_3 = \frac{1 - d_e}{(1 - d_1)(1 - d_2)} = \frac{1 - 0.3583}{(1 - 0.25)(1 - 0.075)} = 0.9250$$

$$d_3 = 1 - 0.9250 = 0.075 = \underline{\underline{7.50\%}}$$

11. $N(\text{retailers}) = L(1 - d_1) = \$5800\ (1 - 0.25) = \underline{\underline{\$4350.00}}$

$N(\text{wholesalers}) = \$4350\ (1 - d_2) = \$4350\ (1 - 0.10) = \underline{\underline{\$3915.00}}$

$N(\text{distributors}) = \$3915\ (1 - d_3) = \$3915\ (1 - 0.075) = \underline{\underline{\$3621.38}}$

12. a. $N = L(1 - d_1)(1 - d_2)(1 - d_3)$
    $= \$11,500\ (1 - 0.25)(1 - 0.075)(1 - 0.05)$
    $= \underline{\underline{\$7579.22}}$

    b. Quantity discount $= d_2 L(1 - d_1)$
    $= 0.075\ (\$11,500)(1 - 0.25)$
    $= \underline{\underline{\$646.88}}$

    c. Joint promotion discount $= d_3 L(1 - d_1)(1 - d_2)$
    $= 0.05\ (\$11,500)(0.75)(0.925)$
    $= \underline{\underline{\$398.91}}$

13. a. $L = \dfrac{N}{(1 - d_1)(1 - d_2)(1 - d_3)} = \dfrac{\$176.72}{(1 - 0.30)(1 - 0.10)(1 - 0.02)} = \underline{\underline{\$286.23}}$

    b. $d_e = \dfrac{L - N}{L} = \dfrac{\$286.23 - \$176.22}{\$286.23} \times 100\% = \underline{\underline{38.26\%}}$

14. $N = L(1 - d_1)(1 - d_2)$

$$1 - d_2 = \frac{N}{L(1 - d_1)} = \frac{\$36.66}{\$48.75(1 - 0.20)} = 0.9400$$

$$d_2 = 1 - 0.9400 = 0.0600 = \underline{\underline{6.00\%}}$$

15. a. $N = L(1 - d_1)(1 - d_2)(1 - d_3)$
    $= \$445\ (1 - 0.25)(1 - 0.10)(1 - 0.05)$
    $= \underline{\underline{\$285.36}}$ per pair

    b. Early-order discount $= d_3 L(1 - d_1)(1 - d_2)$
    $= 0.05\ (\$445)(0.75)(0.90)$
    $= \underline{\underline{\$15.02}}$

    c. $L = \dfrac{N}{(1 - d_1)(1 - d_2)(1 - d_3)} = \dfrac{\$205.20}{(0.75)(0.90)(0.95)} = \underline{\underline{\$320.00}}$

    d. $d_e = \dfrac{L - N}{L} = \dfrac{\$445.00 - \$285.36}{\$445.00} \times 100\% = \underline{\underline{35.87\%}}$

Exercise 4.2 *(concluded)*

16. a. Service discount $= d_2 L(1 - d_1)$
    $$= 0.125(\$1000)(1 - 0.20)$$
    $$= \underline{\$100.00}$$

    b. Advertising and promotion discount $= d_3 L(1 - d_1)(1 - d_2)$
    $$= 0.05(\$1000)(1 - 0.20)(1 - 0.125)$$
    $$= \underline{\$35.00}$$

17. $1 - d_3 = \dfrac{N}{L(1 - d_1)(1 - d_2)} = \dfrac{\$160.00 - 58.15}{\$160.00(1 - 0.25)(1 - 0.125)} = 0.9700$

    $d_3 = 1 - 0.9700 = 0.0300 = \underline{\underline{3.00\%}}$

18. N(Posture-Perfect) $= L(1 - d_1)(1 - d_2)$
    $$= \$440(1 - 0.20)(1 - 0.05)$$
    $$= \$334.40$$

    N(Everest) $= \$480(1 - 0.25)(1 - d_2)$

    For matching prices,
    $$\$480(1 - 0.25)(1 - d_2) = \$334.40$$

    $1 - d_2 = \dfrac{\$334.40}{\$480(0.75)} = 0.9289$

    $d_2 = 1 - 0.9289 = 0.0711 = \underline{7.11\%}$

19. N(Javelin) $= L(1 - d_1)(1 - d_2)$
    $$= L(1 - 0.30)(1 - 0.16667)$$
    $$= 0.58333L$$

    N(Noremco) $= L(1 - d_1)(1 - d_2)(1 - d_3)$
    $$= L(1 - 0.33333)(1 - 0.10)(1 - d_3)$$
    $$= 0.6L(1 - d_3)$$

    For matching discounts,
    $$0.58333L = 0.6L(1 - d_3)$$

    $1 - d_3 = \dfrac{0.58333}{0.6} = 0.97222$

    $d_3 = 1 - 0.97222 = 0.02778 = \underline{2.78\%}$

Exercise 4.3

1. $N - L(1 - d) = \$2365(1 - 0.02) = \underline{\$2317.70}$

2. $\underline{\$2365.00}$ since the payment is on the 16th day after the invoice date.

3. $N = \$815.49(1 - 0.02) = \underline{\$799.18}$

4. $\underline{\$5445.00}$ since the payment is on the 21st day after the invoice date.

5. $\underline{\$3765.25}$ since the payment is on the 17th day after the end of the invoicing month.

6. $N = \$775.50(1 - 0.02) = \underline{\$759.99}$

Exercise 4.3 (continued)

7. <u>$1450.61</u> since payment is on the 11th day after receipt of the goods.

8. N = $995.00(1 – 0.015) = <u>$980.08</u>

9. Payment = (Amount credited)(1 – d)
   = $1365.00(1 – 0.02)
   = <u>$1337.70</u>

   Balance = Invoice amount – Amount credited
   = $2365.00 – $1365.00
   = <u>$1000.00</u>

10. Payment = $1421.32(1 – 0.015) = <u>$1400.00</u>

    Balance = $2365 – $1421.32 = <u>$943.68</u>

11. Amount credited = $\dfrac{\text{Payment}}{1 - d} = \dfrac{\$500}{1 - 0.02} = $ <u>$510.20</u>

    Balance = $815.49 – $510.20 = <u>$305.29</u>

12. Amount credited = $\dfrac{\$3000}{1 - 0.03} = $ <u>$3092.78</u>

    Balance = $5445.00 – $3092.78 = <u>$2352.22</u>

13. Amount credited = Invoice amount – Balance
    = $3765.25 – $2042.28
    = <u>$1722.97</u>

    Payment = $1722.97 (1 – 0.0133333) = <u>$1700.00</u>

14. Amount credited = $775.50 – $293.98 = <u>$481.52</u>

    Payment = $481.52(1 – 0.0125) = <u>$475.50</u>

15. Amount credited = $1450.61 – $943.00 = <u>$507.61</u>

    Cash discount = $507.61 – $500.00 = $7.61

    Discount rate = $\dfrac{\$7.61}{\$507.61} \times 100\% = $ <u>1.50%</u>

16. Amount credited = $995.00 – $285.54 = <u>$709.46</u>

    Cash discount = $709.46 – $700.00 = $9.46

    Discount rate = $\dfrac{\$9.46}{\$709.46} \times 100\% = 1.\overline{3}\% = $ <u>$1\dfrac{1}{3}\%$</u>

Exercise 4.3 (continued)

17. a. April 30 + 15 days = <u>May 15</u>

    b. May 15 + 20 days = <u>June 4</u>

    c. Payment = (Amount credited)(1 − d) = $800(1 − 0.015) = <u>$788.00</u>

    d. Amount credited = $\dfrac{\$800}{1 - 0.015}$ = $812.18

       Balance = $2678.50 − $800.00 − $812.18 = <u>$1066.32</u>

    e. Amount credited = $1066.32 − $800.00 = $266.32

       Amount paid = $266.32 (1 − 0.015) = <u>$262.33</u>

18. a. May 28 + 10 days = <u>June 7</u>

    b. June 7 + 20 days = <u>June 27</u>

    c. Payment = $5000 (1 − 0.02) = <u>$4900.00</u>

    d. Amount credited = $\dfrac{\$5000.00}{1 - 0.02}$ = $5102.04

       Balance = $13,600.00 − $5102.04 = <u>$8497.96</u>

    e. Amount credited = $13,600 − $5000 = $8600

       Payment = $8600 (1 − 0.02) = <u>$8428.00</u>

19. June 20 invoice does not qualify for a cash discount on July 4.

    Payment = $485 + $367(1 − 0.015) + $722(1 − 0.015) = <u>$1557.66</u>

20. The November 2 and November 3 invoices qualify for a 2% cash discount.
    Total payment = $14,200 + $8600 (1 − 0.02) + $11,500 (1 − 0.02) = <u>$33,898</u>

21. a. Amount credited = $\dfrac{\$8000}{1 - 0.02}$ = <u>$8163.27</u>

    b. Balance = $14,772.00 − $8163.27 = <u>$6608.73</u>

22. Total amount credited = $\dfrac{\$900}{1 - 0.025}$ + $\dfrac{\$850}{1 - 0.01}$ + $700

    = $923.08 + $858.59 + $700
    = $2481.67

    Balance owed = $2856.57 − $2481.67 = <u>$374.90</u>

23. Amount credited on first payment = $\dfrac{\$2000}{1 - 0.03}$ = $2061.86

    Balance after first payment = $5400.00 − $2061.86 = $3338.14

    Amount credited on second payment = $3338.14 − $1000 = $2338.14

    Size of second payment = $2338.44 (1 − 0.015) = <u>$2303.07</u>

Exercise 4.3 (concluded)

24. Net amount of invoice $= L(1 - d_1)(1 - d_2)$
$$= 4(\$23,500)(1 - 0.20)(1 - 0.05)$$
$$= \$71,440$$

Amount credited $= \dfrac{\text{Amount paid}}{1 - 0.015} = \dfrac{\$60,000}{0.985} = \$60,913.71$

Balance owed $= \$71,440 - \$60,913.71 = \underline{\$10,526.29}$

25. Invoice amount $= 4(\$3900)(1 - 0.20)(1 - 0.07) + 6(\$4880)(1 - 0.25)(1 - 0.05)$
$$= \$11,606.40 + \$29,280.00$$
$$= \$32,468.40$$

Amount credited $= 0.5(\$32,468.40) = \$16,234.20$
Amount paid $= L(1 - d) = \$16,234.20 \ (1 - 0.025) = \underline{\$15,828.35}$

26. Amount required to settle invoice 535 = $3228.56
Amount required to settle invoice 598 = $2945.31 (1 - 0.02) = $2886.40
Amount to be applied to invoice 678 = $10,000.00 - $3228.56 - $2886.40 = $3885.04

Amount credited to invoice 678 $= \dfrac{\$3885.04}{1 - 0.04} = \$4046.91$

Balance owed on invoice 678 = $6217.69 - $4046.91 = $2170.78

Payment on August 15 to settle invoice 678 = $2170.78 (1 - 0.02) = $\underline{\$2127.36}$

27. Let each of the payments be represented by x.

Balance owed on July 15 $= \$6350 - \dfrac{x}{1 - 0.03} - \dfrac{x}{1 - 0.01}$
$$= \$1043.33$$
Hence,
$$\$6350 - 1.030928x - 1.010101x = \$1043.33$$

$$x = \dfrac{\$6350.00}{1.030928 + 1.010101} = \underline{\$2600.00}$$

The amount of each payment was $2600.00.

28. Let the amount of each payment be represented by x. The total amount credited will be

$$\dfrac{x}{1 - 0.02} + \dfrac{x}{1 - 0.01} + x = \$2956.60$$

$$3.030509x = \$2956.60$$
$$x = \underline{\$975.61}$$

Each of the three payments should be $975.61.

Exercise 4.4

1.

	$
OE	0.4C
+OP	
M	———
+ C	+30
SP	50

  a.   M = $50 − $30 = $20.00 (insert in table)

  b.   OE = 0.4($30) = $12.00 (insert in table)

  c.   OP = M − OE = $20 − $12 = $8.00

  d.   %M(on C) = $\frac{\$20}{\$30}$ × 100% = 66.67%

  e.   %M(on SP) = $\frac{\$20}{\$50}$ × 100% = 40.00%

2.

	$
OE	0.25SP
+OP	
M	———
+ C	+64
SP	96

  a.   M = $96 − $64 = $32.00 (insert in table)

  b.   OE = 0.25($96) = $24.00 (insert in table)

  c.   OP = $32 − $24 = $8.00

  d.   %M(on C) = $\frac{\$32}{\$64}$ × 100% = 50.00%

  e.   %M(on SP) = $\frac{\$32}{\$96}$ × 100% = 33.33%

3.

	$
OE	0.3SP
+OP	
M	———
+ C	+55.65
SP	79.50

  a.   M = $79.50 − $55.65 = $23.85 (insert in table)

  b.   OE = 0.3($79.50) = $23.85 (insert in table)

  c.   OP = $23.85 − $23.85 = $0

  d.   %M(on C) = $\frac{\$23.85}{\$55.65}$ × 100% = 42.86%

  e.   %M(on SP) = $\frac{\$23.85}{\$79.50}$ × 100% = 30.00%

4.

	$
OE	0.5C
+OP	
M	———
+ C	+17.50
SP	29.75

  a.   M = $29.75 − $17.50 = $12.25

  b.   OE = 0.5($17.50) = $8.75

  c.   OP = $12.25 − $8.75 = $3.50

  d.   %M(on C) = $\frac{\$12.25}{\$17.50}$ × 100% = 70.00%

  e.   %M(on SP) = $\frac{\$12.25}{\$29.75}$ × 100% = 41.18%

5.

	$
OE	0.35SP
+OP	
M	———
+ C	+53.90
SP	77.00

  a.   M = $77.00 − $53.90 = $23.10

  b.   OE = 0.35($77.00) = $26.95

  c.   OP = $23.10 − $26.95 = −$3.85 (loss)

  d.   %M(on C) = $\frac{\$23.10}{\$53.90}$ × 100% = 42.86%

  e.   %M(on SP) = $\frac{\$23.10}{\$77.00}$ × 100% = 30.00%

Exercise 4.4 *(continued)*

6.

	$
OE	0.45 C
+OP	
M	
+ C	+23.00
SP	29.90

a. M = $29.90 − $23.00 = $6.90

b. OE = 0.45($23.00) = $10.35

c. OP = $6.90 − $10.35 = −$3.45 (loss)

d. $\%M(\text{on C}) = \dfrac{\$6.90}{\$23.00} \times 100\% = 30.00\%$

e. $\%M(\text{on SP}) = \dfrac{\$6.90}{\$29.90} \times 100\% = 23.08\%$

7.

	$
OE	
+OP	+ 15.35
M	47.45
+ C	+152.50
SP	

OE = $47.45 − $15.35 = $32.10

SP = $47.45 + $152.50 = $199.95

$\%M(\text{on C}) = \dfrac{\$47.45}{\$152.50} \times 100\% = 31.11\%$

$\%M(\text{on SP}) = \dfrac{\$47.45}{\$199.95} \times 100\% = 23.73\%$

8.

	$
OE	18.65
+OP	
M	
+ C	51.30
SP	79.90

M = $79.90 − $51.30 = $28.60

OP = $28.60 − $18.65 = $9.95

$\%M(\text{on C}) = \dfrac{\$28.60}{\$51.30} \times 100\% = 55.75\%$

$\%M(\text{on SP}) = \dfrac{\$28.60}{\$79.90} \times 100\% = 35.79\%$

9.

	$
OE	308
+OP	
M	435
+ C	
SP	1990

OP = $435 − $308 = $127.00

C = $1990 − $435 = $1555.00

$\%M(\text{on C}) = \dfrac{\$435}{\$1555} \times 100\% = 27.97\%$

$\%M(\text{on SP}) = \dfrac{\$435}{\$1990} \times 100\% = 21.86\%$

10.

	$
OE	
+OP	+ 2.45
M	0.5 SP
+ C	
SP	19.90

M = 0.5($19.90) = $9.95

OE = M − OP = $9.95 − $2.45 = $7.50

C = SP − M = $19.90 − $9.95 = $9.95

$\%M(\text{on C}) = \dfrac{\$9.95}{\$9.95} \times 100\% = 100.0\%$

11.

	$
OE	11.25
+OP	+3.75
M	0.38 SP
+ C	
SP	

M = $11.25 + $3.75 = $15.00

$SP = \dfrac{M}{0.38} = \dfrac{\$15.00}{0.38} = \$39.47$

C = SP − M = $39.47 − $15.00 = $24.47

$\%M(\text{on C}) = \dfrac{\$15.00}{\$24.47} \times 100\% = 61.29\%$

Exercise 4.4 *(continued)*

12.

	$
OE	
+OP	+1.37
M	0.9 C
+ C	+8.89
SP	

$M = 0.9C = 0.9(\$8.89) = \underline{\$8.00}$

$SP = M + C = \$8.00 + \$8.89 = \underline{\$16.89}$

$OE = M - OP = \$8.00 - \$1.37 = \underline{\$6.63}$

$\%M(\text{on } SP) = \dfrac{\$8.00}{\$16.89} \times 100\% = \underline{47.37\%}$

13.

	$
OE	3.15
+OP	
M	0.4SP
+ C	+6.60
SP	

$SP = 0.4SP + \$6.60$

$0.6(SP) = \$6.60$

$SP = \underline{\$11.00}$

$M = 0.4(\$11.00) = \underline{\$4.40}$

$OP = M - OE = \$4.40 - \$3.15 = \underline{\$1.25}$

$\%M(\text{on } C) = \dfrac{\$4.40}{\$6.60} \times 100\% = \underline{66.67\%}$

14.

	$
OE	
+OP	+0.14
M	1.5 C
+ C	
SP	0.95

$1.5C + C = \$0.95$

$C = \dfrac{\$0.95}{2.5} = \underline{\$0.38}$

$M = 1.5C = \underline{\$0.57}$

$OE = M - OP = \$0.57 - \$0.14 = \underline{\$0.43}$

$\%M(\text{on } SP) = \dfrac{\$0.57}{\$0.95} \times 100\% = \underline{60.00\%}$

15.

	$
OE	57.00
+OP	33.00
M	
+ C	+273.60
SP	

$C = N = L(1 - d_1)(1 - d_2)$
$= \$380(1 - 0.20)(1 - 0.10)$
$= \$273.60$ (insert in table)

a. $SP = \$57.00 + \$33.00 + \$273.60 = \underline{\$363.60}$

b. $M = \$57.00 + \$33.00 = \$90.00$

$\%M(\text{on } C) = \dfrac{\$90.00}{\$273.60} \times 100\% = \underline{32.89\%}$

c. $\%M(\text{on } SP) = \dfrac{\$90.00}{\$363.60} \times 100\% = \underline{24.75\%}$

d. $SP(\text{break-even}) = C + OE = \$273.60 + \$57.00 = \underline{\$330.60}$

16. $C = N = L(1 - d_1)(1 - d_2) = \$58.00(1 - 0.30)(1 - 0.07) = \$37.76$ (insert in table)

	$	%
OE	14.50	25
+OP		
M		
+ C	+37.76	
SP	58.00	100

a. $OE = 0.25(\$58.00) = \$14.50$ (insert in table)
$OP = \$58.00 - \$37.76 - \$14.50 = \underline{\$5.74}$

b. $M = \$14.50 + \$5.74 = \$20.24$

$\%M(\text{on } C) = \dfrac{\$20.24}{\$37.76} \times 100\% = \underline{53.60\%}$

c. $\%M(\text{on } SP) = \dfrac{\$20.24}{\$58.00} \times 100\% = \underline{34.90\%}$

d. $SP(\text{break-even}) = C + OE = \$37.76 + \$14.50 = \underline{\$52.26}$

17.

	$
M	0.45C
+C	+
SP	$54.95

a. $0.45C + C = \$54.95$

$C = \dfrac{\$54.95}{1.45} = \underline{\$37.90}$

b. $M = \$54.95 - \$37.90 = \$17.05$

$\%M(\text{on } SP) = \dfrac{\$17.05}{\$54.95} \times 100\% = \underline{31.03\%}$

18.

	$	%
M		45
+C	38.50	55
SP		100

a. $\dfrac{\$38.50}{SP} = \dfrac{55}{100}$

$SP = \dfrac{\$38.50}{0.55} = \underline{\$70.00}$

b. $\%M(\text{on } C) = \dfrac{\$70 - \$38.50}{\$38.50} \times 100\% = \underline{81.82\%}$

19.

	%
M	60
+C	40
SP	100

$\dfrac{M}{C} = \dfrac{60}{40} = 1.5$

$\%M(\text{on } C) = \dfrac{M}{C} \times 100\% = \underline{150\%}$

20.

	$
M	1.25C
+C	
SP	

$SP = 1.25C + C = 2.25C$

$\%M(\text{on } SP) = \dfrac{M}{SP} \times 100\% = \dfrac{1.25C}{2.25C} \times 100\% = \underline{55.56\%}$

21.

	$
M	0.85C = $14
+C	
SP	

a. $C = \dfrac{\$14}{0.85} = \$16.47$

$SP = \$14 + \$16.47 = \underline{\$30.47}$

b. $\%M(\text{on } SP) = \dfrac{\$14}{\$30.47} \times 100\% = \underline{45.95\%}$

22.

	$	%
M	12.50	27
+C		73
SP		100

a. $\dfrac{\$12.50}{C} = \dfrac{27}{73}$

$C = \underline{\$33.80}$

b. $\%M(\text{on } C) = \dfrac{\$12.50}{\$33.80} \times 100\% = \underline{36.98\%}$

Exercise 4.4 (concluded)

23.

	$
OE	0.4C
+OP	————
M	
+ C	+15.00
SP	29.50

a. $SP(\text{break-even}) = C + OE$
$= \$15.00 + 0.4(\$15.00)$
$= \underline{\$21.00}$

b. $\text{Average } \%M(\text{on } C) = \dfrac{\text{Total revenue} - \text{Total C}}{\text{Total C}} \times 100\%$

Total C $= 250(\$15) = \$3750$

Total revenue $= 165(\$29.50) + 43\left(\dfrac{2}{3} \times \$29.50\right) + (250 - 165 - 43)\$14.95$

$= \$6341.07$

$\text{Average } \%M(\text{on } C) = \dfrac{\$6341.07 - \$3750}{\$3750} \times 100\% = \underline{69.10\%}$

c. Total OP $=$ Total M $-$ Total OE
$= (\$6341.07 - \$3750) - 0.40(\$3750)$
$= \underline{\$1091.07}$

24. $C = N = L(1 - d_1)(1 - d_2) = \$15(1 - 0.40)(1 - 0.10) = \$8.10$

	$	%
OE	0.55C	
+OP	————	20
M		
+ C	+8.10	
SP		100

$OE = 0.55(\$8.10) = \$4.455$
$SP = \$4.455 + 0.20SP + \$8.10$
$SP - 0.20SP = \$12.555$
$SP = \dfrac{\$12.555}{0.80} = \underline{\$15.69}$

25. $C = N = L(1 - d_1)(1 - d_2) = \$18(1 - 0.30)(1 - 0.05) = \$11.97$

	$	%
OE		20
+OP		12
+ C	11.97	68
SP		100

$\dfrac{\$11.97}{SP} = \dfrac{68}{100}$

$SP = \dfrac{100}{68} \times \$11.97 = \underline{\$17.60}$

Exercise 4.5

1.

	$	%
M	0.5C	
+C	+185	
SP		100
−D	− 60	
RSP		

$M = 0.5C = 0.5(\$185) = \$92.50$
$SP = \$92.50 + \$185 = \underline{\$277.50}$

$\%M(\text{on SP}) = \dfrac{\$92.50}{\$277.50} \times 100\% = \underline{33.33\%}$

$\%D = \dfrac{\$60}{\$277.50} \times 100\% = \underline{21.62\%}$

$RSP = \$277.50 - \$60 = \underline{\$217.50}$

2.

	$	%
M		
+C	+58.50	
SP	95.00	100
−D		−30
RSP		70

$M = \$95 - \$58.50 = \$36.50$

$\%M(\text{on C}) = \dfrac{\$36.50}{\$58.50} \times 100\% = \underline{62.39\%}$

$\%M(\text{on SP}) = \dfrac{\$36.50}{\$95.00} \times 100\% = \underline{38.42\%}$

$D = 0.30(\$95) = \underline{\$28.50}$

$RSP = \$95 - \$28.50 = \underline{\$66.50}$

Exercise 4.5 *(continued)*

3.

	$	%
M		50
+C		+50
SP	49.98	100
−D		−50
RSP		50

$C = 0.5(\$49.98) = \underline{\$24.99} = M$

$\%M(\text{on } C) = \dfrac{\$24.99}{\$24.99} \times 100\% = \underline{100.0\%}$

$D = 0.5(\$49.98) = \underline{\$24.99}$

$RSP = \$49.98 - \$24.99 = \underline{\$24.99}$

4.

	$	%
M	0.3C	
+C	+580	
SP		100
−D		−30
RSP		70

$M = 0.3(\$580) = \$174.00$

$SP = \$174 + \$580 = \underline{\$754.00}$

$\%M(\text{on } SP) = \dfrac{\$174}{\$754} \times 100\% = \underline{23.08\%}$

$D = 0.3(\$754) = \underline{\$226.20}$

$RSP = \$754.00 - \$226.20 = \underline{\$527.80}$

5.

	$	%
M		35
+C	+19.25	+65
SP		100
−D		−25
RSP		75

$\dfrac{\$19.25}{SP} = \dfrac{65}{100}$

$SP = \underline{\$29.62}$

$M = \$29.62 - \$19.25 = \$10.37$

$\%M(\text{on } C) = \dfrac{\$10.37}{\$19.25} \times 100\% = \underline{53.87\%}$

$D = 0.25(\$29.62) = \underline{\$7.41}$

$RSP = \$29.62 - \$7.41 = \underline{\$22.21}$

6.

	$	%
M		25
+C	+249	+75
SP		100
−D		
RSP	249	

$\%M(\text{on } C) = \dfrac{25}{75} \times 100\% = \underline{33.33\%}$

$M = \dfrac{25}{75}C = \dfrac{\$249}{3} = \$83.00$

$SP = \$83 + \$249 = \underline{\$332.00}$

$D = \$332 - \$249 = \underline{\$83.00}$

$\%D = \dfrac{D}{SP} \times 100\% = \dfrac{\$83}{\$332} \times 100\% = \underline{25.00\%}$

7.

	$	%
M	0.75C	
+C		
SP	395	100
−D		−40
RSP		

$0.75C + C = \$395$

$1.75C = \$395$

$C = \underline{\$225.71}$

$\%M(\text{on } SP) = \dfrac{\$395 - \$225.71}{\$395} \times 100\% = \underline{42.86\%}$

$D = 0.40(\$395) = \underline{\$158.00}$

$RSP = \$395 - \$158 = \underline{\$237.00}$

Exercise 4.5 *(continued)*

8.

	$	%
M	0.4C	
+C	⸺	
SP		100
−D		−20
RSP	100	80

$$\frac{D}{\$100} = \frac{20}{80}$$

D = 0.25($100) = $25.00

SP = $100 + $25 = $125.00

0.4C + C = $125.00

1.4C = $125.00

C = $89.29

M = $125 − $89.29 = $35.71

$$\%M(\text{on SP}) = \frac{\$35.71}{\$125} \times 100\% = \underline{28.57\%}$$

9.

	$	%
M		
+C	+37.50	
SP	59.98	100
−D		
RSP	37.50	

a. M = $59.98 − $37.50 = $22.48

$$\%M(\text{on C}) = \frac{\$22.48}{\$37.50} \times 100\% = \underline{59.95\%}$$

b. $\%M(\text{on SP}) = \frac{\$22.48}{\$59.98} \times 100\% = \underline{37.48\%}$

c. D = $59.98 − $37.50 = $22.48

$$\%D = \frac{\$22.48}{\$59.98} \times 100\% = \underline{37.48\%}$$

10. a.

	$
M	0.45C
+C	
SP	⸺
−D	
RSP	C

SP = 0.45C + C = 1.45C

D = SP − RSP = 1.45C − C = 0.45C

$$\%D = \frac{D}{SP} \times 100\% = \frac{0.45C}{1.45C} \times 100\% = \underline{31.03\%}$$

b.

	%
M	45
+C	+55
SP	100
−D	
RSP	55

%D may be deduced quickly by filling in the "plugs" in the % column.

That is, C = RSP = 55% of SP

Therefore, %D = $\underline{45.00\%}$

11.

	$	%
M		45
+C	+96.80	+55
SP		100
−D	⸺	−35
RSP		65

$$\frac{\$96.80}{RSP} = \frac{55}{65}$$

$$RSP = \frac{65}{55} \times \$96.80 = \underline{\$114.40}$$

Exercise 4.5 (concluded)

12 a.

	$	%
SP		100
−D		−30
RSP	100	70

$\dfrac{SP}{\$100} = \dfrac{100}{70}$

$SP = \dfrac{\$100}{0.70} = \underline{\$142.86}$

b.

	$	%
SP		100
−D		−30
RSP	196.49	70

$\dfrac{SP}{\$196.49} = \dfrac{100}{70}$

$SP = \dfrac{\$196.49}{0.70} = \underline{\$280.70}$

13 a.

	$
SP	69.95
−D	
RSP	0.8 (64.95)

$D = \$69.95 - 0.8\,(\$64.95) = \$17.99$

$\%D = \dfrac{\$17.99}{\$69.95} \times 100\% = \underline{25.72\%}$ for merchant C

b.

	$
SP	64.95
−D	
RSP	0.8 (69.95)

$D = \$64.95 - 0.8\,(\$69.95) = \$8.99$

$\%D = \dfrac{\$8.99}{\$64.95} \times 100\% = \underline{13.84\%}$ for merchant D

14.

	$	%
OE	0.4C	
+OP	0.7C	
+ C		
SP		100
− D		
RSP	Break even	

$SP = 0.4C + 0.7C + C = 2.1C$
To break even, $D = OP = 0.7C$

$\%D = \dfrac{0.7C}{2.1C} \times 100\% = \underline{33.33\%}$

Exercise 4.6

1.

	$	%
OE		20
+OP		+15
M		35
+ C	115.70	+65
SP		100
− D		−25
RSP		75
− C	−115.70	−65
−OE		−20
ROP		−10

The % figures for OP, C, RSP, and ROP are easily obtained as the necessary "plugs." Then

$\dfrac{\$115.70}{SP} = \dfrac{65}{100}$

$SP = \dfrac{\$100}{65} \times \$115.70 = \underline{\$178.00}$

$RSP = 0.75\,(SP) = \underline{\$133.50}$

$ROP = -0.10\,(SP) = -\$17.80$

That is, the ROP is a $\underline{\$17.80 \text{ loss}}$.

2.

	$	%
OE		18
+OP		$+15.\overline{3}$
M		$33.\overline{3}$
+ C		$+66.\overline{6}$
SP	147.00	100
– D		$-16.\overline{6}$
RSP		$83.\overline{3}$
– C		$-66.\overline{6}$
–OE		-18
ROP		$-1.\overline{3}$

The % figures for OP, C, RSP, and ROP are easily obtained as the necessary "plugs." Then

$$C = 0.6\overline{6}(\$147.00) = \underline{\$98.00}$$

$$RSP = 0.8\overline{3}(\$147.00) = \underline{\$122.50}$$

$$ROP = -0.01\overline{3}(\$147.00) = -\$1.96$$

That is, the ROP is a $\underline{\$1.96\ loss}$.

3.

	$
OE	
+OP	
M	————
+ C	+37.25
SP	59.60
– D	
RSP	41.72
– C	−37.25
–OE	
ROP	− 2.98

The dollar amounts for D, OE, and M are easily obtained as the necessary "plugs." That is,

$$D = \$59.60 - \$41.72 = \underline{\$17.88}$$

$$OE = \$41.72 - \$37.25 + \$2.98 = \$7.45$$

$$M = \$59.60 - \$37.25 = \$22.35$$

$$\%\,OE\,(of\ C) = \frac{\$7.45}{\$37.25} \times 100\% = \underline{20.00\%}$$

$$\%\,M\,(of\ C) = \frac{\$22.35}{\$37.25} \times 100\% = \underline{60.00\%}$$

4.

	$
OE	0.7C
+OP	————
M	1.5C
+ C	
SP	19.80
– D	
RSP	
– C	
–OE	−0.7C
ROP	2.38

$$1.5C + C = \$19.80$$

$$C = \underline{\$7.92}$$

$$RSP - C - OE = ROP$$

$$RSP - \$7.92 - 0.7(\$7.92) = \$2.38$$

$$RSP = \$2.38 + \$7.92 + 0.7(\$7.92) = \underline{\$15.84}$$

$$\%D = \frac{D}{SP} \times 100\% = \frac{\$19.80 - \$15.84}{\$19.80} \times 100\% = \underline{20.00\%}$$

5.

	$	%
OE	0.5C	25
+OP	————	
M		50
+ C	————	50
SP		100
– D	————	$-33.\overline{3}$
RSP	111.80	$66.\overline{6}$
– C		− 50
–OE	−0.5C	− 25
ROP		− $8.\overline{3}$

The % figures for C and RSP are the necessary "plugs." Then

$$OE = 0.5C = 25\%\ of\ SP\ and$$
$$ROP = 66.\overline{6}\% - 50\% - 25\% = -8.\overline{3}\%\ of\ SP$$

$$\frac{SP}{\$111.80} = \frac{100}{66.\overline{6}}$$

$$SP = \underline{\$167.70}$$

$$C = 0.5(\$167.70) = \underline{\$83.85}$$

$$ROP = -0.08\overline{3}(\$167.70) = -\$13.98$$

The ROP is a $\underline{\$13.98\ loss}$.

6.

	$	%
OE		
+OP		
M		
+ C	+420.00	
SP	575.40	100
– D		–15
RSP		85
– C	–420.00	
–OE		
ROP	11.55	

$RSP = 0.85(SP) = 0.85(\$575.40) = \underline{\$489.09}$

$M = \$575.40 - \$420.00 = \$155.40$

$\%M(\text{of } C) = \dfrac{\$155.40}{\$420.00} \times 100\% = \underline{37.00\%}$

$RSP - C - OE = ROP$

$OE = \$489.09 - \$420.00 - \$11.55 = \$57.54$

$\%OE(\text{of } SP) = \dfrac{\$57.54}{\$575.40} \times 100\% = \underline{10.00\%}$

7. $C = N = L(1 - d_1)(1 - d_2) = \$480(1 - 0.40)(1 - 0.25) = \$216.00$

	$	%
M	1.2C	
+C	+216	
SP		100
–D		–40
RSP		60

a. $M = 1.2C = 1.2(\$216) = \$259.20$

$SP = \$216 + \$259.20 = \$475.20$

$RSP = 0.6(\$475.20) = \underline{\$285.12}$

b. $M(\text{at } RSP) = RSP - C$
$= \$285.12 - \$216.00$
$= \$69.12$

$\%M(\text{on } C) = \dfrac{\$69.12}{\$216.00} \times 100\% = \underline{32.00\%}$

8. $C = N = \$18.60(1 - 0.3\overline{3})(1 - 0.125)(1 - 0.05) = \$10.31$

	$	%
M		55
+C	+10.31	+45
SP		100
–D		–45
RSP		55

a. $\dfrac{\$10.31}{RSP} = \dfrac{45}{55}$

$RSP = \dfrac{55}{45} \times \$10.31 = \underline{\$12.60}$

b. $M(\text{at } RSP) = \$12.60 - \$10.31 = \$2.29$

$\%M(\text{on } RSP) = \dfrac{\$2.29}{\$12.60} \times 100\% = \underline{18.18\%}$

9. $C = N = L(1 - d) = \$360(1 - 0.25) = \$270$

	$	%
OE		16.$\overline{6}$
+OP		15
M		31.$\overline{6}$
+ C	+270	68.$\overline{3}$
SP		100
– D		–20
RSP		80
– C	–270	–68.$\overline{3}$
–OE		–16.$\overline{6}$
ROP		– 5

a. At the break-even point, $D = OP = 15\%$ of SP. Therefore, $\%D = \underline{15\%}$ to break even.

b. Set $\%D = 20\%$ in the table at left. The % column may then be filled in.

$\dfrac{\$270}{ROP} = \dfrac{68.\overline{3}}{-5}$

$ROP = \dfrac{-5}{68.\overline{3}} \times \$270 = -\$19.76$

That is, a <u>loss of \$19.76</u> per unit.

Exercise 4.6 *(continued)*

10.

	$
OE	$0.25C$
+OP	$+0.16C$
M	$0.41\overline{6}C$
+ C	
SP	349
– D	
RSP	

$$0.25C + 0.1\overline{6}\,C + C = \$349$$
$$1.41\overline{6}\,C = \$349$$
$$C = \$246.35$$

a. To break even,

$$D = OP = 0.1\overline{6}(\$246.35) = \underline{\$41.06}$$

b. If RSP = C, then

$$D = \$349.00 - \$246.35 = \$102.65$$

$$\%D = \frac{\$102.65}{\$349.00} \times 100\% = \underline{\underline{29.41\%}}$$

11.

	$
OE	$0.5C$
+OP	$+\ 0.3C$
M	$0.8C$
+ C	$+14.85$
SP	
– D	
RSP	
– C	-14.85
–OE	$-\ 0.5C$
ROP	$-0.25(0.5C)$

$$C = N = \$30(1 - 0.45)(1 - 0.10) = \$14.85$$
$$SP = \$14.85 + 0.8C$$
$$= \$14.85 + 0.8(\$14.85)$$
$$= \$26.73$$

$$SP - D - C - OE = ROP$$
$$\$26.73 - D - \$14.85 - 0.5(\$14.85) = -0.125(\$14.85)$$
$$\$4.455 - D = -\$1.856$$
$$D = \$6.31$$

$$\%D = \frac{\$6.31}{\$26.73} \times 100\% = \underline{\underline{23.61\%}}$$

12.

	$
OE	$0.5\ C$
+OP	$+0.35C$
M	$0.85C$
+ C	$+\ 297$
SP	
– D	
RSP	
– C	-297
–OE	$-0.5C$
ROP	$-0.5(0.5C)$

$$C = N = \$550(1 - 0.40)(1 - 0.10) = \$297.00$$
$$SP = \$297 + 0.85(\$297) = \$549.45$$

$$SP - D - C - OE = ROP$$
$$\$549.45 - D - \$297 - 0.5(\$297) = -0.25(\$297)$$
$$\$103.95 - D = -\$74.25$$
$$D = \$178.20$$

$$\%D = \frac{\$178.20}{\$549.45} \times 100\% = \underline{\underline{32.43\%}}$$

13.

	$	%
OE		25
+OP		+15
M		40
+ C	$+36.72$	+60
SP		100
– D		
RSP	45.90	
– C	-36.72	–60
–OE		25
ROP		

$$C = \$72(1 - 0.40)(1 - 0.15) = \$36.72$$

Fill in the "plugs" for %OP and %C.

a. $\dfrac{\$36.72}{SP} = \dfrac{60}{100}$

$$SP = \$61.20$$

$$\%D = \frac{\$61.20 - \$45.90}{\$61.20} \times 100\% = \underline{\underline{25.00\%}}$$

b. $ROP = \$45.90 - \$36.72 - 0.25(\$61.20)$
$$= \underline{-\$6.12}$$

c. $M(\text{at RSP}) = \$45.90 - \$36.72 = \$9.18$

$$\%M(\text{on C at RSP}) = \frac{\$9.18}{\$36.72} \times 100\% = \underline{\underline{25.00\%}}$$

Exercise 4.6 (continued)

14.

	$	%
OE		12
+OP		
M	171	___
+ C	+204	
SP	375	100
– D	–150	___
RSP	225	
– C	–204	
–OE	___	–12
ROP		

$C = \$360(1 - 0.3\overline{3})(1 - 0.15) = \$204.00$

Fill in the "plugs" for D and M.

a. $\%D = \dfrac{\$150}{\$375} \times 100\% = \underline{\underline{40.00\%}}$

b. $ROP = \$225 - \$204 - 0.12(\$375)$
    $= -\$24.00$
    That is, a <u>loss of \$24.00</u> per sweater.

c. $M(\text{at RSP}) = \$225 - \$204 = \$21.00$

$\%M(\text{on C at RSP}) = \dfrac{\$21}{\$204} \times 100\% = \underline{\underline{10.29\%}}$

15.

	$	%
M		
+C	+665	
SP		100
–D	___	–20
RSP		80
–C	–665	
M(at RSP)	___	

Given: $M(\text{at RSP}) = 0.3\,RSP$

a. $RSP - \$665 = 0.3\,RSP$
      $0.7\,RSP = \$665$
      $RSP = \underline{\underline{\$950.00}}$

b. $\dfrac{SP}{\$950} = \dfrac{100}{80}$

$SP = \underline{\underline{\$1187.50}}$

16.

	$	% (of SP)	% (of RSP)
SP		100	
– D	___	–20	
RSP		80	100
– C	–1425		–67.5
–OE	___		–20
ROP	___	___	12.5

$C = \$2500(1 - 0.4)(1 - 0.05) = \$1425.00$

a. Fill in the "plug" for C in the last column $(100 - 20 - 12.5 = 67.5\%)$.

$\dfrac{RSP}{\$1425} = \dfrac{100}{67.5}$

$RSP = \underline{\underline{\$2111.11}}$

b. $\dfrac{SP}{RSP} = \dfrac{100}{80}$

$SP = \dfrac{100}{80} \times \$2111.11 = \underline{\underline{\$2638.89}}$

17.

	$	% (of SP)	% (of RSP)
SP		100	
– D	___	20	
RSP		80	100
– C	–1428		–60
–OE	___		–25
ROP	___	___	15

$C = \$2400(1 - 0.3)(1 - 0.15) = \$1428.00$

a. The "plug" for C in the last column is 60%.

$\dfrac{RSP}{\$1428} = \dfrac{100}{60}$

$RSP = \$2380.00$

$\dfrac{SP}{RSP} = \dfrac{SP}{\$2380} = \dfrac{100}{80}$

$SP = \underline{\underline{\$2975.00}}$

b. The "one-third-off" special price was
    $\$2975(1 - 0.3\overline{3}) = \$1983.33$

The ROP at this price was
$\$1983.33 - C - OE = \$1983.33 - \$1428 - 0.25(\$2380) = -\$39.67$

There was a <u>loss of \$39.67</u> at the special price.

Exercise 4.6 (concluded)

18.

$C = \$1800(1 - 0.3\overline{3})(1 - 0.05) = \$1140.00$

$$
\begin{array}{ll}
\text{M} & \\
+ \text{ C} \quad \underline{1140} & \\
\text{SP} & \\
- \text{ D} \quad -0.15\,\text{SP} & \\
\overline{\text{RSP}} \quad \overline{0.85\,\text{SP}} & \\
- \text{ C} \quad -1140 & \\
-\text{OE} \quad \underline{-0.3C} & \\
\overline{\text{ROP}} \quad 0.1\overline{6}C &
\end{array}
$$

a. $RSP - C - OE = ROP$
$0.85\,SP - \$1140 - 0.3(\$1140) = 0.1\overline{6}(\$1140)$
$0.85\,SP = \$1672$
$\quad SP = \$1967.06$

$\qquad M + C = SP$
$M + \$1140 = \$1967.06$
$\qquad\quad M = \$827.06$

$\%M\,(\text{on } C) = \dfrac{\$827.06}{\$1140} \times 100\% = \underline{72.55\%}$

b. $ROP = RSP - C - OE = RSP - \$1140 - 0.3(\$1140) = RSP - \$1482$

At an overall discount of 20%,
$\quad ROP = 0.80\,SP - \$1482 = 0.80(\$1967.06) - \$1482 = \underline{\$91.65}$

At an overall discount of 22%, $ROP = 0.78\,SP - \$1482 = \underline{\$52.31}$

At an overall discount of 25%, $ROP = 0.75\,SP - \$1482 = \underline{-\$6.71}$

Review Problems

1. $dL = \$136.92$
$0.28L = \$136.92$
$\qquad L = \$489.00$

$N = \$489.00 - \$136.92 = \underline{\$352.08}$

2. $L = \dfrac{N}{1 - d} = \dfrac{\$155.61}{1 - 0.22} = \$199.50$

$Discount = \$199.50 - \$155.61 = \underline{\$43.89}$

3. $N = L(1 - d) = \$43.00\,(1 - 0.25) = \$32.25$

$Discount = \$44.50 - \$32.25 = \$12.25$

$Discount\ rate = \dfrac{\$12.25}{\$44.50} \times 100\% = \underline{27.5\%}$

4. $L = \dfrac{N}{1 - d} = \dfrac{\$275,995}{1 - 0.045} = \underline{\$289,000}$

5. a. $Fee = 0.029(\$28,476) = \underline{\$825.80}$

b. $dL = \$981.71$

$L = \dfrac{\$981.71}{0.029} = \underline{\$33,852}$

6. $L = \dfrac{N}{1 - d} = \dfrac{1098.6}{1 - 0.009} = 1108.6$

$Decline = 1108.6 - 1098.6 = \underline{10.0\ points}$

7. Beginning price, $L = \dfrac{N}{1 - d} = \dfrac{\$1.10}{1 - 0.78} = \underline{\$5.00}$

Review Problems *(continued)*

8. a. $L = \dfrac{\$199.16}{(1 - 0.22)(1 - 0.07)(1 - 0.05)} = \underline{\underline{\$289.00}}$

    b. $1 - d_e = \dfrac{N}{L} = \dfrac{\$199.16}{\$289.00} = 0.6891$

    $d_e = 1 - 0.6891 = 0.3109 = \underline{31.09\%}$

9. $N = L - \text{discount} = \$249.50 - \$77.85 = \$171.65$

    $\$171.65 = \$249.50(1 - 0.15)(1 - 0.075)(1 - d_3)$

    $ = \$196.169(1 - d_3)$

    $d_3 = 1 - \dfrac{\$171.65}{\$196.169} = 0.1250 = \underline{\underline{12.50\%}}$

10. For matching net prices,

    $\$420(1 - 0.30)(1 - d_2) = \$390(1 - 0.20)(1 - 0.10)$

    $\$294.00(1 - d_2) = \$280.80$

    $d_2 = 1 - \dfrac{\$280.80}{\$294.00} = 0.0449 = \underline{\underline{4.49\%}}$

11. a. 1980 population, $L = \dfrac{N}{(1 - d_1)(1 - d_2)(1 - d_3)}$

    $= \dfrac{9320}{(1 - 0.032)(1 - 0.052)(1 - 0.047)}$

    $= \underline{\underline{10{,}657}}$

    b. 1980–84 decline $= d_1 L = 0.032(10{,}657) = \underline{\underline{341}}$

    1985–89 decline $= d_2(10{,}657 - 341) = 0.052(10{,}316) = \underline{\underline{536}}$

    1990–94 decline $= d_3(10{,}316 - 536) = 0.047(9780) = \underline{\underline{460}}$

12. $\quad d_e = 1 - (1 - d_1)(1 - d_2)(1 - d_3)$

    $0.15 = 1 - (1 - 0.049)(1 - 0.066)(1 - d_3)$

    $1 - d_3 = \dfrac{1 - 0.15}{(1 - 0.049)(1 - 0.066)} = 0.9570$

    $d_3 = 1 - 0.9570 = 0.0430 = \underline{4.30\%}$

    The number of jobs declined by 4.30% in 1992.

13. a. Beginning price, $L = \dfrac{\text{Ending price, } N}{(1 - d_1)(1 - d_2)(1 - d_3)}$

    $= \dfrac{\$0.50}{(1 - 0.40)(1 - 0.60)(1 - 0.70)}$

    $= \underline{\underline{\$6.94}}$

    b. Decline in year 2 $= d_2 L(1 - d_1)$

    $= 0.60(\$6.94)(1 - 0.40)$

    $= \underline{\underline{\$2.50}}$

Review Problems *(continued)*

14. a. March 27 + 10 days = <u>April 6</u>

b. April 6 + 20 days = <u>April 26</u>

c. Amount paid = $6000(1 − 0.02) = <u>$5880.00</u>

d. Amount credited = $\dfrac{\$6000}{1-0.02}$ = $6122.45

Balance owed = $12,600 − $6122.45 = <u>$6477.55</u>

e. Amount credited = $12,600 − $6000 = $6600.00
Amount paid = $6600(1 − 0.02) = <u>$6468.00</u>

15. Total payment = $650 + $790(1 − 0.015) + $465(1 − 0.015) = <u>$1886.18</u>

16. Total amount credited = $\dfrac{\$1100}{1-0.02}$ + $\dfrac{\$900}{1-0.01}$ + $800 = $2831.54

Balance owed = $3691.00 − $2831.54 = <u>$859.46</u>

17. Invoice amount (net of trade discounts)
= 10($1100)(1 − 0.20)(1 − 0.10) + 15($880)(1 − 0.25)(1 − 0.05)
= $17,325

Amount credited = 0.5($17,325) = $8662.50
Amount paid = $8662.50(1 − 0.015) = <u>$8532.56</u>

18.

	$	%
OE		20
+OP		
M	——	—
+ C	+309.83	
SP	459.00	100

C = $459(1 − 0.25)(1 − 0.10) = $309.83

a. OE = 0.2($459.00) = $91.80
M = $459.00 − $309.83 = $149.17

Then, OP = $149.17 − $91.80 = <u>$57.37</u>

b. %M(on C) = $\dfrac{\$149.17}{\$309.83}$ × 100% = <u>48.15%</u>

c. %M(on SP) = $\dfrac{\$149.17}{\$459.00}$ × 100% = <u>32.50%</u>

d. The break-even price is

SP − OP = $459.00 − $57.37 = <u>$401.63</u>

19.

	%
M	55
+C	+45
SP	100

%M(on C) = $\dfrac{55}{45}$ × 100% = <u>122.2%</u>

20.

	$	%
OE		20
+OP		18
M		38
+ C	+9.45	+62
SP		100

C = $15(1 − 0.3)(1 − 0.1) = $9.45

Fill in the "plugs" in the % column.

$\dfrac{\$9.45}{SP} = \dfrac{62}{100}$

SP = $\dfrac{100}{62}$ × $9.45 = <u>$15.45</u>

Review Problems *(continued)*

21.

	$	%
M	40	
+C	+246	60
SP		100
−D		−30
RSP		70

Fill in the "plugs" in the % column.

$$\frac{\$246}{RSP} = \frac{60}{70}$$

$$RSP = \frac{70}{60} \times \$246 = \underline{\$287.00}$$

22.

	$
OE	0.40C
+OP	+0.45C
M	0.85C
+C	+C
SP	1.85C
−D	−0.45C
RSP	1.40C

To break even, D = OP = 0.45C
Fill in the "plugs" in terms of C.

$$\%D = \frac{0.45}{1.85} \times 100\% = \underline{24.32\%}$$

23.

	$
OE	0.20C
+OP	+0.16C
M	0.36C
+C	+C
SP	489
−D	
RSP	

a. $0.3\overline{6}C + C = \$489$

$$C = \frac{\$489}{1.3\overline{6}} = \$357.80$$

To break even,
$$D = OP = 0.1\overline{6}C = 0.1\overline{6}\,(\$357.80) = \underline{\$59.63}$$

b. If RSP = C, then D = M = $0.3\overline{6}C$ and

$$\%D = \frac{0.3\overline{6}C}{1.3\overline{6}C} \times 100\% = \underline{26.83\%}$$

24.

	$	%
OE		20
+OP		+15
M		35
+C	+173.25	+65
SP		100
−D		
RSP	199.00	
−C	−173.25	−65
−OE		−20
ROP		

$C = \$275(1 - 0.3)(1 - 0.1) = \$173.25$
Fill in the "plugs" in the % column for OP and C.

a. $\dfrac{\$173.25}{SP} = \dfrac{65}{100}$

$$SP = \$266.54$$

$$\%D = \frac{\$266.54 - \$199}{\$266.54} \times 100\% = \underline{25.34\%}$$

b. OE = 0.20 ($266.54) = $53.31
   ROP = $199 − $173.25 − $53.31 = −$27.56
   That is, the loss is $27.56.

c. %M (on C at the RSP) = $\dfrac{\$199.00 - \$173.25}{\$173.25} \times 100\% = \underline{14.86\%}$

Review Problems (concluded)

25.

	$	% of SP	% of RSP
SP		100	
−D		−20	
RSP		80	100
−M			−20
C	1750		80

a. $\dfrac{RSP}{1750} = \dfrac{100}{80}$

$RSP = \underline{\$2187.50}$

b. $\dfrac{SP}{RSP} = \dfrac{100}{80}$

$SP = \dfrac{100}{80} \times \$2187.50 = \underline{\$2734.38}$

Self-Test Exercises

1. $N_A = \$196.00\,(1 - 0.20) = \$156.80$

   $N_B = \$186.00\,(1 - 0.1\bar{6}) = \$155.00$

   <u>Source B</u> is $1.80 cheaper.

2. $\text{Discount} = dL$

   $\$337.05 = 0.225L$

   $L = \$1498.00$

   $N = L - dL = \$1498.00 - \$337.05 = \underline{\$1160.95}$

3. Lowest selling price, $L = \dfrac{N}{1-d} = \dfrac{\$160,000}{1 - 0.055} = \underline{\$169,300}$

4. a. $N = \$1195\,(1 - 0.25)(1 - 0.08\bar{3})(1 - 0.05) = \underline{\$780.48}$

   b. $L = \dfrac{\$470.25}{(1 - 0.25)(1 - 0.08\bar{3})(1 - 0.05)} = \underline{\$720.00}$

   c. $d_e = 1 - (1 - 0.25)(1 - 0.083)(1 - 0.05) = 0.3469 = \underline{34.69\%}$

   d. Amount of discount for a January order
   $= d_3 L(1 - d_1)(1 - d_2)$
   $= 0.05(\$1000)(1 - 0.25)(1 - 0.08\bar{3})$
   $= \underline{\$34.38}$

5. a. For the same net cost,
   $L(1 - 0.30)(1 - 0.15) = L(1 - 0.25)(1 - 0.1\bar{6})(1 - d_3)$
   $0.5950 = 0.6250(1 - d_3)$
   $d_3 = 1 - \dfrac{0.5950}{0.6250} = 0.0480 = \underline{4.80\%}$

Self-Test Exercises *(continued)*

   b. For the same net cost,

$$L(1 - 0.30)(1 - 0.15) = L(1 - 0.25)(1 - d_2)$$
$$0.5950 = 0.75(1 - d_2)$$
$$d_2 = 1 - \frac{0.5950}{0.75} = 0.2067 = 20.67\%$$

     Packard needs to increase the second discount by
       $20.67\% - 16.67\% = \underline{4.00\%}$

6. d_1 x Budget before cuts = \$850 million

   Budget before cuts, $L = \dfrac{\$850 \text{ million}}{0.08} = \$10{,}625 \text{ million}$

   Year 2 cut = 0.11(\$10,625 – \$850) million = $\underline{\$1075.25 \text{ million}}$

   Year 3 cut = 0.08 (\$10,625 – \$850 – \$1075.25) million = $\underline{\$695.98 \text{ million}}$

7. Amount credited on Dec. 2 $= \dfrac{\$4000}{1 - 0.03} = \$4123.71$

   Balance owed after Dec. 2 payment = \$7260 – \$4123.71 = \$3136.29

   Payment to settle invoice on Dec. 16 = \$3136.29(1 – 0.015) = $\underline{\$3089.25}$

8. Amount credited = \$887.00 – \$378.09 = \$508.91

   Discount rate $= \dfrac{\$8.91}{\$508.91}$ x 100% = $\underline{1.75\%}$

9. a.

	\$
M	0.3C
+C	+C
SP	87.49

        $0.3C + C = \$87.49$
         $1.3C = \$87.49$
           $C = \underline{\$67.30}$

   b.

	\$	%
M		30
+C	____	+70
SP	87.49	100

     $\dfrac{C}{\$87.49} = \dfrac{70}{100}$

     $C = 0.7 (\$87.49) = \underline{\$61.24}$

10.

	\$	%
OE	33.3	
+OP		+10
M		43.3
+C	+11.70	+56.6
SP		100

    $C = \$19.50(1 - 0.4) = \$11.70$

    a. $\dfrac{\$11.70}{SP} = \dfrac{56.\overline{6}}{100}$

         $SP = \underline{\$20.65}$

    b. $M = \$20.65 - \$11.70 = \$8.95$

       $\%M(\text{on } C) = \dfrac{\$8.95}{\$11.70}$ x 100% = $\underline{76.50\%}$

   c. Break-even price = SP – OP = \$20.65 – 0.1(\$20.65) = $\underline{\$18.59}$

Self-Test Exercises *(continued)*

11.

	$
OE	$0.3\bar{3}C$
+OP	$+0.20C$
M	$0.5\bar{3}C$
+C	$+C$
SP	$1.53C$
−D	
RSP	
−C	$-C$
−OE	$-0.3\bar{3}C$
ROP	$0.10C$

a. Fill in the "plugs" for M and SP. Then
$SP = 1.5\bar{3}C = \underline{153.3\%}$ of cost

b. Given: $ROP = 0.5(OP) = 0.10C$
Then $RSP = C + 0.3\bar{3}C + 0.10C = 1.4\bar{3}C$
and $D = 1.53C - 1.4\bar{3}C = 0.10C$
Therefore,
$\%D = \dfrac{0.10C}{1.53C} \times 100\% = \underline{6.52\%}$

12.

	$	%
OE	22	
+OP		+18
M		40
+C	+216	+60
SP		100
−D		
RSP	270	
−C	−216	−60
−OE		−22
ROP		

$C = \$360(1 - 0.3\bar{3})(1 - 0.10) = \$216.00$
Fill in the "plugs" in the % column for OP and C.

a. $\dfrac{\$216}{SP} = \dfrac{60}{100}$
$SP = \$360.00$

$\%D = \dfrac{\$360 - \$270}{\$360} \times 100\% = \underline{25.00\%}$

b. $OE = 0.22 (\$360) = \$79.20$
$ROP = \$270 - \$216 - \$79.20 = -\$25.20$
That is, the loss is $25.20 per pair.

c. $\%M\text{(on C at RSP)} = \dfrac{\$270 - \$216}{\$216} \times 100\% = \underline{25.00\%}$

13.

	$	%(of SP)	%(of RSP)
SP		100	
−D		−40	
RSP		60	100
−C	−648		−62.5
−OE			−25
ROP			12.5

$C = \$1200(1 - 0.4)(1 - 0.1) = \$648$
Also, $C = 100 - 25 - 12.5$
$= 62.5\%$ of RSP

a. $\dfrac{RSP}{\$648} = \dfrac{100}{62.5}$
$RSP = \$1036.80$

$\dfrac{SP}{\$1036.80} = \dfrac{100}{60}$

$SP = \underline{\$1728.00}$

b. To break even,
$RSP = C + OE = \$648 + 0.25 (\$1036.80) = \$907.20$
$\%D = \dfrac{SP - RSP}{SP} \times 100\% = \dfrac{\$1728 - \$907.20}{\$1728} \times 100\% = \underline{47.50\%}$

5 Applications of Linear Equations

Changes in the Second Edition:

1. This is the revised version of the former Chapter 4. The main change in the chapter is to give "top billing" to the **Contribution Margin Approach to CVP Analysis.** The **Revenue and Cost Function Approach** and the **Graphical Approach** are given less coverage than in the first edition. These changes reflect both the relative usage of the three approaches in business and the preferences expressed by reviewers and survey respondents.

2. Eight new problems involving cost-volume-profit analysis have been added (three to Exercise 5.2 and five to the end-of-chapter Review Problems).

3. The graphical solution of two linear equations in two unknowns has been dropped except for the related case of a **Break-Even Chart**. A typical view is that, although plotting two lines to find the point of intersection is conceptually appealing, the time required and the low degree of precision in the results make the technique impractical.

Exercise 5.1

1.
$$x - y = 2 \quad ①$$
$$3x + 4y = 20 \quad ②$$

$① \times 3$:
$$3x - 3y = 6$$

Subtract:
$$7y = 14$$
$$y = 2$$

Substitute into equation ①:
$$x - 2 = 2$$
$$x = 4$$
$$(x,y) = \underline{(4,2)}$$

Check:
$$\text{LHS of } ② = 3(4) + 4(2) = 20 = \text{RHS of } ②$$

2.
$$y - 3x = 11 \quad ①$$
$$-4y + 5x = -30 \quad ②$$

$① \times 4$:
$$4y - 12x = 44$$

Add:
$$-7x = 14$$
$$x = -2$$

Substitute into equation ①:
$$y - 3(-2) = 11$$
$$y = 11 - 6$$
$$= 5$$
$$(x,y) = \underline{(-2,5)}$$

Check:
$$\text{LHS of } ② = -4(5) + (5)(-2)$$
$$= -30$$
$$= \text{RHS of } ②$$

3.
$$4a - 3b = -3 \quad ①$$
$$5a - b = 10 \quad ②$$

$① \times 1$:
$$4a - 3b = -3$$

$② \times 3$:
$$15a - 3b = 30$$

Subtract:
$$-11a = -33$$
$$a = 3$$

Substitute into equation ②:
$$5(3) - b = 10$$
$$b = 5$$
$$(a,b) = \underline{(3,5)}$$

Check:
$$\text{LHS of } ① = 4(3) - 3(5)$$
$$= -3$$
$$= \text{RHS of } ①$$

Exercise 5.1 *(continued)*

4.

$$7p - 3q = 23 \quad ①$$
$$\underline{-2p - 3q = 5} \quad ②$$

Subtract:
$$9p = 18$$
$$p = 2$$

Substitute into equation ①:

$$7(2) - 3q = 23$$
$$3q = -23 + 14$$
$$q = -3$$
$$(p,q) = \underline{(2,-3)}$$

Check:

$$\text{LHS of } ② = -2(2) - 3(-3)$$
$$= 5$$
$$= \text{RHS of } ②$$

5.

$$y = 2x \quad ①$$
$$\underline{7x - y = 35} \quad ②$$

Add:
$$7x = 2x + 35$$
$$5x = 35$$
$$x = 7$$

Substitute into equation ①:

$$y = 2(7)$$
$$= 14$$
$$(x,y) = \underline{(7,14)}$$

Check:

$$\text{LHS of } ② = 7(7) - 14$$
$$= 49 - 14$$
$$= 35$$
$$= \text{RHS of } ②$$

6.

$$g - h = 17 \quad ①$$
$$\frac{4}{3}g + \frac{3}{2}h = 0 \quad ②$$
$$1.\overline{3}g + 1.5h = 0 \quad ②$$

$$① \times 1.5: \quad \underline{1.5g - 1.5h = 25.5}$$

Add:
$$2.8\overline{3}g = 25.5$$
$$g = 9$$

Substitute into equation ①:

$$9 - h = 17$$
$$h = -8$$
$$(h,g) = \underline{(-8,9)}$$

Check:

$$\text{LHS of } ② = \frac{4}{3}(9) + \frac{3}{2}(-8) = 12 - 12 = 0 = \text{RHS of } ②$$

Exercise 5.1 *(continued)*

7.
$$d = 3c - 500 \quad \text{①}$$
$$0.7c + 0.2d = 550 \quad \text{②}$$

To eliminate d,

① × 0.2:	$-0.6c + 0.2d = -100$
②:	$0.7c + 0.2d = 550$
Subtract:	$-1.3c + 0 = -650$
	$c = 500$

Substitute into ①:
$$d = 3(500) - 500$$
$$= 1000$$
$$(c,d) = \underline{(500, 1000)}$$

Check:
$$\text{LHS of ②} = 0.7(500) + 0.2(1000) = 550 = \text{RHS of ②}$$

8.
$$0.03x + 0.05y = 51 \quad \text{①}$$
$$0.8x - 0.7y = 140 \quad \text{②}$$

To eliminate y,

① × 0.7:	$0.021x + 0.035y = 35.7$
② × 0.05:	$0.04x - 0.035y = 7$
Add:	$0.061x + 0 = 42.7$
	$x = 700$

Substitute into ②:
$$0.8(700) - 0.7y = 140$$
$$-0.7y = -420$$
$$y = 600$$
$$(x,y) = \underline{(700, 600)}$$

Check:
$$\text{LHS of ①} = 0.03(700) + 0.05(600) = 51 = \text{RHS of ①}$$

9.
$$2v + 6w = 1 \quad \text{①}$$
$$10v - 9w = 18 \quad \text{②}$$

To eliminate v,

① × 10:	$20v + 60w = 10$
② × 2:	$20v - 18w = 36$
Subtract:	$0 + 78w = -26$

$$w = -\frac{1}{3}$$

Substitute into ①:
$$2v + 6\left(-\frac{1}{3}\right) = 1$$
$$2v = 1 + 2$$
$$v = \frac{3}{2}$$
$$(v,w) = \underline{\left(\frac{3}{2}, -\frac{1}{3}\right)}$$

Check:
$$\text{LHS of ②} = 10\left(\frac{3}{2}\right) - 9\left(-\frac{1}{3}\right) = 18 = \text{RHS of ②}$$

10.

$$2.5a + 2b = 11 \quad ①$$
$$8a + 3.5b = 13 \quad ②$$

To eliminate b,

$① \times 3.5$: $\quad 8.75a + 7b = 38.5$

$② \times 2$: $\quad \underline{16a + 7b = 26}$

Subtract: $\quad -7.25a + 0 = 12.5$

$$a = -1.724$$

Substitute into ①: $\quad 2.5(-1.724) + 2b = 11$

$$2b = 11 + 4.31$$
$$b = 7.655$$
$$(a,b) = \underline{(-1.72,\ 7.66)}$$

Check:

LHS of ② $= 8(-1.724) + 3.5(7.655)$

$\qquad = 13.00$

$\qquad =$ RHS of ②

11.

$$37x - 63y = 235 \quad ①$$
$$18x + 26y = 468 \quad ②$$

To eliminate x,

$① \times 18$: $666x - 1134y = 4230$

$② \times 37$: $\underline{666x + 962y = 17,316}$

Subtract: $\quad 0 - 2096y = -13,086$

$$y = 6.243$$

Substitute into ①: $\quad 37x - 63(6.243) = 235$

$$37x = 628.3$$
$$x = 16.98$$
$$(x,y) = \underline{(17.0,\ 6.24)}$$

Check:

LHS of ② $= 18(16.98) + 26(6.243) = 468.0 =$ RHS of ②

12.

$$68.9n - 38.5m = 57 \quad ①$$
$$45.1n - 79.4m = -658 \quad ②$$

To eliminate n,

$① \times 45.1$: $3107n - 1736.4m = 2571$

$② \times 68.9$: $\underline{3107n - 5470.7m = -45,336}$

Subtract: $\quad 0 + 3734.3m = 47,907$

$$m = 12.83$$

Substitute into ①: $\quad 68.9n - 38.5(12.83) = 57$

$$68.9n = 551.0$$
$$n = 7.996$$
$$(m,n) = \underline{(12.8,\ 8.00)}$$

Check:

LHS of ② $= 45.1(7.996) - 79.4(12.83) = -658.1 =$ RHS of ②

Exercise 5.1 (continued)

13.

$$0.33e + 1.67f = 292 \quad ①$$
$$1.2\ e + 0.61f = 377 \quad ②$$

To eliminate e,

① ÷ 0.33:	$e + 5.061f = 884.8$	
② ÷ 1.2:	$e + 0.508f = 314.2$	
Subtract:	$0 + 4.552f = 570.6$	
	$f = 125.4$	

Substitute into ①:

$$0.33e + 1.67(125.4) = 292$$
$$0.33e = 82.58$$
$$e = 250.2$$
$$(e,f) = \underline{(250,125)}$$

Check:

LHS of ② = 1.2(250.2) + 0.61(125.4) = 376.7 = RHS of ②

14.

$$318j - 451k = 7.22 \quad ①$$
$$-249j + 193k = -18.79 \quad ②$$

To eliminate k,

① ÷ 451:	$0.7051j - k = 0.01601$	
② ÷ 193:	$-1.2902j + k = -0.09736$	
Add:	$-0.5851j + 0 = -0.08135$	
	$j = 0.1390$	

Substitute into ②:

$$-249(0.1390) + 193k = -18.79$$
$$193k = 15.82$$
$$k = 0.08197$$
$$(j,k) = \underline{(0.139, 0.0820)}$$

Check:

LHS of ① = 318(0.1390) − 451(0.08197)
= 7.23
= RHS of ① within rounding errors.

15. Let the number of regular members be r and the number of student members be s. Then

	$r + s = 583$	①
	$\$1070r + \$428s = \$471,014$	②
① × \$428:	$\$428r + \$428s = \$249,524$	
Subtract:	$\$642r + 0 = \$221,490$	
	$r = 345$	
Substitute into ①:	$345 + s = 583$	
	$s = 238$	

The club had 238 student members and 345 regular members.

16. Let x represent the number of units of product X and y represent the number of units of product Y. Then

	$x + y = 93$	①
	$0.5x + 0.75y = 60.5$	②
① × 0.5:	$0.5x + 0.5\ y = 46.5$	
Subtract:	$0 + 0.25y = 14$	
	$y = 56$	
Substitute into ①:	$x + 56 = 93$	
	$x = 37$	

Therefore 37 units of X and 56 units of Y were produced last week.

17. Let the price per litre of milk be m and the price per dozen eggs be e. Then

$$5m + 4e = \$13.97 \quad ①$$
$$9m + 3e = \$16.83 \quad ②$$

To eliminate e,

① × 3:	15m + 12e =	$41.91
② × 4:	36m + 12e =	$67.32
Subtract:	−21m + 0 =	−$25.41
	m =	$ 1.21

Substitute into ①: $5(\$1.21) + 4e = \$13.97$

$$e = \$ 1.98$$

Milk costs $\underline{\$1.21 \text{ per litre}}$ and eggs cost $\underline{\$1.98 \text{ per dozen}}$.

18. Let M be the number of litres of milk and J be the number of cans of orange juice per week.

$$\$1.10M + \$0.98J = \$42.20 \quad ①$$
$$\$1.15M + \$1.14J = \$45.85 \quad ②$$

To eliminate M,

① × 1.15:	$1.265M + $1.127J =	$48.53
② × 1.1:	$1.265M + $1.254J =	$50.435
Subtract:	0 − $0.127J =	−$ 1.905
	J =	15

Substitution of J = 15 into either equation will give M = 25. Hence $\underline{25 \text{ litres}}$ of milk and $\underline{15 \text{ cans}}$ of orange juice are purchased each week.

19. Let x represent Maurice's investment and y represent Marcel's investment. Then

$$x + y = \$83,000 \quad ①$$
$$y = \left(\frac{4}{3}\right) x - \$8000 \quad ②$$

Rearrange ②:

$$-\left(\frac{4}{3}\right) x + y = -\$8000 \quad ②$$

① − ②:

$$2\frac{1}{3} x + 0 = \$91,000$$

$$x = \$39,000$$

Substitute in ①: $\$39,000 + y = \$83,000$

$$y = \$44,000$$

$\underline{\text{Maurice should invest } \$39,000}$ and $\underline{\text{Marcel should invest } \$44,000}$ in the partnership.

20. Let S represent the price of a box of small envelopes and L represent the price of a box of large envelopes. Then

$$3L + 7S = \$113.30 \quad ①$$
$$L = \$0.50 + 2S \quad ②$$

To eliminate S,

① × 2:	6L + 14S =	$226.60
② × 7:	7L − 14S =	$ 3.50
Add:	13L + 0 =	$230.10
	L =	$17.70

The price of a box of large envelopes is $\underline{\$17.70}$.

Exercise 5.1 *(continued)*

21. Let S represent the selling price of a case of beer and R represent the refund per case of empties. Then

$$871S - 637R = \$12,632.10 \qquad ①$$
$$932S - 805R = \$13,331.70 \qquad ②$$

To eliminate S,

① × 932:	811,772S – 593,684R	=	$11,773,117.20
② × 871:	811,772S – 701,155R	=	$11,611,910.70
Subtract:	0 + 107,471R	=	$ 161,206.50
	R	=	$1.50

The store paid a refund of <u>$1.50</u> per case.

22. Let S represent the number of people who bought single tickets and T represent the number of people who bought at 3-for-$5. Then

$$S + 3T = 3884 \qquad ①$$
$$\$2S + \$5T = \$6925 \qquad ②$$

To eliminate S,

① × $2:	$2S + $6T	=	$7768
②:	$2S + $5T	=	$6925
Subtract:	0 + $1T	=	$ 843
	T	=	843

Hence, <u>843</u> people bought tickets at the 3-for-$5 discount.

23. Let P represent the number of six-packs and C represent the number of single cans sold. Then

$$\$4.35P + \$0.90C = \$178.35 \qquad ①$$
$$6P + C = 225 \qquad ②$$

To eliminate C,

①:	$4.35P + $0.90C	=	$178.35
② × $0.90:	$5.40P + $0.90C	=	$202.50
Subtract:	–$1.05P + 0	=	–$ 24.15
	P	=	23
Substitute into ②:	6(23) + C	=	225
	C	=	87

The store sold <u>23 six-packs</u> and <u>87 single cans</u>.

24. Let P represent the annual salary of a partner and T represent the annual salary of a technician. Then

	7P + 12T	=	$1,086,000	①
	1.05(7P) + 1.08(12T)	=	$1,156,500	②
① × 1.05:	1.05(7P) + 1.05(12T)	=	$1,140,300	
Subtract:	0 + 0.03(12T)	=	$ 16,200	
	T	=	$ 45,000	
Substitute into ①:	7P + 12($45,000)	=	$1,086,000	
	P	=	$ 78,000	

The current annual salaries of a partner and a technician are <u>$78,000</u> and <u>$45,000</u>, respectively.

Exercise 5.1 (concluded)

25. Let P represent the current number of production workers and A the current number of assembly workers. Then

$$\$3400 \ P + \$2800 \ A = \$253,800 \quad ①$$
$$\$3400(0.8P) + \$2800(0.75A) = \$198,000 \quad ②$$

To eliminate P,

① × 0.8:	$\$3400(0.8P) + \$2800(0.8 \ A)$	=	$\$203,040$
②:	$\$3400(0.8P) + \$2800(0.75A)$	=	$\$198,000$
Subtract:	$\$2800(0.05A)$	=	$\$ \ 5040$
	A	=	36
Substitute into ①:	$\$3400P + \$2800(0.8 \times 36)$	=	$\$253,800$
	P	=	45

Therefore, 0.2P = <u>9 production workers</u> and 0.25A = <u>9 assembly workers</u> will be laid off.

Exercise 5.2

Note: All problems will be solved using the contribution margin approach. In addition, alternative solutions using the revenue and cost function approach will be presented for problems 1, 3, 8, 9, and 13.

1. Given: Capacity = 250 units per week
   SP = $20, VC = $12, FC = $1200 per week

   Contribution Margin Approach

   a. CM = SP – VC = $20 – $12 = <u>$8.00</u>

   b. Break-even volume = $\dfrac{FC}{CM} = \dfrac{\$1200}{\$8}$ = <u>150 units per week</u>

   c. (i) At 30 units per week short of breakeven, there will be a <u>loss of</u> 30($8) = <u>$240/week</u>.

   (ii) At 100 units per week above breakeven, there will be a <u>profit of</u> 100($8) = <u>$800/week</u>.

   d. For a net income of $400/week, sales must be

   $$\dfrac{NI}{CM} = \dfrac{\$400}{\$8} = 50 \text{ units above break even}$$

   Hence, sales must be 150 + 50 = <u>200 units per week</u>.

   Revenue/Cost Function Approach

   b. TR = (SP)X = $20X
   TC = (VC)X + FC = $12X + $1200
   To break even, TR = TC
   Then, $20X = $12X + $1200
              X = <u>150 units/week</u>

   c. NI = TR – TC = $20X – $12X – $1200 = $8X – $1200
   (i) If X = 120 units/week,
        NI = $8(120) – $1200 = – $240
   There will be a <u>loss of $240/week</u>.

   (ii) If X = 250 units/week,
        NI = $8(250) – $1200 = <u>$800/week profit</u>.

   d. If NI = $400/week, then

$$\$400 = \$8X - \$1200$$
$$\$1600 = \$8X$$
$$X = \underline{\underline{200 \text{ units/week}}}$$

2. Given: SP = $10, VC = $7.50, FC = $100,000 per year

   a. CM = SP − VC = $\underline{\underline{\$2.50}}$ and CR = $\dfrac{CM}{SP} \times 100\% = \dfrac{\$2.50}{\$10} \times 100\% = \underline{\underline{25\%}}$

   b. To break even, X = $\dfrac{FC}{CM} = \dfrac{\$100,000}{\$2.50} = \underline{\underline{40,000 \text{ bags/year}}}$

   c. If Valley Peat sells 20,000 bags more than break even,

       NI = 20,000($2.50) = $\underline{\underline{\$50,000}}$

   d. For NI = $60,000

$$X = 40,000 \text{ (to break even)} + \frac{\$60,000}{\$2.50} = \underline{\underline{64,000 \text{ bags/year}}}$$

   e. For NI = −$10,000, sales would be

$$\frac{\$10,000}{\$2.50} = 4000 \text{ bags below break even}$$

      That is, X = 40,000 − 4000 = $\underline{\underline{36,000 \text{ bags/year}}}$

      Revenue = (SP)X = $10(36,000) = $\underline{\underline{\$360,000/\text{year}}}$

   f. For each $1000 increase in annual fixed costs, sales must increase by

$$\frac{\$1000}{\$2.50} = \underline{\underline{400 \text{ units}}} \text{ or } \underline{\underline{\$4000}} \text{ to break even.}$$

3. Given: VC = $43, SP = $70, FC = $648,000/year = $54,000/month
       Production capacity = 3200 borgels per month

Contribution Margin Approach

   a. CM = SP − VC = $70 − $43 = $\underline{\underline{\$27}}$

   b. Break-even volume = $\dfrac{FC}{CM} = \dfrac{\$54,000}{\$27} = \underline{\underline{2000 \text{ borgels/month}}}$

   c. At 500 units/month in excess of break even,
      NI = 500(CM) = 500($27) = $\underline{\underline{\$13,500/\text{month}}}$

   d. At 50% of capacity,
      X = 0.5(3200/month) = 1600/month

      This is 400 borgels/month below break even.
      Hence, Reflex will <u>lose</u> 400($27) = $\underline{\underline{\$10,800/\text{month}}}$

Exercise 5.2 (continued)

e. For NI = \$226,800/year = \$18,900/month

$$X = 2000 + \frac{\$18,900}{\$27} = 2700 \text{ units/month}$$

which is $\dfrac{2700}{3200} \times 100\% = \underline{84.4\% \text{ of capacity}}$

f. If SP is \$1 higher while VC and FC are unchanged, then CM will increase \$1 to \$28 and

$$\text{Break-even volume} = \frac{\$54,000}{\$28} = 1929$$

That is, the break-even volume <u>decreases by 71 borgels/month</u> for a \$1 increase in the selling price.

Revenue/Cost Function Approach

b. TR = (SP)X = \$70X
TC = (VC)X + FC = \$43X + \$54,000
At break even, TR = TC
    \$70X = \$43X + \$54,000
    \$27X = \$54,000
       X = <u>2000 borgels/month</u>

c. NI = TR − TC = \$70X − \$43X − \$54,000 = \$27X − \$54,000
If X = 2500 borgels/month,
NI = \$27(2500) − \$54,000 = <u>\$13,500/month</u>

d. At 50% capacity, X = 0.5(3200/month) = 1600/month and
NI = \$27(1600) − \$54,000 = − \$10,800/month.
Reflex will <u>lose \$10,800/month</u> in the recession.

e. For NI = \$226,800/year = \$18,900/month
    \$18,900 = \$27X − \$54,000
    \$72,900 = \$27X
       X = 2700 borgels/month

which is $\dfrac{2700}{3200} \times 100\% = \underline{84.4\% \text{ of capacity}}$

f. If TR = \$71X while costs do not change, then
    \$71X = \$43X + \$54,000 at break even

$$X = \frac{\$54,000}{\$71 - \$43} = 1929$$

The break-even volume decreases 71 borgels/month for a \$1 increase in the selling price.

4. Given: FC = \$450,000/year, VC = \$15, CR = 40%

a. A contribution rate of 40% means that 40¢ of each \$1 of sales is available to pay fixed costs. To pay

FC = \$450,000, the break-even revenue is

$$\frac{\$450,000}{0.40} = \underline{\underline{\$1,125,000}}$$

Exercise 5.2 *(continued)*

b. If 40% of revenue is available for FC, then the other 60% pays VC. That is,
0.60SP = VC = $15.00
Therefore, SP = $15/0.60 = $25

Number of units to break even = $\dfrac{\$1,125,000}{\$25}$ = $\underline{\underline{45,000/year}}$

c. (i) If sales exceed break even by 5000 units,
NI = 5000(CM) = 5000($25 − $15) = $\underline{\$50,000}$

   (ii) The break-even revenue is $1,125,000. Therefore, there will be a <u>loss of $125,000</u>.

d. If the loss is $50,000, sales will be

$\dfrac{\$50,000}{CM}$ = $\dfrac{\$50,000}{\$10}$ = 5000 units below break even.

That is, annual sales will be 45,000 − 5,000 = $\underline{\underline{40,000}}$

e. SP and FC are unchanged, but VC increases $1 to $16.00
The CM drops $1 to $9 and

Break-even volume = $\dfrac{\$450,000}{\$9}$ = 50,000 units

The break-even unit sales increases by 5000 units and the break-even revenue by
5000($25) = $\underline{\$125,000}$.

5. a. (Total) variable costs = Sales − FC − NI
= $400,000 − $100,000 − $60,000
= $\underline{\underline{\$240,000}}$

$X = \dfrac{FC + NI}{CM} = \dfrac{\$100,000 + \$60,000}{\$20}$ = $\underline{\underline{8000 \text{ units}}}$

b. SP = VC + CM = $\dfrac{\$60,000}{4000}$ + $10 = $25

Sales = (SP)X = $25(4000) = $\underline{\$100,000}$
FC = Sales − Variable costs − NI
= $100,000 − $60,000 − $12,500
= $\underline{\$27,500}$

c. Variable costs = Sales − FC − NI
= $360,000 − $90,000 − $60,000
= $\underline{\underline{\$210,000}}$

$CM = \dfrac{FC + NI}{X} = \dfrac{\$90,000 + \$60,000}{5000}$ = $\underline{\underline{\$30.00}}$

Exercise 5.2 *(continued)*

6. a. Sales × CR = FC + NI
       $800,000(0.4) = FC + \$100,000$
       FC = $\underline{\underline{\$220,000}}$

    Variable costs = Sales − FC − NI
    = $800,000 − \$220,000 − \$100,000$
    = $\underline{\underline{\$480,000}}$

    b. FC = Sales − Variable costs − NI
       = $450,000 − \$360,000 − \$47,500$
       = $\underline{\underline{\$42,500}}$

    $$CR = \frac{FC + NI}{Sales} \times 100\% = \frac{\$42,500 + \$47,500}{\$450,000} \times 100\% = \underline{\underline{20.0\%}}$$

    c. Sales × CR = FC + NI
       $0.3 \text{ Sales} = \$180,000 + \$120,000$
       Sales = $\underline{\underline{\$1,000,000}}$

    Variable costs = Sales − FC − NI
    = $1,000,000 − \$180,000 − \$120,000$
    = $\underline{\underline{\$700,000}}$

7. Given: SP = $135, VC = \$110, FC = \$700$ for 15-36 participants

    a. CM = SP − VC = $135 − \$110 = \$25$

       To break even, $X = \dfrac{FC}{CM} = \dfrac{\$700}{\$25} = \underline{\underline{28 \text{ participants}}}$

    b. If X = 36 (8 more than break even),
       NI = 8(CM) = 8($25) = $\underline{\underline{\$200}}$

    c. A loss of $200 will be incurred if there are

       $$\frac{\$200}{CM} = \frac{\$200}{\$25} = 8 \text{ fewer participants than break even}$$

       Hence, the minimum number of participants is 28 − 8 = $\underline{\underline{20}}$.

8. Given: FC = $36,000, SP = \$9$
       Total variable costs of $120,000 on sales of \$180,000$

    Unit sales in September = $\dfrac{Sales}{SP} = \dfrac{\$180,000}{\$9} = 20,000$

    Unit variable cost, VC = $\dfrac{\$120,000}{20,000} = \$6$

    Contribution Margin Approach

    a. Break-even point = $\dfrac{FC}{CM} = \dfrac{\$36,000}{\$9 − \$6} = \underline{\underline{12,000 \text{ units}}}$

    b. Unit sales = $12,000 + \dfrac{\$30,000}{\$3} = \underline{\underline{22,000}}$

Exercise 5.2 *(continued)*

c. We want X when NI = 0.2 Sales = 0.2($9X)
    But also,   NI = $3(X – 12,000)
    Equating the two expressions for NI,
$$\$1.8X = \$3X - \$36,000$$
$$\$36,000 = \$1.2X$$
$$X = \underline{30,000 \text{ units}}$$

d. Unit sales = $12,000 + \dfrac{\$20,000}{\$3} = 18,667$

    $ sales = 18,667($9) = $\underline{\$168,000}$

e. Given: VC = $6(1 – 0.1) = $5.40 while FC and SP are unchanged.

    Then break-even point = $\dfrac{FC}{CM} = \dfrac{\$36,000}{\$9 - \$5.40} = \underline{10,000 \text{ units}}$

Revenue/Cost Function Approach

a. To break even,
$$X = \frac{FC}{SP - VC} = \frac{\$36,000}{\$9 - \$6} = \underline{12,000 \text{ units}}$$

b. In order that NI = $30,000
$$X = \frac{NI + FC}{SP - VC} = \frac{\$30,000 + \$36,000}{\$9 - \$6} = \underline{22,000 \text{ units}}$$

c.
$$NI = 0.2(TR) = (0.2P)X = \$1.80X \quad ①$$
$$NI = (SP - VC)X - FC$$
$$NI = (\$3)X - \$36,000 \quad ②$$
$$① - ②: \quad 0 = \$1.80X - \$3X + \$36,000$$
$$\$1.20X = \$36,000$$
$$X = \underline{30,000 \text{ units}}$$

d. For NI = $20,000,
$$X = \frac{NI + FC}{SP - VC} = \frac{\$20,000 + \$36,000}{\$9 - \$6} = 18,667 \text{ units}$$

    and TR = (SP)X = ($9)18,667 = $\underline{\$168,000}$

e. If VC = $6(1 – 0.10) = $5.40, then to break even,
$$X = \frac{FC}{SP - VC} = \frac{\$36,000}{\$9 - \$5.40} = \underline{10,000 \text{ units}}$$

9. Given: If SP = $23, FC = $2700, then VC = $12 + 0.1($23) = $14.30
            If SP = $28, FC = $2700, then VC = $12 + 0.1($28) = $14.80

Exercise 5.2 (continued)

Contribution Margin Approach

SP = $23	SP = $28

a. CM = $23 − $14.30 = $8.70

   To break even,

   $X = \dfrac{\$2700}{\$8.70} = 310.34 \doteq \underline{311}$

CM = $28 − $14.80 = $13.20

$X = \dfrac{\$2700}{\$13.20} = 204.55 \doteq \underline{205}$

We have rounded up to get the *smallest* number of tickets that will make NI = 0 or a small profit.

b. If 400 tickets are sold,

   NI = $8.70(400 − 310.34)

   = $780

If 300 tickets are sold

NI = $13.20(300 − 204.55)

= $1260

Revenue/Cost Function Approach

a. To break even,

   $X = \dfrac{FC}{P - VC} = \dfrac{\$2700}{\$23 - \$14.30}$

   $\doteq \underline{310\ \text{tickets}}$

$X = \dfrac{\$2700}{\$28 - \$14.80}$

$\doteq \underline{205\ \text{tickets}}$

b. NI = (P − VC)X − FC

   = ($23 − $14.30)400 − $2700

   = $780

NI = (P − VC)X − FC

= ($28 − $14.80)300 − $2700

= $1260

10.

Firm A	Firm B

Firm A

SP = $50, VC = $10

FC = $4000/month

a. CM = $50 − $10 = $40

   Break-even monthly volume

   $= \dfrac{FC}{CM} = \dfrac{\$4000}{\$40} = \underline{100\ \text{units}}$

b. Total costs = (VC)X + FC

   = $1000 + $4000

   = $5000

   20% of costs are <u>variable</u>

   80% of costs are <u>fixed</u>

c. If sales increase 10% (10 units),

   NI increases by

   10(CM) = $400/month

d. If sales decrease 10% (10 units),

   NI decreases by

   10(CM) = $400/month

Firm B

SP = $50, VC = $40

FC = $1000/month

a. CM = $50 − $40 = $10

   Break-even monthly volume

   $= \dfrac{\$1000}{\$10} = \underline{100\ \text{units}}$

b. Total costs = (VC)X + FC

   = $4000 + $1000

   = $5000

   80% of costs are <u>variable</u>

   20% of costs are <u>fixed</u>

c. If sales increase 10% (10 units),

   NI increases by

   10(CM) = $100/month

d. If sales decrease 10% (10 units),

   NI decreases by

   10(CM) = $100/month

A's net income increases more than B's because A's costs increase by only $10(VC) for each additional unit sold while B's costs increase by $40(VC) per unit.

A's net income decreases more than B's because, for each unit decline in sales, A's costs drop by $10 while B's costs drop by $40.

Exercise 5.2 *(continued)*

e. If X = 150 units/month,
   NI = (150 − 100)CM
      = $2000/month
   If X = 50 units/month,
   NI = (50 − 100)CM
      = − $2000/month
   (loss of $2000/month)

e. If X = 150 units/month,
   NI = (150 − 100)CM
      = $500/month
   If X = 50 units/month,
   NI = (50 − 100)CM
      = − $500/month
   (loss of $500/month)

11. Given: SP = $37.50, VC = $13.25, FC = $5600/month
    a. Last year's CM = SP − VC = $37.50 − $13.25 = $24.25

    Last year's break-even volume $= \dfrac{FC}{CM} = \dfrac{\$5600}{\$24.25} = 231$ units/month

    This year, VC = $15, FC = $6000/month. In order that the break-even volume would still be 231 griddles/month,

    $$CM = \dfrac{FC}{\text{Break-even volume}} = \dfrac{\$6000}{231} = \$25.97 \text{ and}$$

    SP = VC + CM = $15 + $25.97 = $40.97

    b. Last year's NI = (CM)X − FC = ($24.25) 300 − $5600 = $1675.00. In order that this year's profit also be $1675/month on sales of 300 griddles/month,

    $1675 = 300CM − $6000

    $$CM = \dfrac{\$7675}{300} = \$25.58$$

    and   SP = CM + VC = $25.58 + $15 = $40.58

12. Given: For last year, NI = $40,000, FC = $130,000/year,
    Total variable costs = $80,000
    a. Last year's sales = Total costs + NI
                        = $80,000 + $130,000 + $40,000
                        = $250,000

    $$CR = \dfrac{\$250,000 - \$80,000}{\$250,000} \times 100\% = 68.00\%$$

    That is, 68¢ of each $1.00 of revenue contributes to the payment of FC and then NI. To break even,
       CR × Sales = FC

    $$\text{Sales} = \dfrac{FC}{CR} = \dfrac{\$130,000}{0.68} = \$191,176$$

    b. In the current year, FC = $140,000 while variable costs remain 32% of sales. Then CR remains 68%.

    $$\text{Break-even sales} = \dfrac{FC}{CR} = \dfrac{\$140,000}{0.68} = \$205,882$$

    c. In order that NI = $50,000,

    $$\text{Sales} = \dfrac{FC + NI}{CR} = \dfrac{\$140,000 + \$50,000}{0.68} = \$279,412$$

Exercise 5.2 *(continued)*

13. Given: SP = $90/tonne, VC = $21 + $12 = $33 per tonne,
FC = $200 + $300 + $225 = $725 per hectare

Contribution Margin Approach

a. CM = SP – VC = $90 – $33 = $57 per tonne

Break-even yield = $\dfrac{FC}{CM}$ = $\dfrac{\$725 \text{ per hectare}}{\$57 \text{ per tonne}}$ = 12.72 tonnes/hectare

b. If SP = $95 per tonne, then CM = $62 per tonne and

Break-even yield = $\dfrac{\$725 \text{ per hectare}}{\$62 \text{ per tonne}}$ = 11.69 tonnes/hectare

The break-even yield is lowered by

12.72 – 11.69 = 1.03 tonnes/hectare

c. (i) If X = 15 tonnes/hectare (2.28 tonnes/hectare *above* break even),
NI = 2.28(CM) = 2.28 ($57) = $130 per hectare

(ii) If X = 10 tonnes/hectare (2.72 tonnes/hectare *below* break even), the loss will be
2.72($57) = $155 per hectare.

Revenue/Cost Function Approach

a. To break even,

X = $\dfrac{FC}{SP - VC}$ = $\dfrac{\$725}{\$90 - \$33}$ = 12.72 tonnes per hectare

b. If SP = $95 per tonne instead of $90 per tonne,

X = $\dfrac{\$725}{\$95 - \$33}$ = 11.69 tonnes per hectare

The break-even tonnage will be reduced by 1.03 tonnes per hectare.

c. (i) NI = (SP – VC)X – FC = ($90 – $33)15 – $725 = $130 per hectare.

(ii) NI = ($90 – $33)10 – $725 = –$155.00 per hectare. That is, a loss of $155 per hectare.

14. Given: NI = – $400,000 on sales of $3 million/year.
Utilization = 60% of capacity
Variable costs = 33.$\overline{3}$% of sales.

a. If variable costs are 33.$\overline{3}$% of sales, then the contribution rate, CR, is 66.$\overline{6}$% of sales.
FC = Sales – Variable costs – NI
= $3 million – 0.3$\overline{3}$($3 million) – (– $400,000)
= $2,400,000

Break-even sales = $\dfrac{FC}{CR}$ = $\dfrac{\$2,400,000}{0.6\overline{6}}$ = $3,600,000

Since sales of $3 million/year represented 60% of capacity,

$\dfrac{\$3 \text{ million}}{\$3.6 \text{ million}}$ = $\dfrac{60\% \text{ of capacity}}{\% \text{ of capacity at break even}}$

% of capacity (break even) = $\dfrac{3.6}{3}$ × 60% = 72%

Exercise 5.2 *(concluded)*

b.

$$\text{Sales at 80\% capacity} = \frac{80}{60} \times \$3 \text{ million} = \$4 \text{ million}$$

which is $400,000 above break even

NI = CR($400,000) = $266,667

c. In order that NI = $700,000

$$\text{Sales} = \$3,600,000 + \frac{\$700,000}{0.6\overline{6}} = \$4,650,000$$

d. The CR gives us this figure directly. That is, CR = $0.6\overline{6}$ means that net income increases by 66 2/3¢ for each $1 of sales (beyond break even).

e. Each $1 of FC requires

$$\frac{\$1}{CR} = \frac{\$1}{0.6\overline{6}} = \$1.50$$

of sales to cover it.

Exercise 5.3

1.

x:	-3	0	6
y:	-6	0	12

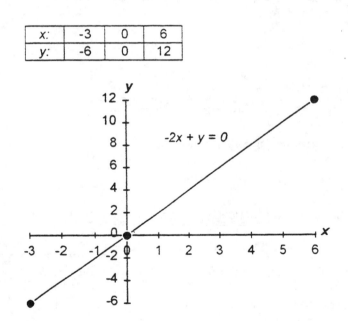

-2x + y = 0

2.

x:	-3	0	6
y:	-2	4	16

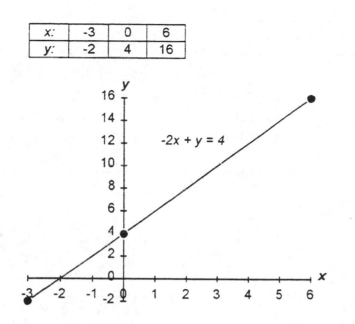

$-2x + y = 4$

3.

x:	-3	0	6
y:	10	4	-8

$2x + y = 4$

4.

x:	-3	0	6
y:	4	4	4

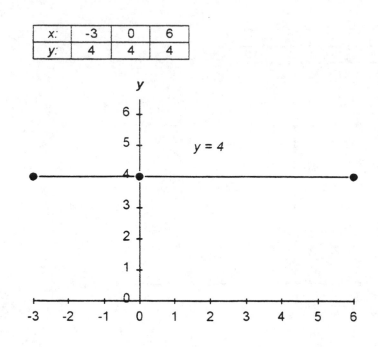

$y = 4$

5.

x:	-8	0	12
y:	-3	3	12

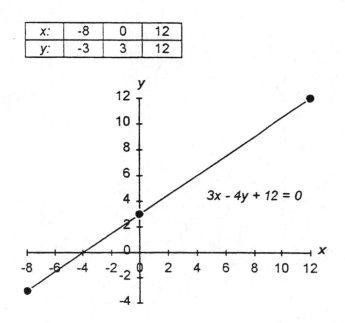

$3x - 4y + 12 = 0$

6.

x:	0	25	50
y:	6000	7500	9000

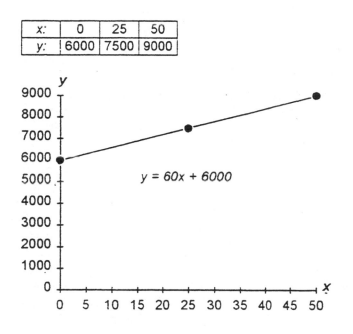

$y = 60x + 6000$

7.

x:	0	3000	6000
y:	5000	18500	32000

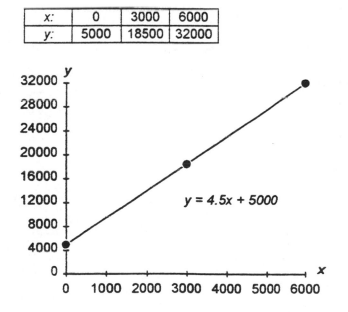

$y = 4.5x + 5000$

Exercise 5.3 (continued)

Graphical solutions to problems 1 and 7 of Exercise 5.2 are presented below.

1. $TR = \$20X$
    $TC = \$1200 + \$12X$

X:	0	250
TR:	$ 0	$5000
TC:	$1200	$4200

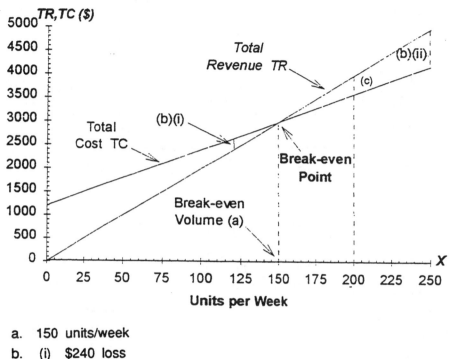

a. 150 units/week

b. (i) $240 loss
    (ii) $800 profit

c. 200 units/week

7. $TR = \$135X$
     $TC = \$700 + \$110X$

X:	15	36
TR:	$2025	$4860
TC:	$2350	$4660

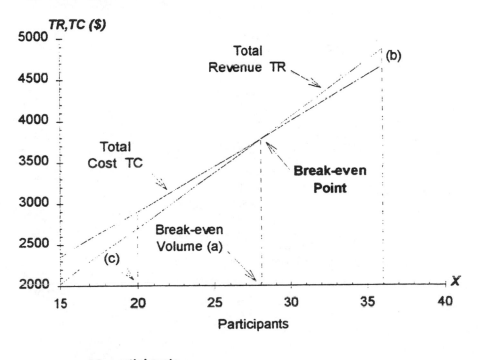

a. 28 participants
b. $200 profit
c. 20 participants

Review Problems

1. a.
$$4a - 5b = 30 \quad ①$$
$$2a - 6b = 22 \quad ②$$

To eliminate a,

$$① \times 1: \quad 4a - 5b = 30$$
$$② \times 2: \quad \underline{4a - 12b = 44}$$
$$\text{Subtract:} \quad 7b = -14$$
$$b = -2$$

Substitute into ①:
$$4a - 5(-2) = 30$$
$$4a = 30 - 10$$
$$a = 5$$
$$\underline{(a, b) = (5, -2)}$$

b.
$$76x - 29y = 1050 \quad ①$$
$$-13x - 63y = 250 \quad ②$$

To eliminate x,

$$① \times 13: \quad 988x - 377y = 13,650$$
$$② \times 76: \quad \underline{-988x - 4788y = 19,000}$$
$$\text{Add:} \quad -5165y = 32,650$$
$$y = -6.321$$

Substitute into ①:
$$76x - 29(-6.321) = 1050$$
$$76x = 1050 - 183.31$$
$$x = 11.40$$
$$\underline{(x, y) = (11.4, -6.32)}$$

2. Let b represent the base salary and r represent the commission rate. Then

$$r(\$27{,}000) + b = \$2815.00 \quad ①$$
$$\underline{r(\$35{,}500) + b = \$3197.50} \quad ②$$
$$\text{Subtract:} \quad -\$8500\, r = -\$382.50$$
$$r = 0.045$$

Substitute into ①:
$$0.045(\$27{,}000) + b = \$2815$$
$$b = \$1600$$

Deanna's base salary is $\underline{\$1600 \text{ per month}}$ and her commission rate is $\underline{4.5\%}$.

3. Let R represent the price per kg for red snapper and L represent the price per kg for lingcod. Then

$$370R + 264L = \$2454.20 \quad ①$$
$$255R + 304L = \$2124.70 \quad ②$$

To eliminate R,

$$① \div 370: \quad R + 0.71351L = \$6.6330$$
$$② \div 255: \quad \underline{R + 1.19216L = \$8.3322}$$
$$\text{Subtract:} \quad -0.47865L = -\$1.6992$$
$$L = \$3.55$$

Substitute into ①:
$$370R + 264(\$3.55) = \$2454.20$$
$$370R = \$1517.00$$
$$R = \$4.10$$

Nguyen was paid $\underline{\$3.55 \text{ per kg for lingcod}}$ and $\underline{\$4.10 \text{ per kg for red snapper}}$.

Review Problems (continued)

4. Let FC represent the fixed costs per month and VC represent the unit variable costs. Then

$$FC + 530 \ VC = \$24,190 \quad ①$$
$$FC + 365 \ VC = \$18,745 \quad ②$$

Subtract:
$$165 \ VC = \$5445$$
$$VC = \$33.00$$

Substitute in ②:
$$FC + 365(\$33) = \$18,745$$
$$FC = \$6700$$

The fixed costs are \$6700/month and unit variable costs are \$33.00.

5. a. NI = Total contribution margin − FC
   = \$300,000 − \$220,000
   = \$80,000

   $$CM = \frac{\$300,000}{150,000} = \$2.00$$

   SP = CM + VC = \$2.00 + \$10.00 = \$12.00

   b. NI = \$900,000 − \$800,000 = \$100,000

   $$CM = \frac{\$900,000}{180,000} = \$5.00$$

   VC = SP − CM = \$25 − \$5 = \$20.00

   c. CM = SP − VC = \$20 − \$14 = \$6.00

   $$Unit \ sales = \frac{Total \ CM}{CM} = \frac{\$120,000}{\$6} = 20,000$$

   NI = Total contribution margin − FC
   \$12,000 = \$120,000 − FC
   FC = \$108,000

6. Given: Total revenue = \$10 million, FC = \$2 million, Total variable costs = \$6 million, X = 1 million

   a. $$CM = \frac{\$10 \ million - \$6 \ million}{1 \ million} = \$4.00$$

   b. $$Break\text{-}even \ point = \frac{FC}{CM} = \frac{\$2,000,000}{\$4.00} = 500,000 \ units$$

   c. To have NI = \$1 million

   $$X = 500,000 + \frac{\$1,000,000}{\$4.00} = 750,000 \ units$$

7. Given: NI = \$6 million on total revenue of \$135 million.
   X = 9000 cars; Break-even volume = 10,000 cars

   a. Since production was 1000 cars below break even,
   1000(CM) = \$6,000,000 loss
   CM = \$6000 loss per car

   b. Since break-even volume = $\frac{FC}{CM}$, then

   FC = 10,000(\$6000) = \$60 million per year

Review Problems (continued)

c. If sales = 12,000 units (2000 more than break even),
NI = 2000(CM) = 2000($6000) = $12 million

8. Given: FC = $45,000 + $7000 + $8000 = $60,000
VC = $8.00 + 0.08($35) = $10.80; SP = $35.00

   a. CM = SP − VC = $35 − $10.80 = $24.20

   $$\text{Break-even volume} = \frac{FC}{CM} = \frac{\$60,000}{\$24.20} = \underline{2479 \text{ books}}$$

   b. If FC = $65,000 and VC = $11.80, then CM = $23.20

   $$\text{and break-even volume} = \frac{\$65,000}{\$23.20} = 2802 \text{ books}$$

   That is, the break-even volume would be raised by

   $$2802 − 2479 = \underline{323 \text{ books}}$$

   c. NI = (CM)X − FC =($24.20)4800 − $60,000 = $56,160

   d. If price is reduced 10%,
   SP = $35(1 − 0.10) = $31.50
   CM = $31.50 − $10.80 = $20.70
   If sales are 15% higher,
   X = 4800(1 + 0.15) = 5520 units
   NI = ($20.70)5520 − $60,000 = $54,264
   Since forecast NI is higher (about $2000) at the higher $35 price, it should be selected.

9. Given: FC = $1.8 million, CR = 45%.

   a. $$\text{Break-even revenue} = \frac{FC}{CR} = \frac{\$1.8 \text{ million}}{0.45} = \underline{\$4.0 \text{ million}}$$

   b. If NI is $100,000 less than break even, revenue will be

   $$\frac{\$100,000}{CR} = \$222,222 \text{ short of break even. That is,}$$

   Revenue = $4,000,000 − $222,222 = $3,777,778

   c. If NI = $300,000, revenue will be

   $$\frac{\$300,000}{0.45} = \$666,667 \text{ above break even. That is,}$$

   Revenue = $4,000,000 + $666,667 = $4,666,667.

   d. Formerly CR = 45%. Then VC = 0.55 SP.
   Now, unit sellilng price = 1.1 SP while VC remains at 0.55 SP. Then

   $$CR = \frac{1.1 \text{ SP} − 0.55 \text{ SP}}{1.1 \text{ SP}} \times 100\% = \underline{50\%}$$

   e. NI = (Total revenue) CR − FC
   = ($4,666,667)0.5 − $1,800,000
   = $533,334

   The operating profit will increase to $533,334.

Review Problems *(concluded)*

10. Given: SP = $100, FC = $200,000, VC = $60.
    Forecast X = 8000 units

   a. CM = SP − VC = $100 − $60 = $40

   Break-even volume = $\dfrac{FC}{CM}$ = $\dfrac{\$200,000}{\$40}$ = <u>5000 units</u>

   b. Volume = 5000 + $\dfrac{NI}{CM}$ = 5000 + $\dfrac{\$100,000}{\$40}$ = <u>7500 units</u>

   c. If sales are 8000 − 5000 = 3000 units above break even,
      NI = 3000(CM) = 3000($40) = <u>$120,000</u>

   d. (i) NI = 8000(CM) − FC
         For each $1 increase in FC, NI will drop $1.
         If FC is 5% ($10,000) higher, NI will be <u>$10,000 lower.</u>

      (ii) If FC is 10% ($20,000) lower, NI will be <u>$20,000 higher.</u>

   e. (i) If VC is 10% ($6) higher, CM = $100 − $66 = $34, and NI = 8000(CM) − FC = 8000($34) − $200,000 = $72,000
         That is, NI will be $120,000 − $72,000 = <u>$48,000 lower.</u>

      (ii) If VC is 5% ($3) lower, CM = $100 − $57 = $43 and NI = 8000($43) − $200,000 = $144,000
         That is, NI will be $144,000 − $120,000 = <u>$24,000 higher.</u>
         Note the "leverage" effect here. That is, % change in NI = − 4(% change in VC)

   f. (i) If SP is 5% ($5) higher, CM = $105 − $60 = $45, and NI = 8000($45) − $200,000 = $160,000
         That is, NI will be $160,000 − $120,000 = <u>$40,000 higher.</u>

      (ii) If SP is 10% ($10) lower, CM = $90 − $60 = $30 and NI = 8000($30) $200,000 = $40,000
         That is, NI will be $120,000 − $40,000 = <u>$80,000 lower.</u>
         Note that the "leverage" effect here is that % change in NI = $6.\overline{6}$(% change in SP) (assuming sales volume does not change).

   g. If X = 8000, VC = 1.1($60) = $66, SP = $100, and
      FC = 0.9($200,000) − $180,000, then
      CM = $100 − $66 = $34 and
      NI = 8000($34) − $180,000 = $92,000
      That is, NI will be $120,000 − $92,000 = <u>$28,000 lower.</u>

Self-Test Exercise

1.
$$3x + 5y = 11 \quad ①$$
$$2x − y = 16 \quad ②$$

To eliminate y,

$$① : \quad 3x + 5y = 11$$
$$② \times 5 : \quad \underline{10x − 5y = 80}$$
Add:
$$13x + 0 \ = 91$$
$$x = 7$$

Substitute into equation ②: 2(7) − y = 16
$$y = −2$$
$$(x,y) = \underline{(7,−2)}$$

2. Let S represent the number of cucumbers sold individually and let F represent the number of packages of 4 cucumbers sold in the promotion. Then

$$S + 4F = 541 \quad \text{①}$$
$$\$0.49S + \$1.47F = \$209.23 \quad \text{②}$$

To eliminate S,

① × $0.49:	$0.49S + $1.96F =	$265.09
②:	$0.49S + $1.47F =	$209.23
Subtract:	0 + $0.49F =	$ 55.86
	F =	114

Hence, a total of 4 x 114 = <u>456 cucumbers</u> were sold on the four-for-the-price-of-three promotion.

3. Let the regular season ticket prices be R for the red sections and B for the blue sections. Then

2500 B + 4500 R =	$50,250	①
2500(1.3B) + 4500(1.2R) =	$62,400	②
① × 1.2: 2500(1.2B) + 4500(1.2R) =	$60,300	
Subtract: 2500(0.1B) + 0 =	$ 2100	
B =	$8.40	

Substitute into ①:

$$2500(\$8.40) + 4500R = \$50,250$$
$$R = \$6.50$$

The ticket prices for the playoffs are

$$1.3 \times \$8.40 = \$10.92 \text{ in the "blues"}$$
$$\text{and } 1.2 \times \$6.50 = \$7.80 \text{ in the "reds."}$$

4. Given: SP = $10 (average revenue per person).
   Plan 1: VC = (0.1 + 0.3) SP = $4, FC = $15,000
   Plan 2: VC = (0.1 + 0.5) SP = $6, FC = $10,000

		Plan 1	Plan 2
a.	CM = SP − VC	$10 − $4 = $6	$10 − $6 = $4
	Break-even point = $\dfrac{FC}{CM}$	$\dfrac{\$15,000}{\$6} = \underline{\underline{2500}}$	$\dfrac{\$10,000}{\$4} = \underline{\underline{2500}}$

b. NI at
   (i) X = 3000:   500($6) = <u>$3000</u>   500($4) = <u>$2000</u>
   (ii) X = 2200:   −300($6) = −$1800   −300($4) = − $1200
                     (loss of $1800)   (loss of $1200)

c. If attendance surpasses the break-even point, the 30% commission rate generates the higher profit. However, if attendance falls short of the 2500 break even, the 30% commission will produce the larger loss.

5. a. Contribution margin, CM = SP − VC = $55 − $12 = $43

   The number of room rentals per month needed to break even is

   $$X = \frac{FC}{CM} = \frac{\$14,000}{\$43} \doteq 326$$

   Full occupancy would be 30 × 30 = 900 rentals per month.

   $$\text{Break-even occupancy} = \frac{326}{900} \times 100\% = \underline{36.2\%}$$

Self-Test Exercise (concluded)

b. (i)   40% occupancy = 0.4 × 900 = 360 rentals per month.

NI = (CM)X – FC = ($43)360 – $14,000 = $1480/month

(ii) 30% occupancy = 0.3 × 900 = 270 rentals per month.

NI = ($43)270 – $14,000 = –$2390

That is, a loss of $2390 per month.

c. In (b)(i), we obtain a net income of $1480/month for a rental rate of $55 and a 40% occupancy.

At a rental rate of $47 per unit, CM = $47 – $12 = $35 per unit.

At a 50% occupancy, X = 450 units/month and

NI = (CM)X – FC = ($35)450 – $14,000 = $1750/month

The owner should reduce the rental rate to $47 per unit per night since the net income will increase by $1750 – $1480 = $270 per month.

6 Simple Interest

Changes in the Second Edition:

1. The main change to Chapter 6 is the splitting of the former Section 6.7 into two sections (Sections 6.7 and 6.8). Section 6.7 is now devoted to the fundamental concept:

    Original loan = Present value of all the payments on the loan

    These changes give more prominence to this important concept while making it easier for the instructor to omit the remaining topics in the former Section 6.7 (by omitting Section 6.8 in the second edition). Some instructors prefer to deal with the general case of Equivalent Payment Streams only in a compound interest environment (Section 8.6).

2. Minor changes include:

    - Changing the method of calculating the number of days in Example 6.2a(ii).

    - Calculating r or t is $S = P(1 + rt)$ by first calculating $I = S - P$ and then rearranging $I = Prt$ (instead of rearranging $S = P(1 + rt)$ to isolate r or t). This change is continued in Chapter 7.

Exercise 6.1

1. $I = Prt = \$1500(0.095)\dfrac{7}{12} = \underline{\$83.13}$

2. $P = \dfrac{I}{rt} = \dfrac{\$328.85}{0.1025\left(\dfrac{11}{12}\right)} = \underline{\$3499.96}$

3. $t = \dfrac{I}{Pr} = \dfrac{\$371.83}{\$4850(0.115)} = 0.6\overline{6}$ year $= \underline{8 \text{ months}}$

4. $r = \dfrac{I}{Pt} = \dfrac{\$548.88}{\$15,000\left(\dfrac{5}{12}\right)} = 0.0875 = \underline{8.75\% \text{ pa}}$

5. $I = Prt = \$6800(0.077)\dfrac{13}{12} = \underline{\$567.23}$

6. $I = Prt = \$25,000(0.011)^3 = \underline{\$825.00}$

7. $t = \dfrac{I}{Pr} = \dfrac{\$511.00}{\$9125(0.008)} = \underline{7 \text{ months}}$

8. $r = \dfrac{I}{Pt} = \dfrac{\$890.00}{\$8900(8)} = 0.0125 = \underline{1.25\% \text{ per month}}$

9. $I = Prt = \$5000(0.055)\dfrac{5}{12} = \underline{\$114.58}$

10. $I = Prt = \$3760(0.015)(3) = \underline{\$169.20}$

11. $P = \dfrac{I}{rt} = \dfrac{\$292.50}{(0.009)5} = \underline{\$6500.00}$

12. $P = \dfrac{I}{rt} = \dfrac{\$500}{0.083\left(\dfrac{5}{12}\right)} = \underline{\$14,457.83}$

13. $r = \dfrac{I}{Pt} = \dfrac{\$214.65}{\$10,600\left(\dfrac{3}{12}\right)} = 0.0810 = \underline{8.10\% \text{ pa}}$

14. $r = \dfrac{I}{Pt} = \dfrac{\$169.05}{\$4830 \ 2 \text{ months}} = 0.0175 = \underline{1.75\% \text{ per month}}$

15. $t = \dfrac{I}{Pr} = \dfrac{\$315.90}{\$2700 \ (0.009) \text{ per month}} = \underline{13 \text{ months}}$

Business Math in Canada, 2/e

Exercise 6.1 *(concluded)*

16. The interest rate actually paid was

$$r = \frac{I}{Pt} = \frac{\$187.50}{\$10,000\left(\frac{5}{12}\right)} = 0.045 = \underline{\underline{4.5\% \text{ pa}}}$$

The interest rate reduction applied for the early redemption was 7.5% − 4.5% = $\underline{\underline{3.0\%}}$

17. Interest on first term deposit = Prt

$$= \$10,000(0.078)\left(\frac{3}{12}\right)$$

$$= \underline{\underline{\$195.00}}$$

Principal amount of second deposit = \$10,195

Interest on second term deposit = $\$10,195(0.078)\left(\frac{3}{12}\right) = \underline{\underline{\$198.80}}$

The interest earned on the second deposit is larger because both the original \$10,000 principal and the \$195 interest earned on the first deposit, earn interest during the second three months.

18. Interest on 6-month deposit = Prt

$$= \$5000(0.058)\left(\frac{6}{12}\right)$$

$$= \$145.00$$

Interest on first 3-month deposit = $\$5000(0.055)\left(\frac{6}{12}\right) = \$68.75$

Principal amount of second 3-month deposit = P + I

$$= \$5000 + \$68.75$$

$$= \$5068.75$$

The second three-month deposit must earn \$145.00 − \$68.75 = \$76.25 to place Randall in the same financial position under either alternative. Hence

$$r = \frac{I}{Pt} = \frac{\$76.25}{\$5068.75\left(\frac{3}{12}\right)} \times 100\% = \underline{\underline{6.02\% \text{ pa}}}$$

Exercise 6.2

1.

Date	Day No.
Oct. 1, 1997	274
June 17, 1997	− 168
Term:	106 days

$I = Prt = \$3800(0.1075)\dfrac{106}{365} = \underline{\underline{\$118.63}}$

2. Number of days = 1(Nov) + 31(Dec) + 31(Jan) + 28(Feb) + 3(Mar) = 94

$$I = Prt = \$7350(0.075)\frac{94}{365} = \underline{\underline{\$141.97}}$$

3. Number of days = 31(Dec) + 31(Jan) + 28(Feb) + 31(Mar) + 30(Apr) + 29(May) = 180

$$I = Prt = \$85,000(0.099)\frac{180}{365} = \underline{\underline{\$4149.86}}$$

Exercise 6.2 *(continued)*

4.

Date	Day no.
July 1 (general)	182
Leap year	+1
July 1, 1996	183
Jan. 7, 1996	−7
Term:	176 days

$I = Prt$

$= \$850(0.14)\dfrac{176}{365}$

$= \underline{\$57.38}$

5.

Date	Day no.
Apr 15, 1995	105
	+366
Apr 15, 1996	471
Oct 16, 1995	−289
Term:	182 days

$I = Prt$

$= \$27,000(0.087)\dfrac{182}{365}$

$= \underline{\$1171.28}$

6.

Date	Day no.	
July 19, 1997		200
Dec 31, 1996	366	
May 21, 1996	−142	
		224
Term:		424 days

$I = Prt$

$= \$14,400(0.1125)\dfrac{424}{365}$

$= \underline{\$1881.86}$

7.

Date	Day no.
July 7 (general)	188
Leap year	+1
July 7, 1996	189
Jan 15, 1996	−15
Term:	174 days

$r = \dfrac{I}{Pt}$

$= \dfrac{\$40.52}{\$1000\left(\dfrac{174}{365}\right)}$

$= 0.085 = \underline{8.5\%}$

8.

Date	Day no.
Apr 14, 1997	104
	+365
Apr 14, 1998	469
Oct 28, 1997	−301
Term:	168 days

$P = \dfrac{I}{rt}$

$= \dfrac{\$67.78}{0.095\left(\dfrac{168}{365}\right)}$

$= \underline{\$1550.11}$

9.

$t = \dfrac{I}{Pr}$

$= \dfrac{\$50.05}{\$1000(0.0725)}$

$= 0.690345$ year

$= 252$ days

Date	Day no.
Nov 16, 1997	320
Term	−252
Start date	68

March 9, 1997 is the 68th day of the year.

10.

$t = \dfrac{I}{Pr}$

$= \dfrac{\$49.42}{\$1000(0.11)}$

$= 0.44927$ year

$= 164$ days

Date	Day no.
March 13, 1998	72
	+365
March 13, 1999	437
Term	−164
Start date (in 1998)	273

September 30, 1998 is the 273rd day of the year.

Exercise 6.2 (continued)

11.

$$t = \frac{I}{Pr}$$

$$= \frac{\$63.91}{\$1000(0.1075)}$$

$$= 0.59451 \text{ year}$$

$$= 217 \text{ days}$$

Date	Day no.
Start (June 26, 1996)	178
Term	+217
	395
Less day no. for Dec 31	−366
End (days after Dec 31, 1996)	29

The end date is <u>January 29, 1997</u>.

12.

$$t = \frac{I}{Pr}$$

$$= \frac{\$32.28}{\$1000(0.077)}$$

$$= 0.41922 \text{ year}$$

$$= 153 \text{ days}$$

Date	Day no.
Start (Apr 18, 1997)	108
Term	+153
End	261

<u>September 18, 1997</u> is the 261st day of the year.

13. No. of days = 5(June) + 31(July) + 31(Aug) + 2(Sept) = 69

$$I = Prt = \$2760 \ (0.0425) \ \frac{69}{365} = \underline{\$22.09}$$

14.

Date	Day no.
End (May 10)	130
Previous Dec 31	365
Start (Oct 30)	−303
	+62
Term:	192 days

$$I = Prt$$

$$= \$2750(0.123) \ \frac{192}{365}$$

$$= \underline{\$48.53}$$

15. $r = \dfrac{I}{Pt} = \dfrac{\$9.70}{\$2146 \left(\dfrac{30}{365} \right)} = 0.0550 = \underline{5.50\% \ pa}$

16. $r = \dfrac{I}{Pt} = \dfrac{\$2.50}{\$329 \left(\dfrac{15}{365} \right)} = 0.1849 = \underline{18.49\% \ pa}$

17. $t = \dfrac{I}{Pr} = \dfrac{\$23.08}{\$2163 \ (0.095)} = 0.11232 \text{ year} = \underline{41 \ days}$

18. $P = \dfrac{I}{rt} = \dfrac{\$124.83}{0.0825 \left(\dfrac{30}{365} \right)} = \underline{\$18,409.27}$

Exercise 6.2 *(continued)*

19.

$$t = \frac{I}{Pr}$$

$$= \frac{\$203.22}{\$6000(0.1075)}$$

= 0.31507 year

= 115 days

Date	Day no.
Start (Nov 23)	327
Term	+115
	442
Less days to Dec 31	−365
End date (after Dec 31)	77

Bruce repaid the loan on the 77th day <u>(March 18)</u> of the following year.

20.

$$t = \frac{I}{Pr}$$

$$= \frac{\$221.92}{\$9000(0.075)}$$

= 0.32877 year

= 120 days

Date	Day no.
March 16, 1995	75
	+366
End (March 16, 1996)	441
Term	−120
Start date (in 1995)	321

November 17 is the 321st day of 1995. Sharon made the term deposit on <u>November 17, 1995</u>.

21.

Interval	Number of days	Int. rate	Interest
Mar 1 to Apr 17	31 + 16 = 47	7.5%	$57.945①
Apr 17 to June 30	14 + 31 + 29 = 74	8.0%	97.315
June 30 to Aug 1	1 + 31 = 32	7.75%	40.767
		Total:	$196.03

$$^①I = Prt = \$6000(0.075)\,\frac{47}{365} = \$57.945$$

22.

Interval	Number of days	Int. rate	Interest
Oct 28 to Dec 2	4 + 30 + 1 = 35	6.3%	$27.185①
Dec 2 to Feb 27	30 + 31 + 26 = 87	5.8%	62.211
Feb 27 to Mar 15	3 + 14 = 17	5.55%	11.632
		Total:	$101.03

$$^①I = Prt = \$4500(0.063)\,\frac{35}{365} = \$27.185$$

Penny will receive a total principal plus interest of
$$\$4500 + \$101.03 = \underline{\$4601.03}$$

In the solutions to problems 21 and 22, the number of days in each interval was determined by adding the number of days in each partial month and full month in the interval. The following solutions to problems 23 and 24 obtain the interval length using the serial numbers for dates in Table 6.2.

Exercise 6.2 (concluded)

23.

Interval	Number of days	Int. rate	Interest
Sept 30 to Nov 2	306 − 273 = 33	10.7%	$29.022①
Nov 2 to Jan 1	1 + 365 − 306 = 60	11.2%	55.233
Jan 1 to Feb 1	32 − 1 = 31	11.0%	28.027
		Total:	$112.28

$$① \ I = Prt = \$3000(0.107)\frac{33}{365} = \$29.022$$

Amount required to pay off the loan on February 1
$$= P + I = \$3000 + \$112.28 = \underline{\$3112.28}$$

24.

Interval	Number of days	Int. rate	Interest
June 3 to July 1	182 − 154 = 28	8.75%	0.00671233P①
July 1 to July 31	212 − 182 = 30	9.00%	0.00739726P
July 31 to Aug 31	243 − 212 = 31	9.50%	0.00806849P
		Total:	0.02217808P

$$① \ I = Prt = P(0.0875)\frac{28}{365} = 0.00671233P$$

Since total interest = $169.66, then

$$0.02217808P = \$169.66$$
$$P = \underline{\$7649.89}$$

The principal amount of the loan was $7649.89.

Exercise 6.3

1. $S = P(1 + rt) = \$2950\left[1 + 0.135\left(\frac{7}{12}\right)\right] = \$2950\,(1.078750) = \underline{\$3182.31}$

2. $S = P(1 + rt) = \$12,800\left[1 + 0.1175\left(\frac{237}{365}\right)\right] = \$12,800\,(1.0762945) = \underline{\$13,776.57}$

3. $P = \dfrac{S}{1 + rt} = \dfrac{\$785.16}{1 + 0.105\left(\frac{23}{365}\right)} = \dfrac{\$785.16}{1.006616} = \underline{\$780.00}$

4. $P = \dfrac{S}{1 + rt} = \dfrac{\$2291.01}{1 + 0.077\left(\frac{360}{365}\right)} = \dfrac{\$2291.01}{1.075945} = \underline{\$2129.30}$

5. $P = \dfrac{S}{1 + rt} = \dfrac{\$15,379.58}{1 + 0.099\left(\frac{11}{12}\right)} = \dfrac{\$15,379.58}{1.0907500} = \underline{\$14,100.00}$

6. $P = \dfrac{S}{1 + rt} = \dfrac{\$7348.25}{1 + 0.0825\left(\frac{14}{12}\right)} = \dfrac{\$7348.25}{1.096250} = \underline{\$6703.08}$

Exercise 6.3 *(continued)*

7. $I = S - P = \$1828.02 - \$1750 = \$78.02$

$$r = \frac{I}{Pt} = \frac{\$78.02}{\$1750 \left(\frac{5}{12}\right)} = 0.1070 = \underline{10.70\%}$$

8. $I = S - P = \$3000 - \$2875.40 = \$124.60$

$$r = \frac{I}{Pt} = \frac{\$124.60}{\$2875.40 \left(\frac{8}{12}\right)} = 0.0650 = \underline{6.50\%}$$

9. $I = S - P = \$798.63 - \$780.82 = \$17.81$

$$r = \frac{I}{Pt} = \frac{\$17.81}{\$780.82 \left(\frac{45}{365}\right)} = 0.1850 = \underline{18.50\%}$$

10. $I = S - P = \$730.30 - \$680 = \$50.30$

$$r = \frac{\$50.30}{\$680 \left(\frac{300}{365}\right)} = 0.0900 = \underline{9.00\%}$$

11. $I = S - P = \$10,000 - \$9625.63 = \$374.37$

$$t = \frac{I}{Pr} = \frac{\$374.37}{\$9625.63(0.078)} = 0.49863 \text{ year} = \underline{182 \text{ days}}$$

12. $I = S - P = \$3646.60 - \$3500 = \$146.60$

$$t = \frac{I}{Pr} = \frac{\$146.60}{\$3500(0.084)} = 0.49864 \text{ year} = \underline{182 \text{ days}}$$

13. $I = S - P = \$8083.33 - \$7760 = \$323.33$

$$t = \frac{I}{Pr} = \frac{\$323.33}{\$7760(0.0625)} = 0.66666 \text{ year} = \underline{8 \text{ months}}$$

14. $I = S - P = \$907.22 - \$859.50 = \$47.72$

$$t = \frac{I}{Pr} = \frac{\$47.72}{\$859.50(0.1025)} = 0.541665 \text{ year} = \underline{6.50 \text{ months}}$$

15. $S = P(1 + rt) = \$4500 \left[1 + 0.119\left(\frac{15}{12}\right)\right] = \$4500 \,(1.148750) = \underline{\$5169.38}$

16. $S = P(1 + rt) = \$17,000 \left[1 + 0.0725\left(\frac{270}{365}\right)\right] = \$17,000(1.0536301) = \underline{\$17,911.71}$

17. $P = \dfrac{S}{1 + rt} = \dfrac{\$20,000}{1 + 0.0675\left(\frac{189}{365}\right)} = \dfrac{\$20,000}{1.0349521} = \underline{\$19,324.57}$

Exercise 6.3 (continued)

18. $P = \dfrac{S}{1 + rt} = \dfrac{\$3701.56}{1 + 0.125\left(\dfrac{7}{12}\right)} = \underline{\underline{\$3450.00}}$

    $I = S - P = \$3701.56 - \$3450.00 = \underline{\underline{\$251.56}}$

19. In effect, there is a $60 interest charge for paying the second $900 after 5 months instead of at the beginning of the year. The annual rate of simple interest is

    $r = \dfrac{I}{Pt} = \dfrac{\$60}{\$900\left(\dfrac{5}{12}\right)} = 0.1600 = \underline{\underline{16.00\%}}$

20. In effect, $107.50 is the "maturity value" on October 1 of an $89.95 "investment" on March 25. The "interest earned" is $107.50 – $89.95 = $17.55. The number of days in the "term" is

    274(for Oct 1) – 84(for Mar 25) = 190

    The annual interest rate implied by the saving is

    $r = \dfrac{I}{Pt} = \dfrac{\$17.55}{\$89.95\left(\dfrac{190}{365}\right)} = 0.3748 = \underline{\underline{37.48\%}}$

21. The $60 higher price for the deferred payment option may be viewed as a $60 interest charge on the cash price of $1535. The implied annual interest rate is

    $r = \dfrac{I}{Pt} = \dfrac{\$60}{\$1535\left(\dfrac{6}{12}\right)} = 0.0782 = \underline{\underline{7.82\%}}$

    If you can earn a rate of return on a six-month investment greater than 7.82%, you would be better off to invest the $1535 now and take A & B's deferred payment option.

22. $I = S - P = \$2614.47 - \$2500 = \$114.47$

    $t = \dfrac{I}{Pr} = \dfrac{\$114.47}{\$2500(0.0875)} = 0.52329 \text{ year} = \underline{\underline{191 \text{ days}}}$

23. $I = S - P = \$2100 - \$2000 = \$100$

    $t = \dfrac{I}{Pr} = \dfrac{\$100}{\$2000(0.1025)} = 0.487805 \text{ year} = \underline{\underline{178.05 \text{ days}}}$

    The balance owed will first exceed $2100 on the 179th day after July 13. From July 13 to December 31 is 365 – 194 = 171 days. Therefore, <u>January 8</u> is the 179th day after July 13.

24. $I = S - P = \$356,041 - \$350,000 = \$6041$

    $t = \dfrac{I}{Pr} = \dfrac{\$6041}{\$350,000(0.075)} = 0.230133 \text{ year} = 84 \text{ days}$

    December 31 to February 28 represents 59 days of the interval. The money was borrowed on the 365 – (84 – 59) = 340th day of the preceding year—that is, on <u>December 6 of the previous year</u>.

Exercise 6.3 *(concluded)*

25.

Sub-interval	Number of days	Cumulative investment	Interest for sub-interval
June 23 to Aug 5	8 + 31 + 4 = 43	$2200	$ 37.581 ①
Aug 5 to Oct 31	27 + 30 + 30 = 87	4000	138.247
Oct 31 to Dec 31	1 + 30 + 30 = 61	5300	128.434
		Total:	$304.26

①$I = Prt = \$2200(0.145)\dfrac{43}{365} = \$37.581$

The total amount required to pay off the loan is
$$\$5300 + \$304.26 = \underline{\$5604.26}$$

26.

Sub-interval	Number of days	Account balance
Jan 1 to Mar 4	31 + 28 + 3 = 62	$3347
Mar 4 to May 24	28 + 30 + 23 = 81	8687
May 24 to June 17	8 + 16 = 24	2568
June 17 to July 1	14	5923
		Total:

①$I = Prt = \$3347(0.04)\dfrac{62}{365} = \$22.741$

Interest of $115.69 was credited to Roger's account on June 30.

27.

Interval	Number of days	Principal	Interest rate	Maturity value
Nov 16 to Apr 1	137①	$7400	6.3%	$ 7574.98②
Dec 30 to Apr 1	93③	6600	5.9%	6699.22
Feb 8 to Apr 1	53④	9200	5.1%	9268.13
			Total:	$23,542.33

①$(365 - 320) + (91 + 1) = 137$ days

②$S = P(1 + rt) = \$7400\left[1 + 0.063\left(\dfrac{137}{365}\right)\right] = \$7574.98$

③$(365 - 364) + 92 = 93$ days
④$92 - 39 = 53$ days

The total amount from the three term deposits on April 1 will be $23,542.33.

Exercise 6.5

1. $P = \dfrac{S}{1 + rt} = \dfrac{\$560}{1 + 0.1075\left(\dfrac{5}{12}\right)} = \underline{\$535.99}$

2. $S = P(1 + rt) = \$1215\left[1 + 0.085\left(\dfrac{7}{12}\right)\right] = \underline{\$1275.24}$

3. $S = P(1 + rt) = \$5230\left[1 + 0.0925\left(\dfrac{174}{365}\right)\right] = \underline{\$5460.62}$

4. $P = \dfrac{S}{1+rt} = \dfrac{\$1480}{1 + 0.0675\left(\dfrac{60}{365}\right)} = \underline{\underline{\$1463.76}}$

5. $I = S - P = \$1975 - \$1936.53 = \$38.47$

   $r = \dfrac{I}{Pt} = \dfrac{\$38.47}{\$1936.53\left(\dfrac{100}{365}\right)} = 0.0725 = \underline{7.25\%}$

6. $I = S - P = \$2508.79 - \$2370 = \$138.79$

   $r = \dfrac{I}{Pt} = \dfrac{\$138.79}{\$2370\left(\dfrac{190}{365}\right)} = 0.1125 = \underline{11.25\%}$

7. $I = S - P = \$850.26 - \$830 = \$20.26$

   $t = \dfrac{I}{Pr} = \dfrac{\$20.26}{\$830(0.099)} = 0.24656 \text{ year} = \underline{90 \text{ days}}$

8. $I = S - P = \$3500 - \$3362.69 = \$137.31$

   $t = \dfrac{I}{Pr} = \dfrac{\$137.31}{\$3362.69(0.1225)} = 0.33333 \text{ year} = \underline{4 \text{ months}}$

9. $I = S - P = \$4850 - \$4574.73 = \$275.27$

   $t = \dfrac{I}{Pr} = \dfrac{\$275.27}{\$4574.73(0.0875)} = 0.68768 \text{ year} = \underline{251 \text{ days}}$

10. $I = S - P = \$2785.60 - \$2740 = \$45.60$

    $t = \dfrac{I}{Pr} = \dfrac{\$45.60}{\$2740(0.135)} = 0.12327 \text{ year} = \underline{45 \text{ days}}$

In problems 11 to 14, calculate the future value of the earlier payment on the date of the later payment. The answer to part "a" will be the larger of this future value or the later payment.

The answer to part "b" is the interest rate that makes the future value of the earlier payment equal to the later payment.

11. a. $S = P(1 + rt) = \$560\left(1 + 0.1075 \times \dfrac{60}{365}\right) = \$569.90 < \$570$

    The <u>later payment</u> has the greater economic value.

    b. If $I = \$570 - \$560 = \$10$,

    $r = \dfrac{I}{Pt} = \dfrac{\$10}{\$560\left(\dfrac{60}{365}\right)} = 0.1086 = \underline{10.86\%}$

    The two payments would be equivalent if the time value of money is 10.86% pa.

Exercise 6.5 (continued)

12. a. $S = \$1215\left(1 + 0.085 \times \dfrac{11}{12}\right) = \$1309.67 > \$1280$

    The _earlier payment_ has the greater economic value.

    b. If $I = \$1280 - \$1215 = \$65$

    $$r = \dfrac{\$65}{\$1215\left(\dfrac{11}{12}\right)} = 0.0584 = \underline{\underline{5.84\%}}$$

    The two payments would be equivalent if the time value of money is 5.84%.

13. a. $S = P(1 + rt) = \$5230(1 + 0.006 \times 5) = \$5386.90 < \$5500$

    The _later payment_ has the larger economic value.

    b. If $I = \$5500 - \$5230 = \$270$,

    $$r = \dfrac{\$270}{\$5230(5)} = 0.0103 = \underline{\underline{1.03\% \text{ per month}}}$$

    The two payments would be equivalent if the time value of money is 1.03% per month.

14. a. $S = P(1 + rt) = \$1480\left(1 + 0.0675 \times \dfrac{150}{365}\right) = \$1521.05 > \$1515$

    The _earlier payment_ has the greater economic value.

    b. If $I = \$1515 - \$1480 = \$35$,

    $$r = \dfrac{I}{Pt} = \dfrac{\$35}{\$1480\left(\dfrac{150}{365}\right)} = 0.0575 = \underline{\underline{5.75\%}}$$

    The two payments would be equivalent if the time value of money is 5.75%.

15. Number of days $= 7 + 31 + 30 = 68$

    $$P = \dfrac{S}{1 + rt} = \dfrac{\$1000}{1 + 0.14\left(\dfrac{68}{365}\right)} = \underline{\underline{\$974.58}}$$

16. Number of days $= 20 + 30 + 31 + 30 + 31 + 12 = 154$

    $$S = P(1 + rt) = \$1000\left[1 + 0.095\left(\dfrac{154}{365}\right)\right] = \underline{\underline{\$1040.08}}$$

17. Victor can expect to pay the maturity value of $450 ninety days later.

    $$S = P(1 + rt) = \$450\left[1 + 0.0675\left(\dfrac{90}{365}\right)\right] = \underline{\underline{\$457.49}}$$

Exercise 6.5 *(continued)*

18. The equivalent (present) value of $1600 on June 15 should be acceptable to both.

$$P = \frac{S}{1 + rt} = \frac{\$1600}{1 + 0.0725\left(\dfrac{61}{365}\right)} = \underline{\$1580.85}$$

19. Duncan Stereo should accept the amount that is equivalent on September 10 to $1195 on the following January 2. That is,

$$P = \frac{S}{1 + rt} = \frac{\$1195}{1 + 0.135\left(\dfrac{114}{365}\right)} = \underline{\$1146.65}$$

20. Equivalent value $= \dfrac{\$5000}{1 + 0.0725\left(\dfrac{120}{365}\right)} = \underline{\$4883.60 \text{ today}}$

$$= \frac{\$5000}{1 + 0.0725\left(\dfrac{90}{365}\right)} = \underline{\$4912.19 \text{ in 30 days}}$$

$$= \frac{\$5000}{1 + 0.0725\left(\dfrac{60}{365}\right)} = \underline{\$4941.11 \text{ in 60 days}}$$

$$= \frac{\$5000}{1 + 0.0725\left(\dfrac{30}{365}\right)} = \underline{\$4970.38 \text{ in 90 days}}$$

$$= \underline{\$5000 \text{ in 120 days}}$$

$$= \$5000\left[1 + 0.0725\left(\dfrac{30}{365}\right)\right] = \underline{\$5029.79 \text{ in 150 days}}$$

$$= \$5000\left[1 + 0.0725\left(\dfrac{60}{365}\right)\right] = \underline{\$5059.59 \text{ in 180 days}}$$

$$= \$5000\left[1 + 0.0725\left(\dfrac{90}{365}\right)\right] = \underline{\$5089.38 \text{ in 210 days}}$$

$$= \$5000\left[1 + 0.0725\left(\dfrac{120}{365}\right)\right] = \underline{\$5119.18 \text{ in 240 days}}$$

Exercise 6.5 *(continued)*

21. Equivalent value $= \dfrac{\$3000}{1 + 0.0675\left(\dfrac{6}{12}\right)} = \underline{\$2902.06 \text{ today}}$

    $= \dfrac{\$3000}{1 + 0.0675\left(\dfrac{4}{12}\right)} = \underline{\$2933.99 \text{ in 2 months}}$

    $= \dfrac{\$3000}{1 + 0.0675\left(\dfrac{2}{12}\right)} = \underline{\$2966.63 \text{ in 4 months}}$

    $= \underline{\$3000 \text{ in 6 months}}$

    $= \$3000\left[1 + 0.0675\left(\dfrac{2}{12}\right)\right] = \underline{\$3033.75 \text{ in 8 months}}$

    $= \$3000\left[1 + 0.0675\left(\dfrac{4}{12}\right)\right] = \underline{\$3067.50 \text{ in 10 months}}$

    $= \$3000\left[1 + 0.0675\left(\dfrac{6}{12}\right)\right] = \underline{\$3101.25 \text{ in 12 months}}$

22. Marpole Furniture should accept a cash price equal to the sum of $\dfrac{\$1845}{2}$ plus the present value of $\dfrac{\$1845}{2}$ six months earlier. That is,

    Cash price $= \$922.50 + \dfrac{\$922.50}{1 + 0.1075\left(\dfrac{6}{12}\right)} = \$922.50 + \$875.44 = \underline{\$1797.94}$

23. The present value of Brian's scholarship 9 months earlier is:

    $P = \dfrac{S}{1 + rt} = \dfrac{\$2100}{1 + 0.0825\left(\dfrac{9}{12}\right)} = \$1977.63$

    which is less than Jody's $2000 scholarship on that date. <u>Jody's scholarship</u> has the greater economic value.

24. Since the down payments are equal, we need only calculate and compare the current economic values of the deferred payments.

    P(of $39,000 payment) $= \dfrac{\$39,000}{1 + 0.075\left(\dfrac{8}{12}\right)} = \$37,142.86$

    P(of $40,000 payment) $= \dfrac{\$40,000}{1 + 0.075(1)} = \$37,209.30$

    Therefore, <u>the $50,000 offer</u> is worth $66.44 more in current dollars.

Exercise 6.5 *(concluded)*

25. For the two offers to be equivalent, their present values must be equal. That is,

$$\frac{\$39{,}000}{1 + r\left(\dfrac{8}{12}\right)} = \frac{\$40{,}000}{1 + r(1)}$$

Divide both sides by 1000 and cross-multiply giving

$$39(1 + r) = 40(1 + 0.6\overline{6}r)$$
$$39 + 39r = 40 + 26.\overline{6}r$$
$$12.\overline{3}r = 1$$
$$r = 0.0811 = \underline{8.11\%}$$

Mr. and Mrs. Chan will be indifferent between the two offers if money can earn 8.11% pa.

26. The time period from March 29 to August 20 is $232 - 88 = 144$ days long.

For \$1348 to earn $\$1389 - \$1348 = \$41$ in 144 days,

$$r = \frac{I}{Pt} = \frac{\$41}{\$1348\left(\dfrac{144}{365}\right)} = 0.0771 = \underline{7.71\%}$$

Exercise 6.6

1. Equivalent value today $= \$500\left[1 + 0.095\left(\dfrac{6}{12}\right)\right] + \dfrac{\$300}{1 + 0.095\left(\dfrac{3}{12}\right)}$

$$= \$523.75 + \$293.04$$
$$= \underline{\$816.79}$$

2. Equivalent value two months from now $= \$1000\left[1 + 0.1025\left(\dfrac{2}{12}\right)\right] + \dfrac{\$1500}{1 + 0.1025\left(\dfrac{3}{12}\right)}$

$$= \$1017.08 + \$1462.52$$
$$= \underline{\$2479.60}$$

3. Equivalent value 90 days from now $= \$900\left[1 + 0.0775\left(\dfrac{240}{365}\right)\right] + 1000\left[1 + 0.0775\left(\dfrac{60}{365}\right)\right]$

$$= \$945.86 + \$1012.74$$
$$= \underline{\$1958.60}$$

4. Equivalent value 30 days from now $= \dfrac{\$2500}{1 + 0.12\left(\dfrac{40}{365}\right)} + \dfrac{\$4000}{1 + 0.12\left(\dfrac{170}{365}\right)}$

$$= \$2467.55 + \$3788.27$$
$$= \underline{\$6255.82}$$

5. Equivalent value today $= \$1000\left[1 + 0.085\left(\dfrac{60}{365}\right)\right] + \dfrac{\$1500}{1 + 0.085\left(\dfrac{10}{365}\right)} + \dfrac{\$2000}{1 + 0.085\left(\dfrac{150}{365}\right)}$

$$= \$1013.97 + \$1496.51 + \$1932.50$$
$$= \underline{\$4442.98}$$

6. Equivalent value 45 days from now

$$= \$1750\left[1 + 0.099\left(\frac{120}{365}\right)\right] + \$1750\left[1 + 0.099\left(\frac{45}{365}\right)\right] + \frac{\$1750}{1 + 0.099\left(\frac{30}{365}\right)}$$

$$= \$1806.96 + \$1771.36 + \$1735.88$$
$$= \underline{\underline{\$5314.20}}$$

7. Equivalent payment three months from now $= \$850\left[1 + 0.0825\left(\frac{8}{12}\right)\right] + \dfrac{\$1140}{1 + 0.0825\left(\frac{1}{12}\right)}$

$$= \$896.75 + \$1132.22$$
$$= \underline{\underline{\$2028.97}}$$

8. Equivalent payment today $= \$850\left[1 + 0.0825\left(\frac{5}{12}\right)\right] + \dfrac{\$1140}{1 + 0.0825\left(\frac{4}{12}\right)}$

$$= \$879.22 + \$1109.49$$
$$= \underline{\underline{\$1988.71}}$$

9. a. Equivalent value today $= \dfrac{\$2000}{1 + 0.10\left(\frac{6}{12}\right)} + \dfrac{\$2000}{1 + 0.10(1)}$

$$= \$1904.76 + \$1818.18$$
$$= \underline{\underline{\$3722.94}}$$

   b. Equivalent value six months from today $= \$2000 + \dfrac{\$2000}{1 + 0.10\left(\frac{6}{12}\right)}$

$$= \$2000 + \$1904.76$$
$$= \underline{\underline{\$3904.76}}$$

   c. The equivalent value of a specified payment stream will be greater at a later date than at an earlier date because of the time value of money.

10. a. Equivalent value today $= \dfrac{\$3000}{1 + 0.09\left(\frac{50}{365}\right)} + \dfrac{\$3000}{1 + 0.09\left(\frac{100}{365}\right)}$

$$= \$2963.46 + \$2927.81$$
$$= \underline{\underline{\$5891.27}}$$

   b. Equivalent value today $= \dfrac{\$3000}{1 + 0.11\left(\frac{50}{365}\right)} + \dfrac{\$3000}{1 + 0.11\left(\frac{100}{365}\right)}$

$$= \$2955.47 + \$2912.23$$
$$= \underline{\underline{\$5867.70}}$$

   c. The ability of money to earn a higher interest rate allows a smaller amount to be economically equivalent to a stream of subsequent payments.

11. a. Economic value today $= \$900\left[1 + 0.095\left(\dfrac{150}{365}\right)\right] + \$1400\left[1 + 0.095\left(\dfrac{80}{365}\right)\right]$

$= \$935.14 + \$1429.15$

$= \underline{\underline{\$2364.29}}$

b. Economic value today $= \dfrac{\$800}{1 + 0.095\left(\dfrac{30}{365}\right)} + \dfrac{\$600}{1 + 0.095\left(\dfrac{75}{365}\right)} + \dfrac{\$1000}{1 + 0.095\left(\dfrac{125}{365}\right)}$

$= \$793.80 + \$588.51 + \$968.49$

$= \underline{\underline{\$2350.80}}$

The \$900 and \$1400 payments have a \$13.49 greater economic value (in today's dollars).

12. a. Economic value today $= \dfrac{\$1000}{1 + 0.075\left(\dfrac{1}{12}\right)} + \dfrac{\$3000}{1 + 0.075\left(\dfrac{3}{12}\right)} + \dfrac{\$2000}{1 + 0.075\left(\dfrac{5}{12}\right)}$

$= \$993.79 + \$2944.79 + \$1939.39$

$= \underline{\underline{\$5877.97}}$

b. Economic value today $= \dfrac{\$3000}{1 + 0.075\left(\dfrac{2}{12}\right)} + \dfrac{\$3000}{1 + 0.075\left(\dfrac{4}{12}\right)}$

$= \$2962.96 + \$2926.83$

$= \underline{\underline{\$5889.79}}$

13. Maturity value of \$750 obligation $= \$750\left[1 + 0.095\left(\dfrac{6}{12}\right)\right] = \$785.63$

Maturity value of \$950 obligation $= \$950[1 + 0.095(1)] = \$1040.25$

Equivalent value in four months of the scheduled payments

$= \$785.63\left[1 + 0.0775\left(\dfrac{6}{12}\right)\right] + \$1040.25$

$= \$816.07 + \$1040.25$

$= \underline{\underline{\$1856.32}}$

Thelma should be willing to accept a payment of \$1856.32 four months from now.

Exercise 6.6 (concluded)

14. The scheduled payments are:

$$\$400\left[1 + 0.135\left(\frac{90}{365}\right)\right] = \$413.32 \text{ today}$$

$$\$400\left[1 + 0.135\left(\frac{150}{365}\right)\right] = \$422.19 \text{ in 60 days}$$

$$\$400\left[1 + 0.135\left(\frac{210}{365}\right)\right] = \$431.07 \text{ in 120 days}$$

The equivalent single payment 30 days from now

$$= \$413.32\left[1 + 0.085\left(\frac{30}{365}\right)\right] + \frac{\$422.19}{1 + 0.085\left(\frac{30}{365}\right)} + \frac{\$431.07}{1 + 0.085\left(\frac{90}{365}\right)}$$

$$= \$416.21 + \$419.26 + \$422.22$$
$$= \underline{\underline{\$1257.69}}$$

Ed should accept a payment of $1257.68 in 30 days.

15. The scheduled payments are:

$$\$6000\left[1 + 0.10\left(\frac{61}{365}\right)\right] = \$6100.27 \text{ on January 14}$$

$$\$6000\left[1 + 0.10\left(\frac{120}{365}\right)\right] = \$6197.26 \text{ on March 14}$$

$$\$6000\left[1 + 0.10\left(\frac{151}{365}\right)\right] = \$6248.22 \text{ on April 14}$$

The equivalent payment on February 14

$$= \$6100.27 + \frac{\$6197.26}{1 + 0.115\left(\frac{59}{365}\right)} + \frac{\$6248.22}{1 + 0.115\left(\frac{90}{365}\right)}$$

$$= \$6100.27 + \$6084.16 + \$6075.93$$
$$= \underline{\underline{\$18,260.36}}$$

Exercise 6.7

1. Let x represent the unknown payment.

Payment	Date	No. of days	Present value
$1000	May 1	31 + 30 = 61	$981.95 ①
1000	June 1	61 + 31 = 92	973.02
x	July 1	92 + 30 = 122	0.9645368x ②

$$①P = \frac{\$1000}{1 + 0.11\left(\frac{61}{365}\right)} = \$981.95$$

$$②P = \frac{x}{1 + 0.11\left(\frac{122}{365}\right)} = 0.9645368x$$

Original loan = Sum of present values of payments
$3000 = $981.95 + $973.02 + 0.9645368x
$1045.03 = 0.9645368x
x = $1083.45

The July 1 payment should be $1083.45.

2. Let x represent the unknown payment.

Payment	Date	No. of days	Present value
$1000	Apr 1	31	$992.00
x	June 1	31 + 30 + 31 = 92	0.9766148x
1000	Aug 1	92 + 30 + 31 = 153	961.70

$3000 = $992.00 + 0.9766148x + $961.70
$1046.30 = 0.9766148x
x = $1071.35

The June 1 payment should be $1071.35.

3. Let x represent the unknown payment.

Payment	Date	No. of days	Present value
x	Apr 13	31 + 12 = 43	0.9881262x ①
$1100	May 27	43 + 18 + 26 = 87	$1073.89 ②
$1100	July 13	87 + 5 + 30 + 12 = 134	1060.30

$$①P = \frac{x}{1 + 0.102\left(\frac{43}{365}\right)} = 0.9881262x$$

$$②P = \frac{\$1100}{1 + 0.102\left(\frac{87}{365}\right)} = \$1073.89$$

Original loan = Present value of all payments
$3000 = 0.9881262x + $1073.89 + $1060.30
$865.81 = 0.9881262x
x = $876.21

The April 13 payment should be $876.21.

Exercise 6.7 *(continued)*

4. Let x represent the unknown payment.

Payment	Date	No. of days	Present value
$500	Mar 31	30	$496.63
$1000	June 15	31 + 30 + 31 + 14 = 106	976.60
x	Aug 31	106 + 16 + 31 + 30 = 183	0.9602799x

$3000 = $496.63 + $976.60 + 0.9602799x
$1526.77 = 0.9602799x
$\qquad$ x = $\underline{\underline{\$1589.92}}$

The August 31 payment should be $1589.92.

5. Let x represent the size of each loan payment. Since the original loan equals the sum of the present values of all of the loan payments, then

$$\$1000 = \frac{x}{1 + 0.09\left(\dfrac{30}{365}\right)} + \frac{x}{1 + 0.09\left(\dfrac{60}{365}\right)}$$

$$= 0.9926571x + 0.9854212x$$
$$= 1.9780783x$$
$$x = \$505.54$$

Each loan payment is $\underline{\$505.54}$.

6. Let x represent the size of each loan payment. Then

$3000 = Sum of present values of all payments

$$= \frac{x}{1 + 0.1025\left(\dfrac{50}{365}\right)} + \frac{x}{1 + 0.1025\left(\dfrac{150}{365}\right)}$$

$$= 0.9861533x + 0.9595794x$$
$$= 1.9457327x$$
$$x = \$1541.84$$

Each loan payment is $\underline{\$1541.84}$.

7. Let x represent the size of each payment. Then

$$\$2500 = \frac{x}{1 + 0.0875\left(\dfrac{2}{12}\right)} + \frac{x}{1 + 0.0875\left(\dfrac{4}{12}\right)} + \frac{x}{1 + 0.0875\left(\dfrac{7}{12}\right)}$$

$$= 0.9856263x + 0.9716599x + 0.9514371x$$
$$= 2.9087233x$$
$$x = \$859.48$$

Each loan payment is $\underline{\$859.48}$.

Exercise 6.7 (continued)

8. Let x represent the size of each payment. Then

$$\$8000 = \frac{x}{1 + 0.115\left(\dfrac{30}{365}\right)} + \frac{x}{1 + 0.115\left(\dfrac{90}{365}\right)} + \frac{x}{1 + 0.115\left(\dfrac{150}{365}\right)}$$

$$= 0.9906364x + 0.9724257x + 0.9548725x$$
$$= 2.9179346x$$
$$x = \$2741.67$$

Each loan payment is $\underline{\$2741.67}$.

9. Let x represent the size of each payment. Then

$$\$5000 = \frac{x}{1 + 0.12\left(\dfrac{100}{365}\right)} + \frac{x}{1 + 0.12\left(\dfrac{150}{365}\right)} + \frac{x}{1 + 0.12\left(\dfrac{200}{365}\right)} + \frac{x}{1 + 0.12\left(\dfrac{250}{365}\right)}$$

$$= 0.9681698x + 0.9530026x + 0.9383033x + 0.9240506x$$
$$= 3.7835263x$$
$$x = \$1321.52$$

Each loan payment is $\underline{\$1321.52}$.

10. Let x represent the size of each payment. Then

$$\$7500 = \frac{x}{1 + 0.099\left(\dfrac{2}{12}\right)} + \frac{x}{1 + 0.099\left(\dfrac{5}{12}\right)} + \frac{x}{1 + 0.099\left(\dfrac{9}{12}\right)} + \frac{x}{1 + 0.099(1)}$$

$$= 0.9837678x + 0.9603842x + 0.9308820x + 0.9099181x$$
$$= 3.7849521x$$
$$x = \$1981.53$$

Each loan payment is $\underline{\$1981.53}$.

11. Let x represent the size of the second replacement payment. The equivalent value on the focal date of the scheduled payments is

$$\$2600\left[1 + 0.0825\left(\frac{80}{365}\right)\right] + \frac{\$3100}{1 + 0.0825\left(\dfrac{10}{365}\right)} = \$2647.01 + \$3093.01 = \$5740.02$$

The equivalent value on the focal date of the replacement payments is

$$\$3000\left[1 + 0.0825\left(\frac{30}{365}\right)\right] + x = \$3020.34 + x$$

For equivalence of the two streams,

$$\$3020.34 + x = \$5740.02$$
$$x = \$2719.68$$

The second payment must be $\underline{\$2719.68}$.

Exercise 6.7 *(concluded)*

12. Let x represent the size of the fourth payment. Then

$$\$10{,}000 = \frac{\$2500}{1 + 0.11\left(\frac{2}{12}\right)} + \frac{\$2500}{1 + 0.11\left(\frac{4}{12}\right)} + \frac{\$2500}{1 + 0.11\left(\frac{6}{12}\right)} + \frac{x}{1 + 0.11\left(\frac{8}{12}\right)}$$

$$= \$2454.99 + \$2411.58 + \$2369.67 + 0.9316770x$$
$$= \$7236.24 + 0.9316770x$$
$$x = \$2966.44$$

The fourth payment should be $\underline{\$2966.44}$.

13. Let x represent the size of each payment. Then

$$\$4000 = \frac{x}{1 + 0.13\left(\frac{4}{12}\right)} + \frac{x}{1 + 0.13\left(\frac{6}{12}\right)} + \frac{x}{1 + 0.13\left(\frac{8}{12}\right)}$$

$$= 0.9584665x + 0.9389671x + 0.9202454x$$
$$= 2.8176790x$$
$$x = \$1419.61$$

Each loan payment is $\underline{\$1419.61}$.

14. Let x represent the size of each payment.

Payment	Date	No. of days	Present value
x	Nov 10	16 + 31 + 9 = 56	0.9822918x
x	Dec 30	56 + 21 + 29 = 106	0.9670027x
x	Feb 28	106 + 2 + 31 + 27 = 166	0.9492724x
		Total:	2.8985669x

Since the original loan = Sum of present values of all payments,

$$\$7500 = 2.8985669x$$
$$x = \underline{\$2587.49}$$

The three payments should each be $2587.49.

15. Let x represent the third payment.

Payment	Date	No. of days	Present value
$2000	June 1	8 + 31 = 39	$1978.86
2000	Aug 1	39 + 30 + 31 = 100	1946.67
x	Oct 1	100 + 31 + 30 = 161	0.9577539x

Since the original loan = Sum of present values of all payments,

$$\$6000 = \$1978.86 + \$1946.67 + 0.9577539x$$

$$\$2074.47 = 0.9577539x$$
$$x = \underline{\$2165.97}$$

The third payment is $2165.97.

Exercise 6.8

1. Let x represent the second replacement payment. The equivalent value on the focal date of the scheduled payments is

$$\$600\left[1 + 0.085\left(\frac{4}{12}\right)\right] + \frac{\$900}{1 + 0.085\left(\frac{11}{12}\right)} = \$617.00 + \$834.94 = \$1451.94$$

The equivalent value on the focal date of the replacement payments is

$$\$800 + \frac{x}{1 + 0.085(1)} = \$800 + 0.921659x$$

The equation of value is

$$\$800.00 + 0.921659x = \$1451.94$$

$$x = \frac{\$651.94}{0.921659}$$

$$= \underline{\underline{\$707.36}}$$

The balance in 12 months will be $707.36.

2. Let x represent the second replacement payment. The equivalent value on the focal date of the scheduled payments is

$$\$1300\left[1 + 0.1125\left(\frac{123}{365}\right)\right] + \frac{\$600}{1 + 0.1125\left(\frac{75}{365}\right)} = \$1349.28 + \$586.44 = \$1935.72$$

The equivalent value on the focal date of the replacement payments is

$$\frac{\$1000}{1 + 0.1125\left(\frac{75}{365}\right)} + \frac{x}{1 + 0.1125\left(\frac{150}{365}\right)} = \$977.41 + 0.9558101x$$

If the two streams are equivalent, we can write the equation of value:

$$\$977.41 + 0.9558101x = \$1935.72$$

$$x = \underline{\underline{\$1002.63}}$$

The balance in 150 days will be $1002.63.

3. Let x represent the size of each replacement payment. The equivalent value on the focal date of the scheduled payment is

$$\$6700\left[1 + 0.099\left(\frac{5}{12}\right)\right] = \$6976.38$$

The equivalent value on the focal date of the replacement payments is

$$x + \frac{x}{1 + 0.099\left(\frac{3}{12}\right)} = x + 0.9758478x$$

The equation of value is

$$1.9758478x = \$6976.38$$

$$x = \underline{\underline{\$3530.83}}$$

The two replacement payments should each be $3530.83.

4. Let x represent the amount of each of the two unknown payments. The equivalent value on the focal date of the scheduled payment is

$$\frac{\$5000}{1 + 0.1375\left(\dfrac{4}{12}\right)} = \$4780.88$$

The equivalent value on the focal date of the replacement payments is

$$\$1000 + \frac{x}{1 + 0.1375\left(\dfrac{3}{12}\right)} + \frac{x}{1 + 0.1375\left(\dfrac{7}{12}\right)} = \$1000 + 0.9667674x + 0.9257473x$$

$$= \$1000 + 1.8925147x$$

Solving the equation of value:

$$\$1000 + 1.8925147x = \$4780.88$$
$$x = \underline{\$1997.81}$$

Each of the two equal replacement payments should be $1997.81.

5. Let x represent the size of each of the three replacement payments. The equivalent value on the focal date of the scheduled payments is

$$\$3000\left[1 + 0.09\left(\dfrac{5}{12}\right)\right] + \$3000 \ = \$3112.50 + \$3000 = \underline{\$6112.50}$$

The equivalent value on the same date of the replacement payments is

$$x + \frac{x}{1 + 0.09\left(\dfrac{2}{12}\right)} + \frac{x}{1 + 0.09\left(\dfrac{4}{12}\right)} = x + 0.9852217x + 0.9708738x = 2.9560955x$$

The equation of value is

$$2.9560955x = \$6112.50$$
$$x = \underline{\$2067.76}$$

The three replacement payments are each $2067.76.

6. Let x represent the size of each of the three replacement payments. The equivalent value on the focal date of the scheduled payments is

$$\$1800\left[1 + 0.105\left(\dfrac{50}{365}\right)\right] + \frac{\$2500}{1 + 0.105\left(\dfrac{50}{365}\right)} = \$1825.89 + \$2464.55 = \$4290.44$$

The equivalent value on the focal date of the replacement payments is

$$x + \frac{x}{1 + 0.105\left(\dfrac{100}{365}\right)} + \frac{x}{1 + 0.105\left(\dfrac{150}{365}\right)} = x + 0.9858204x + 0.9720373x = 2.9578577x$$

The equation of value is $2.9578577x = \$4290.44$
$$x = \underline{\$1450.52}$$

The three replacement payments are each $1450.52.

Exercise 6.8 *(continued)*

7. Let x represent the first replacement payment. The equivalent value on the focal date of the scheduled payments is

$$\frac{\$1500}{1 + 0.0675\left(\frac{4}{12}\right)} + \frac{\$2500}{1 + 0.0675\left(\frac{7}{12}\right)} = \$1466.99 + \$2405.29 = \$3872.28$$

The equivalent value on the focal date of the replacement payments is

$$x + \frac{2x}{1 + 0.0675\left(\frac{3}{12}\right)} = x + 1.9668101x = 2.9668101x$$

For equivalence of the two streams,

$$2.9668101x = \$3872.28$$
$$x = \$1305.20$$

The replacement payments are $\underline{\$1305.20}$ in two months and $\underline{\$2610.40}$ in 5 months.

8. Let x represent the first replacement payment. The equivalent value on the focal date of the scheduled payments is

$$\$850\left[1 + 0.14\left(\frac{110}{365}\right)\right] + \frac{\$1200}{1 + 0.14\left(\frac{130}{365}\right)} = \$885.86 + \$1143.01 = \$2028.87$$

The equivalent value on the focal date of the replacement payments is

$$x + \frac{0.5x}{1 + 0.14\left(\frac{70}{365}\right)} = x + 0.4869264x = 1.4869264x$$

For equivalence of the two streams,

$$1.4869264x = \$2028.87$$
$$x = \underline{\$1364.47}$$

The replacement payments are $\underline{\$1364.47}$ thirty days from now and $\underline{\$682.24}$ in 100 days.

Exercise 6.8 *(continued)*

9. Size of payment due today = $1000\left[1 + 0.11\left(\dfrac{4}{12}\right)\right]$ = $1036.67

    Size of payment due in four months = $1200\left[1 + 0.11\left(\dfrac{8}{12}\right)\right]$ = $1288.00

    The equivalent value on the focal date of the scheduled payments is

    $$\$1036.67 + \frac{\$1288.00}{1 + 0.0875\left(\dfrac{4}{12}\right)} = \$1036.67 + \$1251.50 = \$2288.17$$

    Let x represent the size of each replacement payment. The equivalent value on the focal date of the replacement payments is

    $$\frac{x}{1 + 0.0875\left(\dfrac{6}{12}\right)} + \frac{x}{1 + 0.0875(1)} = 0.9580838x + 0.9195402x = 1.8776240x$$

    For equivalence of the two streams,

    1.8776240x = $2288.17
       x = $1218.65
    Both replacement payments are $\underline{\$1218.65}$.

10. Size of payment due two months ago = $5000\left[1 + 0.08\left(\dfrac{3}{12}\right)\right]$ = $5100.00

    Size of payment due in five months = $3000\left[1 + 0.08\left(\dfrac{10}{12}\right)\right]$ = $3200.00

    Equivalent value on the focal date of the scheduled payments is

    $$\$5100\left[1 + 0.105\left(\dfrac{2}{12}\right)\right] + \frac{\$3200}{1 + 0.105\left(\dfrac{5}{12}\right)} = \$5189.25 + \$3065.87 = \$8255.12$$

    Let x represent the size of each replacement payment. The equivalent value on the focal date of the three replacement payments is

    $$x + \frac{x}{1 + 0.105\left(\dfrac{5}{12}\right)} + \frac{x}{1 + 0.105\left(\dfrac{10}{12}\right)} = x + 0.9580838x + 0.9195402x = 2.8776240x$$

    For equivalence of the two streams,

    2.8776240x = $8255.12
         x = $2868.73

    Each of the three replacement payments should be $\underline{\$2868.73}$.

Exercise 6.8 (continued)

11. Let x represent the size of the second replacement payment. The equivalent value on the focal date of the scheduled payments is

$$\$2600\left[1 + 0.0825\left(\frac{80}{365}\right)\right] + \frac{\$3100}{1 + 0.0825\left(\frac{10}{365}\right)} = \$2647.01 + \$3093.01 = \$5740.02$$

The equivalent value on the focal date of the replacement payments is

$$\$3000\left[1 + 0.0825\left(\frac{30}{365}\right)\right] + x = \$3020.34 + x$$

For equivalence of the two streams,

$$\$3020.34 + x = \$5740.02$$
$$x = \$2719.68$$

The second payment must be $\underline{\$2719.68}$.

12. Let x represent the size of the second replacement payment. The equivalent value on the focal date of the scheduled payments is

$$\$2600\left[1 + 0.0825\left(\frac{50}{365}\right)\right] + \frac{\$3100}{1 + 0.0825\left(\frac{40}{365}\right)} = \$2629.38 + \$3072.22 = \$5701.60$$

The equivalent value on the focal date of the replacement payments is

$$\$3000 + \frac{x}{1 + 0.0825\left(\frac{30}{365}\right)} = \$3000 + 0.9932648x$$

For equivalence of the two streams,

$$\$3000 + 0.9932648x = \$5701.60$$
$$x = \$2719.93$$

The second payment must be $\underline{\$2719.93}$. Note the $0.25 difference between the answers to problems 11 and 12.

13. Let x represent the size of the third payment. The equivalent value on the focal date of the replacement payments is

$$\frac{\$2000}{1 + 0.0975\left(\frac{3}{12}\right)} + \frac{\$1500}{1 + 0.0975\left(\frac{5}{12}\right)} + \frac{x}{1 + 0.0975\left(\frac{8}{12}\right)} = \$1952.41 + \$1441.44 + 0.9389671x$$

For equivalence to $5000 on the focal date,

$$\$3393.85 + 0.9389671x = \$5000$$
$$x = \$1710.55$$

The third payment must be $\underline{\$1710.55}$

Exercise 6.8 (continued)

14. Let x represent the size of the third payment. The equivalent value on the focal date of the $5000 payment scheduled for today is

$$\$5000\left[1 + 0.0975\left(\frac{8}{12}\right)\right] = \$5325.00$$

The equivalent value on the focal date of the replacement payments is

$$\$2000\left[1 + 0.0975\left(\frac{5}{12}\right)\right] + \$1500\left[1 + 0.0975\left(\frac{3}{12}\right)\right] + x = \$2081.25 + \$1536.56 + x$$

For equivalence of the two streams,

$$\$3617.81 + x = \$5325.00$$
$$x = \$1707.19$$

The third payment must be $1707.19. Note that the choice of different focal dates in problems 13 and 14 causes a $3.36 difference in the size of the third payment required for equivalence of the alternative payment streams.

15. Let x represent the size of each replacement payment. The equivalent value on the focal date of the scheduled payment is

$$\$7000\left[1 + 0.13\left(\frac{43}{365}\right)\right] = \$7107.21$$

The equivalent value on the focal date of the replacement payments is

$$x\left[1 + 0.13\left(\frac{81}{365}\right)\right] + x + \frac{x}{1 + 0.13\left(\frac{48}{365}\right)} = 1.0288493x + x + 0.9831915x = 3.0120408x$$

For equivalence of the two streams,

$$3.0120408x = \$7107.21$$
$$x = \$2359.60$$

The size of each of the three payments is $2359.60.

16. Let x represent the amount of the first replacement payment. The equivalent value on the focal date of the scheduled payments is

$$\$3500\left[1 + 0.0825\left(\frac{4}{12}\right)\right] + \frac{\$6100}{1 + 0.0825\left(\frac{4}{12}\right)} = \$3596.25 + \$5936.74 = \$9532.99$$

The equivalent value on the focal date of the replacement payments is

$$x + \frac{0.5x}{1 + 0.0825\left(\frac{5}{12}\right)} = x + 0.4833837x$$

For equivalence of the two streams,

$$1.4833837x = \$9532.99$$
$$x = \$6426.52$$

The replacement payments are $6426.52 one month from now and $3213.26 six months from now

---

Business Math in Canada, 2/e

Exercise 6.8 *(concluded)*

17. Let x represent the size of each of the replacement payments. The amount of the scheduled payment is

$$\$6500\left[1 + 0.09\left(\frac{10}{12}\right)\right] = \$6987.50$$

The equivalent value on the focal date of the scheduled payment is

$$\frac{\$6987.50}{1 + 0.085\left(\frac{3}{12}\right)} = \$6842.11$$

The equivalent value on the focal date of the replacement payments is

$$x + \frac{x}{1 + 0.085\left(\frac{4}{12}\right)} = x + 0.9724473x$$

For equivalence of the two streams,

$$1.9724473x = \$6842.11$$
$$x = \$3468.84$$

The two payments should each be $3468.84.

18. Let x represent the size of the July 1 payment. The amount of the scheduled August 1 payment is

$$\$12,000\left[1 + 0.135\left(\frac{153}{365}\right)\right] = \$12,679.07$$

Its equivalent value on the focal date is

$$\frac{\$12,679.07}{1 + 0.10\left(\frac{31}{365}\right)} = \$12,572.29$$

The equivalent value on the focal date of the replacement payments is

$$x + \frac{2x}{1 + 0.10\left(\frac{123}{365}\right)} = x + 1.9347999x$$

For equivalence of the two streams,

$$2.9347999x = \$12,572.29$$
$$x = \$4283.87$$

The two payments are $4283.87 on July 1 and $8567.74 on November 1.

Review Problems

1. $r = \dfrac{I}{Pt} = \dfrac{\$327.95}{\$21,000\left(\dfrac{120}{365}\right)} = 0.0475 = \underline{\underline{4.75\%}}$

2. Maturity value of the first term deposit is

    $P\left(1 + rt\right) = \$15,000\left[1 + 0.052\left(\dfrac{90}{365}\right)\right] = \$15,192.33$

    Maturity value of the second term deposit is

    $P\left(1 + rt\right) = \$15,192.33\left[1 + 0.052\left(\dfrac{90}{365}\right)\right] = \$15,387.12$

    The total interest earned is $\underline{\$387.12}$.

3. Number of days from November 15, 1996 to June 3, 1997

    $\begin{aligned} &= 16 + 31 + 31 + 28 + 31 + 30 + 31 + 2 \\ &= 200 \end{aligned}$

    Interest owed $= Prt = \$1750\,(0.074)\left(\dfrac{200}{365}\right) = \$70.96$

    Mary owed Jason $\underline{\$70.96}$ for interest.

4. The time period for which the money was borrowed was

    $t = \dfrac{I}{Pr} = \dfrac{\$190.02}{\$7500\,(0.0675)} = 0.37535 \text{ year} = 137 \text{ days}$

    $\underline{\text{March 24, 1998}}$ is the date coming 137 days after November 7, 1997.

5. Number of days from March 16 to November 1

    $\begin{aligned} &= 16 + 30 + 31 + 30 + 31 + 31 + 30 + 31 \\ &= 230 \end{aligned}$

    The amount invested in the term deposit should be

    $P = \dfrac{S}{1 + rt} = \dfrac{\$45,000}{1 + 0.0575\left(\dfrac{230}{365}\right)} = \underline{\underline{\$43,426.53}}$

6. Number of days from September 15 to April 1

    $\begin{aligned} &= 16 + 31 + 30 + 31 + 31 + 28 + 31 \\ &= 198 \end{aligned}$

    Savings "earned" from the early "investment" are

    $\$579.00 - \$499.95 = \$79.05$

    The equivalent annual rate of simple interest is

    $r = \dfrac{I}{Pt} = \dfrac{\$79.05}{\$499.95\left(\dfrac{198}{365}\right)} = 0.2915 = 29.15\%$

    The savings from the early purchase are equivalent to a $\underline{29.15\%}$ per annum rate of simple interest

Review Problems (continued)

7. Number of days from August 18 to January 23 is $14 + 30 + 31 + 30 + 31 + 22 = 158$

    Equivalent value on January 23 is

$$P(1 + rt) = \$1000\left[1 + 0.065\left(\frac{158}{365}\right)\right] = \underline{\$1028.14}$$

8. a. Current economic value of the first offer

$$= \$20,000 + \frac{\$80,000}{1 + 0.06(1)} = \$20,000 + \$75,471.70 = \$95,471.70$$

    Current economic value of the second offer

$$= \$48,000 + \frac{\$48,000}{1 + 0.06\left(\frac{6}{12}\right)} = \$48,000 + \$46,601.94 = \$94,601.94$$

    The first offer is worth $\underline{\$869.75}$ more.

    b. Current economic value of the first offer $= \$20,000 + \dfrac{\$80,000}{1 + 0.09(1)} = \$93,394.50$

    Current economic value of the second offer $= \$48,000 + \dfrac{\$48,000}{1 + 0.09\left(\frac{6}{12}\right)} = \$93,933.01$

    The second offer is worth $\underline{\$538.51}$ more.

9. The equivalent value two months from now of the scheduled payments is

$$\$1000\left[1 + 0.0625\left(\frac{7}{12}\right)\right] + \frac{\$7500}{1 + 0.0625\left(\frac{2}{12}\right)} = \$1036.46 + \$7422.68 = \$8459.14$$

    A single payment of $\underline{\$8459.14}$ two months from now will place the payee in an equivalent financial position.

10. a. The economic value today of the payment stream is

$$\$1800\left[1 + 0.075\left(\frac{150}{365}\right)\right] + \$2800\left[1 + 0.075\left(\frac{90}{365}\right)\right]$$

$$= \$1855.48 + \$2851.78$$
$$= \underline{\$4707.26}$$

    b. The economic value today of the payment stream is

$$\frac{\$1600}{1 + 0.075\left(\frac{30}{365}\right)} + \frac{\$1200}{1 + 0.075\left(\frac{75}{365}\right)} + \frac{\$2000}{1 + 0.075\left(\frac{120}{365}\right)}$$

$$= \$1590.20 + \$1181.79 + \$1951.87$$
$$= \underline{\$4723.86}$$

Review Problems *(continued)*

11. The size of the payment due 3 months ago is

$$\$1200\left[1 + 0.085\left(\frac{6}{12}\right)\right] = \$1251.00$$

The size of the payment due 3 months from now is

$$\$800\left[1 + 0.085\left(\frac{12}{12}\right)\right] = \$868.00$$

The equivalent value four months from now of the scheduled payments is

$$\$1251\left[1 + 0.0675\left(\frac{7}{12}\right)\right] + \$868\left[1 + 0.0675\left(\frac{1}{12}\right)\right]$$

$$= \$1300.26 + \$872.88$$
$$= \$2173.14$$

Tanya should be willing to accept a payment of $\underline{\$2173.14}$ four months from now.

12. The scheduled payments due today, 90 days from now, and 180 days from now are

$$\$500\left[1 + 0.085\left(\frac{90}{365}\right)\right] = \$510.48$$

$$\$500\left[1 + 0.085\left(\frac{180}{365}\right)\right] = \$520.96$$

$$\$500\left[1 + 0.085\left(\frac{270}{365}\right)\right] = \$531.44$$

respectively.

Their combined equivalent value 30 days from now is

$$\$510.48\left[1 + 0.069\left(\frac{30}{365}\right)\right] + \frac{\$520.96}{1 + 0.069\left(\frac{60}{365}\right)} + \frac{\$531.44}{1 + 0.069\left(\frac{150}{365}\right)}$$

$$= \$513.37 + \$515.12 + \$516.78$$
$$= \$1545.27$$

Todd should be willing to accept a single replacement payment of $\underline{\$1545.27}$ thirty days from now.

13. Let x represent the amount of each payment. Then

$$\$9000 = \frac{x}{1 + 0.0725\left(\frac{60}{365}\right)} + \frac{x}{1 + 0.0725\left(\frac{180}{365}\right)} + \frac{x}{1 + 0.0725\left(\frac{300}{365}\right)}$$

$$= 0.9882226x + 0.9654808x + 0.9437621x$$
$$= 2.8974654x$$
$$x = \$3106.16$$

Each loan payment is $\underline{\$3106.16}$.

Review Problems (continued)

14. Let x represent the second replacement payment. The equivalent value on the focal date of the scheduled payments is

$$\$2000\left[1 + 0.0625\left(\frac{90}{365}\right)\right] + \frac{\$3000}{1 + 0.0625\left(\frac{20}{365}\right)} = \$2030.82 + \$2989.76 = \$5020.58$$

The equivalent value on the focal date of the replacement payments is

$$\$3000\left[1 + 0.0625\left(\frac{40}{365}\right)\right] + x = \$3020.55 + x$$

For equivalence of the two streams,

$$\$3020.55 + x = \$5020.58$$
$$x = \$2004.03$$

The second payment must be $\underline{\$2004.03}$.

15. Let x represent the size of each replacement payment. The amount of the scheduled payment due in 4 months is

$$\$6500\left[1 + 0.08\left(\frac{9}{12}\right)\right] = \$6890.00$$

The equivalent value today of this scheduled payment is

$$\frac{\$6890.00}{1 + 0.0725\left(\frac{4}{12}\right)} = \$6727.42$$

The equivalent value today of the replacement payments is

$$x + \frac{x}{1 + 0.0725\left(\frac{6}{12}\right)} = x + 0.9650181x$$

For equivalence of the two payment streams,

$$1.9650181x = \$6727.42$$
$$x = \$3423.59$$

The two replacement payments are each $\underline{\$3423.59}$.

Review Problems (concluded)

16. Let x represent the payment due on July 1. The size of the scheduled August 1 payment is

$$\$7000\left[1 + 0.065\left(\frac{108}{365}\right)\right] = \$7134.63$$

The size of the scheduled December 15 payment is

$$\$7000\left[1 + 0.065\left(\frac{244}{365}\right)\right] = \$7304.16$$

The equivalent value on July 1 of the scheduled payments is

$$\frac{\$7134.63}{1 + 0.08\left(\frac{31}{365}\right)} + \frac{\$7304.16}{1 + 0.08\left(\frac{167}{365}\right)} = \$7086.48 + \$7046.25 = \$14,132.73$$

The equivalent value on July 1 of the rescheduled payments is

$$x + \frac{2x}{1 + 0.08\left(\frac{184}{365}\right)} = x + 1.9224692x$$

For equivalence of the two streams,

$$2.9224692x = \$14,132.73$$
$$x = \$4835.89$$

The rescheduled payments are $\underline{\$4835.89}$ on July 1 and $\underline{\$9671.78}$ on January 1.

Self-Test Exercises

1. The number of days from September 17, 1995 to March 11, 1996 was

$$14 + 31 + 30 + 31 + 31 + 29 + 10 = 176$$

The interest rate earned was

$$r = \frac{I}{Pt} = \frac{\$212.45}{\$3702.40\left(\frac{176}{365}\right)} = 0.1190 = \underline{11.90\%}$$

2. The duration of the loan was

$$t = \frac{I}{Pr} = \frac{\$137.99}{\$3300(0.0925)} = 0.45206 \text{ year} = 165 \text{ days}$$

September 8 comes 165 days after March 27. The loan was repaid on September 8.

3. The number of days from November 19, 1997 to March 3, 1998 is
$$12 + 31 + 31 + 28 + 2 = 104$$

The amount that had to be invested on November 19, 1997 was

$$P = \frac{S}{1 + rt} = \frac{\$10,000}{1 + 0.095\left(\frac{104}{365}\right)} = \underline{\$9736.45}$$

Self-Test Exercises (continued)

4. In effect, Judy will "earn" $1.00 on her $7.95 "investment" in just six weeks. The imputed interest rate is

$$r = \frac{I}{Pt} = \frac{\$1.00}{\$7.95\left(\dfrac{42}{365}\right)} = 1.0932 = \underline{\underline{109.32\%}}$$

5. There are 46 days from April 29 to June 14. The economically equivalent payment on April 29 is

$$P = \frac{S}{1 + rt} = \frac{\$60,000}{1 + 0.076\left(\dfrac{46}{365}\right)} = \$59,430.77$$

Sheldrick should propose to pay $59,430.77.

6. a. The economic value today of the full price due in four months is

$$P = \frac{S}{1 + rt} = \frac{\$3995}{1 + 0.0925\left(\dfrac{4}{12}\right)} = \$3875.51$$

Peter and Reesa will save $25.51 in current dollars by paying the early-booking price.

   b. They will be indifferent between the alternatives at the value of r that makes

$$\$3850 = \frac{\$3995}{1 + r\left(\dfrac{4}{12}\right)}$$

$$\left(\frac{4}{12}\right)r = \frac{\$3995}{\$3850} - 1$$

$$r = 0.1130 = 11.30\%$$

If money could earn 11.30% pa, Peter and Reesa would be indifferent between the two prices.

7. Let x represent the equivalent payment 3 months from now. The equivalent value today of the scheduled payments is

$$\$1200\left[1 + 0.099\left(\frac{7}{12}\right)\right] + \$900\left[1 + 0.099\left(\frac{2}{12}\right)\right] + \frac{\$1500}{1 + 0.099\left(\dfrac{1}{12}\right)}$$

$$= \$1269.30 + \$914.85 + \$1487.73$$
$$= \$3671.88$$

The equivalent value today of the replacement payment is

$$\frac{x}{1 + 0.099\left(\dfrac{3}{12}\right)} = 0.9758478x$$

For equivalence of the two streams,

$$0.9758478x = \$3671.88$$
$$x = \$3762.76$$

The payment 3 months from now should be $3762.76.

Self-Test Exercises (concluded)

8. Let x represent the size of the second rescheduled payment. The maturity value of the loan (due in four months) is

$$\$10,000\left[1 + 0.135\left(\frac{10}{12}\right)\right] = \$11,125$$

Its equivalent value on the focal date is

$$\frac{\$11,125}{1 + 0.095\left(\frac{1}{12}\right)} = \$11,037.62$$

The equivalent value on the focal date of the rescheduled payments is

$$\$3000\left[1 + 0.095\left(\frac{3}{12}\right)\right] + x + \frac{2x}{1 + 0.095\left(\frac{4}{12}\right)} = \$3071.25 + x + 1.9386107x$$

For equivalence of the two streams,

$$\$3071.25 + 2.9386107x = \$11,037.62$$
$$x = \$2710.93$$

The second payment due in 3 months is $\underline{\$2710.93}$ and the third payment due in 7 months is $\underline{\$5421.86}$.

9. a. The equivalent value of the payments today is

$$\frac{\$5000}{1 + 0.09\left(\frac{4}{12}\right)} + \frac{\$5000}{1 + 0.09\left(\frac{8}{12}\right)} = \$4854.37 + \$4716.98 = \underline{\$9571.35}$$

   b. The equivalent value today is

$$\frac{\$5000}{1 + 0.07\left(\frac{4}{12}\right)} + \frac{\$5000}{1 + 0.07\left(\frac{8}{12}\right)} = \$4885.99 + \$4777.07 = \underline{\$9663.06}$$

   The difference between the sum of a stream's nominal payments and its economic value on a prior date, is the amount of interest that the ecominic value can earn up to the dates of the payments. At a lower interest rate, the interest earned will be smaller and the difference will be smaller. Hence, the prior economic value will be larger.

7 Applications of Simple Interest

Changes in the Second Edition:

1. The main change in this chapter is the restriction of demand loan coverage in Section 7.5 to the two most common demand loan arrangements—**Revolving Loans** and **Blended-Payment Loans**. The less common **Straight-Line Loans** and **Fixed-Percentage-Payment Loans** are presented in an appendix.

2. Section 7.5 is also the first instance where spreadsheet templates for solving some problems are available (on the diskette in the sleeve attached to this manual's jacket). The templates are formatted schedules ready for the entry of data and the programming of cells. The directory of blank templates may be copied to students' diskettes or to a master file on a network.

Author's comments:

1. I am inclined (but hesitant because of lack of consensus) to cut back on the coverage of *private* short-term promissory notes of the sort discussed in Section 7.1. I find few instances of their use by businesses and financial institutions, and no instance of a business engaged in discounting *private* promissory notes as a line of business. The aggravation generated in dealing with the "three days grace" seems completely out of proportion to the rarity of private notes and the immateriality of the traditional interest adjustment for the days of grace.

   It seems to me that students are much more likely to encounter short-term notes in the context of money market instruments for which there is no grace period. I would rather use Treasury bills and commercial paper as the primary vehicles for the discussion of short-term debt and investments, and give private promissory notes "second billing."

2. I am also inclined to delete the appendix on the Bank Discount Method of Discounting Promissory Notes. The reason (mentioned in the footnote in that appendix) for including the topic becomes less compelling with each passing year.

Please respond by email (JEROME@MALA.BC.CA) with your thoughts and any information you may have, particularly on the first point.

Exercise 7.1

1. Issue date = May 19 = 139th day of the year (Table 6.2)

   Legal due date = 139 + 120 + 3 = 262nd day of the year = <u>September 19</u>

2. Issue date = June 30 = 181st day of the year (Table 6.2)

   Legal due date = 181 + 90 + 3 = 274th day of the year = <u>October 1</u>

3. Term = October 17 − 3 days − July 6 = 290 − 3 − 187 = <u>100 days</u>

4. Term = January 31 − previous November 14 − 3 days
   $$= (365 + 31) − 318 − 3$$
   $$= \underline{75 \text{ days}}$$

5. Issue date = Feb. 28 − 3 days − 4 months = <u>October 25</u>

6. Issue date = October 3 − 3 days − 9 months
   $$= \text{September 30} − 9 \text{ months}$$
   $$= \underline{\text{December 30}}$$

7. Issue date = September 2 − 3 days − 180 days
   $$= 245 − 183$$
   $$= \text{62nd day}$$
   $$= \underline{\text{March 3}}$$

8. Issue date = March 1 (leap year) − 3 days − 60 days
   $$= (365 + 61) − 63$$
   $$= \text{Day numbered 363}$$

   Hence the issue date is <u>December 29</u> of the preceding year.

9. Interest period = August 30 + 3 days − April 30 = 242 + 3 − 120 = 125 days

   Maturity value, $S = P(1 + rt) = \$1000 \left[1 + 0.095 \left(\dfrac{125}{365}\right)\right] = \underline{\$1032.53}$

10. Maturity value, $S = P(1 + rt) = \$3300 \left[1 + 0.0875 \left(\dfrac{63}{365}\right)\right] = \underline{\$3349.84}$

11. Face value, $P = \dfrac{S}{1 + rt} = \dfrac{\$2667.57}{1 + 0.102 \left(\dfrac{93}{365}\right)} = \underline{\$2600.00}$

12. Interest period = December 3 − August 31 = 337 − 243 = 94 days

    Face value, $P = \dfrac{S}{1 + rt} = \dfrac{\$7644.86}{1 + 0.075 \left(\dfrac{94}{365}\right)} = \underline{\$7500.00}$

13. $I = S − P = \$6388.04 − \$6200 = \$188.04$

    $r = \dfrac{I}{Pt} = \dfrac{\$188.04}{\$6200 \left(\dfrac{123}{365}\right)} = 0.090 = \underline{9.0\%}$

Exercise 7.1 (continued)

14. $I = S - P = \$4445.28 - \$4350 = \$95.28$

$$r = \frac{I}{Pt} = \frac{\$95.28}{\$4350\left(\dfrac{78}{365}\right)} = 0.1025 = \underline{10.25\%}$$

15. $I = S - P = \$5275.22 - \$5200 = \$75.22$

$$t = \frac{I}{Pr} = \frac{\$75.22}{\$5200(0.11)} = 0.131504 \text{ year} = 48 \text{ days}$$

Term = 48 − 3 = 45 days

16. $I = S - P = \$9560.62 - \$9400 = \$160.62$

$$t = \frac{I}{Pr} = \frac{\$160.62}{\$9400(0.099)} = 0.172598 \text{ year} = 63 \text{ days}$$

Term = 63 − 3 = 60 days.

17. Time until maturity = 50 + 3 − 9 = 44 days

$$\text{Proceeds} = \frac{S}{1 + rt} = \frac{\$1000}{1 + 0.10\left(\dfrac{44}{365}\right)} = \underline{\$988.09}$$

18. Time from sale date until maturity = 64 days

$$\text{Proceeds} = \frac{\$6000}{1 + 0.09\left(\dfrac{64}{365}\right)} = \underline{\$5906.79}$$

19. Maturity value $= P(1 + rt) = \$2700\left[1 + 0.10\left(\dfrac{185}{365}\right)\right] = \$2836.85$

Time from sale date until maturity = 84 days

$$\text{Proceeds} = \frac{S}{1 + rt} = \frac{\$2836.85}{1 + 0.12\left(\dfrac{84}{365}\right)} = \underline{\$2760.61}$$

20. Maturity date = October 25 + 120 + 3 days = February 25

Maturity value $= \$3500\left[1 + 0.10\left(\dfrac{123}{365}\right)\right] = \$3617.95$

Time from sale date until maturity = 73 days

$$\text{Proceeds} = \frac{S}{1 + rt} = \frac{\$3617.95}{1 + 0.08\left(\dfrac{73}{365}\right)} = \underline{\$3560.97}$$

21. Maturity value = $9000 $\left[1 + 0.08\left(\dfrac{94}{365}\right)\right]$ = $9185.42

    Time from date of sale until maturity = 94 − 35 = 59 days

    Discount rate, r = $\dfrac{I}{Pt}$ = $\dfrac{\$9185.42 - \$9075.40}{\$9075.40 \times \dfrac{59}{365}}$ = 0.075 = <u>7.5%</u>

22. Maturity value = $4000 $\left[1 + 0.08\left(\dfrac{78}{365}\right)\right]$ = $4068.38

    Time from date of sale until maturity = 78 − 32 = 46 days

    Discount rate, r = $\dfrac{I}{Pt}$ = $\dfrac{\$4068.38 - \$4015.25}{\$4015.25\left(\dfrac{46}{365}\right)}$ = 0.105 = <u>10.5%</u>

23. a. Legal due date = February 28, 1998 + 3 days
    = <u>March 3, 1998</u>

    b. Legal due date = September 29, 1997 + 153 days
    = 272nd day + 153 days
    = (425 − 365) days into 1998
    = 60th day in 1998
    = <u>March 1, 1998</u>

24. a. Legal due date = August 30, 1994 + 3 days
    = <u>September 2, 1994</u>

    b. Legal due date = April 30, 1994 + 123 days
    = 120th day + 123 days
    = 243rd day
    = <u>August 31, 1994</u>

25. Maturity value, S = P (1 + rt) = $1000 $\left[1 + 0.1075\left(\dfrac{123}{365}\right)\right]$ = <u>**$1036.23**</u>

26. Legal due date = May 31 + 3 days = June 3

    Maturity value = $1000 $\left[1 + 0.095\left(\dfrac{154}{365}\right)\right]$ = <u>$1040.08</u>

27. Time from sale date until due date = 93 − 31 = 62 days

    Fair selling price = $\dfrac{S}{1 + rt}$ = $\dfrac{\$3300}{1 + 0.0775\left(\dfrac{62}{365}\right)}$ = <u>$3257.12</u>

Exercise 7.1 *(continued)*

28. Legal due date = March 30, 1994 + 3 days = April 2, 1994.

    Time from sale date until maturity = 365 + 92 − 335 = 122 days.

    $$\text{Proceeds} = \frac{S}{1 + rt} = \frac{\$3300}{1 + 0.1125\left(\frac{122}{365}\right)} = \underline{\underline{\$3180.41}}$$

29. Maturity value = $750 $\left[1 + 0.125\left(\frac{103}{365}\right)\right]$ = $776.46

    Time from settlement date until legal due date = 103 − 26 = 77 days

    $$\text{Settlement amount} = \frac{\$776.46}{1 + 0.0825\left(\frac{77}{365}\right)} = \underline{\underline{\$763.17}}$$

30. Legal due date = August 19 + 3 days = August 22
    Total interest period = 234 − 139 = 95 days

    Maturity value = $2700 $\left[1 + 0.08\left(\frac{95}{365}\right)\right]$ = $2756.22

    Time from June 5 to August 22 = 234 − 156 = 78 days

    $$\text{Price on June 5} = \frac{\$2756.22}{1 + 0.11\left(\frac{78}{365}\right)} = \underline{\underline{\$2692.92}}$$

31. Legal due date = December 30 + 3 days = January 2
    Total interest period = 365 + 2 − 181 = 186 days

    Maturity value = $2900 $\left[1 + 0.135\left(\frac{186}{365}\right)\right]$ = $3099.50

    Time from September 1 to January 2 = 186 − 63 = 123 days

    $$\text{Proceeds} = \frac{\$3099.50}{1 + 0.0975\left(\frac{123}{365}\right)} = \underline{\underline{\$3000.91}}$$

32. Maturity value = $4100 $\left[1 + 0.1025\left(\frac{123}{365}\right)\right]$ = $4241.62

    Time from purchase date until due date = 123 − 22 = 101 days

    $$\text{Price} = \frac{\$4241.62}{1 + 0.12\left(\frac{101}{365}\right)} = \underline{\underline{\$4105.30}}$$

Exercise 7.2

1. a. Price = Present value of payments

$$= \frac{\$500}{1 + 0.09\left(\frac{3}{12}\right)} + \frac{\$500}{1 + 0.09\left(\frac{6}{12}\right)}$$

$$= \$489.00 + \$478.47$$

$$= \underline{\underline{\$967.47}}$$

   b. Price in one month

= Present value, one month from now, of the payments

$$= \frac{\$500}{1 + 0.09\left(\frac{2}{12}\right)} + \frac{\$500}{1 + 0.09\left(\frac{5}{12}\right)}$$

$$= \$492.61 + \$481.93$$

$$= \underline{\underline{\$974.54}}$$

   c. The shorter the time interval until receipt of a specified payment, the closer the economic value will be to the nominal amount of the payment.

2. a. Price = Present value of the payments

$$= \frac{\$1000}{1 + 0.10\left(\frac{60}{365}\right)} + \frac{\$1000}{1 + 0.10\left(\frac{90}{365}\right)}$$

$$= \$983.83 + \$975.94$$

$$= \underline{\underline{\$1959.76}}$$

   b. $\text{Price} = \dfrac{\$1000}{1 + 0.11\left(\frac{60}{365}\right)} + \dfrac{\$1000}{1 + 0.11\left(\frac{90}{365}\right)} = \$982.24 + \$973.59 = \underline{\underline{\$1955.83}}$

   c. When money can earn a higher interest rate, a smaller amount of money will be equivalent to a specified nominal payment at a later date.

3. a. Value of certificate A = Sum of the present values of the payments

$$= \frac{\$1000}{1 + 0.0575\left(\frac{4}{12}\right)} + \frac{\$1000}{1 + 0.0575\left(\frac{8}{12}\right)}$$

$$= \$981.19 + \$963.08$$

$$= \underline{\underline{\$1944.27}}$$

3. b. Value of certificate B $= \dfrac{\$1000}{1 + 0.0575\left(\dfrac{5}{12}\right)} + \dfrac{\$1000}{1 + 0.0575\left(\dfrac{9}{12}\right)}$

$\qquad\qquad\qquad = \$976.60 + \$958.66$

$\qquad\qquad\qquad = \underline{\underline{\$1935.26}}$

c. Since the payments from B are received a month after the respective payments from A, certificate B is not as valuable as certificate A.

4. Value of contract today = Sum of the present values of the payments

$\qquad = \dfrac{\$1500}{1 + 0.105\left(\dfrac{100}{365}\right)} + \dfrac{\$2000}{1 + 0.105\left(\dfrac{150}{365}\right)} + \dfrac{\$1000}{1 + 0.105\left(\dfrac{200}{365}\right)}$

$\qquad = \$1458.06 + \$1917.27 + \$945.60$

$\qquad = \underline{\underline{\$4320.93}}$

5. Maximum price = Sum of the present values of the payments

$\qquad = \dfrac{\$4000}{1 + 0.0925\left(\dfrac{3}{12}\right)} + \dfrac{\$2500}{1 + 0.0925\left(\dfrac{6}{12}\right)} + \dfrac{\$5000}{1 + 0.0925\left(\dfrac{9}{12}\right)}$

$\qquad = \$3909.59 + \$2389.49 + \$4675.63$

$\qquad = \underline{\underline{\$10,974.71}}$

6. Payment due 2 months from now $= \$1800\left[1 + 0.10\left(\dfrac{5}{12}\right)\right] = \$1875.00$

Payment due 7 months from now $= \$1800\left[1 + 0.10\left(\dfrac{10}{12}\right)\right] = \$1950.00$

The price that yields a return of 15% is the present value of the payments, discounted at 15%.

Price $= \dfrac{\$1875}{1 + 0.15\left(\dfrac{2}{12}\right)} + \dfrac{\$1950}{1 + 0.15\left(\dfrac{7}{12}\right)} = \$1829.27 + \$1793.10 = \underline{\underline{\$3622.37}}$

Exercise 7.2 *(concluded)*

7. Number of days from:

March 20 to July 1 = 182 − 79 = 103 days
March 20 to September 1 = 244 − 79 = 165 days

$$\text{Payment on July 1} = \$3000 \left[1 + 0.11\left(\frac{103}{365}\right)\right] = \$3093.12$$

$$\text{Payment on September 1} = \$5000 \left[1 + 0.11\left(\frac{165}{365}\right)\right] = \$5248.63$$

Sale proceeds = Sum of present values of payments

$$= \frac{\$3093.12}{1 + 0.16\left(\frac{103}{365}\right)} + \frac{\$5248.63}{1 + 0.16\left(\frac{165}{365}\right)}$$

$$= \$2959.50 + \$4894.61$$

$$= \underline{\underline{\$7854.11}}$$

Exercise 7.3

1. $\text{Price} = \dfrac{S}{1 + rt} = \dfrac{\$25,000}{1 + 0.07672\left(\frac{91}{365}\right)} = \underline{\underline{\$24,530.79}}$

2. $\text{Price} = \dfrac{S}{1 + rt} = \dfrac{\$100,000}{1 + 0.08560\left(\frac{90}{365}\right)} = \underline{\underline{\$97,932.94}}$

3. Time remaining until maturity = 62 days

$\text{Price} = \dfrac{\$1,000,000}{1 + 0.0710\left(\frac{62}{365}\right)} = \underline{\underline{\$988,083.44}}$

4. Time remaining until maturity = 91 − 37 = 54 days

$\text{Selling price} = \dfrac{\$100,000}{1 + 0.0812\left(\frac{54}{365}\right)} = \underline{\underline{\$98,812.95}}$

Exercise 7.3 *(continued)*

5.

Term	Price
30 days	$\dfrac{\$100,000}{1 + 0.08\left(\dfrac{30}{365}\right)} = \underline{\$99,347}$
60 days	$\dfrac{\$100,000}{1 + 0.08\left(\dfrac{60}{365}\right)} = \underline{\$98,702}$
90 days	$\dfrac{\$100,000}{1 + 0.08\left(\dfrac{90}{365}\right)} = \underline{\$98,066}$

The longer the term of the commercial paper issue, the lower the price paid on the issue date.

6.

Time remaining until maturity	Price
91 days	$\dfrac{\$100,000}{1 + 0.07\left(\dfrac{91}{365}\right)} = \underline{\$98,285}$
61 days	$\dfrac{\$100,000}{1 + 0.07\left(\dfrac{61}{365}\right)} = \underline{\$98,844}$
31 days	$\dfrac{\$100,000}{1 + 0.07\left(\dfrac{31}{365}\right)} = \underline{\$99,409}$
1 day	$\dfrac{\$100,000}{1 + 0.07\left(\dfrac{1}{365}\right)} = \underline{\$99,981}$

As time passes, a T-bill's price rises (finally reaching its face value on the maturity date).

7. Effectively, the interest earned by the buyer will be
$$I = S - P = \$100,000 - \$98,245 = \$1755$$

The corresponding rate of return will be

$$r = \frac{I}{Pt} = \frac{\$1755}{\$98,245\left(\dfrac{90}{365}\right)} = 0.07245 = \underline{7.245\% \text{ pa}}$$

The investment will yield 7.245% pa to the buyer.

Exercise 7.3 (continued)

8. If purchased for $99,000, the T-bill will effectively pay $1000 interest when it matures at $100,000. The time remaining until maturity when the T-bill will have a market value of $99,000 is

$$t = \frac{I}{Pr} = \frac{\$1000}{\$99,000(0.062)} = 0.16292 \text{ year} = 59.5 \text{ days}$$

Since T-bills do not pay interest for a partial day, this T-bill's price will first exceed $99,000 **59 days** before its maturity date.

9. a. The interest effectively earned if held until maturity is

$$I = S - P = \$25,000 - \$24,010 = \$990$$

The corresponding rate of return is

$$r = \frac{I}{Pt} = \frac{\$990}{\$24,010\left(\dfrac{182}{365}\right)} = 0.08269 = \underline{\underline{8.269\% \text{ pa}}}$$

   b. The interest effectively earned during the final 122 days was

$$I = \$25,000 - \$24,425 = \$575$$

The rate of return required by the market was

$$r = \frac{\$575}{\$24,425\left(\dfrac{122}{365}\right)} = 0.07043 = \underline{\underline{7.043\% \text{ pa}}}$$

   c. The original investor earned $24,425 - $24,010 = $415 on a $24,010 investment for 60 days. The rate of return was

$$r = \frac{I}{Pt} = \frac{\$415}{\$24,010\left(\dfrac{60}{365}\right)} = 0.10515 = \underline{\underline{10.515\% \text{ pa}}}$$

10. a. Purchase price $= \dfrac{\$100,000}{1 + 0.085\left(\dfrac{182}{365}\right)} = \underline{\underline{\$95,933.98}}$

   b. (i) Market value $= \dfrac{\$100,000}{1 + 0.09\left(\dfrac{97}{365}\right)} = \underline{\underline{\$97,664.09}}$

   (ii) Market value $= \dfrac{\$100,000}{1 + 0.085\left(\dfrac{97}{365}\right)} = \underline{\underline{\$97,791.00}}$

   (iii) Market value $= \dfrac{\$100,000}{1 + 0.08\left(\dfrac{97}{365}\right)} = \underline{\underline{\$97,918.23}}$

Exercise 7.3 *(continued)*

c. The amount earned in each case was:
   (i)   I = S − P = $97,664.09 − $95,933.98 = $1730.11
   (ii) I = S − P = $97,791.00 − $95,933.98 = $1857.02
   (iii) I = S − P = $97,918.23 − $95,933.98 = $1984.25

The rate of return actually realized in each case was:

(i) $r = \dfrac{I}{Pt} = \dfrac{\$1730.11}{\$95,933.98\left(\dfrac{85}{365}\right)} = 0.07744 = \underline{\underline{7.744\% \text{ pa}}}$

(ii) $r = \dfrac{\$1857.02}{\$95,933.98\left(\dfrac{85}{365}\right)} = 0.08312 = \underline{\underline{8.312\% \text{ pa}}}$

(iii) $r = \dfrac{\$1984.25}{\$95,933.98\left(\dfrac{85}{365}\right)} = 0.08882 = \underline{\underline{8.882\% \text{ pa}}}$

Exercise 7.4

1. a. Maturity value, $S = P(1 + rt) = \$15,000\left[1 + 0.0525\left(\dfrac{120}{365}\right)\right] = \underline{\underline{\$15,258.90}}$

   b. Maturity value $= \$15,258.90\left[1 + 0.0475\left(\dfrac{90}{365}\right)\right] = \underline{\underline{\$15,437.62}}$

2. Maturity amount $= \$20,000\left[1 + 0.05\left(\dfrac{91}{365}\right)\right] = \$20,249.32$

   Proceeds of redemption after 80 days $= \$20,000\left[1 + 0.0325\left(\dfrac{80}{365}\right)\right] = \$20,142.47$

   Extra interest earned = $20,249.32 − $20,142.47 = $\underline{\underline{\$106.85}}$

3. The investor will earn an interest rate differential of 0.375% on $60,000 for 270 days. The amount of additional interest on the single $60,000 GIC will then be

   $Prt = \$60,000\,(0.00375)\left(\dfrac{270}{365}\right) = \underline{\underline{\$166.44}}$

4. Maturity value of the one-year GIC $= \$10,000\,[1 + 0.0675\,(1)] = \$10,675.00$

   Maturity value of the 183-day GIC $= \$10,000\left[1 + 0.06\left(\dfrac{183}{365}\right)\right] = \$10,300.82$

   Maturity value of the 182-day GIC $= \$10,300.82\left[1 + 0.06\left(\dfrac{182}{365}\right)\right] = \$10,609.00$

   Therefore, the investor will earn

   $10,675.00 − $10,609.00 = $\underline{\underline{\$66.00}}$

   more from the one-year GIC.

Exercise 7.4 *(continued)*

5. Maturity value of the 180-day GIC = $15,000 $\left[1 + 0.06\left(\dfrac{180}{365}\right)\right]$ = $15,443.84

Maturity value of the first 90-day GIC = $15,000 $\left[1 + 0.0575\left(\dfrac{90}{365}\right)\right]$ = $15,212.67

Maturity value of the second 90-day GIC = $15,212.67 $\left[1 + 0.0575\left(\dfrac{90}{365}\right)\right]$ = $15,428.36

Therefore, the investor will earn

$15,443.84 − $15,428.36 = $15.48

more from the 180-day GIC.

6. We can pick an arbitrary investment, say $1000, for comparing maturity values. The maturity value of a 180-day GIC

= $1000 $\left[1 + 0.065\left(\dfrac{180}{365}\right)\right]$ = $1032.05

Maturity value of the first 90-day GIC

= $1000 $\left[1 + 0.0625\left(\dfrac{90}{365}\right)\right]$ = $1015.41

If the second 90-day GIC is to have a maturity value of $1032.05, its interest rate must be the solution to

$1032.05 = $1015.41 $\left[1 + r\left(\dfrac{90}{365}\right)\right]$

Solving for r,

$\dfrac{\$1032.05}{\$1015.41} - 1 = r\left(\dfrac{90}{365}\right)$

$r = 0.016388\left(\dfrac{365}{90}\right)$ = 0.06646 = 6.646% pa

Hence, the interest rate on the second 90-day GIC must be 6.646% pa in order that the investor end up in the same financial position.

Exercise 7.4 *(continued)*

7. Number of days from June 1 to September 1 = 30 + 31 + 31 = 92 days

    The redemption value of the term deposit on September 1

    $$= \$12,000 \left[1 + 0.042 \left(\frac{92}{365} \right) \right] = \$12,127.04$$

Date	Amount in savings account
July 1	$\$12,000 \left[1 + 0.04 \left(\frac{30}{365} \right) \right] = \$12,039.45$
August 1	$\$12,039.45 \left[1 + 0.04 \left(\frac{31}{365} \right) \right] = \$12,080.35$
September 1	$\$12,080.35 \left[1 + 0.04 \left(\frac{31}{365} \right) \right] = \$12,121.39$

    Joan will earn

    $$\$12,127.04 - \$12,121.39 = \underline{\underline{\$5.65}}$$

    more from the term deposit up to September 1.

8.

Period (inclusive)	Balance in account	No. of days	Interest earned
Sept. 1–6	$2239	6	$\$2239 \, (0.035) \, \frac{6}{365} = \$1.29$
Sept. 7–9	$2973	3	$\$2973 \, (0.035) \, \frac{3}{365} = \$0.86$
Sept. 10–20	$2673	11	$\$2673 \, (0.035) \, \frac{11}{365} = \$2.82$
Sept. 21–30	$3000	10	$\$3000 \, (0.035) \, \frac{10}{365} = \underline{\$2.88}$

    Interest earned in September = $\underline{\underline{\$7.85}}$

9.

Period (inclusive)	No. of days	Balance	Amount subject to a rate of: 3.25%	4.00%	4.50%
Apr. 1–9	9	$2439	$1000	$1439	
Apr. 10–22	13	3389	1000	2000	$389
Apr. 23–30	8	2839	1000	1889	

    Interest earned from April 1–9 inclusive

    $$= \left[\$1000 \, (0.0325) + \$1439 \, (0.04) \right] \left(\frac{9}{365} \right) = \$2.22$$

    Interest earned from April 10–22 inclusive

    $$= \left[\$1000 \, (0.0325) + \$2000 \, (0.04) + \$389 \, (0.045) \right] \left(\frac{13}{365} \right) = \$4.63$$

    Interest earned from April 23–30 inclusive

    $$= \left[\$1000 \, (0.0325) + \$1889 \, (0.04) \right] \left(\frac{8}{365} \right) = \$2.37$$

    Total interest for April = $2.22 + $4.63 + $2.37 = $\underline{\underline{\$9.22}}$

Exercise 7.4 *(concluded)*

10.

Period (inclusive of end dates)	No. of days	Balance	Amount subject to a rate of: 3.25%	4.00%	Interest
Mar. 1–4	4	$1678	$1678		$0.60
Mar. 5–14	10	978	0		0.00
Mar. 15–22	8	3478	3000	$478	2.56①
Mar. 23–31	9	2578	2578		2.07
			Interest credited for March =		$5.23

$$\text{①Interest} = \left[\$3000\,(0.0325) + \$478\,(0.04)\right]\left(\frac{8}{365}\right) = \$2.56$$

11.

Period (inclusive)	No. of days	Balance (for interest calculation)	Interest rate	Interest
Sept. 1–6	6	$ 8572	3.90%	$ 5.50
Sept. 7–14	8	18,072	4.02%	15.92
Sept. 15–22	8	26,672	5.09%	29.76
Sept. 23–30	8	1672	3.00%	1.10
		Interest credited for September =		$52.28

12. a. The interest rate differential is 0.5%. Using I = Prt, the dollar differential will be

$$\$20,000\,(0.005)\left(\frac{120}{365}\right) = \$32.88$$

The redeemable term deposit will earn $32.88 more than the term deposit if redemption occurs on day 120.

b. There is now a 0.5% differential in favour of alternative (ii). The dollar differential will be

$$\$20,000\,(0.005)\left(\frac{150}{365}\right) = \$41.10$$

in favour of alternative (ii).

c. The interest rate differential conceded is 2.25%. The dollar amount of interest sacrificed will be

$$\$20,000\,(0.0225)\left(\frac{150}{365}\right) = \$184.93$$

Exercise 7.5

1.

Date	Number of days	Interest rate	Interest	Accrued interest	Interest charged to account	Principal repaid (advanced)	Balance
5-Feb						($15,000)	$15,000
29-Feb	24	8.50%	$83.84	$83.84	$83.84		15,000
15-Mar	15	8.50%	52.40	52.40		10,000	5,000
31-Mar	16	8.50%	18.63	71.03	71.03		5,000
30-Apr	30	8.50%	34.93	34.93	34.93		5,000
1-May	1	8.50%	1.16	1.16		(7,000)	12,000
31-May	30	8.50%	83.84	85.00	85.00		12,000

The interest charged to Dr. Robillard's account was $83.84 on February 29, $71.03 on March 31, $34.93 on April 30, and $85.00 on May 31.

2.

Date	Number of days	Interest rate	Interest	Accrued interest	Interest charged to account	Principal repaid (advanced)	Balance
15-Sep							$23,465.72
30-Sep	15	9.75%	$94.02	$94.02		$2,000	21,465.72
15-Oct	15	9.75%	86.01	180.03	$180.03		21,465.72
14-Nov	30	9.75%	172.02	172.02		2,000	19,465.72
15-Nov	1	9.75%	5.20	177.22	177.22		19,465.72
15-Dec	30	9.75%	155.99	155.99	155.99		19,465.72
16-Dec	1	9.75%	5.20	5.20		(2,500)	21,965.72
15-Jan	30	9.75%	176.03	181.23	181.23		21,965.72

3.

Date	Number of days	Interest rate	Interest	Accrued interest	Interest charged to account	Principal repaid (advanced)	Balance
3-Jul						($25,000)	$25,000
20-Jul	17	10.00%	$116.44	$116.44	$116.44		25,000
29-Jul	9	10.00%	61.64	61.64		(30,000)	55,000
5-Aug	7	10.00%	105.48	167.12			55,000
20-Aug	15	9.75%	220.38	387.50	387.50		55,000

The amounts of interest charged on July 20 and August 20 were $116.44 and $387.50, respectively.

4.

Date	Number of days	Interest rate	Interest	Accrued interest	Interest charged to account	Principal repaid (advanced)	Balance
12-Jun							$65,000
30-Jun	18	9.25%	$296.51	$296.51		$10,000	55,000
3-Jul	3	9.25%	41.82	338.33			55,000
12-Jul	9	9.50%	128.84	467.17	$467.17		55,000
29-Jul	17	9.50%	243.36	243.36			55,000
31-Jul	2	10.00%	30.14	273.50		10,000	45,000
12-Aug	12	10.00%	147.95	421.45	421.45		45,000

The interest charges to Delta's current account were $467.17 on July 12 and $421.45 on August 12

Exercise 7.5 (continued)

5.

Date	Number of days	Interest rate	Interest	Accrued interest	Interest charged to account	Principal repaid (advanced)	Balance
7-Oct						($30,000)	$30,000
15-Oct	8	11.75%	$77.26	$77.26	$77.26		30,000
15-Nov	31	11.75%	299.38	299.38	299.38		30,000
24-Nov	9	11.75%	86.92	86.92		(15,000)	45,000
15-Dec	21	11.75%	304.21	391.13	391.13		45,000
17-Dec	2	11.75%	28.97	28.97			45,000
23-Dec	6	11.50%	85.07	114.04		(20,000)	65,000
15-Jan	23	11.50%	471.03	585.07	585.07		65,000

6.

Date	Number of days	Interest rate	Interest	Accrued interest	Interest charged to account	Principal repaid (advanced)	Balance
10-Feb							$770,000
1-Mar	19	11.50%	$4,609.45	$4,609.45		($100,000)	870,000
10-Mar	9	11.50%	2,466.99	7,076.44	$7,076.44		870,000
30-Mar	20	11.50%	5,482.19	5,482.19		125,000	745,000
8-Apr	9	11.50%	2,112.53	7,594.72			745,000
10-Apr	2	12.00%	489.86	8,084.58	8,084.58		745,000
28-Apr	18	12.00%	4,408.77	4,408.77		150,000	595,000
10-May	12	12.00%	2,347.40	6,756.17	6,756.17		595,000

Total interest charged from February 10 to May 10 = $21,917.19

7.

Date	Number of days	Interest rate	Interest	Accrued interest	Interest charged to account	Principal repaid (advanced)	Balance
31-Mar						($30,000)	$30,000
18-Apr	18	10.75%	$159.04	$159.04	$159.04		30,000
28-Apr	10	10.75%	88.36	88.36		(10,000)	40,000
14-May	16	10.75%	188.49	276.85			40,000
18-May	4	11.00%	48.22	325.07	325.07		40,000
1-Jun	14	11.00%	168.77	168.77		(15,000)	55,000
18-Jun	17	11.00%	281.78	450.55	450.55	5,000	50,000
3-Jul	15	11.00%	226.03	226.03		10,000	40,000
18-Jul	15	11.00%	180.82	406.85	406.85		40,000

8.

Date	Number of days	Interest rate	Interest	Accrued interest	Payment made	Principal portion	Balance
3-Jun							$5,000.00
1-Jul	28	12.50%	$47.95	$47.95	$1,000.00	952.05	4,047.95
1-Aug	31	12.50%	42.97	42.97	1,000.00	957.03	3,090.92
1-Sep	31	12.50%	32.81	32.81	1,000.00	967.19	2,123.73
1-Oct	30	12.50%	21.82	21.82	1,000.00	978.18	1,145.55
1-Nov	31	12.50%	12.16	12.16	1,000.00	987.84	157.71
1-Dec	30	12.50%	1.62	1.62	159.33	157.71	0.00

Exercise 7.5 (concluded)

9.

Date	Number of days	Interest rate	Interest	Accrued interest	Payment made	Principal portion	Balance
1-Apr							$6,000.00
1-May	30	11.25%	$ 55.48	$55.48	$1,000.00	$944.52	5,055.48
1-Jun	31	11.25%	48.30	48.30	1,000.00	951.70	4,103.78
7-Jun	6	11.25%	7.59	7.59			4,103.78
1-Jul	24	11.00%	29.68	37.27	1,000.00	962.73	3,141.05
1-Aug	31	11.00%	29.35	29.35	1,000.00	970.65	2,170.40
27-Aug	26	11.00%	17.01	17.01			2,170.40
1-Sep	5	11.25%	3.34	20.35	1,000.00	979.65	1,190.75
1-Oct	30	11.25%	11.01	11.01	1,000.00	988.99	201.76
1-Nov	31	11.25%	$ 1.93	1.93	203.69	201.76	0.00
Total of the interest charges =			$203.69				

10.

Date	Number of days	Interest rate	Interest	Accrued interest	Payment made	Principal portion	Balance
20-Jul							$3,500.00
19-Aug	30	11.25%	$32.36	$32.36			3,500.00
1-Sep	13	11.75%	14.65	47.01	$700.00	$652.99	2,847.01
1-Oct	30	11.75%	27.50	27.50	700.00	672.50	2,174.51
1-Nov	31	11.75%	21.70	21.70	700.00	678.30	1,496.21
2-Nov	1	11.75%	0.48	0.48			1,496.21
1-Dec	29	12.00%	14.27	14.75	700.00	685.25	810.96
1-Jan	31	12.00%	8.27	8.27	700.00	691.73	119.23
1-Feb	31	12.00%	1.22	1.22	120.45	119.23	0.00

11.

Date	Number of days	Interest rate	Interest	Accrued interest	Payment made	Principal portion	Balance
23-Feb							$2,500.00
15-Apr	51	9.00%	$31.44	$31.44	$500.00	$468.56	2,031.44
15-May	30	9.00%	15.03	15.03	500.00	484.97	1,546.47
15-Jun	31	9.00%	11.82	11.82	500.00	488.18	1,058.29
15-Jul	30	9.50%	8.26	8.26	500.00	491.74	566.55
31-Jul	16	9.50%	2.36	2.36			566.55
15-Aug	15	9.75%	2.27	4.63	500.00	495.37	71.18
15-Sep	31	9.75%	0.59	0.59	71.77	71.18	0.00

12.

Date	Number of days	Interest rate	Interest	Accrued interest	Payment made	Principal portion	Balance
13-Sep							$15,000.00
20-Oct	37	11.00%	$167.26	$167.26	$700.00	$532.74	14,467.26
20-Nov	31	11.00%	135.16	135.16	700.00	564.84	13,902.42
26-Nov	6	11.00%	25.14	25.14			13,902.42
20-Dec	24	10.75%	98.27	123.41	700.00	576.59	13,325.83
20-Jan	31	10.75%	121.67	121.67	700.00	578.33	12,747.50
29-Jan	9	10.75%	33.79	33.79			12,747.50
20-Feb	22	11.25%	86.44	120.23	700.00	579.77	12,167.73

Review Problems

1. Legal due date = April 30, 1998 + 3 days = May 3, 1998

   Time (December 31 to May 3) = 123 days

   $$\text{Maturity value} = \$1500 \left[1 + 0.095 \left(\frac{123}{365} \right) \right] = \underline{\underline{\$1548.02}}$$

2. Legal due date = March 30, 1998 + 3 days = April 2, 1998.

   Time (February 1 to April 2) = 92 − 32 = 60 days

   $$\text{Proceeds} = \frac{\$3300}{1 + 0.0725 \left(\frac{60}{365} \right)} = \underline{\underline{\$3261.13}}$$

3. Legal due date = December 30 + 3 days = January 2

   Time (June 30 to January 2) = 2 + 365 − 181 = 186 days

   $$\text{Maturity value} = \$7900 \left[1 + 0.075 \left(\frac{186}{365} \right) \right] = \$8201.93$$

   Time (Sept. 1 to Jan. 2) = 2 + 365 − 244 = 123 days

   $$\text{Proceeds} = \frac{\$8201.93}{1 + 0.0975 \left(\frac{123}{365} \right)} = \underline{\underline{\$7941.02}}$$

4. $$\text{Maturity value} = \$5700 \left[1 + 0.0825 \left(\frac{153}{365} \right) \right] = \underline{\underline{\$5897.12}}$$

   Time (June 18 to August 5) = 217 − 169 = 48 days

   Time remaining until due date = 153 − 48 = 105 days

   $$\text{Price on August 5} = \frac{\$5897.12}{1 + 0.12 \left(\frac{105}{365} \right)} = \underline{\underline{\$5700.34}}$$

5. The maximum price will be the sum of the present values of the payments discounted at the minimum required rate of return. That is,

   $$\text{Price} = \frac{\$4500}{1 + 0.105 \left(\frac{4}{12} \right)} + \frac{\$3000}{1 + 0.105 \left(\frac{8}{12} \right)} + \frac{\$5500}{1 + 0.105 \,(1)}$$

   $$= \$4347.83 + \$2803.74 + \$4977.38$$

   $$= \underline{\underline{\$12{,}128.95}}$$

   The highest price the investor should pay is $12,128.95.

Review Problems (continued)

6. Size of first payment $= \$3200 \left[1 + 0.09 \left(\dfrac{4}{12} \right) \right] = \$3296.00$

   Size of second payment $= \$3200 \left[1 + 0.09 \left(\dfrac{8}{12} \right) \right] = \$3392.00$

   Sum of the present values of the two payments

   $$= \dfrac{\$3296.00}{1 + 0.16 \left(\dfrac{1}{12} \right)} + \dfrac{\$3392.00}{1 + 0.16 \left(\dfrac{5}{12} \right)}$$

   $$= \$3252.63 + \$3180.00$$

   $$= \underline{\underline{\$6432.63}}$$

   The finance company should be prepared to pay $6432.63 today for the loan contract.

7. $\text{Price} = \dfrac{S}{1 + rt} = \dfrac{\$50,000}{1 + 0.06773 \left(\dfrac{91}{365} \right)} = \underline{\underline{\$49,169.71}}$

8. Time remaining until maturity $= 182 - 66 = 116$ days

   $\text{Price} = \dfrac{\$100,000}{1 + 0.0748 \left(\dfrac{116}{365} \right)} = \underline{\underline{\$97,677.99}}$

9. The earnings from the certificate will be

   $I = S - P = \$100,000 - \$98,450 = \$1550$

   The corresponding annual rate of return is

   $r = \dfrac{I}{Pt} = \dfrac{\$1550}{\$98,450 \left(\dfrac{90}{365} \right)} = 0.06385 = \underline{\underline{6.385\%}}$

   The investment will yield the buyer 6.385%.

10. a. $\text{Price} = \dfrac{\$100,000}{1 + 0.065 \left(\dfrac{182}{365} \right)} = \underline{\underline{\$96,860.65}}$

    b.

Market return	Market value
(i) 7%	$\dfrac{\$100,000}{1 + 0.07 \left(\dfrac{97}{365} \right)} = \$98,173.70$
(ii) 6.5%	$\dfrac{\$100,000}{1 + 0.065 \left(\dfrac{97}{365} \right)} = \$98,301.94$
(iii) 6%	$\dfrac{\$100,000}{1 + 0.06 \left(\dfrac{97}{365} \right)} = \$98,430.51$

c. The interest effectively earned in each case was:
   (i)   I = S − P = $98,173.70 − $96,860.65 = $1313.05
   (ii) I = S − P = $98,301.94 − $96,860.65 = $1441.29
   (iii) I = S − P = $98,430.51 − $96,860.65 = $1569.86

The rate of return actually realized in each case was:

(i) $r = \dfrac{I}{Pt} = \dfrac{\$1313.05}{\$96,860.65 \left(\dfrac{85}{365}\right)} = 0.05821 = \underline{\underline{5.821\%}}$

(ii) $r = \dfrac{\$1441.29}{\$98,860.65 \left(\dfrac{85}{365}\right)} = 0.06390 = \underline{\underline{6.390\%}}$

(iii) $r = \dfrac{\$1569.86}{\$98,860.65 \left(\dfrac{85}{365}\right)} = 0.06960 = \underline{\underline{6.960\%}}$

11. In effect, the investor will earn a 0.25% higher rate of return on the single $80,000 GIC. The dollar amount of extra interest earned will be

$$I = Prt = \$80,000 \, (0.0025) \left(\frac{180}{365}\right) = \underline{\underline{\$98.63}}$$

12. Suppose that the amount invested is $1000. Its maturity value in a 120-day GIC will be

$$\$1000 \left[1 + 0.0575 \left(\frac{120}{365}\right)\right] = \$1018.90$$

If instead, the $1000 is invested in a 60-day GIC,

$$\text{Maturity value} = \$1000 \left[1 + 0.055 \left(\frac{60}{365}\right)\right] = \$1009.04$$

For this amount to grow to $1018.90 in another 60 days, the interest rate must be the solution to

$$\$1018.90 = \$1009.04 \left[1 + r \left(\frac{60}{365}\right)\right]$$

$$r = 0.0097717 \left(\frac{365}{60}\right) = 0.05944 = \underline{\underline{5.944\%}}$$

Review Problems (concluded)

13.

Period (inclusive)	No. of days	Balance	3.00%	3.75%	4.25%
			Amount subject to a rate of:		
Jan. 1–13	13	$3678	$1000	$2000	$678
Jan. 14–24	11	878	878		
Jan. 25–31	7	1828	1000	828	

$$I \text{ (Jan. 1–13)} = \left[\$1000 \ (0.03) + \$2000 \ (0.0375) + \$678 \ (0.0425)\right]\left(\frac{13}{365}\right) = \$4.77$$

$$I \text{ (Jan. 14–24)} = \$878 \ (0.03) \ \frac{11}{365} = \$0.79$$

$$I \text{ (Jan. 25–31)} = \left[\$1000 \ (0.03) + \$828 \ (0.0375)\right]\left(\frac{7}{365}\right) = \$1.17$$

Total interest for January = $4.77 + $0.79 + $1.17 = $6.73

14.

Date	Number of days	Interest rate	Interest	Accrued interest	Payment made	Principal portion	Balance
28-Jan							$4,000.00
21-Feb	24	6.75%	$17.75	$17.75	$600.00	$582.25	3,417.75
21-Mar	28	6.75%	17.70	17.70	600.00	582.30	2,835.45
21-Apr	31	6.75%	16.26	16.26	600.00	583.74	2,251.71
15-May	24	6.75%	9.99	9.99			2,251.71
21-May	6	6.50%	2.41	12.40	600.00	587.60	1,664.11
21-Jun	31	6.50%	9.19	9.19	600.00	590.81	1,073.30
5-Jul	14	6.50%	2.68	2.68			1,073.30
21-Jul	16	6.25%	2.94	5.62	600.00	594.38	478.92
21-Aug	31	6.25%	2.54	2.54	481.46	478.92	0.00

15.

Date	Number of days	Interest rate	Interest	Accrued interest	Interest charged to account	Principal repaid (advanced)	Balance
8-Mar						($40,000)	$40,000
24-Mar	16	10.25%	$179.73	$179.73	$179.73		40,000
2-Apr	9	10.25%	101.10	101.10		(15,000)	55,000
24-Apr	22	10.25%	339.79	440.89	440.89		55,000
13-May	19	10.25%	293.46	293.46			55,000
24-May	11	10.50%	174.04	467.50	467.50		55,000
5-Jun	12	10.50%	189.86	189.86		25,000	30,000
24-Jun	19	10.50%	163.97	353.83	353.83		30,000

The first four interest debits were, in order, $179.73, $440.89, $467.50, and $353.93.

Self-Test Exercise

1. Legal due date = June 30, 1996 + 3 days = July 3, 1996

   Time (March 1 to July 3, 1996) = 184 + 1 − (60 + 1) = 124 days

$$\text{Price} = \frac{\$1700}{1 + 0.10 \left(\frac{124}{365}\right)} = \$1644.14$$

Self-Test Exercise *(continued)*

2. Maturity value $= \$8500 \left[1 + 0.09 \left(\dfrac{93}{365} \right) \right] = \$8694.92$

    Time (Nov. 10 to due date) $= 93 - 26 = 67$ days.

    Settlement price (in order to yield 12% pa) $= \dfrac{\$8694.92}{1 + 0.12 \left(\dfrac{67}{365} \right)} = \underline{\$8507.52}$

3. Size of first payment $\quad = \$1900 \left[1 + 0.125 \left(\dfrac{3}{12} \right) \right] = \$1959.38$

    Size of second payment $= \$1900 \left[1 + 0.125 \left(\dfrac{6}{12} \right) \right] = \$2018.75$

    Price = Sum of present values of the payments (discounted at 18%)

    $\quad = \dfrac{\$1959.38}{1 + 0.18 \left(\dfrac{2}{12} \right)} + \dfrac{\$2018.75}{1 + 0.18 \left(\dfrac{5}{12} \right)}$

    $\quad = \$1902.31 + \$1877.91$

    $\quad = \underline{\$3780.22}$

    The finance company should pay \$3780.22 if it requires an 18% rate of return.

4. a. Price $= \dfrac{\$25,000}{1 + 0.09438 \left(\dfrac{91}{365} \right)} = \underline{\$24,425.26}$

    b. The amount earned by the second investor will be

        $I = S - P = \$25,000 - \$24,575 = \$425$

        This will provide a rate of return of

        $r = \dfrac{I}{Pt} = \dfrac{\$425}{\$24,575 \left(\dfrac{57}{365} \right)} = 0.11074 = \underline{11.074\% \text{ pa}}$

    c. During his 34-day holding period, the first investor earned

        $I = S - P = \$24,575 - \$24,425.26 = \$149.74$

        This amount provided a rate of return of

        $r = \dfrac{I}{Pt} = \dfrac{\$149.74}{\$24,425.26 \left(\dfrac{34}{365} \right)} = 0.06581 = \underline{6.581\% \text{ pa}}$

5. Maturity value of the 180-day GIC = $20,000 $\left[1 + 0.065 \left(\frac{180}{365}\right)\right]$ = $20,641.10

Maturity value of the first 90-day GIC = $20,000 $\left[1 + 0.063 \left(\frac{90}{365}\right)\right]$ = $20,310.68

Maturity value of the second 90-day GIC = $20,310.68 $\left[1 + 0.063 \left(\frac{90}{365}\right)\right]$ = $20,626.20

Therefore, Paul will earn

$20,641.10 − $20,626.20 = <u>$14.90</u>

more by buying the 180-day GIC.

6.

Date	Number of days	Interest rate	Interest	Accrued interest	Interest charged to account	Principal repaid (advanced)	Balance
3-Jun						($50,000)	$ 50,000
26-Jun	23	12.00%	$378.08	~~$378.08~~	$378.08		50,000
30-Jun	4	12.00%	65.75	65.75		(40,000)	90,000
5-Jul	5	12.00%	147.95	213.70			90,000
17-Jul	12	12.25%	362.47	576.17		(25,000)	115,000
26-Jul	9	12.25%	347.36	~~923.53~~	923.53		115,000
31-Jul	5	12.50%	196.92	196.92		30,000	85,000
18-Aug	18	12.50%	523.97	720.89		35,000	50,000
26-Aug	8	12.50%	136.99	~~857.88~~	857.88		50,000

7.

Date	Number of days	Interest rate	Interest	Accrued interest	Payment made	Principal portion	Balance
23-May							$15,000.00
15-Jun	23	9.50%	$ 89.79	~~$ 89.79~~	$700.00	$610.21	14,389.79
15-Jul	30	9.50%	112.36	~~112.36~~	700.00	587.64	13,802.15
26-Jul	11	9.50%	39.52	39.52			13,802.15
15-Aug	20	9.25%	69.96	~~109.48~~	700.00	590.52	13,211.63
14-Sep	30	9.25%	100.44	100.44			13,211.63
15-Sep	1	9.75%	3.53	~~103.97~~	700.00	596.03	12,615.60
15-Oct	30	9.75%	101.10	~~101.10~~	700.00	598.90	12,016.70

8 Compound Interest

Changes in the Second Edition:

1. The circumstance in which the compound rate of interest changes in successive compounding periods has been added. **Canada Savings Bonds** and **Variable-Rate GICs** are presented as applications of this case.

2. An appendix has been added providing instructions on the use of the basic financial functions of five popular models of financial calculators. Students are shown how to adapt each of these models to the generic instructions presented in the text.

3. Figure 8.4 has been added to illustrate the effect of the compounding frequency on the maturity value of a lump investment.

4. The expression for the present value of a lump payment is usually expressed in the

   $P = (1 + i)^{-n}$ format instead of the $P = \dfrac{S}{(1 + i)^n}$ format. Two reviewers expressed a preference for

   the negative exponent format since it is closer to the procedure a student ought to employ for efficiently calculating the present value using the y^x function on a calculator. However, in some cases where S is a large number, the division format continues to be used to make a long equation fit on one line.

Exercise 8.1

1. $i = \dfrac{j}{m} = \dfrac{10.8\%}{4} = \underline{\underline{2.7\%}}$ (per quarter)

2. $i = \dfrac{j}{m} = \dfrac{11.75\%}{2} = \underline{\underline{5.875\%}}$ (per half year)

3. $i = \dfrac{j}{m} = \dfrac{10.5\%}{12} = \underline{\underline{0.875\%}}$ (per month)

4. $j = mi = 2\ (4.95\%) = \underline{\underline{9.9\%}}$ compounded semiannually

5. $j = mi = 12\ (0.91667\%) = \underline{\underline{11.0\%}}$ compounded monthly

6. $j = mi = 4\ (2.9375\%) = \underline{\underline{11.75\%}}$ compounded quarterly

7. $m = \dfrac{j}{i} = \dfrac{9.5\%}{2.375\%} = 4$

   That is, <u>quarterly compounding</u>.

8. $m = \dfrac{j}{i} = \dfrac{8.25\%}{4.125\%} = 2$

   That is, <u>semiannual compounding</u>.

9. $m = \dfrac{j}{i} = \dfrac{13.5\%}{1.125\%} = 12$

   That is, <u>monthly compounding</u>.

Exercise 8.2

1. $i = \dfrac{j}{m} = \dfrac{10\%}{2} = 5\%$ (per half year)

   $n = m$ (term in years) $= 2(7) = 14$ compounding periods

   Maturity value, $S = P\ (1 + i)^n = \$5000\ (1.05)^{14} = \underline{\underline{\$9899.66}}$

2. $i = \dfrac{j}{m} = \dfrac{9.5\%}{4} = 2.375\%$ (per quarter)

   $n = m$ (term in years) $= 4(5.5) = 22$ conversion periods

   Maturity value, $S = P\ (1 + i)^n = \$8500\ (1.02375)^{22} = \underline{\underline{\$14{,}245.74}}$

3. $i = \dfrac{j}{m} = \dfrac{7.5\%}{12} = 0.625\%$ (per month)

   $n = m$ (term in years) $= 12(3.25) = 39$ compounding periods

   Maturity value, $S = \$12{,}100\ (1.00625)^{39} = \underline{\underline{\$15{,}428.20}}$

Exercise 8.2 (continued)

4. $i = \dfrac{9.9\%}{1} = 9.9\%$ (per year); $n = 1\,(10) = 10$ periods

Principal, $P = \dfrac{S}{(1 + i)^n} = \dfrac{\$10{,}000}{1.099^{10}} = \underline{\underline{\$3890.66}}$

5. $i = \dfrac{8.5\%}{4} = 2.125\%$ (per quarter); $n = 4\,(2.25) = 9$ periods

Principal, $P = \dfrac{S}{(1 + i)^n} = \dfrac{\$5437.52}{1.02125^9} = \underline{\underline{\$4500.00}}$

6. $i = \dfrac{7.5\%}{2} = 3.75\%$ (per half year); $n = 2\,(3.5) = 7$ periods

Principal, $P = \dfrac{S}{(1 + i)^n} = \dfrac{\$9704.61}{1.0375^7} = \underline{\underline{\$7500.00}}$

7. $i = \dfrac{13\%}{12} = 1.08\overline{3}\%$ (per month); $n = 18$ periods

Principal, $P = \dfrac{S}{(1 + i)^n} = \dfrac{\$8000.00}{1.0108333^{18}} = \underline{\underline{\$6589.58}}$

8. $i = \dfrac{10.5\%}{4} = 2.625\%$ (per quarter); $n = 4\,(4.5) = 18$ periods

Maturity value $= P\,(1 + i)^n = \$2500\,(1.02625)^{18} = \underline{\underline{\$3985.63}}$

9. $i = \dfrac{6.7\%}{1} = 6.7\%$ (per year); $n = 27$ periods

Principal, $P = \dfrac{S}{(1 + i)^n} = \dfrac{\$28{,}801.12}{1.067^{27}} = \underline{\underline{\$5000.00}}$

10. $i = \dfrac{11\%}{12} = 0.91\overline{6}\%$ (per month); $n = 12\,(6.75) = 81$ periods

Maturity value $= P\,(1 + i)^n = \$4400\,(1.00916667)^{81} = \underline{\underline{\$9213.98}}$

11. Maturity value at 11% $= P(1 + i)^n = \$1000(1.11)^{25} = \$13{,}585.46$
    Maturity value at 10% $ = \$1000(1.10)^{25} = \underline{\$10{,}834.71}$

     Difference: $\underline{\underline{\$\ \ 2750.75}}$

    The difference is

    $\dfrac{\$2750.75}{\$10{,}834.71} \times 100\% = \underline{\underline{25.39\%}}$

    of the maturity value at 10% compounded annually.

Exercise 8.2 (continued)

12. Maturity value at 6% = $P(1 + i)^n$ = $1000(1.06)^{25}$ = $4291.87
    Maturity value at 5% = $1000(1.05)^{25}$ = $3386.35

    Difference: $ 905.52

    The difference is

    $$\frac{\$905.52}{\$3386.35} \times 100\% = \underline{26.74\%}$$

    of the maturity value at 5% compounded annually.

13. Maturity value after 25 years = $P(1 + i)^n$ = $1000(1.09)^{25}$ = $8623.08
    Maturity value after 20 years = $1000(1.09)^{20}$ = $5604.41

    Difference: $3018.67

    The difference is

    $$\frac{\$3018.67}{\$5604.41} \times 100\% = \underline{53.86\%}$$

    of the amount after 20 years.

14. Amount after 15 years = $P(1 + i)^n$ = $1000(1.09)^{15}$ = $3642.48
    Amount after 10 years = $1000(1.09)^{10}$ = $2367.36

    Difference: $1275.12

    The difference is

    $$\frac{\$1275.12}{\$2367.36} \times 100\% = \underline{53.86\%}$$

    of the amount after 10 years.

    Note: The equality of the percent differences in problems 13 and 14 is not coincidence. The percent change in the value of the investment in any five-year period will be the same (53.86%). It is a property of compound interest that, for a given interest rate, the percent change in value is the same for all intervals of a given length.

15.

Interest rate	20 years	25 years	30 years
8%	$4660.96	$6848.48	$10,062.66
10%	$6727.50	$10,834.71	$17,449.40

16. The first investment will be worth $1000(1.085)^{30}$ = $11,558.25
    The 16th investment will be worth $1000(1.085)^{15}$ = $ 3399.74

    Difference: $ 8158.51

17. The maturity value of $1000 invested for 30 years at 8% compounded annually is

    $$S = P(1 + i)^n = \$1000(1.08)^{30} = \$10,062.66$$

    The amount that must be invested for 25 years at 8% compounded annually in order to have a maturity value of $10,062.66 is

    $$P = S(1 + i)^{-n} = \$10,062.66(1.08)^{-25} = \underline{\$1469.33}$$

Exercise 8.2 *(continued)*

18.

m	i	n	Maturity amount	
a.	1	$\frac{9\%}{1}$ = 9%	25	$1000 (1.09)^{25} = $8623.08

a. 1 $\dfrac{9\%}{1}$ = 9%   25 $1000 $(1.09)^{25}$ = $\underline{\$8623.08}$

b. 2 $\dfrac{9\%}{2}$ = 4.5%   2(25) = 50 $1000 $(1.045)^{50}$ = $\underline{\$9032.64}$

c. 4 $\dfrac{9\%}{4}$ = 2.25%   4(25) = 100 $1000 $(1.0225)^{100}$ = $\underline{\$9254.05}$

d. 12 $\dfrac{9\%}{12}$ = 0.75%   12(25) = 300 $1000 $(1.0075)^{300}$ = $\underline{\$9408.41}$

19.

m	i	n	Maturity amount

a. 1 $\dfrac{9\%}{1}$ = 9%   5 $1000 $(1.09)^{5}$ = $\underline{\$1538.62}$

b. 2 $\dfrac{9\%}{2}$ = 4.5%   2(5) = 10 $1000 $(1.045)^{10}$ = $\underline{\$1552.97}$

c. 4 $\dfrac{9\%}{4}$ = 2.25%   4(5) = 20 $1000 $(1.0225)^{20}$ = $\underline{\$1560.51}$

d. 12 $\dfrac{9\%}{12}$ = 0.75%   12(5) = 60 $1000 $(1.0075)^{60}$ = $\underline{\$1565.68}$

20.

i	n	Maturity value

a. $\dfrac{8\%}{12}$ = $0.0\overline{6}$%   12 $100 $(1.00\overline{6})^{12}$ = $108.30

b. $\dfrac{8.1\%}{4}$ = 2.025%   4 $100 $(1.02025)^{4}$ = $108.35

c. $\dfrac{8.2\%}{2}$ = 4.1%   2 $100 $(1.041)^{2}$ = $108.37

d.   8.3%   1 $100 $(1.083)^{1}$ = $108.30

The rate that produces the largest interest earnings after one year is <u>8.2% compounded semiannually</u>.

21.

i	n	Maturity value

$\dfrac{12.0\%}{12}$ = 1.0%   12 $100 $(1.01)^{12}$ = $112.68

$\dfrac{12.1\%}{4}$ = 3.025%   4 $100 $(1.03025)^{4}$ = $112.66

$\dfrac{12.2\%}{2}$ = 6.1%   2 $100 $(1.061)^{2}$ = $112.57

$\dfrac{12.3\%}{1}$ = 12.3%   1 $100 $(1.123)^{1}$ = $112.30

An investor would prefer <u>12.0% compounded monthly</u> since it results in the highest maturity value.

Exercise 8.2 (continued)

22. $P = \$3000$; $i = \dfrac{9.5\%}{2} = 4.75\%$; $n = 2\,(1.5) = 3$

    Maturity value, $S = \$3000\,(1.0475)^3 = \underline{\underline{\$3448.13}}$

    Interest charged $= S - P = \$3448.13 - \$3000 = \underline{\underline{\$448.13}}$

23. $P = \$5000$; $i = \dfrac{7.5\%}{12} = 0.625\%$; $n = 12\,(3.5) = 42$

    Maturity value, $S = \$5000\,(1.00625)^{42} = \underline{\underline{\$6495.57}}$

    Interest earned $= S - P = \$6495.57 - \$5000 = \underline{\underline{\$1495.57}}$

24. $i = \dfrac{7.5\%}{2} = 3.75\%$; $n = 2\,(8) = 16$; $S = \$10,000$

    Required investment $= \dfrac{\$10,000}{1.0375^{16}} = \underline{\underline{\$5548.69}}$

25. $i = \dfrac{11\%}{4} = 2.75\%$; $n = 4\,(2\tfrac{1}{4}) = 9$; $S = \$2297.78$

    Principal $= \dfrac{\$2297.78}{1.0275^9} = \underline{\underline{\$1800.00}}$

    Interest $= \$2297.78 - \$1800.00 = \underline{\underline{\$497.78}}$

26.

Principal	i	n	Maturity amount
$3000	2.5%	6	$3000 (1.025)^6 = \$\ 3479.08$
$3500	2.5%	4	$3500 (1.025)^4 = \$\ 3863.35$
$4000	2.5%	2	$4000 (1.025)^2 = \$\ 4202.50$
			Total amount owed = $\underline{\underline{\$11,544.93}}$

27. $P = \$5000$ and $i = \dfrac{8\%}{12} = 0.\overline{6}\%$ in each case.

Grand-child	Age	Time until 19th birthday	n
Donna	12 yr, 7 mo	6 yr, 5 mo	77
Tim	10 yr, 3 mo	8 yr, 9 mo	105
Gary	7 yr, 11 mo	11 yr, 1 mo	133

Donna will receive $\$5000\,(1.00\overline{6})^{77} = \underline{\underline{\$8340.04}}$

Tim will receive $\$5000\,(1.00\overline{6})^{105} = \underline{\underline{\$10,045.40}}$

Gary will receive $\$5000\,(1.00\overline{6})^{133} = \underline{\underline{\$12,099.47}}$

Exercise 8.2 (continued)

28. The data for the three certificates are presented in the following table.

Maturity value	Term	j	m	i	n
$4000	3.5 years	7.75%	2	3.875%	7
$5000	4.5 years	7.75%	2	3.875%	9
$6000	5.5 years	8%	4	2%	22

Michelle should invest:

$$\frac{\$4000}{1.03875^7} = \underline{\underline{\$3065.37}} \text{ in a } 3\frac{1}{2}\text{-year certificate}$$

$$\frac{\$5000}{1.03875^9} = \underline{\underline{\$3551.16}} \text{ in a } 4\frac{1}{2}\text{-year certificate}$$

$$\frac{\$6000}{1.02^{22}} = \underline{\underline{\$3881.03}} \text{ in a } 5\frac{1}{2}\text{-year certificate}$$

29. For the first 2.5 years,

$$i = \frac{13.2\%}{12} = 1.1\%; \; n = 12 \,(2.5) = 30$$

The amount owed after 2.5 years was

$$S = \$5000 \,(1.011)^{30} = \$6942.32$$

For the last two years,

$$i = \frac{10.25\%}{2} = 5.125\%; \; n = 2 \,(2) = 4$$

The total amount required to repay the loan after 4.5 years was

$$S = \$6942.32 \,(1.05125)^4 = \underline{\underline{\$8478.69}}$$

30. For the current GIC,

$$i = \frac{10.5\%}{2} = 5.25\%; \; n = 2 \,(5) = 10$$

Maturity value = $60,000 (1.0525)^{10} = $100,085.76

Maturity value of the second GIC will be:

a. $S = \$100,085.76 \,(1.0525)^{10} = \underline{\underline{\$166,952.66}}$

b. $S = \$100,085.76 \,(1.0575)^{10} = \underline{\underline{\$175,055.62}}$

c. $S = \$100,085.76 \,(1.0475)^{10} = \underline{\underline{\$159,188.84}}$

Exercise 8.2 *(continued)*

31. For the first $1\frac{1}{2}$ years,

$$P = \$2500; \quad i = \frac{7.5\%}{4} = 1.875\%; \quad n = 4\,(1.5) = 6$$

$$S = \$2500\,(1.01875)^6 = \$2794.77$$

For the next two years,

$$P = \$2794.77; \quad i = \frac{6.8\%}{12} = 0.5\overline{6}\%; \quad n = 12\,(2) = 24$$

$$S = \$2794.77\,(1.005\overline{6})^{24} = \$3200.69$$

Total interest earned = $3200.69 − $2500 = <u>$700.69</u>

32. For the first 15 months,

$$P = \$7000; \quad i = \frac{13.5\%}{4} = 3.375\%; \quad n = \frac{15}{3} = 5$$

$$S = \$7000\,(1.03375)^5 = \$8263.72$$

For the next 6 months,

$$P = \$8263.72; \quad i = \frac{12.5\%}{2} = 6.25\%; \quad n = 1$$

Total amount owed = $8263.72 $(1.0625)^1$ = <u>$8780.20</u>

33. For the first $1\frac{1}{2}$ years,

$$P = \$1900; \quad i = \frac{11\%}{2} = 5.5\%; \quad n = 2\,(1.5) = 3$$

Amount owed after $1\frac{1}{2}$ years = $1900 $(1.055)^3$ = $2231.06

Amount owed after $1000 payment = $1231.06

Amount owed today = $1231.06 $(1.055)^4$ = <u>$1525.07</u>

34. Amount owed after $2\frac{1}{2}$ years

$$= P\,(1 + i)^n = \$3000\,(1.025)^5 = \$3394.22$$

Balance owed after payment = $2394.22

Amount owed after another six months

$$= P\,(1 + i)^n = \$2394.22\,(1.025)^1 = \$2454.08$$

Amount owing today (after another two years)

$$= P\,(1 + i)^n = \$2454.08\,(1.0075)^{24} = \underline{\$2936.09}$$

Exercise 8.2 (concluded)

35. Balance after the first payment

$$= P(1+i)^n - \$1000 = \$4000(1.01)^6 - \$1000 = \$3246.08$$

Balance after the second payment

$$= \$3246.08(1.01)^6 - \$1000 = \$2445.78$$

Balance after the third payment

$$= \$2445.78(1.01)^6 - \$1000 = \$1596.24$$

Final payment $= \$1596.24(1.01)^6 = \underline{\underline{\$1694.44}}$

36. Interest $= S - P = P(1+i)^n - P$

$$\$1175.98 = P(1.041)^{17} - P$$

$$= P(1.9799873) - P$$

$$= 0.9799873P$$

Original investment, $P = \dfrac{\$1175.98}{0.9799873} = \underline{\underline{\$1200.00}}$

37. Interest owed $= S - P = P(1+i)^n - P$

$$\$845.56 = P(1.06)^5 - P = 0.3382256P$$

$$P = \underline{\underline{\$2499.99}}$$

Peggy borrowed $2499.99 from her mother.

38. Amount owed after the $2500 payment

$$= P(1+i)^n - \$2500$$

$$= \$10,000(1.009375)^9 - \$2500$$

$$= \$8376.09$$

Amount owed three months later

$$= \$8376.09(1.009375)^3 = \$8613.88$$

Amount owed after the $3000 payment

$$= \$8613.88(1.02875)^2 - \$3000$$

$$= \$6116.30$$

Amount owed six months later

$$= \$6116.30(1.02875)^2$$

$$= \underline{\underline{\$6473.04}}$$

Exercise 8.4

1. Semiannual interest payment $= iP = \dfrac{0.075}{2} \times \$18,000 = \underline{\underline{\$675.00}}$

2. Monthly interest payment $= iP = \dfrac{0.0725}{12} \times \$22,000 = \underline{\underline{\$132.92}}$

Exercise 8.4 (continued)

3. $i = \dfrac{8.25\%}{2} = 4.125\%$; $n = 2(7) = 14$; $P = \$30,000$

    Maturity value, $S = P(1 + i)^n = \$30,000 \ (1.04125)^{14} = \underline{\$52,831.32}$

4. Maturity value $= P(1 + i)^n = \$11,500 \ (1.005625)^{48} = \$15,053.20$

5. Suppose that $1000 is invested for three years at each rate. The maturity value at 7.2% compounded monthly is

    $\$1000 \ (1.006)^{36} = \$1240.30$

    The maturity value at 7.5% compounded semiannually is

    $\$1000 \ (1.0375)^6 = \$1247.18$

    An investor should choose <u>7.5% compounded semiannually</u> since it will produce the larger maturity value.

6. Suppose that $1000 is invested for 6 years at each rate. The maturity value at 10% compounded semi-annually is

    $\$1000 \ (1.05)^{12} = \$1795.86$

    The maturity value at 10.25% compounded annually is

    $\$1000 \ (1.1025)^6 = \$1795.86$

    Since both rates result in the same maturity value, an investor would be <u>indifferent</u> between the two rates.

7. The maturity value at 8.75% compounded annually will be

    $\$10,000 \ (1.0875)^5 = \$15,210.60$

    The maturity value at 8.5% compounded semiannually will be

    $\$10,000 \ (1.0425)^{10} = \$15,162.14$

    The maturity value at 8.25% compounded monthly will be

    $\$10,000 \ (1.006875)^{60} = \$15,084.59$

    An investor will earn

    $\$15,210.60 - \$15,084.59 = \underline{\$126.01}$

    more at 8.75% compounded annually than at 8.25% compounded monthly.

8. Value of $10,000 face value compound interest BC Savings Bond 3 years after its date of issue will be

    $$\begin{aligned} S &= P(1 + i_1)(1 + i_2)(1 + i_3) \\ &= \$10,000(1.0675)(1.06)(1.06) \\ &= \$11,994.43 \end{aligned}$$

    Value of $10,000 face value compound interest Canada Savings Bond 3 years after its date of issue will be

    $$\begin{aligned} S &= \$10,000(1.0525)(1.06)(1.0675) \\ &= \$11,909.56 \end{aligned}$$

    The BC Bond will earn $\underline{\$84.87}$ more.

Exercise 8.4 *(continued)*

9. The value of the BC Bond after two years will be

$$S = \$10,000(1.0675)(1.06) = \$11,315.50$$

Interest earned in year 3 = 0.06($11,315.50) = $678.93.

The value of the CSB after two years will be $11,156.50.
Interest in year 3 = 0.0675($11,156.50) = $753.06.

10. The amount that would have to be invested is

$$P = \frac{S}{(1 + i_1)(1 + i_2)(1 + i_3)}$$

$$= \frac{\$15,000}{(1.0525)(1.06)(1.0675)} = \$12,594.92 \text{ in CSBs}$$

$$= \frac{\$15,000}{(1.0675)(1.06)(1.06)} = \$12,505.80 \text{ in BC Savings Bonds}$$

11. Series CS42 Bonds were issued on November 1, 1987.

   a. Value of a $5000 CS42 bond on November 1, 1991 was

$$S = P(1 + i_1)(1 + i_2)(1 + i_3)(1 + i_4)$$
$$= \$5000(1.09)(1.10\overline{16})(1.109\overline{16})(1.1075) \quad \text{(from Table 8.3)}$$
$$= \$7375.43$$

   b. The bondholder received all accrued interest up to August 1, 1992. To the amount in part a, we need to add 9 months' interest at 7.5% pa.

$$S = P(1 + rt) = \$7375.43 \left(1 + 0.075 \times \frac{9}{12}\right) = \$7790.30$$

   The owner received $7790.30 when she redeemed a $5000 denomination CS42 bond on August 21, 1992.

12. Series CS44 CSBs were issued on November 1, 1989.

   a. The owner received interest for the first 6 full years. The redemption amount was

$$S = P(1 + i_1)...(1 + i_6)$$
$$= \$10,000(1.109\overline{16})(1.1075)(1.075)(1.06)(1.05125)(1.06375)$$
$$= \$15,653.10$$

   b. The bondholder received all accrued interest up to May 1, 1996. To the amount in part a, we need to add 6 months interest at 6.75% pa. The full redemption amount was

$$S = P(1 + rt) = \$15,653.10 \left(1 + 0.0675 \times \frac{6}{12}\right) = \$16,181.39$$

13. The bondholder received interest from the date of issue (November 1, 1988) to March 1, 1996. This period was 7 years, 4 months long. The redemption value was

$$S = P(1 + i_1)...(1 + i_7)(1 + rt)$$
$$= \$300(1.10\overline{16})(1.109\overline{16})(1.1075)(1.075)(1.06)(1.05125)(1.06375)\left(1 + 0.0675 \times \frac{4}{12}\right)$$
$$= \$528.98$$

14. The bondholder received interest from the issue date (November 1, 1990) to June 1, 1997. This period was 6 years, 7 months long. The redemption value was

$$S = P(1 + i_1)...(1 + i_6)(1 + rt)$$

$$= \$500(1.1075)(1.075)(1.06)(1.05125)(1.06375)(1.0675)\left(1 + 0.075 \times \frac{7}{12}\right)$$

$$= \underline{\$786.21}$$

Problem	Value at the end of year 3[1]	Interest earned in year 4[2]	Maturity value at end of year 5[3]
15.	$2484.59	$186.34	$ 2871.26
16.	$6082.38	$410.56	$ 6931.22
17.	$3709.48	$296.76	$ 4326.73
18.	$5551.42	$471.87	$ 6535.28
19.	$9799.49	$881.95	$11,749.59
20.	$3062.54	$245.00	$ 3588.69
21.	$7848.22	$627.86	$ 9154.17
22.	$9381.93	$867.83	$11,274.73

[1]Value at end of year 3 $= P(1 + i_1)(1 + i_2)(1 + i_3)$
[2]Interest earned in year 4 $= i_4$ (Value at end of year 3)
$$= ① \times i_4$$
[3]Maturity value $=$ (Value at end of year 3)$(1 + i_4)(1 + i_5)$
$$= ①(1 + i_4)(1 + i_5)$$

23. Maturity value of the compound-interest RateRiser GIC
$$= P(1 + i_1)...(1 + i_5)$$
$$= \$5000(1.055)(1.06125)(1.0675)(1.07375)(1.08)$$
$$= \$6930.03$$
Interest earned on RateRiser GIC $= \$6930.03 - \$5000 = \underline{\$1930.03}$

Maturity value of fixed-rate compound-interest GIC
$$= P(1 + i)^5 = \$5000(1.0675)^5 = \$6931.22$$
Interest earned on fixed-rate GIC $= \underline{\$1931.22}$

24. Maturity value of $10,000 invested in the RateRiser GIC
$$= \$10,000(1.06)(1.07)(1.08)(1.09)(1.10)(1.11)(1.12)$$
$$= \$18,258.86$$

Maturity value of $10,000 invested in the fixed-rate GIC
$$= \$10,000(1.08)^7$$
$$= \$17,138.24$$

The <u>RateRiser</u> GIC will be <u>worth</u>
$$\$18,258.86 - \$17,138.24 = \underline{\$1120.62} \text{ more at maturity.}$$

Exercise 8.4 *(continued)*

25.   Interest earned in year 4 = i_4(Value at end of year 3)
    $$= i_4\,P(1 + i_1)(1 + i_2)(1 + i_3)$$

    Year 4 interest on $\underline{\text{RateRiser}}$ = 0.09($10,000)(1.06)(1.07)(1.08)
    $$= \underline{\$1102.44}$$

    Year 4 interest on fixed-rate GIC = 0.08($10,000)$(1.08)^3$
    $$= \underline{\$1007.77}$$

26. Initial investment, $P = \dfrac{S}{(1 + i_1)...(1 + i_7)}$

    For the $\underline{\text{RateRiser GIC}}$,

    $$P = \frac{\$20,000}{(1.06)(1.07)(1.08)(1.09)(1.10)(1.11)(1.12)} = \underline{\$10,953.59}$$

    For the $\underline{\text{fixed-rate GIC}}$,
    $$P = \$20,000(1.08)^{-7} = \underline{\$11,669.81}$$

27. Goods costing $100 today will cost
    $$S = P(1 + i)^n = \$100(1 + i)^{20}$$
    twenty years from now if the annual rate of inflation is i.

    a. If i = 0.03, S = $100(1.03)^{20}$ = $\underline{\$180.61}$

    b. If i = 0.05, S = $100(1.05)^{20}$ = $\underline{\$265.33}$

    c. If i = 0.07, S = $100(1.07)^{20}$ = $\underline{\$386.97}$

28. A "basket" of goods costing $1000 today would have cost
    $$P = S(1 + i)^{-n} = \$1000(1 + i)^{-15}$$
    fifteen years ago if the annual rate of inflation was i.

    a. If i = 0.02, S = $1000(1.02)^{-15}$ = $\underline{\$743.01}$

    b. If i = 0.04, S = $1000(1.04)^{-15}$ = $\underline{\$555.26}$

    c. If i = 0.06, S = $1000(1.06)^{-15}$ = $\underline{\$417.27}$

29. To keep pace with inflation, the hourly rate should also grow at i = 3.5% per year. Ten years from now, the hourly rate would then be
    $$S = P(1 + i)^n = \$15(1.035)^{10} = \underline{\$21.16/\text{hour}}$$

30. Today's population of 120,000 follows five years of 3% annual growth. Therefore, the population five years ago was
    $$P = S(1 + i)^{-n} = 120,000(1.03)^{-5} = \underline{103,513}$$

31. The retirement income goal is the nominal amount of $35,000 after 15 years' growth at the projected annual rate of inflation.

    a. $S = P(1 + i)^n = \$35,000(1.03)^{15} = \underline{\$54,529}$

    b. $S = \$35,000(1.045)^{15} = \underline{\$67,735}$

    c. $S = \$35,000(1.06)^{15} = \underline{\$83,880}$

Exercise 8.4 (concluded)

32. The 1997 employment of 80,000 follows 10 years of 3% annual decline. That is,
$$80,000 = P[1 + (-0.03)]^{10}$$
$$= P(0.97)^{10}$$
$$= 0.7374241P$$
$$P = \underline{108,486}$$

108,486 were employed in the forest industry in 1987.

33. Sales for year 3 = $28,600,000 [1 + (-0.04)]^3 = $25,303,450

Sales for year 7 = $25,303,450 (1.08)^4 = $\underline{34,425,064}$

34. Let the rural population in 1989 be represented by P. Then the expected population 10 years later is
$$S = P (1 + i)^n = P [1 + (-0.02)]^{10} = P (0.98^{10}) = 0.8171 \ P$$

That is, the population is expected to decline from P to 81.71% of P. This represents an $\underline{18.29\%}$ loss of rural population.

Exercise 8.5

1. Equivalent value, $S = P (1 + i)^n = \$5000 (1.0825)^4 = \underline{\$6865.65}$

2. $i = \dfrac{9.9\%}{2} = 4.95\%$; $n = 2 (6.5) = 13$

   Equivalent value, $P = S(1 + i)^{-n} = \$7000(1.0495)^{-13} = \underline{\$3735.31}$

3. $i = \dfrac{10.5\%}{4} = 2.625\%$; $n = 4 (2.75) = 11$

   Equivalent value, $P = \$1300(1.02625)^{-11} = \underline{\$977.59}$

4. $i = \dfrac{7.5\%}{12} = 0.625\%$; $n = 12 (3) - 5 = 31$

   Equivalent value, $S = \$3000 (1.00625)^{31} = \underline{\$3639.18}$

5. Equivalent value today of the $1400 payment is
$$\$1400 (1.03)^{12} = \$1996.07$$
   Equivalent value today of the $1800 payment is
$$\$1800(1.03)^{-8} = \$1420.94$$
   Combined equivalent value = $1996.07 + $1420.94 = $\underline{\$3417.01}$

6. Sum of the equivalent values of the payments, three months from now
$$= \$900 (1.008\overline{3})^{18} + \$500(1.008\overline{3})^{-4}$$
$$= \$1045.00 + \$483.67$$
$$= \underline{\$1528.67}$$

7. Sum of the equivalent values of the payments, one year from now
$$= \$1000(1.03875)^{-5} + \$2000(1.03875)^{-9}$$
$$= \$826.88 + \$1420.47$$
$$= \underline{\$2247.35}$$

Exercise 8.5 *(continued)*

8. Sum of the equivalent values of the payments, 2.25 years from now

$$= \$1500 \, (1.0225)^{12} + \$2500(1.0225)^{-9}$$

$$= \$1959.07 + \$2046.30$$

$$= \underline{\$4005.37}$$

9. Sum of the equivalent values of the payments, 6 months from now

$$= \$2100 \, (1.00875)^{24} + \$1300 \, (1.00875)^{6} + \$800(1.00875)^{-18}$$
$$= \$2588.36 + \$1369.76 + \$683.89$$

$$= \underline{\$4642.01}$$

10. Sum of the equivalent values of the payments, 18 months from now

$$= \$750 \, (1.0475)^{3} + \$1000(1.0475)^{-1} + \$1250(1.0475)^{-5}$$

$$= \$862.03 + \$954.65 + \$991.15$$

$$= \underline{\$2807.83}$$

11. The scheduled payments are

$$\$1000 \, (1.0425)^{7} = \$1338.24$$

due in $3\frac{1}{2}$ years and

$$\$2000 \, (1.0425)^{11} = \$3161.31$$

due in $5\frac{1}{2}$ years. The sum of their equivalent values one year from now is

$$\frac{\$1338.24}{1.038755^{5}} + \frac{\$3161.31}{1.038759^{9}} = \$1106.57 + \$2245.26 = \underline{\$3351.83}$$

12. The scheduled payments are

$$\$1500 \, (1.00625)^{15} = \$1646.95$$

due 9 months ago and

$$\$2500 \, (1.00625)^{78} = \$4064.43$$

due in $4\frac{1}{2}$ years. The sum of their equivalent values $2\frac{1}{4}$ years from now is

$$\$1646.95 \, (1.0225)^{12} + \frac{\$4064.43}{1.0225^{9}} = \$2151.00 + \$3326.82 = \underline{\$5477.82}$$

Exercise 8.5 *(continued)*

13. The scheduled payments are

$$\$2100\ (1.0075)^9 = \$2246.08$$

due $1\frac{1}{2}$ years ago,

$$\$1300\ (1.0075)^{27} = \$1590.60$$

due today, and

$$\$800\ (1.0075)^{51} = \$1171.08$$

due in 2 years. The sum of the equivalent values 6 months from now is

$$\$2246.08\ (1.00875)^{24} + \$1590.60\ (1.00875)^6 + \$1171.08(1.00875)^{-18}$$

$$= \$2768.41 + \$1675.95 + \$1001.11$$

$$= \underline{\underline{\$5445.47}}$$

14. The scheduled payments are

$$\$750\ (1.025)^5 = \$848.56$$

due today,

$$\$1000\ (1.025)^{13} = \$1378.51$$

due in 2 years, and

$$\$1250\ (1.025)^{21} = \$2099.48$$

due in four years. The sum of the equivalent values 18 months from now is

$$\$848.56\ (1.0475)^3 + \$1378.51(1.0475)^{-1} + \$2099.48(1.0475)^{-5}$$

$$= \$975.31 + \$1316.00 + \$1664.72$$

$$= \underline{\underline{\$3956.03}}$$

15. Equivalent amount $= \$2000\ (1.0525)^8 = \underline{\underline{\$3011.67}}$

16. Equivalent amount today $= \$3500(1.0225)^{-14} = \underline{\underline{\$2563.19}}$

17. Equivalent amount $= \$2600(1.0075)^{-33} = \underline{\underline{\$2031.83}}$

18. Equivalent amount $= \$2300\ (1.04625)^7 = \underline{\underline{\$3156.28}}$

19. Equivalent payment 6 months from now

$$= \text{Sum of the equivalent values}$$

$$= \$500\ (1.00625)^{10} + \$800(1.00625)^{-6}$$

$$= \$532.14 + \$770.65$$

$$= \underline{\underline{\$1302.79}}$$

20. Equivalent payment one year from now

$$= \$2500\ (1.0175)^3 + \$2500(1.0175)^{-4}$$

$$= \$2633.56 + \$2332.40$$

$$= \underline{\underline{\$4965.96}}$$

21. Current amount to pay taxes = $2250 − $77 = $2173. If invested at 6% compounded monthly for 9 months, the maturity value will be

    $$\$2173\,(1.005)^9 = \$2272.76$$

    Gordon will be

    $$\$2272.76 - \$2250 = \underline{\$22.76}$$

    better off 9 months from now by investing the funds now and paying the taxes 9 months from now. In terms of today's dollars, there is a

    $$\$22.76(1.005)^{-9} = \underline{\$21.76}$$

    advantage to deferring payment and investing the funds.

22. Today's economic value of the Jorgensen offer is

    $$\$10,000 + \$51,000(1.0325)^{-2} = \$57,839.88$$

    Therefore, Gwen should accept the Araki offer because it is worth $160.12 more.

23. The current economic value of the two $12,000 payments is

    $$\$12,000 + \$12,000(1.05)^{-10} = \$19,366.96$$

    The winner should choose the $20,000 payment option. It is worth $633.04 more.

24. The equivalent value, on the date of the fourth-to-last payment, of the three remaining payments is the sum of their present values.

    $$\text{Payout amount} = \$2000(1.0425)^{-2} + \$2000(1.0425)^{-4} + \$2000(1.0425)^{-6}$$
    $$= \$1840.25 + \$1693.27 + \$1558.02$$
    $$= \underline{\$5091.54}$$

25. Current economic value of the March selling price is

    $$\$9300(1.0165)^{-2} = \$9000.53$$

    Deducting the insurance and storage charges, the current net economic value of the March sale alternative is $8500.53. The difference between the alternatives is a negligible $0.53. Ingrid should be indifferent between them.

26. Total price = Sum of the present values

    $$= \$950(1.01375)^{-4} + \$780(1.01375)^{-6} + \$1270(1.01375)^{-5}$$
    $$= \$899.50 + \$718.64 + \$1186.18$$
    $$= \underline{\$2804.32}$$

27. The creditor should accept the economic value, $2\frac{1}{4}$ years from now, of the three scheduled payments. Allowing for a time value of money of 10.5% compounded quarterly, the economic value is

    $$\$2700\,(1.02625)^5 + \$1900\,(1.02625)^3 + \$1100(1.02625)^{-3}$$
    $$= \$3073.47 + \$2053.59 + \$1017.73$$
    $$= \underline{\$6144.79}$$

Exercise 8.5 (continued)

28. The scheduled payments are

$$\$950 \ (1.01)^4 = \$988.57$$

due in four months,

$$\$780 \ (1.01)^6 = \$827.99$$

due in six months, and

$$\$1270 \ (1.01)^5 = \$1334.78$$

due in five months. The total price to be paid for these scheduled payments is the sum of their present values.

$$\text{Total price} = \frac{\$988.57}{1.01375^4} + \frac{\$827.99}{1.01375^6} + \frac{\$1334.78}{1.01375^5} = \underline{\underline{\$2945.55}}$$

29. The scheduled payments are

$$\$2700 \ (1.01)^{21} = \$3327.46$$

due in one year,

$$\$1900 \ (1.01)^{27} = \$2485.60$$

due in $1\frac{1}{2}$ years, and

$$\$1100 \ (1.01)^{45} = \$1721.29$$

due in 3 years. The creditor should accept the sum of the economic values, on the settlement date, of the scheduled payments. Allowing for a time value of money of 10.5% compounded quarterly, this sum is

$$\$3327.46 \ (1.02625)^5 + \$2485.60 \ (1.02625)^3 + \$1721.29(1.02625)^{-3}$$

$$= \$3787.73 + \$2686.52 + \$1592.56$$

$$= \underline{\underline{\$8066.80}}$$

30. Price = Present value of the face value discounted at the market rate of return
    $= S(1 + i)^{-n}$
    $= \$1000(1.0475)^{-44}$
    $= \underline{\underline{\$129.78}}$

31. Price = Present value of the $5000 face value discounted at the buyer's required yield of 8.25% compounded semiannually
    $= S(1 + i)^{-n}$
    $= \$5000(1.04125)^{-39}$
    $= \underline{\underline{\$1033.53}}$

32. Market price of one bond residue $= \$1000(1.05375)^{-30} = \$207.91$

    The number of bond residues that may be purchased with $10,000 is the integer portion of

    $$\frac{\$10,000}{\$207.91} = 48.1$$

    That is, $\underline{\underline{48}}$ bond residues can be purchased.

Exercise 8.5 (continued)

33. Market price of one bond residue = $1000(1.05125)^{-26}$ = $272.67

    The number of bond residues that may be purchased with $12,830 is the integer portion of

    $$\frac{\$12,830}{\$272.67} = 47.05$$

    That is, 47 bond residues can be purchased.

34. Proceeds = Present value of the maturity value

    $$i = \frac{11.5\%}{4} = 2.875\%, \; S = \$6800, \text{ and } n = 3.5(4) = 14$$

    Proceeds = $S(1 + i)^{-n}$ = $6800(1.02875)^{-14}$ = $4572.68

35. $S = \$4900$, $i = 13\%/12 = 1.08\overline{3}\%$, and $n = 2(12) = 24$
    Proceeds = $S(1 + i)^{-n}$ = $4900(1.0108\overline{3})^{-24}$ = $3783.44

36. Proceeds = Present value of the maturity value
    For the maturity value calculation,
    $P = \$8000$, $i = 13.5\%/12 = 1.125\%$, and $n = 4(12) = 48$
    Maturity value = $P(1 + i)^n$ = $8000(1.01125)^{48}$ = $13,686.73

    For the present value (discounting) calculation,
    $S = \$13,686.73$, $i = 12\%/4 = 3\%$, and $n = 21/3 = 7$
    Proceeds = $S(1 + i)^{-n}$ = $13,686.73(1.03)^{-7}$ = $10,489.74

37. Price = Present value of the maturity value
    For the maturity value calculation,
    $P = \$3800$, $i = 11\%/2 = 5.5\%$, and $n = 8(2) = 16$
    Maturity value = $P(1 + i)^n$ = $3800(1.055)^{16}$ = $8950.00

    For the present value calculation,

    $$S = \$8950, \; i = 14\%/4 = 3.5\%, \text{ and } n = \left(8 - 3\frac{1}{4}\right)(4) = 19$$

    Price = $S(1 + i)^{-n}$ = $8950(1.035)^{-19}$ = $4655.39

38. For the first payment, $P = \$2000$, $i = 2.25\%$, and $n = 2(4) = 8$.
    For the second payment, $P = \$1500$, $i = 2.25\%$, and $n = 3(4) = 12$.

    The scheduled payments are
    $S = P(1 + i)^n$ = $2000(1.0225)^8$ = $2389.66 due in 2 years and
    $S = \$1500(1.0225)^{12}$ = $1959.07 due in 3 years.

    The appropriate price to pay is the present value, on the date of purchase, of the scheduled payments. The discount rate should be the yield required by the buyer. That is, $i = 10\%/2 = 5\%$. The first payment is 1.5 years ($n = 3$) and the second payment 2.5 years ($n = 5$) after the purchase date. Thus,

    Price = $2389.66(1.05)^{-3}$ + $1959.07(1.05)^{-5}$
    = $2064.28 + $1534.98
    = $3599.26

Exercise 8.5 (continued)

39. The scheduled payments are

$$\$2500(1.1)^3 = \$3327.50 \text{ and}$$
$$\$2500(1.1)^5 = \$4026.28$$

due 3 and 5 years respectively, after the issue date. The proceeds of the sale of the note will be the sum of the present values, on the date of sale, of the scheduled payments. That is,

$$\text{Proceeds} = \$3327.50(1.0075)^{-16} + \$4026.28(1.0075)^{-40}$$
$$= \$2952.55 + \$2986.08$$
$$= \underline{\$5938.63}$$

40. Let x represent the final loan payment.

$$\text{Loan} = \text{Present value of all payments}$$
$$\$15,000 = \$4000(1.0575)^{-2} + \$4000(1.0575)^{-6} + x(1.0575)^{-10}$$
$$\$15,000 = \$3576.84 + \$2860.08 + 0.57173692x$$
$$x = \underline{\$14,977.31}$$

The third loan payment will be $14,977.31.

41. Let x represent the size of the loan payments.

$$\$4000 = \text{Present value of the payments}$$
$$= x(1.08\overline{3})^{-5} + x(1.08\overline{3})^{-10} + x(1.08\overline{3})^{-15}$$
$$= 0.9593551x + 0.9203622x + 0.8829541x$$
$$x = \underline{\$1447.87}$$

Each of the loan payments is $1447.87.

42. Let x represent the size of each loan payment.

$$\$10,000 = x(1.04)^{-5} + x(1.04)^{-8} + x(1.04)^{-14}$$
$$= 0.82192711x + 0.73069021x + 0.57747508x$$
$$= 2.1300924x$$
$$x = \underline{\$4694.63}$$

The amount of each loan payment is $4694.63.

43. Let x represent the size of the first payment.

$$\$6000 = \text{Present value of both payments}$$
$$= x(1.0225)^{-3} + 0.5x(1.0225)^{-6}$$
$$= 0.9354273x + 0.4375121x$$
$$= 1.3729394x$$
$$x = \$4370.186$$

The first payment is $\underline{\$4370.19}$ and the second payment is $\underline{\$2185.09}$.

44. Let x represent the size of the first payment.

$$\$7500 = \text{Present value of all three payments}$$
$$= x(1.0075)^{-5} + 2x(1.0075)^{-10} + 4x(1.0075)^{-15}$$
$$= 0.9633292x + 1.8560063x + 3.5758902x$$
$$= 6.3952257x$$
$$x = \$1172.75$$

The second payment is 2x = $\underline{\$2345.50}$

Exercise 8.5 *(concluded)*

45. Let x represent the size of each of the first three payments. Then

$$\$9000 = \frac{x}{1.025^8} + \frac{x}{1.025^{16}} + \frac{x}{1.025^{24}} + \frac{\$5169.81}{1.025^{24}}$$

$$= 0.8207466x + 0.6736249x + 0.5528754x + \$2858.26$$

$$= 2.0472469x + \$2858.26$$

$$x = \underline{\$3000.00}$$

Each of the first three payments was $3000.00.

Exercise 8.6

1. Let x represent the replacement payment due in 9 months. The equivalent value of the scheduled payments at a focal date 9 months from today is

   $$\$3000 \, (1.015)^8 + \$2000 \, (1.015)^3 = \$3379.48 + \$2091.36 = \$5470.84$$

   The equivalent value of the replacement payments on the same date is

   $$\$1500 \, (1.015)^3 + x = \$1568.52 + x$$

   The equation of value is

   $$\$1568.52 + x = \$5470.84$$

   $$x = \underline{\underline{\$3902.32}}$$

   The second payment due in 9 months is $3902.32.

2. Let x represent the replacement payment due in two months. The equivalent value of the scheduled payments at a focal date two months from now is

   $$\$1750(1.0075)^9 + \frac{\$2000}{1.0075^9} = \$1871.73 + \$2711.39 = \$4583.12$$

   The equivalent value of the replacement payments on the same date is

   $$x + \$3000(1.0075)^{-10} = x + \$2784.01$$

   The equation of value is

   $$x + \$2784.01 = \$4583.12$$

   $$x = \underline{\underline{\$1799.11}}$$

   The replacement payment due in two months is $1799.11.

3. Let x represent the amount of each replacement payment. At a focal date 9 months from now, the equation of value is

   $$\$1400 \, (1.065)^1 + \$2300(1.065)^{-2} = x + x(1.065)^{-3}$$

   $$\$1491.00 + \$2027.82 = x + 0.8278491x$$

   $$x = \underline{\underline{\$1925.11}}$$

   Each replacement payment should be $1925.11.

Exercise 8.6 *(continued)*

4. Let x represent the size of each replacement payment. With the focal date coinciding with the first replacement payment (three months from now), the equation of value is

    $$\$850(1.0275)^9 + \$1760(1.0275)^3 = x + x(1.0275)^{-2}$$
    $$\$1085.06 + \$1909.23 = x + 0.9471883x$$
    $$\$2994.29 = 1.9471883x$$
    $$x = \underline{\$1537.75}$$

    Each replacement payment should be $1537.75.

5. Let x represent the size of the first replacement payment. At a focal date two months from now, the equation of value is

    $$\$400 \ (1.00875)^{10} + \$650 \ (1.00875)^5 = x + 2x(1.00875)^{-5}$$
    $$\$436.41 + \$678.94 = x + 1.9147508x$$
    $$x = \$382.66$$

    The replacement payments are $\underline{\$382.66}$ in two months and $\underline{\$765.32}$ in seven months.

6. Let x represent the size of the first replacement payment. At a focal date one year from now, the equation of value is

    $$\$2000(1.0625)^1 + \$2000(1.0625)^{-2} = x + 0.5x(1.0625)^{-4}$$
    $$\$2125.00 + \$1771.63 = x + 0.39233247x$$
    $$x = \$2798.63$$

    The replacement payments are $\underline{\$2798.63}$ due in one year and $\underline{\$1399.32}$ due in three years.

7. Let x represent the size of each replacement payment. With today as the focal date, the equation of value is

    $$\$4000 = x + x(1.006)^{-12} + x(1.006)^{-9}$$
    $$= x + 0.9763557x + 0.9475850x$$
    $$x = \underline{\$1539.02}$$

    Each replacement payment should be $1539.02.

8. Let x represent the size of each replacement payment. At a focal date one year from now, the equation of value is

    $$\$5000 \ (1.1075)^1 + \frac{\$10,000}{1.1075^4} = x + \frac{x}{1.1075^2} + \frac{x}{1.1075^4}$$
    $$\$5537.50 + \$6646.99 = x + 0.81529078x + 0.6646991x$$
    $$x = \underline{\$4913.12}$$

    Each replacement payment should be $4913.12.

Exercise 8.6 *(continued)*

9. The scheduled payments are

    $$\$1400\ (1.02625)^1 = \$1436.75$$

    due in three months and

    $$\$2300\ (1.02625)^7 = \$2757.40$$

    due in 21 months.

    Let x represent the amount of each replacement payment. At a focal date 9 months from now, the equation of value is

    $$\$1436.75\ (1.065)^1 + \$2757.40(1.065)^{-2} = x + x(1.065)^{-3}$$

    $$\$1530.14 + \$2431.09 = x + 0.8278491x$$

    $$x = \underline{\$2167.15}$$

    Each replacement payment should be $2167.15.

10. The scheduled payments are

    $$\$2000\ (1.0075)^6 = \$2091.70$$

    due in six months and

    $$\$2000\ (1.0075)^{24} = \$2392.83$$

    due in two years.

    Let x represent the first replacement payment. At a focal date one year from now, the equation of value is

    $$\$2091.70\ (1.0625)^1 + \$2392.83(1.0625)^{-2} = x + 0.5x(1.0625)^{-4}$$

    $$\$2222.44 + \$2119.60 = x + 0.39233247x$$

    $$x = \$3118.53$$

    The replacement payments are $\underline{\$3118.53}$ due in one year and $\underline{\$1559.27}$ due in three years.

11. The scheduled payments are

    $$\$5000\ (1.06)^4 = \$6312.38$$

    due today and

    $$\$10,000\ (1.06)^{14} = \$22,609.04$$

    due in 5 years.

    Let x represent the size of each replacement payment. At a focal date one year from now, the equation of value is

    $$\$6312.38\ (1.1075) + \frac{\$22,609.04}{1.1075^4} = x + \frac{x}{1.1075^2} + \frac{x}{1.1075^4}$$

    $$\$6990.97 + \$15,028.21 = x + 0.81529078x + 0.66469905x$$

    $$x = \underline{\$8878.74}$$

    Each replacement payment should be $8878.74.

12. The scheduled payments are

$$\$1750 \ (1.00875)^8 = \$1876.32$$

due seven months ago and

$$\$2900 \ (1.00875)^{26} = \$3637.23$$

due 11 months from now.

Let x represent the size of the first replacement payment. At a focal date two months from now, the equation of value is

$$\$1876.32 \ (1.0075)^9 + \$3637.23(1.0075)^{-9} = x + \$3000(1.0075)^{-10}$$

$$\$2006.84 + \$3400.67 = x + \$2784.01$$

$$x = \underline{\$2623.50}$$

The replacement payment due in 2 months is $2623.50.

13. In order to compare the two offers, the payments in both streams must first be taken to a common focal date. In order to evaluate and compare the two offers in current dollars, today should be chosen as the focal date.

The current economic value of Mrs. A's offer is

$$\$20,000 + \$40,000(1.02375)^{-4} = \$56,415.34$$

The current economic value of Mr. B's offer is

$$\$15,000 + \$25,000(1.02375)^{-4} + \$25,000(1.02375)^{-8} = \$58,479.53$$

<u>Mr. B's offer</u> should be accepted since its <u>current economic value is $2064 greater</u>.

14. Furniture City should be willing to accept a cash price from a customer that equals the down payment plus the discounted balance from the finance company.

$$\text{Cash price} = 0.25(\$1595) + 0.75(\$1595)(1.15)^{-6} = \underline{\$1492.77}$$

15. The cash price should be compared to the present value of the instalment payment alternative. The appropriate discount rate is the rate of return Henri can earn on invested funds.

    a. Present value $= \$5000 + \$8000(1.035)^{-2} + \$8000(1.035)^{-4} + \$8000(1.035)^{-6}$

$$= \$5000 + \$7468.09 + \$6971.54 + \$6508.01$$

$$= \$25,947.64$$

There is a <u>$947.64 advantage</u> to choosing the <u>cash price</u>.

    b. Present value $= \$5000 + \$8000(1.055)^{-2} + \$8000(1.055)^{-4} + \$8000(1.055)^{-6}$

$$= \$5000 + \$7187.62 + \$6457.73 + \$5801.97$$

$$= \$24,447.32$$

There is a $25,000 − $24,447.32 = <u>$552.68 advantage to the 3-year instalment purchase</u>.

Exercise 8.6 *(continued)*

16. The winner should choose the alternative having the larger current economic value.

    a. Economic value of (1) = $10,000 + $10,000(1.07)$^{-5}$ = $17,129.86

      The economic value of alternative (2) is

      $7000 + $7000(1.07)$^{-5}$ + $7000(1.07)$^{-10}$ + $7000(1.07)$^{-15}$ = $18,086.47

      Alternative (2) should be chosen since it is worth $956.61 more.

    b. Economic value of (1) = $10,000 + $10,000(1.11)$^{-5}$ = $15,934.51

      The economic value of alternative (2) is

      $7000 + $7000(1.11)$^{-5}$ + $7000(1.11)$^{-10}$ + $7000(1.11)$^{-15}$ = $15,082.48

      Alternative (1) should be chosen since it is worth $852.03 more.

17. Let x represent the amount of the second payment. At a focal date five months from now, the equation of value is

    $$\$19{,}000\ (1.015)^9 + \$14{,}000\ (1.015)^3 = \$10{,}000\ (1.015)^5 + x$$
    $$\$21{,}724.41 + \$14{,}639.50 = \$10{,}772.84 + x$$
    $$x = \underline{\$25{,}591.07}$$

    The second payment will be $25,591.07

18. Let x represent the amount of the second replacement payment due 4 years from today. At a focal date four years from today, the equation of value is

    $$\$5000\ (1.0375)^2 + \$7000(1.0375)^{-2} = 0.5x\ (1.0375)^5 + x$$
    $$\$5382.03 + \$6503.12 = 0.6010499x + x$$
    $$x = \$7423.35$$

    The replacement payments are $\underline{\$3711.68}$ due in $1\frac{1}{2}$ years and $\underline{\$7423.35}$ due in four years.

19. Let x represent the size of each replacement payment. At a focal date five years from now, the equation of value is

    $$\$3000\ (1.00625)^{60} + \$3000 = x\ (1.00625)^{48} + x\ (1.00625)^{24} + x$$
    $$\$4359.88 + \$3000 = 1.3485992x + 1.1612920x + x$$
    $$x = \underline{\$2096.90}$$

    Each replacement payment should be $2096.90.

20. Let x represent the size of the second replacement payment. At a focal date 9 months from today, the equation of value is

    $$\$8000\ (1.0275)^8 + \$6000\ (1.0275) = \$4000\ (1.0275)^3 + x + 3x(1.0275)^{-3}$$
    $$\$9939.04 + \$6165.00 = \$4339.16 + x + 2.7655134x$$
    $$x = \$3124.38$$

    The last two replacement payments are $\underline{\$3124.38}$ due in 9 months and $\underline{\$9373.14}$ due in $1\frac{1}{2}$ years.

21. a. Maturity value of loan = $15,000 (1.035)^{18} = $27,862.34

    Let x represent the value of the second replacement payment. At a focal date one year from now, the equation of value is

    $$\$27,862.34(1.05)^{-2} = \$5000(1.05)^2 + x$$
    $$\$25,271.96 = \$5512.50 + x$$
    $$x = \underline{\$19,759.46}$$

    The second payment should be $19,759.46.

    b. The combined future value, two years from now, of the two replacement payments is

    $$\$5000 \ (1.05)^4 + \$19,759.46 \ (1.05)^2 = \$6077.53 + \$21,784.81$$
    $$= \$27,862.34$$

    This is the same amount as the maturity value on this date of the original loan. Therefore, the lender ends up in the same financial position under either alternative.

22. The scheduled payments to Andrea are

    $$\$2000 \ (1.065)^8 = \$3309.99$$

    in one year and

    $$\$1000 \ (1.055)^7 = \$1454.68$$

    in two years.

    Let x represent the size of each replacement payment. At a focal date one year from now, the equation of value is

    $$\$3309.99 + \$1454.68(1.025)^{-4} = x + x(1.025)^{-8}$$
    $$\$3309.99 + \$1317.87 = x + 0.82074657x$$
    $$x = \underline{\$2541.74}$$

    The two replacement payments should each be $2541.74.

23. The scheduled payments are

    $$\$5000 \ (1.008)^{36} = \$6661.15$$

    due in three years and

    $$\$7000 \ (1.008)^{60} = \$11,290.94$$

    due in five years.

    Let x represent the size of the second replacement payment. At a focal date $1\frac{1}{2}$ years from today, the equation of value is

    $$\$6661.15(1.0375)^{-3} + \$11,290.94(1.0375)^{-7} = 0.5x + x(1.0375)^{-5}$$
    $$\$5964.65 + \$8725.96 = 0.5x + 0.83187768x$$
    $$x = \$11,030.00$$

    The payments should be $\underline{\$5515.00}$ in $1\frac{1}{2}$ years and $\underline{\$11,030.00}$ in 4 years.

Exercise 8.6 (concluded)

24. The scheduled payments are

$$\$3000 \ (1.06)^5 = \$4014.68$$

due today and

$$\$3000 \ (1.06)^{15} = \$7189.67$$

due in five years.

Let x represent the size of each of the replacement payments. At a focal date one year from today, the equation of value is

$$\$4014.68 \ (1.00625)^{12} + \frac{\$7189.67}{1.00625^{60}} = x + \frac{x}{1.00625^{24}} + \frac{x}{1.00625^{48}}$$

$$\$4326.35 + \$4947.16 = x + 0.86110985x + 0.7415102x$$

$$x = \underline{\$3563.14}$$

Each of the replacement payments is $3563.14.

25. The scheduled payments are

$$\$8000 \ (1.00625)^{12} = \$8621.06$$

due 15 months ago and

$$\$6000 \ (1.00625)^{33} = \$7369.63$$

due 6 months from now.

Let x represent the amount of the second replacement payment due in 9 months. At a focal date 9 months from today, the equation of value is

$$\$8621.06 \ (1.0275)^8 + \$7369.63 \ (1.0275)^1 = \$4000(1.0275)^3 + x + 3x(1.0275)^{-3}$$

$$\$10,710.64 + \$7572.30 = \$4339.16 + x + 2.7655134x$$

$$x = \$3703.02$$

The last two replacement payments are $\underline{\$3703.02}$ due in 9 months and $\underline{\$11,109.06}$ due in $1\frac{1}{2}$ years.

Review Problems

1. Value of compound-interest CSB after three years

$$= P(1 + i_1)(1 + i_2)(1 + i_3)$$
$$= \$4000(1.0525)(1.06)(1.0675)$$
$$= \$4763.83$$

Maturity value of three-year Bond-Beater GIC

$$= \$4000(1.0575)(1.065)(1.0725)$$
$$= \$4831.56$$

The Bond-Beater GIC earns $4831.56 − $4763.83 = $\underline{\$67.73}$ more than the CSB in the first three years

Review Problems (continued)

2. a. Maturity value $= P(1 + i_1)...(1 + i_4)$
   $= \$8000(1.0525)(1.0575)(1.0625)(1.0675)$
   $= \underline{\$10,099.25}$

   b. Interest earned in year 3 $= i_3 P(1 + i_1)(1 + i_2)$
   $= 0.0625(\$8000)(1.0525)(1.0575)$
   $= \underline{\$556.51}$

   c. Maturity value of fixed-rate GIC $= P(1 + i)^4$
   $= \$8000(1.06)^4$
   $= \$10,099.82$

   The Step-up GIC will earn $\underline{\$0.57\ less}$ than the fixed rate GIC.

3. a. Maturity value $= P(1 + i_1)^2(1 + i_2)^2(1 + i_3)^2$
   $= \$12,000(1.03)^2(1.035)^2(1.04)^2$
   $= \underline{\$14,750.38}$

   b. Interest earned in the second year
   $=$ Value after 2 years $-$ Value after 1 year
   $= \$12,000(1.03)^2(1.035)^2 - \$12,000(1.03)^2$
   $= \$13,637.55 - \$12,730.80$
   $= \underline{\$906.75}$

4. The CS44 CSBs were issued on November 1, 1989.

   a. Redemption value of a \$500 face value bond on November 1, 1995
   $= P(1 + i_1)...(1 + i_6)$
   $= \$500(1.109\overline{16})(1.1075)(1.075)(1.06)(1.05125)(1.06375)$
   $= \underline{\$782.66}$

   b. In addition to the amount in part a, the bond owner is entitled to interest from November 1, 1995 to April 1, 1996 at 6.75% pa. Hence,

   Redemption value $= P(1 + rt)$

   $$= \$782.66 \left(1 + 0.0675 \times \frac{5}{12}\right)$$

   $$= \underline{\$804.67}$$

5. Original principal, $P = S(1 + i)^{-n} = \$2297.78(1.007)^{-19} = \underline{\$2012.56}$

   Interest portion $= \$2297.78 - \$2012.56 = \underline{\$285.22}$

6. Amount owed on June 1 (following graduation)

   $= \$3000\ (1.02)^5 + \$3500\ (1.02)^3 + \$4000\ (1.02)$

   $= \$3312.24 + \$3714.23 + \$4080.00$

   $= \underline{\$11,106.47}$

7. Amount owed after $2\frac{1}{2}$ years $= \$25,000\ (1.0075)^{30} = \$31,281.79$

   Amount owed after 5 years $= \$31,281.79\ (1.04125)^5 = \underline{\$38,288.36}$

Review Problems *(continued)*

8. Amount owed after the $1200 payment one year ago

    $= \$3000 \ (1.02625)^{10} - \$1200$

    $= \$2687.34$

    Balance owed today $= \$2687.34 \ (1.02625)^4 = \underline{\$2980.82}$

9. Equivalent amount $= S(1 + i)^{-n} = \$4800(1.04)^{-9} = \underline{\$3372.42}$

10. Let x represent the original investment. Its maturity value was

    $x \ (1 + i)^n = x \ (1.0055)^{42}$

    Hence,

    $x \ (1.0055)^{42} - x = \$1683.90$

    $1.2590621x - x = \$1683.90$

    $x = \underline{\$6499.99}$

    The original investment was $6499.99.

11. The scheduled payments were

    $\$2400 \ (1.02)^2 = \$2496.96$

    due $1\frac{1}{2}$ years ago,

    $\$1200 \ (1.02)^8 = \$1405.99$

    due today, and

    $\$3000 \ (1.02)^{13} = \$3880.82$

    due in 15 months.

    The sum of their equivalent values 6 months from now is

    $\$2496.96 \ (1.015)^8 + \$1405.99 \ (1.015)^2 + \$3880.82(1.015)^{-3}$

    $= \$2812.81 + \$1448.49 + \$3711.29$

    $= \underline{\$7972.59}$

12. a. Allowing for the ability of money to earn 8% compounded monthly, today's economic value of the 25% down, 75% in six months payment plan is

    $0.25 \ (\$1195) + 0.75(\$1195)(1.00\overline{6})^{-6} = \$1159.97$

    The discounted price is $1155. You should choose the lower economic value alternative. Therefore, <u>pay cash and take the discount</u>.

    b. The economic advantage of the $40 discount alternative is

    $\$1159.97 - \$1155 = \underline{\$4.97}$

Review Problems (continued)

13. For an initial investment P, the maturity value at 7.5% compounded semiannually will be

$$P (1.0375)^{12} = 1.55545 \ P$$

and at 7.75% compounded annually will be

$$P (1.0775)^6 = 1.56496 \ P$$

The <u>7.75% compounded annual</u> rate will result in the larger maturity value.

14. a. Accumulated value of the GIC after 4 years
$$= P(1 + i)^4 = \$1000(1.06)^4 = \$1262.48$$
Interest earned in fifth year = 0.06($1262.48) = <u>$75.75</u>

   b. Amount required five years from now to have the same purchasing power as $1000 today is
$1000(1.04)^5 = $1216.65
Maturity value of GIC = $1262.48 + $75.75 = $1338.23
The percent increase in purchasing power of the funds invested in the GIC will be

$$\frac{\$1338.23 - \$1216.65}{\$1216.65} \times 100\% = \underline{9.99\%}$$

15. The current price of the bond residue is
$$P = S(1 + i)^{-n} = \$1000(1.0395)^{-38} = \underline{\$229.44}$$

The stripped bond residue's value four years from now (at the same market return) will be
$229.44(1.0395)^8 = $312.80
or $1000(1.0395)^{-30} = $312.80
Its value five years from now will be
$229.44(1.0395)^{10} = $338.00
Hence, the increase in value during the fifth year will be
$338.00 − $312.80 = <u>$25.20</u>

16. Maturity value of note = $7000 (1.00875)^{48} = <u>$10,634.29</u>

Proceeds from the sale of the note 18 months after issue

$$= \$10,634.29(1.02375)^{-10} = \underline{\$8409.48}$$

17. The scheduled payments are

$$\$1500 \ (1.02)^8 = \$1757.49$$

two years after the note's date of issue, and

$$\$2500 \ (1.02)^{16} = \$3431.96$$

four years after the date of issue.

The fair market value of the note, 18 months after the issue date, is the present value on the date of sale of the scheduled payments. That is,

Price = $1757.49(1.0525)^{-1} + $3431.96(1.0525)^{-5} = $1669.82 + $2657.25 = <u>$4327.07</u>

18. Equivalent hourly rate 10 years from now will be

$$\$15 \ (1.045)^{10} = \underline{\$23.29/hour}$$

Review Problems *(continued)*

19. If X represents the number employed in 1988, the number employed five years later was forecast to be

$$X (1 + i)^n = X [1 + (-0.035)]^5 = X (0.965)^5 = 0.8368 \ X$$

Number of jobs lost = $X - 0.8368X = 0.1632 \ X$

That is, <u>16.32%</u> of base metal mining jobs were expected to be lost.

20. Let x represent the size of the second replacement payment due in 18 months. At a focal date 18 months from now, the equation of value is

$$\$5000 \ (1.045)^6 + \$5000 \ (1.045)^1 = \$3000 \ (1.045)^3 + x + 2x(1.045)^{-3}$$

$$\$6511.30 + \$5225.00 = \$3423.50 + x + 1.7525932x$$

$$x = \$3019.99$$

The second and third replacement payments are <u>$3019.99</u> due in 18 months and <u>$6039.98</u> due in three years.

21. The original loan equals the combined present value of the payments and the balance. Let x represent the size of each of the three equal payments.

$$\$10,000 = \frac{x}{1.00875^{12}} + \frac{x}{1.00875^{24}} + \frac{x}{1.00875^{36}} + \frac{\$5326.94}{1.00875^{36}}$$

$$\$10,000 = 0.9007358x + 0.8113250x + 0.7307895x + \$3892.87$$

$$2.4428503x = \$6107.13$$

$$x = \underline{\$2500.00}$$

Each of the three payments was $2500.00.

22. The cash price should be compared to the present value of the instalment payment alternative (discounted at the rate of return Carla can earn on invested funds).

    a.   Present value = $7000 + \$10,000(1.035)^{-2} + \$9000(1.035)^{-4} + \$8000(1.035)^{-6}$

$$= \$7000 + \$9335.11 + \$7842.98 + \$6508.01$$

$$= \$30,686.10$$

The <u>cash price has a $686.10 advantage</u>.

    b.   Present value = $7000 + \$10,000(1.05)^{-2} + \$9000(1.05)^{-4} + \$8000(1.05)^{-6}$

$$= \$7000 + \$9070.29 + \$7404.32 + \$5969.72$$

$$= \$29,444.33$$

The <u>3-year instalment plan</u> costs

$$\$30,000 - \$29,444.33 = \underline{\$555.67}$$

less in current dollars.

Review Problems (continued)

23. The maturity amounts of the two loans are

$$\$3000\ (1.05)^{12} = \$5387.57$$

due in two years, and

$$\$1500\ (1.0225)^{14} = \$2048.23$$

due $2\frac{1}{4}$ years from now.

Let x represent the amount of each replacement payment. At a focal date two years from now, the equation of value is

$$\$5387.57 + \$2048.23(1.02)^{-1} = x + x(1.02)^{-6}$$

$$\$5387.57 + \$2008.06 = x + 0.8879714x$$

$$x = \underline{\$3917.24}$$

The two replacement payments should each be $3917.24.

24. The scheduled payments are

$$\$3000\ (1.0225)^6 = \$3428.48$$

due in six months, and

$$\$3000\ (1.0225)^{14} = \$4096.45$$

due $2\frac{1}{2}$ years from today.

Let x represent the size of the first replacement payment due one year from today. At a focal date one year from today, the equation of value is

$$\$3428.48(1.035) + \$4096.45(1.035)^{-3} = x + 0.5x(1.035)^{-2}$$

$$\$3548.47 + \$3694.76 = x + 0.46675535x$$

$$x = \underline{\$4938.27}$$

The two replacement payments are $\underline{\$4938.27}$ due in one year and $\underline{\$2469.14}$ due in two years.

Self-Test Exercise

1. a. Maturity value of RateRiser GIC
$$= P(1 + i_1)...(1 + i_5)$$
$$= \$10{,}000(1.065)(1.07)(1.075)(1.08)(1.085)$$
$$= \underline{\$14{,}354.74}$$

Maturity value of fixed-rate GIC
$$= P(1 + i)^5 = \$10{,}000(1.075)^5 = \underline{\$14{,}356.29}$$

   b. Interest earned in the third year on the RateRiser GIC
$$= i_3\, P(1 + i_1)(1 + i_2)$$
$$= 0.075(\$10{,}000)(1.065)(1.07)$$
$$= \underline{\$854.66}$$

Interest earned in the third year of fixed-rate GIC
$$= i\, P(1 + i)^2 = 0.075(\$10{,}000)(1.075)^2 = \underline{\$866.72}$$

Self-Test Exercise (continued)

2. a. Portfolio value, $S = P(1 + i)^n = \$1000(1.104)^{30} = \underline{\$19,456.84}$

   b. Amount required on December 31, 1993 to have the purchasing power of \$1000 on December 31, 1963
   $$= P(1 + i)^n = \$1000(1.0571)^{30} = \underline{\$5290.32}$$

   c. The percent increase in purchasing power of the funds originally invested in the TSE 300 portfolio is
   $$\frac{\$19,456.84 - \$5290.32}{\$5290.32} \times 100\% = \underline{267.8\%}$$

3. The CS43 bonds were issued on November 1, 1988. On March 14, 1996, the bondholder will receive interest accrued to March 1, 1996 (7 years, 4 months). The amount received was
   $$P(1 + i_1)...(1 + i_7)(1 + irt)$$
   $$= \$1000(1.1016)(1.10916)(1.1075)(1.075)(1.06)(1.05125)(1.06375)\left(1 + 0.0675 \times \frac{4}{12}\right)$$
   $$= \underline{\$1763.25}$$

4. According to the Valuation Principle, the finance company will pay the present value of the two payments discounted at the required rate of return.

   Present value $= \$542.50(1.035)^{-2} + \$542.50(1.035)^{-4}$
   $$= \$506.43 + \$472.76$$
   $$= \underline{\$979.19}$$

5. Value after one year $= \$3000 (1.0075)^{12} = \$3281.42$

   Value after two years $= \$7281.42 (1.02125)^4 = \$7920.35$

   Value after three years $= \$11,420.35 (1.03875)^2 = \underline{\$12,322.58}$

6. Amount owed after the first payment
   $$= \$10,000 (1.0575)^3 - \$1800 = \$10,026.09$$
   Amount owed after two years
   $$= \$10,026.09 (1.0575) = \$10,602.59$$
   Amount owed after the second payment
   $$= \$10,602.59 (1.00895)^6 - \$2400 = \$8784.84$$
   Amount owed after three years
   $$= \$8784.84 (1.00895)^6 = \underline{\$9267.27}$$

7. The economic value today of Offer 1
   $$= \$10,000 + \$15,000(1.05125)^{-1} + \$15,000(1.05125)^{-3}$$
   $$= \$10,000 + \$14,268.73 + \$12,911.40$$
   $$= \underline{\$37,180.13}$$
   The economic value today of Offer 2
   $$= \$8000 + \$17,500(1.05125)^{-2} + \$17,500(1.05125)^{-4}$$
   $$= \$8000 + \$15,835.29 + \$14,328.94$$
   $$= \underline{\$38,164.23}$$
   Donnelly should accept Offer 2. Its current economic value is almost \$1000 more than that of Offer 1.

Self-Test Exercise *(concluded)*

8. Maturity value of the Escalator GIC

    $= P(1 + i_1)...(1 + i_5)$
    $= \$10{,}000(1.06)(1.065)(1.075)(1.085)(1.095)$
    $= \$14{,}418.09$

    Maturity value of the regular fixed-rate GIC
    $= P(1 + i)^n = \$10{,}000(1.075)^5 = \$14{,}356.29$

    The <u>Escalator GIC will earn</u>

    $\$14{,}418.09 - \$14{,}356.29 = \underline{\$61.80 \text{ more}}$

9. Maturity value of note $= \$6000\ (1.0075)^{36} = \$7851.87$

    Selling price $= S(1 + i)^{-n} = \$7851.87(1.055)^{-4} = \underline{\$6338.16}$

10. Let L represent the current level of waste discharge. The level after 5 years is to be

    $L\ (1 + i)^n = L\ [1 + (-0.10)]^5 = L\ (0.9)^5 = 0.5905\ L$

    The target level is <u>59.05%</u> of the current level.

11. Let x represent the size of the replacement payments due two and four years from now. At a focal date two years from now, the equation of value is

    $$\$2300\ (1.04875)^7 + \frac{\$3100}{1.04875^2} = \$2000\ (1.04875)^4 + x + \frac{x}{1.04875^4}$$

    $$\$3209.46 + \$2818.50 = \$2419.46 + x + 0.8266317x$$

    $$x = \underline{\$1975.49}$$

    The second and third payments should be $1975.49.

12. Let x represent the size of each loan payment.

    $$\$6500 = x(1.009375)^{-3} + x(1.009375)^{-6} + x(1.009375)^{-12}$$

    $$= 0.9723942x + 0.9455505x + 0.8940658x$$

    $$= 2.8120105x$$

    $$x = \underline{\$2311.51}$$

    Each loan payment should be $2311.51.

9 Compound Interest: Further Topics and Applications

Changes in the Second Edition:

1. The case of a **Fractional Number of Conversion Periods** (Section 9.1 in the first edition) is now combined with the topic **Solving for the Number of Conversion Periods,** *n.*

2. The most efficient keystroke sequence for evaluating the algebraic formula for *n* is presented in a "Tip."

3. As previously mentioned in the Chapter 2 preamble, the brief discussion of logarithms has been moved to an appendix in this chapter since this is the first instance where logarithms are used in the mathematics of finance.

Exercise 9.1

1. $P = \$3400$, $S = \$4297.91$, $n = 3$

   $i = \left(\dfrac{S}{P}\right)^{\frac{1}{n}} - 1 = \left(\dfrac{\$4297.91}{\$3400}\right)^{\frac{1}{3}} - 1 = 0.08125 = 8.125\%$

   Nominal rate = 8.125% compounded annually.

2. $P = \$1000$, $S = \$4016.94$, $n = 20$

   $i = \left(\dfrac{S}{P}\right)^{\frac{1}{n}} - 1 = \left(\dfrac{\$4016.94}{\$1000}\right)^{\frac{1}{20}} - 1 = 0.0720 = 7.20\%$

   Nominal rate = 7.20% compounded annually.

3. $i = \left(\dfrac{S}{P}\right)^{\frac{1}{n}} - 1 = \left(\dfrac{\$2299.16}{\$1800}\right)^{\frac{1}{11}} - 1 = 0.022500$

   Nominal rate = $4i$ = 0.0900 = 9.00% compounded quarterly

4. $i = \left(\dfrac{S}{P}\right)^{\frac{1}{n}} - 1 = \left(\dfrac{\$13,048.66}{\$6100}\right)^{\frac{1}{15}} - 1 = 0.05200$

   Nominal rate = $2i$ = 0.1040 = 10.40% compounded semiannually

5. $i = \left(\dfrac{S}{P}\right)^{\frac{1}{n}} - 1 = \left(\dfrac{\$1165.79}{\$950}\right)^{\frac{1}{29}} - 1 = 0.0070833$

   Nominal rate = $12i$ = 0.0850 = 8.50% compounded monthly

6. $i = \left(\dfrac{S}{P}\right)^{\frac{1}{n}} - 1 = \left(\dfrac{\$10,440.32}{\$4300}\right)^{\frac{1}{8.5}} - 1 = 0.11000$

   Nominal rate = i = 11.00% compounded annually

7. $P = \$4600$, $n = 100$, $S = \$332,000$

   $i = \left(\dfrac{S}{P}\right)^{\frac{1}{n}} - 1 = \left(\dfrac{\$332,000}{\$4600}\right)^{\frac{1}{100}} - 1 = 0.0437 = \underline{4.37\%}$

   The bequest earned 4.37% compounded annually.

8. $P = \$10,000$, $S = \$3,540,000$, $n = 41$

   $i = \left(\dfrac{S}{P}\right)^{\frac{1}{n}} - 1 = \left(\dfrac{\$3,540,000}{\$10,000}\right)^{\frac{1}{41}} - 1 = 0.1539 = 15.39\%$

   The Templeton Growth Fund has realized a 15.39% compound annual return over the 41-year period.

9. $P = \$2550/\text{month}$, $S = \$4475/\text{month}$, $n = 11$

   $i = \left(\dfrac{S}{P}\right)^{\frac{1}{n}} - 1 = \left(\dfrac{\$4475}{\$2550}\right)^{\frac{1}{11}} - 1 = 0.0525 = 5.25\%$

   Anders' salary has grown at an equivalent rate of 5.25% compounded annually.

Exercise 9.1 *(continued)*

10. P = $42.4 billion, S = $115 billion, n = 11

$$i = \left(\frac{S}{P}\right)^{\frac{1}{n}} - 1 = \left(\frac{\$115}{\$42.4}\right)^{\frac{1}{11}} - 1 = 0.0949 = 9.49\%$$

Consumer credit grew at a rate of <u>9.49% compounded annually</u>.

11. P = $70,000, n = 17, S = $260,000

$$i = \left(\frac{S}{P}\right)^{\frac{1}{n}} - 1 = \left(\frac{\$260,000}{\$70,000}\right)^{\frac{1}{17}} - 1 = 0.0802 = 8.02\%$$

The value of the home increased at the rate of <u>8.02% compounded annually</u>.

12. P = 53,500, S = 64,300, n = 8

$$i = \left(\frac{S}{P}\right)^{\frac{1}{n}} - 1 = \left(\frac{64,300}{53,500}\right)^{\frac{1}{8}} - 1 = 0.0233 = 2.33\%$$

The city's population grew at a <u>2.33% compounded annual rate</u> during the eight-year period.

13. P = 1, S = 14, n = 10

$$i = \left(\frac{S}{P}\right)^{\frac{1}{n}} - 1 = \left(\frac{14}{1}\right)^{\frac{1}{10}} - 1 = 0.3020 = 30.20\%$$

Mutual fund assets grew at a rate of <u>30.20% compounded annually</u>.

14. For the Atlantic provinces,

$$i = \left(\frac{2.337}{2.030}\right)^{\frac{1}{22}} - 1 = 0.00642 = \underline{0.642\%}$$

For British Columbia,

$$i = \left(\frac{3.273}{2.107}\right)^{\frac{1}{22}} - 1 = 0.0202 = \underline{2.02\%}$$

Averaged over the 22-year period, the Atlantic provinces' population grew at 0.642% per year and British Columbia's population grew at 2.02% per year.

15. $$i = \left(\frac{S}{P}\right)^{\frac{1}{n}} - 1 = \left(\frac{70}{100}\right)^{\frac{1}{6}} - 1 -0.0577 = \underline{-5.77\%}$$

The number of steel workers declined at <u>5.77% per year</u>.

16. $$i = \left(\frac{S}{P}\right)^{\frac{1}{n}} - 1 = \left(\frac{210.6}{97.2}\right)^{\frac{1}{10}} - 1 = 0.0804 = \underline{8.04\%}$$

The average rate of inflation during the 1970's was 8.04% compounded annually.

17. $$i = \left(\frac{S}{P}\right)^{\frac{1}{n}} - 1 = \left(\frac{119.5}{67.2}\right)^{\frac{1}{10}} - 1 = 0.0593 = \underline{5.93\%}$$

The average rate of inflation during the 1980's was 5.93% compounded annually.

Exercise 9.1 (continued)

18. Maturity value of note, $S = P(1 + i)^n$

$$= \$3800 \, (1.0475)^8$$

$$= \$5508.28$$

Based on proceeds of $4481,

$$i = \left(\frac{S}{P}\right)^{\frac{1}{n}} - 1 = \left(\frac{\$5508.28}{\$4481}\right)^{\frac{1}{6}} - 1 = 0.0350 = \underline{3.50\%}$$

The buyer will realize a rate of return of 4 (3.50%) = <u>14.0% compounded quarterly</u> on her investment.

19. Maturity value = $P(1 + i)^n = \$6000(1.055)^6 = \$8273.06$. The purchase price is the present value, 21 months before maturity, of the maturity value.

$$i = \left(\frac{S}{P}\right)^{\frac{1}{n}} - 1 = \left(\frac{\$8273.06}{\$6854.12}\right)^{\frac{1}{21}} - 1 = 0.00900 = 0.90\%$$

The nominal discount rate was 12i = <u>10.80% compounded monthly</u>.

20. *Method 1*

In terms of the 1971 base value of 100, the CPI in 1990 was

$$1980 \text{ CPI(1971 base)} \times \frac{1990 \text{ CPI(1986 base)}}{1980 \text{ CPI(1986 base)}} = 210.6 \times \frac{119.5}{67.2} = 374.5$$

With P = 97.2, S = 374.5, and n = 20,

$$i = \left(\frac{S}{P}\right)^{\frac{1}{n}} - 1 = \left(\frac{374.5}{97.2}\right)^{\frac{1}{20}} - 1 = 0.0698 = \underline{6.98\%}$$

Method 2

In problems 16 and 17, we found that the equivalent annual inflation rate in the seventies was 8.04% and in the eighties was 5.93%. This means that a basket of goods costing $100 in 1970 cost

$$\$100(1.0804)^{10}(1.0593)^{10} = \$385.51$$

in 1990. The equivalent annual rate of inflation for the entire 20 years was

$$i = \left(\frac{\$385.51}{\$100}\right)^{\frac{1}{20}} - 1 = 0.0698 = \underline{6.98\%}$$

21. a. For the TSE 300 stock portfolio,

$$i = \left(\frac{S}{P}\right)^{\frac{1}{n}} - 1 = \left(\frac{\$10,791}{\$1000}\right)^{\frac{1}{20}} - 1 = 0.1263 = \underline{12.63\%}$$

For the 3-month Treasury bill portfolio,

$$i = \left(\frac{\$6964}{\$1000}\right)^{\frac{1}{20}} - 1 = 0.1019 = \underline{10.19\%}$$

b. The purchasing power of each portfolio's 1995 value in terms of 1975 dollars is the present value, 20 years earlier, of the 1995 value discounted at the rate of inflation.

Purchasing power of TSE 300 portfolio in 1975 dollars

$$= S(1 + i)^{-n} = \$10{,}791(1.0588)^{-20} = \underline{\$3441.78}$$

Purchasing power of T-bill portfolio in 1975 dollars

$$= \$6964(1.0588)^{-20} = \underline{\$2221.16}$$

c. Real rate of return on the TSE 300 portfolio was

$$i = \left(\frac{S}{P}\right)^{\frac{1}{n}} - 1 = \left(\frac{\$3441.78}{\$1000}\right)^{\frac{1}{20}} - 1 = 0.0637 = \underline{6.37\%}$$

Real rate of return on the T-bill portfolio was

$$i = \left(\frac{\$2221.16}{\$1000}\right)^{\frac{1}{20}} - 1 = 0.0407 = \underline{4.07\%}$$

22. a. For the S & P stock portfolio,

$$i = \left(\frac{\$15{,}238}{\$1000}\right)^{\frac{1}{20}} - 1 = 0.1459 = \underline{14.59\%}$$

For the 3-month Treasury bill portfolio,

$$i = \left(\frac{\$4304}{\$1000}\right)^{\frac{1}{20}} - 1 = 0.0757 = \underline{7.57\%}$$

b. Purchasing power of the S & P 500 portfolio in 1975 dollars

$$= S(1 + i)^{-n} = \$15{,}238(1.054)^{-20} = \$5322.50$$

Purchasing power of the T-bill portfolio in 1975 dollars

$$= \$4304(1.054)^{-20} = \$1503.35$$

c. Real rate of return on the S & P 500 portfolio was

$$i = \left(\frac{\$5322.50}{\$1000}\right)^{\frac{1}{20}} - 1 = 0.0872 = \underline{8.72\%}$$

Real rate of return on the T-bill portfolio was

$$i = \left(\frac{\$1503.35}{\$1000}\right)^{\frac{1}{20}} - 1 = 0.0206 = \underline{2.06\%}$$

23. a. Equivalent compound annual change in the TSE 300 Index was

$$i = \left(\frac{S}{P}\right)^{\frac{1}{n}} - 1 = \left(\frac{4620}{4100}\right)^{\frac{1}{8}} - 1 = 0.0150 = \underline{1.50\%}$$

Equivalent compound annual change in the S & P 500 Index was

$$i = \left(\frac{560}{335}\right)^{\frac{1}{8}} - 1 = 0.0663 = \underline{6.63\%}$$

Exercise 9.1 (continued)

b. Eight-year percent increase in prices of US stocks

$$= \frac{560 - 335}{335} \times 100\% = 67.16\%$$

Eight-year percent increase in prices of Canadian stocks

$$= \frac{4620 - 4100}{4100} \times 100\% = 12.68\%$$

Therefore, US stocks outperformed Canadian stocks by a factor of $\frac{67.16\%}{12.68\%} = 5.30$

24. Suppose the amount invested was $100. The amount after two years was

$$S = P(1 + i)^n = \$100 (1.06)^4 = \$126.248$$

The amount after three further years was

$$S = \$126.248 (1.10)^3 = \$168.04$$

The annually compounded return that would produce the same maturity amount after 5 years is

$$i = \left(\frac{S}{P}\right)^{\frac{1}{n}} - 1 = \left(\frac{\$168.04}{\$100}\right)^{\frac{1}{5}} - 1 = 0.1094 = \underline{\underline{10.94\%}}$$

25. Suppose the initial investment in the portfolio was $100. Its value after 5 years would have been $100(1 + i_1)...(1 + i_5) = \$100(1.20(0.80)(1.0)(1.20)(0.80) = \$92.16$. The annually compounded rate of return that would have produced the same final value is

$$i = \left(\frac{S}{P}\right)^{\frac{1}{n}} - 1 = \left(\frac{\$92.16}{\$100}\right)^{\frac{1}{5}} - 1 = -0.0162 = \underline{\underline{-1.62\%}}$$

26. Let x represent the initial value of the portfolio. The value after five years was

$$x (1.20)(1.15)(0.90)(1.25)(0.95) = 1.474845x$$

The annually compounded return that would produce the same value after five years is

$$i = \left(\frac{S}{P}\right)^{\frac{1}{n}} - 1 = \left(\frac{1.474875x}{1.00x}\right)^{\frac{1}{5}} - 1 = 0.0808 = \underline{\underline{8.08\%}}$$

27. $100 invested for the last 3 years would have grown to $100(1.363)(1.038)(1.141) = $161.43. The 3-year equivalent annually compounded return was

$$i = \left(\frac{S}{P}\right)^{\frac{1}{n}} - 1 = \left(\frac{\$161.43}{\$100}\right)^{\frac{1}{3}} - 1 = \underline{\underline{17.31\%}}$$

$100 invested for the last 5 years would have grown to $100(1.303)(1.152)(1.363) \times (1.038)(1.141) = $242.31. The 5-year equivalent annually compounded return was

$$i = \left(\frac{\$242.31}{\$100}\right)^{\frac{1}{5}} - 1 = 0.1936 = \underline{\underline{19.36\%}}$$

$100 invested for all 10 years would have grown to $100(1.197)...(1.141) = $323.43. The 10-year equivalent annually compounded return was

$$i = \left(\frac{\$323.43}{\$100}\right)^{\frac{1}{10}} - 1 = 0.1245 = \underline{\underline{12.45\%}}$$

Exercise 9.1 *(concluded)*

28. $100 invested for the last 3 years would have grown to 100(1.203)(0.906)(1.309)$ = $142.67. The <u>3-year</u> equivalent annually compounded <u>return</u> was

$$i = \left(\frac{S}{P}\right)^{\frac{1}{n}} - 1 = \left(\frac{\$142.67}{\$100}\right)^{\frac{1}{3}} - 1 = 0.1258 = \underline{12.58\%}$$

$100 invested for the last 5 years would have grown to 142.67(1.043)(1.819) = $270.67. The <u>5-year</u> equivalent annually compounded <u>return</u> was

$$i = \left(\frac{\$270.67}{\$100}\right)^{\frac{1}{5}} - 1 = 0.2204 = \underline{22.04\%}$$

$100 invested for the entire 10 years would have grown to 270.67 (1.105)(1.441) x (0.945)(0.977)(1.291) = $513.72. The <u>10-year</u> equivalent annually compounded <u>return</u> was

$$i = \left(\frac{\$513.72}{\$100}\right)^{\frac{1}{10}} - 1 = 0.1778 = \underline{17.78\%}$$

Exercise 9.2

1. $n = \dfrac{\ln\left(\dfrac{S}{P}\right)}{\ln(1+i)} = \dfrac{\ln\left(\dfrac{\$4483.92}{\$1100}\right)}{\ln(1.063)} = \dfrac{1.4052}{0.061095} = 23.00 \text{ periods}$

   Since the compounding period is one year, the term is <u>23 years.</u>

2. $n = \dfrac{\ln\left(\dfrac{S}{P}\right)}{\ln(1+i)} = \dfrac{\ln\left(\dfrac{\$8481.61}{\$4625}\right)}{\ln(1.07875)} = \dfrac{0.60642}{0.075803} = 8.00 \text{ periods}$

   Since the compounding period is one year, the term is <u>8 years.</u>

3. $n = \dfrac{\ln\left(\dfrac{S}{P}\right)}{\ln(1+i)} = \dfrac{\ln\left(\dfrac{\$10,365.39}{\$5670}\right)}{\ln(1.0475)} = \dfrac{0.603283}{0.046406} = 13.0 \text{ periods}$

   Total time = 13 (6 months) = <u>6 years, 6 months</u>

4. $n = \dfrac{\ln\left(\dfrac{S}{P}\right)}{\ln(1+i)} = \dfrac{\ln\left(\dfrac{\$3172.42}{\$2000}\right)}{\ln(1.0875)} = \dfrac{0.46135}{0.083881} = 5.50 \text{ periods}$

   Total time = 5.5 (1 year) = <u>5 years, 6 months</u>

5. $n = \dfrac{\ln\left(\dfrac{S}{P}\right)}{\ln(1+i)} = \dfrac{\ln\left(\dfrac{\$3837.30}{\$2870}\right)}{\ln(1.0083)} = \dfrac{0.290457}{0.0082988} = 35.00 \text{ periods}$

   Total time = 35 (1 month) = <u>2 years, 11 months</u>

Exercise 9.2 *(continued)*

6. $n = \dfrac{\ln\left(\dfrac{S}{P}\right)}{\ln(1+i)} = \dfrac{\ln\left(\dfrac{\$4456.90}{\$3250}\right)}{\ln(1.01875)} = \dfrac{0.315798}{0.018576} = 17.00$ periods

   Total time = 17 (3 months) = <u>4 years, 3 months</u>

7. $n = \dfrac{\ln\left(\dfrac{S}{P}\right)}{\ln(1+i)} = \dfrac{\ln\left(\dfrac{\$3252}{\$2150}\right)}{\ln(1.03)} = 14.00$ periods (quarters)

   The time interval before the scheduled payment is $3\dfrac{1}{2}$ years.

8. $n = \dfrac{\ln\left(\dfrac{S}{P}\right)}{\ln(1+i)} = \dfrac{\ln\left(\dfrac{\$1609.90}{\$1450}\right)}{\ln(1.0075)} = 14$ periods

   Marilyn made the equivalent payment 14 months after the scheduled date, that is, on <u>May 1 of the following year.</u>

9. $n = \dfrac{\ln\left(\dfrac{S}{P}\right)}{\ln(1+i)} = \dfrac{\ln\left(\dfrac{\$10,000}{\$2603.35}\right)}{\ln(1.0475)} = 29$ periods

   The time remaining until the maturity date is $14\dfrac{1}{2}$ years.

10. a. $n = \dfrac{\ln\left(\dfrac{S}{P}\right)}{\ln(1+i)} = \dfrac{\ln\left(\dfrac{40,000}{32,500}\right)}{\ln(1.03)} = 7.0246$ periods

    Each compounding period is one year. The partial period is $0.0246 \times 12 = 0.295$ months. Rounded to the nearest month, it will take <u>7 years</u> for the population to grow from 32,500 to 40,000.

    b. $n = \dfrac{\ln\left(\dfrac{S}{P}\right)}{\ln(1+i)} = \dfrac{\ln\left(\dfrac{32,500}{40,000}\right)}{\ln(1-0.03)} = 6.8170$ periods

    The partial period is $12(0.8170) = 9.8$ months. Rounded to the nearest month, it will take <u>6 years, 10 months</u> for the population to decline from 40,000 to 32,500.

Exercise 9.2 *(continued)*

11. a. $n = \dfrac{\ln\left(\dfrac{S}{P}\right)}{\ln(1+i)} = \dfrac{\ln(2)}{\ln(1.084)} = 8.5937$ periods

Each period is one year. The partial period is $12(0.5937) = 7.12$ months. Rounded to the nearest month, the investment will double in <u>8 years, 7 months</u>.

b. $n = \dfrac{\ln(2)}{\ln(1.0525)} = 13.5464$ periods

Each period is 6 months. The partial period is $6(0.5464) = 3.28$ months. Rounded to the nearest month, the investment will double in <u>6 years, 9 months</u>.

12. a. $n = \dfrac{\ln\left(\dfrac{S}{P}\right)}{\ln(1+i)} = \dfrac{\ln(3)}{\ln(1.09)} = 12.748$ periods

Since each period is one year, the investment will triple in <u>12 years, 9 months</u>.

b. $n = \dfrac{\ln(3)}{\ln(1.02)} = 55.478$ periods

Each period is 3 months. The partial period is $3(0.478) = 1.43$ months. Rounded to the nearest month, the investment will triple in <u>13 years, 10 months</u>.

13. a. $n = \dfrac{\ln\left(\dfrac{S}{P}\right)}{\ln(1+i)} = \dfrac{\ln(4)}{\ln(1.08)} = 18.013$ periods

Rounded to the nearest quarter, it will take <u>18 years</u> for the investment to quadruple.

b. $n = \dfrac{\ln(4)}{\ln(1.045)} = 31.495$ periods

Each period is 6 months (2 quarters). The investment will quadruple in $2(31.495) = 62.99$ quarters $= 15\frac{3}{4}$ years rounded to the nearest quarter.

14. a. $n = \dfrac{\ln\left(\dfrac{S}{P}\right)}{\ln(1+i)} = \dfrac{\ln(0.5)}{\ln(1-0.03)} = 22.757$ periods

Each period is one year. The partial period is $12(0.757) = 9.1$ months. Rounded to the nearest month, money will lose half its purchasing power in <u>22 years, 9 months</u>.

b. $n = \dfrac{\ln(0.5)}{\ln(1-0.06)} = 11.202$ periods

Each period is one year. The partial period is $12(0.202) = 2.43$ months. Rounded to the nearest month, money will lose half its purchasing power in <u>11 years, 2 months</u>.

Exercise 9.2 *(continued)*

15. a. $n = \dfrac{\ln\left(\dfrac{S}{P}\right)}{\ln(1 + i)} = \dfrac{\ln(0.10)}{\ln(1 - 0.04)} = 56.406$ periods

Each period is one year. The partial period is $12(0.406) = 4.87$ months. Rounded to the nearest month, money will lose 90% of its purchasing power in <u>56 years, 5 months</u>.

b. $n = \dfrac{\ln(0.10)}{\ln(1 - 0.10)} = 21.854$ periods

Each period is one year. The partial period is $12(0.854) = 10.3$ months. Rounded to the nearest month, money will lose 90% of its purchasing power in <u>21 years, 10 months</u>.

16. The early settlement figure of $3383.33 represents the present value, on the settlement date, of the loan's maturity value.

Maturity value $= P(1 + i)^n = \$3,000\left(1 + \dfrac{0.076}{4}\right)^{12} = \$3760.20$

The number of 3-month compounding periods between the settlement date and the maturity date was

$n = \dfrac{\ln\left(\dfrac{S}{P}\right)}{\ln(1 + i)} = \dfrac{\ln\left(\dfrac{\$3760.20}{\$3383.33}\right)}{\ln\left(1 + \dfrac{0.08}{4}\right)} = \dfrac{0.105612}{0.0198026} = 5.333$

Therefore, the loan was settled 5.333×3 months $= 16$ months before maturity, or $36 - 16 = $ <u>20 months</u> into the three-year term.

17. Maturity value, $S = P(1 + i)^n = \$2600(1.1225)^3 = \$3677.33$, Price $= \$3283.57$

The number of compounding periods between the discount date and maturity is

$n = \dfrac{\ln\left(\dfrac{S}{P}\right)}{\ln(1 + i)} = \dfrac{\ln\left(\dfrac{\$3677.33}{\$3283.57}\right)}{\ln(1.00875)} = 13.0$ periods

The discounting took place $36 - 13 = $ <u>23 months</u> after the issue date.

18. Maturity value $= P(1 + i)^n = \$4500(1.0225)^{20} = \$7022.29$, Proceeds $= \$6055.62$

The number of compounding periods between the discount date and maturity date is

$n = \dfrac{\ln\left(\dfrac{S}{P}\right)}{\ln(1 + i)} = \dfrac{\ln\left(\dfrac{\$7022.29}{\$6055.62}\right)}{\ln(1.00875)} = 17.0$ periods

The note was sold <u>1 year and 5 months</u> before maturity.

Exercise 9.2 *(continued)*

19. The number of months required for $4000 invested at 7.5% compounded monthly to grow to $5000 is

$$n = \frac{\ln\left(\dfrac{\$5000}{\$4000}\right)}{\ln(1.00625)} = 35.8144$$

The partial month is $0.8144(30 \text{ days}) = 24.43$ days. To the nearest day, $5000 will be the equivalent payment <u>2 years, 11 months, and 24 days</u> after the scheduled payment date.

20. The number of calendar quarters over which $6000 must be discounted to have a present value of $5000 is

$$n = \frac{\ln\left(\dfrac{\$6000}{\$5000}\right)}{\ln\left(1 + \dfrac{0.08}{4}\right)} = 9.2069$$

The number of days in the partial quarter is $0.2069(91 \text{ days}) = 18.8$ days. To the nearest day, $5000 is the equivalent value <u>2 years, 3 months, and 19 days</u> before the $6000 scheduled payment.

21. $416.71 represents the present value of $1000 on the purchase date. The number of half-years between the purchase date and maturity date was

$$n = \frac{\ln\left(\dfrac{\$1000}{\$416.71}\right)}{\ln\left(1 + \dfrac{0.0786}{2}\right)} = 22.70878$$

The partial period was $0.70878(182 \text{ days}) = 129.0$ days long. Therefore, Wilf purchased the stripped bond <u>11 years and 129 days</u> before its maturity date.

22. The purchase price is the present value of the face value. The number of compounding periods (half-years) over which the face value is discounted is

$$n = \frac{\ln\left(\dfrac{\$5000}{\$1073.36}\right)}{\ln\left(1 + \dfrac{0.0727}{2}\right)} = 43.093327$$

The partial period is $0.093327(182 \text{ days}) = 17.0$ days long. The total time remaining until maturity is <u>21 years, 6 months, and 17 days</u>.

Exercise 9.2 *(concluded)*

23. The $9380.24 payout figure represents the present value on the prepayment date of the loan's maturity value (discounted at 10% compounded quarterly). The maturity value was

$$S = P(1 + i)^n = \$7500 \left(1 + \frac{0.09}{4}\right)^{16} = \$10,707.16$$

The number of compounding periods (calendar quarters) between prepayment and maturity was

$$n = \frac{\ln\left(\frac{S}{P}\right)}{\ln(1 + i)} = \frac{\ln\left(\frac{\$10,707.16}{\$9380.24}\right)}{\ln\left(1 + \frac{0.07}{4}\right)} = 7.62639$$

The partial period was
   0.62639(91 days) = 57.0 days long
Hence, the loan was prepaid <u>1 year, 9 months, and 57 days</u> before maturity.

Exercise 9.3

	Maturity value of $100 in 1 year	Equivalent interest rate*

1. $110 $i = \left(\dfrac{\$110}{\$100}\right)^{\frac{1}{2}} - 1 = 0.04881$

   $j = 2i = \underline{9.76\% \text{ csa}}$

2. $110 $i = \left(\dfrac{\$110}{\$100}\right)^{\frac{1}{4}} - 1 = 0.02411$

   $j = 4i = \underline{9.65\% \text{ cq}}$

3. $110 $i = \left(\dfrac{\$110}{\$100}\right)^{\frac{1}{12}} - 1 = 0.007974$

   $j = 12i = \underline{9.57\% \text{ cm}}$

4. $S = \$100 \, (1.05)^2 = \$110.25$ $j = \underline{10.25\% \text{ ca}}$

5. $S = \$100 \, (1.05)^2 = \$110.25$ $i = \left(\dfrac{\$110.25}{\$100}\right)^{\frac{1}{4}} - 1 = 0.02470$

   $j = 4i = \underline{9.88\% \text{ cq}}$

6. $S = \$100 \, (1.05)^2 = \$110.25$ $i = \left(\dfrac{\$110.25}{\$100}\right)^{\frac{1}{12}} - 1 = 0.008165$

   $j = 12i = \underline{9.80\% \text{ cm}}$

7. $S = \$100 \, (1.025)^4 = \$110.38$ $j = \underline{10.38\% \text{ ca}}$

8. $S = \$100 \, (1.025)^4 = \$110.38$ $i = \left(\dfrac{\$110.38}{\$100}\right)^{\frac{1}{2}} - 1 = 0.05062$

   $j = 2i = \underline{10.12\% \text{ csa}}$

*ca = compounded annually; cq = compounded quarterly; csa = compounded semiannually; cm = compounded monthly.

Exercise 9.3 (continued)

	Maturity value of $100 in 1 year	Equivalent interest rate*

9. $S = \$100\ (1.025)^4 = \$110.38$

$i = \left(\dfrac{\$110.38}{\$100}\right)^{\frac{1}{12}} - 1 = 0.008264$

$j = 12i = \underline{9.92\%\ cm}$

10. $S = \$100\ (1.008\overline{3})^{12} = \$110.47$

$j = \underline{10.47\%\ ca}$

11. $S = \$100\ (1.008\overline{3})^{12} = \$110.47$

$i = \left(\dfrac{\$110.47}{\$100}\right)^{\frac{1}{2}} - 1 = 0.05105$

$j = 2i = \underline{10.21\%\ csa}$

12. $S = \$100\ (1.008\overline{3})^{12} = \$110.47$

$i = \left(\dfrac{\$110.47}{\$100}\right)^{\frac{1}{4}} - 1 = 0.02521$

$j = 4i = \underline{10.08\%\ cq}$

13. $S = \$100\ (1.045)^2 = \$109.20$

$j = i = \underline{9.20\%\ ca}$

14. $S = \$100\ (1.025)^4 = \$110.38$

$j = i = \underline{10.38\%\ ca}$

15. $S = \$100\ (1.0825) = \$108.25$

$i = \left(\dfrac{\$108.25}{\$100}\right)^{\frac{1}{12}} - 1 = 0.006628$

$j = 12i = \underline{7.95\%\ cm}$

16. $S = \$100\ (1.01)^{12} = \$112.68$

$i = \left(\dfrac{\$112.68}{\$100}\right)^{\frac{1}{2}} - 1 = 0.06151$

$j = 2i = \underline{12.30\%\ csa}$

17. $S = \$100\ (1.0375)^2 = \$107.64$

$i = \left(\dfrac{\$107.64}{\$100}\right)^{\frac{1}{4}} - 1 = 0.01858$

$j = 4i = \underline{7.43\%\ cq}$

18. $S = \$100\ (1.02875)^4 = \$112.01$

$i = \left(\dfrac{\$112.01}{\$100}\right)^{\frac{1}{12}} - 1 = 0.00949$

$j = 12i = \underline{11.39\%\ cm}$

19. $S = \$100\ (1.02125)^4 = \$108.77$

$i = \left(\dfrac{\$108.77}{\$100}\right)^{\frac{1}{2}} - 1 = 0.004293$

$j = 2i = \underline{8.59\%\ csa}$

20. $S = \$100\ (1.00875)^{12} = \$111.02$

$i = \left(\dfrac{\$111.02}{\$100}\right)^{\frac{1}{4}} - 1 = 0.02648$

$j = 4i = \underline{10.59\%\ cq}$

21. a. $S = \$100\ (1.045)^2 = \$109.20$

$j = i = \underline{9.20\%\ ca}$

    b. $S = \$100\ (1.0225)^4 = \$109.31$

$j = i = \underline{9.31\%\ ca}$

    c. $S = \$100\ (1.0075)^{12} = \$109.38$

$j = i = \underline{9.38\%\ ca}$

Exercise 9.3 *(continued)*

	Maturity value of $100 in 1 year	Equivalent interest rate*

22. a. $S = \$109.00$

$i = \left(\dfrac{\$109}{\$100}\right)^{\frac{1}{12}} - 1 = 0.00721$

$j = 12i = \underline{8.65\% \text{ cm}}$

b. $S = \$100 \,(1.045)^2 = \$109.20$

$i = \left(\dfrac{\$109.20}{\$100}\right)^{\frac{1}{12}} - 1 = 0.00736$

$j = 12i = \underline{8.84\% \text{ cm}}$

c. $S = \$100 \,(1.0225)^4 = \$109.31$

$i = \left(\dfrac{\$109.31}{\$100}\right)^{\frac{1}{12}} - 1 = 0.00744$

$j = 12i = \underline{8.93\% \text{ cm}}$

23. $S = \$100 \,(1.0375)^2 = \$107.64$

$i = \left(\dfrac{\$107.64}{\$100}\right)^{\frac{1}{12}} - 1 = 0.006155$

$j = 12i = \underline{7.39\% \text{ cm}}$

24. $S = \$100 \,(1.0375)^2 = \$107.64$

$j = i = \underline{7.64\% \text{ ca}}$

25. $S = \$100 \,(1.01)^{12} = \$112.68$

$i = \left(\dfrac{\$112.68}{\$100}\right)^{\frac{1}{2}} - 1 = 0.06152$

$j = 2i = \underline{12.30\% \text{ csa}}$

26. $S = \$100 \,(1.0475)^2 = \$109.73$

$i = \left(\dfrac{109.73}{\$100}\right)^{\frac{1}{12}} - 1 = 0.00776$

$j = 12i = \underline{9.32\% \text{ cm}}$

27. $S = \$108.25$

$i = \left(\dfrac{\$108.25}{\$100}\right)^{\frac{1}{2}} - 1 = 0.04043$

$j = 2i = \underline{8.09\% \text{ csa}}$

and

$i = \left(\dfrac{\$108.25}{\$100}\right)^{\frac{1}{12}} - 1 = 0.006628$

$j = 12i = \underline{7.95\% \text{ cm}}$

28. $S = \$100 \,(1.0375)^2 = \$107.64$

$i = \left(\dfrac{\$107.64}{\$100}\right)^{\frac{1}{12}} - 1 = 0.00615$

$j = 12i = \underline{7.39\% \text{ cm}}$

and

$j = \underline{7.64\% \text{ ca}}$

Exercise 9.4

1. $f = (1 + i)^m - 1 = \left(1 + \dfrac{0.15}{2}\right)^2 - 1 = 0.1556 = \underline{15.56\%}$

2. $f = (1 + i)^m - 1 = \left(1 + \dfrac{0.15}{4}\right)^4 - 1 = 0.1587 = \underline{15.87\%}$

3. $f = (1 + i)^m - 1 = \left(1 + \dfrac{0.15}{12}\right)^{12} - 1 = 0.1608 = \underline{16.08\%}$

4. $f = (1 + i)^m - 1 = \left(1 + \dfrac{0.075}{2}\right)^2 - 1 = 0.0764 = \underline{7.64\%}$

5. $f = (1 + i)^m - 1 = \left(1 + \dfrac{0.075}{4}\right)^4 - 1 = 0.0771 = \underline{7.71\%}$

6. $f = (1 + i)^m - 1 = \left(1 + \dfrac{0.075}{12}\right)^{12} - 1 = 0.0776 = \underline{7.76\%}$

Digression

Problems 7 to 12 and 17 to 20 require the calculation of the nominal rate (j) given the effective interest rate (f). Rather than rearrange formula (9-3) to isolate i in each case, we will do it below for the general case and just use the new version of (9-3) in each case. Since

$$f = (1 + i)^m - 1$$

then

$$1 + f = (1 + i)^m$$

Taking the "mth root" of both sides is equivalent to raising both sides to the exponent $\dfrac{1}{m}$. This gives

$$(1 + f)^{\frac{1}{m}} = 1 + i$$

Therefore,

$$\boxed{i = (1 + f)^{\frac{1}{m}} - 1}$$

7. $i = (1 + f)^{\frac{1}{m}} - 1 = 1.15^{\frac{1}{2}} - 1 = 0.07238 = 7.238\%$

    $j = mi = 2(7.238\%) = \underline{14.48\% \text{ csa}}$

8. $i = (1 + f)^{\frac{1}{m}} - 1 = 1.15^{\frac{1}{4}} - 1 = 0.03556 = 3.556\%$

    $j = mi = 4(3.556\%) = \underline{14.22\% \text{ cq}}$

9. $i = (1 + f)^{\frac{1}{m}} - 1 = 1.15^{\frac{1}{12}} - 1 = 0.01171 = 1.171\%$

    $j = mi = 12(1.171\%) = \underline{14.06\% \text{ cm}}$

Exercise 9.4 (continued)

10. $i = (1 + f)^{\frac{1}{m}} - 1 = 1.075^{\frac{1}{2}} - 1 = 0.03682 = 3.682\%$

    $j = mi = 2(3.682\%) = \underline{7.36\% \text{ csa}}$

11. $i = (1 + f)^{\frac{1}{m}} - 1 = 1.075^{\frac{1}{4}} - 1 = 0.01824 = 1.824\%$

    $j = mi = 4(1.824\%) = \underline{7.30\% \text{ cq}}$

12. $i = (1 + f)^{\frac{1}{m}} - 1 = 1.075^{\frac{1}{12}} - 1 = 0.006045 = 0.6045\%$

    $j = mi = 12(0.6045\%) = \underline{7.25\% \text{ cm}}$

13. $f = (1 + i)^m - 1 = \left(1 + \dfrac{0.12}{12}\right)^{12} - 1 = 0.1268 = \underline{\underline{12.68\%}}$

14. $f = (1 + i)^m - 1 = \left(1 + \dfrac{0.18}{12}\right)^{12} - 1 = 0.1956 = \underline{\underline{19.56\%}}$

15. $f = (1 + i)^m - 1 = \left(1 + \dfrac{0.115}{4}\right)^{4} - 1 = 0.1201 = \underline{\underline{12.01\%}}$

16. $f = (1 + i)^m - 1 = \left(1 + \dfrac{0.099}{2}\right)^{2} - 1 = 0.1015 = \underline{\underline{10.15\%}}$

17. $i = (1 + f)^{\frac{1}{m}} - 1 = 1.1025^{\frac{1}{2}} - 1 = 0.0500 = 5.00\%$

    $j = mi = 2(5.00\%) = \underline{\underline{10.00\% \text{ csa}}}$

18. $i = (1 + f)^{\frac{1}{m}} - 1 = 1.14^{\frac{1}{4}} - 1 = 0.03330 = 3.330\%$

    $j = mi = 4(3.330\%) = \underline{\underline{13.32\% \text{ cq}}}$

19. $i = (1 + f)^{\frac{1}{m}} - 1 = 1.10^{\frac{1}{12}} - 1 = 0.007974 = 0.7974\%$

    $j = mi = 12(0.7974\%) = \underline{\underline{9.57\% \text{ cm}}}$

20. $i = (1 + f)^{\frac{1}{m}} - 1 = 1.20^{\frac{1}{12}} - 1 = 0.01531 = 1.531\%$

    $j = mi = 12(1.531\%) = \underline{\underline{18.37\% \text{ cm}}}$

21. Since the interest is collected each month, we have monthly compounding. The effective rate being charged is

    $f = (1 + i)^m - 1 = 1.018^{12} - 1 = 0.2387 = \underline{\underline{23.87\%}}$

22. Since the interest is charged each month, we have monthly compounding.

    $f = (1 + i)^m - 1 = 1.024^{12} - 1 = 0.3292 = \underline{\underline{32.92\%}}$

Exercise 9.4 *(continued)*

23. Since the interest is charged each month, we have monthly compounding.

$$f = (1 + i)^m - 1 = 1.02^{12} - 1 = 0.2682 = \underline{\underline{26.82\%}}$$

24. Since the interest is paid monthly, we have monthly compounding.

$$f = (1 + i)^m - 1 = \left(1 + \frac{0.04}{12}\right)^{12} - 1 = 0.0407 = \underline{\underline{4.07\%}}$$

25. $f = (1 + i)^m - 1 = \left(1 + \dfrac{0.089}{2}\right)^2 - 1 = 0.0910 = \underline{\underline{9.10\%}}$

26. Because of the 3% compounding every quarter, the annual growth rate will exceed 4(3%) = 12%. The actual annual growth is

$$f = (1 + i)^m - 1 = 1.03^4 - 1 = 0.1255 = \underline{\underline{12.55\%}}$$

27. The fundamental question is: "What annually compounded rate of return would produce the same growth in $2\frac{1}{2}$ years (30 months)?" In this case,

$$f = i = \left(\frac{S}{P}\right)^{\frac{1}{n}} - 1 = \left(\frac{\$6450}{\$5000}\right)^{\frac{1}{2.5}} - 1 = 0.1072 = \underline{\underline{10.72\%}}$$

28. The essential question is: "What annually compounded rate of interest would produce the same maturity value after 2.25 years (27 months)?" This rate is

$$f = i = \left(\frac{S}{P}\right)^{\frac{1}{n}} - 1 = \left(\frac{\$3810}{\$3000}\right)^{\frac{1}{2.25}} - 1 = 0.1121 = \underline{\underline{11.21\%}}$$

29. f (bank) = $(1.01028\bar{3})^{12} - 1 = 0.1296 = 12.96\%$
    f (credit union) = $(1.0625)^2 - 1 = 0.1289 = 12.89\%$

    Lisa should choose the <u>credit union loan</u> since it has the lower effective interest rate.

30. f (semiannual compounding) = $(1.0375)^2 - 1 = 0.0764 = 7.64\%$
    f (monthly compounding) = $(1.0061\bar{6})^{12} - 1 = 0.0766 = 7.66\%$

    Craig should choose the <u>monthly compounded GIC</u> since it has a slightly higher effective rate.

31. f (semiannual compounding) = $(1.0475)^2 - 1 = 0.0973 = 9.73\%$
    f (monthly compounding) = $(1.0078\bar{3})^{12} - 1 = 0.0982 = 9.82\%$

    Camille should choose the <u>bank loan</u> since it carries the lower effective rate of interest.

32. f (ABC) = $(1.013)^{12} - 1 = 0.1677 = \underline{\underline{16.77\%}}$

    f (DEF) = $(1.04)^4 - 1 = 0.1699 = \underline{\underline{16.99\%}}$

Exercise 9.4 *(concluded)*

33. For annual compounding,

$$j = i = f = \underline{7.75\% \text{ ca}}$$

For semiannual compounding,

$$i = (1 + f)^{\frac{1}{m}} - 1 = (1.0775)^{\frac{1}{2}} - 1 = 0.03803$$

$$j = 2i = \underline{7.61\% \text{ csa}}$$

For monthly compounding,

$$i = (1.0775)^{\frac{1}{12}} - 1 = 0.006240$$

$$j = 12i = \underline{7.49\% \text{ cm}}$$

34. For monthly compounding,

$$i = (1.07)^{\frac{1}{12}} - 1 = 0.005654$$

$$j = 12i = \underline{6.78\% \text{ cm}}$$

For semiannual compounding,

$$i = (1.07)^{\frac{1}{2}} - 1 = 0.03441$$

$$j = 2i = \underline{6.88\% \text{ csa}}$$

For annual compounding,

$$j = i = f = \underline{7\% \text{ ca}}$$

35. $f \text{ (old)} = (1.015)^{12} - 1 = 0.1956$

$f \text{ (new)} = 0.2156$

$i \text{ (new)} = (1 + f)^{\frac{1}{m}} - 1 = 1.2156^{\frac{1}{12}} - 1 = 0.01640$

The monthly compounded rate should be changed to $12i = \underline{19.68\%}$

36. $f \text{ (old)} = (1.017)^{12} - 1 = 0.2242$

$f \text{ (new)} = 0.1942$

$f \text{ (new)} = (1 + f)^{\frac{1}{m}} - 1 = 1.1942^{\frac{1}{12}} - 1 = 0.0149$

The monthly periodic rate should be dropped to $\underline{1.49\% \text{ per month}}$.

Exercise 9B

1. Current (simple) yield $= \dfrac{\text{One year}}{\text{Holding period}} \times$ Holding-period return

$$= \frac{365 \text{ days}}{7 \text{ days}} \times 0.111\%$$

$$= \underline{5.79\%}$$

Effective yield, $f = (1 + i)^m - 1$

$$= (1.00111)^{\frac{365}{7}} - 1$$

$$= 0.0596$$

$$= \underline{5.96\%}$$

Exercise 9B *(continued)*

2. Current (simple) yield $= \dfrac{\text{One year}}{\text{Holding period}} \times$ Holding-period return

    $= \dfrac{365 \text{ days}}{7 \text{ days}} \times 0.097\%$

    $= \underline{5.06\%}$

    Effective annualized yield, $f = (1 + i)^m - 1$

    $= (1.00097)^{\frac{365}{7}} - 1$

    $= 0.05185$

    $= \underline{5.19\%}$

3. The return for the most recent 7-day holding period was

    $5.62\% \times \dfrac{\text{Holding period}}{\text{One Year}} = 5.62\% \times \dfrac{7 \text{ days}}{365 \text{ days}} = 0.10778\%$

    The corresponding effective (annualized) yield is

    $f = (1 + i)^m - 1 = (1.0010778)^{\frac{365}{7}} - 1 = 0.05778 = \underline{5.78\%}$

4. The return for the most recent 7 days was

    $6.17\% \times \dfrac{7 \text{ days}}{365 \text{ days}} = 0.11833\%$

    The corresponding effective (annualized) yield is

    $f = (1 + i)^m - 1 = (1.0011833)^{\frac{365}{7}} - 1 = 0.06361 = \underline{6.36\%}$

5. a. Holding-period return $= \dfrac{40 \text{ days}}{365 \text{ days}} \times 6.7\% = 0.73425\%$

    The corresponding effective annualized rate of return is

    $f = (1 + i)^m - 1 = (1.0073425)^{\frac{365}{40}} - 1 = 0.06903 = \underline{6.90\%}$

    b. Holding-period return $= \dfrac{160}{365} \times 6.7\% = 2.9370\%$

    $f = (1.029370)^{\frac{365}{160}} - 1 = 0.06826 = \underline{6.83\%}$

6. Holding-period return $= \dfrac{125}{365} \times 8.6\% = 2.9452\%$

    The corresponding effective annualized rate of return is

    $f = (1 + i)^m - 1 = (1.029452)^{\frac{365}{125}} - 1 = 0.0885 = \underline{8.85\%}$

7. Holding-period return $= \dfrac{\$600 - \$550}{\$550} \times 100\% = 9.0909\%$

    The corresponding effective annualized yield was

    $f = (1 + i)^m - 1 = (1.090909)^{\frac{365}{83}} - 1 = 0.46615 = \underline{46.62\%}$

Exercise 9B (continued)

8. Holding-period return = $\dfrac{\$84{,}300 - \$78{,}900}{\$78{,}900}$ x 100% = 6.8441%

   Simple annualized rate of return = $\dfrac{12}{2}$ x 6.8441% = <u>41.06%</u>

   The effective annualized rate of return was

   $$f = (1 + i)^m - 1 = (1.068441)^{\frac{12}{2}} - 1 = 0.48766 = \underline{48.77\%}$$

9. Increase in one month = $\dfrac{\$333.81 - \$331.12}{\$331.12}$ x 100% = 0.81239%

   Simple annualized rate = $\dfrac{12 \text{ months}}{1 \text{ month}}$ x 0.81239% = <u>9.75%</u>

   Effective annualized rate = $(1.0081239)^{\frac{12}{1}} - 1 = 0.10196 = \underline{10.20\%}$

10. Percent change during 50 days = $\dfrac{3748 - 3852}{3852}$ x 100% = −2.700%

    Simple annualized rate = $\dfrac{365 \text{ days}}{50 \text{ days}}$ (−2.700%) = <u>−19.71%</u>

    Effective annualized rate = $(1 - 0.027)^{\frac{365}{50}} - 1 = -0.1811 = \underline{-18.11\%}$

    That is, the TSE 300 index declined at a simple annualized rate of 19.71% and an effective annualized rate of 18.11%.

11. Percent change during 3 months = $\dfrac{\$12.56 - \$12.86}{\$12.86}$ x 100% = −2.3328%

    Simple annualized rate = $\dfrac{12 \text{ months}}{3 \text{ months}}$ (−2.3328%) = <u>−9.33%</u>

    Effective annualized rate = $(1 - 0.023328)^{\frac{12}{3}} - 1 = \underline{-9.01\%}$

    The shares in the mutual fund declined at a simple annual rate of 9.33% and an effective annual rate of 9.01%.

12. The compound or effective increase in house prices for the year will be

    $$f = (1 + i)^m - 1 = (1.08)^{\frac{12}{7}} - 1 = 0.1410 = \underline{14.10\%}$$

13. The simple annualized rate of inflation was

    $$\dfrac{12 \text{ months}}{2 \text{ months}} \text{ x } 1\% = \underline{6\%}$$

    The effective annualized rate of inflation was

    $$(1.01)^{\frac{12}{2}} - 1 = 0.0615 = \underline{6.15\%}$$

14. The percent increase in the CPI in the second quarter was

    $$\dfrac{132.1 - 131.2}{131.2} \text{ x } 100\% = 0.68598\%$$

    The effective annualized rate of inflation was

    $$(1 + i)^m - 1 = (1.0068598)^4 - 1 = 0.0277 = \underline{2.77\%}$$

15.   The discounter pays out $170 now and gets back the full $200 when the tax refund is received. The holding-period return is

$$\frac{\$30}{\$170} \times 100\% = 17.647\%$$

   a.   If the holding period is 25 days, the discounter's effective annualized rate of return is

$$f = (1 + i)^m - 1 = (1.17647)^{\frac{365}{25}} - 1 = 9.727 = \underline{972.7\%}$$

   b.   If the holding period is 50 days,

$$f = (1.17647)^{\frac{365}{50}} - 1 = 2.275 - \underline{227.5\%}$$

16.   In effect, Jennifer earns $8.95 – $7.49 = $1.46 by "investing" $7.49 for 5 weeks.

   Holding-period rate of return $= \dfrac{\$1.46}{\$7.49} \times 100\% = 19.493\%$

   Simple annualized rate of return $= \dfrac{52 \text{ weeks}}{5 \text{ weeks}} \times 19.493\% = \underline{202.7\%}$

   The corresponding effective annualized "return on investment" is

$$f = (1 + i)^m - 1 = (1.19493)^{\frac{52}{5}} - 1 = 5.373 = \underline{537.3\%}$$

17.   An early "investment" of $265 avoids payment of $295 45 days later.

   Holding-period rate of return $= \dfrac{\$30}{\$265} \times 100\% = 11.321\%$

   Simple annualized rate of return $= \dfrac{365 \text{ days}}{45 \text{ days}} \times 11.321\% = \underline{91.83\%}$

   Effective annualized rate $= (1.11321)^{\frac{365}{45}} - 1 = 1.387 = \underline{138.7\%}$

18.   Number of days in the interval November 15 to January 20 is
        $16 + 31 + 19 = 66$
        By paying on November 15, Melanie and David earn 6% on their "investment" in a 66-day period. The effective annualized "return on investment" is

$$f = (1 + i)^m - 1 = (1.06)^{\frac{365}{66}} - 1 = 0.3802 = \underline{38.02\%}$$

19. a. $56 spent now saves $65 – $56 = $9 six months from now. The 6-month "return on investment" is

$$\frac{\$9}{\$56} \times 100\% = 16.071\%$$

   The effective annualized rate of return is

$$f = (1 + i)^m - 1 = (1.16071)^{\frac{12}{6}} - 1 = 0.3472 = \underline{34.72\%}$$

   b.   If the 6-month subscription rate is $67, the 6-month "return on investment" will be

$$\frac{\$11}{\$56} \times 100\% = 19.643\%$$

   and $f = 1.19643^2 - 1 = 0.4314 = \underline{43.14\%}$

Exercise 9B (concluded)

20. Paying $671 now instead of $739 in 6 months saves $68. The 6-month "return on investment" is

$$\frac{\$68}{\$671} \times 100\% = 10.1341$$

The effective annualized rate of return is

$$f = (1 + i)^m - 1 = (1.101341)^{\frac{12}{6}} - 1 = 0.2130 = \underline{21.30\%}$$

21. The alternatives are to pay 97% of the invoiced amount after 10 days or to pay 100% after 90 days. Each $97 paid after 10 days avoids payment of $100 another 80 days later. The 80-day "holding-period return" is

$$\frac{\$3}{\$97} \times 100\% = 3.0928\%$$

Simple annualized rate $= \dfrac{365 \text{ days}}{80 \text{ days}} \times 3.0928\% = \underline{14.11\%}$

Effective annualized rate $= (1.030928)^{\frac{365}{80}} - 1 = 0.1491 = \underline{14.91\%}$

22. The alternatives are to pay 98.5% of the invoiced amount on the 10th day of the following month or pay 100% on the 30th day. Each $98.50 paid on the 10th day avoids payment of $100 20 days later. The 20-day "holding-period rate of return" is

$$\frac{\$1.50}{\$98.50} \times 100\% = 1.52284\%$$

Simple annualized rate $= \dfrac{365 \text{ days}}{20 \text{ days}} \times 1.52284\% = 27.79\%$

Effective annualized rate $= (1.0152284)^{\frac{365}{20}} - 1 = 0.3176 = \underline{31.76\%}$

Review Problems

1. P = $10,000, S = $43,679, n = 7

$$i = \left(\frac{S}{P}\right)^{\frac{1}{n}} - 1 = \left(\frac{\$43,679}{\$10,000}\right)^{\frac{1}{7}} - 1 = 0.2344 = 23.44\%$$

Nominal rate = <u>23.44% compounded annually</u>

2. $i = \left(\dfrac{S}{P}\right)^{\frac{1}{n}} - 1 = \left(\dfrac{\$10.40}{\$6.75}\right)^{\frac{1}{9}} - 1 = 0.0492 = \underline{4.92\%}$

Maxine's wages have grown at a compound annual rate of 4.92% over the last 9 years.

3. $i = \left(\dfrac{S}{P}\right)^{\frac{1}{n}} - 1 = \left(\dfrac{\$485,000}{\$165,000}\right)^{\frac{1}{8}} - 1 = 0.1443 = \underline{14.43\%}$

Sales grew at a compound annual rate of 14.43% during the 8-year period.

Review Problems (continued)

4. Each $100 invested grew to $153 after 5 years. The purchasing power of the $153 in terms of beginning-of-year-one dollars was

$$\$153 \times \frac{\text{Beginning CPI}}{\text{Ending CPI}} = \$153 \times \frac{121.6}{135.3} = \$137.51$$

The real annually compounded rate of return on the portfolio was

$$i = \left(\frac{S}{P}\right)^{\frac{1}{n}} - 1 = \left(\frac{\$137.51}{\$100}\right)^{\frac{1}{5}} - 1 = 0.0658 = \underline{6.58\%}$$

5. The value, after five years, of an initial $100 investment was

$$\$100\,(1 - 0.13)(1 + 0.18)(1 + 0.05)(1 + 0.24)(1 - 0.05) = \$126.98$$

The five-year compound annual return was

$$i = \left(\frac{S}{P}\right)^{\frac{1}{n}} - 1 = \left(\frac{\$126.98}{\$100}\right)^{\frac{1}{5}} - 1 = 0.0489 = \underline{4.89\%}$$

6. $100 invested for the last 3 years would have grown to

$$\$100\,(1.167)(1.149)(1.316) = \$176.46$$

The 3-year equivalent annually compounded <u>return</u> was

$$i = \left(\frac{S}{P}\right)^{\frac{1}{n}} - 1 = \left(\frac{\$176.46}{\$100}\right)^{\frac{1}{3}} - 1 = 0.2084 = \underline{20.84\%}$$

$100 invested for the last 5 years would have grown to

$$\$176.46\,(1.283)(1.290) = \$292.05$$

The 5-year equivalent annually compounded <u>return</u> was

$$i = \left(\frac{\$292.05}{\$100}\right)^{\frac{1}{5}} - 1 = 0.2391 = \underline{23.91\%}$$

$100 invested for the entire 10 years would have grown to

$$\$292.05\,(1.103)(1 - 0.023)(1.228)(1.159)(1 - 0.099) = \$403.58$$

The 10-year equivalent annually compounded <u>return</u> was

$$i = \left(\frac{\$403.58}{\$100}\right)^{\frac{1}{10}} - 1 = 0.1497 = \underline{14.97\%}$$

7. $$n = \frac{\ln\left(\frac{S}{P}\right)}{\ln(1 + i)} = \frac{\ln\left(\frac{\$895.67}{\$800}\right)}{\ln(1.006\overline{6})} = \frac{0.11296}{0.0066445} = 17.00 \text{ periods}$$

Terry made the payment 17 months after March 1, that is, on <u>August 1 of the following year.</u>

8. $$n = \frac{\ln\left(\frac{S}{P}\right)}{\ln(1 + i)} = \frac{\ln\left(\frac{\$100,000}{\$19,725.75}\right)}{\ln(1.0425)} = \frac{1.62325}{0.041622} = 39 \text{ periods}$$

Since each compounding period is 6 months, <u>19.5 years</u> remain until maturity of the stripped bond.

Review Problems *(continued)*

9. Maturity value = $P(1 + i)^n = \$4500 (1.0575)^8 = \$7038.10$

The number of compounding periods between the discount date and the maturity date is

$$n = \frac{\ln\left(\dfrac{S}{P}\right)}{\ln(1 + i)} = \frac{\ln\left(\dfrac{\$7038.10}{\$5697.84}\right)}{\ln(1.02375)} = \frac{0.21125}{0.023472} = 9.00 \text{ periods}$$

Therefore, the discounting took place

$16 - 9 = 7 \text{ periods} = \underline{1.75 \text{ years}}$

after the issue date.

10. The annual rate of population decline for the 1987 to 1992 period is

$$i = \left(\frac{S}{P}\right)^{\frac{1}{n}} - 1 = \left(\frac{14{,}500}{17{,}500}\right)^{\frac{1}{5}} - 1 = -0.03691 = -3.691\%$$

If the population continues to decline at the same annual rate, it will take

$$n = \frac{\ln\left(\dfrac{S}{P}\right)}{\ln(1 + i)} = \frac{\ln\left(\dfrac{11{,}500}{14{,}500}\right)}{\ln(1 - 0.03691)} = \frac{-0.2318}{-0.03761} = 6.164 \text{ years}$$

for the population to drop another 3000 to 11,500. To the nearest month, it will take **6 years, 2 months.**

11. The number of half years for $10,000 invested at 8% compounded semiannually to grow to $12,000 is

$$n = \frac{\ln\left(\dfrac{S}{P}\right)}{\ln(1 + i)} = \frac{\ln\left(\dfrac{\$12{,}000}{\$10{,}000}\right)}{\ln\left(1 + \dfrac{0.08}{2}\right)} = \frac{\ln 1.2}{\ln 1.04} = 4.6486$$

The number of days in the partial half year is

$0.6486 (182 \text{ days}) = 118.0$

To the nearest day, it will take 2 years and 118 days for the $10,000 to grow to $12,000.

12. $f = (1 + i)^m - 1 = (1.01625)^4 - 1 = 0.06660 = 6.660\%$

For equivalent monthly compounding,

$i = (1 + f)^{\frac{1}{m}} - 1 = 1.06660^{\frac{1}{12}} - 1 = 0.00539$

$j = 12i = \underline{6.465\% \text{ compounded monthly.}}$

Review Problems *(concluded)*

13. $f = (1 + i)^m - 1 = (1.00875)^{12} - 1 = 0.1102 = 11.02\%$

    For equivalent semiannual compounding,

    $i = (1 + f)^{\frac{1}{m}} - 1 = 1.1102^{\frac{1}{2}} - 1 = 0.05366$

    $j = 2i = \underline{10.73\%\ \text{compounded semiannually.}}$

    For any nominal interest rate below 10.73%, you should choose semiannual compounding.

14. $f = (1 + i)^m - 1 = (1.035)^2 - 1 = 0.0712$

    For equivalent monthly compounding,

    $i = (1 + f)^{\frac{1}{m}} - 1 = 1.0712^{\frac{1}{12}} - 1 = 0.00575$

    $j = 12i = \underline{6.90\%\ \text{compounded monthly.}}$

    For equivalent annual compounding,

    $j = f = \underline{7.12\%\ \text{compounded annually.}}$

15. $f = (1 + i)^m - 1 = (1.015)^{12} - 1 = 0.1956 = \underline{19.56\%}$

16. $f = (1 + i)^m - 1 = (1.0025)^{12} - 1 = 0.0304 = \underline{3.04\%}$

17. $f = (1 + i)^m - 1 = (1.0345)^2 - 1 = 0.0702 = \underline{7.02\%}$

18. $f = \left(\dfrac{S}{P}\right)^{\frac{1}{n}} - 1 = \left(\dfrac{\$21{,}805}{\$15{,}000}\right)^{\frac{1}{4.5}} - 1 = 0.0867 = \underline{8.67\%}$

19. $f\ (\text{bank}) = (1 + i)^m - 1 = 1.04375^2 - 1 = 0.08941 = 8.941\%$

    $f\ (\text{broker}) = (1.0071\overline{6})^{12} - 1 = 0.08947 = 8.947\%$

    Camille should take the <u>bank mortgage</u> since its effective interest rate is lower.

20. $f\ (\text{old}) = (1.015)^{12} - 1 = 0.1956 = 19.56\%$

    $f\ (\text{new}) = 19.56\% - 2\% = 17.56\%$

    $i\ (\text{new}) = (1 + f)^{\frac{1}{m}} - 1 = (1.1756)^{\frac{1}{12}} - 1 = 0.01357$

    The monthly (periodic) rate should be reduced to <u>1.357% per month.</u>

Self-Test Exercise

1. $P = \$85,000$, $S = \$215,000$, $n = 13$

   The compound annual rate of appreciation of the home has been

   $$i = \left(\frac{S}{P}\right)^{\frac{1}{n}} - 1 = \left(\frac{\$215,000}{\$85,000}\right)^{\frac{1}{13}} - 1 = 0.0740 = \underline{7.40\%}$$

2. $P = 109.6$, $S = 133.8$, $n = 8.5$

   The average compound annual inflation rate was

   $$i = \left(\frac{S}{P}\right)^{\frac{1}{n}} - 1 = \left(\frac{133.8}{109.6}\right)^{\frac{1}{8.5}} - 1 = 0.0237 = \underline{2.37\%}$$

3. Suppose the company began the five-year period with sales of 1000 units/year. (The answer to the problem will not depend on the initial number chosen since the given information is in terms of proportional (percentage) changes.) After the first 5 years, annual sales will be

   $$S = P(1 + i)^n = 1000(1 - 0.10)^5 = 590.49 \text{ units/year}$$

   a. To return to 1000 units/year over the subsequent 5 years, the compound annual growth of sales must be

   $$i = \left(\frac{S}{P}\right)^{\frac{1}{n}} - 1 = \left(\frac{1000}{590.45}\right)^{\frac{1}{5}} - 1 = 0.1111 = \underline{11.11\%}$$

   b. If sales grow at 10% per year, it will take

   $$n = \frac{\ln(S/P)}{\ln(1 + i)} = \frac{\ln(1000/590.45)}{\ln(1.1111)} = 5.527 \text{ years}$$

   or $\underline{5 \text{ years and } 6 \text{ months}}$ (to the nearest month) to return to the original level of sales.

4. In terms of beginning dollars, the $54,230 has a purchasing power of only

   $$\$54,230 \times \frac{\text{Beginning CPI}}{\text{Ending CPI}} = \$54,230 \times \frac{100}{126.5} = \$42,869.57$$

   The portfolio's annually compounded real rate of return was

   $$i = \left(\frac{S}{P}\right)^{\frac{1}{n}} - 1 = \left(\frac{\$42,869.57}{\$35,645}\right)^{\frac{1}{6}} - 1 = 0.0312 = \underline{3.12\%}$$

5. Terminal value of $100 invested for the last 3 years

   $$= \$100(1 - 0.162)(1 - 0.041)(1 + 1.154) = \$173.10$$

   Terminal value of $100 invested for the last 5 years

   $$= \$173.10(1 - 0.059)(1 - 0.113) = \$144.48$$

   Terminal value of $100 invested for all 10 years

   $$= \$144.48(1 - 0.027)(1.101)(1 - 0.297)(1.226)(1.340) = \$178.76$$

Self-Test Exercise

The corresponding equivalent annually compounded rates of return are

$$i = \left(\frac{\$173.10}{\$100}\right)^{\frac{1}{3}} - 1 = 0.2007 = \underline{\underline{20.07\%}} \text{ for the last } \underline{3 \text{ years}}$$

$$i = \left(\frac{\$144.48}{\$100}\right)^{\frac{1}{5}} - 1 = 0.0764 = \underline{\underline{7.64\%}} \text{ for the last } \underline{5 \text{ years}}$$

$$i = \left(\frac{\$178.76}{\$100}\right)^{\frac{1}{10}} - 1 = 0.0598 = \underline{\underline{5.98\%}} \text{ for the last } \underline{10 \text{ years}}$$

6. The number of compounding periods (quarters) for $100 to grow to $250 at 9% compounded quarterly is

$$n = \frac{\ln\left(\frac{S}{P}\right)}{\ln(1+i)} = \frac{\ln\left(\frac{\$250}{\$100}\right)}{\ln(1.0225)} = 41.180$$

The partial period is 0.180 (3 months) = 0.54 months. Rounded to the nearest month, it will take an investment $\underline{10 \text{ years and } 4 \text{ months}}$ to increase by 150% if it earns 9% compounded quarterly.

7. Maturity value of debt = $\$5600 (1.042)^6 = \$7167.94$
   The number of months before maturity when the loan was settled was

$$n = \frac{\ln\left(\frac{S}{P}\right)}{\ln(1+i)} = \frac{\ln\left(\frac{\$7167.94}{\$6569.19}\right)}{\ln\left(1 + \frac{0.075}{12}\right)} = 14.000$$

Hence, the loan was settled $36 - 14 = \underline{22 \text{ months}}$ into the 3-year term.

8. The purchase price is the present value of the $10,000 face value discounted at 7.67% csa. The number of half years until maturity is

$$n = \frac{\ln\left(\frac{S}{P}\right)}{\ln(1+i)} = \frac{\ln\left(\frac{\$10,000}{\$3658.46}\right)}{\ln\left(1 + \frac{0.0767}{2}\right)} = 26.7198$$

The partial period is 0.7198 (182 days) = 131.00 days. Therefore, the bond will mature $\underline{13 \text{ years and } 131 \text{ days}}$ after the date of purchase.

9. $f = 8.375\%$. For semiannual compounding,

$$i = (1 + f)^{\frac{1}{m}} - 1 = 1.08375^{\frac{1}{2}} - 1 = 0.04103$$

$$j = 2i = \underline{8.21\% \text{ compounded semiannually}}$$

Choose the semiannually compounded GIC if the nominal rate exceeds 8.21% compounded semiannually.

Self-Test Exercise *(concluded)*

10. $f \text{ (GMAC)} = (1 + i)^m - 1 = (1.0290)^4 - 1 = 0.12114$

    $f \text{ (bank)} = (1.009583\overline{3})^{12} - 1 = 0.12126$

    $f \text{ (credit union)} = (1.05875)^2 - 1 = 0.12095$

    Janet should choose the <u>credit union loan</u> since it carries the lowest effective rate of interest.

11. $f = i = \left(\dfrac{S}{P}\right)^{\frac{1}{n}} - 1 = \left(\dfrac{\$7900}{\$6000}\right)^{2.75} - 1 = 0.1052 = \underline{10.52\%}$

    The investment earned an effective rate of 10.52% during the 33-month period.

10   Ordinary Annuities: Future Value and Present value

Changes in the Second Edition

Consumer credit, formerly covered in chapter 10, is now the subject of Chapter 18. Consumer Credit has been moved out of the flow of core topics because it is an area that is not covered in a majority of business math courses. Furthermore, one of the topics in Consumer Credit can be more readily handled with a knowledge of annuities.

Coverage of annuities (Chapters 11, 12, and 13 in the first edition) has been restructured among four chapters (10, 11, 12, and 13). However, these chapters are, on average, shorter than the former annuity chapters, occupying a total of 141 pages compared to 164 pages in the first edition.

The usual sequence of annuity topics in most texts (including the first edition of this text) is: ordinary simple annuities, simple annuities due, ordinary general annuities, and general annuities due. As each type of annuity is discussed in turn, the exposition typically presents a variety of scenarios illustrating the calculation of each of the five variables (present value, future value, payment size, number of payments, and interest rate) from given values of the other variables. This traditional approach tends to have the following consequences.

- Students do not develop the habit, as an *intentional* early step in solving an annuity problem, of determining the type of annuity involved. The type of annuity is self-evident from the topic at hand. Later, in a problem where the annuity type is not apparent from a broader context, students all too frequently present a correct solution for the wrong type of annuity.
- Students' interest lags at the instructor and text repeat the cycle of calculating each annuity variable for each successive type of annuity.
- Because the general annuity case is often presented as "just like the simple annuity case except that the interest rate per compounding period must be replaced by the effective interest rate per payment interval," students tend to view the interest rate *per compounding period* as the fundamental interest rate variable in annuity calculations. They ought to see the interest rate *per payment interval* as fundamental, and perform the necessary calculation to obtain its value.

Survey respondents and colleagues have commented on the use (in the first edition and in other texts) of the symbol f to represent both the effective (annual) rate of interest and the effective interest rate per payment interval in annuity formulas. They said that this dual usage of f tends to confuse students. Indeed the conceptual similarity of the two quantities increases the potential for confusion. Therefore, we have retained f as the symbol for the effective (annual) rate interest and have introduced p to present the interest rate per payment interval.

We believe that the reorganized treatment of annuities addresses all of the preceding concerns. In Chapter 11, we begin by formulating the future value of an *ordinary* annuity in terms of p, the interest rate per payment interval. Then (in Section 10.3) we deal with how p is determined given that interest rates are normally quoted as nominal annual rates. If it happens that the compounding interval equals the payment interval, then p simply equals i, the interest rate per payment interval. Otherwise, we must calculate the value of p from $p = (1+i)^c - 1$ (which is derived using an inferential argument). By taking this approach it is clear that p, the interest rate per payment interval, is the fundamental interest rate variable for annuities. Furthermore, students begin to develop the habit of looking for indications in the problem's wording of the type of annuity.

Section 10.4 discusses the present value of an *ordinary* annuity in terms of p. At this point, students are able to calculate the present value and future value of both *ordinary simple* annuities and *ordinary general* annuities.

In Chapter 11, we develop the simple mathematical adjustment needed to extend future value and present value calculations to annuities *due*. Students are then able to handle present value and future value applications involving any of the four types of annuities.

In Chapter 12, we turn to the calculation of each of the other three variables: payment size (R), number of payments (n), and interest rate per payment interval (p). As each variable is considered, all four types of annuity are "fair game." Under this approach, the calculation of each of these values is addressed once (for all four types of annuity) instead of four times if each type of annuity is taught in sequence.

Perpetuities and deferred annuities are presented (again in terms of p) in Chapter 13.

Another matter regarding notation was raised in reviews and surveys. Some instructors expressed a strong dislike for the use of the shorthand "angle" notation at this level of mathematics. (The notation has its origin in actuarial science.) Therefore, it has been dropped from the text except for some advanced topics in Chapters 15 and 16.

Exercise 10.2

1. Given: R = $500, n = 13, p = i = 11.5%

$$S_n = R \left[\frac{(1 + p)^n - 1}{p} \right] = \$500 \left(\frac{1.115^{13} - 1}{0.115} \right) = \underline{\underline{\$13,551.86}}$$

2. Given: R = $100, n = 5.5(4) = 22, $p = i = \dfrac{10\%}{4} = 2.5\%$

$$S_n = \$100 \left(\frac{1.025^{22} - 1}{0.025} \right) = \underline{\underline{\$2886.29}}$$

3. Given: R = $75, n = 2.5(12) = 30, $p = i = \dfrac{8\%}{12} = 0.6\overline{6}\%$

$$S_n = \$75 \left(\frac{1.00\overline{6}^{\,30} - 1}{0.006} \right) = \underline{\underline{\$2481.66}}$$

4. Given: R = $2000, n = 12.5(2) = 25, $p = i = \dfrac{7.5\%}{2} = 3.75\%$

$$S_n = \$2000 \left(\frac{1.00375^{25} - 1}{0.00375} \right) = \underline{\underline{\$80,542.25}}$$

5. Given: R = $175, n = 8.25(12) = 99, $p = i = \dfrac{11\%}{12} = 0.91\overline{6}\%$

$$S_n = \$175 \left(\frac{1.0091\overline{6}^{\,99} - 1}{0.0091\overline{6}} \right) = \underline{\underline{\$28,023.46}}$$

6. Given: R = $700, n = 7.75(4) = 31, $p = i = \dfrac{9\%}{4} = 2.25\%$

$$S_n = \$700 \left(\frac{1.0225^{31} - 1}{0.0225} \right) = \underline{\underline{\$30,901.26}}$$

7. Given: R = $3500, n = 19(2) = 38, $p = i = \dfrac{9.25\%}{2} = 4.625\%$

$$S_n = \$3500 \left(\frac{1.04625^{38} - 1}{0.04625} \right) = \underline{\underline{\$346,122.02}}$$

8. Given: R = $435, n = 6(12) + 7 = 79, $p = \dfrac{8.5\%}{12} = 0.708\overline{3}\%$

$$S_n = \$435 \left(\frac{1.00708\overline{3}^{\,79} - 1}{0.007083} \right) = \underline{\underline{\$45,843.56}}$$

9. a. Given: R = $1000, p = 10%, n = 5 payments

$$S_n = \$1000 \left(\frac{1.10^5 - 1}{0.10} \right) = \underline{\underline{\$6105.10}}$$

   Similarly,

   b. $S_n = \underline{\underline{\$15,937.43}}$ for n = 10

   c. $S_n = \underline{\underline{\$31,772.48}}$ for n = 15

   d. $S_n = \underline{\underline{\$57,275.48}}$ for n = 20

 e. $S_n = \underline{\$98,347.06}$ for $n = 25$

 f. $S_n = \underline{\$164,494.02}$ for $n = 30$

10. a. Given: $n = 20$, $R = \$1000$, $p = 9\%$

$$S_n = \$1000 \left(\frac{1.09^{20} - 1}{0.09}\right) = \underline{\$51,160.12}$$

Similarly,

 b. $S_n = \underline{\$57,275.00}$ for $p = 10\%$

 c. $S_n = \underline{\$64,202.83}$ for $p = 11\%$

 d. $S_n = \underline{\$72,052.44}$ for $p = 12\%$

11. a. (i) $S = P(1 + i)^n = \$5000(1.08)^8 = \underline{\$9254.65}$

   (ii) $S_n = R\left[\dfrac{(1 + p)^n - 1}{p}\right] = \$910\left(\dfrac{1.08^8 - 1}{0.08}\right) = \underline{\$9679.33}$

   (iii) $S_n = \$1675\left(\dfrac{1.08^5 - 1}{0.08}\right) = \underline{\$9826.56}$

 b. (i) $S = \$5000(1.10)^8 = \underline{\$10,717.94}$

   (ii) $S_n = \$910\left(\dfrac{1.10^8 - 1}{0.10}\right) = \underline{\$10,406.66}$

   (iii) $S_n = \$1675\left(\dfrac{1.10^5 - 1}{0.10}\right) = \underline{\$10,226.04}$

At the lower (8%) interest rate, the five-payment annuity has the largest economic value while the lump payment has the lowest economic value. At the higher (10%) interest rate, the ranking of the economic values is reversed.

12. Given: $R = \$60$, $n = 5(12) = 60$, $p = i = \dfrac{6\%}{12} = 0.5\%$

$$S_n = \$60\left(\frac{1.005^{60} - 1}{0.005}\right) = \underline{\$4186.20}$$

Josie will have $4186.20 after 5 years.

13. For the first 2 years, $R = \$1200$, $n = 8$, $p = i = 2.5\%$. The future value after 2 years is

$$S_n = \$1200\left(\frac{1.025^8 - 1}{0.025}\right) = \$10,483.34$$

For the next 3 years,

$P = \$10,483.34$, $n = 12$, $R = \$1200$, $p = i = 2.25\%$

The combined future value of these amounts at the end of the three years is

$$\$10,483.24(1.0225)^{12} + \$1200\left(\frac{1.0225^{12} - 1}{0.0225}\right)$$

$$= \$13,691.77 + \$16,322.67$$

$$= \underline{\$30,014.43}$$

14. The amount currently in Herb's RRSP is

$$S_n = \$2000 \left(\frac{1.0475^{16} - 1}{0.0475} \right) = \$46,365.73$$

For the next 7 years,

$$P = \$46,365.73, \; R = \$1500, \; n = 7(4) = 28, \; p = i = \frac{8\%}{4} = 2\%$$

The amount in the RRSP 7 years from now will be

$$\$46,365.73(1.02)^{28} + \$1500 \left(\frac{1.02^{28} - 1}{0.02} \right)$$

$$= \$80,723.85 + \$55,576.82$$
$$= \underline{\$136,300.67}$$

15. After 10 years, Marika's RRSP will be worth

$$\$18,000(1.045)^{20} + \$2000 \left(\frac{1.045^{20} - 1}{0.045} \right) = \$43,410.85 + \$62,742.85$$

$$= \$106,153.70$$

After a further 5 years, it will be worth

$$\$106,153.70(1.0075)^{60} + \$300 \left(\frac{1.0075^{60} - 1}{0.0075} \right)$$

$$= \$166,202.83 + \$22,627.24$$
$$= \underline{\$188,830.07}$$

16. If contributions start this year, the amount in the RRSP 30 years from now will be

$$S_n = \$1000 \left(\frac{1.08^{30} - 1}{0.08} \right) = \$113,283$$

If contributions start in the sixth year and continue for 25 years, the RRSP will be worth

$$S_n = \$1000 \left(\frac{1.08^{25} - 1}{0.08} \right) = \$73,106$$

The RRSP will be worth $113,283 - \$73,106 = \underline{\$40,177}$ more as a result of the first 5 years' contributions.

17. The difference will arise from the future value of the first payment. Its future value 39 years later will be

$$S = P(1 + i)^n = \$1000(1.08)^{39} = \underline{\$20,115.29}$$

Hence, the RRSP will be worth $20,115.39 more as a result of starting the contributions one year earlier.

Exercise 10.2 *(concluded)*

18. If $3000 is contributed at the end of the next 30 years,

$$S_n = \$3000 \left(\frac{1.08^{30} - 1}{0.08} \right) = \$339,850$$

If $6000 is contributed in each of the last 15 years,

$$S_n = \$6000 \left(\frac{1.08^{15} - 1}{0.08} \right) = \$162,913$$

The $3000 contribution for 30 years will result in $339,850 − $162,913 = $176,937 more in the RRSP. This is more than twice as much as with the alternative plan.

19. The amount in Leona's plan at age 30 was

$$S_n = \$3000 \left(\frac{1.08^{10} - 1}{0.08} \right) = \$43,459.69$$

The amount in her plan at age 65 will be

$$S = P(1 + i)^n = \$43,459.69(1.08)^{35} = \underline{\$642,566}$$

The amount in John's plan at age 65 will be

$$S_n = \$3000 \left(\frac{1.08^{35} - 1}{0.08} \right) = \underline{\$516,950}$$

Leona will have $642,566 − $516,950 = $125,616 more than John in her RRSP at age 65.

Exercise 10.3

1. $i = \dfrac{\text{Nominal interest rate}}{\text{Compounding frequency}} = \dfrac{10\%}{4} = 2.50\%$

$c = \dfrac{\text{Compounding frequency}}{\text{Payment frequency}} = \dfrac{4}{1} = 4$

$p = (1 + i)^c - 1 = 1.025^4 - 1 = 0.10381 = \underline{10.318\%}$

2. $i = \dfrac{9\%}{12} = 0.75\%; \ c = \dfrac{12}{4} = 3$

$p = 1.0075^3 - 1 = 0.02267 = \underline{2.267\%}$

3. $i = \dfrac{8\%}{4} = 2\%; \ c = \dfrac{4}{2} = 2$

$p = 1.02^2 - 1 = 0.0404 = \underline{4.040\%}$

4. $i = \dfrac{7.5\%}{12} = 0.625\%; \ c = \dfrac{12}{1} = 12$

$p = 1.00625^{12} - 1 = 0.07763 = \underline{7.763\%}$

5. $i = \dfrac{11\%}{4} = 2.75\%; \ c = \dfrac{4}{12} = 0.\overline{3}$

$p = 1.0275^{0.\overline{3}} - 1 = 0.00908 = \underline{0.908\%}$

6. $i = \dfrac{9.5\%}{2} = 4.75\%; \quad c = \dfrac{2}{12} = 0.1\overline{6}$

    $p = 1.0475^{0.1\overline{6}} - 1 = 0.00776 = \underline{0.776\%}$

7. $i = \dfrac{7.75\%}{1} = 7.75\%; \quad c = \dfrac{1}{4} = 0.25$

    $p = 1.0775^{0.25} - 1 = 0.01884 = \underline{1.884\%}$

8. $i = \dfrac{9.25\%}{1} = 9.25\%; \quad c = \dfrac{1}{2} = 0.5$

    $p = 1.0925^{0.5} - 1 = 0.04523 = \underline{4.523\%}$

9. $i = \dfrac{10.25\%}{1} = 10.25\%; \quad c = \dfrac{1}{12} = 0.08\overline{3}$

    $p = 1.1025^{0.08\overline{3}} - 1 = 0.00816 = \underline{0.816\%}$

10. $i = \dfrac{8.5\%}{2} = 4.25\%; \quad c = \dfrac{2}{4} = 0.5$

    $p = 1.0425^{0.5} - 1 = 0.02103 = \underline{2.103\%}$

11. $i = \dfrac{11.5\%}{1} = 11.5\%; \quad c = \dfrac{1}{4} = 0.25; \quad n = 11(4) = 44$

    $p = 1.115^{0.25} - 1 = 0.027587273$

    $S_n = \$400 \left(\dfrac{1.027587273^{44} - 1}{0.027587273} \right) = \underline{\$33,515.32}$

12. $i = \dfrac{10\%}{4} = 2.5\%; \quad n = 6.5(12) = 78; \quad c = \dfrac{4}{12} = 0.\overline{3}$

    $p = 1.025^{0.\overline{3}} - 1 = 0.008264838$

    $S_n = \$150 \left(\dfrac{1.08264838^{78} - 1}{0.008264838} \right) = \underline{\$16,339.57}$

13. $i = \dfrac{8\%}{12} = 0.\overline{6}\%; \quad n = 3.5(2) = 7; \quad c = \dfrac{12}{2} = 6$

    $p = 1.00\overline{6}^{6} - 1 = 0.040672622$

    $S_n = \$2750 \left(\dfrac{1.040672622^{7} - 1}{0.040672622} \right) = \underline{\$21,764.70}$

14. $i = \dfrac{7.5\%}{2} = 3.75\%; \quad n = 13.5(4) = 54; \quad c = \dfrac{2}{4} = 0.5$

    $p = 1.0375^{0.5} - 1 = 0.018577439$

    $S_n = \$1500 \left(\dfrac{1.018577439^{54} - 1}{0.018577439} \right) = \underline{\$137,421.49}$

Exercise 10.3 *(continued)*

15. $i = \dfrac{10.5\%}{12} = 0.875\%;\; n = 17;\; c = \dfrac{12}{1} = 12$

$p = 1.00875^{12} - 1 = 0.11020345$

$S_n = \$3500 \left(\dfrac{1.11020345^{17} - 1}{0.11020345} \right) = \underline{\underline{\$156{,}049.64}}$

16. $i = \dfrac{9\%}{4} = 2.25\%;\; n = 8.5(2) = 17;\; c = \dfrac{4}{2} = 2$

$p = 1.0225^{2} - 1 = 0.04550625$

$S_n = \$950 \left(\dfrac{1.04550625^{17} - 1}{0.04550625} \right) = \underline{\underline{\$23{,}607.90}}$

17. $R = \$500;\; n = 8(4) = 32;\; i = \dfrac{9\%}{12} = 0.75\%;\; c = \dfrac{12}{4} = 3$

$p = 1.0075^{3} - 1 = 0.022669172$

The amount in the RESP after 8 years will be

$S_n = \$500 \left(\dfrac{1.022669172^{32} - 1}{0.022669172} \right) = \underline{\underline{\$23{,}135.41}}$

Of this amount,

$\$23{,}135.41 - 32(\$500) = \underline{\underline{\$7135.41}}$

will be interest.

18. a. $S = P(1 + i)^n = \$5000(1.045)^{16} = \underline{\underline{\$10{,}111.85}}$

b. $R = \$900;\; i = 4.5\%;\; n = 8;\; c = \dfrac{2}{1} = 2$

$p = 1.045^{2} - 1 = 0.092025$

$S_n = \$900 \left(\dfrac{1.092025^{8} - 1}{0.092025} \right) = \underline{\underline{\$9998.73}}$

c. $R = \$400;\; i = 4.5\%;\; n = 20;\; c = \dfrac{2}{4} = 0.5$

$p = 1.045^{0.5} - 1 = 0.022252415$

$S_n = \$400 \left(\dfrac{1.022252415^{20} - 1}{0.022252415} \right) = \underline{\underline{\$9939.94}}$

Exercise 10.3 (continued)

19. a. $R = \$1000$, $n = 25$, $p = i = 9\%$

$$S_n = \$1000 \left(\frac{1.09^{25} - 1}{0.09} \right) = \underline{\underline{\$84,700.90}}$$

b. $R = \$1000$; $n = 25$; $i = \dfrac{9\%}{4} = 2.25\%$; $c = \dfrac{4}{1} = 4$

$p = 1.0225^4 - 1 = 0.093083319$

$$S_n = \$1000 \left(\frac{1.093083319^{25} - 1}{0.093083319} \right) = \underline{\underline{\$88,673.74}}$$

c. $R = \$1000$; $n = 25$; $i = \dfrac{9\%}{12} = 0.75\%$, $c = \dfrac{12}{1} = 12$

$p = 1.0075^{12} - 1 = 0.093806898$

$$S_n = \$1000 \left(\frac{1.093806898 - 1}{0.093806898} \right) = \underline{\underline{\$89,635.35}}$$

20. For the case of month-end contributions of $300,

$R = \$300$; $n = 300$; $i = \dfrac{8.5\%}{2} = 4.25\%$, $c = \dfrac{2}{12} = 0.1\overline{6}$

$p = 1.0425^{0.1\overline{6}} - 1 = 0.0069610621$

The amount in the RRSP after 25 years will be

$$S_n = \$300 \left(\frac{1.0069610621^{300} - 1}{0.0069610621} \right) = \underline{\underline{\$302,244.75}}$$

For year-end contributions of $3600,

$R = \$3600$; $n = 25$; $i = 4.25\%$, $c = \dfrac{2}{1} = 2$

$p = 1.0425^2 - 1 = 0.08680625$

The amount in the RRSP after 25 years will be

$$S_n = \$3600 \left(\frac{1.08680625^{25} - 1}{0.08680625} \right) = \underline{\underline{\$290,846.96}}$$

The RRSP will be worth $\underline{\underline{\$11,397.79}}$ more with monthly contributions.

Exercise 10.3 *(continued)*

21. $R = \$1000$; $n = 25(4) = 100$

    If the RRSP earns 9% compounded monthly,

    $i = \dfrac{9\%}{12} = 0.75\%$; $c = \dfrac{12}{4} = 3$; $p = 1.0075^3 - 1 = 0.022669172$

    $S_n = \$1000 \left(\dfrac{1.022669172^{100} - 1}{0.022669172} \right) = \underline{\underline{\$370,918.47}}$

    If the RRSP earns 9% compounded annually,

    $i = 9\%$; $c = \dfrac{1}{4} = 0.25$, $p = 1.09^{0.25} - 1 = 0.021778181$

    $S_n = \$1000 \left(\dfrac{1.021778181^{100} - 1}{0.021778181} \right) = \underline{\underline{\$350,032.94}}$

    With monthly compounding, the RRSP will be worth $\$370,918.47 - \$350,032.94 = \underline{\underline{\$20,885.53}}$ more.

22. For the first $8\dfrac{1}{2}$ years,

    $R = \$600$; $n = 8.5(2) = 17$; $i = \dfrac{9\%}{4} = 2.25\%$; $c = \dfrac{4}{2} = 2$

    $p = 1.0225^2 - 1 = 0.045506250$

    and the future value at the end of the $8\dfrac{1}{2}$ years is

    $S_n = \$600 \left(\dfrac{1.045506250^{17} - 1}{0.045506250} \right) = \underline{\underline{\$14,910.25}}$

    For the next $11\dfrac{1}{2}$ years,

    $R = \$600$; $n = 11.5(2) = 23$; $p = i = \dfrac{8\%}{2} = 4\%$; $P = \$14,910.25$

    The combined future value at the end of the 20 years is

    $\$14,910.25(1.04)^{23} + \$600 \left(\dfrac{1.04^{23} - 1}{0.04} \right) = \$36,749.52 + \$21,970.73$

    $= \underline{\underline{\$58,720.25}}$

Exercise 10.3 (continued)

23. For the first $12\frac{1}{2}$ years,

$$R = \$100; \ n = 12.5(12) = 150; \ i = \frac{7\%}{4} = 1.75\%; \ c = \frac{4}{12} = 0.\overline{3}$$

$$p = 1.0175^{0.\overline{3}} - 1 = 0.005799633$$

$$S_n = \$100 \left(\frac{1.005799633^{150} - 1}{0.005799633} \right) = \$23,808.21$$

For the next $12\frac{1}{2}$ years,

$$P = \$23,808.21; \ R = \$100; \ n = 150; \ i = \frac{8\%}{2} = 4\%; \ c = \frac{2}{12} = 0.1\overline{6}$$

$$p = 1.04^{0.1\overline{6}} - 1 = 0.0065581969$$

The combined future value after 25 years will be

$$\$23,808.21(1.04)^{25} + \$100 \left(\frac{1.0065581969^{150} - 1}{0.0065581969} \right) = \$63,468.79 + \$25,400.83$$

$$= \underline{\underline{\$88,869.62}}$$

24. a. Economic value = $\underline{\$10,000}$ since the due date coincides with the focal date.

   b. $R = \$800; \ n = 9; \ i = \frac{9\%}{2} = 4.5\%, \ c = \frac{2}{1} = 2$

   $$p = 1.045^2 - 1 = 0.092025$$

   $$S_n = \$800 \left(\frac{1.092025^9 - 1}{0.092025} \right) = \underline{\underline{\$10,505.66}}$$

   c. $R = \$330; \ n = 24; \ i = 4.5\%; \ c = \frac{2}{4} = 0.5$

   $$p = 1.045^{0.5} - 1 = 0.022252415$$

   $$S_n = \$330 \left(\frac{1.022252415^{24} - 1}{0.022252415} \right) = \underline{\underline{\$10,319.82}}$$

   The nine annual payments of $800 have the highest economic value and the single payment of $10,000 has the lowest economic value.

Exercise 10.3 (continued)

25. For the first 10 years,

$$R = \$1000; \ n = 10; \ i = \frac{7.5\%}{12} = 0.625\%; \ c = \frac{12}{1} = 12$$

$$p = 1.00625^{12} - 1 = 0.077632599$$

$$S_n = \$1000 \left(\frac{1.077632599^{10} - 1}{0.077632599} \right) = \underline{\$14,324.71}$$

For the next 15 years,

$$P = \$14,324.71; \ R = \$1000; \ i = \frac{8\%}{2} = 4\%; \ c = \frac{2}{1} = 2; \ n = 15$$

$$p = 1.04^2 - 1 = 0.0816$$

The combined future value after 25 years will be

$$\$14,324.71(1.04)^{30} + \$1000 \left(\frac{1.0816^{15} - 1}{0.0816} \right) = \underline{\$73,953.35}$$

26. For the first 5 years,

$$R = \$300; \ n = 5(12) = 60; \ i = \frac{8\%}{2} = 4\%; \ c = \frac{2}{12} = 0.1\overline{6}$$

$$p = 1.04^{0.1\overline{6}} - 1 = 0.0065581969$$

$$S_n = \$300 \left(\frac{1.0065581969^{60} - 1}{0.0065581969} \right) = \underline{\$21,968.43}$$

For the subsequent 10 years,

$$R = \$2000; \ n = 10(4) = 40; \ i = 4\%; \ c = \frac{2}{4} = 0.5; \ P = \$21,968.43$$

$$p = 1.04^{0.5} - 1 = 0.019803903$$

The combined future value after 15 years will be

$$\$21,968.43(1.04)^{20} + \$2000 \left(\frac{1.019803903^{40} - 1}{0.019803903} \right) = \underline{\$168,427.29}$$

27. For the past 9 years,

$$R = \$2000; \ n = 9; \ i = \frac{8\%}{4} = 2\%; \ c = \frac{4}{1} = 4$$

$$p = 1.02^4 - 1 = 0.082432160$$

The current value of Gloria's RRSP is

$$S_n = \$2000 \left(\frac{1.08243216^9 - 1}{0.08243216} \right) = \underline{\$25,230.14}$$

For the next 15 years,

$$R = \$2000; \ n = 30; \ i = 2\%; \ c = \frac{4}{2} = 2; \ P = \$25,230.14$$

$$p = 1.02^2 - 1 = 0.0404$$

The total amount in the RRSP 15 years from now will be

$$\$25,230.14(1.02)^{60} + \$2000 \left(\frac{1.0404^{30} - 1}{0.0404} \right) = \underline{\$195,703.18}$$

Exercise 10.3 *(concluded)*

28.

8% compounding quarterly   **7% compounding semiannually**

$3000 per year $500 per month

For the first 7 years,

$R = \$3000; \ n = 7; \ i = \dfrac{8\%}{4} = 2; \ c = 4; \ p = 1.02^4 - 1 = 0.082432160$

For the next 5 years,

$R = \$500; \ n = 60; \ i = 2\%; \ c = 0.\overline{3}; \ p = 1.02^{0.\overline{3}} - 1 = 0.0066227096$

For the last 13 years,

$R = \$500; \ n = 156; \ i = 3.5\%; \ c = 0.1\overline{6}; \ p = 1.035^{0.1\overline{6}} - 1 = 0.00575003948$

Amount in RRSP after 7 years will be

$\$3000 \left(\dfrac{1.08243216^7 - 1}{0.08243216} \right) = \underline{\underline{\$26{,}968.51}}$

Amount in RRSP after 12 years will be

$\$26{,}968.51(1.02)^{20} + \$500 \left(\dfrac{1.0066227096^{60} - 1}{0.0066227096} \right) = \underline{\underline{\$76{,}761.75}}$

Amount in RRSP after 25 years will be

$\$76{,}761.75(1.035)^{26} + \$500 \left(\dfrac{1.0057500395^{156} - 1}{1.0057500395} \right) = \underline{\underline{\$313{,}490.72}}$

Exercise 10.4

1. Given: $R = \$500; \ n = 13, \ p = i = 11.5\%$

$A_n = R \left[\dfrac{1 - (1 + p)^{-n}}{p} \right] = \$500 \left(\dfrac{1 - 1.115^{-13}}{0.115} \right) = \underline{\underline{\$3291.74}}$

2. Given: $R = \$100, \ n = 22, \ p = i = \dfrac{10\%}{4} = 2.5\%$

$A_n = \$100 \left(\dfrac{1 - 1.025^{-22}}{0.025} \right) = \underline{\underline{\$1676.54}}$

3. Given: $R = \$75, \ n = 2.5(12) = 30, \ p = i = \dfrac{8\%}{12} = 0.\overline{6}\%$

$A_n = \$75 \left(\dfrac{1 - 1.00\overline{6}^{-30}}{0.00\overline{6}} \right) = \underline{\underline{\$2033.16}}$

4. Given: $R = \$2000, \ n = 12.5(2) = 25, \ p = i = \dfrac{7.5\%}{2} = 3.75\%$

$A_n = \$2000 \left(\dfrac{1 - 1.0375^{-25}}{0.0375} \right) = \underline{\underline{\$32{,}086.41}}$

Exercise 10.4 *(continued)*

5. Given: $R = \$175$, $n = 8.25(12) = 99$, $p = i = \dfrac{11\%}{12} = 0.91\overline{6}$

$$A_n = \$175\left(\dfrac{1 - 1.0091\overline{6}^{-99}}{0.0091\overline{6}}\right) = \underline{\underline{\$11,355.21}}$$

6. Given: $R = \$700$, $n = 7.75(4) = 31$, $p = i = \dfrac{9\%}{4} = 2.25\%$

$$A_n = \$700\left(\dfrac{1 - 1.0225^{-31}}{0.0225}\right) = \underline{\underline{\$15,502.92}}$$

7. Given: $R = \$1240$, $n = 9.5(2) = 19$, $p = i = \dfrac{9.9\%}{2} = 4.95\%$

$$A_n = \$1240\left(\dfrac{1 - 1.0495^{-19}}{0.0495}\right) = \underline{\underline{\$15,047.05}}$$

8. Given: $R = \$350$, $n = 11(12) + 5 = 137$, $p = i = \dfrac{8.75\%}{12} = 0.7291\overline{6}\%$

$$A_n = \$350\left(\dfrac{1 - 1.0072916\overline{6}^{-137}}{0.0072916\overline{6}}\right) = \underline{\underline{\$30,259.20}}$$

9. Given: $R = \$400$, $i = \dfrac{11.5\%}{1} = 11.5\%$, $n = 11(4) = 44$, $c = \dfrac{1}{4} = 0.25$

$p = 1.115^{0.25} - 1 = 0.027587273$

$$A_n = \$400\left(\dfrac{1 - 1.027587273^{-44}}{0.027587273}\right) = \underline{\underline{\$10,120.92}}$$

10. Given: $R = \$150$, $i = \dfrac{10\%}{4} = 2.5\%$, $n = 6.5(12) = 78$, $c = \dfrac{4}{12} = 0.\overline{3}$

$p = 1.025^{0.\overline{3}} - 1 = 0.008264838$

$$A_n = \$150\left(\dfrac{1 - 1.008264838^{-78}}{0.008264838}\right) = \underline{\underline{\$8598.45}}$$

11. Given: $R = \$2750$, $i = \dfrac{8\%}{12} = 0.\overline{6}\%$, $n = 3.5(2) = 7$, $c = \dfrac{12}{2} = 6$

$p = 1.00\overline{6}^{6} - 1 = 0.040672622$

$$A_n = \$2750\left(\dfrac{1 - 1.040672622^{-7}}{0.040672622}\right) = \underline{\underline{\$16,464.70}}$$

12. Given: $R = \$1500$, $i = \dfrac{7.5\%}{2} = 3.75\%$, $n = 13.5(4) = 54$, $c = \dfrac{2}{4} = 0.5$

$p = 1.0375^{0.5} - 1 = 0.018577439$

$$A_n = \$1500\left(\dfrac{1 - 1.018577439^{-54}}{0.018577439}\right) = \underline{\underline{\$50,859.93}}$$

Exercise 10.4 *(continued)*

13. Given $R = \$3500$, $i = \dfrac{10.5\%}{12} = 0.875\%$, $n = 17$, $c = \dfrac{12}{1} = 12$

$p = 1.00875^{12} - 1 = 0.110203450$

$A_n = \$3500 \left(\dfrac{1 - 1.11020345^{-17}}{0.11020345} \right) = \underline{\$26,388.76}$

14. Given: $R = \$950$, $i = \dfrac{9\%}{4} = 2.25\%$, $n = 8.5(2) = 17$, $c = \dfrac{4}{2} = 2$

$p = 1.0225^2 - 1 = 0.045506250$

$A_n = \$950 \left(\dfrac{1 - 1.04550625^{-17}}{0.04550625} \right) = \underline{\$11,079.10}$

15. $R = \$1000$ and $p = i = 10\%$ in all parts.

    a. $A_n = \$1000 \left(\dfrac{1 - 1.10^{-5}}{0.10} \right) = \underline{\$3790.79}$

    Similarly,
    b. For $n = 10$, $A_n = \underline{\$6144.57}$
    c. For $n = 20$, $A_n = \underline{\$8513.56}$
    d. For $n = 30$, $A_n = \underline{\$9426.91}$
    e. For $n = 100$, $A_n = \underline{\$9999.27}$
    f. For $n = 1000$, $A_n = \underline{\$10,000.00}$

16: $R = \$1000$ and $n = 20$ in all parts.

    a. For $p = i = 5\%$

    $A_n = \$1000 \left(\dfrac{1 - 1.05^{-20}}{0.05} \right) = \underline{\$12,462.21}$

    Similarly,

    b. For $p = i = 10\%$, $A_n = \underline{\$8513,56}$
    c. For $p = i = 11\%$, $A_n = \underline{\$7963.33}$
    d. For $p = i = 15\%$, $A_n = \underline{\$6259.33}$

17. The current economic value is the present value of future expenditures discounted at 8% compounded annually.

    $R = \$5$ million, $n = 5(4) = 20$, $i = 8\%$, $c = \dfrac{1}{4} = 0.25$

    $p = 1.08^{0.25} - 1 = 0.019426547$

    Substituting these values into formula (10–4),

    $A_n = \$5 \text{ million} \left(\dfrac{1 - 1.019426547^{-20}}{0.019426547} \right) = \underline{\$82,211,000}$

    to the nearest \$1000.

Exercise 10.4 *(continued)*

18. The economic value of the contract at the date of termination is the present value of the remaining payments. Substitution of

$R = \$30,000$, $n = 12(3) = 36$, $p = i = 7.5\%/12 = 0.625\%$
into formula (10–4) gives

$$A_n = \$30,000 \left(\frac{1 - 1.00625^{-36}}{0.00625} \right) = \underline{\underline{\$964,437}}$$

The settlement amount is $964,437.

19. The $21.6 million figure is the sum of all the monthly payments over the 7 years. That is,

$$36(\$200,000) + 48(\$300,000) = \$21,600,000$$

The current economic value of the deal is the present value of all the payments discounted at 7% compounded annually. The corresponding interest rate per payment interval is

$$p = 1.07^{0.08\overline{3}} - 1 = 0.00565414537$$

The present value, three years from now, of the last 48 payments is

$$A_n = \$300,000 \left(\frac{1 - 1.00565414537^{-48}}{0.00565414537} \right) = \underline{\underline{\$12,580,405}}$$

The present value today of this amount and the first 36 payments is

$$\frac{\$12,580,405}{1.07^3} + \$200,000 \left(\frac{1 - 1.00565414537^{-36}}{1.00565414537} \right) = \underline{\underline{\$16,767,320}}$$

The current economic value of the deal is $16,767,320.

20. For the first 6 years, $p = i = 4\%$

For the subsequent 9 years, $p = i = 5\%$

The present value, 6 years from now, of the last 18 payments is

$$A_n = \$2000 \left(\frac{1 - 1.05^{-18}}{0.05} \right) = \underline{\underline{\$23,379.17}}$$

The present value (today) of this amount and the first 12 payments is

$$\$2000 \left(\frac{1 - 1.04^{-12}}{0.04} \right) + \frac{\$23,379.17}{1.04^{12}} = \underline{\underline{\$33,372.71}}$$

21. For the first 5 years, $i = 0.625\%$, $c = \dfrac{12}{2} = 6$, and $p = 1.00625^6 - 1 = 0.038090843$

For the subsequent 10 years, $i = 9\%$, $c = \dfrac{1}{2} = 0.5$, and $p = 1.09^{0.5} - 1 = 0.044030651$

The present value, 5 years from now, of the last 20 payments is

$$A_n = \$2000 \left(\frac{1 - 1.044030651^{-20}}{0.044030651} \right) = \underline{\underline{\$26,235.78}}$$

The present value (today) of this amount and the first 10 payments is

$$\frac{\$26,235.78}{1.00625^{60}} + \$2000 \left(\frac{1 - 1.038090843^{-10}}{0.038090843} \right) = \$18,052.63 + \$16,377.07 = \underline{\underline{\$34,429.70}}$$

Exercise 10.4 (concluded)

22. For the first annuity, R = $800 quarterly, n = 4.5(4) = 18, and $p = i = \dfrac{8\%}{4} = 2\%$.

   For the second annuity, R = $2000 semiannually,

   $i = 2\%$, n = 4.5(2) = 9, $c = \dfrac{4}{2} = 2$, $p = 1.02^2 - 1 = 0.0404$

   The present value, $4\frac{1}{2}$ years from now, of the 9 semi-annual payments is

   $$A_n = \$2000 \left(\frac{1 - 1.0404^{-9}}{0.0404}\right) = \underline{\$14{,}843.60}$$

   The present value (today) of this amount and the first 18 quarterly payments is

   $$\frac{\$14{,}843.60}{1.02^{18}} + \$800 \left(\frac{1 - 1.02^{-18}}{0.02}\right) = \underline{\$22{,}386.51}$$

23. For the first annuity, R = $500 monthly, n = 2.5(12) = 30,

   $i = 3.5\%$, $c = \dfrac{2}{12} = 0.1\overline{6}$, $p = 1.035^{0.1\overline{6}} - 1 = 0.0057500395$

   For the second annuity, R = $2000 quarterly, n = 3.5(4) = 14,

   $i = 3.5\%$, $c = \dfrac{2}{4} = 0.5$, $p = 1.035^{0.5} - 1 = 0.017349497$

   The present value, $2\frac{1}{2}$ years from now, of the second annuity is

   $$A_n = \$2000 \left(\frac{1 - 1.017349497^{-14}}{0.017349497}\right) - \underline{\$24{,}670.34}$$

   The present value (today) of this amount and the first annuity is

   $$\frac{\$24{,}670.34}{1.035^5} + \$500 \left(\frac{1 - 1.0057500395^{-30}}{0.0057500395}\right) = \underline{\$34{,}513.13}$$

Exercise 10.5

1. The amount required to purchase an annuity is the present value of the payments discounted at the rate of return earned by the purchase price. If j = 8% compounded monthly for a 20-year term,

   n = 20(12) = 240, $p = i = 0.\overline{6}\%$, and

   $$A_n = \$3000 \left(\frac{1 - 1.00\overline{6}^{-240}}{0.00\overline{6}}\right) = \underline{\$358{,}662.88}$$

   Similarly,

j	Term	A_n
8% compounded monthly	25 years	$388,693.57
9% compounded monthly	20 years	$333,434.86
9% compounded monthly	25 years	$357,484.87

Exercise 10.5 (continued)

2. The economic value of the contract is the present value of the payments discounted at the time value of money.

R = \$100,000, n = 12(10) = 120, p = i = 0.75%, and

$$A_n = \$100,000 \left(\frac{1 - 1.0075^{-120}}{0.0075} \right) = \underline{\underline{\$7,894,169}}$$

The current economic value of Skoroften's contract is \$7,894,169.

3. a. The value placed on a 25% interest in the partnership was the present value of all the payments (discounted at the interest rate charged on the purchase price.) The payments form an ordinary general annuity with R = \$537.66, n = 144, i = 4%, c = 0.1$\overline{6}$, and p = 1.04$^{0.1\overline{6}}$ − 1 = 0.0065581969

$$A_n = \$537.66 \left(\frac{1 - 1.0065581969^{-144}}{0.0065581969} \right) = \underline{\underline{\$50,000}}$$

The implied value of the entire partnership is

4(\$50,000) = $\underline{\underline{\$200,000}}$

b. Total interest = Total payments − Principal
= 144(\$537.66) − \$50,000
= $\underline{\underline{\$27,423.04}}$

4. The amount required to purchase the annuity will be the present value of the payments discounted at the rate of return on the annuity.

R = \$2500, n = 20(12) = 240, i = 8.75%, c = $\dfrac{1}{12}$ = 0.08$\overline{3}$, and

p = 1.0875$^{0.08\overline{3}}$ − 1 = 0.0070146116

$$A_n = \$2500 \left(\frac{1 - 1.0070146116^{-240}}{0.0070146116} \right) = \underline{\underline{\$289,817.81}}$$

5. Colin and Marie should accept the offer that has the higher current economic value—that is, the one with the larger present value. The present value of the multiple-payment offer is

$$\$1000 + \$2000 \left(\frac{1 - 1.05^{-4}}{0.05} \right) = \underline{\underline{\$8091.90}}$$

They should accept the multiple-payment offer since it is worth \$191.90 more.

6. Since we are purchasing the building, we should choose the option having the lower economic or present value. The present value of the multiple-payment option is

$$\$10,000 + \$2500 \left(\frac{1 - 1.02^{-16}}{0.02} \right) = \underline{\underline{\$43,944.27}}$$

Hence, the multiple payment alternative has a \$45,000 − \$43,944.27 = \$1055.73 economic advantage.

7. The offer having the higher current economic value is preferred. The present value of Mrs. Martel's offer is

$$\$1900 + \$1900 \left(\frac{1 - 1.05^{-4}}{0.05} \right) = \underline{\underline{\$8637.31}}$$

Therefore, Mrs. Martel's offer is worth \$137.31 more in current dollars.

Exercise 10.5 *(continued)*

8. Osgood should accept a cash price that would put it in the same financial position as selling the refrigerator on credit and then discounting the conditional sale contract. The latter amount is

$$\$199 + \$199 \left(\frac{1 - 1.015^{-5}}{0.015} \right) = \underline{\underline{\$1150.75}}$$

Osgood should accept a cash offer of $1150.75.

9. The amount required to fund each annuity is the present value of the annuity discounted at the interest rate the money can earn. For both annuities,

$$R = \$200 \text{ monthly and } p = i = \frac{9.75\%}{12} = 0.8125\%$$

for the 30-year annuity,

$$A_n = \$200 \left(\frac{1 - 1.008125^{-360}}{0.008125} \right) = \underline{\underline{\$23,278.70}}$$

For the 20-year annuity, A_n = $21,085.55. It requires only $23,278.70 − $21,085.55 = $\underline{\underline{\$2193.15}}$ more to fund the extra 10 years. (This is only about 10% more.)

10. The investor will pay the present value of the remaining 14 semiannual payments of $4000 discounted at the required rate of return.

a. $i = 8\%$, $c = \frac{1}{2} = 0.5$, and $p = 1.08^{0.5} - 1 = 0.039230485$

$$A_n = \$4000 \left(\frac{1 - 1.039230485^{-14}}{0.039230485} \right) = \underline{\underline{\$42,467.95}}$$

Similarly,

b. $i = 10\%$, $c = 0.5$, $p = 0.048808848$, $A_n = \underline{\underline{\$39,897.84}}$

c. $i = 12\%$, $c = 0.5$, $p = 0.058300524$, $A_n = \underline{\underline{\$37,574.33}}$

11. Household Finance paid the present value of the scheduled payments discounted at the required rate of return of 19.5% compounded monthly.

$R = \$250$, $n = 15$, $p = i = 1.625\%$

$$\text{Price, } A_n = \$250 \left(\frac{1 - 1.01625^{-15}}{0.01625} \right) = \underline{\underline{\$3304.30}}$$

12. Selling price = Down payment + Present value of the monthly payments

$$R = \$160.70, \ n = 3.5(12) = 42, \ i = \frac{12\%}{4} = 3\%, \ c = \frac{4}{12} = 0.\overline{3}$$

$p = 1.03^{0.\overline{3}} - 1 = 0.0099016340$

$$A_n = \$160.70 \left(\frac{1 - 1.0099016340^{-42}}{0.0099016340} \right) = \underline{\underline{\$5499.94}}$$

Thus, the selling price was

$$\$2000 + \$5499.94 = \underline{\underline{\$7499.94}}$$

Exercise 10.5 (continued)

13. The $1000 purchase requires a $100 down payment plus monthly payments of $900/12 = $75. Flemmings should be willing to accept a cash amount equal to the present value of the payments discounted at the rate of return which Flemmings can earn on this money. That is,

$$\text{Cash price} = \$100 + \$75 \left(\frac{1 - 1.00958\overline{3}^{-12}}{0.00958\overline{3}} \right) = \underline{\underline{\$946.36}}$$

14. The finance company will pay the present value of the payments discounted at the required return of 20% compounded quarterly. The present value, 3 months from now, of the six payments is

$$A_n = \$569 \left(\frac{1 - 1.05^{-6}}{0.05} \right) = \$2888.07$$

The present value of this amount today is

$$P = S(1 + i)^{-n} = \$2888.07(1.05)^{-1} = \underline{\underline{\$2750.54}}$$

15. The economic values of the two annuities must be calculated and compared at the *same* focal date. Their ranking will be the same at any focal date. Calculations will be minimized if the date 10 years from now is chosen as the focal date. The economic value of the $1000 annuity on that date is its future value. The economic value of the $2500 annuity on that date is its present value.

For the $1000 annuity,

$$S_n = \$1000 \left(\frac{1.10^{10} - 1}{0.10} \right) = \$15,937.42$$

For the $2500 annuity,

$$A_n = \$2500 \left(\frac{1 - 1.10^{-10}}{0.10} \right) = \$15,361.42$$

<u>The $1000 annuity has the greater economic value.</u>

16. The appropriate price to pay is the present value of the future payments discounted at the required rate of return. Hence,

$$\text{Price} = \$50 \left(\frac{1 - 1.045^{-30}}{0.045} \right) + \$1000(1.045)^{-30} = \underline{\underline{\$1081.44}}$$

17. The highest price is the price that provides the lowest acceptable rate of return (10.5% compounded monthly). This price is the present value of all payments from the mortgage discounted at 10.5% compounded monthly. For the annuity component of the payments,

$$R = \$800, \quad i = \frac{10.5\%}{12} = 0.875\%, \quad n = 3.5(12) = 42$$

$$\text{Price} = \$800 \left(\frac{1 - 1.00875^{-42}}{0.00875} \right) + \$45,572(1.00875)^{-42} = \underline{\underline{\$59,623.78}}$$

Exercise 10.5 *(continued)*

18. The maximum price is the present value of the payments discounted at the lowest acceptable rate of return.

    The present value, 5 years from now, of the subsequent 7 years' payments is

    $$A_n = \$500 \left(\frac{1 - 1.0075^{-84}}{0.0075} \right) = \$31{,}076.98$$

    Today's present value of this amount and the first 5 years' payment is

    $$\$31{,}076.98(1.00\overline{6})^{-60} + \$500 \left(\frac{1 - 1.00\overline{6}^{-60}}{0.00\overline{6}} \right) = \underline{\$45{,}518.41}$$

19. Choose the alternative having the higher current economic value (present value). The present value, $12\frac{1}{2}$ years from now, of the $1500 payment is

    $$A_n = \$1500 \left(\frac{1 - 1.006875^{-150}}{0.006875} \right) = \$140{,}111.69$$

    Today's present value of this amount and the $1000 payments is

    $$\frac{\$140{,}111.69}{1.006875^{150}} + \$1000 \left(\frac{1 - 1.006875^{-150}}{0.006875} \right) = \underline{\$143{,}542.76}$$

    Choose the $150,000 cash prize since it has the greater economic value.

20. a. Purchase price = Down payment + Present value of monthly payments

    For the monthly payments, $n = 36$ and $p = i = \dfrac{10\%}{12} = 0.8\overline{3}\%$

    $$\text{Purchase price} = \$2000 + \$224.58 \left(\frac{1 - 1.008\overline{3}^{-27}}{0.008\overline{3}} \right) = \underline{\$8960.01}$$

    b. Payout amount = Balance after 9 payments
    = Present value of remaining 27 payments

    $$= \$224.58 \left(\frac{1 - 1.008\overline{3}^{-27}}{0.008\overline{3}} \right) = \underline{\$5409.83}$$

21. a. Original loan = Present value of all payments

    $$\text{Original loan} = \$1333.28 \left(\frac{1 - 1.05375^{-40}}{0.05375} \right) = \underline{\$21{,}750.01}$$

    b. Payout amount = Principal balance
    = Present value of remaining 23 payments

    $$= \$1333.28 \left(\frac{1 - 1.05375^{-23}}{0.05375} \right) = \underline{\$17{,}365.12}$$

Exercise 10.5 *(concluded)*

22. The fair market value (FMV) of a share is the present value of future dividends and the redemption payment, discounted at the market's required rate of return.

    a. $FMV = \$1.00 \left(\dfrac{1 - 1.0175^{-61}}{0.0175}\right) + \$50(1.0175)^{-61} = \underline{\$54.66}$

    b. $FMV = \$1.00 \left(\dfrac{1 - 1.02^{-61}}{0.02}\right) + \$50(1.02)^{-61} = \underline{\$50.00}$

    c. $FMV = \$1.00 \left(\dfrac{1 - 1.0225^{-61}}{0.0225}\right) + \$50(1.0225)^{-61} = \underline{\$45.87}$

23. The economic values of the two alternatives are their respective present values at age 65. Let R represent the monthly pension payment at age 65. If the CPP payments start at age 68, they will be 1.18R. The present value, at age 68, of the expected 12 years' payments of 1.18R is

    $$A_n = 1.18R \left(\dfrac{1 - 1.00625^{-144}}{0.00625}\right) = 129.11R$$

    The present value at age 65 of this amount is

    $$129.11R(1.00625)^{-36} = 89.36R$$

    The present value at age 65 of 15 years' payments of R per month is

    $$A_n = R \left(\dfrac{1 - 1.00625^{-180}}{0.00625}\right) = 107.87R$$

    Hence, the pension-at-age-65 option has a

    $$\dfrac{107.87R - 89.36R}{89.36R} \times 100\% = \underline{20.7\%}$$

    higher economic value.

24. The economic values of the two alternatives are their respective present values at age 55. Let R represent the normal monthly pension payment at age 60. If she elects to receive the pension at age 55, she will receive 0.85R per month.

    The present value at age 60 of the expected 23 years' payments of R is

    $$A_n = R \left(\dfrac{1 - 1.00625^{-276}}{0.00625}\right) = 131.34R$$

    The present value at age 55 of this amount is

    $$131.34R(1.00625)^{-60} = 90.37R$$

    The present value at age 55 of 28 years' payments of 0.85R per month is

    $$A_n = 0.85R \left(\dfrac{1 - 1.00625^{-336}}{0.00625}\right) = 119.24R$$

    Hence, the pension-at-age-55 option has a

    $$\dfrac{119.24R - 90.37R}{90.37R} \times 100\% = \underline{31.9\%}$$

    higher economic value.

Review Problems

1. Since it is a purchase transaction, choose the option having the lower current economic value—that is, the lower present value. For the multiple-payment option, the present value of the payments is

$$\$10,000 + \$1000 \left(\frac{1 - 1.00625^{-60}}{0.00625} \right) = \$59,905.31$$

Choose the five-year-payment option since its cost is $94.69 less in current dollars.

2. The amount of the lost wages plus interest at the end of the two-year period was

$$S_n = \$5500 \left(\frac{1.005^{24} - 1}{0.005} \right) = \$124,095.76$$

The amount with additional interest to the judgement date is

$$S = \$124,095.76(1.005)^9 = \$129,793.07$$

3. a. The value placed on half of the partnership is the present value of Dr. Wilson's payments discounted at 7% compounded semiannually.

$$R = \$714.60, \ n = 15(12) = 180, \ i = 3.5\%, \ c = \frac{2}{12} = 0.1\overline{6}, \ p = 1.035^{0.1\overline{6}} - 1 = 0.0057500395$$

$$A_n = \$714.60 \left(\frac{1 - 1.0057500395^{-180}}{0.0057500395} \right) = \$80,000.05$$

The implied value of the partnership was $160,000.

   b. Total interest $= 180(\$714.60) - \$80,000 = \$48,628$

4. The minimum amount is the present value of the payments, discounted at 7% compounded semiannually.

$$R = \$1000, \ n = 12(12) = 144, \ i = 3.5\%, c = \frac{2}{12} = 0.1\overline{6}, \ p = 1.035^{0.1\overline{6}} - 1 = 0.0057500395$$

$$A_n = \$1000 \left(\frac{1 - 1.0057500395^{-144}}{0.0057500395} \right) = \$97,745.91$$

5. For the first 2 years,

$$R = \$300, \ n = 2(12) = 24, \ p = i = \frac{9\%}{12} = 0.75\%$$

For the subsequent 3 years,

$$R = \$300, \ n = 36, \ p = i = \frac{7.5\%}{12} = 0.625\%$$

The future value 2 years from now of the first 24 payments is

$$S_n = \$300 \left(\frac{1.0075^{24} - 1}{0.0075} \right) = \$7856.54$$

The future value, 5 years from now, of this amount and the last 36 payments is

$$\$7856.54(1.00625)^{36} + \$300 \left(\frac{1.00625^{36} - 1}{0.00625} \right) = \$21,901.45$$

Review Problems *(continued)*

6. The amount in the RRSP will be the future value of the payments. For monthly contributions,

$R = \$500$, $n = 20(12) = 240$, $i = \dfrac{7.5\%}{2} = 3.75\%$, $c = \dfrac{2}{12} = 0.1\overline{6}$,

$p = 1.0375^{0.1\overline{6}} - 1 = 0.0061545239$

$S_n = \$500 \left(\dfrac{1.0061545239^{240} - 1}{0.0061545239} \right) = \$273,000.71$

For annual contributions,
$R = \$6000$, $n = 20$, $i = 3.75\%$, $c = 2$
$p = 1.0375^2 - 1 = 0.076406250$

$S_n = \$6000 \left(\dfrac{1.0764062^{20} - 1}{0.07640625} \right) = \$263,882.50$

The value of the RRSP will be

$\$273,000.71 - \$263,882.50 = \underline{\underline{\$9118.21}}$

larger with monthly contributions.

7. For the past 7 years,

$R = \$3000$, $n = 7(2) = 14$, $p = i = 4.5\%$

The amount currently in Charlene's RRSP is

$S_n = \$3000 \left(\dfrac{1.045^{14} - 1}{0.045} \right) = \$56,796.33$

For the next 5 years,

$R = \$2000$, $n = 5(4) = 20$, $p = i = \dfrac{7.5\%}{4} = 1.875\%$

The amount is the RRSP 5 years from now will be

$\$56,796.33(1.01875)^{20} + \$2000 \left(\dfrac{1.01875^{20} - 1}{0.01875} \right) = \underline{\underline{\$130,346.18}}$

8. If \$3000 is contributed every 6 months for 20 years,

$S_n = \$3000 \left(\dfrac{1.04^{40} - 1}{0.04} \right) = \$285,076.55$

If \$6000 is contributed every 6 months for the last 10 years,

$S_n = \$6000 \left(\dfrac{1.04^{20} - 1}{0.04} \right) = \$178,668.47$

The early start results in

$\dfrac{\$285,076.55 - \$178,668.47}{\$178,668.47} \times 100\% = \underline{\underline{59.56\%}}$

more funds in the RRSP after 20 years.

Review Problems (continued)

9. The appropriate amount to pay is the present value of all remaining payments, discounted at the required rate of return.

$R = \$900$, $n = 2.75(12) = 33$, $p = i = \dfrac{7.2\%}{12} = 0.6\%$

$$\text{Price} = \$900 \left(\frac{1 - 1.006^{-33}}{0.006} \right) + \$37,886(1.006)^{-33}$$

$$= \$26,871.69 + \$31,098.93$$

$$= \underline{\$57,970.62}$$

10. The appropriate price to pay is the present value of the payments discounted at the required rate of return. The present value, 5 years from now, of the last 7 years' payments is

$$A_n = \$1500 \left(\frac{1 - 1.0225^{-28}}{0.0225} \right) = \$30,911.74$$

Today's present value of this amount and the first 5 years' payments is

$$\frac{\$30,911.74}{1.02^{20}} + \$1500 \left(\frac{1 - 1.02^{-20}}{0.02} \right) = \underline{\$45,329.87}$$

The appropriate price to pay is $45,329.87.

11. a. The original amount of the loan is the present value of all the payments.

$$\text{Original loan} = \$587.33 \left(\frac{1 - 1.007^{-180}}{0.007} \right) = \underline{\$59,999.80}$$

b. Balance after $7\dfrac{1}{2}$ years = Present value of remaining payments

$$= \$587.33 \left(\frac{1 - 1.00875^{-60}}{0.00875} \right)$$

$$= \underline{\$39,119.37}$$

12. Amount in the RRSP = Future value of all contributions. For the first 15 years' contributions,

$R = \$2000$, $n = 15(4) = 60$, $i = 4\%$, $c = \dfrac{2}{4} = 0.5$

$p = 1.04^{0.5} - 1 = 0.019803903$

The amount in the RRSP after 15 years will be

$$S_n = \$2000 \left(\frac{1.019803903^{60} - 1}{0.019803903} \right) = \underline{\$226,561.15}$$

For the subsequent 10 years' contributions,

$R = \$1000$, $n = 10(12) = 120$, $i = 4\%$, $c = \dfrac{2}{12} = 0.1\overline{6}$

$p = 1.04^{0.1\overline{6}} - 1 = 0.0065581969$

The future value, 25 years from now, of all the payments will be

$$\$226,561.15(1.04)^{20} + \$1000 \left(\frac{1.0065581969^{120} - 1}{0.0065581969} \right)$$

$$= \$496,423.38 + \$181,623.57$$

$$= \underline{\$678,046.95}$$

Self-Test Exercise

1. a. $R = \$1000$, $n = 20(2) = 40$, $p = i = \dfrac{8.5\%}{2} = 4.25\%$

$$S_n = \$1000 \left(\frac{1.0425^{40} - 1}{0.0425} \right) = \underline{\underline{\$100{,}822.83}}$$

   b. $R = \$2000$, $n = 20$, $p = i = 8.5\%$

$$S_n = \$2000 \left(\frac{1.085^{20} - 1}{0.085} \right) = \underline{\underline{\$96{,}754.03}}$$

2. a. Purchase price = Down payment + Present value of the monthly payments

$$= \$9{,}000 + \$812.47 \left(\frac{1 - 1.00875^{-60}}{0.00875} \right)$$

$$= \$9000 + \$37{,}800.03$$
$$= \underline{\underline{\$46{,}800.03}}$$

   b. Payout amount = Principal balance after 24 payments

$$= \text{Present value of remaining 36 payments}$$

$$= \$812.47 \left(\frac{1 - 1.00875^{-36}}{0.00875} \right)$$

$$= \underline{\underline{\$24{,}997.20}}$$

3. The finance company will pay an amount equal to the present value of the 15 payments discounted at its required rate of return.

$R = \$180.50$, $n = 15$, $i = \dfrac{21\%}{2} = 10.5\%$, $c = \dfrac{2}{12} = 0.1\overline{6}$

$p = 1.105^{0.1\overline{6}} - 1 = 0.016780120$

$$\text{Price} = \$180.50 \left(\frac{1 - 1.01678012^{-15}}{0.01678012} \right) = \underline{\underline{\$2376.15}}$$

The finance company will pay \$2376.15 for the contract.

4. The amount (future value) in Dr. Krawchuk's RRSP when he left general practice was

$$S_n = \$2000 \left(\frac{1.025^{24} - 1}{0.025} \right) = \$64{,}698.08$$

After a further 2.5 years with no further contributions, this amount grew to

$$S = \$64{,}698.08(1.025)^{10} = \underline{\underline{\$82{,}819.01}}$$

Self-Test Exercise *(concluded)*

5. The bond's fair market value (FMV) is the present value of the interest payments and the face value payment discounted at the market's prevailing rate of return. That is,

$$FMV = \$231.25 \left(\frac{1 - 1.039^{-29}}{0.039} \right) + \$5000(1.039)^{-29}$$

$$= \$3974.40 + \$1648.61$$

$$= \underline{\underline{\$5623.01}}$$

6. The current economic value of the award is the present value of all the payments discounted at the time value of money.

The present value, 5 years from now, of the 120 monthly payments of $1000 is

$$A_n = \$1000 \left(\frac{1 - 1.00875^{-120}}{0.00875} \right) = \underline{\underline{\$74,109.76}}$$

The present value today of this amount and the 60 monthly payments of $800 is

$$\$74,109.76(1.00875)^{-60} + \$800 \left(\frac{1 - 1.00875^{-60}}{0.00875} \right) = \underline{\underline{\$81,160.11}}$$

The economic value of the award, one month before the first payment, is $81,160.11.

7. For the first 30 months,

$$R = \$800, \ n = \frac{30}{3} = 10, \ p = i = \frac{10\%}{4} = 2.5\%$$

For the subsequent $7(12) - 30 = 54$ months,

$$R = \$800, \ n = \frac{54}{3} = 18, \ i = \frac{9\%}{2} = 4.5\%, \ c = \frac{2}{4} = 0.5$$

$$p = 1.045^{0.5} - 1 = 0.022252415$$

The future value, 30 months from now, of the first 10 payments is

$$S_n = \$800 \left(\frac{1.025^{10} - 1}{0.025} \right) = \$8962.71$$

The future value, 7 years from now, of this amount and the last 18 payments is

$$\$8962.71(1.045)^9 + \$800 \left(\frac{1.022252415^{18} - 1}{0.022252415} \right)$$

$$= \$13,319.44 + \$17,475.68$$

$$= \underline{\underline{\$30,795.12}}$$

11 Annuities Due: Future Value and Present Value

Changes in the Second Edition:

1. The major changes have already been covered in the lengthy preamble to the Chapter 10 solutions.

2. Figure 11.3 (Annuity Classification Flowchart) and Table 11.1 (Summary of Formulas) are new.

Exercise 11.1

1. Given: R = $400, n = 11, p = i = 11.5%

    $$S_n(\text{due}) = R\left[\frac{(1+p)^n - 1}{p}\right](1+p) = \$400\left(\frac{1.115^{11} - 1}{0.115}\right)(1.115) = \underline{\$8964.56}$$

2. Given: R = $150, n = 6.5(4) = 26, p = i = $\frac{10\%}{4}$ = 2.5%

    $$S_n(\text{due}) = \$150\left(\frac{1.025^{26} - 1}{0.025}\right)(1.025) = \underline{\$5536.80}$$

3. Given: R = $275, n = 3.5(12) = 42, p = i = $\frac{8\%}{12}$ = $0.\overline{6}$%

    $$S_n(\text{due}) = \$275\left(\frac{1.00\overline{6}^{42} - 1}{0.00\overline{6}}\right)(1.00\overline{6}) = \underline{\$13,366.94}$$

4. Given: R = $1500, n = 13.5(2) = 27, p = i = $\frac{7.5\%}{2}$ = 3.75%

    $$S_n(\text{due}) = \$1500\left(\frac{1.0375^{27} - 1}{0.0375}\right)(1.0375) = \underline{\$70,631.32}$$

5. Substitute R = $325, n = 7.25(12) = 87, p = i = $\frac{11\%}{12}$ = $0.91\overline{6}$%

    into formula (11-1) giving
    $$S_n(\text{due}) = \underline{\$43,362.43}$$

6. Substitute R = $950, n = 8.75(4) = 35, p = i = $\frac{9\%}{4}$ = 2.25%

    into formula (11-1) giving
    $$S_n(\text{due}) = \underline{\$50,891.14}$$

7. Substitute R = $329, n = 8.5(2) = 17, p = i = $\frac{8.75\%}{2}$ = 4.375%

    into formula (11-1) giving
    $$S_n(\text{due}) = \underline{\$8404.79}$$

8. Substitute R = $1000, n = 25, p = i = 7.25%
    into formula (11-1) giving
    $$S_n(\text{due}) = \underline{\$70,319.10}$$

9. Substitute R = $500, n = 12(4) = 48, i = 11%, c = $\frac{1}{4}$ = 0.25

    into formulas (10-2) and (11-1) giving
    p = 2.6433327% and $S_n(\text{due}) = \underline{\$48,508.71}$

10. Substitute R = $200, n = 7.5(12) = 90, i = $\frac{10\%}{4}$ = 2.5%, c = $\frac{4}{12}$ = $0.\overline{3}$

    into formulas (10-2) and (11-1) giving
    p = 0.8264838% and $S_n(\text{due}) = \underline{\$26,779.44}$

Exercise 11.1 (continued)

11. Substitute $R = \$3000$, $n = 4.5(2) = 9$, $i = \dfrac{8\%}{12} = 0.\bar{6}\%$, $c = \dfrac{12}{2} = 6$

   into formulas (10-2) and (11-1) giving
   $p = 4.067622\%$ and $S_n(\text{due}) = \underline{\$33,130.87}$

12. Substitute $R = \$1700$, $n = 11.5(4) = 46$, $i = \dfrac{7.5\%}{2} = 3.75\%$, $c = \dfrac{2}{4} = 0.5$

   into formulas (10-2) and (11-1) giving
   $p = 1.8577439\%$ and $S_n(\text{due}) = \underline{\$124,153.12}$

13. Substitute $R = \$2500$, $n = 16$, $i = \dfrac{10.5\%}{12} = 0.875\%$, $c = \dfrac{12}{1} = 12$

   into formulas (10-2) and (11-1) giving
   $p = 11.0203450\%$ and $S_n(\text{due}) = \underline{\$108,964.03}$

14. Substitute $R = \$750$, $n = 6.5(2) = 13$, $i = \dfrac{9\%}{4} = 2.25\%$, $c = \dfrac{4}{2} = 2$

   into formulas (10-2) and (11-1) giving
   $p = 4.5506250\%$ and $S_n(\text{due}) = \underline{\$13,498.78}$

15. The balance in the account on March 1, 1997 is the future value of all the previous deposits in the account. With March 1 as the focal date, the payments form a simple annuity due having $R = \$200$, $n = 19$, and $p = i = \dfrac{6.75\%}{12} = 0.5625\%$.

$$S_n(\text{due}) = \$200\left(\frac{1.005625^{19}-1}{0.005625}\right)(1.005625) = \underline{\$4021.14}$$

   Interest portion = Amount in account - Deposits
   $$= \$4021.14 - 19(\$200)$$
   $$= \underline{\$221.14}$$

16. With August 1, 2017 as the focal date, the RRSP contributions form a simple annuity due. The amount in the RRSP will be the future value of previous contributions. Substitution of
   $R = \$1500$, $n = 27.5(2) = 55$, $p = i = \dfrac{8.5\%}{2} = 4.25\%$

   into formula (11-1) gives
   $$S_n(\text{due}) = \underline{\$326,252.08}$$

   Interest portion = Amount in RRSP - Contributions
   $$= \$326,252.08 - 55(\$1500)$$
   $$= \underline{\$243,752.08}$$

17. a. Substitute $R = \$5000$, $n = 25$, $p = i = 8\%$
   into formulas (10-1) and (11-1) giving
   $$S_n = \$365,529.70 \text{ and } S_n(\text{due}) = \$394,772.08$$
   Hence, there will be
   $$\$394,772.08 - \$365,529.70 = \underline{\$29,242.38}$$
   more in the RRSP after 25 years if the contributions are made at the beginning of each year.

Exercise 11.1 *(concluded)*

b. Substitute R = $5000, n = 25, $i = 0.\bar{6}\%$, $c = \dfrac{12}{1} = 12$

   into formulas (10-2), (10-1), and (11-1) giving
   p = 8.29995067%, S_n = $381,940.58, and S_n(due) = $413,641.46

   Now, beginning-of-year contributions will result in
   $413,641.46 - $381,940.58 = $31,700.88
   more in the RRSP after 25 years.

18. Substitute R = $2000, n = 25(2) = 50, $i = 8.25\%$, $c = \dfrac{1}{2} = 0.5$

   into formulas (10-2) and (11-1) giving
   p = 4.0432602% and S_n(due) = $321,965.55
   The value of the RRSP in 25 years will be $321,965.55.

19. The amount in the RRSP will be the future value of all the contributions. The amount in the RRSP after 10 years is obtained by substituting

   $R = \$2000, n = 10, i = \dfrac{8\%}{4} = 2\%, c = \dfrac{4}{1} = 4$

   into formulas (10-2) and (11-1) giving
   p = 8.2432160% and S_n(due) = $31,725.99
   The amount after 25 years is the future value of $31,725.99 an additional 15 years later plus the future value of the last 15 years' contributions. That is,

   $\text{Amount} = \$4000 \left(\dfrac{1.08243216^{15}-1}{0.08243216} \right)(1.08243216) + \$31,725.99 \,(1.08243216)^{15}$

   $= \$223,904.52$

20. The amount in Fay's RRSP on her 31st birthday was

   $S_n(\text{due}) = \$3000 \left(\dfrac{1.08^{10}-1}{0.08} \right)(1.08) = \$46,936.46$

   The future value of this amount at age 65 (34 years later) will be
   $S = \$46,936.46 \,(1.08)^{34} = \$642,566.41$

   The amount in Fred's RRSP on his 65th birthday will be

   $S_n(\text{due}) = \$3000 \left(\dfrac{1.08^{34}-1}{0.08} \right)(1.08) = \$513,950.41$

   Fay will have $642,566.41 - $513,950.41 = $128,616.00
   more in her RRSP at age 65 than Fred will have at age 65.

Exercise 11.2

1. Given: R = $400, n = 11, $p = i = 11.5\%$

   $A_n(\text{due}) = R \left[\dfrac{1-(1+p)^{-n}}{p} \right](1+p) = \$400 \left(\dfrac{1-1.115^{-11}}{0.115} \right)(1.115) = \$2707.11$

2. Given: R = $150, n = 6.5(4) = 26, $p = i = \dfrac{10\%}{4} = 2.5\%$

   $A_n(\text{due}) = \$150 \left(\dfrac{1-1.025^{-26}}{0.025} \right)(1.025) = \$2913.66$

Exercise 11.2 (continued)

3. Given: $R = \$275$, $n = 3.5(12) = 42$, $p = i = \dfrac{8\%}{12} = 0.\bar{6}\%$

$$A_n(\text{due}) = \$275 \left(\dfrac{1-1.00\bar{6}^{-42}}{0.00\bar{6}}\right)(1.00\bar{6}) = \underline{\$10,111.90}$$

4. Given: $R = \$1500$, $n = 13.5(2) = 27$, $p = i = \dfrac{7.5\%}{2} = 3.75\%$

$$A_n(\text{due}) = \$1500 \left(\dfrac{1-1.0375^{-27}}{0.0375}\right)(1.0375) = \underline{\$26,140.78}$$

5. Substitute $R = \$325$, $n = 7.25(12) = 87$, $p = i = \dfrac{11\%}{12} = 0.91\bar{6}\%$

   into formula (11-2) giving
   $A_n(\text{due}) = \underline{\$19,603.86}$

6. Substitute $R = \$950$, $n = 8.75(4) = 35$, $p = i = \dfrac{9\%}{4} = 2.25\%$

   into formula (11-2) giving
   $A_n(\text{due}) = \underline{\$23,357.48}$

7. Substitute $R = \$329$, $n = 8.5(2) = 17$, $p = i = \dfrac{8.75\%}{2} = 4.375\%$

   into formula (11-2) giving
   $A_n(\text{due}) = \underline{\$4058.70}$

8. Substitute $R = \$1000$, $n = 25$, $p = i = 7.25\%$
   into formula (11-2) giving
   $A_n(\text{due}) = \underline{\$12,221.96}$

9. Substitute $R = \$500$, $n = 12(4) = 48$, $i = 11\%$, $c = \dfrac{1}{4} = 0.25$

   into formulas (10-2) and (11-2) giving
   $p = 2.6433327\%$ and $A_n(\text{due}) = \underline{\$13,865.77}$

10. Substitute $R = \$200$, $n = 7.5(12) = 90$, $i = \dfrac{10\%}{4} = 2.5\%$, $c = \dfrac{12}{2} = 6$

    into formulas (10-2) and (11-2) giving
    $p = 0.8264838\%$ and $A_n(\text{due}) = \underline{\$12,766.90}$

11. Substitute $R = \$3000$, $n = 4.5(2) = 9$, $i = \dfrac{8\%}{12} = 0.\bar{6}\%$, $c = \dfrac{12}{2} = 6$

    into formulas (10-2) and (11-2) giving
    $p = 4.0672622\%$ and $A_n(\text{due}) = \underline{\$23,142.25}$

12. Substitute $R = \$1700$, $n = 11.5(4) = 46$, $i = \dfrac{7.5\%}{2} = 3.75\%$, $c = \dfrac{2}{4} = 0.5$

    into formulas (10-2) and (11-2) giving
    $p - 1.8577439\%$ and $A_n(\text{duo}) = \underline{\$53,230.16}$

13. Substitute $R = \$2500$, $n = 16$, $i = \dfrac{10.5\%}{12} = 0.875\%$, $c = \dfrac{12}{1} = 12$

    into formulas (10-2) and (11-2) giving
    $p = 11.0203450\%$ and $A_n(\text{due}) = \underline{\$20,457.00}$

Exercise 11.2 (continued)

14. Substitute $R = \$750$, $n = 6.5(2) = 13$, $i = \dfrac{9\%}{4} = 2.25\%$, $c = \dfrac{4}{2} = 2$

    into formulas (10-2) and (11-2) giving
    $p = 4.5506250\%$ and $A_n(\text{due}) = \underline{\$7569.17}$

15. The economic value of the jackpot on the date of the first payment is the present value of the payments discounted at the time value of money. The twenty payments constitute on annuity due.

    a. Substitution of $R = \$4.38$ million, $n = 20$, $p = i = 7\%$ into formula (11-2)
       gives $A_n(\text{due}) = \underline{\$49.65 \text{ million}}$. If money was worth 7% compounded annually,
       the economic value of the jackpot was \$49.65 million (not 20 x \$4.38 million = \$87.6 million.)

    b. Similarly, if $p = i = 9\%$, we obtain
       $A_n(\text{due}) = \underline{\$43.58 \text{ million}}$
       for the jackpot's economic value on the date of the first payment.

16. The current economic value of the grants is their present value. The payments form a general annuity due having
    $R = \$100,000$, $n = 10$, $i = \dfrac{7.5\%}{12} = 0.625\%$, $c = \dfrac{12}{1} = 12$ and

    $p = 1.00625^{12} - 1 = 0.077632599$.
    Then

    $$A_n(\text{due}) = \$100,000 \left(\frac{1 - 1.077632599^{-10}}{0.077632599} \right) (1.077632599) = \underline{\$730,885.63}$$

17. The current economic value of Mrs. Martel's offer is the present value of her payments. The payments form a simple annuity due having
    $R = \$1900$, $n = 5$, $p = i = 5\%$

    $$A_n(\text{due}) = \$1900 \left(\frac{1 - 1.05^{-5}}{0.05} \right) (1.05) = \$8637.31$$

    <u>Mrs. Martels offer is worth</u>

    $\$8637.31 - \$8500 = \underline{\$137.31}$
    <u>more</u> in current dollars.

18. Osgood Appliance Centre should accept a cash price that will put Osgood in the same financial position as if the refrigerator were sold on a conditional sale contract with the contract being sold at a discount to the finance company. The price that the finance company would pay for all 6 payments is their present value (discounting at 18% compounded monthly). The 6 payments form a simple annuity due having
    $R = \$199$, $n = 6$, and $p = i = \dfrac{18\%}{12} = 1.5\%$

    Then

    $$A_n(\text{due}) = \$199 \left(\frac{1 - 1.015^{-6}}{0.015} \right) (1.015) = \underline{\$1150.75}$$
    Osgood should accept a cash price of \$1150.75.

Business Math in Canada, 2/e

Exercise 11.2 (continued)

19. a. The landlord should accept a lump payment that is economically equivalent to the 12 monthly payments. This amount is the present value of the payments. The payments form a simple annuity due having

$$R = \$900, n = 12, p = i = \frac{9\%}{12} = 0.75\%$$

$$A_n(\text{due}) = \$900\left(\frac{1-1.0075^{-12}}{0.0075}\right)(1.0075) = \underline{\$10,368.61}$$

b. We will compare the amounts the landlord will have at the year-end under two scenarios:
(i) The lump payment is invested at 9% compounded monthly;
(ii) Monthly payments are invested (when received) at 9% compounded monthly.

The accumulated amounts after 1 year will be
(i) $S = P(1+i)^n = \$10,368.61\ (1.0075)^{12} = \$11,341.25$

(ii) $S_n(\text{due}) = \$900\left(\frac{1.0075^{12}-1}{0.0075}\right)(1.0075) = \$11,341.25$

Either way, the landlord will have $11,341.25 at the end of the year.

20. The required amount of money is the present value of the payments. The payments form a general annuity due having

$$R = \$1200, n = 15(12) = 180, i = 4.5\%, c = \frac{2}{12} = 0.1\overline{6} \text{ and}$$

$$p = 1.045^{0.1\overline{6}} - 1 = 0.0073631230$$

$$A_n(\text{due}) = \$1200\left(\frac{1-1.007363123^{-180}}{0.007363123}\right)(1.007363123) = \underline{\$120,339.78}$$

$120,339.78 will sustain the withdrawals.

21. a. The initial long-term liability reported is the present value of all the lease payments discounted at the firm's interest rate to borrow funds. The lease payments form a simple annuity due having

$$R = \$2100, n = 5(4) = 20, \text{ and } p = i = \frac{13\%}{4} = 3.25\%$$

$$A_n(\text{due}) = \$2100\left(\frac{1-1.0325^{-20}}{0.0325}\right)(1.0325) = \underline{\$31,524.95}$$

The initial lease liability will be $31,524.95.

b. The liability remaining at the end of the 4th year will be the present value of the remaining 4 payments.
That is,

$$\text{Lease liability} = \$2100\left(\frac{1-1.0325^{-4}}{0.0325}\right)(1.0325) = \underline{\$8011.65}$$

22. a. The initial lease liability is the present value of all payments discounted at the cost of borrowing. The payments form a simple annuity due having

$$R = \$1700, n = 5(12) = 60, \text{ and } p = i = \frac{11.25\%}{12} = 0.9375\%$$

Then

$$\text{Lease liability} = \$1700\left(\frac{1-1.009375^{-60}}{0.009375}\right)(1.009375) = \underline{\$78,470.45}$$

Exercise 11.2 *(continued)*

b. After the first year, 48 payments remain and

$$\text{Lease liability} = \$1700 \left(\frac{1-1.009375^{-48}}{0.009375}\right)(1.009375) = \$66,081.22$$

The reduction in the liability during the first year is
$$\$78,470.45 - \$66,081.22 = \$12,389.23$$

23. The current economic value of the annuity due is the present value of all the payments. The calculation must be done in two steps because of the change in the time value of money.
The present value, 3 years from now, of the last 10 payments is

$$A_n(\text{due}) = \$700 \left(\frac{1-1.025^{-10}}{0.025}\right)(1.025) = \$6279.61$$

The present value to-day of this amount and the first 3 years' payments is

$$\frac{\$6279.61}{1.0225^{12}} + \$700 \left(\frac{1-1.0225^{-12}}{0.0225}\right)(1.0225) = \$12,262.47$$

24. The ranking does not depend on where the focal date is set. The choice of 8 years from now as the focal date will minimize the calculations required to determine each stream's economic value on the focal date.

a. (i) The \$10,000 is already at the focal date.
(ii) Economic value = $S_n(\text{due})$

$$= \$850 \left(\frac{1.08^8-1}{0.08}\right)(1.08)$$
$$= \$9764.42$$

(iii) Economic value = $A_n(\text{due})$

$$= \$1700 \left(\frac{1-1.08^{-8}}{0.08}\right)(1.08)$$
$$= \$10,550.83$$

The \$1700 annuity has the largest economic value and the \$850 annuity has the lowest value.

b. (i) The \$10,000 payment is already at the focal date.
(ii) Economic value = $S_n(\text{due})$

$$= \$850 \left(\frac{1.10^8-1}{0.10}\right)(1.10)$$
$$= \$10,692.56$$

(iii) Economic value = $A_n(\text{due})$

$$= \$1700 \left(\frac{1-1.10^{-8}}{0.10}\right)(1.10)$$
$$= \$9976.31$$

The ranking in part a is reversed. The \$850 annuity now has the largest economic value and the \$1700 annuity has the lowest value.

Exercise 11.2 *(concluded)*

25. If the two policies provide the same coverage, select the policy whose stream of premiums has the lower present value.

Paul Revere Insurance Co.

The present value, on the client's 31st birthday, of all subsequent premiums up to age 65 is

$$A_n(\text{due}) = \$78.17 \left(\frac{1-1.0075^{-408}}{0.0075} \right)(1.0075) = \$10,002.82$$

The present value, on the client's 26th birthday, of this amount and the first 5 years' premiums is

$$\frac{\$10,002.82}{1.0075^{60}} + \$54.83 \left(\frac{1-1.0075^{-60}}{0.0075} \right)(1.0075) = \underline{\underline{\$9049.96}}$$

Provident Insurance Co.

The present value, on the client's 26th birthday, of all premiums to age 65 is

$$A_n(\text{due}) = \$69.35 \left(\frac{1-1.0075^{-468}}{0.0075} \right)(1.0075) = \underline{\underline{\$9033.82}}$$

These calculations show that <u>the current economic value of the Provident premiums is</u> a negligible <u>$16.13 less than the current economic value of the Paul Revere premiums.</u> The insurance broker's approach of comparing the totals of the nominal premiums is flawed because it ignores the time value of money.

Review Problems

1. a. Initial liability = Present value of all lease payments

$$= \$1900 \left(\frac{1-1.00875^{-60}}{0.00875} \right)(1.00875)$$

$$= \underline{\underline{\$89,170.65}}$$

   b. Liability after the first year
      = Present value of the remaining 48 payments

$$= \$1900 \left(\frac{1-1.00875^{-48}}{0.00875} \right)(1.00875)$$

$$= \$74,858.28$$

   The reduction in the liability during the first year will be $89,170.65 - $74,858.28 = $\underline{\underline{\$14,312.37}}$

2. Minimum amount = Present value of the withdrawals
   The withdrawals constitute a general annuity due having

   $R = \$1000$, $n = 12(12) = 144$, $i = 3.5\%$, $c = \dfrac{2}{12} = 0.1\overline{6}$, and

   $p = 1.035^{0.1\overline{6}} - 1 = 0.0057500395$.
   Hence,

$$A_n(\text{due}) = \$1000 \left(\frac{1-1.0057500395^{-144}}{0.0057500395} \right)(1.0057500395) = \underline{\underline{\$98,307.96}}$$

   The minimum amount required is $98,307.96.

3. The economic value of an annuity at its beginning is its present value.
   The present value, 5 years from now, of the last 9 payments is

$$A_n(\text{due}) = \$1500 \left(\frac{1-1.05^{-9}}{0.05} \right)(1.05) = \$11,194.82$$

   Today's present value of this amount and the first 10 payments is

$$\frac{\$11,194.82}{1.045^{10}} + \$1500 \left(\frac{1-1.045^{-10}}{0.045} \right)(1.045) = \underline{\underline{\$19,611.84}}$$

Review Problems *(continued)*

4. The total amount in the RRSP after 30 years will be the future value of all the contributions. The future value, 10 years from now, of the $4000 contributions will be

$$S_n(due) = \$4000\left(\frac{1.0825^{10}-1}{0.0825}\right)(1.0825) = \$63,476.43$$

The future value, 30 years from now, of this amount and the $6000 contributions will be

$$\$63,476.43\ (1.0825)^{20} + \$6000\left(\frac{1.0825^{20}-1}{0.0825}\right)(1.0825) = \underline{\underline{\$615,447.79}}$$

5. a. The single equivalent payment at the beginning of the year is the present value of the schedule payments.

$$A_n(due) = \$1000\left(\frac{1-1.00\bar{6}^{-12}}{0.00\bar{6}}\right)(1.00\bar{6}) = \underline{\underline{\$11,572.42}}$$

The landlord should accept a single payment of $11,572.42.

b. Compare the amounts accumulated after one year if all rental payments are invested at 8% compounded monthly.
For the normal monthly payments

$$S_n(due) = \$1000\left(\frac{1.00\bar{6}^{12}-1}{0.00\bar{6}}\right)(1.00\bar{6}) = \$12,532.93$$

For the alternative initial "lump" payment of $11,572.42
$$S = \$11,572.42\ (1.00\bar{6})^{12} = \$12,532.93$$
In either case, the landlord will be in the same financial position at the end of the year.

6. The amount in the RRSP from contributions in the first 5 years
= Future value of all contributions – Future value of last 20 years' contributions

$$= \$5000\left(\frac{1.08^{25}-1}{0.08}\right)(1.08) - \$5000\left(\frac{1.08^{20}-1}{0.08}\right)1.08$$
$$= \$394,772.08 - \$247,114.61$$
$$= \$147,657.47$$
This difference is
$$\frac{\$147,657.47}{\$394,772.08}\ \times\ 100\% = \underline{37.4\%}$$
of the value of the RRSP after 25 years.

7. The $4000 payments form an ordinary simple annuity having
$$R = \$4000,\ n = 5(4) = 20,\ p = i = \frac{7.5\%}{4} = 1.875\%$$

The $2500 payments form a general annuity due having
$$R = \$2500,\ n = 15(12) = 180,\ i = 1.875\%,\ c = \frac{4}{12} = 0.\bar{3},\ and$$

$$p = 1.01875^{0.\bar{3}}-1 = 0.0062113394$$

The amount required to purchase these annuities is their present value on the purchase date.

Step 1: Calculate the present value, 5 years from now, of the $2500-payment annuity
$$A_n(due) = \$2500\left(\frac{1-1.0062113394^{-180}}{0.0062113394}\right)(1.0062113394) = \$272,132.00$$

Review Problems *(concluded)*

Step 2: Calculate today's present value of the amount from step 1 and the $4000-payment annuity.

$$\frac{\$272,132.00}{1.01875^{20}} + \$4000 \left(\frac{1-1.01875^{-20}}{0.01875}\right)(1.01875) = \underline{\$253,885.59}$$

The amount required to purchase the annuity is $253,885.59.

Self-Test Exercise

1. a. The payments form an annuity due having
    $$R = \$1000, n = 20(2) = 40, p = i = \frac{8.5\%}{2} = 4.25\%$$

    $$S_n(\text{due}) = \$1000 \left(\frac{1.0425^{40}-1}{0.0425}\right)(1.0425) = \underline{\$105,107.80}$$

    b.
    $$S_n(\text{due}) = \$2000 \left(\frac{1.085^{20}-1}{0.085}\right)(1.085) = \underline{\$104,978.12}$$

2. Choose the payment plan with the lower economic value.
    The present value of the monthly payments for 1 year is

    $$A_n(\text{due}) = \$33.71 \left(\frac{1-1.008\overline{3}^{-12}}{0.008\overline{3}}\right)(1.008\overline{3}) = \$386.63$$

    This is $0.87 less than the single payment falling on the focal date.
    The monthly payment plan is slightly cheaper.

3. a. The initial long-term lease liability
    = Present value of all lease payments

    $$= \$200,000 \left(\frac{1-1.05375^{-14}}{0.05375}\right)(1.05375)$$

    $$= \underline{\$2,037,008}$$

    b. Liability = Present value of remaining payments

    $$= \$200,000 \left(\frac{1-1.05375^{-7}}{0.05375}\right)(1.05375)$$

    $$= \underline{\$1,203,077}$$

4. For the first 30 months, the payments form a simple annuity due having
    $$R = \$800, n = \frac{30}{3} = 10, p = i = \frac{10\%}{4} = 2.5\%$$

    For the next 4.5 years, the payments for a general annuity due having
    $$R = \$800, n = 4.5(4) = 18, i = 4.5\%, c = \frac{2}{4} = 0.5, \text{ and}$$

    $$p = 1.045^{0.5}-1 = 0.022252415$$

    The future value, 30 months from now, of the first 10 payments is

    $$S_n(\text{due}) = \$800 \left(\frac{1.025^{10}-1}{0.025}\right)(1.025) = \$9186.77$$

    The future value, 7 years from now, of this amount and the remaining 18 payments is

    $$\$9186.77(1.045)^9 + \$800 \left(\frac{1.022252415^{18}-1}{0.022252415}\right)(1.022252415)$$

    $$= \$13,652.41 + \$17,864.56$$

    $$= \underline{\$31,516.97}$$

12 Annuities: Payment Size, Term, and Interest Rate

Changes in the Second Edition:

1. The major changes have already been covered in the lengthy preamble to the Chapter 10 solutions.

2. The mathematics prerequisite for some college business programs is such that some students are not able to comfortably manipulate logarithms. Therefore, formulas are presented (and derived in an appendix) for the direct calculation of n. (In the first edition, the approach was to substitute known numerical values in a future value formula or in a present value formula, and then rearrange the resulting equation to solve for n.)

3. In colleges where the algebraic approach is emphasized, the calculation of the interest rate per payment interval is usually either omitted or performed using the financial functions on a calculator. Therefore, the numerical (trial–and–error) approach is illustrated only in an appendix in the second edition.

Exercise 12.1

1. Given: $S_n = \$76,055$, $n = 13$, $p = i = 10.5\%$

$$\$76,055 = R\left(\frac{1.105^{13}-1}{0.105}\right)$$
$$R = \underline{\underline{\$3000.00}}$$

2. Given: $S_n = \$35,790$, $n = 5.5(4) = 22$, $p = i = \dfrac{10\%}{4} = 2.5\%$

$$\$35,790 = R\left(\frac{1.025^{22}-1}{0.025}\right)$$
$$R = \underline{\underline{\$1240.00}}$$

3. Given: $S_n = \$4357$, $n = 2.5(12) = 30$, $p = i = \dfrac{7.5\%}{12} = 0.625\%$

$$\$4357 = R\left(\frac{1.00625^{30}-1}{0.00625}\right)$$
$$R = \underline{\underline{\$132.50}}$$

4. Given: $S_n = \$50,000$, $n = 12.5(2) = 25$, $p = i = \dfrac{8\%}{2} = 4\%$

$$\$50,000 = R\left(\frac{1.04^{25}-1}{0.04}\right)$$
$$R = \underline{\underline{\$1200.60}}$$

5. Given: $A_n = \$20,832$, $n = 8.25(12) = 99$, $p = i = \dfrac{13.5\%}{12} = 1.125\%$

$$\$20,832 = R\left(\frac{1-1.01125^{-99}}{0.01125}\right)$$
$$R = \underline{\underline{\$349.99}}$$

6. Given: $A_n = \$35,531$, $n = 7.75(4) = 31$, $p = i = \dfrac{9.9\%}{4} = 2.475\%$

$$\$35,531 = R\left(\frac{1-1.02475^{-31}}{0.02475}\right)$$
$$R = \underline{\underline{\$1655.00}}$$

7. Given: $A_n = \$20,049$, $n = 19(2) = 38$, $p = i = \dfrac{9.25\%}{2} = 4.625\%$

$$\$20,049 = R\left(\frac{1-1.04625^{-38}}{0.04625}\right)$$
$$R = \underline{\underline{\$1130.00}}$$

8. Given: $A_n = \$35,104$, $n = 6(12) + 7 = 79$, $p = i = \dfrac{8.4\%}{12} = 0.7\%$

$$\$35,104 = R\left(\frac{1-1.007^{-79}}{0.007}\right)$$
$$R = \underline{\underline{\$580.00}}$$

9. Given: A_n (due) $= \$25,000$, $n = 8.5(2) = 17$, $p = i = \dfrac{9.5\%}{2} = 4.75\%$

$$\$25,000 = R\left(\frac{1-1.0475^{-17}}{0.0475}\right)(1.0475)$$
$$R = \underline{\underline{\$2077.58}}$$

Exercise 12.1 (continued)

10. Given: A_n (due) = \$50,000, n = 12, p = i = 8.9%

$$\$50,000 = R \left(\frac{1-1.089^{-12}}{0.089} \right) (1.089)$$
$$R = \underline{\$6379.61}$$

11. Given: S_n (due) = \$100,000, n = 15.25(4) = 61, p = i = $\frac{9\%}{4}$ = 2.25%

$$\$100,000 = R \left(\frac{1.0225^{61}-1}{0.0225} \right) (1.0225)$$
$$R = \underline{\$762.57}$$

12. Given: S_n (due) = \$30,000, n = 7(12) + 9 = 93, p = i = $\frac{8.25\%}{12}$ = 0.6875%

$$\$30,000 = R \left(\frac{1.006875^{93}-1}{0.006875} \right) (1.006875)$$
$$R = \underline{\$229.86}$$

13. Given: A_n = \$25,000, n = 8.5(4) = 34, i = $\frac{9.5\%}{2}$ = 4.75%, c = $\frac{2}{4}$ = 0.5

Then   p = $1.0475^{0.5}-1$ = 0.023474475

and $$\$25,000 = R \left(\frac{1-1.023474475^{-34}}{0.023474475} \right)$$
$$R = \underline{\$1075.51}$$

14. Given: A_n = \$50,000, n = 12(12) = 144, i = 8.9%, c = $\frac{1}{12}$ = 0.08$\overline{3}$

Then   p = $1.089^{0.08\overline{3}}-1$ = 0.0071302873

and $$\$50,000 = R \left(\frac{1-1.0071302873^{-144}}{0.0071302873} \right)$$
$$R = \underline{\$556.59}$$

15. Given: S_n = \$100,000, n = 15, i = $\frac{9\%}{4}$ = 2.25%, c = 4

Then   p = 1.0225^4-1 = 0.093083319

and $$\$100,000 = R \left(\frac{1.093083319^{15}-1}{0.093083319} \right)$$
$$R = \underline{\$3324.24}$$

16. Given: S_n = \$30,000, n = 7(2) = 14, i = $\frac{8.25\%}{12}$ = 0.6875%, c = 6

Then   p = 1.006875^6-1 = 0.041965517

and $$\$30,000 = R \left(\frac{1.041965517^{14}-1}{0.041965517} \right)$$
$$R = \underline{\$1618.08}$$

17. Given: A_n (due) = \$30,000, n = 10.5(4) = 42, i = 4.25%, c = $\frac{2}{4}$ = 0.5

Then   p = $1.0425^{0.5} - 1$ = 2.1028893%

$$\$30,000 = R \left(\frac{1-1.021028893^{-42}}{0.021028893} \right) (1.021028893)$$
$$R = \underline{\$1060.28}$$

Exercise 12.1 (continued)

18. Given: A_n (due) = \$45,000, $n = 11(12) = 132$, $i = 9.9\%$, $c = \frac{1}{12} = 0.08\overline{3}$

    Then $\quad p = 1.099^{0.08\overline{3}} - 1 = 0.007897747$

    $\$45,000 = R \left(\dfrac{1-1.007897747^{-132}}{0.007897747} \right) (1.007897747)$

    $R = \underline{\$545.86}$

19. Given: S_n (due) = \$150,000, $n = 16$, $i = \dfrac{11\%}{4} = 2.75\%$, $c = 4$

    Then $\quad p = 1.0275^4 - 1 = 0.114621259$

    $\$150,000 = R \left(\dfrac{1.114621259^{16}-1}{0.114621259} \right) (1.114621259)$

    $R = \underline{\$3298.84}$

20. Given: S_n (due) = \$25,000, $n = 15$, $i = \dfrac{8.25\%}{12} = 0.6875\%$, $c = 6$

    Then $\quad p = 1.006875^6 - 1 = 0.041965517$

    $\$25,000 = R \left(\dfrac{1.041965517^{15}-1}{0.041965517} \right) (1.041965517)$

    $R = \underline{\$1180.85}$

21. a. Given: $S_n = \$200,000$, $n = 25$, $p = i = 8\%$

    $\$200,000 = R \left(\dfrac{1.08^{25}-1}{0.08} \right)$

    $R = \underline{\$2735.76}$

    b. Given: $S_n = \$200,000$, $n = 25$, $p = i = 10\%$

    $\$200,000 = R \left(\dfrac{1.10^{25}-1}{0.10} \right)$

    $R = \underline{\$2033.61}$

22. a. Given: $S_n = \$200,000$, $n = 25$, $p = i = 9\%$

    $\$200,000 = R \left(\dfrac{1.09^{25}-1}{0.09} \right)$

    $R = \underline{\$2361.25}$

    b. Given: $S_n = \$200,000$, $n = 30$, $p = i = 9\%$

    $\$200,000 = R \left(\dfrac{1.09^{30}-1}{0.09} \right)$

    $R = \underline{\$1467.27}$

23. a. Given: S_n (due) = \$200,000, $n = 20$, $p = i = 9\%$

    $\$200,000 = R \left(\dfrac{1.09^{20}-1}{0.09} \right) (1.09)$

    $R = \underline{\$3586.51}$

Exercise 12.1 (continued)

b.   Given: $S_n = \$200{,}000$, $n = 20$, $p = i = 9\%$

$$\$200{,}000 = R\left(\frac{1.09^{20}-1}{0.09}\right)$$
$$R = \underline{\underline{\$3909.30}}$$

24. a.   Given: A_n (due) $= \$200{,}000$, $n = 20$, $p = i = 9\%$

$$\$200{,}000 = R\left(\frac{1-1.09^{-20}}{0.09}\right)(1.09)$$
$$R = \underline{\underline{\$20{,}100.27}}$$

b.   Given: $A_n = \$200{,}000$, $n = 20$, $p = i = 9\%$

$$\$200{,}000 = R\left(\frac{1-1.09^{-20}}{0.09}\right)$$
$$R = \underline{\underline{\$21{,}909.30}}$$

25. a.   Given: $A_n = \$20{,}000$, $n = 10(12) = 120$, $p = i = \frac{7.5\%}{12} = 0.625\%$

$$\$20{,}000 = R\left(\frac{1-1.00625^{-120}}{0.00625}\right)$$
$$R = \underline{\underline{\$237.40}}$$

b.   Given: $A_n = \$20{,}000$, $n = 20(12) = 240$, $p = i = 0.625\%$

$$\$20{,}000 = R\left(\frac{1-1.00625^{-240}}{0.00625}\right)$$
$$R = \underline{\underline{\$161.12}}$$

26. a.   Given: $A_n = \$25{,}000$, $n = 10(4) = 40$, $p = i = \frac{10\%}{4} = 2.5\%$

$$\$25{,}000 = R\left(\frac{1-1.025^{-40}}{0.025}\right)$$
$$R = \underline{\underline{\$995.91}}$$

b.   Given: $A_n = \$25{,}000$, $n = 40$, $p = i = \frac{8\%}{4} = 2\%$

$$\$25{,}000 = R\left(\frac{1-1.02^{-40}}{0.02}\right)$$
$$R = \underline{\underline{\$913.89}}$$

27. a.   Given: S_n (due) $= \$4000$, $n = 12$, $p = i = \frac{6\%}{12} = 0.5\%$

$$\$4000 = R\left(\frac{1.005^{12}-1}{0.005}\right)(1.005)$$
$$R = \underline{\underline{\$322.65}}$$

b.   Given: S_n (due) $= \$4000$, $n = 24$, $p = i = 0.5\%$

$$\$4000 = R\left(\frac{1.005^{24}-1}{0.005}\right)(1.005)$$
$$R = \underline{\underline{\$156.50}}$$

Exercise 12.1 *(continued)*

28. Original loan = Present value of all the payments

    For every case, $A_n = \$20,000$, $p = i = \dfrac{12\%}{12} = 1\%$

    a. For $n = 5(12) = 60$, $\$20,000 = R\left(\dfrac{1-1.01^{-60}}{0.01}\right)$

    $R = \underline{\$444.89}$

    Total interest $= 60\,(\$444.89) - \$20,000 = \underline{\$6693.40}$

Similarly,

   b. For $n = 120$, $R = \underline{\$286.94}$, Total interest $= \underline{\$14,432.80}$

   c. For $n = 180$, $R = \underline{\$240.03}$, Total interest $= \underline{\$23,205.40}$

   d. For $n = 240$, $R = \underline{\$220.22}$, Total interest $= \underline{\$32,852.80}$

   e. For $n = 300$, $R = \underline{\$210.64}$, Total interest $= \underline{\$43,192.00}$

29. Original loan = Present value of all payments

    The payments in this case form a general annuity due with

    $n = 7.5(2) = 15$, $i = \dfrac{10.5\%}{12} = 0.875\%$, $c = \dfrac{12}{2} = 6$ and

    $p = 1.00875^6 - 1 = 0.053661924$

    $\$20,000 = R\left(\dfrac{1-1.053661924^{-15}}{0.053661924}\right)$

    $R = \underline{\$1974.83}$

    The semiannual payment is $1974.83.

30. The $500,000 target is the future value of the semiannual contributions.

    a. The contributions form a simple annuity due having

    $S_n\,(\text{due}) = \$500,000$, $n = 9(2) = 18$, $p = i = \dfrac{7.5\%}{2} = 3.75\%$

    $\$500,000 = R\left(\dfrac{1.0375^{18}-1}{0.0375}\right)(1.0375)$

    $R = \underline{\$19,227.29}$

    b. Now $S_n = \$500,000$, $n = 18$, $p = 3.75\%$ and

    $\$500,000 = R\left(\dfrac{1.0375^{18}-1}{0.0375}\right)$

    $R = \underline{\$19,948.31}$

31. The future value of the payments is $500,000. The payments form a general annuity due having

    $S_n\,(\text{due}) = \$500,000$, $n = 5(4) = 20$, $i = 0.6875\%$, $c = \dfrac{12}{4} = 3$ and $p = 1.006875^3 - 1 = 0.020767122$

    $\$500,000 = R\left(\dfrac{1.020767122^{20}-1}{0.020767122}\right)(1.020767122)$

    $R = \underline{\$20,006.16}$

    Triex should make quarterly payments of $20,006.16.

Exercise 12.1 *(continued)*

32. Given: $S_n = \$30,000$, $n = 4(12) = 48$, $i = \dfrac{5.5\%}{2} = 2.75\%$, $c = \dfrac{2}{12} = 0.1\overline{6}$

Then $p = 1.0275^{0.1\overline{6}} - 1 = 0.004531682$

$$\$30,000 = R\left(\frac{1.004531682^{48} - 1}{0.004531682}\right)$$

$$R = \underline{\underline{\$560.90}}$$

Brenda and Tom must save $560.90 each month.

33. The $300,000 balance is the present value of the payments which form an ordinary general annuity.

$A_n = \$300,000$, $n = 20(4) = 80$, $i = 8\%$, $c = \dfrac{1}{4} = 0.25$.

Then $p = 1.08^{0.25} - 1 = 0.019426547$ and

$$\$300,000 = R\left(\frac{1 - 1.019426547^{-80}}{0.019426547}\right)$$

$$R = \underline{\underline{\$7419.89}}$$

Henry's quarterly payments will be $7419.89.

34. With the instalment payment option, the insurance company effectively lends the annual premium to the customer. The customer repays the loan with 12 monthly payments including interest at 15% compounded monthly. We have

A_n (due) $= \$100$, $n = 12$, $p = i = \dfrac{15\%}{12} = 1.25\%$

$$\$100 = R\left(\frac{1 - 1.0125^{-12}}{0.0125}\right)(1.0125)$$

$$R = \underline{\underline{\$8.91}}$$

The monthly premium per $100 of annual premium is $8.91.

35. The present value of the lease payments discounted at the lessor's required rate of return equals the capital cost of the equipment. Therefore,

A_n (due) $= \$8500$, $n = 3(12) = 36$, $p = i = \dfrac{18\%}{12} = 1.5\%$, and

$$\$8500 = R\left(\frac{1 - 1.015^{-36}}{0.015}\right)(1.015)$$

$$R = \underline{\underline{\$302.75}}$$

The lease rate will be $302.75 at the beginning of each month for 3 years.

36. The present value of the equivalent payments is $10,000.

$A_n = \$10,000$, $n = 2(4) = 8$, $p = i = \dfrac{7.5\%}{4} = 1.875\%$

$$\$10,000 = R\left(\frac{1 - 1.01875^{-8}}{0.01875}\right)$$

$$R = \underline{\underline{\$1357.75}}$$

Quarterly payments of $1357.75 for 2 years would be equivalent to $10,000 today.

37. The future value of the replacement payments is $25,000.

$S_n = \$25,000$, $n = 11$, $p = i = \dfrac{5.4\%}{12} = 0.45\%$

$\$25,000 = R \left(\dfrac{1.0045^{11}-1}{0.0045} \right)$

$R = \underline{\$2222.05}$

Eleven monthly payments of $2222.05 are economically equivalent to the scheduled payment of $25,000.

38. a. The contributions form a simple annuity due having

$S_n \text{ (due)} = \$700,000$, $n = 30$, $p = i = 8\%$

$\$700,000 = R \left(\dfrac{1.08^{30}-1}{0.08} \right)(1.08)$

$R = \underline{\$5721.48}$

b. With $n = 25$ instead of $n = 30$,

$\$700,000 = R \left(\dfrac{1.08^{25}-1}{0.08} \right)(1.08)$

$R = \underline{\$8865.88}$

39. With the contributions at the beginning of each year,

$S_n \text{ (due)} = \$500,000$, $n = 27$, $p = i = 9\%$

$\$500,000 = R \left(\dfrac{1.09^{27}-1}{0.09} \right)(1.09)$

$R = \underline{\$4465.55}$

With the contributions at the end of each year,

$S_n = \$500,000$, $n = 27$, $p = i = 9\%$

$\$500,000 = R \left(\dfrac{1.09^{27}-1}{0.09} \right)$

$R = \underline{\$4867.45}$

The annual contributions must be $4867.45 − $4465.55 = $\underline{\$401.90}$ larger if made at the end of the year instead of the beginning.

40. The present value of the payments discounted at the required rate of return must equal the capital cost.

$A_n \text{ (due)} = \$20,000$, $n = 5(4) = 20$, $p = i = \dfrac{16\%}{4} = 4\%$

$\$20,000 = R \left(\dfrac{1-1.04^{-20}}{0.04} \right)(1.04)$

$R = \underline{\$1415.03}$

CompuLease must charge $1415.03 at the beginning of each quarter of the 5–year lease.

41. Initial lease liability = Present value of all lease payments. The lease payments form a simple annuity due having

$A_n \text{ (due)} = \$43,000$, $n = 5(12) = 60$, $p = i = \dfrac{13.5\%}{12} = 1.125\%$

$\$43,000 = R \left(\dfrac{1-1.01125^{-60}}{0.01125} \right)(1.01125)$

$R = \underline{\$978.42}$

The monthly lease payment is $978.42.

Exercise 12.1 *(continued)*

42. With payments at the end of each year,
$S_n = \$600{,}000$, $n = 32$, $i = 4\%$, $c = 2$, and $p = 1.04^2 - 1 = 0.0816$

$$\$600{,}000 = R\left(\frac{1.0816^{32}-1}{0.0816}\right)$$

$$R = \$4330.26$$

If payments are made at the beginning of each year,

$$\$600{,}000 = R\left(\frac{1.0816^{32}-1}{0.0816}\right)(1.0816)$$

$$R = \$4003.57$$

The annual contributions will have to be
$\$4330.26 - \$4003.57 = \underline{\$326.69}$
larger if they are made at the year-end.

43. The present value of the lease payments discounted at the required rate of return must equal the capital cost of the equipment.

a. A_n (due) $= \$25{,}000$, $n = 5(12) = 60$, $i = \frac{18\%}{4} = 4.5\%$, $c = \frac{4}{12} = 0.\overline{3}$

$p = 1.045^{0.\overline{3}} - 1 = 0.014780462$

$$\$25{,}000 = R\left(\frac{1-1.014780462^{-60}}{0.014780462}\right)(1.014780462)$$

$$R = \underline{\$622.06}$$

The monthly lease payment is $\$622.06$.

b. A_n (due) $= \$25{,}000$, $n = 5(2) = 10$, $i = 4.5\%$, $c = \frac{4}{2} = 2$

$p = 1.045^2 - 1 = 0.092025$

$$\$25{,}000 = R\left(\frac{1-1.092025^{-10}}{0.092025}\right)(1.092025)$$

$$R = \underline{\$3599.09}$$

The semiannual lease payment is $\$3599.09$.

44. a. Original loan = Present value of 14 quarterly payments + Present value of $\$150{,}000$

$$\$200{,}000 = R\left(\frac{1-1.0275^{-14}}{0.0275}\right) + \$150{,}000\,(1.0275)^{-14}$$

Solving for R gives $R = \underline{\$8476.23}$

b. Original loan = Present value of 28 quarterly payments + Present value of balance after 7 years

$$\$200{,}000 = \$8476.23\left(\frac{1-1.0275^{-28}}{0.0275}\right) + \frac{\text{Balance}}{1.0275^{28}}$$

$$= \$164{,}022.06 + \text{Balance}\,(0.467852273)$$

Balance $= \underline{\$76{,}900.21}$

45. a. Original loan = Present value of all payments

$A_n = \$50{,}000$, $n = 60$, $i = 5.5\%$, $c = \frac{2}{12} = 0.1\overline{6}$, and

$p = 1.055^{0.1\overline{6}} - 1 = 0.89633939$

$$\$50{,}000 = R\left(\frac{1-1.0089633939^{-60}}{0.0089633939}\right)$$

$$R = \underline{\$1081.05}$$

The monthly payment is $\$1081.05$.

Exercise 12.1 (continued)

b. Payout amount = Present value of remaining payments

$$= \$1081.05 \left(\frac{1-1.0089633939^{-36}}{0.0089633939} \right)$$

$$= \underline{\$33,137.29}$$

46. Amount in the trust account on 19th birthday

= Present value on 19th birthday of monthly payments

$$\$5000 \, (1.0825)^{19} = R \left(\frac{1-1.00625^{-48}}{0.00625} \right)$$

$$R = \underline{\$545.18}$$

The monthly payment will be $545.18.

47. Future value, 10 years from now, of retiring allowance

= Present value, 10 years from now, of the 15-year annuity

Viewed from the focal date, the annuity is a simple annuity due.

Putting the word equation into mathematics,

$$\$25,000 \, (1.0875)^{10} = R \left(\frac{1-1.0225^{-60}}{0.0225} \right) (1.0225)$$

$$R = \underline{\$1727.32}$$

Elizabeth can expect payments of $1727.32 at the beginning of each quarter.

48. The future value, 9 years from now, of contributions = Present value, 9 years from now, of payments to daughter

$$R \left(\frac{1.04125^{18}-1}{0.04125} \right) (1.04125) = \$3000 \left(\frac{1-1.04125^{-8}}{0.04125} \right) (1.04125)$$

$$= \$20,923.28$$

Solving for R gives R = $\underline{\$774.60.}$

The Friedrichs must make semiannual contributions of $774.60.

49. The future value, 4 years from now, of quarterly amounts saved

= Present value, 4 years from now, of the $3000 monthly payments.

$$R \left(\frac{1.015^{16}-1}{0.015} \right) = \$3000 \left(\frac{1-0.0035^{-12}}{0.0035} \right)$$

The solution is R = $\underline{\$1962.61.}$ Tim and Justine must pay $1962.61 into the fund at the end of every calendar quarter.

50. a. The future value of the contributions after 30 years is to be $600,000. The future value of contributions after 25 years = Present value, 25 years from now, of $600,000.

$$R \left(\frac{1.035^{50}-1}{0.035} \right) = \$600,000 \, (1.035)^{-10}$$

Solving for R gives R = $\underline{\$3247.01}$

b. $600,000 = Present value of the annuity payments = $R \left(\frac{1-1.006^{300}}{0.006} \right)$

$$R = \underline{\$4317.53}$$

They can expect $4317.53 at the end of each month for 25 years.

Exercise 12.1 (continued)

51. Amount required in the RRSP 28 years from now
    = Present value, 28 years from now, of the annuity payments.
    The latter amount is

$$\$6000 \left(\frac{1-1.00625^{-300}}{0.00625}\right) = \$811,917.68$$

The amount in the RRSP 10 years from now will be

$$\$7000 \left(\frac{1.075^{10}-1}{0.075}\right) = \$99,029.61$$

The future value, 28 years from now, of this amount and the contributions for years 11 to 28 inclusive is to be \$811,917.68. Hence

$$\$99,029.61(1.075)^{18} + R \left(\frac{1.075^{18}-1}{0.075}\right) = \$811,917.68$$

The solution is R = $\underline{\underline{\$12,554.29}}$ at each year-end for years 11 to 28 inclusive.

52. a. The nominal amount in the RRSP should be
    $$S = \$500,000(1.05)^{30} = \underline{\$2,160,971}$$

    b. The contributions form an ordinary general annuity having
    $$S_n = \$2,160,971, n = 30(4) = 120, i = 4.25\%, c = \frac{2}{4} = 0.5,$$

    and $p = 1.0425^{0.5}-1 = 0.021028893$

    $$\$2,160,971 = R \left(\frac{1.021028893^{120}-1}{0.021028893}\right)$$

    $$R = \underline{\underline{\$4075.72}}$$

    Dr. Collins should make quarterly contributions of \$4075.72.

53. Present value of instalment payments = \$1900.
    For payments at the beginning of each quarter,

    $$A_n \text{ (due)} = \$1900, n = 4, i = 7.5\%, c = \frac{2}{4} = 0.5, \text{ and}$$

    $$p = 1.075^{0.5}-1 = 0.036822068$$

    $$\$1900 = R \left(\frac{1-1.036822068^{-4}}{0.036822068}\right)(1.036822068)$$

    $$R = \underline{\underline{\$501.07}}$$

    For payments at the beginning of each month,

    $$A_n \text{ (due)} = \$1900, n = 12, i = 7.5\%, c = \frac{2}{12} = 0.1\overline{6}, \text{ and}$$

    $$p = 1.075^{0.1\overline{6}}-1 = 0.012126379$$

    $$\$1900 = R \left(\frac{1-1.012126379^{-12}}{0.012126379}\right)(1.012126379)$$

    $$R = \underline{\underline{\$169.04}}$$

    The payments are \$501.07 quarterly or \$169.04 monthly.

Exercise 12.1 (continued)

54. The amount required, 23 years from now, to purchase the annuity is

$$A_n = \$4000 \left(\frac{1 - 1.0055^{-300}}{0.0055} \right) = \$586,967.19$$

The initial investment, 23 years earlier, required to reach this amount is

$$P = \frac{S}{(1 + i)^n} = \frac{\$586,967.19}{1.0125^{92}} = \$187,184.93$$

The remaining $\$225,000 - \$187,184.93 = \$37,815.07$ of the inheritance can be viewed as the amount funding quarterly withdrawals for the next 23 years. The size of these withdrawals is the value of R in

$$\$37,815.07 = R \left(\frac{1 - 1.0125^{-92}}{0.0125} \right)$$

$$R = \underline{\$694.01}$$

Connie and Rich can withdraw $\$694.01$ at the end of each quarter.

55. The amount, 33 years from now, that will have the purchasing power of 300,000 current dollars is

$$S = P(1 + i)^n = \$300,000 (1.05)^{33} = \$1,500,956.60.$$

This amount is the future value of the required RRSP contributions.

Hence,

$$\$1,500,956.60 = R \left(\frac{1.085^{33} - 1}{0.085} \right)$$

$$R = \underline{\$9269.72}$$

56. The amount required in the RESP 12.5 years from now is the present value of the subsequent payments from the RESP. That is,

$$A_n = \$5000 \left(\frac{1 - 1.0425^{-12}}{0.0425} \right) = \$46,251.97$$

This amount also represents the future value of the contributions.

$$S_n = \$46,251.97 = R \left(\frac{1.0425^{25} - 1}{0.0425} \right)$$

$$R = \underline{\$1073.72}$$

Ken and Barbara must make semiannual contributions of $\$1073.72$.

57. a. The future value, 17 years from now, of the RRSP
= Present value, 17 years from now, of the annuity.
The amount in the RRSP 17 years from now will be

$$\$31,000(1.0875)^{17} + \$5000 \left(\frac{1.0875^{17} - 1}{0.0875} \right) = \$309,703.87$$

This amount will purchase a 20-year annuity whose monthly payments is the solution to

$$\$309,703.87 = R \left(\frac{1 - 1.006875^{-240}}{0.006875} \right)$$

$$R = \underline{\$2638.88}$$

b. The purchasing power in current dollars of one payment is
$$P = S (1 + i)^{-n} = \$2638.88 (1.04)^{-17} = \underline{\$1354.73}$$

58. The amount, 20 years from now, that will have the purchasing power of $\$6000$ (in today's dollars) is
$$S = P (1 + i)^n = \$6000(1.045)^{20} = \$14,470.28.$$
Present value, 20 years from now, of the 25-year annuity
= Future value, 20 years from now, of the RRSP

The former amount is $A_n = \$14,470.28 \left(\dfrac{1 - 1.02^{100}}{0.02} \right) = \$623,645.22$

Exercise 12.1 *(concluded)*

The semiannual RRSP contributions needed to accumulate this amount after 20 years is the value of R in

$$\$54{,}000(1.04)^{40} + R\left(\frac{1.04^{40}-1}{0.04}\right) = \$623{,}645.22$$

$$R = \underline{\$3834.66}$$

59. Future value, today, of the contributions to the RRSP = Present value, today, of the RRIF withdrawals. The amount in the RRSP 10 years ago was

$$\$500\left(\frac{1.025^{40}-1}{0.025}\right)(1.025) = \$34{,}543.81$$

The amount currently in the RRSP is

$$\$34{,}543.81(1.03)^{40} + \$500\left(\frac{1.03^{40}-1}{0.03}\right)(1.03) = \$151{,}514.86$$

The maximum beginning-of-month withdrawal for the next 15 years is the value of R satisfying

$$\$151{,}514.86 = R\left(\frac{1-1.006875^{-180}}{0.006875}\right)(1.006875)$$

$$R = \underline{\$1459.87}$$

Exercise 12.2

1. Given: $A_n = \$50{,}000$, $R = \$4352.53$, $p = i = \dfrac{9.5\%}{2} = 4.75\%$

$$n = -\frac{\ln\left(1 - \dfrac{pA_n}{R}\right)}{\ln\ (1+p)}$$

$$= -\frac{\ln\left(1 - \dfrac{0.0475 \times \$50{,}000}{\$4352.53}\right)}{\ln\ (1.0475)}$$

$$= -\frac{-0.78891}{0.046406}$$

$$= 17.00$$

The annuity consists of 17 semiannual payments. Its term is $\dfrac{17}{2} = 8.5$ years = $\underline{\underline{8\ \text{years and 6 months.}}}$

2. Given: $S_n = \$100{,}000$, $R = \$900.46$, $p = i = 8.9\%$

$$n = \frac{\ln\left(1 + \dfrac{pS_n}{R}\right)}{\ln\ (1+p)}$$

$$= \frac{\ln\left(1 + \dfrac{0.089 \times \$100{,}000}{\$900.46}\right)}{\ln\ (1.089)}$$

$$= \frac{2.38228}{0.085260}$$

$$= 28.00$$

The annuity has 28 annual payments. Its term is $\underline{\underline{28\ \text{years.}}}$

Exercise 12.2 (continued)

3. Given: $A_n = \$200,000$, $R = \$5807.91$, $p = i = \dfrac{9\%}{4} = 2.25\%$

$$n = -\dfrac{\ln\left(1 - \dfrac{0.0225 \times \$200,000}{\$5807.91}\right)}{\ln(1.0225)} = 67.00$$

There are 67 payments in the annuity requiring 67 calendar quarters = $\dfrac{67}{4}$ years
= <u>16 years and 9 months.</u>

4. Given: $S_n = \$30,000$, $R = \$209.59$, $p = i = \dfrac{8.25\%}{12} = 0.6875\%$

$$n = \dfrac{\ln\left(1 - \dfrac{0.006875 \times \$30,000}{\$209.59}\right)}{\ln(1.006875)} = 100.00$$

The annuity has 100 payments requiring 100 months = <u>8 years and 4 months.</u>

5. Given: $A_n = \$100,000$, $R = \$10,000$, $p = i = 8.75\%$

$$n = -\dfrac{\ln\left(1 - \dfrac{0.0875 \times \$100,000}{\$10,000}\right)}{\ln(1.0875)} = 24.79$$

The annuity consists of 25 annual payments with the last payment smaller than $10,000. The annuity's term is <u>25 years.</u>

6. Given: $A_n = \$100,000$, $R = \$1000$, $p = i = \dfrac{9\%}{12} = 0.75\%$

$$n = -\dfrac{\ln\left(1 - \dfrac{0.0075 \times \$100,000}{\$1000}\right)}{\ln(1.0075)} = 185.53$$

The annuity contains 186 monthly payments with the last payment smaller than $1000. The annuity's term is 186 months = $\dfrac{186}{12}$ years = 15.5 years = <u>15 years and 6 months</u>

7. Given: $S_n = \$100,000$, $R = \$5000$, $p = i = \dfrac{7.5\%}{2} = 3.75\%$

$$n = \dfrac{\ln\left(1 + \dfrac{0.0375 \times \$100,000}{\$5000}\right)}{\ln(1.0375)} = 15.20$$

The annuity consists of 16 semiannual payments with the last payment smaller than $5000. The term of the annuity is 16 half years = <u>8 years.</u>

8. Given: $S_n = \$100,000$, $R = \$3,000$, $p = i = \dfrac{10\%}{4} = 2.5\%$

$$n = \dfrac{\ln\left(1 + \dfrac{0.025 \times \$100,000}{\$3000}\right)}{\ln(1.025)} = 24.55$$

The annuity has 25 quarterly payments requiring $\dfrac{25}{4}$ years = 6.25 years = <u>6 years and 3 months</u>

Exercise 12.2 *(continued)*

9. Given: S_n (due) = \$117,896, R = \$3000.00, p = i = 8.75%

$$n = \frac{\ln\left[1 + \dfrac{pS_n \text{ (due)}}{R(1+p)}\right]}{\ln(1+p)}$$

$$= \frac{\ln\left[1 + \dfrac{0.0875 \times \$117,896}{\$3000(1.0875)}\right]}{\ln(1.0875)}$$

$$= \frac{1.42599}{0.083881}$$

$$= 17.00$$

The annuity contains 17 annual payments. The term is 17 years (with the last payment occurring one year before the end of the annuity's term).

10. Given: S_n (due) = \$22,500, R = \$150.75, p = i = $\dfrac{9\%}{12}$ = 0.75%

$$n = \frac{\ln\left[1 + \dfrac{0.0075 \times \$22,500}{\$150.75(1.0075)}\right]}{\ln(1.0075)} = 100.00$$

The annuity has 100 monthly payments requiring $\dfrac{100}{12}$ years = $8.\overline{3}$ years = <u>8 years and 4 months</u>

11. Given: A_n (due) = \$13,405, R = \$1000, p = i = $\dfrac{7.5\%}{2}$ = 3.75%

$$n = -\frac{\ln\left[1 - \dfrac{pA_n \text{ (due)}}{R(1+p)}\right]}{\ln(1+p)}$$

$$= -\frac{\ln\left[1 - \dfrac{0.0375 \times \$13,405}{\$1000(1.0375)}\right]}{\ln(1.0375)}$$

$$= -\frac{-0.66265}{0.036814}$$

$$= 18.00$$

The annuity has 18 semiannual payments. Therefore, its term is <u>9 years</u>.

12. Given: A_n (due) = \$20,000, R = \$858.67, p = i = $\dfrac{10\%}{4}$ = 2.5%

$$n = -\frac{\ln\left[1 - \dfrac{0.025 \times \$20,000}{\$858.67(1.025)}\right]}{\ln(1.025)} = 34.00$$

The annuity consists of 34 quarterly payments. Its term is $\dfrac{34}{4}$ years = 8.5 years = <u>8 years and 6 months.</u>

Exercise 12.2 (continued)

13. Given: $S_n = \$74,385$, $R = \$1200$, $i = 8.75\%$, $c = \dfrac{1}{4} = 0.25$

$$p = (1 + i)^c - 1 = 1.0875^{0.25} - 1 = 0.02119179$$

$$n = \frac{\ln\left(1 + \dfrac{0.02119179 \times \$74,385}{\$1200}\right)}{\ln(1.02119179)} = 40.00$$

The 40 quarterly payments require a term of <u>10 years</u>.

14. Given: $S_n = \$22,500$, $R = \$1075.68$, $i = \dfrac{9\%}{12} = 0.75\%$, $c = \dfrac{12}{2} = 6$

$$p = (1 + i)^c - 1 = 1.0075^6 - 1 = 0.04585224$$

$$n = \frac{\ln\left(1 + \dfrac{0.04585224 \times \$22,500}{\$1075.68}\right)}{\ln(1.04585224)} = 15.00$$

The annuity consists of 15 semiannual payments requiring <u>7 years and 6 months</u>.

15. Given: $A_n = \$5825.85$, $R = \$1000$, $i = \dfrac{7.5\%}{2} = 3.75\%$, $c = 2$

$$p = (1 + i)^c - 1 = 1.0375^2 - 1 = 0.0764025$$

$$n = -\frac{\ln\left(1 - \dfrac{0.0764025 \times \$5825.85}{\$1000}\right)}{\ln(1.0764025)} = 8.00$$

The annuity has 8 annual payments. Its term is <u>8 years</u>.

16. Given: $A_n = \$20,000$, $R = \$358.87$, $i = \dfrac{10\%}{4} = 2.5\%$, $c = \dfrac{4}{12} = 0.\overline{3}$

$$p = (1 + i)^c - 1 = 1.025^{0.\overline{3}} - 1 = 0.008264838$$

$$n = -\frac{\ln\left(1 - \dfrac{0.008264838 \times \$20,000}{\$358.87}\right)}{\ln(1.008264838)} = 75.00$$

The annuity has 75 monthly payments. Its term is $\dfrac{75}{12}$ years = 6.25 years = <u>6 years and 3 months</u>.

Exercise 12.2 *(continued)*

17. Given: S_n (due) = \$58,898.50, R = \$1200, i = 10.25%, $c = \frac{1}{4} = 0.25$

$p = (1 + i)^c - 1 = 1.1025^{0.25} - 1 = 0.02469508$

$$n = \frac{\ln\left(1 + \dfrac{0.02469508 \times \$58,898.50}{\$1200\,(1.02469508)}\right)}{\ln\,(1.02469508)} = 32.00$$

The annuity has 32 quarterly payments. Its term is <u>8 years.</u>

18. Given: S_n (due) = \$30,000, R = \$636.22, $i = \frac{9\%}{12} = 0.75\%$, $c = \frac{12}{2} = 6$

$p = (1 + i)^c - 1 = 1.0075^6 - 1 = 0.04585224$

$$n = \frac{\ln\left(1 + \dfrac{0.04585224 \times \$30,000}{\$636.22\,(1.04585224)}\right)}{\ln\,(1.04585224)} = 25.00$$

The annuity has 25 semiannual payments. Its term is <u>12 years and 6 months.</u>

19. Given: A_n (due) = \$6601.13, R = \$1000, $i = \frac{8.5\%}{2} = 4.25\%$, $c = 2$

$p = (1 + i)^c - 1 = 1.0425^2 - 1 = 0.08680625$

$$n = -\frac{\ln\left(1 - \dfrac{0.08680625 \times \$6601.13}{\$1000\,(1.08680625)}\right)}{\ln\,(1.08680625)} = 9.00$$

The annuity has 9 annual payments taking <u>9 years.</u>

20. Note: The payment interval given in the text should be "1 month" instead of "6 months".

Given: A_n (due) = \$20,000, R = \$236.18, $i = \frac{12\%}{4} = 3\%$, $c = \frac{4}{12} = 0.\overline{3}$

$p = (1 + i)^c - 1 = 1.03^{0.3} - 1 = 0.009901634$

$$n = -\frac{\ln\left(1 - \dfrac{0.009901634 \times \$20,000}{\$236.18\,(1.009901634)}\right)}{\ln\,(1.009901634)} = 180.00$$

The annuity has 180 monthly payments taking $\frac{180}{12}$ years = 15 years

Exercise 12.2 (continued)

21. The deposits form an ordinary simple annuity whose future value,
    S_n, is $10,000. With R = $100 and $p = i = \dfrac{5.25\%}{12} = 0.4375\%$,

$$n = \frac{\ln\left(1 + \dfrac{pS_n}{R}\right)}{\ln\ (1 + p)} = \frac{\ln\left(1 + \dfrac{0.004375 \times \$10,000}{0.004375}\right)}{\ln\ (1.004375)} = 83.131$$

Since 0.131 of $100 paid 0.131 month after the 83rd payment would make S_n = $10,000, it is probable that interest accruing during the 84th month will be sufficient to reach the $10,000 goal before the 84th deposit of $100 is made. The amount accumulated after 83 deposits will be

$$S_n = R\left[\frac{(1+p)^n - 1}{p}\right] = \$100\left(\frac{1.004375^{83} - 1}{0.004375}\right) = \$9981.19$$

The additional fraction of a month needed for this amount to grow to $10,000 is

$$n = \frac{\ln\left(\dfrac{S}{P}\right)}{\ln\ (1 + i)} \quad \frac{\ln\left(\dfrac{\$10,000}{\$9981.19}\right)}{\ln\ (1.004375)} = 0.431$$

Therefore, it will require a total of 83.43 months or 6 years and 11.43 months to accumulate $10,000.

22. The withdrawals constitute an ordinary simple annuity whose present value, A_n, is $10,000.
    With R = $100 and $p = i = \dfrac{5.25\%}{12} = 0.4375\%$,

$$n = -\frac{\ln\left(\dfrac{1 - pA_n}{R}\right)}{\ln\ (1+p)} = -\frac{\ln\left(1 - \dfrac{0.004375 \times \$10,000}{\$100}\right)}{\ln\ (1.004375)} = 131.80$$

The $10,000 can sustain the $100 withdrawals for 132 months or 11 years. (The last withdrawal will be less than $100.)

23. The purchase price represents the present value of the annuity. Hence, A_n = $300,000 with R = $2500
    and $p = i = \dfrac{7.5\%}{12} = 0.625\%$.

$$n = -\frac{\ln\left(1 - \dfrac{0.00625 \times \$300,000}{\$2500}\right)}{\ln\ (1.00625)} = 222.50$$

The annuity will have 223 monthly payments. Its term will be 223 months or 18 years and 7 months.

Exercise 12.2 (continued)

24. In each case, the contributions form an ordinary simple annuity whose future value is to be $100,000. With R = $1000 and $p = i = 8\%$,

$$n = \frac{\ln\left(1 + \frac{0.08 \times \$100{,}000}{\$1000}\right)}{\ln(1.08)} = 28.550$$

We will now determine whether interest accruing during the 29th year will cause the total amount accumulated to reach $100,000 before the 29th contribution is made. After 28 contributions,

$$S_n = \$1000\left(\frac{1.08^{28}-1}{0.08}\right) = \$95{,}338.82$$

The time required for interest only to cause this amount to reach $100,000 is

$$n = \frac{\ln\left(\frac{S}{P}\right)}{\ln(1+i)} = \frac{\ln\left(\frac{\$100{,}000}{\$95{,}338.82}\right)}{\ln(1.08)} = 0.620 \text{ years}$$

Therefore, 28 contributions of $1000 will have a future value of $100,000 after 28.620 years.

With R = $1100 and $p = i = 8\%$,

$$n = \frac{\ln\left(1 + \frac{0.08 \times \$100{,}000}{\$1100}\right)}{\ln(1.08)} = 27.455$$

In this case, $100,000 will be reached before the 28th payment is made. The amount accumulated after 27 payments will be

$$S_n = \$1100\left(\frac{1.08^{27}-1}{0.08}\right) = \$96{,}085.85$$

The extra time required for this amount to grow to $100,000 is

$$n = \frac{\ln\left(\frac{S}{P}\right)}{\ln(1+i)} = \frac{\ln\left(\frac{\$100{,}000}{\$96{,}085.85}\right)}{\ln(1.08)} = 0.519 \text{ years}$$

Therefore, 27 contributions of $1100 will have a future value of $100,000 after 27.519 years. The $1000 annual contributions take

(28.620 − 27.519) years = 1.101 years = <u>1 year and 37 days</u>

longer to reach $100,000.

Exercise 12.2 *(continued)*

25. The original loan equals the present value of the loan payments.
    With $A_n = \$100,000$, $R = \$1000$, and $p = i = \dfrac{10.5\%}{12} = 0.875\%$,

    the number of payments required to pay off the loan is

    $$n = -\frac{\ln\left(1 - \dfrac{0.00875 \times \$100,000}{\$1000}\right)}{\ln(1.00875)} = 238.69$$

    That is, it will take 239 months to pay off the loan (with the last payment smaller than the others).

    With R increased to $1100 per month,

    $$n = -\frac{\ln\left(1 - \dfrac{0.00875 \times \$100,000}{\$1100}\right)}{\ln(1.00875)} = 182.16$$

    The loan will be paid off in only 183 months. Therefore, the $1000 payments will take
    (239 – 183) months = 56 months = <u>4 years and 8 months</u> longer to pay off the loan.

26. The original loan equals the present value of the loan payments.
    With $A_n = \$100,000$, $R = \$1000$, and $p = i = \dfrac{10.5\%}{12} = 0.875\%$,

    the number of payments required to pay off the loan is

    $$n = -\frac{\ln\left(1 - \dfrac{0.00875 \times \$100,000}{\$1000}\right)}{\ln(1.00875)} = 238.69$$

    That is, the loan will be paid off after 239 payments (with the last payment smaller than the others). With
    the interest rate reduced to $p = i = \dfrac{9.75\%}{12} = 0.8125\%$,

    $$n = -\frac{\ln\left(1 - \dfrac{0.008125 \times \$100,000}{\$1000}\right)}{\ln(1.008125)} = 206.86$$

    The loan will be paid off after only 207 payments.
    Therefore, it will take (239 – 207) months = 32 months = <u>2 years and 8 months</u> longer to pay off the loan
    at the higher interest rate.

27. $200,000 will be the future value of the annual $2000 contributions.

    a. The contributions form a simple annuity due with
       S_n (due) = $200,000, R = $2000, $p = i = 9\%$.
       The required number of contributions is

       $$n = \frac{\ln\left[1 + \dfrac{0.09 \times \$200,000}{\$2000\,(1.09)}\right]}{\ln(1.09)} = 25.82$$

       Rounded to the nearest year, it will take 26 years.

Exercise 12.2 *(continued)*

b. Now the contributions form an ordinary simple annuity.

$$n = \frac{\ln\left[1 + \dfrac{0.09 \times \$200,000}{\$2000}\right]}{\ln\,(1.09)} = 26.72$$

Rounded to the nearest year, it will take <u>27 years</u>.

28. The initial amount in the fund represents the present value of the withdrawals.

   a. A_n (due) = \$200,000, R = \$20,000, $p = i = 9\%$

   The number of withdrawals will be

$$n = -\frac{\ln\left[1 - \dfrac{0.09 \times \$200,000}{\$20,000\,(1.09)}\right]}{\ln\,(1.09)} = 20.27$$

   There will be 21 withdrawals with the <u>last withdrawal</u> (less than \$20,000) occurring <u>20 years from now</u>.

   b. A_n = \$200,000, R = \$20,000, $p = i = 9\%$.

   The number of withdrawals will be

$$n = -\frac{\ln\left(1 - \dfrac{0.09 \times \$200,000}{\$20,000}\right)}{\ln\,(1.09)} = 26.72$$

   There will be 27 withdrawals with the <u>last withdrawal</u> (less than \$20,000) occurring <u>27 years from now</u>.

29. The future value of Kim's contributions must be \$8000. The contributions form a simple annuity due having S_n (due) = \$8000, R = \$300, and $p = i = \dfrac{5.25\%}{12} = 0.4375\%$. The number of contributions will be

$$n = \frac{\ln\left(1 + \dfrac{0.004375 \times \$8000}{\$300}\right)}{\ln\,(1.004375)} = 25.173$$

   Kim will reach the goal with his 26th deposit (which can be less than \$300) occurring <u>25 months from today</u>.

30. The lease liability is the present value of the lease payments (discounted at the firm's cost of borrowing). That is, A_n (due) = \$11,622.73, R = \$295, $p = i = \dfrac{10.5\%}{12} = 0.875\%$.

   The number of lease payments is

$$n = -\frac{\ln\left(1 - \dfrac{0.00875 \times \$11,622.73}{\$295\,(1.00875)}\right)}{\ln\,(1.00875)} = 48.00$$

   The lease has 48 monthly payments. Its term is <u>4 years</u>.

Exercise 12.2 *(continued)*

31. The purchase price of the annuity is the present value of the annuity payments. In this case, the payments form an ordinary general annuity having

$A_n = \$200{,}000$, $R = \$5000$, $i = \dfrac{8.5\%}{2} = 4.25\%$, $c = \dfrac{2}{4} = 0.5$

$p = (1 + i)^c - 1 = 1.0425^{0.5} - 1 = 0.02102889$

The number of payments that the annuity will provide is

$$n = -\dfrac{\ln\left(1 - \dfrac{0.02102889 \times \$200{,}000}{\$5000}\right)}{\ln(1.02102889)} = 88.41$$

The 89 quarterly payments will last for $\dfrac{89}{4}$ years = 22.25 years = <u>22 years and 3 months</u>

32. The $40,000 savings target is the future value of the monthly contributions which form an ordinary general annuity. Hence,

$S_n = \$40{,}000$, $R = \$700$, $i = \dfrac{7.5\%}{2} = 3.75\%$, $c = \dfrac{2}{12} = 0.1\overline{6}$

$p = (1 + i)^c - 1 = 1.0375^{0.1\overline{6}} - 1 = 0.006154524$

The required number of contributions is

$$n = \dfrac{\ln\left(1 + \dfrac{0.006154524 \times \$40{,}000}{\$700}\right)}{\ln(1.006154524)} = 49.12$$

Accrued interest part way through the 50th month will result in the target being reached. It will take <u>between 49 months and 50 months.</u>

33. The present value of all the payments equals the purchase price. Since the down payment equals the monthly payment, it can be included with the later payments by treating them all as an annuity due. That is,

A_n (due) $= \$1395$, $R = \$50$, $p = i = \dfrac{13.5\%}{12} = 1.125\%$

The number of payments (including the down payment) will be

$$n = -\dfrac{\ln\left[1 - \dfrac{0.01125 \times \$1395}{\$50(1.01125)}\right]}{\ln(1.01125)} = 33.22$$

The final payment will be the 34th payment (smaller than $50) made 33 months or <u>2 years and 9 months</u> after the date of purchase.

Exercise 12.2 *(continued)*

34. The purchase price is the present value of the remaining payments discounted at the investor's required rate of return. Viewed from the date of purchase, the payments form a simple annuity due with

$$A_n \text{ (due)} = \$13{,}372, \ R = \$500, \ p = i = \frac{9.75\%}{12} = 8.125\%$$

The number of remaining payments is

$$n = -\frac{\ln\left[1 - \dfrac{0.08125\ (\$13{,}372)}{\$500\ (1.08125)}\right]}{\ln\ (1.08125)} = 30.00$$

The investor will receive <u>30 payments</u>.

35. The \$100,000 fund equals the present value of the withdrawals which form a simple annuity due having $p = i = \dfrac{9\%}{12} = 0.75\%$. With R = \$900,

$$n = -\frac{\ln\left[1 - \dfrac{0.0075\ (\$100{,}000)}{\$900\ (1.0075)}\right]}{\ln\ (1.0075)} = 234.91$$

The fund will provide 235 monthly payments (with the final payment smaller than \$900).
With R = \$1000,

$$n = -\frac{\ln\left(1 - \dfrac{0.0075\ (\$100{,}000)}{\$1000\ (1.0075)}\right)}{\ln\ (1.0075)} = 182.58$$

The fund will provide 183 monthly payments of \$1000 (except for the smaller final payment). Therefore, the \$900 payments can be sustained for (235 − 183) months = 52 months = <u>4 years and 4 months</u> longer.

36. The monthly deposits form a simple annuity due whose future value is to be \$100,000.
With $S_n \text{ (due)} = \$100{,}000, \ R = \$220, \ p = i = \dfrac{6\%}{12} = 0.5\%,$

$$n = \frac{\ln\left[1 + \dfrac{0.005\ (\$100{,}000)}{\$220\ (1.005)}\right]}{\ln\ (1.005)} = 237.02$$

The 238th deposit of \$220 will cause the accumulated amount to pass \$100,000.
If the monthly deposits are only \$200,

$$n = \frac{\ln\left[1 + \dfrac{0.005\ (\$100{,}000)}{\$200\ (1.005)}\right]}{\ln\ (1.005)} = 250.46$$

The 251st deposit of \$200 will cause the total amount to surpass \$100,000. The larger deposits take (251 − 238) months = <u>13 months</u> less to reach the savings target.

Exercise 12.2 *(continued)*

37. The RRSP contributions constitute a simple annuity due whose future value is to be $150,000. That is,
    S_n (due) = $150,000, R = $1000, $p = i = \dfrac{8\%}{2} = 4\%$

    The number of contributions required is

    $$n = \frac{\ln\left[1 + \dfrac{0.04\,(\$150,000)}{\$1000\,(1.04)}\right]}{\ln\,(1.04)} = 48.76$$

    Hence, 49 contributions will be required to accumulate $150,000. If, however, the funds earn $p = i = \dfrac{10\%}{2} = 5\%$ every 6 months,

    $$n = \frac{\ln\left[1 + \dfrac{0.05\,(\$150,000)}{\$1000\,(1.05)}\right]}{\ln\,(1.05)} = 42.98$$

    That is, 43 contributions will be required. At the lower rate of return, 49 – 43 = <u>6 more contributions</u> will be needed to reach $150,000.

38. The future value (7 years from now) of the $10,000 lump investment equals the present value (7 years from now) of the withdrawals. Viewed from the focal date (7 years from now), the withdrawals form a simple annuity due. The future value of the $10,000 is
    $S = P\,(1 + i)^n = \$10,000\,(1.00\overline{6})^{84} = \$17,474.22$

    With A_n (due) = $17,474.22, R = $500, $p = i = 0.\overline{6}\%$,

    $$n = -\frac{\ln\left[1 - \dfrac{0.00\overline{6}\,(\$17,474.22)}{\$500\,(1.00\overline{6})}\right]}{\ln\,(1.00\overline{6})} = 39.62$$

    There can be 40 withdrawals with the last one being less than $500. <u>The last payment will occur 39 months (3 years and 3 months) after the grandson starts college.</u>

39. The economic value at age 65 of each annuity is the present value of the payments discounted at the time value of money. For the 25-year-term annuity, R = $386, n = 12(25) = 300, and $p = i = \dfrac{8\%}{12} = 0.\overline{6}\%$

    $$A_n = \$300\left[\frac{1 - (1.00\overline{6})^{-300}}{0.00\overline{6}}\right] = \$50,011.91$$

    For payments of $485 per month to have the same economic value,

    $$n = -\frac{\ln\left[1 - \dfrac{0.00\overline{6}\,(\$50,011.91)}{\$485}\right]}{\ln\,(1.00\overline{6})} = 175.03$$

    Therefore, if the man receives more than 175 payments, the life annuity will have the larger economic value. <u>He must live more than 175 months (14 years and 7 months) beyond age 65. That is, he must live beyond age 79 years and 7 months.</u>

Exercise 12.2 *(continued)*

40. The economic value at age 60 of each annuity is the present value of the payments discounted at the time value of money.

For the 30-year term annuity, R = \$367, n = 12(30) = 360, $p = i = \dfrac{8\%}{12} = 0.\overline{6}\%$

$$A_n = \$367 \left[\frac{1 - 1.00\overline{6}^{-360}}{0.00\overline{6}} \right] = \$50{,}016.04$$

For payments of \$405 per month to have the same economic value,

$$n = -\frac{\ln\left[1 - \dfrac{0.00\overline{6}\,(50{,}016.04)}{\$405} \right]}{\ln\,(1.00\overline{6})} = 260.87$$

Therefore, if the woman receives more than 260 payments, the life annuity will have the larger economic value. She must live more than 260 months (21 years and 8 months) beyond age 60. That is, she must **live beyond age 81 years and 8 months.**

41. The future value (25 years from now) of the RRSP contributions will equal the present value of the annuity payments. The RRSP contributions form a simple annuity due with

R = \$500, n = 100, $p = i = \dfrac{8.5\%}{4} = 2.125\%$, and

$$S_n \text{ (due)} = \$500 \left(\frac{1.02125^{100} - 1}{0.02125} \right) (1.02125) = \$172{,}736.60$$

The annuity payments form a simple annuity due having

A_n (due) = \$172,736.60, R = \$1500, $p = i = \dfrac{7.5\%}{12} = 0.625\%$

The number of monthly payments will be

$$n = -\frac{\ln\left[1 - \dfrac{0.00625\,(\$172{,}736.60)}{\$1500\,(1.00625)} \right]}{\ln\,(1.00625)} = 201.62$$

The annuity's term will be 202 months or **16 years and 10 months.**

42. The loan "draws" constitute a general annuity due whose future value is \$1,000,000. That is,

S_n (due) = \$1,000,000, R = \$10,000, $i = \dfrac{12\%}{4} = 3\%$, $c = \dfrac{4}{12} = 0.\overline{3}$

$$p = (1 + i)^c - 1 = 1.03^{0.\overline{3}} - 1 = 0.009901634$$

The number of draws will be

$$n = \frac{\ln\left[1 + \dfrac{0.009901634\,(\$1{,}000{,}000)}{\$10{,}000\,(1.009901634)} \right]}{\ln\,(1.009901034)} = 69.35$$

The 70th draw, occurring 69 months or 5 years and 9 months after the first draw, will cause the credit limit to be reached.

Exercise 12.2 *(continued)*

43. a. The loan payments form an ordinary general annuity whose present value is $50,000. That is,
$A_n = \$50,000$, $R = \$500$, $i = \dfrac{10.25\%}{2} = 5.125\%$, $c = \dfrac{2}{12} = 0.1\overline{6}$

$p = (1 + i)^c - 1 = 1.05125^{0.1\overline{6}} - 1 = 0.008364780$

The number of monthly payments is

$$n = -\dfrac{\ln\left[1 - \dfrac{0.008364780\,(\$50,000)}{\$500}\right]}{\ln(1.008364780)} = 217.38$$

It will take 218 months or <u>18 years and 2 months</u> to repay the loan.

b. If the monthly payments are $550 instead of $500,

$$n = -\dfrac{\ln\left[1 - \dfrac{0.008364780\,(\$50,000)}{\$550}\right]}{\ln(1.008364780)} = 171.54$$

Only 172 payments will be required. The time to repay the loan will be reduced by
$(218 - 172)$ months = 46 months = <u>3 years and 10 months</u>.

44. a. The monthly borrowings of $350 form a general annuity due. The amount owed after 2.5 years is the future value of the borrowings. That is,
$R = \$350$, $n = 12(2.5) = 30$, $i = \dfrac{6\%}{2} = 3\%$, $c = \dfrac{2}{12} = 0.1\overline{6}$

$p = (1 + i)^c - 1 = 1.03^{0.1\overline{6}} - 1 = 0.004938622$

$$S_n\,(\text{due}) = \$350\left(\dfrac{1.004938622^{30} - 1}{0.004938622}\right)(1.004938622) = \$11,343.49$$

The amount owed was $11,343.49.

b. The amount owed is the present value of the payments which form an ordinary general annuity having
$A_n = \$11,343.49$, $R = \$175$, $p = 0.4938622\%$.
The number of monthly payments will be

$$n = -\dfrac{\ln\left[1 - \dfrac{0.004938622 \times \$11,343.49}{\$175}\right]}{\ln(1.004938622)} = 78.32$$

The time required to pay off the loan is 79 months or 6 years and 7 months. This will be
6 years + 7 months + 2 years + 6 months = <u>9 years and 1 month</u> after entering college.

Exercise 12.2 *(continued)*

45. With the focal date at the date of purchase of the annuity, the future value of the RRSP contributions equals the present value of the annuity payments.
The quarterly annuity payments form a simple annuity due having

$$R = \$12{,}865, \; n = 4(20) = 80, \; p = i = \frac{8\%}{4} = 2\%$$

$$A_n \text{ (due)} = \$12{,}865 \left(\frac{1 - 1.02^{-80}}{0.02}\right) 1.02 = \$521{,}539.43$$

The RRSP contributions form a simple annuity due with

$$S_n \text{ (due)} = \$521{,}539.43, \; R = \$3000, \; p = i = \frac{8\%}{2} = 4\%$$

The number of semiannual contributions was

$$n = \frac{\ln\left[1 + \dfrac{0.04 \times \$521{,}539.43}{\$3000\,(1.04)}\right]}{\ln(1.04)} = 52.00$$

Dr. Weisburg contributed to her RRSP for <u>26 years.</u>

46. The semiannual contributions form an ordinary general annuity having

$$R = \$2000, \; i = \frac{9.75\%}{12} = 0.8125\%, \text{ and } c = \frac{12}{2} = 6. \text{ Then}$$

$$p = (1 + i)^c - 1 = 1.008125^6 - 1 = 0.04975103$$

The combined future value of the initial \$56,000 and the annuity payments is to be \$250,000. The number of contributions required is the value of n in

$$\$56{,}000\,(1.04975103)^n + \$2000 \left(\frac{1.04975103^n - 1}{1.04975103}\right) = \$250{,}000$$

An algebraic solution requires the trial-and-error method (see Appendix 12B). The solution is n = 22.74. With contributions occurring at the end of each interval, it is not clear whether interest accruing during the 23rd interval will be sufficient to reach the \$250,000 target. Substituting n = 22 in the left side of the above equation gives an amount of \$239,746. Adding one period's (half-year's) interest at 4.975103% gives \$251,674 (to the nearest dollar). Therefore, <u>22 contributions (but almost 23 half years)</u> will be required to reach \$250,000.

Exercise 12.2 *(continued)*

47. The future value at age 62 of the severance settlement equals the present value of the annuity.
    For the future value calculation, P = $27,000, i = 8.5%, and n = 9.
    Then
    $$S = P (1 + i)^n = \$27,000 \ (1.085)^9 = \$56,264.10$$

    The monthly annuity payments constitute a general annuity due having

    $$A_n \text{ (due)} = \$56,264.10, \ R = \$491.31, \ i = 8.5\%, \ c = \frac{1}{12} = 0.08\overline{3}$$

    $$p = (1 + i)^c - 1 = 1.085^{0.08\overline{3}} - 1 = 0.006821493$$

    The number of monthly payments is

    $$n = -\frac{\ln\left[1 - \dfrac{0.006821493 \ (\$56,264.10)}{\$491.31 \ (1.006821493)}\right]}{\ln \ (1.006821493)} = 220.00$$

    The term of the annuity is 220 months or <u>18 years and 4 months.</u>

48. With the focal date at the date of purchase of the annuity, the future value of the RRSP contributions
    equals the present value of the annuity payments.
    The monthly annuity payments form a general annuity due having

    $$R = \$3509, \ n = 12(25) = 300, \ i = \frac{8\%}{2} = 4\%, \ c = \frac{2}{12} = 0.1\overline{6}$$

    $$p = (1 + i)^c - 1 = 1.04^{0.1\overline{6}} - 1 = 0.006558197$$

    The present value of the annuity is

    $$A_n \text{ (due)} = \$3509 \left(\frac{1 - 1.006558197^{-300}}{0.006558197}\right)(1.006558197) = \$462,781.77$$

    The RRSP contributions also form a general annuity due having

    $$S_n \text{ (due)} = \$462,781.77, \ R = \$2500, \ i = 8\%, \ c = \frac{1}{2} = 0.5$$

    $$p = (1 + i)^c - 1 = 1.08^{0.5} - 1 = 0.039230485$$

    The number of semiannual contributions was

    $$n = \frac{\ln\left[1 + \dfrac{0.039230485 \ (\$462,781.77)}{\$2500 \ (1.039230485)}\right]}{\ln \ (1.039230485)} = 54.00$$

    Therefore, Mr. van der Linden contributed to his RRSP for $\frac{54}{2}$ = 27 years.

Exercise 12.3

1. Given: $A_n = \$27{,}207.34$, $R = \$4000$, $n = 10$
   Then $p = 7.70\%$ per year
   $\underline{\underline{j = mp = 7.70\% \text{ compounded annually}}}$
   $\underline{\underline{f = 7.70\%}}$

2. Given: $A_n = \$100{,}000$, $R = \$6918.51$, $n = 2(12.5) = 25$
   Then $p = 4.7495\%$ per half year
   $j = mp = 2(4.7495\%) = \underline{\underline{9.50\% \text{ compounded semiannually}}}$
   $f = (1 + p)^m - 1 = 1.047495^2 - 1 = \underline{\underline{9.72\%}}$

3. Given: $A_n = \$50{,}000$, $R = \$2377.16$, $n = 4(7.75) = 31$
   Then $p = 2.625\%$ per quarter
   $j = mp = 4(2.625\%) = \underline{\underline{10.50\% \text{ compounded quarterly}}}$
   $f = (1 + p)^m - 1 = 1.02625^4 - 1 = \underline{\underline{10.92\%}}$

4. Given: $A_n = \$35{,}820$, $R = \$500{,}00$, $n = 12(8.75) = 105$
   Then $p = 0.77583\%$ per month
   $j = mp = 12(0.7758\%) = \underline{\underline{9.31\% \text{ compounded monthly}}}$
   $f = (1 + p)^m - 1 = 1.007758^{12} - 1 = \underline{\underline{9.72\%}}$

5. Given: $S_n = \$500{,}000$, $R = \$3030.02$, $n = 2(25) = 50$
   Then $p = 4.250\%$ per half year
   $j = mp = 2(4.250\%) = \underline{\underline{8.50\% \text{ compounded semiannually}}}$
   $f = (1 + p)^m - 1 = 1.0425^2 - 1 = \underline{\underline{8.68\%}}$

6. $S_n = \$291{,}955$, $R = \$2500$, $n = 4(13.25) = 53$
   Then $p = 2.750\%$ per quarter
   $j = mp = 4(2.750\%) = \underline{\underline{11.00\% \text{ compounded quarterly}}}$
   $f = (1 + p)^m - 1 = 1.0275^4 - 1 = \underline{\underline{11.46\%}}$

7. $S_n = \$100{,}000$, $R = \$251.33$, $n = 12(15) + 5 = 185$
   Then $p = 0.75\%$ per month
   $j = mp = 12(0.75\%) = \underline{\underline{9.00\% \text{ compounded monthly}}}$
   $f = (1 + p)^m - 1 = 1.0075^{12} - 1 = \underline{\underline{9.38\%}}$

8. $S_n = \$138{,}809$, $R = \$775$, $n = 12(9.25) = 111$
   Then $p = 0.8125\%$ per month
   $j = mp = 12(0.8125\%) = \underline{\underline{9.75\% \text{ compounded monthly}}}$
   $f = (1 + p)^m - 1 = 1.008125^{12} - 1 = \underline{\underline{10.20\%}}$

9. $S_n \text{ (due)} = \$75{,}000$, $R = \$1557.78$, $n = 2(11.5) = 23$
   Then $p = 5.75\%$ per half year
   $j = mp = 2(5.75\%) = \underline{\underline{11.50\% \text{ compounded semiannually}}}$
   $f = (1 + p)^m - 1 = 1.0575^2 - 1 = \underline{\underline{11.83\%}}$

10. $A_n \text{ (due)} = \$18{,}143$, $R = \$2000$, $n = 18$
    Then $p = 9.90\%$ per year
    $\underline{\underline{j = mp = 1(9.90\%) = 9.90\% \text{ compounded annually}}}$
    $\underline{\underline{f = 9.90\%}}$

Exercise 12.3 (continued)

11. S_n (due) = \$37,670, R = \$500.00, n = 4(9.5) = 38

Then p = 3.25% per quarter

$\quad$ j = mp = 4(3.25%) = <u>13.00% compounded quarterly</u>

$\quad$ f = $(1 + p)^m - 1$ = $1.0325^4 - 1$ = <u><u>13.65%</u></u>

12. A_n (due) = \$45,000, R = \$533.42, n = 12(13) + 8 = 164

Then p = 0.9375% per month

$\quad$ j = mp = 12(0.9375%) = <u>11.25% compounded monthly</u>

$\quad$ f = $(1 + p)^m - 1$ = $1.009375^{12} - 1$ = <u><u>11.85%</u></u>

13. S_n = \$75,000, R = \$318.07, n = 12(11) = 132

Then p = 0.81648% per month

$\quad$ j = mp = 12(0.81648%) = <u>9.80% compounded monthly</u>

$\quad$ f = $(1 + p)^m - 1$ = $1.0081648^{12} - 1$ = <u><u>10.25%</u></u>

14. A_n = \$48,215, R = \$5000, n = 20

Then p = 8.243% per year

$\quad$ j = mp = 1(8.243%) = <u>8.24% compounded annually</u>

$\quad$ f = <u><u>8.24%</u></u>

15. S_n (due) = \$75,000, R = \$357.29, n = 12(10) = 120

Then p = 0.85645%

$\quad$ j = mp = 12(0.85645%) = <u>10.28% compounded monthly</u>

$\quad$ f = $(1 + p)^m - 1$ = $1.0085645^{12} - 1$ = <u><u>10.78%</u></u>

16. A_n (due) = \$39,936, R = \$5000, n = 25

Then p = 13.648% per year

$\quad$ j = mp = 1(13.648%) = <u>13.65% compounded annually</u>

$\quad$ f = <u><u>13.65%</u></u>

17. The purchase price represents the present value of the annuity.

That is, A_n = \$100,000 with R = \$830 and n = 12(20) = 240.

Then p = 0.65803% per month

$\quad$ j = mp = 12(0.65803%) = <u>7.90% compounded monthly</u>

$\quad$ f = $(1 + p)^m - 1$ = $1.0065803^{12} - 1$ = <u><u>8.19%</u></u>

18. The future value of the payments is \$7727.62.

That is, S_n = \$7727.62 with R = \$200 and n = 12(3) = 36. Then

$\quad$ p = 0.400% per month

$\quad$ j = mp = 12(0.400%) = <u>4.80% compounded monthly</u>

$\quad$ f = $(1 + p)^m - 1$ = $1.004^{12} - 1$ = <u><u>4.91%</u></u>

19. The accumulated amount represents the future value of the contributions.

That is, S_n = \$65,727.82 with R = \$2000 and n = 2 (10.5) = 21. Then

$\quad$ p = 4.251% per half year

$\quad$ j = mp = 2(4.251%) = <u>8.50% compounded semiannually</u>

$\quad$ f = $(1 + p)^m - 1$ = $1.0425^{12} - 1$ = <u><u>8.68%</u></u>

Exercise 12.3 *(continued)*

20. The original loan is the present value of the loan payments.
    That is, A_n = $5000, R = $302.07, and n = 4(5.5) = 22. Then
    $$p = 2.625\% \text{ per quarter}$$
    $$j = mp = 4(2.625\%) = \underline{10.50\% \text{ compounded quarterly}}$$
    $$f = (1 + p)^m - 1 = 1.02625^4 - 1 = \underline{10.92\%}.$$

21. The original loan equals the present value of the loan payments.
    That is, A_n = $9000, R = $234.36, and n = 12(4)= 48. Then p = 0.9500% per month
    $$j = mp = 12(0.950\%) = \underline{11.40\% \text{ compounded monthly}}$$
    $$f = (1 + p)^m - 1 = 1.009500^{12} - 1 = \underline{12.01\%}$$

22. The purchase price of the conditional sale contract represents the present value of the payments.
    That is, A_n = $1050 with R = $100 and n = 12. Then
    $$p = 2.11661\% \text{ per month}$$
    $$f = (1 + p)^m - 1 = 1.0211661^{12} - 1 = \underline{28.58\%}$$

23. The payments form an annuity due whose present value equals the purchase price.
    That is, A_n (due) = $1500 with R = $400 and n = 4. Then
    $$p = 4.4800\% \text{ per quarter}$$
    $$f = (1 + p)^m - 1 = 1.04480^4 - 1 = \underline{19.16\%}$$

24. The contributions form an annuity due whose future value is $223,000.
    That is, S_n (due) = $223,000 with R = $2500 and n = 2(14) = 28. Then
    $$p = 7.1860\% \text{ per half year}$$
    $$f = (1 + p)^m - 1 = 1.07186^2 - 1 = \underline{14.89\%}$$

25. The six payments of $1000 form an annuity due whose present value is $5500.
    That is, A_n (due) = $5500 with R = $1000 and n = 6. Then f = p - $\underline{3.62\%}$.

26. The initial purchase price equals the present value of the annuity payments.
    That is, A_n = $150,000 with R = $1200 and n = 12(20) = 240. Then
    $$p = 0.61736\% \text{ per month}$$
    $$f = (1 + p)^m - 1 = 1.0061736^{12} - 1 = \underline{7.67\%}$$

27. The settlement represents the future value, at the end of the 2 years, of the lost wages.
    Since monthly wages are paid at each month's end, the payments form an ordinary annuity with
    A_n = $103,600, R = $4000, and n = 12(2) = 24. Then
    $$p = 0.65576\% \text{ per month}$$
    $$f = (1 + p)^m - 1 = 1.0065576^{12} - 1 = \underline{8.16\%}$$

28. The amount in the RRSP represents the future value of the contributions.
    Hence, S_n (due) = $434,960 with R = $1500 and n = 4(20) = 80. Then
    $$p = 2.75\% \text{ per quarter}$$
    $$j = mp = 4(2.75\%) = \underline{11.00\% \text{ compounded quarterly}}$$
    $$f = (1 + p)^m - 1 = 1.0275^4 - 1 = \underline{11.46\%}$$

Exercise 12.3 *(continued)*

29. The lease liability is the present value of the lease payments.
    That is, A_n (due) = \$13,824, R = \$450, and n = 12(3) = 36. Then
    $$p = 0.9375\% \text{ per month}$$
    $$j = mp = 12(0.9375\%) = \underline{11.25\% \text{ compounded monthly}}$$

30. The purchase price is the present value of the payments.
    That is, A_n (due) = \$1195, R = \$110, and n = 12. Then
    $$p = 1.863\% \text{ per month}$$
    $$f = (1 + p)^m - 1 = 1.01863^{12} - 1 = \underline{24.79\%}$$

31. The \$131,483 total represents the future value of the semiannual contributions.
    That is, S_n (due) = \$131,483 with R = \$2000 and n = 2(13) = 26. Then
    $$p = 6.30\% \text{ per half year}$$
    $$j = mp = 2(6.30\%) = \underline{12.60\% \text{ compounded semiannually}}$$
    $$f = (1 + p)^m - 1 = 1.0630^2 - 1 = \underline{13.00\%}$$

32. The four quarterly payments form an annuity due. The interest rate being charged by the golf club is the discount rate that makes the present value of the payments equal to the single membership payment of \$1714. That is, A_n (due) = \$1714 with R = \$449.40 and n = 4. Then
    $$p = 3.2703\% \text{ per quarter}$$
    $$f = (1 + p)^m - 1 = 1.032703^4 - 1 = \underline{13.74\%}$$

33. By paying 12(\$29.50) = \$354 now, the Stapletons avoid paying 1.1(\$29.50) = \$32.45 at the end of each of the next 12 months. Their "return on investment" is the discount rate that makes the present value of n = 12 payments of R = \$32.45 equal to A_n = \$354. This rate is
    $$p = 1.498\% \text{ per month or}$$
    $$f = (1 + p)^m - 1 = 1.01498^{12} - 1 = \underline{19.53\%}$$

34. The implied interest rate is the discount rate that makes the present value of the n = 6 payments of R = \$60 equal to A_n (due) = \$300. This rate is
    $$p = 7.931\% \text{ per 2–month interval or}$$
    $$f = (1 + p)^m - 1 = 1.07931^6 - 1 = \underline{58.08\%}$$

35. The interest rate being charged is the discount rate that makes the present value of n = 12 payments of R = \$13 equal to A_n = \$120. This rate is
    $$p = 4.287\% \text{ per month or}$$
    $$f = (1 + p)^{12} - 1 = 1.04287^{12} - 1 = \underline{65.48\%}$$

36. By paying \$39.95 now, the subscriber avoids paying \$15.95 at the beginning of each of the next 3 years. The "return on investment" is the discount rate that makes the present value of n = 3 payments of R = \$15.95 equal to A_n (due) = \$39.95. This rate is
    $$j = p = \underline{21.26\% \text{ compounded annually}}$$

37. The interest rate being charged is the discount rate that makes the present value of n = 12 payments of R = \$38.82 equal to A_n (due) = \$447.50. This rate is
    $$p = 0.7389\% \text{ per month or}$$
    $$f = (1 + p)^m - 1 = 1.007389^{12} - 1 = \underline{9.24\%}$$

Exercise 12.3 *(continued)*

38. Consider an arbitrary amount, say $100, of annual premium. The choice is between paying $100 today or paying $(0.25 \times \$100) + (0.03 \times \$100) = \$28.00$ at the beginning of each quarter. The implied interest rate being charged under the second alternative is the discount rate that makes the present value of $n = 4$ payments of $R = \$28.00$ equal to A_n (due) = $100. This rate is

   $p = 8.122\%$ per quarter or

   $f = (1 + p)^m - 1 = 1.08122^4 - 1 = \underline{36.67\%}$

39. In each case, the interest rate being charged is the discount rate that makes the present value of the premium payments for one year equal to A_n (due) = $666.96.
   a. For $R = \$341.32$ and $n = 2$, the rate is

   $p = 4.815\%$ per half year or

   $f = 1.04815^2 - 1 = \underline{9.86\%}$

   b. For $R = \$172.62$ and $n = 4$, the rate is

   $p = 2.361\%$ per quarter or

   $f = 1.02361^4 - 1 = \underline{9.78\%}$

   c. For $R = \$58.85$ and $n = 12$, the rate is

   $p = 1.057\%$ per month or

   $f = 1.01057^{12} - 1 = \underline{13.45\%}$

40. In each case, the interest rate being charged is the discount rate that makes the present value of the premium payments equal to A_n (due) = $470.
   a. For semiannual payments of $R = \$244.40$, $n = 2$ and the rate is

   $p = 8.333\%$ per half year or

   $f = 1.08333^2 - 1 = \underline{17.36\%}$

   b. For quarterly payments of $R = \$123.37$, $n = 4$ and the rate is

   $p = 3.350\%$ per quarter or

   $f = 1.03350^4 - 1 = \underline{14.09\%}$

   c. For monthly payments of $R = \$42.30$, $n = 12$ and the rate is

   $p = 1.431\%$ per month or

   $f = \underline{18.59\%}$

41. The buyer can choose between:
   (i) borrowing $17,000 at 2.9% compounded monthly;
   (ii) taking the cash rebate and borrowing $16,000 at market rates.
   The effective rate of interest under option (i) is the interest rate on a $16,000 loan that has the same monthly payments as the option (i) loan.

   Step 1: Determine the monthly payments under option (i).
   Step 2: Calculate p for an option (ii) loan whose monthly payments are the same as for the option (i) loan.
   Step 3: Convert p from step 2 to an effective rate, f.
   Step 1: $A_n = \$17,000$, $n = 12$, $p = i = \dfrac{2.9\%}{12} = 0.24\overline{16}\%$

   Substitution in formula (10–4) gives $R = \$1439.02$
   Step 2: $A_n = \$16,000$, $n = 12$, $R = \$1439.02$. Then $p = 1.1935\%$ per month
   Step 3: $f = (1 + p)^m - 1 = 1.011935^{12} - 1 = 15.30\%$
   The effective interest rate on the "2.9%" loan was $\underline{15.30\%}$.

Exercise 12.3 *(concluded)*

42. The customer can choose between:
    (i) borrowing $10,000 at 4.9% compounded monthly;
    (ii) taking the $1250 cash rebate and borrowing $8750 at market rates.
    The effective interest rate under option (i) is the interest rate on an $8750 loan that has the same monthly payment as the option (i) loan.

    Step 1: Determine the monthly payments under option (i).
    $$A_n = \$10,000, \; n = 48, \; p = i = \frac{4.9\%}{12} = 0.408\overline{3}\%$$

    Substitution in formula (10–4) gives R = $229.84.
    Step 2: Calculate p for an option (ii) loan where
    $A_n = \$8750, n = 48, R = \$229.84.$ The solution is p = 0.9887% per month
    Step 3: Convert p to an effective rate, f.
    $$f = (1 + p)^m - 1 = 1.009887^{12} - 1 = \underline{\underline{12.53\%}}$$
    The effective interest rate on the "4.9%" loan was $\underline{\underline{12.53\%}}$.

Exercise 12c

1. a.

x	y
2.5	−0.375
x_i	0
3.0	0.500

    Setting up the proportion for interpolating,
    $$\frac{x_i - 2.5}{3.0 - 2.5} = \frac{0 - (-0.375)}{0.500 - (-0.375)}$$
    $$\frac{x_i - 2.5}{0.5} = \frac{0.375}{0.875} = 0.4286$$

    $x_i = 0.5(0.4286) + 2.5 = \underline{2.714}$

    b.

x	y
2.0	−1.000
x_i	−0.55
2.5	−0.375

    The proportion for interpolating is
    $$\frac{x_i - 2.0}{2.5 - 2.0} = \frac{-0.55 - (-1.000)}{-0.375 - (-1.000)}$$
    $$\frac{x_i - 2.0}{0.5} = \frac{0.45}{0.625} = 0.720$$

    $x_i = 0.5(0.720) + 2.0 = \underline{2.360}$

    c.

x	y
3.0	0.500
3.15	y_i
3.5	1.625

    The proportion for interpolating is
    $$\frac{3.15 - 3.5}{3.0 - 3.5} = \frac{y_i - 1.625}{0.500 - 1.625}$$
    $$\frac{y_i - 1.625}{-1.125} = \frac{-0.35}{-0.5} = 0.70$$

    $y_i = -1.125(0.70) + 1.625 = \underline{0.8375}$

2.

Interest rate	Monthly payment
10.5%	$10.92
10.7%	m_i
11.5%	$11.51

    The monthly payment per $1000 is approximately the value of m_i in
    $$\frac{m_i - \$10.92}{\$11.51 - \$10.92} = \frac{10.7\% - 10.5\%}{11.5\% - 10.5\%}$$
    $$\frac{m_i - \$10.92}{\$0.59} = 0.2$$

    $m_i - 0.2(\$0.59) + \$10.92 = \$11.038$
    On a $64,500 loan, the monthly payment will be about 64.5 ($11.038) = $\underline{\underline{\$711.95}}$

Exercise 12c *(concluded)*

3.

Loan duration	Monthly rate
$\begin{cases} 5 \text{ yr} \\ 6.5 \\ 7 \end{cases}$	$\begin{cases} \$20.91 \\ m_i \\ \$16.25 \end{cases}$

The monthly payment per $1000 is approximately the value of m_i in

$$\frac{m_i - \$20.91}{\$16.25 - \$20.91} = \frac{6.5 - 5}{7 - 5}$$

$$\frac{m_i - \$20.91}{-\$4.66} = 0.75$$

$m_i = 0.75 \, (-\$4.66) + \$20.91 = \$17.415$

On a $77,400 loan, the monthly payment will be about 77.4 ($17.415) = <u>$1347.92</u>

4.

Loan duration	Monthly rate
$\begin{cases} 4 \text{ yr} \\ 4.25 \\ 5 \end{cases}$	$\begin{cases} \$25.96 \\ m_i \\ \$21.86 \end{cases}$

The monthly payment per $1000 is approximately the value of m_i in

$$\frac{m_i - \$25.96}{\$21.86 - \$25.96} = \frac{4.25 - 4}{5 - 4}$$

$$\frac{m_i - \$25.96}{-\$4.10} = 0.25$$

$m_i = 0.25 \, (-\$4.10) + \$25.96 = \$24.935$

On a $59,800 loan, the monthly payment will be about 59.8 ($24.935) = <u>$1491.11</u>

Review Problems

1. Given: $S_n = \$500,000$, $p = i = \dfrac{7.75\%}{2} = 3.875\%$

   a. For $n = 2(20) = 40$,
   $$\$500,000 = R \left(\frac{1.03875^{40} - 1}{0.03875} \right)$$
   $$R = \underline{\underline{\$5418.78}}$$
   Semiannual investments of $5418.78 are required.

   b. For $n = 2(30) = 60$,
   $$\$500,000 = R \left(\frac{1.03875^{60} - 1}{0.03875} \right)$$
   $$R = \underline{\underline{\$2204.89}}$$
   Semiannual investments of $2204.89 are required.

2. Given: $A_n = \$50,000$, $p = i = \dfrac{8.25\%}{12} = 0.6875\%$

   a. For $n = 12(15) = 180$,
   $$\$50,000 = R \left(\frac{1 - 1.006875^{-180}}{0.006875} \right)$$
   $$R = \underline{\underline{\$485.07}}$$

   b. For $n = 12(30) = 360$
   $$\$50,000 = R \left(\frac{1 - 1.006875^{-360}}{0.006875} \right)$$
   $$R = \underline{\underline{\$375.63}}$$

Review Problems (continued)

3. The $300,000 in the fund represents the present value of the withdrawals.

   a. A_n (due) = $300,000, n = 25, p = i = 7.75\%$

   $$\$300{,}000 = R\left(1 - \frac{1.0775^{-25}}{0.0775}\right)(1.0775)$$

   $$R = \$25{,}527.54$$

   b. $A_n = \$300{,}000$, n = 25, p = i = 7.75\%$

   $$\$300{,}000 = R\left(1 - \frac{1.0775^{-25}}{0.0775}\right)$$

   $$R = \$27{,}505.93$$

4. The quarterly deposits form a simple annuity due having
   S_n (due) = $100,000 and $p = i = \dfrac{6\%}{4} = 1.5\%$

   With R = $1000,

   $$n = \frac{\ln\left[1 + \dfrac{0.015\,(\$100{,}000)}{\$1000\,(1.015)}\right]}{\ln\,(1.015)} = 60.94$$

   It will take 61 deposits of $1000 to accumulate $100,000. Similarly, with R = $1100, we obtain n = 57.20. The 58th deposit will cause the savings to surpass $100,000. Hence, it will take
   61 − 58 = 3 more deposits of the smaller amount.

5. The selling price of the annuity represents the present value of the annuity payments.
   Hence, A_n = $100,000 where R = $802.76 and n = 12(20) = 240. The rate of return being earned is

   $p = 0.62114\%$ per month
   $j = mp = 12\,(0.62114\%) = 7.45\%$ compounded monthly
   $f = (1 + p)^m − 1 = 1.0062114^{12} − 1 = 7.71\%$

6. The purchase price of the annuity equals the present value of the payments. The payments form an
   ordinary simple annuity having A_n = $400,000, R = $4500, and $p = i = \dfrac{7.2\%}{12} = 0.6\%$.

   $$n = -\frac{\ln\left(1 - \dfrac{0.006 \times \$400{,}000}{\$4500}\right)}{\ln\,(1.006)} = 127.4$$

   The annuity will deliver 128 monthly payments requiring 10 years and 8 months.

7. The accumulated amount is the future value of the contributions which form an ordinary annuity. That is,

   S_n = $205,064, R = $2000, n = 4(13.75) = 55

   Then $p = 2.125\%$ per quarter
   $f = (1 + p)^m − 1 = 1.02125^4 − 1 = 8.775\%$

Review Problems *(continued)*

8. The original loan is the present value of all payments.
   That is, $A_n = \$12{,}000$ where $R = \$1204.55$ and $n = 2(7) = 14$.

   Then $p = 4.900\%$ per half year
   $$j = mp = 2(4.90\%) = \underline{9.80\% \text{ compounded semiannually}}$$
   $$f = (1 + p)^m - 1 = 1.049^2 - 1 = \underline{10.04\%}$$

9. The contributions form an annuity due having

   $$S_n \text{ (due)} = \$316{,}000, \ R = \$3500, \ n = 2(17) = 34$$
   Then $\qquad p = 5.0513\%$ per half year
   $$f = (1 + p)^m - 1 = 1.050513^2 - 1 = 10.36\%$$

10. The original loan equals the present value of all payments.
    With $A_n = \$100{,}000$, $p = i = \dfrac{9\%}{12} = 0.75\%$, and $R = \$1000$,

    $$n = -\frac{\ln\left[1 - \dfrac{0.0075\,(\$100{,}000)}{\$1000}\right]}{\ln(1.0075)} = 185.5$$

    Hence, 186 monthly payments are required to pay off the loan. If the payments are increased to $1050, we obtain $n = 167.7$. That is, only 168 payments will be required to pay off the loan. Therefore, it takes $186 - 168 = \underline{18 \text{ months longer}}$ to pay off the loan with the smaller payments.

11. The interest rate earned is the discount rate that makes the purchase price of the annuity equal to the present value of the annuity payments. With $A_n = \$100{,}000$, $R = \$739$ per month, and $n = 12(20) = 240$, we obtain

    $$p = 0.53234\% \text{ per month}$$
    $$j = mp = 12(0.53234\%) = \underline{6.39\% \text{ compounded monthly}}$$
    $$f = (1 + p)^m - 1 = 1.0053234^{12} - 1 = \underline{6.58\%}$$

12. The contributions form a simple annuity due.

    a. For S_n (due) $= \$500{,}000$ with $R = \$5000$ and $p = i = 8\%$,

    $$n = \frac{\ln\left[1 + \dfrac{0.08\,(\$500{,}000)}{\$5000\,(1.08)}\right]}{\ln(1.08)} = 27.66$$

    That is, $\underline{28 \text{ contributions}}$ are required.

    b. To accumulate $1,000,000, we obtain $n = 35.87$. That is, 36 contributions in total will be required. Therefore, only $36 - 28 = \underline{8 \text{ additional contributions}}$ are required to accumulate the second $500,000.

Review Problems *(continued)*

13. The purchase price equals the present value of the annuity payments discounted at the rate of return earned by the funds that remain invested. The payments form an ordinary general annuity having

$$A_n = \$175{,}000, \ R = \$4000, \ i = \frac{7\%}{2} = 3.5\%, \ c = \frac{2}{4} = 0.5$$

$$p = (1 + i)^c - 1 = 1.035^{0.5} - 1 = 0.0173495$$

$$n = -\frac{\ln\left[1 - \dfrac{0.0173495\,(\$175{,}000)}{\$4000}\right]}{\ln(1.0173495)} = 82.74$$

The payments will continue for 83 calendar quarters or <u>20 years and 9 months.</u>

14. The rate of return is the discount rate that makes the price paid equal to the present value of the monthly payments.

For $A_n = \$1934$, $R = \$175$, and $n = 12$,
$\quad p = 1.2902\%$ per month and
$\quad f = (1 + p)^m - 1 = 1.012902^{12} - 1 = \underline{16.63\%}$

15. The interest rate being charged is the discount rate that makes the present value of four quarterly payments equal to the annual dues payment.

With A_n (due) = \$1410, $R = \$368.28$, and $n = 4$, we obtain

$\quad p = 3.00\%$ per quarter
$\quad f = (1 + p)^m - 1 = 1.03^4 - 1 = \underline{12.55\%}$

16. The quarterly payments form a general annuity due having
$$S_n \text{ (due)} = \$800{,}000, \ n = 4(4) = 16, \ i = \frac{6.75\%}{12} = 0.5625\%, \ c = \frac{12}{4} = 3$$

$$p = (1 + i)^c - 1 = 1.005625^3 - 1 = 0.0169701$$

Solve for R in

$$\$800{,}000 = R\left(\frac{1.0169701^{16} - 1}{0.0169701}\right) 1.0169701$$

$$R = \underline{\$43{,}206.05}$$

The quarterly payments should be \$43,206.05.

17. The contributions form a simple annuity due having
    S_n (due) = $200,000 and R = $300

    If $p = i = \dfrac{8\%}{12} = 0.\overline{6}\%$,

    $$n = \frac{\ln\left[1 + \dfrac{0.00666667\,(\$200,000)}{\$300\,(1.0066667)}\right]}{\ln(1.00666667)} = 254.22$$

    That is, 255 contributions will be required.
    If $p = i = \dfrac{10\%}{12} = 0.8\overline{3}\%$, then n = 225.73

    That is, 226 contributions will be required.
    Therefore, at the lower rate of return, 255 − 226 = 29 more contributions will be required.

18. The lease liability equals the present value of the remaining lease payments. The lease payments form an annuity due having A_n (due) = $26,244, R = $750, and n = 12(3.5) = 42.

    Solving for p, we obtain
    p = 0.925% per month
    j = mp = 12 (0.925%) = 11.10% compounded monthly

19. The interest rate being charged is the discount rate that makes the present value of the payments equal to the purchase price. The payments form an annuity due with
    A_n (due) = $1395, n = 12, and R = $125. Then
    p = 1.348% per month
    $f = (1 + p)^m - 1 = 1.01348^{12} - 1 = 17.43\%$

20. By paying $59.95 now, the subscriber avoids paying $23.95 at the beginning of each of the next 3 years. The "return on investment" is the discount rate that makes the present value of
    n = 3 payments of R = $23.95 equal to A_n (due) = $59.95. This rate is
    j = p = 21.35% compounded annually.

21. The interest rate charged is the discount rate that makes the present value of 12 monthly payments equal to the annual premium. The monthly payments form an annuity due having
    A_n (due) = $716, n = 12, and R = $62.50. Solving for the discount rate gives

    p = 0.855% per month
    $f = (1 + p)^m - 1 = 1.00855^{12} - 1 = 10.76\%$.

22. The original loan equals the present value of the loan payments which form an ordinary general annuity.
    We have A_n = $90,000, n = 2(10) = 20, $i = \dfrac{9.75\%}{12} = 0.8125\%$, $c = \dfrac{12}{2} = 6$

    $p = (1 + i)^c - 1 = 1.008125^6 - 1 = 0.049751027$

    Solve for R in

    $$\$90,000 = R\left(\frac{1 - 1.049751027^{-20}}{0.049751027}\right)$$

    R = $7206.60

Review Problems (continued)

23. a. The contributions form a simple annuity due having
$$S_n \text{ (due)} = \$1,000,000, \; n = 31, \; p = i = 8\%$$
Then
$$\$1,000,000 = R \left(\frac{1.08^{31} - 1}{0.08} \right) (1.08)$$

$$R = \underline{\underline{\$7506.74}}$$

b. If instead, n = 26, we obtain R = $\underline{\underline{\$11,580.67}}$

24. a. The original loan equals the combined present value of 5 years' payments and the $75,000 balance. Using both formulas (8 – 2) and (10 – 4) with $n = 4(5) = 20$ and $p = i = \frac{9.5\%}{4} = 2.375\%$,

$$\$100,000 = R \left(\frac{1 - 1.02375^{-20}}{0.02375} \right) + \frac{\$75,000}{1.02375^{20}}$$

Solving for R gives R = $\underline{\underline{\$3366.05}}$.

b. After 10 years (n = 40 payments), the balance will be the value of S in

$$\$100,000 = \$3366.05 \left(\frac{1 - 1.02375^{-40}}{0.02375} \right) + \frac{S}{1.02375^{40}}$$

$$S = \underline{\underline{\$35,022.49}}$$

The balance after 10 years will be $35,022.49.

25. a. Use formula (8 – 2) to adjust P = $400,000 for n = 25 years of inflation at $i = 4\%$ per year.

$$S = P(1 + i)^n = \$400,000 \, (1.04)^{25} = \underline{\underline{\$1,066,335}}$$

Mr. Braun should have $1,066,335 in his RRSP 25 years from now to have the same purchasing power as $400,000 current dollars.

b. The contributions form an ordinary general annuity having
$$S_n = \$1,066,335, \; n = 4(25) = 100, \; i = \frac{7.5\%}{2} = 3.75\%, \text{ and } c = \frac{2}{4} = 0.5. \text{ Then}$$
$$p = (1 + i)^c - 1 = 1.0375^{0.5} - 1 = 0.01857744$$

$$\$1,066,335 = R \left(\frac{1.01857744^{100} - 1}{0.01857744} \right)$$

$$R = \underline{\underline{\$3737.03}}$$

Mr. Braun should make quarterly contributions of $3737.03.

Review Problems *(continued)*

26. a. Original loan = Present value of all payments

$A_n = \$65{,}000$, $R = \$600$, $i = \dfrac{9.5\%}{2} = 4.75\%$, $c = \dfrac{2}{12} = 0.1\overline{6}$

$$p = (1 + i)^c - 1 = 1.0475^{0.1\overline{6}} - 1 = 0.007764383$$

$$n = -\frac{\ln\left(1 - \dfrac{0.007764383\,(\$65{,}000)}{\$600}\right)}{\ln\,(1.007764383)} = 237.86$$

The loan will be paid off after 238 months or <u>19 years and 10 months</u>.

   b. If $R = \$650$ instead of \$600, $n = 193.69$. That is, the loan will be paid off after 194 months or 16 years and 2 months. The time to repay the loan will be reduced by
   (19 years + 10 months) − (16 years + 2 months) = <u>3 years, 8 months</u>

27. The economic value of each annuity is the present value of the payments discounted at the time value of money. For the 20-year-term annuity,

$R = \$394$, $n = 12(20) = 240$, $p = i = \dfrac{7.2\%}{12} = 0.6\%$

$$A_n = \$394\left(\frac{1 - 1.006^{-240}}{0.006}\right) = \$50{,}041.32$$

Next calculate n in order for the life annuity ($R = \$440$) to have the same present value.

$$n = -\frac{\ln\left[1 - \dfrac{0.006\,(\$50{,}041.32)}{\$440}\right]}{\ln\,(1.006)} = 191.72$$

The man must live at least 192 months (16 years) beyond age 70. That is, he must live to at least age <u>86 years</u>.

28. a. The loan advances form a general annuity due having
   $R = \$250$, $n = 12(3.5) = 42$, $i = \dfrac{5\%}{2} = 2.5\%$, $c = \dfrac{2}{12} = 0.1\overline{6}$
   The amount owed after $3\frac{1}{2}$ years is the future value of the advances.

$$p = (1 + i)^c - 1 = 1.025^{0.1\overline{6}} - 1 = 0.004123915$$

$$S_n\text{ (due)} = \$250\left(\frac{1.004123915^{42} - 1}{0.004123915}\right)(1.004123915)$$

$$= \$11{,}485.68$$

Review Problems *(continued)*

b. The loan payments form an ordinary general annuity having
$A_n = \$11,485.68$, $R = \$200$, and $p = 0.004123915$

$$n = -\frac{\ln\left[1 - \dfrac{0.004123915\,(\$11,485.68)}{\$200}\right]}{\ln\,(1.004123915)} = 65.67$$

It requires 66 monthly payments taking <u>5 years and 6 months</u> to pay off the loan.

29. By "investing" 4 ($10.75) = $43 now, Mrs. Ciminelli avoids spending $12.50 at the end of each of the next 4 quarters. The "rate of return on investment" is the discount rate that makes $43 the present value of $n = 4$ payments of $R = \$12.50$. The rate obtained is

$p = 6.318\%$ per quarter or
$f = (1 + p)^m - 1 = 1.06318^4 - 1 = \underline{27.77\%}$

30. With $R = \$5000$, $n = 25$, and $p = i = 10\%$,

$$S_n\,(\text{due}) = \$5000\left(\frac{1.10^{25} - 1}{0.10}\right)(1.10) = \$540,908.83$$

To have the same future value with $p = i = 8\%$,

$$\$540,908.83 = R\left(\frac{1.08^{25} - 1}{0.08}\right)(1.08)$$

$$R = \$6850.90$$

The annual contributions must, therefore, be increased by

$$\frac{\$6850.90 - \$5000}{\$5000} \times 100\% = \underline{37.0\%}$$

to offset the 2% per annum lower rate of return.

31. With the focal date at 25 years from now,
(Future value of RRSP contributions) = (Present value of annuity payments)
Both cash flow streams are simple annuities due.
For the RRSP contributions, $R = \$2000$, $n = 50$, $p = i = \dfrac{8\%}{2} = 4\%$.

$$S_n\,(\text{due}) = \$2000\left(\frac{1.04^{50} - 1}{0.04}\right)(1.04) = \$317,547.53$$

For the income annuity, $A_n\,(\text{due}) = \$317,547.53$, $R = \$2500$, and $p = i = \dfrac{7.5\%}{12} = 0.625\%$

$$n = -\frac{\ln\left(1 - \dfrac{0.00625\,(\$317,547.53)}{\$2500\,(1.00625)}\right)}{\ln\,(1.00625)} = 249.67$$

The annuity will deliver 250 payments with the last payment occurring 249 months = <u>20 years and 9 months</u> after the start of the annuity.

Review Problems (continued)

32. The present value of the lease payments discounted at the required rate of return must equal the capital cost of the leased equipment.

    a. The lease payments form a general annuity due having

$$A_n \text{ (due)} = \$35{,}000, \ n = 12(5) = 60, \ i = \frac{16\%}{2} = 8\%, \ c = \frac{2}{12} = 0.1\overline{6}$$

$$p = (1 + i)^c - 1 = 1.08^{0.1\overline{6}} - 1 = 0.012909457$$

$$\$35{,}000 = R \left(\frac{1 - 1.012909457^{-60}}{0.012909457} \right)(1.012909457)$$

$$R = \underline{\$830.97}$$

    b. The lease payments now form a simple annuity due having

$$A_n \text{ (due)} = \$35{,}000, \ n = 2(5) = 10, \ p = i = \frac{16\%}{2} = 8\%$$

$$\$35{,}000 = R \left(\frac{1 - 1.08^{-10}}{0.08} \right)(1.08)$$

$$R = \underline{\$4829.66}$$

33. With the focal date at 10 years from now,
       (Combined future value of \$125,000 and contributions) = (Present value of \$500,000)

We can calculate the right side of this equation using formula (8 –2) with S = \$500,000, $i = 8\%$, and n = 5.

$$P = \frac{S}{(1 + i)^n} = \frac{\$500{,}000}{1.08^5} = \$340{,}291.60$$

The RRSP contributions form an ordinary general annuity having

$$n = 2(10) = 20, \ i = 8\%, \ c = \frac{1}{2} = 0.5$$

$$p = (1 + i)^c - 1 = 1.08^{0.5} - 1 = 0.039230485$$

Returning to the initial equation,

$$\$125{,}000 \ (1.08)^{10} + R \left(\frac{1.039230485^{20} - 1}{0.039230485} \right) = \$340{,}291.60$$

Solving for R, we obtain R = $\underline{\$2383.97}$

Noreen should make semiannual contributions of \$2383.97 for the next 10 years.

Review Problems *(concluded)*

34. With the focal date at 30 years from now,

  (Future value of RRSP contributions) = (Present value of income annuity payments)

  We can calculate the right side where the payments form an ordinary simple annuity having

  $R = \$7000$, $n = 12(25) = 300$, $p = i = \dfrac{7.5\%}{12} = 0.625\%$

  $A_n = \$7000 \left(\dfrac{1 - 1.00625^{-300}}{0.00625} \right) = \$947{,}237.29$

  An expression for the left side of the equation can be developed in two steps.

  Step 1: Calculate the amount in the RRSP 10 years from now.

  $R = \$5000$, $n = 10$, $p = i = 8\%$

  $S_n = \$5000 \left(\dfrac{1.08^{10} - 1}{0.08} \right) = \$72{,}432.81$

  Step 2: Write an expression for the combined future value, 30 years from now, of the step 1 amount and twenty annual contributions of R. The left side of the initial equation becomes

  $\$72{,}432.81 \, (1.08)^{20} + R \left(\dfrac{1.08^{20} - 1}{0.08} \right)$

  Next form the equation and solve for R giving R = $13,321.79

  Yvette must make year–end contributions of $13,321.79 for the 20 years in question.

35. The nominal amount desired at age 60 is

  $S = P \, (1 + i)^n = \$250{,}000 \, (1.04)^{29} = \$779{,}662.86$

  This amount represents the future value of the RRSP contributions. That is,

  $S_n = \$779{,}662.86$ where $n = 29$ and $p = i = 8\%$. Then

  $\$779{,}662.86 = R \left(\dfrac{1.08^{29} - 1}{0.08} \right)$

  $R = \$7499.21$

  Justin should make annual contributions of $7499.21.

Self–Test Exercise

1. a. The loan payments form an ordinary simple annuity with

   $A_n = \$30{,}000$, $n = 12(8) = 96$, $p = i = \dfrac{11.25\%}{12} = 0.9375\%$

   $\$30{,}000 = R \left(\dfrac{1 - 1.009375^{-96}}{0.009375} \right)$

   $R = \$475.31$

Self–Test Exercise *(continued)*

b. Now $30,000 is the combined present value of n = 60 payments and the $10,000 balance. That is,

$$\$30{,}000 = R\left(\frac{1 - 1.009375^{-60}}{0.009375}\right) + \frac{\$10{,}000}{1.009375^{60}}$$

Solving for R gives R = $531.10.

2. With A_n = $65,000, R = $625, and $p = i = \dfrac{10.5\%}{12} = 0.875\%$,

$$n = -\;\frac{\ln\left[1 - \dfrac{0.00875\,(\$65{,}000)}{\$625}\right]}{\ln(1.00875)} = 276.40$$

Thus, 277 payments are required to satisfy the loan. With R reduced to $600, we obtain n = 339.18. That is, 340 payments are required. The larger payments will pay off the loan
   (340 − 277) months = 63 months = 5 years and 3 months sooner.
The interest savings are approximately
   339.18 ($600) − 276.40 ($625) = $30,758.

3. The present value of the lease payments discounted at the required rate of return must equal the capital cost of the equipment. The proposed lease payments form a general annuity due having
   A_n (due) = $7650, n = 12(4) = 48, $i = \dfrac{15\%}{4} = 3.75\%$, $c = \dfrac{4}{12} = 0.\overline{3}$

$$p = (1 + i)^c - 1 = 1.0375^{0.\overline{3}} - 1 = 0.012346926$$

$$\$7650 = R\left(\frac{1 - 1.012346926^{-48}}{0.012346926}\right)1.012346926$$

   R = $209.61

The beginning-of-month lease payments should be $209.61.

4. Given: R = $2000, n = 2(20) = 40, S_n = $250,000
   Then   p = 5.140% per half year and
          $f = (1 + p)^m - 1 = 1.0514^2 - 1 = 10.54\%$

5. The payments form an ordinary general annuity having
   S_n = $15,000, n = 4(8.5) = 34, $i = 7.5\%$, and $c = \dfrac{1}{4} = 0.25$

$$p = (1 + i)^c - 1 = 1.075^{0.25} - 1 = 0.01824460$$

$$\$15{,}000 = R\left(\frac{1.01824460^{34} - 1}{0.01824460}\right)$$

   R = $322.49

Quarterly payments of $322.49 are required.

Self–Test Exercise (continued)

6. The sale price represents the present value of the remaining payments discounted at the yield required by the buyer. Viewed from the date of sale, the payments form an ordinary general annuity with

$A_n = \$7147.52$, $R = \$500$, $i = \dfrac{15\%}{12} = 1.25\%$, $c = \dfrac{12}{4} = 3$

$p = (1 + i)^c - 1 = 1.0125^3 - 1 = 0.037970703$

Then

$$n = -\dfrac{\ln\left[1 - \dfrac{0.037970703\,(\$7147.52)}{\$500}\right]}{\ln(1.037970703)} = 21.00$$

Since 21 quarterly payments remain, the note has 21 (0.25 year) = 5.25 years = 5 years and 3 months remaining in its term.

7. a. The original loan equals the present value of all the payments. The payments form an ordinary general annuity having

$A_n = \$90,000$, $n = 12(20) = 240$, $i = \dfrac{7.9\%}{2} = 3.95\%$, $c = \dfrac{2}{12} = 0.1\overline{6}$

$p = (1 + i)^c - 1 = 1.0395^{0.1\overline{6}} - 1 = 0.006477527$

$\$90,000 = R\left(\dfrac{1 - 1.006477527^{-240}}{0.006477527}\right)$

$R = \$740.13$

b. If $R = \$800$ instead of $\underline{\$740.13}$,

$$n = -\dfrac{\ln\left[1 - \dfrac{0.006477527\,(\$90,000)}{\$800}\right]}{\ln(1.006477527)} = 202.06$$

It will take 203 months or 16 years and 11 months to pay off the loan.

8. With the focal date at her 62nd birthday,
   (Future value of RRSP contributions) = (Present value of the annuity payments)
   Viewed from the focal date, both payment streams form simple annuities due.
   For the present value calculation,

$R = \$3500$, $n = 12(20) = 240$, $p = i = \dfrac{7.5\%}{12} = 0.625\%$

$A_n \text{ (due)} = \$3500 \left(\dfrac{1 - 1.00625^{-240}}{0.00625}\right)(1.00625) = \$437,177.85$

For the RRSP contributions, $S_n \text{ (due)} = \$437,177.85$
$n = 4(27) = 108$, and $p = i = \dfrac{8\%}{4} = 2\%$. Then

$\$437,177.85 = R\left(\dfrac{1.02^{108} - 1}{0.02}\right)(1.02)$

$R = \$1144.74$

Each quarterly contribution should be $1144.74.

Self–Test Exercise *(continued)*

9. With the focal date set at the date Jeff entered college,
   (Future value of RESP contributions) = (Present value of withdrawals)
   Both payment streams form simple annuities due. For the RESP contributions,
   $R = \$50$, $n = 12(14) + 5 = 173$, and $p = i = \dfrac{8.25\%}{12} = 0.6875\%$. Then

   $$S_n \text{ (due)} = \$50 \left(\frac{1.006875^{175} - 1}{0.006875} \right)(1.006875) = \$16{,}634.93$$

   For the monthly withdrawals, A_n (due) = \$16,634.93, $R = \$500$, and $p = i = 0.6875\%$. Then

   $$n = -\frac{\ln\left[1 - \dfrac{0.006875\,(\$16{,}634.93)}{\$500\,(1.006875)}\right]}{\ln(1.006875)} = 37.61$$

   The payments will run for 38 months or <u>3 years and 2 months</u>.

10. With the focal date at the date of the last \$500 contribution,
    (Future value of the contributions) = (Present value of \$13,232.56)
    For evaluating the right side, $S = \$13{,}232.56$, $i = \dfrac{7.5\%}{4} = 1.875\%$, $n = 4(3) = 12$

    Then $P = S(1 + i)^{-n} = \$13{,}232.56\,(1.01875)^{12} = \$10{,}588.45$

    For the quarterly contributions, $S_n = \$10{,}588.45$, $R = \$500$, and $p = i = 1.875\%$

    Then

    $$n = \frac{\ln\left[1 + \dfrac{0.01875\,(\$10{,}588.45)}{\$500}\right]}{\ln(1.01875)} = \underline{\underline{18.0}}$$

    Eighteen contributions of \$500 were made.

11. The implied interest rate is the discount rate that makes the present value of four 3-month memberships equal to the price of a 1-year membership. With A_n (due) = \$250, $n = 4$, and $R = \$80$, we can obtain

    $p = 19.443\%$ per quarter and
    $f = (1 + p)^m - 1 = 1.19443^4 - 1 = \underline{103.54\%}$

12. To build in an interest rate of 16% compounded semiannually, the present value of 12 monthly premium payments discounted at this rate equals the annual premium. The monthly payments form a general annuity due having
    A_n (due) = \$100, $n = 12$, $i = \dfrac{16\%}{2} = 8\%$, and $c = \dfrac{2}{12} = 0.1\overline{6}$

    $$p = (1 + i)^c - 1 = 1.08^{0.1\overline{6}} - 1 = 0.012909457$$

    $$\$100 = R\left(\frac{1 - 1.012909457^{-12}}{0.012909457} \right)(1.012909457)$$

    $$R = \underline{\$8.93}$$

    The monthly premium per \$100 of annual premium should be \$8.93.

Self–Test Exercise (continued)

13. The effective interest rate on the $20,000 loan is the interest rate on an $18,000 loan that has the same monthly payment as has the $20,000 loan.

Step 1: Determine the monthly payment on the $20,000 loan.
$$A_n = \$20{,}000, \; n = 48, \; p = i = \frac{5.9\%}{12} = 0.491\overline{6}\%$$

$$\$20{,}000 = R \left(\frac{1 - 1.00491\overline{6}^{-48}}{0.00491\overline{6}} \right)$$

$$R = \$468.78$$

Step 2: Calculate p for an $18,000 loan having R = $468.78 and n = 48. The solution is p = 0.9505345%
Step 3: Convert p to the corresponding effective rate, f.
$$f = (1 + p)^m - 1 = 1.0095050535^{12} - 1 = \underline{12.02\%}$$

The effective rate of interest on the "5.9%" loan was 12.02%.

13 Other Annuities

Changes in the Second Edition:

1. The major changes have already been covered in the lengthy preamble to the Chapter 10 solutions.
2. There is no consensus on whether deferred annuities should be developed as a separate topic with their own set of formulas, or whether they should be handled in a two-step procedure using mathematical tools already learned for determining equivalent values of annuities and lump amounts. Instructors who hold the latter view can skip the exposition in Section 13.2, and merely use Exercise 13.2 as a source of problems to illustrate and apply this approach.

Exercise 13.1

1. With the focal date set at the date the bequest was received, the scholarship payments form a simple perpetuity due having

    A (due) = $125,000 and p = i = 7.5%

    Rearrange formula (13–2) to isolate R giving

    $$R = \frac{pA\,(due)}{1 + p} = \frac{0.075 \times \$125,000}{1.075} = \$8720.93$$

    An $8720.93 scholarship can be awarded every August.

2. The required amount is the present value of the payments which form a simple perpetuity due having

    $$R = \$2000 \text{ and } p = i = \frac{8\%}{4} = 2\%$$

    $$A\,(due) = \frac{R}{p}\,(1 + p) = \frac{\$2000}{0.02}\,(1.02) = \underline{\$102,000}$$

    $102,000 is required to fund the perpetuity.

3. The amount required to fund a perpetuity is the present value of the payments. The difference between A (due) and A is just the amount of the first payment of the perpetuity due. More formally,

    $$A\,(due) - A = A\,(1 + p) - A = A + Ap - A = Ap = R$$

    The answer to both part a and part b is R = $\underline{\$10,000}$

4. The initial amount required is the present value of the payments.
   The payments form an ordinary simple perpetuity having

    $$R = \$500 \text{ and } p = i = \frac{7.5\%}{12} = 0.625\%$$

    $$A = \frac{R}{p} = \frac{\$500}{0.00625} = \underline{\$80,000}$$

5. The fair market value of the shares is the present value of the dividend payments discounted at the rate of return required by the financial market. Since the first dividend will be received in 6 months, the dividend stream forms an ordinary simple perpetuity.

    a. Share price = $A = \frac{R}{p} = \frac{\$2}{0.045} = \underline{\$44.44}$

    b. Share price = $A = \frac{R}{p} = \frac{\$2}{0.05} = \underline{\$40.00}$

6. a. The price equals the present value of the dividends discounted at the required rate of return. Since the next dividend is about to be paid, the dividends form a simple perpetuity due with R = $3.00 and p = i = 4.5%.

    $$\text{Price} = A\,(due) = \frac{R}{p}\,(1 + p) = \frac{\$3.00}{0.045}\,(1.045) = \underline{\$69.67}$$

Exercise 13.1 *(continued)*

b. Rearranging formula (13–2) to isolate p,

$$pA \text{ (due)} = R + Rp$$

$$p [A \text{ (due)} - R] = R$$

$$p = \frac{R}{A \text{ (due)} - R} = \frac{\$3.00}{\$78 - \$3} = 0.04 = 4.0\% \text{ per half-year}$$

$$j = mp = 2 \text{ (4.0\%)} = \underline{8.0\% \text{ compounded semiannually}}.$$

7. The required endowment equals the present value of the annual payments which form an ordinary simple perpetuity.

$$A = \frac{R}{p} = \frac{\$5000}{0.07} = \$71,428.57$$

The amount required from the Real Estate Foundation is

$$0.5 \text{ (\$71,428.57)} = \underline{\$35,714.29}$$

8. The scholarship payouts form an ordinary simple perpetuity having R = 10($2000) = $20,000.

a. Required amount $= A = \dfrac{R}{p} = \dfrac{\$20,000}{0.0725} = \underline{\$275,862.07}$

b. If p = 7.6%,

Required amount $= \dfrac{\$20,000}{0.076} = \$263,157.89$

Therefore,

$$\$275,862.07 - \$263,157.89 = \underline{\$12,704.18}$$

less money is needed.

c. If A = $200,000 and p = *i* = 7.6%, then

$$R = Ap = \$200,000 \text{ (0.076)} = \underline{\$15,200.}$$

Only $15,200 of scholarships can be awarded annually.

9. The owner should be willing to accept the economic value of the stream of future payments. This economic value equals the present value of the future payments. Viewed from a focal date at the time of the next scheduled payment, the payments form a simple perpetuity due.

$$A \text{ (due)} = \frac{R}{p} \text{ (1 + p)} = \frac{\$500}{0.09} \text{ (1.09)} = \underline{\$6055.56}$$

The landowner should be willing to accept $6055.56.

---

10. The amount required to fund each payment stream equals the present value of the payment stream. For the perpetuity due, R = $1000 and $p = i = \frac{7\%}{4} = 1.75\%$. Then

$$A \text{ (due)} = \frac{\$1000}{0.0175}(1.0175) = \$58,142.86$$

For the annuity due, R = $1000, n = 4(30) = 120, and p = 1.75%.
$$A_n \text{ (due)} = \$1000\left(\frac{1 - 1.0175^{-120}}{0.0175}\right)(1.0175) = \$50,892.39$$

Therefore, only $58,142.86 − $50,892.39 = $7250.47 more is needed to fund the perpetuity due.

11. The required amount equals the present value of the payments which form a general perpetuity due having
$$R = \$2000,\ i = \frac{8\%}{4} = 2\% \text{ and } c = \frac{4}{1} = 4$$

$$p = (1 + i)^c - 1 = 1.02^4 - 1 = 0.082432160$$

$$A \text{ (due)} = \frac{\$2000}{0.08243216}(1.08243216) = \underline{\$26,262.38}$$

12. The additional annual scholarships form an ordinary general perpetuity having
$$A = \$37,500,\ i = \frac{9\%}{2} = 4.5\%, \text{ and } c = 2$$

$$p = (1 + i)^c - 1 = 1.045^2 - 1 = 0.09202500$$

$$R = pA = 0.092025\,(\$37,500) = \underline{\$3450.94}$$

The $37,500 will support an additional $3450.94 of annual awards in perpetuity.

13. Just before a payment, the balance will be A (due). Just after a payment, the balance will be A (due) - R. The payments form a general perpetuity having
$$R = \$500,\ i = 8\%, \text{ and } c = \frac{1}{12} = 0.08\overline{3}$$

$$p = (1 + i)^c - 1 = 1.08^{0.08\overline{3}} - 1 = 0.006434030$$

$$A \text{ (due)} = \frac{\$500}{0.00643403}(1.00643403) = \$78,211.79$$

The balance fluctuates between $77,711.79 and $78,211.79.

14. A fair settlement is the current economic value of the future payments. This economic value equals the present value of the future payments discounted at the time value of money. With the valuation date at the next payment date, the payments form a general perpetuity due having

$$R = \$400,\ i = 9\%, \text{ and } c = \frac{1}{2} = 0.5$$

$$p = (1 + i)^c - 1 = 1.09^{0.5} - 1 = 0.04403065$$

$$A \text{ (due)} = \frac{\$400}{0.04403065}(1.04403065) = \underline{\$9484.58}$$

A fair lump settlement on the next payment date is $9484.58.

Exercise 13.1 *(continued)*

15. Price = $500 + Present value of quarterly payments
    The quarterly payments form a general perpetuity due having

    $R = \$15$, $i = 6.5\%$, and $c = \dfrac{1}{4} = 0.25$

    $p = (1 + i)^c - 1 = 1.065^{0.25} - 1 = 0.0158683$

    $A \text{ (due)} = \dfrac{\$15}{0.0158683} \, (1.0158683) = \$960.28$

    Price = $500 + $960.28 = $1460.28

16. With the focal date at the date of the first scholarship,
    (Future value of donated funds) = (Present value of annual scholarships)
    The scholarships form a simple perpetuity due having

    $R = \$2000$, $p = i = 7.8\%$, and

    $A \text{ (due)} = \dfrac{\$2000}{0.078} \, (1.078) = \$27{,}641.03$

    The $20,856 total of donations must be invested long enough to grow to $27,641.03. Formula (9–2) can be used to calculate the number of compounding intervals required.

    $$n = \dfrac{\ln\left(\dfrac{S}{P}\right)}{\ln(1 + i)} = \dfrac{\ln\left(\dfrac{\$27{,}641.03}{\$20{,}856}\right)}{\ln(1.078)} = 3.750$$

    Since each compounding period is 1 year, the funds must be invested for 3 years and 9 months before the first scholarship can be awarded.

17. With the focal date 3 years from now,
    (Future value of $1 million donation) = (Present value of perpetuity)
    The left side is

    $S = P(1 + i)^n = \$1{,}000{,}000(1.02)^{12} = \$1{,}268{,}241.80$

    The payments form a simple perpetuity due having

    $A \text{ (due)} = \$1{,}268{,}241.80$ and $p = i = 2\%$

    $\$1{,}268{,}241.80 = \dfrac{R}{0.02} \, (1.02)$

    $R = \$24{,}867.49$

    Quarterly payments of $24,867.49 will be made.

Exercise 13.1 *(continued)*

18. a. The payments form a simple perpetuity due having R = $5000 and $p = i = \dfrac{8.5\%}{2} = 4.25\%$. Their present value today is

$$A \, (\text{due}) = \frac{\$5000}{0.0425} \, (1.0425) = \underline{\underline{\$122,647.06}}$$

b. The present value, 1 year from now, of the payments is the amount calculated in part a. The present value today is

$$P = \frac{S}{(1 + i)^n} = \frac{\$122,647.06}{1.0425^2} = \underline{\underline{\$112,850.90}}$$

c. The present value, 5 years from now, of the payments is the amount calculated in part a. The present value today is

$$P = \frac{\$122,647.06}{1.0425^{10}} = \underline{\underline{\$80,890.31}}$$

19. In every case, the amount that must be invested is the present value today of the future payments. The payments, once begun, form a general perpetuity having

$$i = \frac{7.5\%}{2} = 3.75\%, \ c = \frac{2}{4} = 0.5, \text{ and } p = 1.0375^{0.5} - 1 = 0.018577439$$

a. $$A \, (\text{due}) = \frac{\$1000}{0.018577439} (1.018577439) = \underline{\underline{\$54,828.73}}$$

b. $$A = \frac{\$1000}{0.018577439} = \underline{\underline{\$53,828.73}}$$

c. The present value, one year from now, of the payments is the amount calculated in part a. The present value today is

$$P = \frac{S}{(1 + i)^n} = \frac{\$54,828.73}{1.0375^2} = \underline{\underline{\$50,936.84}}$$

20. With the focal date 3 years from now,
     (Future value of $1,000,000 donation) = (Present value of the monthly payments)
    The left side of the equation is

$$S = P \, (1 + i)^n = \$1,000,000(1.006)^{36} = \$1,240,301.61$$

Viewed from the focal date, the payments form a simple perpetuity due having A (due) = $1,240,301.61 and $p = i = 0.6\%$. Hence,

$$\$1,240,301.61 = \frac{R}{0.006} \, (1.006)$$

$$R = \underline{\underline{\$7397.43}}$$

The museum can expect monthly payments of $7397.43.

Exercise 13.1 *(concluded)*

21. With the focal date 4 years from now,

    (Future value of quarterly contributions) = (Present value of monthly payments)

    The contributions form an ordinary simple annuity having

    $$R = \$34{,}650, \quad n = 4\,(4) = 16, \quad \text{and} \quad p = i = \frac{9\%}{4} = 2.25\%$$

    Then

    $$S_n = \$34{,}650 \left(\frac{1.0225^{16} - 1}{0.0225} \right) = \$658{,}537.04$$

    The monthly payments form a simple perpetuity due having

    $$A\,(\text{due}) = \$658{,}537.04 \quad \text{and} \quad p = i = \frac{7.5\%}{12} = 0.625\%$$

    Then

    $$\$658{,}537.04 = \frac{R}{1.00625}\,(1.00625)$$

    $$R = \underline{\$4090.29}$$

22. The amount required to fund each payment stream equals the present value of the payment stream. For the perpetuity due,

    $$R = \$500, \quad i = \frac{8\%}{4} = 2\% \quad \text{and} \quad c = \frac{4}{12} = 0.\overline{3}$$

    $$p = (1 + i)^c - 1 = 1.02^{0.\overline{3}} - 1 = 0.006622710$$

    $$A\,(\text{due}) = \frac{\$500}{0.00662271}\,(1.00662271) = \$75{,}997.80$$

    For the annuity due, $n = 12\,(30) = 360$, $R = \$500$, and $p = 0.00662271$.

    $$A_n\,(\text{due}) = \$500 \left(\frac{1 - 1.00662271^{-360}}{0.00662271} \right)(1.00662271) = \$68{,}938.19$$

    Therefore, only $\$75{,}997.80 - \$68{,}938.19 = \underline{\$7059.61}$ more is needed to fund the perpetuity due.

23. The total amount forwarded from the court equals the present value of the quarterly payments. The former amount is

    $$S = P(1 + i)^n = \$500{,}000\,(1.025)^3 = \$538{,}445.31$$

    The quarterly payments form an ordinary general perpetuity having

    $$A = \$538{,}445.31, \quad i = \frac{7.8\%}{2} = 3.9\%, \quad \text{and} \quad c = \frac{2}{4} = 0.5$$

    $$p = (1 + i)^c - 1 = 1.039^{0.5} - 1 = 0.019313494$$

    $$R = pA = 0.019313494\,(\$538{,}445.31) = \underline{\$10{,}399.26}$$

    The hospice will receive quarterly payments of $10,399.26.

Exercise 13.2

1. Given: R = \$2000, $p = i = \dfrac{7\%}{2} = 3.5\%$, n = 2(10) = 20, d = 2(5) = 10

$$A_n \text{ (def)} = \$2000 \left[\frac{1 - 1.035^{-20}}{0.035\,(1.035)^{10}} \right] = \underline{\underline{\$20,150.88}}$$

2. Given: R = \$750, $p = i = \dfrac{8\%}{4} = 2\%$, n = 4(5) = 20, d = 4(3.5) = 14

$$A_n \text{ (def)} = \$750 \left[\frac{1 - 1.02^{-20}}{0.02\,(1.02)^{14}} \right] = \underline{\underline{\$9294.26}}$$

3. Given: R = \$500, $p = i = \dfrac{9\%}{12} = 0.75\%$, n = 12(3.5) = 42, d = 12(2.75) = 33

$$A_n \text{ (def)} = \$500 \left[\frac{1 - 1.0075^{-42}}{0.0075\,(1.0075)^{33}} \right] = \underline{\underline{\$14,032.77}}$$

4. Given: $p = i = 7.75\%$, d = 4, n = 10, A_n (def) = \$20,000

$$\$20,000 = R \left[\frac{1 - 1.0775^{-10}}{0.0775\,(1.0775)^{4}} \right]$$

$$R = \underline{\underline{\$3972.46}}$$

5. Given: $p = i = \dfrac{9.5\%}{2} = 4.75\%$, d = 2(6) = 12, n = 2(7.5) = 15, A_n (def) = \$25,000

$$\$25,000 = R \left[\frac{1 - 1.0475^{-15}}{0.0475\,(1.0475)^{12}} \right]$$

$$R = \underline{\underline{\$4132.71}}$$

6. Given: $p = i = \dfrac{10\%}{4} = 2.5\%$, d $= \dfrac{27}{3} = 9$, n = 4(20) = 80, A_n (def) = \$50,000

$$\$50,000 = R \left[\frac{1 - 1.025^{-80}}{0.025\,(1.025)^{9}} \right]$$

$$R = \underline{\underline{\$1812.48}}$$

7. Given: R = \$1500, $p = i = 7.9\%$, n = 8, A_n (def) = \$6383.65

$$d = \frac{ln \left[\dfrac{\$1500\,(1 - 1.079^{-8})}{0.079\,(\$6383.65)} \right]}{ln\,(1.079)} = 4.00$$

The period of deferral is <u>4 years.</u>

Exercise 13.2 *(continued)*

8. Given: $R = \$1076.71$, $p = i = \dfrac{7\%}{4} = 1.75\%$, $n = 4(12.5) = 50$, A_n (def) = $\$30{,}000$

$$d = \frac{ln\left[\dfrac{\$1076.71\,(1 - 1.0175^{-50})}{0.0175\,(\$30{,}000)}\right]}{ln\,(1.0175)} = 10.00$$

The period of deferral is 10 quarters or 2 years and 6 months.

9. Given: $R = \$400$, $p = i = \dfrac{9.75\%}{12} = 0.8125\%$, $n = 180$, A_n (def) = $\$33{,}173.03$

$$d = \frac{ln\left[\dfrac{\$400\,(1 - 1.008125^{-180})}{0.008125\,(\$33{,}173.03)}\right]}{ln\,(1.008125)} = 16.00$$

The period of deferral is 16 months or 1 year and 4 months.

10. Given: $R = \$9427.11$, $p = i = 8.7\%$, $d = 7$, An (def) = $\$40{,}000$

$$n = -\frac{ln\left[1 - \dfrac{0.087\,(1.087)^7\,\$40{,}000}{\$9427.11}\right]}{ln\,(1.087)} = 13.00$$

The term of the annuity is 13 years.

11. Given: $R = \$2500$, $p = i = 4.25\%$, $d = 2(4.5) = 9$, A_n (def) = $\$25{,}550.39$

$$n = -\frac{ln\left[1 - \dfrac{0.0425\,(1.0425)^9\,\$25{,}550.39}{\$2500}\right]}{ln\,(1.0425)} = 24.00$$

The term of the annuity is 24 half-years or 12 years.

12. Given: $R = \$253.89$, $p = i = \dfrac{6.75\%}{12} = 0.5625\%$, $d = 66$, A_n (def) = $\$15{,}000$

$$n = -\frac{ln\left[1 - \dfrac{0.005625\,(1.005625)^{66}\,\$15{,}000}{\$253.89}\right]}{ln\,(1.005625)} = 117.00$$

The term of the annuity is 117 months or 9 years and 9 months.

Exercise 13.2 (continued)

13. Given: R = \$2000, $i = \dfrac{7\%}{4} = 1.75\%$, n = 20, d = 10, $c = \dfrac{4}{2} = 2$

$p = (1 + i)^c - 1 = 1.0175^2 - 1 = 0.035306250$

$A_n \text{ (def)} = \$2000 \left[\dfrac{1 - 1.03530625^{-20}}{0.03530625 \, (1.03530625)^{10}} \right]$

$= \underline{\$20{,}035.79}$

14. Given: R = \$750, $i = \dfrac{8.25\%}{12} = 0.6875\%$, n = 20, d = 14, $c = \dfrac{12}{4} = 3$

$p = (1 + i)^c - 1 = 1.006875^3 - 1 = 0.020767122$

$A_n \text{ (def)} = \$750 \left[\dfrac{1 - 1.020767122^{-20}}{0.020767122 \, (1.020767122)^{14}} \right] = \underline{\underline{\$9129.22}}$

15. Given: R = \$500, $i = \dfrac{9\%}{4} = 2.25\%$, n = 42, d = 33, $c = \dfrac{4}{12} = 0.\overline{3}$

$p = (1 + i)^c - 1 = 1.0225^{0.\overline{3}} - 1 = 0.007444443$

$A_n \text{ (def)} = \$500 \left[\dfrac{1 - 1.007444443^{-42}}{0.007444443 \, (1.007444443)^{33}} \right] = \underline{\underline{\$14{,}074.16}}$

16. Given: $i = \dfrac{7.5\%}{12} = 0.625\%$, d = 8, n = 20, $c = \dfrac{12}{2} = 6$, $A_n \text{ (def)} = \$20{,}000$

$p = (1 + i)^c - 1 = 1.00625^6 - 1 = 0.038090843$

$\$20{,}000 = R \left[\dfrac{1 - 1.038090843^{-20}}{0.038090843 \, (1.038090843)^8} \right]$

$R = \underline{\underline{\$1951.24}}$

17. Given: $i = \dfrac{9.5\%}{2} = 4.75\%$, d = 72, n = 90, $c = \dfrac{2}{12} = 0.1\overline{6}$, $A_n \text{ (def)} = \$25{,}000$

$p = (1 + i)^c - 1 = 1.0475^{0.1\overline{6}} - 1 = 0.007764383$

$\$25{,}000 = R \left[\dfrac{1 - 1.007764383^{-90}}{0.007764383 \, (1.007764383)^{72}} \right]$

$R = \underline{\underline{\$675.54}}$

Exercise 13.2 *(continued)*

18. Given: $i = \dfrac{10\%}{4} = 2.5\%$, d = 27, n = 240, c = $\dfrac{4}{12} = 0.\bar{3}$, A_n (def) = $50,000

$$p = (1 + i)^c - 1 = 1.025^{0.\bar{3}} - 1 = 0.008264838$$

$$\$50,000 = R \left[\frac{1 - 1.008264838^{-240}}{0.008264838 \, (1.008264838)^{27}} \right]$$

$$R = \underline{\$599.19}$$

19. Given: R = $1500, i = 7.9%, n = 32, c = $\dfrac{1}{4}$ = 0.25, A_n (def) = $28,355.14

$$p = (1 + i)^c - 1 = 1.079^{0.25} - 1 = 0.019190487$$

$$d = \frac{ln \left[\dfrac{\$1500 \, (1 - 1.019190487^{-32})}{0.019190487 \, (\$28,355.14)} \right]}{ln \, (1.019190487)} = 12.00$$

The period of deferral is 12 quarters or 3 years.

20. Given: R = $356.83, i = 1.75%, n = 150, c = $\dfrac{4}{12}$ = 0.$\bar{3}$, A_n (def) = $30,000

$$p = (1 + i)^c - 1 = 1.0175^{0.\bar{3}} - 1 = 0.005799633$$

$$d = \frac{ln \left[\dfrac{\$356.83 \, (1 - 1.005799633^{-150})}{0.005799633 \, (\$30,000)} \right]}{ln \, (1.005799633)} = 30.00$$

The period of deferral is 30 months or 2 years and 6 months.

21. Given: R = $400, i = 0.8125%, n = 30, c = $\dfrac{12}{2}$ = 6, A_n (def) = $4608.07

$$p = (1 + i)^c - 1 = 1.008125^6 - 1 = 0.04975103$$

$$d = \frac{ln \left[\dfrac{\$400 \, (1 - 1.04975103^{-30})}{0.04975103 \, (\$4608.07)} \right]}{ln \, (1.04975103)} = 6.00$$

The period of deferral is 6 half-years or 3 years.

Exercise 13.2(continued)

22. Given: $R = \$3764.77$, $i = 8.7\%$, $d = 14$, $c = 0.5$, A_n (def) $= \$40,000$

$$p = (1 + i)^c - 1 = 1.087^{0.5} - 1 = 0.04259292$$

$$n = -\frac{\ln\left[1 - \dfrac{0.04259292\,(1.04259292)^{14}\,\$40,000}{\$3764.77}\right]}{\ln\,(1.04259292)} = 40.00$$

The term of the annuity is 40 half-years or <u>20 years.</u>

23. Given: $R = \$2500$, $i = 4.25\%$, $d = 18$, $c = 0.5$, A_n (def) $= \$37,958.58$

$$p = (1 + i)^c - 1 = 1.0425^{0.5} - 1 = 0.02102889$$

$$n = -\frac{\ln\left[1 - \dfrac{0.02102889\,(1.02102889)^{18}\,\$37,958.58}{\$2500}\right]}{\ln\,(1.02102889)} = 30.00$$

The term of the annuity is 30 quarters or <u>7 years and 6 months.</u>

24. Given: $R = \$752.43$, $i = 0.5625\%$, $d = 22$, $c = 3$, A_n (def) $= \$15,000$

$$p = (1 + i)^c - 1 = 1.005625^3 - 1 = 0.01697010$$

$$n = -\frac{\ln\left[1 - \dfrac{0.0169701\,(1.0169701)^{22}\,\$15,000}{\$752.43}\right]}{\ln\,(1.0169701)} = 40.00$$

The term of the annuity is 40 quarters or <u>10 years.</u>

25. Today's economic value of the future payments is their present value (discounting at the time value of money). Viewing the payments as a deferred ordinary simple annuity,

$R = \$1500$, $n = 4(11) = 44$, $d = 4(5.75) = 23$, $p = i = \dfrac{9\%}{4} = 2.25\%$

Then use formula (13-3) to obtain

$$A_n\text{ (def)} = \$1500\left[\frac{1 - 1.0225^{-44}}{0.0225\,(1.0225)^{23}}\right] = \underline{\underline{\$24,949.52}}$$

26. The amount that must be invested now to generate the future payments is the present value of the payments. With $R = \$200$, $n = 60$, $d = 12(3.5) = 42$, and $p = i = \dfrac{7.5\%}{12} = 0.625\%$,

$$A_n\text{ (def)} = \$200\left[\frac{1 - 1.00625^{-60}}{0.00625\,(1.00625)^{42}}\right] = \underline{\underline{\$7682.97}}$$

Exercise 13.2 *(continued)*

27. The amount that must be invested is the present value of the deferred annuity's payments. With

    $R = \$5000$, $n = 4(5) = 20$, $d = 4(9.5) = 38$, and $p = i = \dfrac{6\%}{4} = 1.5\%$,

    $$A_n (\text{def}) = \$5000 \left[\frac{1 - 1.015^{-20}}{0.015 \, (1.015)^{38}} \right] = \underline{\underline{\$48,752.43}}$$

28. The price paid will be the present value of the payments discounted at the required rate of return. Since the first payment is due in 6 months, the period of deferral is 5 months (in order to treat the payments as a deferred ordinary annuity). With $R = \$231$, $n = 15$, $d = 5$, and $p = i = \dfrac{18\%}{12} = 1.5\%$

    $$A_n (\text{def}) = \$231 \left[\frac{1 - 1.015^{-15}}{0.015 \, (1.015)^5} \right] = \underline{\underline{\$2861.17}}$$

29. The amount that must be invested equals the present value of the deferred ordinary general annuity. With

    $R = \$2500$, $n = 4(15) = 60$, $d = 4(6) = 24$, $i = 4.5\%$, $c = \dfrac{2}{4} = 0.5$

    $p = (1 + i)^c - 1 = 1.045^{0.5} - 1 = 0.022252415$

    $$A_n (\text{def}) = \$2500 \left[\frac{1 - 1.022252415^{-60}}{0.022252415 \, (1.022252415)^{24}} \right] = \underline{\underline{\$48,559.18}}$$

30. The inheritance's current economic value is the present value of the deferred general annuity. Since the first payment is 4.5 years from now, the period of deferral is 4.25 years (if we wish to treat the payments as a deferred ordinary annuity). With $R = \$2000$, $n = 4(20) = 80$, $d = 4(4.25) = 17$, $i = \dfrac{9\%}{12} = 0.75\%$, $c = \dfrac{12}{4} = 3$,

    $p = (1 + i)^c - 1 = 1.0075^3 - 1 = 0.022669172$

    $$A_n (\text{def}) = \$2000 \left[\frac{1 - 1.022669172^{-80}}{0.022669172 \, (1.022669172)^{17}} \right] = \underline{\underline{\$50,239.76}}$$

31. The present value, on the date of sale, of the monthly payments equals 85% of the purchase price. Viewing the payments as a deferred ordinary general annuity with

    $R = \$2700$, $n = 12(20) = 240$, $d = 14$, $i = 9\%$, $c = \dfrac{1}{12} = 0.08\overline{3}$

    $p = (1 + i)^c - 1 = 1.09^{0.08\overline{3}} - 1 = 0.007207323$

    $$A_n (\text{def}) = \$2700 \left[\frac{1 - 1.007207323^{-240}}{0.007207323 \, (1.007207323)^{14}} \right] = \underline{\underline{\$327,454.29}}$$

Exercise 13.2 (continued)

32. The amount in the RRSP at age 54 equals the present value (on Brice's 54th birthday) of the annuity payments. That is, A_n (def) = $154,000 with n = 12(20) = 240, d = 12(11) = 132, and $p = i = \frac{8.25\%}{12} = 0.6875\%$. Solve for R in

$$\$154,000 = R\left[\frac{1 - 1.006875^{-240}}{0.006875\ (1.006875)^{132}}\right]$$

$$R = \$3241.66$$

The annuity payments will be $3241.66 per month.

33. $22,000 is the present value (on the date the funds were invested in the RRSP) of the withdrawals from the RRIF. That is, A_n (def) = $22,000 with n = 4(20) = 80, d = 4(15) = 60, and $p = i = \frac{8.5\%}{4} = 2.125\%$. Solve for R in

$$\$22,000 = R\left[\frac{1 - 1.02125^{-80}}{0.02125\ (1.02125)^{60}}\right]$$

$$R = \$2027.98$$

Each quarterly RRIF withdrawal will be $2027.98.

34. The original loan equals the present value of the loan payments. Then A_n (def) = $3 million with n = 2(15) = 30, d = 2(2.5) = 5, and $p = i = \frac{6\%}{2} = 3\%$.

    a. Solve for R in

    $$\$3,000,000 = R\left[\frac{1 - 1.03^{-30}}{0.03(1.03)^5}\right]$$

    $$R = \$177,435.91$$

    b. Total interest = Total of payments – Principal
       = 30 ($177,435.91) – $3,000,000
       = $2,323,077.30

35. a. The original price equals the present value of the payments discounted at the rate of interest charged to the customer. That is, A_n (def) = $995 with n = 8, d = 3, and $p = i = 1\%$.
       Solve for R in

    $$\$995 = R\left[\frac{1 - 1.01^{-8}}{0.01(1.01)^3}\right]$$

    $$R = \$133.98$$

    b. The amount that Al's Warehouse will receive from the sale of the contract equals the present value of the payments discounted at the finance company's required rate of return. With

    R = $133.98, n = 8, d = 3, and $p = i = \frac{15.6\%}{12} = 1.3\%$

    $$A_n\ (\text{def}) = \$133.98\left[\frac{1 - 1.013^{-8}}{0.013(1.013)^3}\right] = \$973.31$$

Exercise 13.2 (continued)

36. a. The balance owed after the down payment is
$1700 (1 − 0.15) = $1445.00.
This balance equals the present value of the 12 deferred payments. That is, A_n (def) = $1445 with

n = 12, d = 5, $i = \dfrac{14\%}{2} = 7\%$, and $c = \dfrac{2}{12} = 0.1\bar{6}$. Then

$p = (1 + i)^c − 1 = 1.07^{0.1\bar{6}} − 1 = 0.011340260$ and

$$\$1445 = R\left[\frac{1 − 1.01134026^{-12}}{0.01134026(1.01134026)^5}\right]$$

R = $136.99

The customer's monthly payments are $136.99.

b. The price paid by the finance company will be the present value of the 12 payments discounted at the finance company's required yield. With R = $136.99, n = 12, d = 5, $i = 16\%$, and $c = \dfrac{1}{12} = 0.08\bar{3}$, then

$p = (1 + i)^c − 1 = 1.16^{0.08\bar{3}} − 1 = 0.012445138$ and

$$A_n \text{ (def)} = \$136.99\left[\frac{1 − 1.012445138^{-12}}{0.012445138\,(1.012445138)^5}\right] = \$1427.23$$

The finance company will pay $1427.23 for the contract.

37. The present value (on the purchase date) of the deferred annuity payments equals $85,000. That is, A_n (def) = $85,000 with n = (2)20 − 40, d = 2(9) = 18, $i = 8.25\%$, $c = \dfrac{1}{2} = 0.5$. Then

$p = (1 + i)^c − 1 = 1.0825^{0.5} − 1 = 0.040432602$

Solve for R in

$$\$85,000 = R\left[\frac{1 − 1.040432602^{-40}}{0.040432602\,(1.040432602)^{18}}\right]$$

R = $8821.74

The semiannual payments will be $8821.74.

38. a. The original loan equals the present value of the payments. Hence, A_n (def) = $2.5 million with

n = 4(20) = 80, $i = \dfrac{12\%}{2} = 6\%$, and $c = \dfrac{2}{4} = 0.5$. For the loan payments to be viewed as an ordinary annuity following the period of deferral, d = 5.

$p = (1 + i)^c − 1 = 1.06^{0.5} − 1 = 0.029563014$

Solve for R in

$$\$2,500,000 = R\left[\frac{1 − 1.029563014^{-80}}{0.029563014\,(1.029563014)^5}\right]$$

R = $94,704.91

Exercise 13.2 (continued)

b. If the payments are $1.1R = \$104,175.40$, then

$$n = -\dfrac{\ln\left[\dfrac{1 - 0.029563014\,(1.029563014)^5\,\$2,500,000}{\$104,175.40}\right]}{\ln(1.029563014)} = 58.99$$

That is, 59 payments will pay off the loan. Hence, $80 - 59 = \underline{\underline{21}}$ fewer payments will be required to pay off the loan.

39. The initial investment equals the present value of the monthly withdrawals. Hence, $A_n\text{(def)} = \$10,000$ with $R = \$300$, $p = i = \dfrac{7.5\%}{12} = 0.625\%$, and $d = 3(12) + 5 = 41$ (to make the payments an ordinary annuity when viewed from the end of the period of deferral). Then

$$n = -\dfrac{\ln\left[\dfrac{1 - 0.00625\,(1.00625)^{41}\,\$10,000}{\$300}\right]}{\ln(1.00625)} = 50.28$$

The fund will provide $\underline{\underline{51}}$ monthly withdrawals (with the last one less than $300).

40. The original loan equals the present value of the loan payments. Thus, $A_n\text{(def)} = \$8000$ with $R = \$200$, $p = i = \dfrac{4.5\%}{12} = 0.375\%$, and $d = 2(12) + 11 = 35$ (in order to treat the payments as an ordinary annuity following the period of deferral). Then

$$n = -\dfrac{\ln\left[\dfrac{1 - 0.00375\,(1.00375)^{35}\,\$8000}{\$200}\right]}{\ln(1.00375)} = 50.10$$

The loan requires 51 monthly payments. Measured from the date of the first payment, it will take 50 months or $\underline{4\ \text{years and 2 months}}$ to pay off the loan.

41. Since the interest rate during the period of deferral differs from the interest rate during the term of the annuity, formula (13-3a) cannot be used. The most straightforward approach is a two-step solution using the idea that, at a focal date 3 years ago,
  (Future value of $17,000 placed in the RRSP) = (Present value of the RRIF withdrawals).
The amount on the left side is

$$S = P(1 + i)^n = \$17,000\,(1.05)^{18} = \$40,912.53$$

On the right side, we have $A_n\text{(due)} = \$40,912.53$, $R = \$1000$, and $p = i = \dfrac{8\%}{4} = 2\%$. Using formula (11-2a),

$$n = -\dfrac{\ln\left[\dfrac{1 - 0.02\,(\$40,912.53)}{\$1000\,(1.02)}\right]}{\ln(1.02)} = 81.83$$

There will be 82 withdrawals with the last one occurring 81 quarters or $\underline{\underline{20\ \text{years and 3 months}}}$ after the first withdrawal.

Exercise 13.2 (continued)

42.   In order for the additional profits to repay the initial investment and provide a return on investment of 15% compounded quarterly, then the present value (on the date of purchase of the patent) of the additional profits discounted at 15% compounded quarterly must be $150,000. Hence

A_n (def) = $150,000 with R = $28,000, d = 4(2.5) = 10, and $p = i = \dfrac{15\%}{4} = 3.75\%$. The required number of quarters each having a $28,000 profit is

$$n = -\frac{ln\left[1 - \dfrac{0.0375\,(1.0375)^{10}\,\$150,000}{\$28,000}\right]}{ln\,(1.0375)} = 9.31$$

Hence, the profits from 10 quarters are required. Measured from the date of purchase of the patent, it will take 2.5 years + 2.5 years = 5 years to recover the investment along with the required rate of return.

43.   The original loan equals the present value of the payments. The payments form a deferred general annuity having A_n (def) = $20,000, $i = 8\%$, $c = \dfrac{1}{12} = 0.08\bar{3}$, R = $300, and d = 23. Then

$$p = (1 + i)^c - 1 = 1.08^{0.08\bar{3}} - 1 = 0.006434030 \text{ and}$$

$$n = -\frac{ln\left[1 - \dfrac{0.00643403\,(1.00643403)^{23}\,\$20,000}{\$300}\right]}{ln\,(1.00643403)} = 107.18$$

The 108th payment will extinguish the debt. It will occur 23 + 108 = 131 months or 10 years and 11 months after the date the $20,000 was originally borrowed.

44.   Since the interest rate during the period of deferral differs from the rate during the term of the annuity, we will not use formula (13-3a). Instead, with the focal date at 6 years from now, use the idea

     (Future value of the RRSP) = (Present value of the annuity payments)

The left side is

$$S = P\,(1 + i)^n = \$139,000\,(1.085)^6 = \$226,773.98$$

On the right side we have A_n = $226,773.98, R = $5000, $i = \dfrac{7.5\%}{12} = 0.625\%$, and $c = \dfrac{12}{4} = 3$. Then

$$p = (1 + i)^c - 1 = 1.00625^3 - 1 = 0.01886743 \text{ and}$$

$$n = -\frac{ln\left[1 - \dfrac{0.01886743\,(\$226,773.98)}{\$5000}\right]}{ln\,(1.01886743)} = 103.58$$

There will be 104 payments lasting 104 quarters or 26 years after the purchase of the annuity.

Exercise 13.2 *(continued)*

45. The initial deposit equals the present value of the withdrawals. Hence, A_n (def) = \$10,000 with R = \$1000, $n = 40$, and $p = i = \dfrac{8.5\%}{2} = 4.25\%$. Then

$$d = \frac{ln\left[\dfrac{\$1000\,(1 - 1.0425^{-40})}{0.0425\,(\$10,000)}\right]}{ln\,(1.0425)} = 15.52$$

The period of deferral is 15.52 half-years or 7 years and 9 months to the nearest month. Formula (13-3b) assumes that the payments form an ordinary annuity following the period of deferral. Therefore, the first withdrawal occurs 6 months after the period of deferral. The \$10,000 deposit must be made 8 years and 3 months before the first withdrawal.

46. The initial deposit equals the present value of the withdrawals. Hence, A_n (def) = \$19,665 with R = \$1000, $i = \dfrac{9.5\%}{2} = 4.75\%$, $n = 60$, and $c = \dfrac{2}{4} = 0.5$. Then

$$p = (1 + i)^c - 1 = 1.0475^{0.5} - 1 = 0.023474475 \text{ and}$$

$$d = \frac{ln\left[\dfrac{\$1000\,(1 - 1.023474475^{-60})}{0.023474475\,(\$19,665)}\right]}{ln\,(1.023474475)} = 21.00$$

The period of deferral is 21 quarters long. The deposit must be made 22 quarters or 5 years and 6 months before the first withdrawal.

47. The original loan equals the present value of the payments. Thus, A_n (def) = \$35,000 with R = \$1573.83, $n = 4(12) = 48$, and $p = i = \dfrac{10\%}{4} = 2.5\%$. Then

$$d = \frac{ln\left[\dfrac{\$1573.83\,(1 - 1.025^{-48})}{0.025\,(\$35,000)}\right]}{ln\,(1.025)} = 9.00$$

The period of deferral was 9 quarters long. The interval between the date of the loan and the first payment was 10 quarters or 2 years and 6 months.

48. The amount paid for the conditional sale contract equals the present value of the monthly payments discounted at the finance company's required rate of return. That is A_n (def) = \$3975 with R = \$256.96, $p = i = \dfrac{18\%}{12} = 1.5\%$, and $n = 20$. Then

$$d = \frac{ln\left[\dfrac{\$256.96\,(1 - 1.015^{-20})}{0.015\,(\$3975)}\right]}{ln\,(1.015)} = 7.00$$

The period of deferral is 7 months. The interval between the date of sale and the first payment is 8 months.

Exercise 13.2 *(continued)*

49. The initial amount in the RRSP equals the present value of the annuity. Thus, A_n (def) = \$160,360 with $R = \$2000$, $n = 12(25) = 300$, and $p = i = \dfrac{7.5\%}{12} = 0.625\%$. Then

$$d = \frac{ln\left[\dfrac{\$2000\,(1 - 1.00625^{-300})}{0.00625(\$160,360)}\right]}{ln\,(1.00625)} = 84.00$$

The period of deferral is 84 months. Therefore, the funds must be left to grow in the RRSP for <u>7 years</u> before buying the annuity.

50. The initial amount in the RRSP equals the present value of the annuity. Thus, A_n (def) = \$142,470 with $R = \$1700$, $i = \dfrac{8.75\%}{2} = 4.375\%$, $c = \dfrac{2}{12} = 0.1\overline{6}$, and $n = 12(25) = 300$.

Then

$$p = (1 + i)^c - 1 = 1.04375^{0.1\overline{6}} - 1 = 0.007162193 \text{ and}$$

$$d = \frac{ln\left[\dfrac{\$1700\,(1 - 1.007162193^{-300})}{0.007162193\,(\$142,470)}\right]}{ln\,(1.007162193)} = 54.00$$

The period of deferral is 54 months. Therefore, the funds must be left in the RRSP for <u>4 years and 6 months</u> before purchasing the annuity.

51. The company providing the larger monthly payments offers the better rate of return. We will calculate the monthly payments from Liberty Standard (based on its quoted rate of return of 8% compounded annually). Then we will compare this amount to the \$1205 per month quoted by Northwest Mutual.

    The purchase price of any annuity equals the present value of the annuity payments. For the Liberty Standard case, we have A_n (def) = \$100,000 with $n = 12(20) = 240$, $d = 12(5) = 60$, $i = 8\%$, and $c = \dfrac{1}{12} = 0.08\overline{3}$.

Then

$$p = (1 + i)^c - 1 = 1.08^{0.08\overline{3}} - 1 = 0.006434030$$

Solve for R in

$$\$100,000 = R\left[\frac{1 - 1.00643403^{-240}}{0.006434030\,(1.006434030)^{60}}\right]$$

$$R = \$1203.60$$

Since <u>Northwest Mutual</u> makes slightly larger payments, it offers the better rate of return.

Exercise 13.2 *(concluded)*

52. Heath and Company should choose the lease having the smaller economic value. The current economic value of each lease is the present value of the lease payments discounted at the time value of money. For the lease on the current premises, R = $2100, n = 12(7) = 84, p = $i = \dfrac{10.5\%}{12}$ = 0.875%. Then

$$A_n \text{ (due)} = \$2100 \left[\frac{1 - 1.00875^{-84}}{0.00875} \right] (1.00875) = \$125{,}640$$

For the lease on the new premises, the payments form a deferred annuity having R = $2500, n = 12(6) = 72, d = 11, and p = i = 0.875%. Then

$$A_n \text{ (def)} = \$2500 \left[\frac{1 - 1.00875^{-72}}{0.00875 \,(1.00875)^{11}} \right] = \$120{,}962$$

Therefore, Heath should accept the lease on the new location since it represents a saving (in current dollars) of

$$\$125{,}640 - \$120{,}962 = \$4678$$

Exercise 13.3

1. Step 1: Calculate the original payment size using the idea that the original loan equals the present value of the payments. That is, A_n = $20,000 with n = 120 and p = $i = \dfrac{12.75\%}{12}$ = 1.0625%.

$$\$20{,}000 = R \left(\frac{1 - 1.010625^{-120}}{0.010625} \right)$$

$$R = \$295.68$$

Step 2: Calculate the balance after 1 year using the idea that the original loan equals the present value of 12 payments plus the present value of the balance. That is,

$$\$20{,}000 = \$295.68 \left(\frac{1 - 1.010625^{-12}}{0.010625} \right) + \frac{\text{Balance}}{1.010625^{12}}$$

Balance = $18,941.78

Step 3: Calculate the number of monthly payments of
1.15($295.68) = $340.03
whose present value is $18,941.78. Using formula (10-4a),

$$n = -\frac{\ln \left[1 - \dfrac{0.010625\,(\$18{,}941.78)}{\$340.03} \right]}{\ln (1.010625)} = 84.79$$

The total time required to pay off the loan will be
(12 + 85) months = 8 years and 1 month.
Therefore, the loan will be paid off 1 year and 11 months sooner.

Exercise 13.3 (continued)

2. a. The economic value on May 23, 1992 was the present value of the 20 annual payments discounted at the time value of money. The payments form a general annuity due having $n = 20$, $i = 3.5\%$, $c = 2$, and

$$R = \frac{\$9,346,862}{20} = \$467,343.10$$

Then $p = (1 + i)^c - 1 = 1.035^2 - 1 = 0.07122500$ and

$$A_n \text{ (due)} = \$467,343.10 \left(\frac{1 - 1.071225^{-20}}{0.071225} \right) 1.071225$$

$$= \$5,253,554$$

The economic value of the jackpot on the date of the win was $5,253,554.

b. The lump amount calculated in part a is economically equivalent to the annuity payments. Thus, we can answer this part by finding the date on which the amount from part a, invested at 7% compounded semiannually, will have a future value of $9,346,862. Using formula (9-2), the required number of compounding intervals is

$$n = \frac{ln \left(\dfrac{S}{P} \right)}{ln (1 + i)} = \frac{ln \left(\dfrac{\$9,346,862}{\$5,253,554} \right)}{ln (1.035)} = 16.75$$

The total time period is 16.75 half-years or 8 years and 4.5 months. This period ends in early October, 2000.

3. The combined future value of the initial $67,000 and the semiannual contributions is to be $500,000. The contributions form an ordinary general annuity having $R = \$4000$, $i = \dfrac{9\%}{4} = 2.25\%$, and $c = \dfrac{4}{2} = 2$. Then

$$p = (1 + i)^c - 1 = 1.0225^2 - 1 = 0.045506250 \text{ and}$$

$$\$67,000 \, (1.04550625)^n + \$4000 \left(\frac{1.04550625^n - 1}{0.04550625} \right) = \$500,000$$

Solving for n gives n = 29.97. Therefore, Sheila must make 30 contributions requiring 15 years.

4. The required amount equals the combined present value on the purchase date of the two annuities.

Step 1: Calculate the present value, 10 years after the purchase date, of the $2500 per month annuity. With
$R = \$2500$, $i = \dfrac{8.5\%}{4} = 2.125\%$, $c = \dfrac{4}{12} = 0.\overline{3}$, and $n = 120$,

$$p = (1 + i)^c - 1 = 1.02125^{0.\overline{3}} - 1 = 0.007033744 \text{ and}$$

$$A_n \text{ (due)} = \$2500 \left(\frac{1 - 1.007033744^{-120}}{0.007033744} \right) 1.007033744$$

$$= \$203,576.63$$

Step 2: Calculate the combined present value (on the purchase date) of the Step 1 result and the $5000 per quarter annuity. With R = $5000, p = i = 2.125%, and n = 4(10) = 40, the combined present value is

$$\frac{\$203{,}576.63}{1.02125^{40}} + \$5000 \left(\frac{1 - 1.02125^{-40}}{0.02125} \right) = \underline{\$221{,}616.32}$$

5. The combined future value, 10 years from now, of the initial $133,000 and the semiannual contributions is to be $350,000. With the focal date placed 7 years from now, an equivalent statement is

(Combined future value of $133,000 and contributions) = (Present value of $350,000)

The right side of the equation is

$$P = \frac{S}{(1 + i)^n} = \frac{\$350{,}000}{1.0825^3} = \$275{,}920.73$$

The RRSP contributions form an ordinary general annuity having

$$n = 2(7) = 14,\ i = 8.25\%,\ \text{and}\ c = \frac{1}{2} = 0.5$$
$$p = (1 + i)^c - 1 = 1.0825^{0.5} - 1 = 0.04043260$$

Putting the initial word equation into mathematics,

$$\$133{,}000 (1.0404326)^{14} + R \left(\frac{1.0404326^{14} - 1}{0.0404326} \right) = \$275{,}920.73$$

Solving for R gives
$$R = \underline{\$2412.64}$$

Natalie must contribute $2412.64 every 6 months to reach her goal.

6. The present value, on the date of purchase of the equipment, of the lease payments discounted at the required rate of return, is to be 90% of the capital investment.

Shifting the focal date from the date of purchase to the beginning of the lease, we can re-state the preceding idea as

(Present value of lease payments) = (Future value of 90% of $40,000)

With the lease payments at the beginning of each month, they form a general annuity due having

$$n = 12(5) = 60,\ i = \frac{16\%}{2} = 8\%,\ c = \frac{2}{12} = 0.1\overline{6}\ \text{and}$$

$$p = (1 + i)^c - 1 = 1.08^{0.1\overline{6}} - 1 = 0.01290946$$

Expressing the word equation in mathematics,

$$R \left(\frac{1 - 1.01290946^{-60}}{0.01290946} \right) 1.01290946 = \$36{,}000 (1.01290946)^3$$

Solving for R gives R = $\underline{\$888.25}$

The monthly lease payment will be $888.25.

Exercise 13.3 (continued)

7.   The preferred option is the one having the lower economic value. If the economic value, 5 years from now, of today's purchase price and the annual property taxes is less than the future purchase price, the current purchase will be financially advantageous.

   The annual property taxes form an ordinary general annuity having R = $9000, n = 5, i = 6%, and c = 2. Then
   $$p = (1 + i)^c - 1 = 1.06^2 - 1 = 0.1236000$$

   The combined future value, 5 years from now, of the purchase price and property tax payments is

   $$\$450,000 \ (1.1236)^5 + \$9000 \left(\frac{1.1236^5 - 1}{0.1236} \right) = \underline{\underline{\$863,467}}$$

   The price, 5 years from today, would have to exceed $863,467 for it to be financially advantageous to purchase the property today.

8.   If the combined present value of the next 3 years' dividends and the stock's price (3 years from now) discounted at 13% compounded annually, equals $37.50, the current buyer will earn 13% compounded annually.

   The dividends form an ordinary general annuity having
   R = $1.00, n = 4(3) = 12, i = 13%, and c = $\frac{1}{4}$ = 0.25. Then
   $$p = 1.13^{0.25} - 1 = 0.0310260$$
   Putting the initial criterion into mathematics,

   $$\$1.00 \left(\frac{1 - 1.031026^{-12}}{0.031026} \right) + \frac{\text{Future price}}{1.031026^{12}} = \$37.50$$

   Solving for the future price, we obtain future price = $\underline{\underline{\$39.83}}$.

9.   The amount in the RRSP after 25 years will be the future value of all the contributions.

   For the first 10 years, the contributions form an ordinary general annuity having R = $1000, n = 40,
   i = 4.25%, c = $\frac{2}{4}$ = 0.5, and p = $1.0425^{0.5} - 1 = 0.021028893$. The amount in the RRSP after 10 years will be

   $$\$1000 \left(\frac{1.021028893^{40} - 1}{0.021028893} \right) = \$61,767.70$$

   For the last 15 years, the contributions form an ordinary general annuity having R = $1000, n = 180,
   i = 4.25%, c = $\frac{2}{12}$ = $0.1\overline{6}$, and p = $1.0425^{0.1\overline{6}} - 1 = 0.006961062$. The combined future value, 25 years from now, of these contributions and the $61,767.70 will be

   $$\$61,767.70 \ (1.006961062)^{180} + \$1000 \left(\frac{1.006961062^{180} - 1}{0.006961062} \right) = \underline{\underline{\$572,376.63}}$$

   Gayle will have $572,376.63 in her RRSP after 25 years.

Exercise 13.3 *(continued)*

10. The initial investment (cost) will be recovered and a semiannually compounded return of 13% earned if the present value of the monthly fuel savings, discounted at 13% compounded semiannually, equals the initial cost.

    The monthly fuel savings form a general annuity due having A_n (due) = $1300, n = 60, i = 6.5\%$ and $c = 0.1\overline{6}$. Then

    $$p = 1.065^{0.1\overline{6}} - 1 = 0.01055107 \quad \text{and}$$

    $$\$1300 = R \left(\frac{1 - 1.01055107^{-60}}{0.01055107} \right) 1.01055107$$

    Solving for R gives $\quad R = \underline{\$29.05}$

    The reduction in the monthly cost of fuel must be $29.05.

11. The sum of the balances currently owed on the two existing loans equals the present value of the payments on the consolidated loan.

    Step 1: Calculate the monthly payment on the $8500 loan.
    $$A_n = \$8500, n = 36, p = i = 1.125\%$$

    $$\$8500 = R \left(\frac{1 - 1.01125^{-36}}{0.01125} \right)$$

    $$R = \$288.45$$

    Step 2: Calculate the balance after 11 payments.

    $$\$8500 = \$288.45 \left(\frac{1 - 1.01125^{-11}}{0.01125} \right) + \frac{\text{Balance}}{1.01125^{11}}$$

    Balance = $6255.50

    Step 3: Calculate the balance on the second loan.
    Balance = Present value of remaining payments
    where $R = \$338.70, n = 38$ payments remain, $i = 6.5\%, c = 0.1\overline{6}, p = 1.065^{0.1\overline{6}} - 1 = 0.010551074$

    $$\text{Balance} = \$338.70 \left(\frac{1 - 1.010551074^{-38}}{0.010551074} \right) = \$10,558.09$$

    Step 4: Calculate the monthly payment on the consolidated loan.
    Initial loan = $6255.50 + \$10,558.09 = \$16,813.59.$
    Hence, $A_n = \$16,813.59, n = 60$, and $p = i = 0.9375\%.$
    Solve for R in

    $$\$16,813.59 = R \left(\frac{1 - 1.009375^{-60}}{0.009375} \right)$$

    $$R = \underline{\$367.67}$$

    The monthly payment on the consolidated loan would be $367.67.

Exercise 13.3 *(continued)*

12. a. The extra make-up payment will be the future value, at the end of the 15th month, of (missed) payments 12, 13, and 14.

    Step 1: Calculate the size of the monthly payment where A_n = $10,000, p = i = 0.9375%, and n = 72.

    $$\$10,000 = R\left(\frac{1 - 1.009375^{-72}}{0.009375}\right)$$

    $$R = \$191.62$$

    Step 2: Calculate the future value, at the end of the 15th month, of payments 12, 13, and 14.

    $$S_n \text{ (due)} = \$191.62 \left(\frac{1.009375^3 - 1}{0.009375}\right)1.009375 = \underline{\$585.71}$$

    Therefore, $585.71 paid along with the 15th payment will make up for the three missed payments.

    b. We must recalculate the payments so that the present value of 72 – 14 = 58 payments equals the balance owed after 14 months.

    Step 1: Calculate the balance after 11 payments.

    $$\$10,000 = \$191.62 \left(\frac{1 - 1.009375^{-11}}{0.009375}\right) + \frac{\text{Balance}}{1.009375^{11}}$$

    Balance = $8871.52

    Step 2: Calculate the balance after 14 months. This will be the future value, 3 months later, of the step 1 result.

    $$S = \$8871.52 \, (1.009375)^3 = \$9123.38$$

    Step 3: Calculate the new monthly payment such that
    A_n = $9123.38 with n = 58 and p = i = 0.9375%.

    $$\$9123.38 = R\left(\frac{1 - 1.009375^{-58}}{0.009375}\right)$$

    $$R = \underline{\$204.64}$$

    The new monthly payment will be $204.64.

13. a. The total of the nominal costs is
    $$6(\$8400) + 6(\$5400) + 5(\$7200) + 2(\$9600) = \underline{\$138,000}$$

b. The economic value, at the date of birth, of all costs is their present value.

Years	Monthly cost ($)	No. of months
1 – 6	700	72
7 – 12	450	72
13 – 17	600	60
18 – 19	800	24

The present value, at the beginning of the 18th year, of the last 2 years' costs is

$$A_n = \$800 \left(\frac{1 - 1.005^{-24}}{0.005} \right)$$

$$= \$18,050.29$$

The present value, at the beginning of the 13th year, of the last 7 years' costs is

$$\$600 \left(\frac{1 - 1.005^{-60}}{0.005} \right) + \frac{\$18,050.29}{1.005^{60}} = \$44,417.32$$

The present value, at the beginning of the 7th year, of the last 13 years' costs is

$$\$450 \left(\frac{1 - 1.005^{-72}}{0.005} \right) + \frac{\$44,417.32}{1.005^{72}} = \$58,169.51$$

The present value, at the birth date, of all the costs is

$$\$700 \left(\frac{1 - 1.005^{-72}}{0.005} \right) + \frac{\$58,169.51}{1.005^{72}} = \$82,857.57$$

c. The economic value, at age 19, of the expenditures is the future value of all the expenditures. This is most easily determined by calculating the future value, 19 years later, of the result in part b.

$$S = P (1 + i)^n = \$82,857.57 (1.005)^{228} = \underline{\underline{\$258,342}}$$

14. The total amount needed in the Pelyks' RRSPs at retirement is the present value, at the beginning of 2005, of all the annuity payments discounted at

$$p = (1 + i)^c - 1 = 1.04^{0.1\overline{6}} - 1 = 0.6558197\% \text{ per month.}$$

The present value, at the beginning of 2020, of the next 11 years' payments is

$$\$10,000 \left(\frac{1 - 1.006558197^{-132}}{0.006558197} \right) = \$881,407.83$$

The present value, at the beginning of 2015, of the next 16 years' payments is

$$\$7500 \left(\frac{1 - 1.006558197^{-60}}{0.006558197} \right) + \frac{\$881,407.83}{1.006558197^{60}} = \$966,474.64$$

The present value, at the beginning of 2010, of the next 21 years' payments is

$$\$6000 \left(\frac{1 - 1.006558197^{-60}}{0.006558197} \right) + \frac{\$966,474.64}{1.006558197^{60}} = \$949,737.31$$

Exercise 13.3 (continued)

The present value, at the beginning of 2005, of all the annuity payments is

$$\$5000 \left(\frac{1 - 1.006558197^{-60}}{0.006558197} \right) + \frac{\$949,737.31}{1.006558197^{60}} = \underline{\underline{\$888,959.89}}$$

The Pelyks will need $888,959.89 in their RRSPs at the beginning of 2005.

15.   Step 1: Calculate the customer's monthly payments. Since no interest is charged during the first 6 months, $2000 is owed when the first of the 6 monthly payments is made. Then A_n (due) = $2000 with n = 6 and p = i = 1.25%. Solve for R in

$$\$2000 = R \left(\frac{1 - 1.0125^{-6}}{0.0125} \right) (1.0125)$$

$$R = \$309.39$$

The price that Afco will pay is the present value, on the date of the sale, of the 6 payments discounted at 18% compounded semiannually.

Step 2: Calculate the present value, 6 months from the date of sale, of the payments which form a general annuity due having i = 9%, c = 0.1$\overline{6}$, and

$$p = 1.09^{0.1\overline{6}} - 1 = 0.014466592$$

$$A_n \text{ (due)} = \$309.39 \left(\frac{1 - 1.014466592^{-6}}{0.014466592} \right) 1.014466592$$

$$= \$1791.42$$

Step 3: Calculate the present value, on the date of sale, of the amount calculated in step 2.

$$P = \frac{S}{(1 + i)^n} = \frac{\$1791.42}{1.09^1} = \underline{\underline{\$1643.51}}$$

Pioneer will receive $1643.51 from Afco on the sale of the contract.

16.   The value of the RRSP will be the combined future value of the two contribution annuities.
       The quarterly contributions form a general annuity due having R = $1000, n = 92, i = 4.75%, c = 0.5, and p = $1.0475^{0.5} - 1$ = 0.023474475%

$$S_n \text{ (due)} = \$1000 \left(\frac{1.023474475^{92} - 1}{0.023474475} \right) 1.023474475$$

$$= \$325,010.10$$

The annual contributions form an ordinary general annuity having R = $2000, i = 4.75%, c = 2, n = 23, and p = $1.0475^2 - 1$ = 0.097256250

$$S_n = \$2000 \left(\frac{1.09725625^{23} - 1}{0.09725625} \right) = \$153,295.07$$

The total amount in the RRSP will be
       $325,010 + $153,295 = $\underline{\underline{\$478,305}}$

Exercise 13.3 (continued)

17. With the focal date at Reg's 60th birthday,
   (Future value of RRSP contributions) = (Present value of all annuity payments).
   The right side can be calculated in two steps.

   Step 1: Calculate the present value at age 70 of the 20-year annuity having R = $6000, n = 240, and p = i = 0.625%. Then

   $$A_n = \$6000 \left(\frac{1 - 1.00625^{-240}}{0.00625} \right) = \$744,792.79$$

   Step 2: Calculate the present value at age 60 of the 10-year annuity and the step 1 result.

   $$\$5000 \left(\frac{1 - 1.00625^{-120}}{0.00625} \right) + \frac{\$744,792.79}{1.00625^{120}} = \$773,861.02$$

   Step 3: Calculate the RRSP contributions so that
   S_n (due) = $773,861.02 with n = 4(30) = 120, i = 4.25%, c = 0.5 and
   p = $1.0425^{0.5} - 1 = 0.021028893$. Solve for R in

   $$\$773,861.02 = R \left(\frac{1.021028893^{120} - 1}{0.021028893} \right) 1.021028893$$

   $$R = \$1429.49$$

   The quarterly RRSP contributions must be $1429.49.

18. a. With the focal date 17 years from now,
   (Combined future value of $31,000 and contributions) = (Present value of annuity payments)

   For the contribution annuity, R = $5000, n = 17, and p = i = 8.75%. The amount in the RRSP 17 years from now will be

   $$\$31,000 (1.0875)^{17} + \$5000 \left(\frac{1.0875^{17} - 1}{0.0875} \right) = \$309,703.87$$

   For the income annuity, A_n = $309,703.87, n = 240, and p = i = 0.6875%. Solve for R in

   $$\$309,703.87 = R \left(\frac{1 - 1.006875^{-240}}{0.006875} \right)$$

   $$R = \$2638.88$$

   Cynthia will receive monthly payments of $2638.88.

   b. The purchasing power in today's dollars is the present value of $2638.88 discounted at 4% per year for 17 years. This amount is

   $$P = \frac{S}{(1 + i)^n} = \frac{\$2638.88}{1.04^{17}} = \$1354.73$$

Exercise 13.3 (concluded)

19. The car buyer will be indifferent between the alternatives if the payments during the 4 year-term of each loan are the same.

Step 1: Calculate the monthly payment on $20,000 financed at 6.9% compounded monthly for 4 years. Solve for R when $A_n = \$20,000$, $n = 48$, and $p = i = 0.575\%$.

$$\$20,000 = R\left(\frac{1 - 1.00575^{-48}}{0.00575}\right)$$

$$R = \$478.00$$

Step 2: Calculate the initial loan at 10.5% compounded monthly that would have the same payments on a 4-year term. This amount is the present value of the payments discounted at $p = i = 0.875\%$.

$$A_n = \$478.00\left(\frac{1 - 1.00875^{-48}}{0.00875}\right) = \$18,669.31$$

Step 3: Calculate the cash rebate. For indifference, the rebate must reduce the net price to $18,669.31.
Rebate = $20,000 − $18,669.31 = $\underline{\$1330.69}$

20. With the focal date at 20 years from now,
    (Combined future value of $54,000 and semiannual contributions)
    = (Present value of 25-year annuity)

Step 1: Calculate the nominal amount of the income annuity payments.

$$S = P (1 + i)^n = \$6000 (1.045)^{20} = \$14,470.28$$

Step 2: Calculate the present value of the 25-year annuity having $R = \$14,470.28$, $n = 4(25) = 100$, and $p = i = 2\%$.

$$A_n = \$14,470.28\left(\frac{1 - 1.02^{-100}}{0.02}\right) = \$623,645.22$$

Step 3: Calculate the RRSP contributions with $n = 40$ and $p = i = 4\%$. Solve for R in

$$\$54,000 (1.04)^{40} + R\left(\frac{1.04^{40} - 1}{0.04}\right) = \$623,645.22$$

$$R = \underline{\$3834.66}$$

Mr. Parmar must make semiannual contributions of $3834.66.

Review Problems

1. The amount required to fund an annuity or a perpetuity is the present value of the payments. For a perpetuity having R = $1000 and p = i = 8%,

    $$A = \frac{R}{p} = \frac{\$1000}{0.08} = \$12,500$$

    For the annuity having R = $1000, n = 25, and p = i = 8%,

    $$A_n = \$1000 \left(\frac{1 - 1.08^{-25}}{0.08} \right) = \$10,674.78$$

    Therefore, only

    $$\frac{\$12,500 - \$10,674.78}{\$10,674.78} \times 100\% = \underline{17.10\%}$$

    more funds are needed to fund the perpetuity.

2. The fair market value of a share is the present value of future dividends discounted at the rate of return required by the market. On a date just after a dividend is paid, the dividends form an ordinary simple perpetuity.

    a. $A = \frac{R}{p} = \frac{\$1.25}{0.02} = \underline{\$62.50}$

    The fair market value is $62.50 per share.

    b. $A = \frac{\$1.25}{0.0225} = \underline{\$55.56}$

    The fair market value is $55.56 per share.

3. The required amount is the present value of the deferred annuity. With R = $500, n = 5(12) = 60, d = 48, and p = i = $\frac{7.2\%}{12}$ = 0.6%,

    $$A_n \text{ (def)} = \$500 \left[\frac{1 - 1.006^{-60}}{0.006 \,(1.006)^{48}} \right] = \underline{\$18,858.53}$$

    Therefore, $18,858.53 invested now will provide the desired payments.

4. The finance company will pay the present value of the payments discounted at its required rate of return. The payments form a deferred annuity having R = $249, n = 12, d = 5, and p = i = $\frac{16.5\%}{12}$ = 1.375%. Its present value is

    $$A_n \text{ (def)} = \$249 \left[\frac{1 - 1.01375^{-12}}{0.01375 \,(1.01375)^{5}} \right] = \underline{\$2556.57}$$

    The finance company will pay $2556.57 for the contract.

5. The amount required to fund any of the cash flow streams equals today's present value of the payment stream.

    a. The payments form a simple perpetuity due.

    $$A \text{ (due)} = \frac{R}{p} (1 + p) = \frac{\$2000}{0.02} (1.02) = \underline{\$102,000}$$

Review Problems (*continued*)

b. The payments form a deferred simple perpetuity. The present value today equals the present value, one year earlier, of the part a result. This amount is

$$P = \frac{S}{(1 + i)^n} = \frac{\$102{,}000}{1.02^4} = \underline{\$94{,}232.23}$$

c. The present value today equals the present value, 5 years earlier, of the part a result. That is,

$$P = \frac{\$102{,}000}{1.02^{20}} = \underline{\$68{,}643.08}$$

6. The fair market value of a share is the present value of future dividends discounted at the market's required rate of return. The present value, 5 years from now, of annual dividends of $2 in perpetuity is

$$A = \frac{R}{p} = \frac{\$2.00}{0.14} = \$14.286$$

Today's combined present value of the preceding amount and five annual dividends of $3.00 is

$$\frac{\$14.286}{1.14^5} + \$3.00 \left(\frac{1 - 1.14^{-5}}{0.14} \right) = \underline{\$17.72}$$

The fair market value of a share is $17.72.

7. With the focal date set at the date of the first scholarship payment,
   (Future value of the donations) = (Present value of the annual scholarships).
   Viewed from the focal date, the scholarships form a general perpetuity due having R = $3000,
   $i = \frac{7.8\%}{12} = 0.65\%$, c = 12, and $p = (1 + i)^c - 1 = 1.0065^{12} - 1 = 0.0808498$. Then

$$A \text{ (due)} = \frac{R}{p} (1 + p) = \frac{\$3000}{0.0808498} (1.0808498) = \$40{,}105.84$$

The number of months required for $27,830 to grow to $40,105.84 it

$$n = \frac{\ln\left(\dfrac{S}{P} \right)}{\ln (1 + i)} = \frac{\ln\left(\dfrac{\$40{,}105.84}{\$27{,}830} \right)}{\ln (1.0065)} = 56.40$$

The funds must be invested for 57 months or <u>4 years and 9 months</u> before the first scholarship can be paid out.

8. With a focal date at age 65,
   (Future value of amount in RRSP) = (Present value of the annuity)
   The left side of the equation is
   $S = P (1 + i)^n = \$195{,}000 (1.007)^{108} = \$414{,}207.00$

   Then the retirement annuity has $A_n = \$414{,}207.00$, n = 240, and $p = i = \frac{7.2\%}{12} = 0.6\%$. The size of each payment is the value of R in

$$\$414{,}207.00 = R \left[\frac{1 - 1.006^{-240}}{0.006} \right]$$

$$R = \underline{\$3261.26}$$

Review Problems (*continued*)

9. With a focal date 3 years from today

(Future value of $30,000) = (Present value of quarterly withdrawals)

The left side of the equation is

$$S = P(1 + i)^n = \$30,000 \, (1.0175)^{12} = \$36,943.18$$

For the simple annuity due on the right side of the equation, A_n (due) = $36,943.18, $p = i = 1.75\%$, and $R = \$2000$. Then the number of payments is

$$n = -\frac{ln\left[1 - \dfrac{0.0175 \, (\$35,943.18)}{\$2000 \, (1.0175)}\right]}{ln \, (1.0175)} = 22.035$$

There can be <u>23 withdrawals</u> (with the last one being only about 0.035 x $2000 = $70).

10. With the focal date set at the date of the first payment,

(Future value of original principal) = (Present value of loan payments)

The amount on the right side is

$$A_n(\text{due}) = \$425.10 \left[\frac{1 - 1.0075^{-120}}{0.0075}\right](1.0075) = \$33,809.80$$

On the left side of the equation, we have S = $33,809.80, P = $30,000, and $i = 0.75\%$. Then the number of compounding intervals is

$$n = \frac{ln\left(\dfrac{S}{P}\right)}{ln \, (1 + i)} = \frac{ln\left(\dfrac{\$33,809.80}{\$30,000}\right)}{ln \, (1.0075)} = 16.00$$

Therefore, the time interval between the date of the loan and the first payment was <u>16 months</u>.

11. The amount required to fund each payment stream is the present value of the payment stream. For each payment stream, R = $500, $i = 1.75\%$, $c = \dfrac{4}{12} = 0.\overline{3}$, and $p = 1.0175^{0.\overline{3}} - 1 = 0.005799633$. For the perpetuity due,

$$A \, (\text{due}) = \frac{\$500}{0.005799633} \, (1.005799633) = \$86,712.36$$

For the annuity due,

$$A_n(\text{due}) = \$500 \left(\frac{1 - 1.005799633^{-300}}{0.005799633}\right) 1.005799633$$

$$= \$71,414.20$$

Hence,

$$\$86,712.36 - \$71,414.20 = \underline{\$15,298.16}$$

more is required to fund the perpetuity.

Review Problems (*continued*)

12. The current economic value equals today's present value of the future payments. The payments form a deferred general annuity having R = $2500, n = 4(20) = 80, d = 20, $i = \frac{6\%}{12} = 0.5\%$, $c = \frac{12}{4} = 3$, and p = $1.005^3 - 1 = 0.015075125$.

Then

$$A_n \text{ (def)} = \$2500 \left[\frac{1 - 1.015075125^{-80}}{0.015075125 \, (1.015075125)^{20}} \right] = \underline{\$85,804.68}$$

The current economic value of the inheritance is $85,804.68.

13. The present value of the payments will be 0.9 ($1450) = $1305. The payments form a deferred general annuity with A_n(def) = $1305, n = 12, d = 5, $i = 6.5\%$, $c = 0.1\overline{6}$ and p = $(1 + i)^c - 1 = 1.065^{0.1\overline{6}} - 1 = 0.010551074$. Solve for R in

$$\$1305 = R \left[\frac{1 - 1.010551074^{-12}}{0.010551074 \, (1.010551074)^5} \right]$$

$$R = \underline{\$122.62}$$

The monthly payment will be $122.62.

14. The purchase price of the annuity equals the present value of the annuity. The payments form a deferred general annuity having A_n(def) = $120,000, n = 50, d = 16, $i = 7.25\%$, $c = \frac{1}{2} = 0.5$, and

$$p = (1 + i)^c - 1 = 1.0725^{0.5} - 1 = 0.03561576$$

Solve for R in

$$\$120,000 = R \left[\frac{1 - 1.03561576^{-50}}{0.03561576 \, (1.03561576)^{16}} \right]$$

$$R = \underline{\$9055.67}$$

The annuity payments will be $9055.67.

15. With the focal date at 5 years from now,
  (Future value of RRSP) − (Present value of annuity)
  The amount on the left side is
  S = P $(1 + i)^n$ = $188,000 $(1.08)^5$ = $276,233.68
  Then the annuity has A_n = $276,233.68, R = $6000, $i = \frac{7.5\%}{12} = 0.625\%$, $c = \frac{12}{4} = 3$, and
  p = $(1 + i)^c - 1 = 1.00625^3 - 1 = 0.01886743$
  The number of quarterly payments is

$$n = - \frac{ln \left[1 - \dfrac{0.01886743 \, (\$276,233.68)}{\$6000} \right]}{ln \, (1.01886743)} = 108.59$$

The term of the annuity will be 109 quarters or <u>27 years and 3 months</u>.

Review Problems (*concluded*)

16. a. The extra make-up payment will be the future value, at the end of the 36th month, of (missed) payments 33, 34, and 35.

Step 1: Calculate the size of the monthly payment where $A_n = \$30,000$, $n = 120$, and $p = i = 0.875\%$. Solve for R in

$$\$30,000 = R \left[\frac{1 - 1.00875^{-120}}{0.00875} \right]$$

$$R = \$404.80$$

Step 2: Calculate the future value, at the end of the 36th month, of scheduled payments 33, 34, and 35.

$$S_n \text{ (due)} = \$404.80 \left[\frac{1.00875^3 - 1}{0.00875} \right] (1.00875) = \underline{\underline{\$1235.78}}$$

Therefore, $1235.78 paid along with the 36th payment will replace the missed payments.

b. We must recalculate the payments so that the present value of $120 - 35 = 85$ payments equals the balance owed after 35 months.

Step 1: Calculate the balance after 32 payments.

$$\$30,000 = \$404.80 \left[\frac{1 - 1.00875^{-32}}{0.00875} \right] + \frac{Balance}{1.00875^{32}}$$

Balance = $24,771.18

Step 2: Calculate the balance after 35 months. This will be the future value, 3 months later, of the step 1 result.

$$S = \$24,771.18 \, (1.00875)^3 = \$25,427.13$$

Step 3: Calculate the new monthly payment such that
$A_n = \$25,417.13$ with $n = 85$ and $p = i = 0.875\%$

$$\$25,427.13 = R \left(\frac{1 - 1.00875^{-85}}{0.00875} \right)$$

$$R = \underline{\underline{\$425.30}}$$

The new monthly payment will be $425.30.

Self-Test Exercise

1. With the focal date at the date of the first perpetuity payment,
   (Future value of $50,000 donation) = (Present value of payments)
   The amount on the left side of the equation is
   $$S = P (1 + i)^n = \$50,000 (1.0375)^{10} = \$72,252.20$$
   For the perpetuity on the right side,
   A (due) = $72,252.20 and $p = i = 3.75\%$
   Solve for R in

   $$\$72,252.20 = \frac{R}{0.0375} (1.0375)$$

   $$R = \$2611.53$$

   The semiannual payments in perpetuity will be $2611.53.

2. The amount required to fund the perpetuity is today's present value of the deferred perpetuity. The present value, 2 years from now, of the annual scholarships is

   $$A \text{ (due)} = \frac{R}{p} (1 + p) = \frac{\$5000}{0.0825} (1.0825) = \$65,606.06$$

   The present value of this amount 2 years earlier is

   $$P = \frac{S}{(1 + i)^n} = \frac{\$65,606.06}{1.0825^2} = \$55,987.12$$

   Mrs. McTavish must pay $55,987.12 to establish the perpetual scholarship fund.

3. The monthly payments form a general perpetuity due having A (due) = $200,000, $i = \frac{7.5\%}{12} = 3.75\%$, $c = \frac{2}{12} = 0.1\overline{6}$ and

   $$p = (1 + i)^c - 1 = 1.0375^{0.1\overline{6}} - 1 = 0.006154524$$
   The size of each payment is the value of R in

   $$\$200,000 = \frac{R}{0.006154524} (1.006154524)$$

   $$R = \$1223.38$$

   Each monthly payment will be $1223.38.

4. a. The nominal amount required in her RRSP will be the future value of $300,000 compounded at the rate of inflation. That is, she will require
   $$S = P (1 + i)^n = \$300,000 (1.04)^{30} = \$973,019.25.$$

   b. The future value, 30 years from now, of all her RRSP contributions is to be $973,019.25. The amount in her RRSP 5 years from now will be

   $$S_n = \$3000 \left(\frac{1.08^5 - 1}{0.08} \right) = \$17,599.80$$

Self-Test Exercise (continued)

The combined future value, 30 years from now, of the preceding amount and the subsequent 25 years' contributions must be $973,019.25. Therefore,

$$\$17{,}599.80\,(1.08)^{25} + R\left(\frac{1.08^{25}-1}{0.08}\right) = \$973{,}019.25$$

Solving for R gives R = $11,660.99.

Jeanette's year-end contributions for the subsequent 25 years must be $11,660.99.

c. The purchase price of the annuity equals the present value of the annuity payments. With A_n = $973,019.25, n = 12(30) = 360, and $p = i = \dfrac{8.25\%}{12} = 0.6875\%$, we have

$$\$973{,}019.25 = R\left(\frac{1 - 1.006875^{-360}}{0.006875}\right)$$

$$R = \$7309.97$$

The monthly annuity payments will be $7309.97.

5. The amount required to fund each payment stream is the present value of the payments. For the perpetuity due,

$$A\,(\text{due}) = \frac{R}{p}(1 + p) = \frac{\$1000}{0.035}\,(1.035) = \$29{,}571.43$$

For the 30-year annuity due,

$$A_n(\text{due}) = \$1000\left(\frac{1 - 1.035^{-60}}{0.035}\right)(1.035) = \$25{,}817.80$$

Therefore,

$$\frac{\$29{,}571.43 - \$25{,}817.80}{\$25{,}817.80} \times 100\% = 14.54\%$$

more money is required to fund the perpetuity due than the 30-year annuity due.

6. The selling price (original loan) equals the present value of the payments. The payments form a deferred simple annuity having R = $226.51, n = 12, d = 3, and $p = i = \dfrac{16.5\%}{12} = 1.375\%$. Then

$$A_n(\text{def}) = \$226.51\left[\frac{1 - 1.01375^{-12}}{0.01375\,(1.01375)^3}\right] = \$2390.05$$

The selling price of the stereo system was $2390.05.

7. The original loan equals the present value of the loan payments. Viewed from the date of the loan, the payments form a deferred simple annuity having $A_n(\text{def})$ = $3,500,000, R = $40,000, $p = i = 0.75\%$, and d = 23. The number of payments will be

$$n = -\frac{\ln\left[1 - \dfrac{0.0075\,(1.0075)^{23}\,\$3{,}500{,}000}{\$40{,}000}\right]}{\ln(1.0075)} = 202.22$$

To extinguish the loan, 203 monthly payments will be required. Measured from the date of the first payment, this will take 202 months or 16 years and 10 months.

Self-Test Exercise *(continued)*

8. Viewed from the date each trust is set up, the payments each child will receive constitute a deferred general annuity whose present value is $20,000. That is, $A_n(def) = \$20,000$, $n = 4(15) = 60$, $i = \dfrac{9.25\%}{2}$ $= 4.625\%$, $c = \dfrac{2}{4} = 0.5$ and

$$p = (1 + i)^c - 1 = 1.04625^{0.5} - 1 = 0.02286363$$

Lena will receive her first payment in 5 years. The period of deferral is 4.75 years and $d = 19$. Her quarterly payments will be the value of R in

$$\$20,000 = R \left[\frac{1 - 1.02286363^{-60}}{0.02286363\ (1.02286363)^{19}} \right]$$

$$R = \underline{\underline{\$946.39}}$$

Axel will receive his first payment in 9.5 years. The period of deferral is 9.25 years and $d = 37$. His quarterly payment will be the solution to

$$\$20,000 = R \left[\frac{1 - 1.02286363^{-60}}{0.02286363\ (1.02286363)^{37}} \right]$$

$$R = \underline{\underline{\$1421.64}}$$

Lena will receive quarterly payments of $946.39 and Axel will receive quarterly payments of $1421.64.

9. Our strategy will be to determine how much is left in Martha's RRSP at age 70. This amount will also be the present value of the (unknown) payments in the third annuity.

   Step 1: Calculate the amount in the RRSP at age 60. With $R = \$5000$, $n = 24$, $i = 8\%$, $c = 0.5$ and $p = 1.08^{0.5} - 1 = 0.039230485$, the combined future value of the initial $97,000 and the subsequent contributions will be

$$\$97,000\ (1.039230485)^{24} + \$5000 \left[\frac{1.039230485^{24} - 1}{0.039230485} \right] 1.039230485$$

$$= \$244,262.50 + \$201,084.53$$
$$= \$445,347.03$$

   Step 2: Calculate the amount in the RRSP at age 65 (just before the purchase of the second annuity). This will be the future value, after a further 5 years, of half the step 1 result. That is,

$$S = \$222,673.51\ (1.08)^5 = \$327,180.44$$

   Step 3: Calculate the amount available at age 70 to purchase the third annuity. This will be the future value, after a further 5 years, of half the step 2 result. That is,

$$S = \$163,590.22\ (1.08)^5 = \$240,367.70$$

   Step 4: Calculate the payments in the first annuity purchased for $222,673.52. Solve for R_1 in

$$\$222,673.52 = R_1 \left(\frac{1 - 1.00625^{-240}}{0.00625} \right)$$

$$R_1 = \$1793.84$$

Step 5: Calculate the payments in the second annuity purchased for $163,590.22. Solve for R_2 in

$$\$163{,}590.22 = R_2 \left(\frac{1 - 1.00625^{-240}}{0.00625} \right)$$

$$R_2 = \$1317.87$$

Step 6: Calculate the payments in the third annuity purchased for $240,367.70. Solve for R_3 in

$$\$240{,}367.70 = R_3 \left(\frac{1 - 1.00625^{-240}}{0.00625} \right)$$

$$R_3 = \$1936.39$$

Step 7: Calculate the total monthly incomes at ages 67 and 72.
Monthly income at age 67 = $R_1 + R_2$ = $\underline{\$3111.71}$.
Monthly income at age 72 = $R_1 + R_2 + R_3$ = $\underline{\$5048.10}$.

14 Amortization of Loans

Changes in the Second Edition:

1. The Retrospective Method for calculating the balance owed on a blended payment loan is introduced earlier, and is routinely used in preference to the Prospective Method because of the latter method's imprecision when periodic payments are rounded to the nearest cent.
   In the sections on mortgage loans:
2. Figures 14.3 (changing composition of mortgage payments over the amortization period) and 14.4 (declining mortgage balance over the amortization period) are new.
3. The determination of the amount of a mortgage loan for which an applicant can qualify is a new topic.
4. The coverage of mortgage prepayment privileges and prepayment penalties is expanded.

Exercise 14.1

Note: The solutions to problems 1 to 6 inclusive all involve the same steps. A detailed solution is given below for only problem 1. Solution outlines are presented for problems 2 to 6.

1. Given: $A_n = \$12,000$, $n = 4(3) = 12$, $p = i = \dfrac{10.5\%}{4} = 2.625\%$

Solve for R in $\quad \$12,000 = R\left(\dfrac{1 - 1.02625^{-12}}{0.02625}\right)$

$$R = \$1178.72$$

Principal portion of the fifth payment (R_5)
= Balance after payment 4 − Balance after payment 5

$$= \left[\$12,000\ (1.02625)^4 - \$1178.72\left(\dfrac{1.02625^4 - 1}{0.02625}\right)\right]$$

$$- \left[\$12,000\ (1.02625)^5 - \$1178.72\left(\dfrac{1.02625^5 - 1}{0.02625}\right)\right]$$

$$= \$8406.69 - \$7448.64$$
$$= \underline{\underline{\$958.05}}$$

Interest portion of the ninth payment (R_9)
= p x Balance after payment 8

$$= 0.02625\left[\$12,000\ (1.02625)^8 - \$1178.72\left(\dfrac{1.02625^8 - 1}{0.02625}\right)\right]$$

$$= \underline{\underline{\$116.05}}$$

2. Given: $A_n = \$40,000$, $n = 12(8) = 96$, $p = i = \dfrac{11\%}{12} = 0.91\overline{6}\%$

Solve for R in

$$\$40,000 = R\left(\dfrac{1 - 1.0091\overline{6}^{-96}}{0.0091\overline{6}}\right)$$

$$R = \$628.34$$

Principal in R_{75} = Balance after R_{74} − Balance after R_{75}
$\qquad\qquad\quad = \$12,466.90 - \$11,952.84$
$\qquad\qquad\quad = \underline{\underline{\$514.06}}$

Interest in R_{43} = p x Balance after R_{42}
$\qquad\qquad\quad = 0.0091\overline{6}\ (\$26,667.82)$
$\qquad\qquad\quad = \underline{\underline{\$244.46}}$

3. Given: $A_n = \$14,000$, $n = 2(6) = 12$, $p = i = \dfrac{12.5\%}{2} = 6.25\%$

Solve for R in

$$\$14,000 = R\left(\dfrac{1 - 1.0625^{-12}}{0.0625}\right)$$

$$R = \$1692.84$$

Principal in R_8 = Balance after R_7 – Balance after R_8
= \$7082.64 – \$5832.46
= \$1250.18

Interest in $R_{10'}$ = p x Balance after R_9
= 0.0625 (\$4504.15)
= \$281.51

4. Given: A_n = \$25,000, n = 4(5) = 20, $p = i = \dfrac{11\%}{4}$ = 2.75%

Solve for R in

$$\$25,000 = R \left(\frac{1 - 1.0275^{-20}}{0.0275} \right)$$

$$R = \$1641.79$$

Principal in R_{15} = Balance after R_{14} – Balance after R_{15}
= \$8968.13 – \$7572.97
= \$1395.16

Interest in R_6 = p x Balance after R_5
= 0.0275 (\$19,958.80)
= \$548.87

5. Given: A_n = \$45,000, n = 12(15) = 180, $p = i = \dfrac{9.75\%}{12}$ = 0.8125%

Solve for R in

$$\$45,000 = R \left(\frac{1 - 1.008125^{-180}}{0.008125} \right)$$

$$R = \$476.71$$

Principal in R_{117} = Balance after R_{116} – Balance after R_{117}
= \$23,717.69 – \$23,433.69
= \$284.00

Interest in R_{149} = p x Balance after R_{148}
= 0.008125 (\$13,386.31)
= \$108.76

6. Given: A_n = \$30,000, n = 12(10) = 120, $p = i = \dfrac{12\%}{12}$ = 1%

Solve for R in

$$\$30,000 = R \left(\frac{1 - 1.01^{-120}}{0.01} \right)$$

$$R = \$430.41$$

Principal in R_{99} = Balance after R_{98} – Balance after R_{99}
= \$8462.55 – \$8116.77
= \$345.78

Exercise 14.1 (continued)

Interest in R_{41} = p × Balance after R_{40}
  = 0.01 ($23,624.73)
  = $236.25

Note: The steps in the solutions to problems 7 to 14 inclusive are the same as in problems 1 to 6 except for the additional step of calculating p since p ≠ *i*.

7. Given: A_n = $7000, n = 10, $i = \frac{10\%}{2} = 5\%$, $c = \frac{2}{1} = 2$

$$p = (1 + i)^c - 1 = 1.05^2 - 1 = 0.1025$$

Solve for R in

$$\$7000 = R \left(\frac{1 - 1.1025^{-10}}{0.1025} \right)$$

$$R = \$1151.48$$

Principal in R_7 = Balance after R_6 – Balance after R_7
  = $3630.38 – $2851.02
  = $779.36

Interest in R_4 = p × Balance after R_3
  = 0.1025 ($5560.05)
  = $569.91

8. Given: A_n = $9000, n = 8, $i = \frac{11\%}{12} = 0.91\overline{6}$, $c = \frac{12}{1} = 12$

$$p = (1 + i)^c - 1 = 1.009\overline{16}^{12} - 1 = 0.11571884$$

Solve for R in

$$\$9000 = R \left(\frac{1 - 1.11571884^{-8}}{0.11571884} \right)$$

$$R = \$1784.71$$

Principal in R_4 = Balance after R_3 – Balance after R_4
  = $6502.31 – $5470.03
  = $1032.28

Interest in R_7 = p × Balance after R_6
  = 0.11571884 ($3033.31)
  = $351.01

9. Given: A_n = $10,000, n = 2(7) = 14, i = 9.5%, $c = \frac{1}{2} = 0.5$

$$p = (1 + i)^c - 1 = 1.095^{0.5} - 1 = 0.04642248$$

Solve for R in

$$\$10,000 = R \left(\frac{1 - 1.04642248^{-14}}{0.04642248} \right)$$

$$R = \$987.26$$

Exercise 14.1 *(continued)*

Principal in R_6 = Balance after R_5 – Balance after R_6
$$= \$7130.48 - \$6474.24$$
$$= \underline{\underline{\$656.24}}$$

Interest in R_{10} = p x Balance after R_9
$$= 0.04642248\ (\$4316.99)$$
$$= \underline{\underline{\$200.41}}$$

10. Given: $A_n = \$25{,}000$, n = 12(5) = 60, $i = 10.25\%$, $c = \dfrac{1}{12} = 0.08\overline{3}$

$p = (1 + i)^c - 1 = 1.1025^{0.08\overline{3}} - 1 = 0.008164846$
Solve for R in
$$\$25{,}000 = R\left(\frac{1 - 1.008164846^{-60}}{0.008164846}\right)$$

$$R = \underline{\underline{\$528.69}}$$

Principal in R_{38} = Balance after R_{37} – Balance after R_{38}
$$= \$11{,}045.57 - \$10{,}607.06$$
$$= \underline{\underline{\$438.51}}$$

Interest in R_4 = p x Balance after R_3
$$= 0.008164846\ (\$24{,}018.32)$$
$$= \underline{\underline{\$196.11}}$$

11. Given: $A_n = \$70{,}000$, n = 4(12) = 48, $i = \dfrac{10.75\%}{2} = 5.375\%$, $c = \dfrac{2}{4} = 0.5$

$p = (1 + i)^c - 1 = 1.05375^{0.5} - 1 = 0.026523258$
Solve for R in
$$\$70{,}000 = R\left(\frac{1 - 1.026523258^{-48}}{0.026523258}\right)$$

$$R = \underline{\underline{\$2595.38}}$$

Principal in R_{11} = Balance after R_{10} – Balance after R_{11}
$$= \$61{,}665.39 - \$60{,}705.58$$
$$= \underline{\underline{\$959.81}}$$

Interest in R_{30} = p x Balance after R_{29}
$$= 0.026523258\ (\$38{,}346.16)$$
$$= \underline{\underline{\$1017.07}}$$

12. Given: $A_n = \$4000$, n = 24, $i = \dfrac{13\%}{4} = 3.25\%$, $c = \dfrac{4}{12} = 0.\overline{3}$

$p = (1 + i)^c - 1 = 1.0325^{0.\overline{3}} - 1 = 0.010718046$
Solve for R in
$$\$4000 = R\left(\frac{1 - 1.010718046^{-24}}{0.010718046}\right)$$

$$R = \underline{\underline{\$189.91}}$$

Principal in R_{21} = Balance after R_{20} – Balance after R_{21}
$$= \$739.65 - \$557.67$$
$$= \underline{\underline{\$181.98}}$$

$$\begin{aligned}\text{Interest in } R_{13} &= p \times \text{Balance after } R_{12} \\ &= 0.010718046\ (\$2127.73) \\ &= \underline{\$22.81}\end{aligned}$$

13. Given: $A_n = \$45{,}000$, $n = 12(15) = 180$, $i = 5.25\%$, $c = \dfrac{2}{12} = 0.1\overline{6}$

$$p = 1.0525^{0.1\overline{6}} - 1 = 0.0085645151$$

Solve for R in

$$\$45{,}000 = R\left(\frac{1 - 1.0085645151^{-180}}{0.0085645151}\right)$$

$$R = \$491.24$$

$$\begin{aligned}\text{Principal in } R_{117} &= \text{Balance after } R_{116} - \text{Balance after } R_{117} \\ &= \$24{,}125.22 - \$23{,}840.60 \\ &= \underline{\$284.62}\end{aligned}$$

$$\begin{aligned}\text{Interest in } R_{149} &= p \times \text{Balance after } R_{148} \\ &= 0.0085645151\ (\$13{,}698.05) \\ &= \underline{\$117.32}\end{aligned}$$

14. Given: $A_n = \$30{,}000$, $n = 2(10) = 20$, $i = \dfrac{12\%}{4} = 3\%$, $c = \dfrac{4}{2} = 2$

$$p = 1.03^2 - 1 = 0.0609$$

Solve for R in

$$\$30{,}000 = R\left(\frac{1 - 1.0609^{-20}}{0.0609}\right)$$

$$R = \$2634.68$$

$$\begin{aligned}\text{Principal in } R_{19} &= \text{Balance after } R_{18} - \text{Balance after } R_{19} \\ &= \$4824.28 - \$2483.40 \\ &= \underline{\$2340.88}\end{aligned}$$

$$\begin{aligned}\text{Interest in } R_9 &= p \times \text{Balance after } R_8 \\ &= 0.0609\ (\$21{,}980.14) \\ &= \underline{\$1338.59}\end{aligned}$$

15. Given: $A_n = \$14{,}000$, $n = 2(6) = 12$, $p = i = \dfrac{12.5\%}{2} = 6.25\%$

Solve for R in

$$\$14{,}000 = R\left(\frac{1 - 1.0625^{-12}}{0.0625}\right)$$

$$R = \underline{\$1692.84}$$

Principal paid in year 2
= Balance after year 1 − Balance after year 2
= Balance after R_2 − Balance after R_4
= $12,313.20 − $10,408.97
= $\underline{\$1904.23}$

Interest paid in year 5
    = Total payments in year 5 – Principal paid in year 5
    = 2R – (Balance after year 4 – Balance after year 5)
    = 2 ($1692.84) – (Balance after R_8 – Balance after R_{10})
    = 2 ($1692.84) – ($5832.46 – $3092.82)
    = $\underline{\$646.04}$

16. Given: $A_n = \$25,000$, $n = 4(5) = 20$, $p = i = \dfrac{11\%}{4} = 2.75\%$

    Solve for R in
    $$\$25,000 = R\left(\frac{1 - 1.0275^{-20}}{0.0275}\right)$$
        R = $1641.79

    Principal paid in year 4 = Balance after R_{12} – Balance after R_{16}
                = $11,647.44 – $6139.43
                = $\underline{\$5508.01}$

    Interest paid in year 2 = 4R – Principal paid in year 2
                = 4R – (Balance after R_4 – Balance after R_8)
                = 4 ($1641.79) – ($21,022.48 – $16,589.04)
                = $\underline{\$2133.72}$

17. Given: $A_n = \$45,000$, $n = 12(15) = 180$, $p = i = \dfrac{9.75\%}{12} = 0.8125\%$

    Solve for R in
    $$\$45,000 = R\left(\frac{1 - 1.008125^{-180}}{0.008125}\right)$$
        R = $\underline{\$476.71}$

    Principal paid in year 11 = Balance after R_{120} – Balance after R_{132}
                = $22,567.76 – $18,885.95
                = $\underline{\$3681.81}$

    Interest paid in year 6 = 12R – (Balance after R_{60} – Balance after R_{72})
                = 12 ($476.71) – ($36,454.50 – $34,188.82)
                = $\underline{\$3454.84}$

18. Given: $A_n = \$30,000$, $n = 12(10) = 120$, $p = i = \dfrac{12\%}{12} = 1\%$

    Solve for R in
    $$\$30,000 = R\left(\frac{1 - 1.01^{-120}}{0.01}\right)$$
        R = $430.41

    Principal paid in year 3 = Balance after R_{24} – Balance after R_{36}
                = $26,482.39 – $24,382.34
                = $\underline{\$2100.05}$

Interest paid in year 8 = $12R$ – (Balance after R_{84} – Balance after R_{96})

= 12 ($430.41) – ($12,959.03 – $9143.88)

= $\underline{\underline{\$1349.77}}$

19. Given: A_n = $25,000, n = 12(5) = 60, i = 10.25%, $c = \dfrac{1}{12} = 0.08\overline{3}$

$p = 1.1025^{0.08\overline{3}} – 1 = 0.81648460\%$

Solve for R in

$\$25,000 = R\left(\dfrac{1 – 1.008164846^{-60}}{0.008164846}\right)$

$R = \underline{\underline{\$528.69}}$

Principal paid in year 2 = Balance after R_{12} – Balance after R_{24}

= $20,925.42 – $16,433.20

= $\underline{\underline{\$4492.22}}$

Interest paid in year 4 = $12R$ – (Balance after R_{36} – Balance after R_{48})

= 12 ($528.69) – ($11,480.52 – $6020.20)

= $\underline{\underline{\$883.96}}$

20. Given: A_n = $70,000, n = 4(12) = 48, i = 5.375%, $c = \dfrac{2}{4} = 0.5$

$p = 1.05375^{0.5} – 1 = 0.026523258$

Solve for R in

$\$70,000 = R\left(\dfrac{1 – 1.026523258^{-48}}{0.026523258}\right)$

$R = \$2595.38$

Principal paid in year 9 = Balance after R_{32} – Balance after R_{36}

= $33,484.52 – $26,378.95

= $\underline{\underline{\$7105.57}}$

Interest paid in year 4 = $4R$ – (Balance after R_{12} – Balance after R_{16})

= 4 ($2595.38) – ($59,720.31 – $55,510.88)

= $\underline{\underline{\$6172.09}}$

21. Given: A_n = $4000, n = 12(7) = 84, $i = \dfrac{13\%}{4} = 3.25\%, c = \dfrac{4}{12} = 0.\overline{3}$

$p = 1.0325^{0.\overline{3}} – 1 = 0.010718046$

Solve for R in

$\$4000 = R\left(\dfrac{1 – 1.010718046^{-84}}{0.010718046}\right)$

$R = \$72.47$

Principal paid in year 6 = Balance after R_{60} – Balance after R_{72}

= $1526.15 – $811.65

= $\underline{\underline{\$714.50}}$

Interest paid in year 3 = $12R$ – (Balance after R_{24} – Balance after R_{36})

= 12 ($72.47) – ($3194.81 – $2708.04)

= $\underline{\underline{\$382.87}}$

Exercise 14.1 *(continued)*

22. Given $A_n = \$45,000$, $n = 12(15) = 180$, $i = \dfrac{10.5\%}{2} = 5.25\%$, $c = \dfrac{2}{12} = 0.1\overline{6}$

$p = 1.0525^{0.1\overline{6}} - 1 = 0.0085645151$

Solve for R in

$$\$45,000 = R\left(\dfrac{1 - 1.0085645151^{-180}}{0.0085645151}\right)$$

$R = \$491.24$

Principal paid in year 5 = Balance after R_{48} − Balance after R_{60}
$= \$38,749.12 - \$36,743.94$
$= \underline{\$2005.18}$

Interest paid in year 10 = $12R$ − (Balance after R_{108} − Balance after R_{120})
$= 12\,(\$491.24) - (\$26,316.87 - \$22,972.04)$
$= \underline{\$2550.05}$

23. Given: $A_n = \$37,000$, $p = i = \dfrac{10.8\%}{2} = 5.4\%$, $n = 2(10) = 20$

Solve for R in

$$\$37,000 = R\left(\dfrac{1 - 1.054^{-20}}{0.054}\right)$$

$R = \$3070.50$

a. Principal in R_6 = Balance after R_5 − Balance after R_6
$= \$31,026.22 - \$29,631.14$
$- \underline{\$1395.08}$

b. Interest in R_{16} = $p \times$ Balance after R_{15}
$= 0.054\,(\$13,147.90)$
$= \underline{\$709.99}$

c. Principal paid by R_6 to R_{15} inclusive
$= $ Balance after R_5 − Balance after R_{15}
$= \$31,026.22 - \$13,147.90$
$= \underline{\$17,878.32}$

d. Interest paid in year 3 = $2R$ − (Balance after R_4 − Balance after R_6)
$= 2\,(\$3070.50) - (\$32,349.83 - \$29,631.14)$
$= \underline{\underline{\$3422.31}}$

24. Given: $A_n = \$25,000$, $p = i = \dfrac{8\%}{4} = 2\%$, $n = 4(10) = 40$

Solve for R in

$$\$25,000 = R\left(\dfrac{1 - 1.02^{-40}}{0.02}\right)$$

$R = \$913.89$

a. Interest in R_{25} = $p \times$ Balance after R_{24}
$= 0.02\,(\$12,408.70)$
$= \underline{\$248.17}$

b. Principal in R_{13} = Balance after R_{12} – Balance after R_{13}
$$= \$19{,}448.87 - \$18{,}923.96$$
$$= \underline{\underline{\$524.91}}$$

c. Interest paid by R_{11} to R_{20} inclusive
$$= 10R - (\text{Balance after } R_{10} - \text{Balance after } R_{20})$$
$$= 10\ (\$913.89) - (\$20{,}468.02 - \$14{,}943.56)$$
$$= \underline{\underline{\$3614.44}}$$

d. Principal paid in year 2 = Balance after R_4 – Balance after R_8
$$= \$23{,}294.11 - \$21{,}447.59$$
$$= \underline{\underline{\$1846.52}}$$

25. Given: $A_n = \$6000$, $i = \dfrac{12.75\%}{12} = 1.0625\%$, n = 4(4) = 16, $c = \dfrac{12}{4} = 3$

$p = 1.010625^3 - 1 = 0.032214871$
Solve for R in
$$\$6000 = R\left(\frac{1 - 1.032214871^{-16}}{0.032214871}\right)$$

$$R = \underline{\underline{\$485.79}}$$

a. Interest in R_5 = p x Balance after R_4
$$= 0.032214871\ (\$4772.24)$$
$$= \underline{\underline{\$153.74}}$$

b. Principal in R_{11} = Balance after R_{10} – Balance after R_{11}
$$= \$2612.40 - \$2210.77$$
$$= \underline{\underline{\$401.63}}$$

c. Interest paid by R_5 to R_{12} inclusive
$$= 8R - (\text{Balance after } R_4 - \text{Balance after } R_{12})$$
$$= 8\ (\$485.79) - (\$4772.24 - \$1796.20)$$
$$= \underline{\underline{\$910.28}}$$

d. Principal paid in year 2 = Balance after R_4 – Balance after R_8
$$= \$4772.24 - \$3378.45$$
$$= \underline{\underline{\$1393.79}}$$

26. Given: $A_n = \$225{,}000$, $i = \dfrac{9.5\%}{2} = 4.75\%$, n = 12(25) = 300, $c = \dfrac{2}{12} = 0.1\bar{6}$

$p = 1.0475^{0.1\bar{6}} - 1 = 0.00776438315$
Solve for R in
$$\$225{,}000 = R\left(\frac{1 - 1.00776438315^{-300}}{0.00776438315}\right)$$

$$R = \underline{\underline{\$1937.31}}$$

a. Principal in R_{206} = Balance after R_{205} – Balance after R_{206}
$$= \$129{,}843.27 - \$128{,}914.11$$
$$= \underline{\underline{\$929.16}}$$

Exercise 14.1 (continued)

b. Interest in R_{187} = p x Balance after R_{186}
$$= 0.00776438315 \ (\$146,197.96)$$
$$= \underline{\$1135.14}$$

c. Principal paid by R_{50} to R_{100} inclusive
$$- \text{Balance after } R_{49} - \text{Balance after } R_{100}$$
$$= \$213,704.64 - \$196,388.92$$
$$= \underline{\$17,315.72}$$

d. Interest paid in year 14 = 12R – (Balance after R_{156} – Balance after R_{168})
$$= 12 \ (\$1937.31) - (\$167,592.23 - \$159,624.98)$$
$$= \underline{\$15,280.47}$$

27. Given: $A_n = \$1000$, n = 6, $p = i = \dfrac{15\%}{12} = 1.25\%$

Solve for R in
$$\$1000 = R \left(\frac{1 - 1.0125^{-6}}{0.0125} \right)$$
$$R = \$174.03$$

Payment number	Payment	Interest portion	Principal portion	Principal balance
0				$1000.00
1	$174.03	$12.50	$161.53	838.47
2	174.03	10.48	163.55	674.92
3	174.03	8.44	165.59	509.33
4	174.03	6.37	167.66	341.67
5	174.03	4.27	169.76	171.91
6	174.06	2.15	171.91	0.00
	Total:	$44.21		

28. Given: $A_n = \$8000$, n = 8, $p = i = \dfrac{10\%}{4} = 2.5\%$

Solve for R in
$$\$8000 = R \left(\frac{1 - 1.025^{-8}}{0.025} \right)$$
$$R = \$1115.74$$

Payment number	Payment	Interest portion	Principal portion	Principal balance
0				$8000.00
1	$1115.74	$200.00	$915.74	7084.26
2	1115.74	177.11	938.63	6145.63
3	1115.74	153.64	962.10	5183.53
4	1115.74	129.59	986.15	4197.38
5	1115.74	104.93	1010.81	3186.57
6	1115.74	79.66	1036.08	2150.49
7	1115.74	53.76	1061.98	1088.51
8	1115.72	27.21	1088.51	0.00
	Total:	$925.90		

Exercise 14.1 *(continued)*

29. Given: $A_n = \$9000$, $n = 6$, $i = 12.75\%$, $c = \dfrac{1}{2} = 0.5$

$p = 1.1275^{0.5} - 1 = 0.061838029$

Solve for R in

$$\$9000 = R\left(\frac{1 - 1.061838029^{-6}}{0.061838029}\right)$$

$R = \$1840.85$

Payment number	Payment	Interest portion	Principal portion	Principal balance
0				$9000.00
1	$1840.85	$556.54	$1284.31	7715.69
2	1840.85	477.12	1363.73	6351.96
3	1840.85	392.79	1448.06	4903.90
4	1840.85	303.25	1537.60	3366.30
5	1840.85	208.17	1632.68	1733.62
6	1840.82	107.20	1733.62	0.00

30. Given: $A_n = \$50,000$, $n = 7$, $i = \dfrac{11.5\%}{2} = 5.75\%$, $c = \dfrac{2}{1} = 2$

$p = 1.0575^2 - 1 = 0.11830625$

Solve for R in

$$\$50,000 = R\left(\frac{1 - 1.11830625^{-7}}{0.11830625}\right)$$

$R = \$10,897.11$

Payment number	Payment	Interest portion	Principal portion	Principal balance
0				$50,000.00
1	$10,897.11	$5915.31	$4981.80	45,018.20
2	10,897.11	5325.93	5571.18	39,447.02
3	10,897.11	4666.83	6230.28	33,216.74
4	10,897.11	3929.75	6967.36	26,249.38
5	10,897.11	3105.47	7791.64	18,457.74
6	10,897.11	2183.67	8713.44	9744.30
7	10,897.11	1152.81	9744.30	0.00
	Total:	$26,279.77		

Exercise 14.1 (continued)

31. Given: $A_n = \$8000$, $n = 8$, $p = i = 2.5\%$

Solve for R in

$$\$8000 = R\left(\frac{1 - 1.025^{-8}}{0.025}\right)$$

$$R = \$1115.74$$

Payment number	Payment	Interest portion	Principal portion	Principal balance
0				$8000.00
1	$1115.74	$200.00	$915.74	7084.26
2	1115.74	177.11	938.63	6145.63
3	2615.74	153.64	2462.10	3683.53
4	1115.74	92.09	1023.65	2659.88
5	1115.74	66.50	1049.24	1610.64
6	1115.74	40.27	1075.47	535.17
7	548.55	13.38	535.17	0.00
	Total:	$742.99		

32. Given: $A_n = \$50,000$, $n = 7$, $i = 5.75\%$, $c = 2$

$p = 1.0575^2 - 1 = 0.11830625$

Solve for R in

$$\$50,000 = R\left(\frac{1 - 1.11830625^{-7}}{0.11830625}\right)$$

$$R = \$10,897.11$$

Payment number	Payment	Interest portion	Principal portion	Principal balance
0				$50,000.00
1	$10,897.11	$5915.31	$4981.80	45,018.20
2	20,897.11	5325.93	15,571.18	29,447.02
3	10,897.11	3483.77	7413.34	22,033.68
4	10,897.11	2606.72	8290.39	13,743.29
5	10,897.11	1625.92	9271.19	4472.10
6	5001.18	529.08	4472.10	0.00
	Total:	$19,486.73		

Interest saved = $26,279.77 − $19,486.73 = $6793.04.

Exercise 14.1 (continued)

33. Given: $A_n = \$60,000$, $n = 12(6) = 72$, $p = i = \dfrac{10.5\%}{12} = 0.875\%$

Solve for R in

$$\$60,000 = R\left(\frac{1 - 1.100875^{-72}}{0.00875}\right)$$

R = \$1126.74

Payment number	Payment	Interest portion	Principal portion	Principal balance
0				$60,000.00
1	$1126.74	$525.00	$601.74	59,398.26
2	1126.74	519.73	607.01	58,791.25
42				29,616.38
43	1126.74	259.14	867.60	28,748.78
44	1126.74	251.55	875.19	27,873.59
70				2224.07
71	1126.74	19.46	1107.28	1116.79
72	1126.56	9.77	1116.79	0.00

34. Given: $A_n = \$24,000$, $n = 60$, $i = \dfrac{11\%}{2} = 5.5\%$, $c = \dfrac{2}{12} = 0.1\overline{6}$

$p = 1.055^{0.1\overline{6}} - 1 = 0.008963392$

Solve for R in

$$\$24,000 = R\left(\frac{1 - 1.008963392^{-60}}{0.008963392}\right)$$

R = \$518.90

Payment number	Payment	Interest portion	Principal portion	Principal balance
0				$24,000.00
1	$518.90	$215.12	$303.78	23,696.22
2	518.90	212.40	306.50	23,389.72
29				13,990.31
30	518.90	125.40	393.50	13,596.81
31	518.90	121.87	397.03	13,199.78
58				1024.27
59	518.90	9.18	509.72	514.55
60	519.16	4.61	514.55	0.00

Total interest = 59 ($518.90) + $519.16 − $24,000 = $7134.26

Exercise 14.1 *(concluded)*

35. a. For an 8-year amortization on the original loan,

$A_n = \$60{,}000$, $n = 12(8) = 96$, $p = i = \dfrac{10.5\%}{12} = 0.875\%$

The payments during the first 4-year term are the value of R satisfying

$$\$60{,}000 = R\left(\frac{1 - 1.00875^{-96}}{0.00875}\right)$$

$$R = \$926.40$$

The balance at the end of the first 4-year term will be
Balance after $R_{48} = \$36{,}182.82$

For the second 4-year term, $A_n = \$36{,}182.82$, $n = 48$, and $p = i = 0.75\%$. Solve for R in

$$\$36{,}182.82 = R\left(\frac{1 - 1.0075^{-48}}{0.0075}\right)$$

$$R = \$900.41$$

b. Interest in $R_{23} = p \times$ Balance after R_{22}
$= 0.00875\,(\$50{,}308.51)$
$= \underline{\$440.20}$

c. The 53rd payment overall is the 5th payment in the second 4-year term. Then
Principal in $R_{53} =$ Balance after R_4 in second term
$\qquad -$ Balance after R_5 in second term
$= \$33{,}638.22 - \$32{,}990.09$
$= \underline{\$648.13}$

36. a. Given: $A_n = \$12{,}000$, Balance after $R_{24} = \$10{,}000$, $i = 5.5\%$, $c = 0.1\overline{6}$
$p = 1.055^{0.1\overline{6}} - 1 = 0.008963394$
Solve for R in

$$\$12{,}000 = R\left(\frac{1 - 1.008963394^{-24}}{0.008963394}\right) + \left(\frac{\$10{,}000}{1.008963394^{24}}\right)$$

$$R = \underline{\$182.62}$$

b. Interest in $R_9 = p \times$ Balance after R_8
$= 0.008963394\,(\$11{,}380.35)$
$= \underline{\$102.01}$

c. Principal in $R_{16} =$ Balance after $R_{15} -$ Balance after R_{16}
$= \$10{,}800.65 - \$10{,}714.84$
$= \underline{\$85.81}$

Exercise 14.2

1. Given: $A_n = \$12{,}000$, $R = \$1000$, $p = i = \dfrac{10.5\%}{4} = 2.625\%$

$$n = -\frac{ln\left(1 - \dfrac{pA_n}{R}\right)}{ln\,(1 + p)} = -\frac{ln\left[1 - \dfrac{0.02625\,(\$12{,}000)}{0.02625}\right]}{ln\,(1.02625)} = 14.601168$$

Principal in R_9 = Balance after R_8 − Balance after R_9
$$= \$5989.21 - \$5146.42$$
$$= \underline{\underline{\$842.79}}$$

Interest in R_5 = p x Balance after R_4
$$= 0.02625\,(\$9150.21)$$
$$= \underline{\underline{\$240.19}}$$

Final payment = $(1 + p)$ x Balance after R_{14}
$$= 1.02625\,(\$588.82)$$
$$= \underline{\underline{\$604.28}}$$

2. Given: $A_n = \$40{,}000$, $R = \$600$, $p = i = \dfrac{11\%}{12} = 0.91\bar{6}\%$

$$n = -\frac{ln\left[\dfrac{1 - 0.00916\,(\$40{,}000)}{\$600}\right]}{ln\,(1.00916)} = 103.50369$$

Principal in R_{43} = Balance after R_{42} − Balance after R_{43}
$$= \$28{,}111.73 - \$27{,}769.42$$
$$= \underline{\underline{\$342.31}}$$

Interest in R_{77} = p x Balance after R_{76}
$$= 0.00916\,(\$14{,}527.85)$$
$$= \underline{\underline{\$133.17}}$$

Final payment = $(1 + p)$ x Balance after R_{103}
$$= 1.00916\,(\$300.15)$$
$$= \underline{\underline{\$302.90}}$$

3. Given: $A_n = \$14{,}000$, $R = \$1200$, $p = i = \dfrac{12.5\%}{2} = 6.25\%$

$$n = -\frac{ln\left[1 - \dfrac{0.0625\,(\$14{,}000)}{\$1200}\right]}{ln\,1.0625} = 21.54655$$

Principal in R_7 = Balance after R_6 − Balance after R_7
$$= \$11{,}718.70 - \$11{,}251.12$$
$$= \underline{\underline{\$467.58}}$$

Interest in R_{12} = p x Balance after R_{11}
$$= 0.0625\,(\$9069.71)$$
$$= \underline{\underline{\$566.86}}$$

Exercise 14.2 (continued)

Final payment = (1 + p) x Balance after R_{21}
= 1.0625 ($625.76)
= **$664.87**

4. Given: A_n = $25,000, R = $500, i = 10.25%, c = $\frac{1}{12}$ = 0.08$\overline{3}$

$p = 1.1025^{0.08\overline{3}} - 1 = 0.008164846$

$$n = -\frac{ln\left[1 - \dfrac{0.008164846\,(\$25,000)}{\$500}\right]}{ln\,(1.008164846)} = 64.52014$$

Principal in R_{11} = Balance after R_{10} – Balance after R_{11}
= $21,930.10 – $21,609.16
= **$320.94**

Interest in R_{41} = p x Balance after R_{40}
= 0.008164846 ($11,070.01)
= **$90.38**

Final payment = (1 + p) x Balance after R_{64}
= 1.008164846 ($258.47)
= **$260.58**

5. Given: A_n = $70,000, R = $2500, i = $\frac{10.75\%}{2}$ = 5.375%, c = $\frac{2}{4}$ = 0.5

$p = 1.05375^{0.5} - 1 - 0.026523258$

$$n = -\frac{ln\left[1 - \dfrac{0.026523258\,(\$70,000)}{\$2500}\right]}{ln\,(1.026523258)} = 51.85052$$

Principal in R_{30} = Balance after R_{29} – Balance after R_{30}
= $42,432.98 – $41,058.44
= **$1374.54**

Interest in R_{11} = p x Balance after R_{10}
= 0.026523258 ($62,741.47)
= **$1664.11**

Final payment = (1 + p) x Balance after R_{51}
= 1.026523258 ($2075.41)
= **$2130.46**

Exercise 14.2 *(continued)*

6. Given: $A_n = \$4000$, $R = \$150$, $i = \dfrac{13\%}{4} = 3.25\%$, $c = \dfrac{4}{12} = 0.\overline{3}$

$$p = 1.0325^{0.\overline{3}} - 1 = 0.010718046$$

$$n = -\frac{\ln\left[1 - \dfrac{0.010718046\,(\$4000)}{\$150}\right]}{\ln\,(1.010718046)} = 31.57416$$

Principal in R_{14} = Balance after R_{13} − Balance after R_{14}
$\qquad\qquad\quad$ = \$2514.16 − \$2391.11
$\qquad\qquad\quad$ = $\underline{\underline{\$123.05}}$

Interest in R_{22} = p x Balance after R_{21}
$\qquad\qquad\quad$ = 0.010718406 (\$1492.01)
$\qquad\qquad\quad$ = $\underline{\underline{\$15.99}}$

Final payment = (1 + p) x Balance after R_{31}
$\qquad\qquad\quad$ = 1.010718406 (\$85.40)
$\qquad\qquad\quad$ = $\underline{\underline{\$86.32}}$

7. Given: $A_n = \$45{,}000$, $R = \$500$, $i = \dfrac{10.5\%}{2} = 5.25\%$, $c = \dfrac{2}{12} = 0.1\overline{6}$

$$p = 1.0525^{0.1\overline{6}} - 1 = 0.0085645151$$

$$n = -\frac{\ln\left[1 - \dfrac{0.0085645151\,(\$45{,}000)}{\$500}\right]}{\ln\,(1.0085645151)} = 172.74622$$

Principal in R_{149} = Balance after R_{148} − Balance after R_{149}
$\qquad\qquad\quad$ = \$11,107.22 − \$10,702.35
$\qquad\qquad\quad$ = $\underline{\underline{\$404.87}}$

Interest in R_{117} = p x Balance after R_{116}
$\qquad\qquad\quad$ = 0.0085645151 (\$22,397.44)
$\qquad\qquad\quad$ = $\underline{\underline{\$191.82}}$

Final payment = (1 + p) x Balance after R_{172}
$\qquad\qquad\quad$ = 1.0085645151 (\$370.34)
$\qquad\qquad\quad$ = $\underline{\underline{\$373.51}}$

Exercise 14.2 *(continued)*

8. Given: $A_n = \$30,000$, $R = \$2500$, $i = \dfrac{12\%}{4} = 3\%$, $c = \dfrac{4}{2} = 2$

$$p = 1.03^2 - 1 = 0.0609$$

$$n = -\frac{ln\left[1 - \dfrac{0.0609\,(\$30,000)}{\$2500}\right]}{ln\,(1.0609)} = 22.19814$$

Principal in R_9 = Balance after R_8 − Balance after R_9
= \$23,317.45 − \$22,237.48
= \$1079.97

Interest in R_{19} = p x Balance after R_{18}
= 0.0609 (\$9022.31)
= \$549.46

Final payment = (1 + p) x Balance after R_{22}
= 1.0609 (\$478.04)
= \$507.15

9. Given: $A_n = \$37,000$, $p = i = \dfrac{10.8\%}{2} = 5.4\%$, $R = \$3000$

  a. Principal in R_{16} = Balance after R_{15} − Balance after R_{16}
= \$14,715.80 − \$12,510.45
= \$2205.35

  b. Interest in R_6 = p x Balance after R_5
= 0.054 (\$31,418.90)
= \$1696.62

  c. Principal in payments 8 to 14 inclusive
= Balance after R_7 − Balance after R_{14}
= \$28,741.76 − \$16,808.16
= \$11,933.60

  d. Interest in year 5 = 2R − (Principal in year 5)
= 2R − (Balance after R_8 − Balance after R_{10})
= 2 (\$3000) − (\$27,293.82 − \$24,159.14)
= \$2865.32

10. Given: $A_n = \$27,000$, $R = \$1000$, $p = i = \dfrac{8\%}{4} = 2\%$

  a. Interest in R_{16} = p x Balance after R_{15}
= 0.02 (\$19,045.03)
= \$380.90

  b. Principal in R_{33} = Balance after R_{32} − Balance after R_{33}
= \$6655.57 − \$5788.68
= \$866.89

Exercise 14.2 *(continued)*

c. Interest in payments 20 to 25 inclusive
= 6R – Principal in payments 20 to 25 inclusive
= 6R – (Balance after R_{19} – Balance after R_{25})
= 6 ($1000) – ($16,493.34 – 12,266.06)
= $1772.72

d. Principal in year 6 = Balance after R_{20} – Balance after R_{24}
= $15,823.21 – $13,005.94
= $2817.27

11. Given: A_n = $6000, R = $500, $i = \dfrac{12.75\%}{12}$ = 1.0625%, $c = \dfrac{12}{4}$ = 3

$p = 1.010625^3 - 1 = 0.032214871$

a. Interest in R_{11} = p x Balance after R_{10}
= 0.032214871 ($2447.83)
= $78.86

b. Principal in R_6 = Balance after R_5 – Balance after R_6
= $4364.40 – $4005.00
= $359.40

c. Interest in payments 3 to 9 inclusive
= 7R – (Principal in payments 3 to 9 inclusive)
= 7R – (Balance after R_2 – Balance after R_9)
= 7 ($500) – ($5376.70 – $2855.83)
= $979.13

d. Principal in year 3 = Balance after R_8 – Balance after R_{12}
= $3251.09 – $1591.97
= $1659.12

12. Given: A_n = $225,000, R = $2000, $i = \dfrac{9.5\%}{2}$ = 4.75%, $c = \dfrac{2}{12}$ = $0.1\overline{6}$

$p = 1.0475^{0.1\overline{6}} - 1 = 0.0077643832$

a. Principal in R_{137} = Balance after R_{136} – Balance after R_{137}
= $164,290.70 – $163,566.31
= $724.39

b. Interest in R_{204} = p x Balance after R_{203}
= 0.0077643832 ($100,941.91)
= $783.75

c. Principal in payments 145 to 156 inclusive
= Balance after R_{144} – Balance after R_{156}
= $158,335.67 – $148,682.91
= $9652.76

Exercise 14.2 (continued)

   d. Interest in year 20 = 12R − Principal in year 20

$$= 12R − (\text{Balance after } R_{228} − \text{Balance after } R_{240})$$
$$= 12\ (\$2000) − (\$67{,}526.60 − \$49{,}042.09)$$
$$= \underline{\$5515.49}$$

13. Given: $A_n = \$1000$, $R = \$200$, $p = i = \dfrac{15\%}{12} = 1.25\%$

Payment number	Payment	Interest portion	Principal portion	Principal balance
0				$1000.00
1	$200.00	$12.50	$187.50	812.50
2	200.00	10.16	189.84	622.66
3	200.00	7.78	192.22	430.44
4	200.00	5.38	194.62	235.82
5	200.00	2.95	197.05	38.77
6	39.25	0.48	38.77	0.00
	Total:	$39.25		

14. Given: $A_n = \$7500$, $R = \$1000$, $p = i = \dfrac{10\%}{4} = 2.5\%$

Payment number	Payment	Interest portion	Principal portion	Principal balance
0				$7500.00
1	$1000.00	$187.50	$812.50	6687.50
2	1000.00	167.19	832.81	5854.69
3	1000.00	146.37	853.63	5001.06
4	1000.00	125.03	874.97	4126.09
5	1000.00	103.15	896.85	3229.24
6	1000.00	80.73	919.27	2309.97
7	1000.00	57.75	942.25	1367.72
8	1000.00	34.19	965.81	401.91
9	411.96	10.05	401.91	0.00
	Total:	$911.96		

15. Given: $A_n = \$9000$, $R = \$2000$, $i = 12.75\%$, $c = \dfrac{1}{2} = 0.5$

$$p = 1.1275^{0.5} − 1 = 0.061838029$$

Payment number	Payment	Interest portion	Principal portion	Principal balance
0				$9000.00
1	$2000.00	$556.54	$1443.46	7556.54
2	2000.00	467.28	1532.72	6023.82
3	2000.00	372.50	1627.50	4396.32
4	2000.00	271.86	1728.14	2668.18
5	2000.00	164.99	1835.01	833.17
6	884.69	51.52	833.17	0.00

Exercise 14.2 (continued)

16. Given: $A_n = \$50{,}000$, $R = \$12{,}000$, $i = \dfrac{11.5\%}{2} = 5.75\%$, $c = \dfrac{2}{1} = 2$

$p = 1.0575^2 - 1 = 0.11830625$

Payment number	Payment	Interest portion	Principal portion	Principal balance
0				$50,000.00
1	$12,000.00	$5915.31	$6,084.69	43,915.31
2	12,000.00	5195.46	6,804.54	37,110.77
3	12,000.00	4390.44	7609.56	29,501.21
4	12,000.00	3490.18	8,509.82	20,991.39
5	12,000.00	2483.41	9,516.59	11,474.80
6	12,000.00	1357.54	10,642.46	832.34
7	930.81	98.47	832.34	0.00
	Total:	$22,930.81		

17. Given: $A_n = \$7500$, $R = \$1000$, $p = i = 2.5\%$

Payment number	Payment	Interest portion	Principal portion	Principal balance
0				$7500.00
1	$1000.00	$187.50	$812.50	6687.50
2	1000.00	167.19	832.81	5854.69
3	2000.00	146.37	1853.63	4001.06
4	1000.00	100.03	899.97	3101.09
5	1000.00	77.53	922.47	2178.62
6	1000.00	54.47	945.53	1233.09
7	1000.00	30.83	969.17	263.92
8	270.52	6.60	263.92	0.00
	Total:	$770.52		

18. Given: $A_n = \$50{,}000$, $R = \$12{,}000$, $i = 5.75\%$, $c = 2$

$p = 1.0575^2 - 1 = 0.11830625$

Payment number	Payment	Interest portion	Principal portion	Principal balance
0				$50,000.00
1	$12,000.00	$5915.31	$6084.69	43,915.31
2	22,000.00	5195.46	16,804.54	27,110.77
3	12,000.00	3207.37	8792.63	18,318.14
4	12,000.00	2167.15	9832.85	8485.29
5	9489.15	1003.86	8485.29	0.00
	Total:	$17,489.15		

Interest savings = Total interest in problem 16 − $17,489.15 = $5441.66

---

19. Given: $A_n = \$60,000$, $R = \$1000$, $p = i = \dfrac{10.5\%}{12} = 0.875\%$

Payment number	Payment	Interest portion	Principal portion	Principal balance
0				$60,000.00
1	$1000.00	$525.00	$475.00	59,525.00
2	1000.00	520.84	479.16	59,045.84
⋮	⋮	⋮	⋮	⋮
55				26,629.91
56	1000.00	233.01	766.99	25,862.92
57	1000.00	226.30	773.70	25,089.22
⋮	⋮	⋮	⋮	⋮
84				1435.19
85	1000.00	12.56	987.44	447.75
86	451.67	3.92	447.75	0.00

20. Given: $A_n = \$24,000$, $R = \$500$, $i = \dfrac{11\%}{2} = 5.5\%$, $c = \dfrac{2}{12} = 0.1\overline{6}$

$p = 1.055^{0.1\overline{6}} - 1 = 0.008963394$

Payment number	Payment	Interest portion	Principal portion	Principal balance
0				$24,000.00
1	$500.00	$215.12	$284.88	23,715.12
2	500.00	212.57	287.43	23,427.69
⋮	⋮	⋮	⋮	⋮
27	500.00			15,341.31
28	500.00	137.51	362.49	14,978.82
29	500.00	134.26	365.74	14,613.08
⋮	⋮	⋮	⋮	⋮
62				515.85
63	500.00	4.62	495.38	20.47
64	20.65	0.18	20.47	0.00

Total interest = 63 ($500) + $20.65 − $24,000 = <u>$7520.65</u>

21. For the first 4 years, $A_n = \$60,000$, $R = \$1000$, and $p = i = 0.875\%$.

a. Balance after 4 years = Balance after R_{48}
     = $31,815.74

This balance equals the present value of the remaining monthly payments of $1000 with i = 0.75%. The number of remaining payments is

$$n = -\dfrac{\ln\left[1 - \dfrac{0.0075\,(\$31,815.74)}{\$1000}\right]}{\ln(1.0075)} = 36.48549$$

Exercise 14.2 *(concluded)*

The loan requires 37 payments taking 3 years and one month. The loan will be paid off <u>7 years and one month after the loan was received.</u>

b.   Final payment = (1 + p) x Balance after 36 payments in the second term

= 1.0075 ($482.80)

= $486.42

c.   Interest in R_{32} = p x Balance after R_{31} in the first term

= 0.00875 ($43,168.37)

= $377.72

d.   Principal in R_{58}= Balance after R_9 in the second term − Balance after R_{10} in the second term

= $24,754.09 − $23,939.75

= $814.34

Exercise 14.3

1.   The principal reduction in any 5-year period equals the decrease in the loan balance during the period.
Step 1: Calculate the monthly payment.
Step 2: Calculate the balance owed at the end of each 5-year interval.
Step 3: Calculate the principal reduction in each 5-year interval.

Step 1: A_n = $100,000, n = 300, i = 4.1%, c = $0.1\overline{6}$

$p = 1.041^{0.1\overline{6}} - 1 = 0.0067194397$

Solve for R in

$$\$100,000 = R \left(\frac{1 - 1.0067194397^{-300}}{0.0067194397} \right)$$

R = $776.02

Step 2:

Payment number	Balance after payment
60	$92,340.18
120	80,892.29
180	63,782.96
240	38,212.40
360	0

Step 3:

Interval	Reduction in principal
1 – 5 years	$100,000 − $92,340.18 = <u>$7660</u>
6 – 10 years	$92,340.18 − $80,892.29 = <u>$11,448</u>
11 – 15 years	$80,892.29 − $63,782.96 = <u>$17,109</u>
16 – 20 years	$63,782.96 − $38,212.40 = <u>$25,571</u>
21 – 25 years	<u>$38,212</u>

Exercise 14.3 (continued)

2. Given: $A_n = \$100{,}000$, $i = 4.5\%$, and $c = 0.1\overline{6}$

    $p = 1.045^{0.1\overline{6}} - 1 = 0.0073631230$

    a. For each of $n = 180$, 240, and 300, solve for R in

    $$\$100{,}000 = R \left(\frac{1 - 1.007363123^{-n}}{0.007363123} \right)$$

    $R = \underline{\$1004.52}$ for a 15-year amortization
    $R = \underline{\$889.19}$ for a 20-year amortization
    $R = \underline{\$827.98}$ for a 25-year amortization

    b. % increase $= \dfrac{\$889.19 - \$827.98}{\$827.98} \times 100\% = \underline{7.39\%}$

    c. % increase $= \dfrac{\$1004.52 - \$827.98}{\$827.98} \times 100\% = \underline{21.32\%}$

d. Amortization	Total interest paid
15 years	180 ($1004.52) – $100,000 = $\underline{\$80{,}813.60}$
20 years	240 ($889.19) – $100,000 = $\underline{\$113{,}405.60}$
25 years	300 ($827.98) – $100,000 = $\underline{\$148{,}394.00}$

3. Given: $A_n = \$100{,}000$, $n = 300$, $c = 0.1\overline{6}$

    a. For each of $i = 4\%$, 4.5%, and 5%, calculate p and R

$i(\%)$	$p(\%)$	$R(\$)$
4	0.65581969	763.21
4.5	0.73631230	827.98
5	0.81648460	894.49

    b. % difference $= \dfrac{\$894.49 - \$827.98}{\$827.98} \times 100\% = \underline{8.03\%}$

c. $j(\%\text{ csa})$	Total interest paid
8	300 ($763.21) – $100,000 = $\underline{\$128{,}963}$
9	300 ($827.98) – $100,000 = $\underline{\$148{,}394}$
10	300 ($894.49) – $100,000 – $\underline{\$168{,}347}$

    (These answers ignore the fact that the 300th payment will differ slightly from all the others.)

Exercise 14.3 *(continued)*

4. In each case, the maximum loan is the present value of the $1000 payments discounted at the interest rate on the loan.

   Given: $R = \$1000$, $i = 4.125\%$, $c = 0.1\overline{6}$

   $p = 1.04125^{0.1\overline{6}} - 1 = 0.0067597303$

Amortization period	n	Maximum loan
a. 15 years	180	$A_n = \$103,938$
b. 20 years	240	$A_n = \$118,567$
c. 25 years	300	$A_n = \$128,332$

5. The maximum loan equals the present value of the $1000 payments discounted at the interest rate on the loan.
   Given: $R = \$1000$, $n = 300$, $c = 0.1\overline{6}$

	j	i	p	Maximum loan
a.	8% csa	4%	0.65581969%	$A_n = \$131,025$
b.	9% csa	4.5%	0.73631230%	$A_n = \$120,776$

6. a. Given: $A_n = \$100,000$, $i = 4.25\%$, $n = 240$, $c = 0.1\overline{6}$

   $p = 1.0425^{0.1\overline{6}} - 1 = 0.0069610621$

   Solve for R in

   $$\$100,000 = R\left(\frac{1 - 1.0069610621^{-240}}{0.0069610621}\right)$$

   $$R = \$858.56$$

   b. Given: $A_n = \$100,000$, $i = 4.75\%$, $n = 300$, $c = 0.1\overline{6}$

   $p = 1.0475^{0.1\overline{6}} - 1 = 0.0077643832$

   Solve for R in

   $$\$100,000 = R\left(\frac{1 - 1.0077643832^{-300}}{0.0077643832}\right)$$

   $$R = \$861.03$$

7. Step 1: Calculate the payment size for the first 5-year term.
   Step 2: Calculate the balance after 5 years.
   Step 3: Calculate the payment upon renewal.
   Step 4: Calculate the difference between Step 1 and Step 3 results.

Exercise 14.3 *(continued)*

Step 1: Given: $A_n = \$100,000$, $n = 300$, $i = 4.25\%$, $c = 0.1\overline{6}$

$$p = 1.0425^{0.1\overline{6}} - 1 = 0.0069610621$$

Solve for R giving R = $795.36

Step 2: Balance after $R_{60} = \$92,639.33$

Step 3: Now $A_n = \$92,639.33$, $n = 240$, $i = 4.75\%$, $c = 0.1\overline{6}$

$$p = 1.0475^{0.1\overline{6}} - 1 = 0.0077643832$$

Solve for R giving R = $852.50

Step 4: Increase in payment size = $852.50 − $795.36 = $57.14

8.　　Step 1: Calculate the payment for the first 3-year term.
　　　Step 2: Calculate the balance after 3 years.
　　　Step 3: Calculate the payment upon renewal.
　　　Step 4: Calculate the difference between the Step 1 and Step 3 results.

Step 1: Given: $A_n = \$100,000$, $n = 240$, $i = 4.5\%$, $c = 0.1\overline{6}$

$$p = 1.045^{0.1\overline{6}} - 1 = 0.0073631230$$

Solve for R giving R = $889.19

Step 2: Balance after $R_{36} = \$93,724.31$

Step 3: Now $A_n = \$93,724.31$, $n = 204$, $i = 4\%$, $c = 0.1\overline{6}$

$$p = 1.04^{0.1\overline{6}} - 1 = 0.0065581969$$

Solve for R giving R = $834.63

Step 4: Decrease in payment size = $889.19 − $834.63 = $54.56

9. a. Given: $A_n = \$80,000$, $i = 5.25\%$, $n = 300$, $c = 0.1\overline{6}$

$$p = 1.0525^{0.1\overline{6}} - 1 = 0.0085645151$$

Solve for R giving R = $742.66

Balance after $R_{36} = \$77,587.44$

b. Now $A_n = \$77,587.44$, $i = 4.75\%$, $n = 264$, $c = 0.1\overline{6}$

$$p = 1.0475^{0.1\overline{6}} - 1 = 0.0077643832$$

Solve for R giving R = $692.26.

Exercise 14.3 (continued)

10. a. Step 1: Calculate the payment size for the first 5-year term.
    Step 2: Calculate the balance after 5 years.
    Step 3: Calculate the payment size on mortgage renewal.
    Step 4: Calculate the balance after the second 5-year term.
    Step 5: Calculate the difference between the step 2 and step 4 results.

    Step 1: $A_n = \$60,000$, $i = 5.625\%$, n = 300, c = $0.1\overline{6}$

    $p = 1.05625^{0.1\overline{6}} - 1 = 0.0091625380$

    Solve for R giving R = \$587.85

    Step 2: Balance after R_{60} = \$56,970.94

    Step 3: $A_n = \$56,970.94$, $i = 5\%$, n = 240, c = $0.1\overline{6}$

    $p = 1.05^{0.1\overline{6}} - 1 = 0.0081648460$

    Solve for R giving R = \$542.17

    Step 4: Balance after R_{60} = \$51,039.19

    Step 5: Principal reduction = \$56,970.94 − \$51,039.19 = <u>\$5931.75</u>

    b. Return to step 3 in part a. Calculate the balance after the 60th payment in the second 5-year term where $A_n = \$56,970.94$, $i = 5\%$, R = \$587.85, c = $0.1\overline{6}$ and p = 0.0081648460.

    Balance = \$47,520.70

    Principal reduction = \$56,970.94 − \$47,520.70 = <u>\$9450.24</u>

11. a. Given: $A_n = \$40,000$, $p = i = 0.8125\%$, n = 180
    Solve for R giving R = \$423.75
    Rounded monthly payment = \$430
    Balance after 4 years = Balance after 48 payments of \$430
    = <u>\$33,866.00</u>

    b. On renewal, $A_n = \$33,866.00$, n = 132, $p = i = 0.75\%$
    Solve for R giving R = \$405.06
    Rounded monthly payment = <u>\$410.00</u>

Exercise 14.3 *(continued)*

12. Given: $A_n = \$95{,}000$, $i = 5.375\%$, $n = 4(20) = 80$, $c = \dfrac{2}{4} = 0.5$

$p = 1.05375^{0.5} - 1 = 0.026523258$

Solve for R giving R = $2873.65
Rounded quarterly payment = $2900
The number of quarterly payments of $2900 needed to pay off the loan is

$$n = -\dfrac{ln\left[1 - \dfrac{0.026523258\,(\$95{,}000)}{\$2900}\right]}{ln\,(1.026523258)} = 77.60564$$

Therefore, 78 payments are required to pay off the loan.

Final payment = $(1 + p)$ x Balance after R_{77}
$$= (1.026523258)\,\$1719.81$$
$$= \underline{\$1765.43}$$

13. a. Given: $A_n = \$27{,}000$, $i = 5.625\%$, $n = 120$, $c = 0.1\overline{6}$

$p = 1.05625^{0.1\overline{6}} - 1 = 0.009162538$

Solve for R giving R = $371.85
Rounded payment = $380.00
Balance after 60 payments of $380 = $16,456.38

b. For the second 5-year term, $A_n = \$16{,}456.38$, $i = 5.25\%$, $n = 60$, $c = 0.1\overline{6}$, and $p = 0.0085645151$.
Solve for R giving R = $351.90
Rounded monthly payment = $360.00
The number of monthly payments of $360 needed to pay off the balance owed is

$$n = -\dfrac{ln\left[1 - \dfrac{0.0085645151\,(\$16{,}456.38)}{\$360}\right]}{ln\,(1.0085645151)} = 58.25044$$

Final payment = $(1 + p)$ x Balance after 58 payments
$$= 1.0085645151\,(\$89.68)$$
$$= \underline{\$90.45}$$

14. a. GDS ratio must be $\leq 33\%$. Let R represent the monthly mortgage payment. Then

$$\text{GDS ratio} = \dfrac{R + \$200 + \$120}{\$6000} \leq 0.33$$

That is,

$$R \leq 0.33\,(\$6000) - \$320 = \$1660$$

The TDS ratio must be $\leq 42\%$. That is,

$$\text{TDS ratio} = \dfrac{R + \$500 + \$200 + \$120}{\$6000} \leq 0.42$$

Therefore,

$$R \leq 0.42\ (\$6000) - \$820 = \$1700$$

The GDS ratio is the more restrictive ratio for the Delgados.

With R = $1660, n = 300, i = 4.3%, and c = $0.1\overline{6}$,

$$p = 1.043^{0.1\overline{6}} - 1 = 0.0070415385$$

The maximum mortgage loan is

$$A_n = \$1660\ \left(\frac{1 - 1.0070415385^{-300}}{0.0070415385} \right) = \$207,021$$

Rounded to the nearest $100, the maximum mortgage loan (on the basis of the Delgados' income) is $207,000.

b. For the maximum conventional mortgage loan,

$$\$207,000 = 0.75\ \text{(Home value)}$$
$$\text{Home value} = \$276,000$$
$$\text{Minimum down payment} = 0.25\ \text{(Home value)}$$
$$= 0.25\ (\$276,000)$$
$$= \$69,000$$

15. a. GDS ratio must be ≤ 35%. Let R represent the monthly mortgage payment. Then

$$\text{GDS ratio} = \frac{R + \$175 + \$100}{\$5000} \leq 0.35$$

That is,

$$R \leq 0.35\ (\$5000) - \$275 = \$1475$$

The TDS ratio must be ≤ 42%. That is,

$$\text{TDS ratio} = \frac{R + \$600 + \$175 + \$100}{\$5000} \leq 0.42$$

Therefore,

$$R \leq 0.42\ (\$5000) - \$875 = \$1225$$

The TDS ratio is the more restrictive ratio for the Archibalds.

With R = $1225, n = 300, i = 4.125%, and c = $0.1\overline{6}$,

$$p = 1.04125^{0.1\overline{6}} - 1 = 0.0067597303$$

The maximum mortgage loan is

$$A_n = \$1225\ \frac{1 - 1.0067597303^{-300}}{0.0067597303} = \$157,207$$

Rounded to the nearest $100, the maximum mortgage loan (based on income) is $157,200.

b. For the maximum CMHC-insured mortgage loan and minimum down payment,
$157,200 = 0.95 (Maximum home price)

Maximum home price $= \dfrac{\$157{,}200}{0.95} = \$165{,}474$

Rounded to the nearest $100, the maximum price they can pay is <u>$165,500</u>.

16. Given: $A_n = \$75{,}000$, R = $683.52, n = 300, c = $0.1\overline{6}$.
Solve for p in

$$\$75{,}000 = \$683.52\left[\dfrac{1-(1+p)^{-300}}{p}\right]$$

$$p = 0.008364753$$

Then
$$i = (1+p)^{1/c} - 1 = 1.008364753^6 - 1 = 0.05125$$

Nominal rate, $j = 2i = 2\,(5.125\%) = $ <u>10.25% compounded semiannually.</u>

17. a. Given: $A_n = \$100{,}000$, $i = 4.375\%$, n = 300, c = $0.1\overline{6}$

$p = 1.04375^{0.16} - 1 = 0.0071621929$
Solve for R giving R = <u>$811.61</u>

b. Weekly payment = 0.25 ($811.61) = $202.90
With weekly payments, $A_n = \$100{,}000$, R = $202.90, $i = 4.375\%$, and $c = \dfrac{2}{52} = 0.038461538$.
Then
$$p = 1.04375^{0.038461538} - 1 = 0.0016482799$$
and

$$n = -\dfrac{ln\left[1 - \dfrac{0.0016482799\,(\$100{,}000)}{\$202.90}\right]}{ln\,(1.0016482799)} = 1015.98$$

Therefore, 1016 weekly payments will be required. The loan will be paid off after <u>19 years and 28 weeks</u>. The amortization period is reduced by almost $5\frac{1}{2}$ years.

18. Given: $A_n = \$100{,}000$, $i = 4.1\%$, n = 300, c = $0.1\overline{6}$

$p = 1.041^{0.1\overline{6}} - 1 = 0.0067194397$

Solve for R giving R = $776.02
Balance after 1 year = Balance after 12 payments
$= \$98{,}703.88$

Exercise 14.3 (continued)

a. Balance after $5000 prepayment = $93,703.88
   The number of payments required to pay off this balance is

$$n = -\frac{ln\left[1 - \dfrac{0.0067194397\ (\$93,703.88)}{\$776.02}\right]}{ln\ (1.0067194397)} = 249.06$$

   The total time to pay off the loan will be 250 + 12 = 262 months. The amortization period will be shortened by 38 months or <u>3 years and 2 months</u>.

b. Balance after $10,000 prepayment = $88,703.88.
   The number of additional payments needed to pay off this balance is n = 218.208. That is, the total time to pay off the loan will be 219 + 12 = 231 months. The amortization period will be shortened by 69 months or <u>5 years and 9 months</u>.

19. This problem is the same as problem 18 except that the initial amortization period is now 20 years. A briefer solution will be presented in this case.
    Given: A_n = $100,000, i = 4.1%, n = 240, c = 0.1$\bar{6}$, p = 0.67194397%
    Solve for R giving R = $840.39
    Balance after 12 payments = $97,902.25.

a. Balance after $5000 prepayment = $92,902.25
   Solve for n giving n = 202.77.
   A total of 203 + 12 = 215 payments (months) will be required to pay off the loan. The amortization period will be reduced by 240 – 215 = 25 months = <u>2 years and 1 month</u>.

b. Balance after $10,000 prepayment = $87,902.25
   Solve for n giving n = 181.20.
   A total of 182 + 12 = 194 payments (months) will be required to pay off the loan. The amortization period will be reduced by 240 – 194 = 46 months = <u>3 years and 10 months</u>.

20. Given: A_n = $100,000, i = 4%, n = 300, c = 0.1$\bar{6}$
    p = $1.040^{.1\bar{6}} - 1$ = 0.0065581969
    Solve for R giving R = $763.21.
    Balance after 12 payments = $98,663.80

a. Increased payment = 1.05 ($763.21) = $801.37
   Solve for remaining n giving n = 252.01
   Total time to pay off loan = 253 + 12 = 265 months
   Reduction of amortization period = (300 – 265) months
   = 35 months
   = <u>2 years and 11 months</u>

b. Increased payment = 1.10 ($763.21) = $839.53
   Solve for remaining n giving n = 225.32
   Total time to pay off loan = 226 + 12 = 238 months
   Reduction of amortization period = (300 – 238) months
   = 62 months
   = <u>5 years and 2 months</u>

Exercise 14.3 *(continued)*

21.   Given: $A_n = \$100,000$, $i = 4\%$, n = 240, c = $0.1\overline{6}$
        $p = 1.04^{0.1\overline{6}} - 1 = 0.0065581969$
        Solve for R giving R = $828.36
        Balance after 12 payments = $97,853.18

   a.   Increased payment = 1.05 ($828.36) = $869.78
        Solve for remaining n giving n = 204.80
        Total time to pay off loan = 205 + 12 = 217 months
        Reduction of amortization period = (240 − 217) months
                                       = 23 months
                                       = 1 year and 11 months

   b.   Increased payment = 1.10 ($828.36) = $911.20
        Solve for remaining n giving n = 186.38
        Total time to pay off loan = 187 + 12 = 199 months
        Reduction of amortization period = (240 − 199) months
                                       = 41 months
                                       = 3 years and 5 months

22.   Given: $A_n = \$100,000$, $i = 4.25\%$, n = 300, c = $0.1\overline{6}$
        $p = 1.0425^{0.1\overline{6}} - 1 = 0.0069610621$
        Solve for R giving R = $795.36
        Balance after 10th payment = $98,975.79
        Balance after extra payment = $98,180.43
        Solve for remaining n giving n = 282.69
        Total time to pay off loan = 283 + 10 = 293 months
        Amortization period is shortened by 300 − 293 = 7 months.

23.   Given: $A_n = \$100,000$, $i = 4.4\%$, n = 240, c = $0.1\overline{6}$
        $p = 1.044^{0.1\overline{6}} - 1 = 0.0072023949$
        Solve for R giving R = $876.89
        Balance after 8th payment = $98,714.75
        Balance after extra payment = $97,837.86
        Solve for remaining n giving n = 226.79
        Total time to pay off loan = 227 + 8 = 235 months
        Amortization period is reduced by 240 − 235 = 5 months.

24.   Given: $A_n = \$100,000$, $i = 4.375\%$, n = 240, c = $0.1\overline{6}$
        $p = 1.04375^{0.1\overline{6}} - 1 = 0.0071621929$
        Solve for R giving R = $873.82
        Balance after 8th payment = $98,707.13
        Interest for 9th month = 0.0071621929 ($98,707.13) = $706.96
        Balance after 9th month = $98,707.13 + $706.96 = $99,414.09
        Solve for remaining n giving n = 236.32
        Total time to pay off loan = 237 + 9 = 246 months
        The amortization period will be lengthened by 6 months.

Exercise 14.3 *(continued)*

25. Given: A_n = $100,000, i = 4.125%, n = 300, c = $0.1\overline{6}$
    $p = 1.04125^{0.1\overline{6}} - 1 = 0.0067597303$
    Solve for R giving R = $779.23
    Balance after 11th payment = $98,824.99
    Interest for the 12th month = 0.0067597303 ($98,824.99) = $668.03
    Balance after 12th month = $98,824.99 + $668.03 = $99,493.02
    Solve for remaining n giving n = 295.15
    Total time to pay off loan = 296 + 12 = 308 months
    The amortization period will be lengthened by <u>8 months</u>.

26. Given: A_n = $100,000, i = 4.55%, n = 240, c = $0.1\overline{6}$
    $p = 1.0455^{0.1\overline{6}} - 1 = 0.0074434390$
    Solve for R giving R = $895.37
    Balance after 12 payments = $98,111.62
    Balance after $10,000 lump payment = $88,111.62
    Balance after 12 more payments = $85,116.79
    Monthly payments beginning in third year = 1.1 ($895.37) = $984.91
    Solve for remaining n giving n = 138.995
    Total time to pay off loan = 139 + 24 = 163 months
    The amortization period will be reduced by 240 – 163 = 77 months or <u>6 years and 5 months</u>.

27. Given: A_n = $100,000, i = 4.4%, n = 300, c = $0.1\overline{6}$
    $p = 1.044^{0.1\overline{6}} - 1 = 0.0072023949$
    Solve for R giving R = $814.88
    Balance after 12 payments = $98,818.23
    Monthly payments beginning in 2nd year = 1.1 ($814.88) = $896.37
    Balance after 12 more payments = $96,512.61
    Balance after lump payment = $86,512.61
    Solve for remaining n giving n = 165.52
    Total time to pay off loan = 166 + 24 = 190 months
    The amortization period will be reduced by (300 – 190) months = 110 months = <u>9 years and 2 months</u>.

28. Given: A_n = $70,000, i = 5.75%, n = 240, c = $0.1\overline{6}$
    $p = 1.0575^{0.1\overline{6}} - 1 = 0.0093614858$
    Solve for R giving R = $733.70.
    Balance after 32 payments = $67,090.80
    Balance after $5000 prepayment = $62,090.80

  a. Solve for remaining n giving n = 168.636
     Total time to repay loan = 169 + 32 = 201 months
     The amortization period will be shortened by (240 – 201) months = 39 months = <u>3 years and 3 months</u>

  b. Balance after 4 years
       = Balance 16 payments after $5000 prepayment
       = <u>$59,472.83</u>

Exercise 14.3 *(continued)*

29.   Given: $A_n = \$120{,}000$, $i = 4.95\%$, $n = 300$, $c = 0.1\overline{6}$

      $p = 1.0495^{0.1\overline{6}} - 1 = 0.0080848171$

Solve for R giving R = \$1065.32

Balance after 2 years = \$117,491.15

Balance after \$5000 prepayment = \$112,491.15

  a. Solve for remaining n giving n = 238.707

     Total time to repay loan = 239 + 24 = 263 months

     The amortization period will be shortened by

       (300 − 263) months = 37 months = <u>3 years and 1 month.</u>

  b. Balance after 5 years

     = Balance 3 years after \$5000 prepayment

     = <u>\$106,008.91</u>

30.   Given: $A_n = \$100{,}000$, $n = 300$, $p = i = 0.75\%$

Solve for R giving R = \$839.20

  a. Balance after 1 year = \$98,884.32

     The last 23 years of payments will pay off principal amounting to

$$A_n = \$839.20 \left(\frac{1 - 1.0075^{-276}}{0.0075} \right) = \$97{,}664.51$$

     The lump payment after 1 year must reduce the balance by

      \$98,884.32 − \$97,664.51 = <u>\$1219.81</u>

  b. Balance after 10 years = \$82,738.53.

     The last 14 years of payments will pay off

$$A_n = \$839.20 \left(\frac{1 - 1.0075^{-168}}{0.0075} \right) = \$80{,}004.77$$

     The lump payment after 10 years must reduce the balance by

      \$82,738.53 − \$80,004.77 = <u>\$2733.76.</u>

31.   Given: $A_n = \$100{,}000$, $i = 5.125\%$, $n = 240$, $c = 0.1\overline{6}$

      $p = 1.05125^{0.1\overline{6}} - 1 = 0.0083647796$

Solve for R giving R = \$967.52

Balance after 3 years = Balance after 36th payment

               = \$94,521.68

Payment size beginning in year 4 = 1.10 (\$967.52) = \$1064.27

  a. Number of payments of \$1064.27 needed to pay off \$94,521.68 is n = 163.063.

     Total time to pay off loan = 164 + 36 = 200 months

     Reduction in amortization period = 240 − 200 = 40 months or <u>3 years and 4 months.</u>

   b. Balance after 5 years
       = Balance 24 payments after balance reaches $94,521.68
       = $87,282.67

32.   Given: A_n = $69,000, R = $800, i = 5.25%, c = $0.1\overline{6}$
        p = $1.0525^{0.1\overline{6}} - 1 = 0.0085645151$
        Number of payments of $800 required to pay off loan is

$$n = -\frac{ln\left[1 - \dfrac{0.0085645151\,(\$69,000)}{\$800}\right]}{ln\,(1.0085645151)} = 157.368$$

        The amortization period is 158 months.
        Balance after 3 years = $60,228.64.

   a. Payment size beginning in year 4 = 1.1 ($800) = $880.
       Number of payments of $880 needed to pay off $60,228.64 is n = 103.458. The total time to pay off
       the loan is 104 + 36 = 140 months or 11 years and 8 months.

   b. Balance after 5 years
       = Balance 2 years after payments rise to $880
       = $50,571.13

33.   Originally, A_n = $83,000, n = 300, i = 4.95%, c = $0.1\overline{6}$
        p = $1.0495^{0.1\overline{6}} - 1 = 0.0080848171$
        Solve for R giving R = $736.84
        Balance after 2 years = $81,264.88
        Monthly payment starting in year 3 = $736.84 + $50 = $786.84
        Balance an additional 24 payments later = $77,841.37
        Balance after $5000 prepayment = $72,841.37

   a. Number of payments of $786.84 to pay off the $72,841.37 balance is n = 171.393. Overall, the
       amortization period has been reduced by
          300 − (172 + 24 + 24) = 80 months = 6 years and 8 months

   b. Balance after 5 years
       = Balance 12 payments after balance reached $72,841.37
       = $70,357.69

34.   Given: A_n = $66,000, i = 6%, n = 240, c = $0.1\overline{6}$
        p = $1.06^{0.1\overline{6}} - 1 = 0.0097587942$
        Solve for R giving R = $713.44
        The balance after 3 years (36 payments) is $63,025.42.
        Refinancing the mortgage requires prepayment of the entire balance. The 3 months' interest penalty
        would be
          3 (0.0097587942) $63,025.42 = $1845.16

Exercise 14.3 *(concluded)*

35.   Given: $A_n = \$90,000$, $i = 5.5\%$, n = 240, c = $0.1\overline{6}$
        $p = 1.055^{0.1\overline{6}} - 1 = 0.0089633939$
Solve for R giving R = \$914.08
Balance after 27 payments = \$86,736.42
Amount subject to prepayment penalty
       = \$86,736.42 − 0.1 (\$90,000) = \$77,736.42
Prepayment penalty = 3 (0.0089633939) \$77,736.42
               = \$2090.35
Total amount required to settle mortgage = \$86,736.42 + \$2090.35
                        = <u>\$88,826.77</u>

Exercise 14.4

1.   The monthly payments are based on
        $A_n = \$21,500$, n = 60, and $p = i = 1.125\%$
Solving for R gives R = \$494.71
Since the borrower receives only \$20,000, the effective interest rate per payment interval is the value of p satisfying

$$\$20,000 = \$494.71 \left[\frac{1 - (1 + p)^{-60}}{p} \right]$$

The solution is p = 0.013985 per month.
The effective cost of borrowing is
     $f = (1 + p)^m - 1 = 1.013985^{12} - 1 = 0.18135 = \underline{18.135\%}$.

2.   Monthly payments are based on
        $A_n = \$63,000$, n = 300, $i = 4\%$, and c = $0.1\overline{6}$
          $p = 1.04^{0.1\overline{6}} - 1 = 0.0065581969$
Solve for R giving R = \$480.82.
Balance after 60 payments = \$58,045.86
Since the borrower actually receives only \$60,000, the effective interest rate per payment interval is the value of p satisfying

$$\$60,000 = \$480.82 \left[\frac{1 - (1 + p)^{-60}}{p} \right] + \frac{\$58,045.86}{(1 + p)^{60}}$$

The solution is p = 0.0075830 per month.
The effective cost of borrowing is
     $f = (1 + p)^m - 1 = 1.0075830^{12} - 1 = 0.09489 = \underline{9.489\%}$.

3.   Monthly payments are based on
        $A_n = \$105,000$, n = 180, $i = 5.4\%$, and c = $0.1\overline{6}$.
          $p = 1.054^{0.1\overline{6}} - 1 = 0.0088039370$
Solve for R giving R = \$1164.89.

Exercise 14.4 *(continued)*

a. Balance after 60 payments = $86,097.64
The effective interest rate per payment interval is the value of p satisfying

$$\$100{,}000 = \$1164.89 \left[\frac{1-(1+p)^{-60}}{p}\right] + \frac{\$86{,}097.64}{(1+p)^{60}}$$

p = 0.00994354 per month

The effective annual cost of borrowing is
$f = (1+p)^m - 1 = 1.00994354^{12} - 1 = \underline{12.607\%}.$

b. Balance after 120 payments = $54,114.42
Solve for p in

$$\$100{,}000 = \$1164.89 \left[\frac{1-(1+p)^{-120}}{p}\right] + \frac{\$54{,}114.42}{(1+p)^{120}}$$

p = 0.00959692 per month

The effective cost of borrowing is
$f = 1.00959692^{12} - 1 = \underline{12.144\%}.$

c. Solve for p in

$$\$100{,}000 = \$1164.89 \left[\frac{1-(1+p)^{-180}}{p}\right]$$

p = 0.00954005 per month

The effective cost of borrowing is
$f = 1.00954005^{12} - 1 = \underline{12.068\%}$

4. Monthly payments are based on
$A_n = \$77{,}500$, n = 240, $i = 6\%$, and $c = 0.1\overline{6}$
$p = 1.06^{0.1\overline{6}} - 1 = 0.0097587942$
Solve for R giving R = $837.75.

a. Balance after 36 payments = $74,007.19
The effective interest rate per payment interval is the value of p satisfying

$$\$75{,}000 = \$837.75 \left[\frac{1-(1+p)^{-36}}{p}\right] + \frac{\$74{,}007.19}{(1+p)^{36}}$$

p = 0.0108676 per month

The effective (annual) cost of borrowing is
$f = (1+p)^m - 1 = 1.0108676^{12} - 1 = \underline{13.850\%}$

Exercise 14.4 (continued)

b. Balance after 84 payments = $66,976.94
   Solve for p in

$$\$75,000 = \$837.75 \left[\frac{1 - (1 + p)^{-84}}{p} \right] + \frac{\$66,976.94}{(1 + p)^{84}}$$

   p = 0.0103653 per month
   The effective cost of borrowing is
   f = $1.0103653^{12} - 1 = \underline{13.172\%}$

c. Solve for p in

$$\$75,000 = \$837.75 \left[\frac{1 - (1 + p)^{-240}}{p} \right]$$

   p = 0.0101898 per month
   The effective cost of borrowing is
   f = $1.0101898^{12} - 1 = \underline{12.937\%}$

5. The payments on the loan from the mortgage broker are based on
   $A_n = \$82,200$, $i = 5.125\%$, n = 120, and c = $0.1\overline{6}$
   p = $1.05125^{0.1\overline{6}} - 1 = 0.0083647796$
   Solving for R gives R = $1088.00

a. Balance after 60 payments = $51,162.08
   The effective rate per payment interval is the solution to

$$\$80,000 = \$1088.00 \left[\frac{1 - (1 + p)^{-60}}{p} \right] + \frac{\$51,162.08}{(1 + p)^{60}}$$

   The solution is p = 0.009049832.
   The effective cost of borrowing on the brokered loan is
   f = $1.009049832^{12} - 1 = 11.417\%$
   The effective rate on the trust company loan is
   f = $(1 + i)^m - 1 = 1.05375^2 - 1 = 11.039\%$
   The trust company loan's effective rate is 0.378% lower.

b. The effective interest rate per payment interval on the brokered loan is the solution to

$$\$80,000 = \$1088.00 \left[\frac{1 - (1 + p)^{-120}}{p} \right]$$

   The solution is p = 0.00890817.
   The effective cost of borrowing is
   f = $1.00890817^{12} - 1 = 11.229\%$
   compared to f = 11.039% for the trust company loan.
   The effective cost of borrowing from the trust company is 0.190% lower.

Exercise 14.4 *(continued)*

6.   Payments on the loan from the mortgage broker are based on
$$A_n = \$93{,}000, \; n = 240, \; i = 5.125\%, \text{ and } c = 0.1\overline{6}.$$
$$p = 1.05125^{0.1\overline{6}} - 1 = 0.0083647796$$
Solving for R gives R = \$899.80.
Balance after 84 payments = \$78,237.79
The effective rate per payment interval is the solution to

$$\$90{,}000 = \$899.80 \left[\frac{1 - (1 + p)^{-84}}{p} \right] + \frac{\$78{,}237.79}{(1 + p)^{84}}$$

The solution is p = 0.00894741.
The effective annual rate on the loan <u>from broker M</u> is

$$f = 1.00894741^{12} - 1 = \underline{\underline{11.281\%}}.$$

The effective annual rate on the loan <u>from bank B</u> is

$$f = 1.05375^2 - 1 = \underline{\underline{11.039\%}}.$$

The effective annual rate on the loan <u>from credit union C</u> is

$$f = 1.00875^{12} - 1 = \underline{\underline{11.020\%}}.$$

7.   With $A_n = \$40{,}000, \; n = 40, \; i = 3.5\%, \; c = 0.5,$ and
$$p = 1.035^{0.5} - 1 = 0.017349497,$$
the quarterly payments are R = \$1395.12.

    a.   The fair market value (FMV) of the mortgage equals the present value of the 40 payments discounted at the prevailing market rate of interest. The market rate per payment interval is
$$p = 1.0525^{0.5} - 1 = 0.025914226$$

$$\text{FMV} = A_n = \$1395.12 \left[\frac{1 - 1.025914226^{-40}}{0.025914226} \right] = \underline{\underline{\$34{,}488.28}}$$

    b.   The market rate per payment interval is
$$p = 1.045^{0.5} - 1 = 0.022252415$$
The present value of the 40 payments discounted at this rate is $A_n = \underline{\underline{\$36{,}699.09}}$.

8.   The fair market value (FMV) of the mortgage equals the present value of the cash flows from the mortgage, discounted at the prevailing market rate on mortgages with similar terms.
Step 1: Calculate the balance owed at the end of the 2 years.
Step 2: Calculate the combined present value of this balance and 2 years' payments discounted at the market rate.

    Step 1: $A_n = \$55{,}000, \; R = \$500, \; i = 3.75\%, \; c = 0.1\overline{6}$
$$p = 1.0375^{0.1\overline{6}} - 1 = 0.0061545239$$
Balance after 24 payments = \$50,836.85

    Step 2: The market rate per payment interval is
$$p = 1.0475^{0.1\overline{6}} - 1 = 0.0077643832$$

$$\text{FMV} = A_n = \$500 \left[\frac{1 - 1.0077643832^{-24}}{0.0077643832} \right] + \frac{\$50{,}836.85}{1.0077643832^{24}} = \underline{\underline{\$53{,}134.08}}$$

Exercise 14.4 *(continued)*

9. The fair market value (FMV) of a mortgage equals the present value of the remaining cash flows discounted at the prevailing market rate.

Step 1: Calculate the payments on the mortgage having
A_n = \$60,000, i = 6%, n = 240, and c = 0.1$\overline{6}$.
$$p = 1.06^{0.1\overline{6}} - 1 = 0.0097587942$$
Solving for R gives R = \$648.58

Step 2: Calculate the balance at the end of the 5-year term.
Balance after 60 payments = \$54,890.27.

Step 3: Calculate the combined present value of the step 2 balance and the remaining 39 payments discounted at the prevailing market rate.

a. At a market rate of
$$p = 1.055^{0.1\overline{6}} - 1 = 0.0089633939$$

$$FMV = \$648.58 \left[\frac{1 - 1.0089633939^{-39}}{0.0089633939} \right] + \frac{\$54,890.27}{1.0089633939}$$

$$= \$60,024.46$$

b. Similarly, at a market rate of
$$p = 1.06^{0.1\overline{6}} - 1 = 0.0097587942$$
FMV = \$58,538.34

c. At a market rate of
$$p = 1.065^{0.1\overline{6}} - 1 = 0.010551074$$
FMV = \$57,100.64

10. The price the investor should pay is the present value of the remaining cash flows discounted at the required rate of return.

Step 1: Calculate the mortgage's balance at the end of the 4-year term.
A_n = \$45,000, R = \$500, i = 5%, c = 0.1$\overline{6}$
$$p = 1.05^{0.16} - 1 = 0.0081648460$$
Balance after 48 payments = \$37,247.01

Step 2: Calculate the combined present value of the step 1 balance and the remaining 28 payments discounted at the investor's required rate of return.

a. For a return of 11% compounded semiannually,
$$p = 1.055^{0.1\overline{6}} - 1 = 0.0089633939$$

$$Price = \$500 \left[\frac{1 - 1.0089633939^{-28}}{0.0089633939} \right] + \frac{\$37,247.01}{1.0089633939^{28}}$$

$$= \$41,344.97$$

Exercise 14.4 (continued)

   b. For a return of 10% compounded semiannually,
      $p = 1.05^{0.1\overline{6}} - 1 = 0.0081648460$
      Price = A_n = $\underline{\$42,132.25}$

   c. For a return of 9% compounded semiannually,
      $p = 1.045^{0.1\overline{6}} - 1 = 0.0073631230$
      Price = A_n = $\underline{\$42,940.02}$

11.   Equivalent cash value = Cash payment + Fair market value of vendor take-back mortgage

   Step 1: Calculate payments on the take-back mortgage.
      A_n = $95,000, n = 120, i = 4%, c = 0.1$\overline{6}$
      $p = 1.04^{0.1\overline{6}} - 1 = 0.0065581969$
      Solving for R gives R = $1146.09.

   Step 2: Calculate the present value of these payments discounted at the prevailing market rate (10.25% compounded semiannually).
      $p = 1.05125^{0.1\overline{6}} - 1 = 0.0083647796$

      $A_n = \$1146.09 \left[\dfrac{1 - 1.0083647796^{-120}}{0.0083647796} \right] = \$86,588.89$

   Equivalent cash value = $75,000 + $86,588.89 = $\underline{\$161,588.89}$

12.   Equivalent cash value = Cash payment + Fair market value of vendor take-back mortgage

   a. Step 1: Calculate the balance after 5 years.
         With A_n = $95,000, R = $1146.09, and p = 0.65581969%,
         Balance after 60 payments = $56,697.22

      Step 2: Calculate the combined present value of the step 1 balance and the first 60 payments discounted at p = 0.83647796%.
            Present value = $88,289.54
            Equivalent cash value = $75,000 + $88,289.54 = $\underline{\$163,289.54}$

   b. Similarly, balance after 12 payments = $88,491.84
      FMV of take-back mortgage = $93,107.55
      Equivalent cash value = $75,000 + $93,107.55 = $\underline{\$168,107.55}$

13.   Equivalent cash value = Cash payment + Market value of the vendor take-back mortgage

   Step 1: Calculate the balance at the end of the 5-year term.
      A_n = $100,000, i = 4%, R = $750, c = 0.1$\overline{6}$
      $p = 1.04^{0.1\overline{6}} - 1 = 0.0065581969$
      Balance after 60 payments = $93,103.36

Step 2: Calculate the combined present value of the step 1 balance and the first 60 payments discounted at

$$p = 1.05125^{0.1\overline{6}} - 1 = 0.0083647796$$

$$\text{Market value} = \$750 \left[\frac{1 - 1.0083647796^{-60}}{0.0083647796} \right] + \frac{\$93,103.36}{1.0083647796^{60}}$$

$$= \$91,749.57$$

Equivalent cash value = $50,000 + $91,749.57 = $141,749.57
Offer M is worth $1749.50 more (in current dollars).

14. Cash value = Down payment + Market value of mortgage

Step 1: Calculate the monthly payment on the proposed mortgage
$A_n = \$120,000$, $i = 4.25\%$, n = 240, c = 0.1\overline{6}
$p = 1.0425^{0.1\overline{6}} - 1 = 0.0069610621$
Solve for R giving R = $1030.27.

Step 2: The market value of the mortgage is the present value of these payments discounted at
$p = 1.0525^{0.1\overline{6}} - 1 = 0.0085645151$
This present value is $A_n = \$104,758.30$.
The cash value of the offer is $60,000 + $104,758.30 = $164,758.30.

15. Step 1: Calculate the size of the mortgage payments.
$A_n = \$80,000$, n = 300, $i = 5.25\%$, and c = 0.1\overline{6}
$p = 1.0525^{0.1\overline{6}} - 1 = 0.0085645151$
Solve for R giving R = $742.66

Step 2: Calculate the balance after 2 years.
Balance after 24 payments = $78,475.18.

Step 3: Calculate 3 months' interest on the step 2 balance.
Case "a" penalty = 3 (0.0085645151) $78,475.18
$= \$2016.30$

Step 4: Calculate the current market value of the mortgage by discounting remaining payments at
$p = 1.045^{0.1\overline{6}} - 1 = 0.0073631230$
Balance at end of 5-year term = $75,514.67

$$\text{FMV} = \$742.66 \left[\frac{1 - 1.007363123^{-36}}{0.007363123} \right] + \frac{\$75,514.67}{1.007363123^{36}}$$

$$= \$81,397.91$$

Step 5: Calculate the case "b" prepayment penalty.
Penalty = $81,397.91 − $78,475.18 = $2922.73
The larger of the alternative penalties is $2922.73.

Exercise 14.4 (continued)

16. Step 1: Calculate the monthly mortgage payment.
    A_n = $75,000, n = 300, i = 4.5%, and c = $0.1\bar{6}$
    p = $1.045^{0.1\bar{6}} - 1$ = 0.0073631230
    Solve for R giving R = $620.98.

    Step 2: Calculate the balance after 19 payments.
    Balance after 19 payments = $73,603.55

    Step 3: Calculate 3 months' interest on the step 2 balance.
    Case "a" penalty = 3 (0.007363123) $73,603.55
    $\qquad\qquad$ = $1625.86

    Step 4: Calculate the current market value of the mortgage by discounting remaining payments at
    p = $1.04^{0.1\bar{6}} - 1$ = 0.0065581969
    Balance at end of 5-year term = $69,837.20
    The fair market value of the mortgage is

    $$\$620.98 \left[\frac{1 - 1.0065581969^{-41}}{0.0065581969} \right] + \frac{\$69,837.20}{1.0065581969^{41}} = \$75,679.49$$

    Step 5: Calculate the case "b" prepayment penalty.
    Penalty = $75,679.49 − $73,603.55 = $2075.94
    The larger of the two alternative penalties is $2075.94.

17. The expected market value of the property in 15 years is
    S = P $(1 + i)^n$ = $150,000 $(1.06)^{15}$ = $359,483.73
    The future value, after 15 years, of the monthly reverse mortgage payments is to be
    S_n = 0.7 ($359,483.73) = $251,638.61
    With i = 5.5%, n = 12(15) = 180, c = $0.1\bar{6}$,
    p = $1.055^{0.1\bar{6}} - 1$ = 0.0089633939,
    the monthly payment is the solution to

    $$\$251,638.61 = R \left(\frac{1.0089633939^{180} - 1}{0.0089633939} \right)$$

    $$R = \underline{\$566.16}$$

    The monthly reverse mortgage payment can be $566.16.

18. For the reverse mortgage advances,
    R = $700, i = 5.25%, c = $0.1\bar{6}$,
    p = $1.0525^{0.1\bar{6}} - 1$ = 0.0085645151

    a. After 5 years (n = 60), balance owed on mortgage will be

    $$S_n = \$700 \left(\frac{1.0085645151^{60} - 1}{0.0085645151} \right) = \$54,605$$

    Expected market value of home is
    S = P $(1 + i)^n$ = $160,000 $(1.06)^5$ = $214,116

    $$\frac{\text{Debt}}{\text{Market value}} = \frac{\$54,605}{\$214,116} \times 100\% = \underline{25.50\%}$$

Exercise 14.4 *(continued)*

b. Similarly, after 10 years,

$$\frac{\text{Debt}}{\text{Market value}} = \frac{\$145,692}{\$286,536} \times 100\% = \underline{50.85\%}$$

c. Similarly, after 15 years,

$$\frac{\text{Debt}}{\text{Market value}} = \frac{\$297,633}{\$383,449} \times 100\% = \underline{77.62\%}$$

19. From Example 14.4f, part b, the balance owed on the reverse mortgage after n months will be

$$S_n = \$600 \left(\frac{1.0087640531^n - 1}{0.0087640531} \right)$$

The expected market value of the home after n months is
$$S = \$130,000 (1 + p)^n$$
where $p = 1.07^{0.08\overline{3}} - 1 = 0.005654145$
Equate the expressions for S_n and 0.7S, and solve for n.
The solution is n = 173.0 months.
It will take 173 months or <u>14 years and 5 months</u> for the amount owed to reach 70% of the home's market value. (Comparing this result to the answer in Example 14.4f, we see that a 1% higher rate of appreciation in the property's value extends the duration of the monthly mortgage advances by 2 years and 11 months.)

20. Since $45,000 = 0.3 (Current appraised value)

$$\text{Current appraised value} = \frac{\$45,000}{0.3} = \$150,000$$

Expected market value of home after N years is
$$\$150,000 (1.06)^N$$
Amount owed on the mortgage after N years will be
$$\$45,000 (1.05625)^{2N}$$

	Years later (N)	Amount owed	Market value	Equity	Equity as a % of market value
a.	5	$77,782	$200,734	$122,952	61.25%
b.	10	134,446	268,627	134,181	49.95%
c.	15	232,388	359,484	127,096	35.36%
d.	20	401,681	481,070	79,389	16.50%

21. The current appraised value of Mrs. Yokoyama's home is

$$\frac{\$50,000}{0.3} = \$166,667$$

The expected market value of the home after 10 years of appreciation at i per year is

$$\$166,667 (1 + i)^{10}$$

The amount owed on the loan after 10 years is

$$S = \$50,000 (1.0525)^{20} = \$139,127$$

	Annual rate (i)	Amount owed	Market value	Equity	Equity as a % of market value
a.	4%	$139,127	$246,707	$107,580	43.61%
b.	6%	139,127	298,475	159,348	53.39%
c.	8%	139,127	359,821	220,694	61.33%

22. Let V represent the property's current appraised value, and let x represent the maximum loan-to-value ratio.

    The amount owed on the home after 19 + 7 = 26 years will be

    $$S = P (1 + i)^n = xV (1.0525)^{52}$$

    The expected value of the home in 26 years is

    $$S = P (1 + i)^n = V (1.05)^{26}$$

    Solve for the value of x that makes

    $$xV (1.0525)^{52} = V (1.05)^{26}$$

    $$x = \frac{1.05^{26}}{1.0525^{52}} = \frac{3.5557}{14.3070} \times 100\% = \underline{\underline{24.85\%}}$$

    The maximum loan-to-loan ratio is 24.85%.

23. The solution proceeds as for problem 22 with the change that the expected market value of the property after 26 years is

    $$S = V (1.07)^{26}$$

    Then

    $$x = \frac{1.07^{26}}{1.0525^{52}} = \frac{5.8074}{14.3070} \times 100\% = \underline{\underline{40.59\%}}$$

    If the property appreciates at 7% per year instead of 5% per year, the maximum loan-to-loan value ratio can be 40.59% instead of 24.85%.

24. a. The amount owed on the loan after 24 years will be

    $$S = P (1 + i)^n = \$45,000 (1.05625)^{48} = \$622,322$$

    The expected market value of the home in 24 years is

    $$S = \$150,000 (1.06)^{24} = \$607,340$$

    The lender's loss (in nominal dollars 24 years from now) will be

    $$\$622,322 - \$607,340 = \underline{\underline{\$14,982}}$$

  b. The amount owed on the loan in 20 years will be

    $$S = \$45,000 (1.05625)^{40} = \$401,681$$

    The expected market value of the property in 20 years is

    $$S = \$150,000 (1.05)^{20} = \$397,995$$

    The lender's loss will be

    $$\$401,681 - \$397,995 = \underline{\underline{\$3686}}$$

Exercise 14.4 *(concluded)*

25. After N years, the market value of the property is expected to be

$166,667 $(1.06)^N$

and the amount owed on the loan will be

$50,000 $(1.0525)^{2N}$

Solve for the value of N that makes these two amounts equal.

$166,667 $(1.06)^N$ = $50,000 $(1.0525)^{2N}$

$$1.06^N = 0.3 \, (1.0525)^{2N}$$

$$N \ln (1.06) = \ln (0.3) + 2N \ln (1.0525)$$

$$N = \frac{\ln (0.3)}{\ln (1.06) - 2 \ln (1.0525)} = 27.32$$

The lender will start to lose money after 27.32 years or <u>27 years, 4 months.</u>

Note: Students unfamiliar with logarithms can use the trial-and-error method to solve the equation for N.

26. The interest rate on the annuity will be
10.75% − 1.5% = 9.25% compounded semiannually.
The purchase price of the annuity equals the present value of the annuity payments. With
A_n = $35,000, i = 4.625%, n = 180, and c = 0.1$\overline{6}$,
then p = $1.04625^{0.1\overline{6}} - 1$ = 0.007563853.
Solving for R gives R = <u>$356.59.</u>
The annuitant can expect monthly payments of $356.59.

Review Problems

1. Amount to be paid off = $1150 (1 − 0.25) = $862.50.
The present value of the six payments is $862.50.
A_n = $862.50, n = 6, p = i = 0.9375%.
Solving for R gives R = $148.50.

Payment number	Payment	Interest portion	Principal portion	Principal balance
0				$862.50
1	$148.50	$8.09	$140.41	722.09
2	148.50	6.77	141.73	580.36
3	148.50	5.44	143.06	437.30
4	148.50	4.10	144.40	292.90
5	148.50	2.75	145.75	147.15
6	148.53	1.38	147.15	0.00
	Total:	$28.53		

Review Problems *(continued)*

2.   Given: $A_n = \$7000$, $n = 6$, $i = 10.75\%$, $c = 0.5$,
        $p = 1.1075^{0.5} - 1 = 0.052378259$
        Solving for R gives R = $1389.63

Payment number	Payment	Interest portion	Principal portion	Principal balance
0				$7000.00
1	$1389.63	$366.65	$1022.98	5977.02
2	1389.63	313.07	1076.56	4900.46
3	1389.63	256.68	1132.95	3767.51
4	1389.63	197.34	1192.29	2575.22
5	1389.63	134.89	1254.74	1320.48
6	1389.64	69.16	1320.48	0.00

3.   Given: $A_n = \$28,000$, $p = i = 2.625\%$, $n = 28$
        Solving for R gives R = $1424.62

   a.   Principal in R_6 = Balance after R_5 – Balance after R_6
             = \$24,366.06 – \$23,581.05
             = <u>$785.01</u>

   b.   Interest in R_{22} = p x Balance after R_{21}
             = 0.02625 (\$9002.63)
             = <u>$236.32</u>

   c.   Principal paid by R_{10} to R_{15} inclusive
           = Balance after R_9 – Balance after R_{15}
           = \$21,100.20 – \$15,520.67
           = <u>$5579.53</u>

   d.   Interest paid in year 2 = 4R – (Balance after R_4 – Balance after R_8)
                          = 4 (\$1424.62) – (\$25,130.99 – \$21,948.67)
                          = <u>$2516.16</u>

4.   Given: $A_n = \$180,000$, $i = 3.75\%$, $n = 240$, $c = 0.1\overline{6}$,
        $p = 1.0375^{0.1\overline{6}} - 1 = 0.0061545239$
        Solve for R giving R = $1437.48

   a.   Principal in R_{134} = Balance after R_{133} – Balance after R_{134}
              = \$112,426.25 – \$111,680.70
              = <u>$745.55</u>

   b.   Interest in R_{210} = p x Balance after R_{209}
              = 0.0061545239 (\$40,457.65)
              = <u>$249.00</u>

   c.   Principal paid by R_{75} to R_{100} inclusive
           = Balance after R_{74} – Balance after R_{100}
           = \$149,218.50 – \$134,630.29
           = <u>$14,588.21</u>

Review Problems (continued)

d. Interest paid in year 6 = 12R − (Balance after R_{60} − Balance after R_{72})
   = 12 ($1437.48) − ($156,161.32 − $150,247.21)
   = $11,335.65

5. Given: A_n = $60,000, p = i = 5.25%, R = $10,000

Payment number	Payment	Interest portion	Principal portion	Principal balance
0				$60,000.00
1	$10,000.00	$3150.00	$6850.00	53,150.00
2	10,000.00	2790.38	7209.62	45,940.38
3	10,000.00	2411.87	7588.13	38,352.25
4	10,000.00	2013.49	7986.51	30,365.74
5	10,000.00	1594.20	8405.80	21,959.94
6	10,000.00	1152.90	8847.10	13,112.84
7	10,000.00	688.42	9311.58	3801.26
8	4000.83	199.57	3801.26	0.00
	Total:	$14,000.83		

6. Given: A_n = $60,000, p = i = 5.25%, R = $10,000.
   Balloon payment of $5000 is paid along with R_3.

Payment number	Payment	Interest portion	Principal portion	Principal balance
0				$60,000.00
1	$10,000.00	$3150.00	$6850.00	53,150.00
2	10,000.00	2790.38	7209.62	45,940.38
3	15,000.00	2411.87	12,588.13	33,352.25
4	10,000.00	1750.99	8249.01	25,103.24
5	10,000.00	1317.92	8682.08	16,421.16
6	10,000.00	862.11	9137.89	7283.27
7	7665.64	382.37	7283.27	0.00
	Total:	$12,665.64		

Interest saved = $14,000.83 − $12,665.64 = $1335.19

7. Given: A_n = $45,000, p = i = 0.625%, R = $500

a. Interest in R_{37} = p x Balance after R_{36}
   = 0.00625 ($36,199.39)
   = $226.25

b. Principal in R_{92} = Balance after R_{91} − Balance after R_{92}
   = $18,297.28 − $17,911.63
   = $385.65

c. Interest paid by R_{85} to R_{96} inclusive
   = 12R − (Balance after R_{84} − Balance after R_{96})
   = 12 ($500) − ($20,930.53 − $16,344.81)
   = $1414.28

Review Problems (continued)

d. Principal paid in year 5 = Balance after R_{48} − Balance after R_{60}
$$= \$32{,}799.03 - \$29{,}134.70$$
$$= \underline{\$3664.33}$$

8.   Given: $A_n = \$80{,}000$, $p = i = 0.8125\%$, R = \$1200

Payment number	Payment	Interest portion	Principal portion	Principal balance
0				$80,000.00
1	$1200.00	$650.00	$550.00	79,450.00
2	1200.00	645.53	554.47	78,895.53
|	|	|	|	|
|	|	|	|	|
40				54,127.03
41	1200.00	439.78	760.22	53,366.81
42	1200.00	433.61	766.39	52,600.42
|	|	|	|	|
|	|	|	|	|
95				1674.48
96	1200.00	13.61	1186.39	488.09
97	492.06	3.97	488.09	0.00

9.   Given: $A_n = \$90{,}000$, $i = 4.625\%$, n = 240, c = 0.1$\overline{6}$
   $p = 1.04625^{0.1\overline{6}} - 1 = 0.0075638530$
   Solving for R gives R = \$814.19.

a.   Balance after 5 years = Balance after R_{60} = $\underline{\$79{,}914.89}$

b.   For renewal of the loan after 5 years,
   $A_n = \$79{,}914.89$, n = 180, $i = 5.25\%$, c = 0.1$\overline{6}$
   $p = 1.0525^{0.1\overline{6}} - 1 = 0.0085645151$
   Solving for R gives R = $\underline{\$872.38}$

10.   Given: R = \$802.23, n = 300, $A_n = \$95{,}000$, c = 0.1$\overline{6}$
   The interest rate per one-month payment interval is the value of p satisfying

$$\$95{,}000 = \$802.23 \left[\frac{1 - (1 + p)^{-300}}{p} \right]$$
$$p = 0.007563889$$

   The equivalent interest rate for 6 months is
   $i = (1 + p)^6 - 1 = 1.007563889^6 - 1 = 0.046250$
   The corresponding nominal annual rate is
   $j = 2i = 2\,(4.625\%) = \underline{9.25\%\text{ compounded semiannually}}$

11.   Given: $A_n = \$25{,}000$, $p = i = 0.8125\%$, n = 120
   Solve for R giving R = \$326.93.
   The "rounded" payment is \$330.
   Balance after 36 payments of \$330 = $\underline{\$19{,}719.03}$

Review Problems *(continued)*

12. Given: $A_n = \$95,000$, $i = 4.75\%$, $n = 300$, $c = 0.1\overline{6}$

$p = 1.0475^{0.1\overline{6}} - 1 = 0.0077643832$

a. Solving for R gives R = $817.98
Balance after 36 payments = $91,676.88
Balance after $3000 prepayment = $88,676.88
The number of additional payments required to pay off this balance is

$$n = -\frac{\ln\left[1 - \dfrac{0.0077643832\,(\$88,676.88)}{\$817.98}\right]}{\ln(1.0077643832)} = 238.348$$

The total time required to pay off the loan is
239 + 36 = 275 months.
The prepayment reduces the amortization period by
300 − 275 = 25 months = <u>2 years and 1 month</u>.

b. Balance at end of 5-year term
= Balance 2 years after $3000 prepayment
= <u>$85,275.98</u>

13. Given: $A_n = \$110,000$, $n = 300$, $i = 5.125\%$, $c = 0.1\overline{6}$

$p = 1.05125^{0.1\overline{6}} - 1 = 0.0083647796$

a. Solving for R gives R = $1002.50.
Balance after 24 payments = $107,820.65
Monthly payment after 10% increase = 1.1 ($1002.50) = $1102.75
The number of these payments required to pay off the balance is

$$n = -\frac{\ln\left[1 - \dfrac{0.0083647796\,(\$107,820.65)}{\$1102.75}\right]}{\ln(1.0083647796)} = 204.44$$

The total time required to pay off the loan is
205 + 24 = 229 months.
Hence, the larger payments reduce the amortization period by 300 − 229 = 71 months or <u>5 years and 11 months</u>.

b. Balance at end of 5-year term
= Balance after 36 payments of $1102.75
= <u>$99,423.78</u>

Review Problems *(continued)*

14. Given: $A_n = \$72,000$, $i = 5\%$, n = 240, c = $0.1\overline{6}$
$p = 1.05^{0.1\overline{6}} - 1 = 0.0081648460$
Solve for R giving R = $685.20
Balance after 31 payments = $68,582.29
Amount subject to prepayment penalty
= $68,582.29 − 0.10 ($72,000)
= $61,382.29
Three months' interest penalty = 3 (0.0081648460) $61,382.29
= $1503.53
Amount required to pay off mortgage = $68,582.29 + $1503.53
= $70,085.82

15. Monthly payments are based on
$A_n = \$46,500$, n = 180, $i = 5.125\%$, and c = $0.1\overline{6}$
$p = 1.05125^{0.1\overline{6}} - 1 = 0.0083647796$
Solving for R gives R = $500.77.

a. Balance after 36 payments = $41,825.79
The effective interest rate per payment interval is the solution to

$$\$45,000 = \$500.77 \left[\frac{1 - (1 + p)^{-36}}{p} \right] + \frac{\$41,825.79}{(1 + p)^{36}}$$

p = 0.0094748617

The effective annual cost of borrowing is
$f = (1 + p)^m - 1 = 1.0094748617^{12} - 1 = \underline{11.981\%}$

b. Balance after 60 payments = $37,833.30
Solve for p in

$$\$45,000 = \$500.77 \left[\frac{1 - (1 + p)^{-60}}{p} \right] + \frac{\$37,833.30}{(1 + p)^{60}}$$

p = 0.0091225854

The effective annual cost of borrowing is
$f = 1.0091225854^{12} - 1 = \underline{11.513\%}$

16. Given: $A_n = \$60,000$, $i = 5.5\%$, n = 300, c = $0.1\overline{6}$
$p = 1.055^{0.1\overline{6}} - 1 = 0.0089633939$
Solve for R giving R = $577.52
Ms. Finch can expect to receive the fair market value of the mortgage which equals the present value of the remaining cash flows discounted at the prevailing market rate.
Balance after 29 payments = $58,691.32

a. If the market rate is 10% compounded semiannually,
$i = 5\%$, c = $0.1\overline{6}$, and $p = 1.05^{0.1\overline{6}} - 1 = 0.0081648460$

$$\text{Price} = \$577.52 \left(\frac{1 - 1.008164846^{-31}}{0.008164846} \right) + \frac{\$58,691.32}{1.008164846^{31}}$$

$$= \underline{\$61,374.33}$$

Review Problems (continued)

b. Similarly, if the market rate is 12% csa,
   $i = 6\%$, $c = 0.1\overline{6}$, and $p = 0.009758794$
   and the fair market value is $58,818.22$.

17. Cash value of the Conlins' offer
    = Cash payment + Fair market value of take-back mortgage
    Step 1: Calculate the balance after 5 years.
    $A_n = \$130,000$, $i = 3.75\%$, $c = 0.1\overline{6}$, $R = \$1000$
    $p = 1.0375^{0.1\overline{6}} - 1 = 0.0061545239$
    Balance after 60 payments = $115,544.04$

    Step 2: Calculate the combined present value of the step 1 balance and the first 60 payments
    discounted at
    $p = 1.0425^{0.1\overline{6}} - 1 = 0.0069610621$.
    Present value = $125,115.19$

    Step 3: Cash value of Conlin's offer = $65,000 + $125,115.19
    = $190,115.19$

    The Sharpe offer should be accepted since it is worth $884.81 more in current dollars.

18. The current appraised value of the Eubank home is

    $$\frac{\$51,000}{0.3} = \$170,000$$

    The expected market value of the home after N years is

    $$S = P (1 + i)^n = \$170,000 (1.05)^N$$

    The amount owed on the loan after N years will be

    $$\$51,000 (1.05375)^{2N}$$

Years later	Amount owed	Market value	Equity	Equity as a % of market value
a.	10	$145,319	$276,912	$131,593	47.52%
b.	20	414,070	451,061	36,991	8.20%
c.	25	698,955	575,680	−123,275	

    The lender's projected loss if the last surviving spouse lives 25 years is $123,275.

Review Problems *(concluded)*

19.   Let V represent the property's current appraised value, and let x represent the maximum loan-to-value ratio. The amount owed on the mortgage after 20.5 years will be

$$S = P(1 + i)^n = xV(1.04875)^{41}$$

In order to project the home's value after 20.5 years, we need the semiannually compounded equivalent of 5% compounded annually.

$$i = 1.05^{0.5} - 1 = 2.469508\%$$

The forecast value of the home in 20.5 years is

$$S = P(1 + i)^n = V(1.0246951)^{41}$$

The maximum loan-to-value ratio is the value of x satisfying

$$xV(1.04875)^{41} = V(1.0246951)^{41}$$

$$x = \frac{1.0246951^{41}}{1.04875^{41}} \times 100\% = \underline{\underline{38.62\%}}$$

The maximum initial loan-to-value ratio is 38.62%.

Self–Test Exercise

1.   Given: $A_n = \$16,000$, n = 60, $p = i = 0.9\%$
Solve for R giving R = \$346.29.

a.   Interest in $R_{29} = p \times$ Balance after R_{28}
$= 0.009\ (\$9590.86)$
$= \$86.32$

b.   Principal in $R_{46} =$ Balance after $R_{45} -$ Balance after R_{46}
$= \$4838.34 - \$4535.59$
$= \$302.75$

c.   Principal paid in year 2 = Balance after $R_{12} -$ Balance after R_{24}
$= \$13,448.68 - \$10,607.76$
$= \underline{\underline{\$2840.92}}$

d.   Interest paid in year 3 = 12R – (Balance after $R_{24} -$ Balance after R_{36})
$= 12\ (\$346.29) - (\$10,607.76 - \$7444.37)$
$= \underline{\underline{\$992.09}}$

2.   Given: $A_n = \$6400$, $i = 5\%$, n = 48, $c = 0.1\overline{6}$
$p = 1.05^{0.1\overline{6}} - 1 = 0.0081648460$
Solve for R giving R = \$161.70

Self-Test Exercise *(continued)*

Payment number	Payment	Interest portion	Principal portion	Principal balance
0				$6400.00
1	$161.70	$52.26	$109.44	6290.56
2	161.70	51.36	110.34	6180.22
⋮	⋮	⋮	⋮	⋮
⋮	⋮	⋮	⋮	⋮
33				2274.13
34	161.70	18.57	143.13	2131.00
35	161.70	17.40	144.30	1986.70
⋮	⋮	⋮	⋮	⋮
⋮	⋮	⋮	⋮	⋮
46				319.47
47	161.70	2.61	159.09	160.38
48	161.69	1.31	160.38	0.00

3. Given: $A_n = \$255{,}000$, $R = \$7500$, $i = 10\%$, $c = 0.25$

$p = 1.10^{0.25} - 1 = 0.024113689$

a. The number of payments needed to pay off the loan is

$$n = -\frac{\ln\left[1 - \dfrac{0.024113689\,(\$255{,}000)}{\$7500}\right]}{\ln(1.024113689)} = 71.935698$$

Final payment = $(1 + p) \times$ Balance after 71 payments
= 1.024113689 ($6857.73)
= $7023.10

b. Interest in $R_{27} = p \times$ Balance after R_{26}
= 0.024113689 ($206,927.51)
= $4989.79

c. Principal in $R_{53} =$ Balance after R_{52} − Balance after R_{53}
= $117,607.45 − $112,943.40
= $4664.05

d. Principal paid by payments 14 to 20 inclusive
= Balance after R_{13} − Balance after R_{20}
= $234,656.98 − $220,795.17
= $13,861.81

e. Interest paid in year 6 = 4R − (Balance after R_{20} − Balance after R_{24})
= 4 ($7500) − ($220,795.17 − $211,772.02)
= $20,976.85

4.   Initially, A_n = \$45,000, n = 300, i = 6.5%, and c = 0.1$\overline{6}$.
    p = $1.065^{0.1\overline{6}}$ − 1 = 0.010551074
    Solve for R giving R = \$496.08
    Balance after 60 payments = \$43,230.80
    At the first renewal,
        A_n = \$43,230.80, n = 240, i = 5.875%, c = 0.1$\overline{6}$,
            p = $1.05875^{0.1\overline{6}}$ − 1 = 0.0095602377
    Solving for R again gives R = \$460.20
    Balance after a further 60 payments = $\underline{\$39,453.90}$

5. A_n = \$87,000, i = 4.75%, n = 240, c = 0.1$\overline{6}$
    p = $1.0475^{0.1\overline{6}}$ − 1 = 0.0077643832
    Solving for R gives R = \$800.60

   a.   Balance after 16 payments = \$84,877.53
       Balance after \$4000 prepayment = \$80,877.53
       The number of additional payments required to pay off this balance is

$$n = -\frac{ln\left[1 - \dfrac{0.0077643832\,(\$80,877.53)}{\$800.60}\right]}{ln\,(1.0077643832)} = 198.357$$

   Total time to pay off loan = 199 + 16 = 215 months. Hence, the \$4000 prepayment shortens the amortization period by 240 − 215 = 25 months or $\underline{2\text{ years and 1 month}}$.

   b.   Balance after 3 years = Balance 20 months after \$4000 prepayment
                            = $\underline{\$77,157.87}$

6.   The monthly mortgage payments are based on
        A_n = \$110,000, i = 5.5%, n = 300, c = 0.1$\overline{6}$
            p = $1.055^{0.1\overline{6}}$ − 1 = 0.0089633939
    Solving for R gives R = \$1058.78
    The balance after 60 payments will be \$104,247.98. The effective cost of borrowing per payment interval is the value of p satisfying

$$\$106,700 = \$1058.78\left[\frac{1 - (1 + p)^{-60}}{p}\right] + \frac{\$104,247.98}{(1 + p)^{60}}$$

$$p = 0.009638292$$

   The effective annual cost of borrowing is
       f = $(1 + p)^{12}$ − 1 = 1.009638292^{12} − 1 = $\underline{12.199\%}$

Self-Test Exercise *(continued)*

7.   Cash value of Mrs. Jones's offer = Cash payment
        + Fair market value (FMV) of the take-back mortgage.
     The vendor take-back mortgage has
     $A_n = \$90{,}000$, $R = \$700$, $i = 3.75\%$, and $c = 0.1\overline{6}$
        $p = 1.0375^{0.1\overline{6}} - 1 = 0.0061545239$
     Balance after 36 payments = \$84,132.61
     The FMV of the mortgage is the combined present value of this balance and the 36 payments
     discounted at the prevailing market rate on 3-year term mortgages. The market rate per payment
     interval is
        $p = 1.0475^{0.1\overline{6}} - 1 = 0.0077643832$

$$\text{FMV} = \$700 \left(\frac{1 - 1.0077643832^{-36}}{0.0077643832} \right) + \frac{\$84{,}132.61}{1.0077643832^{36}}$$

   $$= \$85{,}596.33$$

   Rounded to the nearest dollar, the equivalent cash value of Mrs. Jones's offer is
      $\$100{,}000 + \$85{,}596 = \underline{\$185{,}596}$

8.   The amount owed on the mortgage after 12.5 years will be

   $$S = P(1 + i)^n = \$30{,}000 (1.055)^{25} = \$114{,}401.77$$

   The current market value of Mr. Lamelin's home is

   $$\frac{\$30{,}000}{0.27} = \$111{,}111$$

   The market value is expected to grow at the 6-month periodic rate of

   $$i = (1.07)^{0.5} - 1 = 3.4408043\%$$

   After 12.5 years, the market value is expected to be

   $$\$111{,}111 (1.034408043)^{25} = \$258{,}854$$

   After paying off the mortgage,

   $$\$258{,}854 - \$114{,}402 = \underline{\$144{,}452}$$

   will pass to Mr. Lamelin's estate.

9.   Let V = Current appraised value of the property

        x = Maximum initial loan-to-value ratio

   The amount owed after 18 years will be

   $$S = P(1 + i)^n = xV (1.055)^{36}$$

   The expected market value of the property after 18 years is

   $$V (1.06)^{18}$$

   The maximum loan-to-value ratio is the value of x satisfying

   $$xV (1.055)^{36} = V (1.06)^{18}$$

   $$x = \frac{1.06^{18}}{1.055^{36}} = \frac{2.8543}{6.8721} \times 100\% = \underline{41.54\%}$$

   The maximum loan-to-value ratio for a 70-year-old man is 41.54%.

15 Bonds and Sinking Funds

Changes in the Second Edition:

1. The former Section 15.2 (Valuation of Bonds) has been split into three sections:
   - 15.2 Bond Price on an Interest Payment Date
   - 15.3 Yield to Maturity on an Interest Payment Date
   - 15.4 Bond Price on Any Date

2. One of the mathematical steps in calculating a bond's market value between interest payment dates (Section 15.4) has been changed to make the procedure exactly the same as employed in the bond market. The procedure used in the first edition was slightly simpler but produced a small error — the price of a $1000 face value bond was typically 10 to 20 cents too high (and occasionally around $0.50 too high).

3. The short sub-section on Callable Bonds has been deleted because very few courses have the time to go beyond basic topics.

4. The angle notation for annuities is introduced for the first time in Section 15.6.

Exercise 15.2

1. Given: F = $1000, b = $\dfrac{12.25\%}{2}$ = 6.125%, p = $\dfrac{9.75\%}{2}$ = 4.875%

    Time until maturity = (June 1, 2003) − (June 1, 1986) = 17 years

    Fb = $61.25 and n = 34

    Bond price = 61.25\left(\dfrac{1 - 1.04875^{-34}}{0.04875}\right)$ + $\dfrac{\$1000}{1.04875^{34}}$ = $\underline{\underline{\$1205.58}}$

2. Given: F = $1000, b = $\dfrac{16\%}{2}$ = 8%, p = $\dfrac{10\%}{2}$ = 5%

    Time until maturity = (March 15, 2007) − (Sept. 15, 1989) = $17\frac{1}{2}$ years

    Fb = $80.00 and n = 35

    Bond price = $80 $\left(\dfrac{1 - 1.05^{-35}}{0.05}\right)$ + $\dfrac{\$1000}{1.05^{35}}$ = $\underline{\underline{\$1491.23}}$

3. Given: F = $1000, b = $\dfrac{9.30\%}{2}$ = 4.65%, p = $\dfrac{10.60\%}{2}$ = 5.30%

    Time until maturity = (Jan. 1, 2002) − (July 1, 1987) = $14\frac{1}{2}$ years

    Fb = $46.50 and n = 29

    Bond price = $46.50 $\left(\dfrac{1 - 1.053^{-29}}{0.053}\right)$ + $\dfrac{\$1000}{1.053^{29}}$ = $\underline{\underline{\$904.79}}$

4. Given: F = $1000, b = $\dfrac{9.75\%}{2}$ = 4.875%, p = $\dfrac{11.5\%}{2}$ = 5.75%

    Time until maturity = (Sept. 20, 2006) − (Sept. 20, 1987) = 19 years

    Fb = $48.75 and n = 38

    Bond price = $48.75 $\left(\dfrac{1 - 1.0575^{-38}}{0.0575}\right)$ + $\dfrac{\$1000}{1.0575^{38}}$ = $\underline{\underline{\$866.01}}$

5. Given: F = $1000, b = 4.75%, p = 5.75%

    Time until maturity = (Aug. 1, 2006) − (Aug. 1, 1990) = 16 years

    Fb = $47.50 and n = 32

    Bond price = $47.50 $\left(\dfrac{1 - 1.0575^{-32}}{0.0575}\right)$ + $\dfrac{\$1000}{1.0575^{32}}$ = $\underline{\underline{\$855.15}}$

6. Given: F = $1000, b = 4.85%, p = 5.95%

    Time until maturity = (July 1, 2009) − (Jan. 1, 1990) = $19\frac{1}{2}$ years

    Fb = $48.50 and n = 39

    Bond price = $48.50 $\left(\dfrac{1 - 1.0595^{-39}}{0.0595}\right)$ + $\dfrac{\$1000}{1.0595^{39}}$ = $\underline{\underline{\$834.53}}$

Exercise 15.2 *(continued)*

7. Given: F = $1000, b = 7.125%, p = 4.50%

    Time until maturity = (June 1, 2009) − (June 1, 1992) = 17 years

    Fb = $71.25 and n = 34

    Bond price = $71.25 $\left(\dfrac{1 - 1.045^{-34}}{0.045}\right) + \dfrac{\$1000}{1.045^{34}} = \underline{\underline{\$1452.73}}$

8. Given: F = $1000, b = 6.0%, p = 4.55%

    Time until maturity = (Apr. 1, 2005) − (Oct. 1, 1991) = $13\frac{1}{2}$ years

    Fb = $60.00 and n = 27

    Bond price = $60 $\left(\dfrac{1 - 1.0455^{-27}}{0.0455}\right) + \dfrac{\$1000}{1.0455^{27}} = \underline{\underline{\$1222.83}}$

9. For all four bonds, F = $1000, b = 5%, and p = 4%

    n = 10, 20, 30, and 50 for bonds A, B, C, and D, respectively.

    Price of A = $50 $\left(\dfrac{1 - 1.04^{-10}}{0.04}\right) + \dfrac{\$1000}{1.04^{10}} = \underline{\underline{\$1081.11}}$

    Price of B = $50 $\left(\dfrac{1 - 1.04^{-20}}{0.04}\right) + \dfrac{\$1000}{1.04^{20}} = \underline{\underline{\$1135.90}}$

    Similarly, price of C = $\underline{\underline{\$1172.92}}$ and price of D = $\underline{\underline{\$1214.82}}$

    The results demonstrate that, for a given difference

        "Coupon rate − Market rate",

    the bond premium gets larger for longer maturities.

10. For all four bonds, F = $1000, b = 5%, and p = 6%

    n = 10, 20, 30, and 50 for bonds E, F, G, and H, respectively.

    Price of E = $50 $\left(\dfrac{1 - 1.06^{-10}}{0.06}\right) + \dfrac{\$1000}{1.06^{10}} = \underline{\underline{\$926.40}}$

    Price of F = $50 $\left(\dfrac{1 - 1.06^{-20}}{0.06}\right) + \dfrac{\$1000}{1.06^{20}} = \underline{\underline{\$885.30}}$

    Similarly, price of G = $\underline{\underline{\$862.35}}$ and price of H = $\underline{\underline{\$842.38}}$

    The results demonstrate that, for a given difference

        "Market rate − Coupon rate",

    the bond discount gets larger for longer maturities.

Exercise 15.2 *(continued)*

11. For all three bonds, F = $1000, n = 40, and p = 4.5%

    b = 5%, 5.5%, and 6% for bonds J, K, and L, respectively.

    $$\text{Price of J} = \$50 \left(\frac{1 - 1.045^{-40}}{0.045} \right) + \frac{\$1000}{1.045^{40}} = \$1092.01$$

    $$\text{Price of K} = \$55 \left(\frac{1 - 1.045^{-40}}{0.045} \right) + \frac{\$1000}{1.045^{40}} = \$1184.02$$

    $$\text{Price of L} = \$60 \left(\frac{1 - 1.045^{-40}}{0.045} \right) + \frac{\$1000}{1.045^{40}} = \$1276.02$$

    The results demonstrate that, other variables remaining unchanged, the greater the spread

    "Coupon rate – Market rate",

    the larger the bond premium.

12. For all three bonds, F = $1000, n = 40, and p = 4.5%

    b = 4%, 3.5%, and 3% for bonds, M, N, and Q, respectively.

    $$\text{Price of M} = \$40 \left(\frac{1 - 1.045^{-40}}{0.045} \right) + \frac{\$1000}{1.045^{40}} = \$907.99$$

    $$\text{Price of N} = \$35 \left(\frac{1 - 1.045^{-40}}{0.045} \right) + \frac{\$1000}{1.045^{40}} = \$815.98$$

    $$\text{Price of Q} = \$30 \left(\frac{1 - 1.045^{-40}}{0.045} \right) + \frac{\$1000}{1.045^{40}} = \$723.98$$

    The results demonstrate that, other variables remaining unchanged, the greater the spread

    "Market rate – Coupon rate",

    the larger the bond discount.

13. For both bonds, F = $1000, n = 24, and p = 5%

    b = 4% and 6% for bonds E and F, respectively.

    $$\text{Price of E} = \$40 \left(\frac{1 - 1.05^{-24}}{0.05} \right) + \frac{\$1000}{1.05^{24}} = \$862.01$$

    $$\text{Price of F} = \$60 \left(\frac{1 - 1.05^{-24}}{0.05} \right) + \frac{\$1000}{1.05^{24}} = \$1137.99$$

Exercise 15.2 *(continued)*

14. Given: F = $1000, b = 5%, and n = 30
    When the market rate was p = 5%, the bond traded at face value ($1000) since p = b.

   a. If p rises to 5.5%, the price will drop to

$$\$50\left(\frac{1-1.055^{-30}}{0.055}\right) + \frac{\$1000}{1.055^{30}} = \$927.33$$

   The price change will be

$$V_f - V_i = \$927.33 - \$1000 = -\$72.67$$

   That is, the price will drop by $72.67.

   b. If p rises to 6%, the price will drop to

$$\$50\left(\frac{1-1.06^{-30}}{0.06}\right) + \frac{\$1000}{1.06^{30}} = \$862.35$$

   The price change will be

$$\$862.35 - \$1000 = -\$137.65$$

   That is, the price will drop by $137.65.

   c. If p falls to 4.5%, the price will rise to

$$\$50\left(\frac{1-1.045^{-30}}{0.045}\right) + \frac{\$1000}{1.045^{30}} = \$1081.44$$

   The price change will be $1081.44 - $1000 = $81.44

   That is, the price will rise by $81.44.

   d. If p falls to 4%, the price will rise to

$$\$50\left(\frac{1-1.04^{-30}}{0.04}\right) + \frac{\$1000}{1.04^{30}} = \$1172.92$$

   The price change will be $1172.92 - $1000 = $172.92

   That is, the price will rise by $172.92.

   e. $\frac{\text{Price change in part b}}{\text{Price change in part a}} = \frac{-\$137.65}{-\$72.67} = 1.89$

   The ratio of the price changes is less than the ratio (2.0) of the interest rate changes.

   f. The price change (−$72.67) resulting from a 1% interest rate increase is smaller in magnitude than the price change ($81.44) resulting from a 1% interest rate decrease.

Exercise 15.2 (continued)

15. All three bonds have F = $1000 and b = 5%.
    n = 10, 20, and 50 for bonds G, H, and J, respectively.
    When p = 5% (= b), all bonds will be priced at par ($1000). If p becomes 5.5%,

$$\text{Price of G} = \$50 \left(\frac{1 - 1.055^{-10}}{0.055} \right) + \frac{\$1000}{1.055^{10}} = \$962.31$$

$$\text{Price of H} = \$50 \left(\frac{1 - 1.055^{-20}}{0.055} \right) + \frac{\$1000}{1.055^{20}} = \$940.25$$

$$\text{Price of J} = \$50 \left(\frac{1 - 1.055^{-50}}{0.055} \right) + \frac{\$1000}{1.055^{50}} = \$915.34$$

The prices of bonds G, H, and J drop by $37.69, $59.75, and $84.66, respectively. The longer the maturity of a bond, the more sensitive is its price to a given change in the market rate of return.

16. For both bonds, F = $1000 and n = 30.
    b = 4% for bond K and b = 6% for bond L.

a. When p = 5%,

$$\text{Price of K} = \$40 \left(\frac{1 - 1.05^{-30}}{0.05} \right) + \frac{\$1000}{1.05^{30}} = \$846.28$$

$$\text{Price of L} = \$60 \left(\frac{1 - 1.05^{-30}}{0.05} \right) + \frac{\$1000}{1.05^{30}} = \$1153.72$$

When p = 4.5%

$$\text{Price of K} = \$40 \left(\frac{1 - 1.045^{-30}}{0.045} \right) + \frac{\$1000}{1.045^{30}} = \$918.56$$

$$\text{Price of L} = \$60 \left(\frac{1 - 1.045^{-30}}{0.045} \right) + \frac{\$1000}{1.045^{30}} = \$1244.33$$

K's price rises by $918.56 − $846.28 = $72.28 and

L's price rises by $1244.33 − $1153.72 = $90.61.

b. K's price rises by $\dfrac{\$72.28}{\$846.28} \times 100\% = 8.54\%$

L's price rises by $\dfrac{\$90.61}{\$1153.72} \times 100\% = 7.85\%$

c. The results in part b demonstrate that the lower coupon rate bond (K) will have a proportionately larger price change for a given change in the prevailing market rate. In general, the price of a low-coupon bond is more sensitive to a change in the market rate than the price of a higher coupon rate bond.

Exercise 15.2 *(continued)*

17. Given: F = $1000, b = 4.75%, n = 27, p = 4.1%

$$\text{Bond price} = \$47.50 \left(\frac{1 - 1.041^{-27}}{0.041} \right) + \frac{\$1000}{1.041^{27}} = \$1104.96$$

Bond premium = $1104.96 − $1000 = <u>$104.96</u>

18. Given: F = $1000, b = 5.625%, n = 17, p = 4.25%

$$\text{Bond price} = \$56.25 \left(\frac{1 - 1.0425^{-17}}{0.0425} \right) + \frac{\$1000}{1.0425^{17}} = \$1164.08$$

Bond premium = $1164.08 − $1000 = <u>$164.08</u>

19. Given: F = $1000, b = 4.5%, n = 32, p = 5.1%

$$\text{Bond price} = \$45 \left(\frac{1 - 1.051^{-32}}{0.051} \right) + \frac{\$1000}{1.051^{32}} = \$906.30$$

Bond discount = $1000 − $906.30 = <u>$93.70</u>

20. Given: F = $1000, b = 4.125%, n = 43, p = 4.85%

$$\text{Bond price} = \$41.25 \left(\frac{1 - 1.0485^{-43}}{0.0485} \right) + \frac{\$1000}{1.0485^{43}} = \$870.02$$

Bond discount − $1000 − $870.02 − <u>$129.98</u>

21. Given: F = $10,000, b = 4.375%, n = 2(25−3) = 44, p = 4.05%

a. $$\text{Price} = \$437.50 \left(\frac{1 - 1.0405^{-44}}{0.0405} \right) + \frac{\$10,000}{1.0405^{44}} = \underline{\underline{\$10,662.58}}$$

b. Percent capital gain $= \dfrac{\text{Selling price} - \text{Purchase price}}{\text{Purchase price}} \times 100\%$

$$= \frac{\$662.58}{\$10,000} \times 100\%$$

$$= 6.62\%$$

22. Given: F = $1000, b = 4.25%, n = 2 $\left(20 - 4\frac{1}{2} \right)$ = 31, p = 4.8%

a. $$\text{Price} = \$42.50 \left(\frac{1 - 1.048^{-31}}{0.048} \right) + \frac{\$1000}{1.048^{31}} = \$912.20$$

Proceeds from the sale of 20 bonds = <u>$18,244.00</u>

b.   Percent capital gain $= \dfrac{\text{Current price} - \text{Purchase price}}{\text{Purchase price}} \times 100\%$

$$= \frac{\$912.20 - \$1000}{\$1000} \times 100\%$$

$$= -8.78\%$$

That is, there would be a <u>capital loss of 8.78%</u>.

23. Given: b = 5.25%, n = 2(20 − 3) = 34
The percent capital gain will be the same for all bond denominations. Use F = $1000.

a.   If p = 4.5%,

$$\text{Price} = \$52.50 \left(\frac{1 - 1.045^{-34}}{0.045} \right) + \frac{\$1000}{1.045^{34}} = \$1129.35$$

Percent capital gain $= \dfrac{\$1129.35 - \$1000}{\$1000} \times 100\% = \underline{\underline{12.94\%}}$

b.   If p = 5.25% (= b), the bond's price will be F (= $1000). Then, percent capital gain = <u>0%</u>

c.   If p = 6%,

$$\text{Price} = \$52.50 \left(\frac{1 - 1.06^{-34}}{0.06} \right) + \frac{\$1000}{1.06^{34}} = \$892.24$$

Percent capital gain $= \dfrac{\$892.24 - \$1000}{\$1000} \times 100\% = \underline{\underline{-10.78\%}}$

24. Given: b = 5.5%, n = 2 (25 − 2½) = 45

The percent capital gain will be the same for all bond denominations. Use F = $1000.

a.   If p = 6%,

$$\text{Price} = \$55 \left(\frac{1 - 1.06^{-45}}{0.06} \right) + \frac{\$1000}{1.06^{45}} = \$922.72$$

Percent capital gain $= \dfrac{\$922.72 - \$1000}{\$1000} \times 100\% = \underline{\underline{-7.73\%}}$

b.   If p = 5.5% (= b), the bond's price will be at par ($1000). Then, percent capital gain = <u>0%</u>

c.   If p = 5%,

$$\text{Price} = \$55 \left(\frac{1 - 1.05^{-45}}{0.05} \right) + \frac{\$1000}{1.05^{45}} = \$1088.87$$

Percent capital gain $= \dfrac{\$1088.87 - \$1000}{\$1000} \times 100\% = \underline{\underline{8.89\%}}$

Exercise 15.2 (continued)

25. The answer will not depend on the bond's face value.
Use F = $1000.
When the bond was purchased, b = 5%, n = 40, and p = 9.25%.

$$\text{Purchase price} = \$50 \left(\frac{1 - 1.0925^{-40}}{0.0925} \right) + \frac{\$1000}{1.0925^{40}} = \$553.89$$

When the bond was sold, p = 4.85% and n = 31.

$$\text{Selling price} = \$50 \left(\frac{1 - 1.0485^{-31}}{0.0485} \right) + \frac{\$1000}{1.0485^{31}} = \$1023.80$$

In effect, a $553.89 investment purchased an annuity paying $50 every six months for $4\frac{1}{2}$ years, and a lump amount of $1023.80 at the end of the $4\frac{1}{2}$ years. The rate of total return is the discount rate that makes $553.89 equal to the present value of the payments received.
Solve for p in

$$\$553.89 = \$50 \left[\frac{1 - (1 + p)^{-9}}{p} \right] + \frac{\$1023.80}{(1 + p)^9}$$

$$p = 14.246\% \text{ per 6 months.}$$

The nominal annual rate of total return was

$$j = 2p = \underline{\underline{28.49\% \text{ compounded semiannually.}}}$$

26. The answer will be the same for any denomination of bond. Use F = $1000.
At the time of purchase, b = 5%, n = 44, and p = 5.5%.

$$\text{Purchase price} = \$50 \left(\frac{1 - 1.055^{-44}}{0.055} \right) + \frac{\$1000}{1.055^{44}} = \$917.71$$

At the time of sale, n = 40 and p = 9.25%.

$$\text{Selling price} = \$50 \left(\frac{1 - 1.0925^{-40}}{0.0925} \right) + \frac{\$1000}{1.0925^{40}} = \$553.89$$

The rate of total return on investment during the holding period is the discount rate that makes the initial investment ($917.71) equal to the present value of the payments received. The investor received four semiannual payments of $50 and a lump amount of $553.89 at the end of the 2 years. Solve for p in

$$\$917.71 = \$50 \left[\frac{1 - (1 + p)^{-4}}{p} \right] + \frac{\$553.89}{(1 + p)^4}$$

$$p = -5.284\% \text{ per 6 months}$$

The nominal annual rate of total return was j = 2p = $\underline{\underline{-10.57\% \text{ compounded semiannually.}}}$

Exercise 15.3

1. Given: F = $1000, n = 30, b = 5%, and price = $900
   The yield to maturity (YTM) is 2p where p is the solution to

   $$\$900 = \$50 \left[\frac{1 - (1 + p)^{-30}}{p} \right] + \frac{\$1000}{(1 + p)^{30}}$$

   p = 5.704% per 6 months

   YTM = 2p = 11.41% compounded semiannually.

2. Given: F = $1000, n = 30, b = 5%, and price = $1100
   The yield to maturity (YTM) is 2p where p is the solution to

   $$\$1100 = \$50 \left[\frac{1 - (1 + p)^{-30}}{p} \right] + \frac{\$1000}{(1 + p)^{30}}$$

   p = 4.394% per 6 months

   YTM = 2p = 8.79% compounded semiannually.

3. For both bonds, F = $1000, b = 4.5%, and price = $950. For bond A, n = 10 and

   $$\$950 = \$45 \left[\frac{1 - (1 + p)^{-10}}{p} \right] + \frac{\$1000}{(1 + p)^{10}}$$

   Solving for p gives p = 5.152% per 6 months. Then
   YTM = 2p = 10.30% compounded semiannually.

   For bond C, n = 40 and

   $$\$950 = \$45 \left[\frac{1 - (1 + p)^{-40}}{p} \right] + \frac{\$1000}{(1 + p)^{40}}$$

   Solving for p gives p = 4.783% per 6 months. Then YTM = 2p = 9.57% compounded semiannually.

4. For both bonds, F = $1000, b = 4.5%, and price = $1050. For bond D, n = 10 and

   $$\$1050 = \$45 \left[\frac{1 - (1 + p)^{-10}}{p} \right] + \frac{\$1000}{(1 + p)^{10}}$$

   Solving for p gives p = 3.887% per 6 months. Then
   YTM = 2p = 7.77% compounded semiannually.

   For bond E, n = 40 and

   $$\$1050 = \$45 \left[\frac{1 - (1 + p)^{-40}}{p} \right] + \frac{\$1000}{(1 + p)^{40}}$$

   Solving for p gives p = 4.239% per 6 months. Then
   YTM = 2p = 8.48% compounded semiannually.

Business Math in Canada, 2/e

Exercise 15.3 (continued)

5. Currently, p = b. Consequently, the bond currently trades at par ($1000).
   a. Price = $1020, n = 6, b = 5%, F = $1000
      YTM = 2p where

$$\$1020 = \$50\left[\frac{1 - (1 + p)^{-6}}{p}\right] + \frac{\$1000}{(1 + p)^6}$$

Solving for p gives p = 4.611%.
   YTM = 2p = 9.22% compounded semiannually.
Therefore, the YTM <u>decreased by</u> 10.00% − 9.22% = <u>0.78% compounded semiannually.</u>

   b. Price = $1020, n = 30, b = 5%, F = $1000
      Now solve for p in

$$\$1020 = \$50\left[\frac{1 - (1 + p)^{-30}}{p}\right] + \frac{\$1000}{(1 + p)^{30}}$$

   p = 4.872%

   YTM = 2p = 9.74% compounded semiannually.
   The YTM decreased by 0.26% compounded semiannually.

6. a. Initially, F = $1000, b = 5.5%, n = 4, and p = 5% = $\dfrac{\text{YTM}}{2}$

$$\text{Price} = \$55\left(\frac{1 - 1.05^{-4}}{0.05}\right) + \frac{\$1000}{1.05^4} = \$1017.73$$

   If the bond price abruptly falls $25 to $992.73, the new YTM will be 2p where p is the solution to

$$\$992.73 = \$55\left[\frac{1 - (1 + p)^{-4}}{p}\right] + \frac{\$1000}{(1 + p)^4}$$

   p = 5.709%

   YTM = 2p = 11.42% compounded semiannually.
   Therefore, the YTM <u>increases by</u> 11.42% − 10.00% = <u>1.42% compounded semiannually.</u>

   b. Initially, F = $1000, b = 5.5%, n = 24, and p = 5% = $\dfrac{\text{YTM}}{2}$

$$\text{Price} = \$55\left(\frac{1 - 1.05^{-24}}{0.05}\right) + \frac{\$1000}{1.05^{24}} = \$1068.99$$

   If the bond price abruptly falls $25 to $1043.99, the new YTM will be 2p where p is the solution to

$$\$1043.99 = \$55\left[\frac{1 - (1 + p)^{-24}}{p}\right] + \frac{\$1000}{(1 + p)^{24}}$$

   p = 5.176%

   YTM = 2p = 10.35% compounded semiannually. Therefore, the $25 price decline in the longer maturity
   bond corresponds to only a <u>0.35% increase in the YTM.</u>

Exercise 15.3 *(concluded)*

7. Given: F = $1000, b = 5.625%, n = 13, price = $761.50.
   The YTM is 2p where p is the solution to

   $$\$761.50 = \$56.25 \left[\frac{1 - (1 + p)^{-13}}{p} \right] + \frac{\$1000}{(1 + p)^{13}}$$

   $$p = 8.772\%$$

   Hence, the YTM = 2p = <u>17.54% compounded semiannually.</u>

Exercise 15.4

1. Given: F = $1000, b = 6.125%, p = 4.875%
   (June 1, 2003) − (June 1, 1992) = 22 half-years
   (June 15, 1992) − (June 1, 1992) = 14 days
   (Dec. 1, 1992) − (June 1, 1992) = 183 days

   $$\text{Price (June 1, 1992)} = \$61.25 \left(\frac{1 - 1.04875^{-22}}{0.04875} \right) + \frac{\$1000}{1.04875^{22}} = \$1166.43$$

   $$\text{Price (June 15, 1992)} = \$1166.43 \,(1.04875)^{14/183} = \underline{\$1170.69}$$

2. Given: F = $1000, b = 8.0%, p = 5%
   (March 15, 2007) − (Sept. 15, 1988) = 37 half-years
   (Oct. 5, 1988) − (Sept. 15, 1988) = 20 days
   (Mar. 15, 1989) − (Sept. 15, 1988) = 181 days

   $$\text{Price (Sept. 15, 1988)} = \$80 \left(\frac{1 - 1.05^{-37}}{0.05} \right) + \frac{\$1000}{1.05^{37}} = \$1501.34$$

   $$\text{Price (Oct. 5, 1988)} = \$1501.34 \,(1.05)^{20/181} = \underline{\$1509.46}$$

3. Given: F = $1000, b = 4.65%, p = 5.3%
   (Jan. 1, 2002) − (Jan. 1, 1987) = 30 half-years
   (Apr. 15, 1987) − (Jan. 1, 1987) = 104 days
   (July 1, 1987) − (Jan. 1, 1987) = 181 days

   $$\text{Price (Jan. 1, 1987)} = \$46.50 \left(\frac{1 - 1.053^{-30}}{0.053} \right) + \frac{\$1000}{1.053^{30}} = \$903.41$$

   $$\text{Price (Apr. 15, 1987)} = \$930.62 \,(1.053)^{104/181} = \underline{\$930.62}$$

4. Given: F = $1000, b = 4.875%, p = 5.75%
   (Sept. 20, 2006) − (Mar. 20, 1989) = 35 half-years
   (June 1, 1989) − (Mar. 20, 1989) = 73 days
   (Sept. 20, 1989) − (Mar. 20, 1989) = 184 days

   $$\text{Price (Mar. 20, 1989)} = \$48.75 \left(\frac{1 - 1.0575^{-35}}{0.0575} \right) + \frac{\$1000}{1.0575^{35}} = \$869.33$$

   $$\text{Price (June 1, 1989)} = \$869.33 \,(1.0575)^{73/184} = \underline{\$888.83}$$

Exercise 15.4 (continued)

5. Given: F = $1000, b = 4.75%, p = 5.75%
   (Aug. 1, 2006) − (Aug. 1, 1990) = 32 half-years
   (Dec. 15, 1990) − (Aug. 1, 1990) = 136 days
   (Feb. 1, 1991) − (Aug. 1, 1990) = 184 days

   $$\text{Price (Aug. 1, 1990)} = \$47.50 \left(\frac{1 - 1.0575^{-32}}{0.0575}\right) + \frac{\$1000}{1.0575^{32}} = \$855.15$$

   Price (Dec. 15, 1990) = $855.15 $(1.0575)^{136/184}$ = $\underline{\$891.23}$

6. Given: F = $1000, b = 4.85%, p = 5.95%
   (July 1, 2009) − (Jan. 1, 1990) = 39 half-years
   (Apr. 9, 1990) − (Jan. 1, 1990) = 98 days
   (July 1, 1990) − (Jan. 1, 1990) = 181 days

   $$\text{Price (Jan. 1, 1990)} = \$48.50 \left(\frac{1 - 1.0595^{-39}}{0.0595}\right) + \frac{\$1000}{1.0595^{39}} = \$834.53$$

   Price (Apr. 9, 1990) = $834.53 $(1.0595)^{98/181}$ = $\underline{\$861.06}$

7. Given: F = $1000, b = 7.125%, p = 4.5%
   (June 1, 2009) − (June 1, 1992) = 34 half-years
   (June 25, 1992) − (June 1, 1992) = 24 days
   (Dec. 1, 1992) − (June 1, 1992) = 183 days

   $$\text{Price (June 1, 1992)} = \$71.25 \left(\frac{1 - 1.045^{-34}}{0.045}\right) + \frac{\$1000}{1.045^{34}} = \$1452.73$$

   Price (June 25, 1992) = $1452.73 $(1.045)^{24/183}$ = $\underline{\$1461.14}$

8. Given: F = $1000, b = 6.0%, p = 4.55%
   (Apr. 1, 2005) − (Oct. 1, 1991) = 27 half-years
   (Dec. 20, 1991) − (Oct. 1, 1991) = 80 days
   (Apr. 1, 1992) − (Oct. 1, 1991) = 183 days

   $$\text{Price (Oct. 1, 1991)} = \$60 \left(\frac{1 - 1.0455^{-27}}{0.0455}\right) + \frac{\$1000}{1.0455^{27}} = \$1222.83$$

   Price (Dec. 20, 1991) = $1222.83 $(1.0455)^{80/183}$ = $\underline{\$1246.85}$

9. Given: F = $1000, b = 5.5%, p = 4.95%
   (Oct. 15, 2011) − (Apr. 15, 1992) = 39 half-years
   (June 11, 1992) − (Apr. 15, 1992) = 57 days
   (Oct. 15, 1992) − (Apr. 15, 1992) = 183 days

   $$\text{Price (Apr. 15, 1992)} = \$55 \left(\frac{1 - 1.0495^{-39}}{0.0495}\right) + \frac{\$1000}{1.0495^{39}} = \$1094.23$$

   Price (June 11, 1992) = $1094.23 $(1.0495)^{57/183}$ = $\underline{\$1110.82}$

Exercise 15.4 (continued)

10. Given: F = $1000, b = 4.25%, p = 5.6%
    (June 1, 2011) − (Dec. 1, 1989) = 43 half-years
    (Apr. 27, 1990) − (Dec. 1, 1989) = 147 days
    (June 1, 1990) − (Dec. 1, 1989) = 182 days

    Price (Dec. 1, 1989) = $42.50 $\left(\dfrac{1-1.056^{-43}}{0.056}\right) + \dfrac{\$1000}{1.056^{43}}$ = $782.08

    Price (Apr. 27, 1990) = $782.08 $(1.056)^{147/182}$ = $\underline{\$817.27}$

11. Given: F = $1000, b = 4.625%, p = 8.5%
    (Jan. 6, 2004) − (July 6, 1981) = 45 half-years
    (Aug. 8, 1981) − (July 6, 1981) = 33 days
    (Jan. 6, 1982) − (July 6, 1981) = 184 days

    Price (July 6, 1981) = $46.25 $\left(\dfrac{1-1.085^{-45}}{0.085}\right) + \dfrac{\$1000}{1.085^{45}}$ = $555.72

    Price (Aug. 8, 1981) = $555.72 $(1.085)^{33/184}$ = $\underline{\$563.91}$

12. Given: F = $1000, b = 7.75%, p = 4.6%
    (Mar. 15, 2007) − (Mar. 15, 1986) = 42 half-years
    (June 4, 1986) − (Mar. 15, 1986) = 81 days
    (Sept. 15, 1986) − (Mar. 15, 1986) = 184 days

    Price (Mar. 15, 1986) = $77.50 $\left(\dfrac{1-1.046^{-42}}{0.046}\right) + \dfrac{\$1000}{1.046^{42}}$ = $1581.22

    Price (June 4, 1986) = $1581.22 $(1.046)^{81/184}$ = $\underline{\$1612.84}$

13. Given: F = $1000, b = 4.5%, p = 5%
    (Mar. 15, 2012) − (Mar. 15, 1993) = 38 half-years
    (Sept. 15, 1993) − (Mar. 15, 1993) = 184 days

    Price (Mar. 15, 1993) = $45 $\left(\dfrac{1-1.05^{-38}}{0.05}\right) + \dfrac{\$1000}{1.05^{38}}$ = $\underline{\$915.66}$

Date	No. days since Mar. 15, 1993	Price
Apr. 15, 1993	31	$915.66 $(1.05)^{31/184}$ = $\underline{\$923.22}$
May 15, 1993	61	$915.66 $(1.05)^{61/184}$ = $\underline{\$930.59}$
June 15, 1993	92	$915.66 $(1.05)^{92/184}$ = $\underline{\$938.27}$
July 15, 1993	122	$915.66 $(1.05)^{122/184}$ = $\underline{\$945.77}$
Aug. 15, 1993	153	$915.66 $(1.05)^{153/184}$ = $\underline{\$953.57}$

Price after interest payment on Sept. 15, 1993

= $45 $\left(\dfrac{1-1.05^{-37}}{0.05}\right) + \dfrac{\$1000}{1.05^{37}}$ = $\underline{\$916.44}$

Exercise 15.4 *(continued)*

14. Given: F = $1000, b = 5.5%, p = 4.8%
(Nov. 20, 2006) – (May 20, 1993) = 27 half-years
(Nov. 20, 1993) – (May 20, 1993) = 184 days

$$\text{Price (May 20, 1993)} = \$55\left(\frac{1-1.048^{-27}}{0.048}\right) + \frac{\$1000}{1.048^{27}} = \underline{\underline{\$1104.71}}$$

Date	No. days since May 20, 1993	Price
June 20, 1993	31	$1104.71 (1.048)$^{31/184}$ = $\underline{\underline{\$1113.47}}$
July 20, 1993	61	$1104.71 (1.048)$^{61/184}$ = $\underline{\underline{\$1122.01}}$
Aug. 20, 1993	92	$1104.71 (1.048)$^{92/184}$ = $\underline{\underline{\$1130.91}}$
Sept. 20, 1993	123	$1104.71 (1.048)$^{123/184}$ = $\underline{\underline{\$1139.88}}$
Oct. 20, 1993	153	$1104.71 (1.048)$^{153/184}$ = $\underline{\underline{\$1148.63}}$

Price after interest payment on Nov. 20, 1993

$$= \$55\left(\frac{1-1.048^{-26}}{0.048}\right) + \frac{\$1000}{1.048^{26}} = \underline{\underline{\$1102.73}}$$

15. Given: F = $5000, b = 4.5%, Maturity date = Aug. 1, 2006
    p = 5.75% on the date of purchase (Apr. 25, 1990)
    p = 4.4% on the date of sale (Dec. 27, 1991)

a. Step 1: Determine the purchase price.
    (Aug. 1, 2006) – (Feb. 1, 1990) = 33 half-years
    (Apr. 25, 1990) – (Feb. 1, 1990) = 83 days
    (Aug. 1, 1990) – (Feb. 1, 1990) = 181 days

$$\text{Price (Feb. 1, 1990)} = \$225\left(\frac{1-1.0575^{-33}}{0.0575}\right) + \frac{\$5000}{1.0575^{33}} = \$4084.82$$

$$\text{Price (Apr. 25, 1990)} = \$4084.82 (1.0575)^{83/181} = \$4190.90$$

Step 2: Determine the selling price.
    (Aug. 1, 2006) – (Aug. 1, 1991) = 30 half-years
    (Dec. 27, 1991) – (Aug. 1, 1991) = 148 days
    (Feb. 1, 1992) – (Aug. 1, 1991) = 184 days

$$\text{Price (Aug. 1, 1991)} = \$225\left(\frac{1-1.044^{-30}}{0.044}\right) + \frac{\$5000}{1.044^{30}} = \$5082.41$$

$$\text{Price (Dec. 27, 1991)} = \$5082.41 (1.044)^{148/184} = \$5261.52$$

Step 3: Calculate the capital gain.
    Capital gain = $5261.52 – $4190.90 = $\underline{\underline{\$1070.62}}$

b. Percent capital gain $= \frac{\$1070.62}{\$4190.90} \times 100\% = \underline{\underline{25.55\%}}$

Exercise 15.4 (continued)

16. Given: F = $10,000, b = 7%, Maturity date = June 15, 2009
    p = 4.5% on the date of purchase (Mar. 20, 1987)
    p = 5.75% on the date of sale (Apr. 20, 1990)

a.   Step 1: Determine the purchase price.
         (June 15, 2009) – (Dec. 15, 1986) = 45 half-years
         (Mar. 20, 1987) – (Dec. 15, 1986) = 95 days
         (June 15, 1987) – (Dec. 15, 1986) = 182 days

$$\text{Price (Dec. 15, 1986)} = \$700 \left(\frac{1 - 1.045^{-45}}{0.045} \right) + \frac{\$10,000}{1.045^{45}} = \$14,789.09$$

Price (Mar. 20, 1987) = $14,789.09 (1.045)^{95/182} = $15,132.82

Step 2: Determine the selling price.
    (June 15, 2009) – (Dec. 15, 1989) = 39 half-years
    (Apr. 20, 1990) – (Dec. 15, 1989) = 126 days
    (June 15, 1990) – (Dec. 15, 1989) = 182 days

$$\text{Price (Dec. 15, 1989)} = \$700 \left(\frac{1 - 1.0575^{-39}}{0.0575} \right) + \frac{\$10,000}{1.0575^{39}} = \$11,928.27$$

Price (Apr. 20, 1990) = $11,928.27 (1.0575)^{126/182} = $12,399.01

Step 3: Calculate the capital gain.
    Capital gain = $12,399.01 – $15,132.82 = – $2733.81
    That is, a <u>capital loss of $2733.81</u>.

b.   Percent capital gain = $\dfrac{- \$2733.81}{\$15,132.82}$ x 100% = –18.07%

That is, the <u>capital loss is 18.07%</u>.

17. Quoted price = Flat price – Accrued interest
    August 1 – May 15 = 78 days
    November 15 – May 15 = 184 days
    Accrued interest = Prt = Fbt = $1000 (0.055)$\dfrac{78}{184}$ = $23.32

    Quoted price = $1065.50 – $23.32 = $1042.18
    The quoted price is <u>104.22%</u> of face value.

18. Given: F = $5000, Fb = $200, flat price = $4860 on September 17.
         Interest payment dates are June 1 and December 1.
    September 17 – June 1 = 108 days
    December 1 – June 1 = 183 days

    Accrued interest = $200 $\left(\dfrac{108}{183} \right)$ = $118.03

    Quoted price = $4860 – $118.03 = $4741.97
    This quoted price is <u>94.84% of face value</u>.

---

476   *Business Math in Canada, 2/e*

Exercise 15.4 (continued)

19. Given: Quoted price (on Oct. 23) = 108.50% of face value
    $F = \$1000$, $b = 5.25\%$ paid on Mar. 1 and Sept. 1
    October 23 – September 1 = 52 days
    March 1 – September 1 = 181 days

    Accrued interest to Oct. 23 = $\$52.50\left(\dfrac{52}{181}\right) = \$15.08$

    Flat price = Quoted price + Accrued interest
    $\quad = \$1085.00 + \$15.08$
    $\quad = \underline{\underline{\$1100.08}}$

20. The flat price was calculated in problem 3 to be \$930.62. It was also determined in the solution to problem 3 that 104 days of the 181-day interest payment interval had elapsed. Hence,

    Accrued interest = $\$46.50\left(\dfrac{104}{181}\right) = \$26.72$

    Quoted price = Flat price – Accrued interest
    $\quad = \$930.62 - \$26.72$
    $\quad = \underline{\underline{\$903.90}}$

21. In the solution to problem 4, it was determined that the flat price on June 1, 1989 was \$888.83 and that 73 days of the 184-day interest payment interval had elapsed. Hence,

    Accrued interest = $\$48.75\left(\dfrac{73}{184}\right) = \$19.34$

    Quoted price = Flat price – Accrued interest
    $\quad = \$888.83 - \$19.34$
    $\quad = \underline{\underline{\$869.49}}$

22. a. Given: $F = \$1000$, $b = 3.25\%$, $p = 3.796\%$ on Oct. 6, 1995
       Maturity date = June 1, 2004
       (June 1, 2004) – (June 1, 1995) = 18 half-years
       (Oct. 6, 1995) – (June 1, 1995) = 127 days
       (Dec. 1, 1995) – (June 1, 1995) = 183 days

       Price (June 1, 1995) = $\$32.50\left(\dfrac{1 - 1.03796^{18}}{0.03796}\right) + \dfrac{\$1000}{1.03796^{18}} = \$929.72$

       Flat price (Oct. 6, 1995) = $\$929.72\,(1.03796)^{127/183} = \$954.07$

       Quoted price (Oct. 6, 1995) = $\$954.07 - \$32.50\left(\dfrac{127}{183}\right) = \$931.52$

       That is, quoted price = $\underline{\underline{93.15\% \text{ of face value.}}}$

Exercise 15.4 (continued)

b. Given: F = $1000, b = 5.25%, p = 4.0175% on Oct. 6, 1995

        Maturity date = March 15, 2021

(March 15, 2021) – (Sept. 15, 1995) = 51 half-years

(Oct. 6, 1995) – (Sept. 15, 1995) = 21 days

(Mar. 15, 1996) – (Sept. 15, 1995) = 182 days

$$\text{Price (Sept. 15, 1995)} = \$52.50 \left(\frac{1 - 1.040175^{-51}}{0.040175} \right) + \frac{\$1000}{1.040175^{51}} = \$1265.63$$

Flat price (Oct. 6, 1995) = $1265.63 (1.040175)^{21/182} = $1271.40

$$\text{Quoted price (Oct. 6, 1995)} = \$1271.40 - \$52.50 \left(\frac{21}{182} \right) = \$1265.34$$

That is, quoted price = <u>126.53% of face value</u>.

c. Given: F = $1000, b = 4.8%, p = 4.262% on Oct. 6, 1995

        Maturity date = Jan. 30, 2022

Following the same procedure as in parts a and b,

No. of payments remaining = 53

Length of payment interval = 184 days

Elapsed time = 68 days

Price (July 30, 1995) = $1112.41

Flat price (Oct. 6, 1995) = $1112.41 (1.04262)^{68/184} = $1129.70

$$\text{Quoted price (Oct. 6, 1995)} = \$1129.70 - \$48 \left(\frac{68}{184} \right) = \$1111.96$$

That is, quoted price = <u>111.20% of face value</u>.

d. Given: F = $1000, b = 4.125%, p = 3.6705% on Oct. 6, 1995

        Maturity date = March 22, 2000

No. of remaining payments = 9

Length of payment interval = 182 days

Elapsed time = 14 days

Price (Sept. 22, 1995) = $1034.31

Flat price (Oct. 6, 1995) = $1034.31 (1.036705)^{14/182} = $1037.18

$$\text{Quoted price (Oct. 6, 1995)} = \$1037.18 - \$41.25 \left(\frac{14}{182} \right) = \$1034.01$$

That is, quoted price = <u>103.40% of face value</u>.

e. Given: F = $1000, b = 5%, p = 4.115% on Oct. 6, 1995

        Maturity date = Oct. 17, 2014

No. of remaining payments = 39

Length of payment interval = 183 days

Elapsed time = 172 days

Price (Apr. 17, 1995) = $1170.44

Flat price (Oct. 6, 1995) = $1170.44 (1.04115)^{172/183} = $1215.65

$$\text{Quoted price (Oct. 6, 1995)} = \$1215.65 - \$50 \left(\frac{172}{183} \right) = \$1168.66$$

That is, quoted price = <u>116.87% of face value</u>.

Exercise 15.4 *(concluded)*

f. Given: F = $1000, b = 5.175%, p = 4.1845% on Oct. 6, 1995
    Maturity date = December 15, 2009
    No. of remaining payments = 29
    Length of payment interval = 183 days
    Elapsed time = 113 days
    Price (June 15, 1995) = $1164.61
    Flat price (Oct. 6, 1995) = $1164.61 $(1.041845)^{113/183}$ = $1194.47

    Quoted price (Oct. 6, 1995) = $1194.47 − $51.75 $\left(\dfrac{113}{183}\right)$ = $1162.52

    That is, quoted price = 116.25% of face value.

g. Given: F = $1000, b = 4.725%, p = 4.3185% on Oct. 6, 1995
    Maturity date = March 20, 2018
    No. of remaining payments = 45
    Length of payment interval = 182 days
    Elapsed time = 16 days
    Price (Sept. 20, 1995) = $1080.09
    Flat price (Oct. 6, 1995) = $1080.09 $(1.043185)^{16/182}$ = $1084.11

    Quoted price (Oct. 6, 1995) = $1084.11 − $47.25 $\left(\dfrac{16}{182}\right)$ = $1079.96

    That is, quoted price = 108.00% of face value.

Exercise 15.5

1. Given: F = $1000, b = 4.5%, n = 6, p = 4%

    Bond price = $45 $\left(\dfrac{1-1.04^{-6}}{0.04}\right)$ + $\dfrac{\$1000}{1.04^6}$ = $\underline{\underline{\$1026.21}}$

Coupon number	Coupon payment	Interest on book value	Premium amortized	Book value of bond	Unamortized premium
0	—	—	—	$1026.21	$26.21
1	$45.00	$41.05	$3.95	1022.26	22.26
2	45.00	40.89	4.11	1018.15	18.15
3	45.00	40.73	4.27	1013.88	13.88
4	45.00	40.56	4.44	1009.44	9.44
5	45.00	40.38	4.62	1004.82	4.82
6	45.00	40.18	4.82	1000.00	0.00
	$270.00	$243.79	$26.21		

Exercise 15.5 (continued)

2. Given: F = $5000, b = 5.5%, n = 7, p = 4.75%

$$\text{Purchase price} = \$275 \left(\frac{1 - 1.0475^{-7}}{0.0475} \right) + \frac{\$5000}{1.0475^{7}} = \underline{\underline{\$5218.97}}$$

Coupon number	Coupon payment	Interest on book value	Premium amortized	Book value of bond	Unamortized premium
0	—	—	—	$5218.97	$218.97
1	$275.00	$247.90	$27.10	5191.87	191.87
2	275.00	246.61	28.39	5163.48	163.48
3	275.00	245.27	29.73	5133.75	133.75
4	275.00	243.85	31.15	5102.60	102.60
5	275.00	242.37	32.63	5069.97	69.97
6	275.00	240.82	34.18	5035.79	35.79
7	275.00	239.21	35.79	5000.00	0.00
	$1925.00	$1706.03	$218.97		

3. Given: F = $1000, b = 5%, n = 24, p = 4.4%

$$\text{Purchase price} = \$50 \left(\frac{1 - 1.044^{-24}}{0.044} \right) + \frac{\$1000}{1.044^{24}} = \underline{\underline{\$1087.85}}$$

Coupon number	Coupon payment	Interest on book value	Premium amortized	Book value of bond	Unamortized premium
0	—	—	—	$1087.85	$87.85
1	$50.00	$47.87	$2.13	1085.72	85.72
2	50.00	47.77	2.23	1083.49	83.49
3	50.00	47.67	2.33	1081.16	81.16
⏐	⏐	⏐	⏐	⏐	⏐
				1016.52	16.52
22	50.00	44.73	5.27	1011.25	11.25
23	50.00	44.50	5.50	1005.75	5.75
24	50.00	44.25	5.75	1000.00	0.00
	$1200.00	$1112.15	$87.85		

4. Given: F = $10,000, b = 6.5%, n = 33, p = 5%

$$\text{Purchase price} = \$650 \left(\frac{1 - 1.05^{-33}}{0.05} \right) + \frac{\$10,000}{1.05^{33}} = \underline{\underline{\$12,400.38}}$$

Exercise 15.5 (continued)

Coupon number	Coupon payment	Interest on book value	Premium amortized	Book value of bond	Unamortized premium
0	—	—	—	$12,400.38	$2400.38
1	$650.00	$620.02	$29.98	12,370.40	2370.40
2	650.00	618.52	31.48	12,338.92	2338.92
3	650.00	616.95	33.05	12,305.87	2305.87
I	I	I	I	I	I
				10,408.49	408.49
31	650.00	520.42	129.58	10,278.91	278.91
32	650.00	513.95	136.05	10,142.86	142.86
33	650.00	507.14	142.86	10,000.00	0.00
	$21,450.00	$19,049.62	$2400.38		

5. Given: F = $1000, b = 4%, n = 6, p = 4.75%

$$\text{Purchase price} = \$40 \left(\frac{1 - 1.0475^{-6}}{0.0475} \right) + \frac{\$1000}{1.0475^6} = \underline{\$961.63}$$

Coupon number	Coupon payment	Interest on book value	Discount amortized	Book value of bond	Unamortized discount
0	—	—	—	$961.63	$38.37
1	$40.00	$45.68	$5.68	967.31	32.69
2	40.00	45.95	5.95	973.26	26.74
3	40.00	46.23	6.23	979.49	20.51
4	40.00	46.53	6.53	986.02	13.98
5	40.00	46.84	6.84	992.86	7.14
6	40.00	47.14	7.14	1000.00	0.00
	$240.00	$278.37	$38.37		

6. Given: F = $5000, b = 4.5%, n = 5, p = 5.5%

$$\text{Purchase price} = \$225 \left(\frac{1 - 1.055^{-5}}{0.055} \right) + \frac{\$5000}{1.055^5} = \$4786.49$$

Coupon number	Coupon payment	Interest on book value	Discount amortized	Book value of bond	Unamortized discount
0	—	—	—	$4786.49	$213.51
1	$225.00	$263.26	$38.26	4824.75	175.25
2	225.00	265.36	40.36	4865.11	134.89
3	225.00	267.58	42.58	4907.69	92.3I
4	225.00	269.92	44.92	4952.61	47.39
5	225.00	272.39	47.39	5000.00	0.00
	$1125.00	$1338.51	$213.51		

Exercise 15.5 (concluded)

7. Given: F = $1000, b = 4.25%, n = 22, p = 5.2%

$$\text{Purchase price} = \$42.50\left(\frac{1-1.052^{-22}}{0.052}\right) + \frac{\$1000}{1.052^{22}} = \$877.20$$

Coupon number	Coupon payment	Interest on book value	Discount amortized	Book value of bond	Unamortized discount
0	—	—	—	$877.20	$122.80
1	$42.50	$45.61	$3.11	880.31	119.69
2	42.50	45.78	3.28	883.59	116.41
3	42.50	45.95	3.45	887.04	112.96
I	I	I	I	I	I
				974.23	25.77
20	42.50	50.66	8.16	982.39	17.61
21	42.50	51.08	8.58	990.97	9.03
22	42.50	51.53	9.03	1000.00	0.00
	$935.00	$1057.80	$122.80		

8. Given: F = $10,000, b = 4.3%, n = 29, p = 5%

$$\text{Purchase price} = \$430\left(\frac{1-1.05^{-29}}{0.05}\right) + \frac{\$10,000}{1.05^{29}} = \$8940.12$$

Coupon number	Coupon payment	Interest on book value	Discount amortized	Book value of bond	Unamortized discount
0	—	—	—	$8940.12	$1059.88
1	$430.00	$447.01	$17.01	8957.13	1042.87
2	430.00	447.86	17.86	8974.99	1025.01
3	430.00	448.75	18.75	8993.74	1006.26
I	I	I	I	I	I
				9809.37	190.63
27	430.00	490.47	60.47	9869.84	130.16
28	430.00	493.49	63.49	9933.33	66.67
29	430.00	496.67	66.67	10,000.00	0.00
	$12,470.00	$13,529.88	$1059.88		

Exercise 15.6

1. S_n = $12,000,000, n = 20, p = 3.5%

   a. Solve for R in

   $$\$12,000,000 = R\,s_{\overline{20}|\,3.5\%}$$
   $$R = \underline{\$424,333}$$

   b. The balance after the 12th interval (and payment) will be

   $$S_n = \$424,333\,s_{\overline{12}|\,3.5\%} = \underline{\$6,196,094}$$

Exercise 15.6 *(continued)*

2. $S_n = \$7,000,000$, $n = 20$, $p = 1.5\%$

   a. Solve for R in

$$\$7,000,000 = R\ s_{\overline{20}|1.5\%}$$
$$R = \underline{\$302,720}$$

   b. The balance after the 6th interval (and payment) will be

$$S_n = \$302,720\ s_{\overline{6}|1.5\%} = \underline{\$1,885,810}$$

3. $S_n = \$15,000,000$, $n = 15$, $p = 6.5\%$

   a. Solve for R in

$$\$15,000,000 = R\ s_{\overline{15}|6.5\%}$$
$$R = \underline{\$620,292}$$

   b. The balance after the 11th interval will be

$$S_n = \$620,292\ s_{\overline{11}|6.5\%} = \underline{\$9,534,856}$$

4. $S_n = \$8,000,000$, $p = 0.625\%$, $n = 120$

   a. Solve for R in

$$\$8,000,000 = R\ s_{\overline{120}|0.625\%}$$
$$R = \underline{\$44,961}$$

   b. The balance after the 65th interval will be

$$S_n = \$44,961\ s_{\overline{65}|0.625\%} = \underline{\$3,591,708}$$

5. $S_n(\text{due}) = \$6,000,000$, $p = 0.4375\%$, $n = 60$

   a. Solve for R in

$$\$6,000,000 = R\ s_{\overline{60}|0.4375\%}\ (1.004375)$$
$$R = \underline{\$87,284}$$

   b. The balance at the end of the 27th interval will be

$$S_n(\text{due}) = \$87,284\ s_{\overline{27}|0.4375\%}\ (1.004375) = \underline{\$2,506,640}$$

6. $S_n(\text{due}) = \$10,000,000$, $p = 1.625\%$, $n = 40$

   a. Solve for R in

$$\$10,000,000 = R\ s_{\overline{40}|1.625\%}\ (1.01625)$$
$$R = \underline{\$176,578}$$

   b. The balance at the end of the 28th interval will be

$$S_n(\text{due}) = \$176,578\ s_{\overline{28}|1.625\%}\ (1.01625) = \underline{\$6,299,093}$$

Exercise 15.6 (continued)

7. $S_n(\text{due}) = \$18,000,000$, $n = 30$, $p = 3.375\%$

    a. Solve for R in

    $$\$18,000,000 = R\; s_{\overline{30}|3.375\%}\;(1.03375)$$
    $$R = \underline{\$344,297}$$

    b. The balance at the end of the 19th interval will be

    $$S_n(\text{due}) = \$344,297\; s_{\overline{19}|3.375\%}\;(1.03375) = \underline{\$9,268,208}$$

8. $S_n(\text{due}) = \$5,000,000$, $n = 10$, $p = 5.75\%$

    a. Solve for R in

    $$\$5,000,000 = R\; s_{\overline{10}|5.75\%}\;(1.0575)$$
    $$R = \underline{\$362,947}$$

    b. The balance at the end of the 8th interval will be

    $$S_n(\text{due}) = \$362,947\; s_{\overline{8}|5.75\%}\;(1.0575) = \underline{\$3,764,889}$$

9. $S_n = \$10,000,000$, $n = 20$, $p = 3.5\%$, $2b = 10\%$

    a. $\$10,000,000 = R\; s_{\overline{20}|3.5\%}$

    $$R = \underline{\$353,611}$$

    b. Annual interest payment $= 0.10\; (\$10,000,000) = \$1,000,000$

    Annual cost of debt $= 2\; (\$353,611) + \$1,000,000 = \underline{\$1,707,222}$

    c. The balance after the 12th interval (6 years) will be

    $$S_n = \$353,611\; s_{\overline{12}|3.5\%} = \underline{\$5,163,414}$$

    Book value of debt $= \$10,000,000 - \$5,163,414 = \underline{\$4,836,586}$

10. $S_n = \$8,000,000$, $n = 10$, $p = 3\%$, $2b = 8.5\%$

    a. $\$8,000,000 = R\; s_{\overline{10}|3\%}$

    $$R = \underline{\$697,844}$$

    b. Annual cost of debt $= 2R + (2b)\; \$8,000,000$

    $$= 2\; (\$697,844) + 0.085\; (\$8,000,000)$$
    $$= \underline{\$2,075,688}$$

    c. Book value of debt $= \$8,000,000 - \$697,844\; s_{\overline{6}|3\%}$

    $$= \underline{\$3,486,059}$$

Exercise 15.6 (continued)

11. $S_n = \$15,000,000$, $n = 30$, $p = 3.25\%$, $2b = 9\%$

    a. $\$15,000,000 = R \, s_{\overline{30}|3.25\%}$

            $R = \underline{\$302,726}$

    b. Annual cost of debt $= 2R + (2b)\,(\$15,000,000)$

                        $= 2\,(\$302,726) + 0.09\,(\$15,000,000)$

                        $= \underline{\$1,955,452}$

    c. Book value of debt $= \$15,000,000 - \$302,726 \, s_{\overline{21}|3.25\%}$

                        $= \underline{\$6,081,667}$

12. $S_n = \$12,000,000$, $n = 20$, $p = 3.75\%$, $2b = 10.5\%$

    a. $\$12,000,000 = R \, s_{\overline{20}|3.75\%}$

            $R = \underline{\$413,545}$

    b. Annual cost of debt $= 2R + 2b\,(\$12,000,000)$

                        $= 2\,(\$413,545) + 0.105\,(\$12,000,000)$

                        $= \underline{\$2,087,090}$

    c. Book value of debt $= \$12,000,000 - \$413,545 \, s_{\overline{15}|3.75\%}$

                      $= \underline{\$3,871,502}$

13. $S_n = \$7,000,000$, $n = 10$, $p = 2.875\%$, $2b = 8\%$

    a. $\$7,000,000 = R \, s_{\overline{10}|2.875\%}$

             $R = \underline{\$614,137}$

    b. Annual cost of debt $= 2R + 2b\,(\$7,000,000)$

                        $= 2\,(\$614,137) + 0.08\,(\$7,000,000)$

                        $= \underline{\$1,788,274}$

    c. Book value of debt $= \$7,000,000 - \$614,137 \, s_{\overline{7}|2.875\%}$

                      $= \underline{\$2,311,969}$

14. $S_n = \$9,000,000$, $n = 20$, $p = 3.25\%$, $2b = 9.25\%$

    a. $\$9,000,000 = R \, s_{\overline{20}|3.25\%}$

            $R = \underline{\$326,510}$

    b. Annual cost of debt $= 2R + 2b\,(\$9,000,000)$

                        $= 2\,(\$326,510) + 0.0925\,(\$9,000,000)$

                        $= \underline{\$1,485,520}$

Exercise 15.6 *(continued)*

c. Book value of debt = $9,000,000 - $326,510 $s_{\overline{18}|3.25\%}$

$= \underline{\underline{\$1,180,178}}$

15. $S_n = \$11,000,000$, $n = 30$, $p = 3.75\%$, $2b = 10.25\%$

a. $\$11,000,000 = R\, s_{\overline{30}|3.75\%}$

$R = \underline{\underline{\$204,464}}$

b. Annual cost of debt = $2R + 2b$ ($11,000,000)

$= 2\,(\$204,464) + 0.1025\,(\$11,000,000)$

$= \underline{\underline{\$1,536,428}}$

c. Book value of debt = $11,000,000 - $204,464 $s_{\overline{19}|3.75\%}$

$= \underline{\underline{\$5,478,509}}$

16. $S_n = \$10,000,000$, $n = 20$, $p = 3.5\%$, $2b = 9.75\%$

a. $\$10,000,000 = R\, s_{\overline{20}|3.5\%}$

$R = \underline{\underline{\$353,611}}$

b. Annual cost of debt = $2R + 2b$ ($10,000,000)

$= 2\,(\$353,611) + 0.0975\,(\$10,000,000)$

$= \underline{\underline{\$1,682,222}}$

c. Book value of debt = $10,000,000 - $353,611 $s_{\overline{11}|3.5\%}$

$= \underline{\underline{\$5,352,847}}$

17. $S_n = \$800,000$, $n = 6$, $p = 3.5\%$

$\$800,000 = R\, s_{\overline{6}|3.5\%}$

$R = \$122,135$

Payment interval number	Payment (at end)	Interest earned	Increase in the fund	Balance in fund (end of interval)
0	—	—	—	$0
1	$122,135	$0	$122,135	122,135
2	122,135	4275	126,410	248,545
3	122,135	8699	130,834	379,379
4	122,135	13,278	135,413	514,792
5	122,135	18,018	140,153	654,945
6	122,135	22,923	145,058	800,003
		Total: $67,193	$800,003	

Total interest = $800,003 - 6\,($122,135$) = \underline{\underline{\$67,193}}$

Exercise 15.6 (continued)

18. $S_n = \$675,000$, $n = 6$, $p = 6\%$

$\$675,000 = R\ s_{\overline{6}|6\%}$

$R = \$96,770$

Payment interval number	Payment (at end)	Interest earned	Increase in the fund	Balance in fund (end of interval)
0	—	—	—	$0
1	$96,770	$0	$96,770	96,770
2	96,770	5806	102,576	199,346
3	96,770	11,961	108,731	308,077
4	96,770	18,485	115,255	423,332
5	96,770	25,400	122,170	545,502
6	96,770	32,730	129,500	675,002
		Total: $94,382	$675,002	

Total interest = $675,002 − 6 ($96,770) = $94,382

19. $S_n(due) = \$1,000,000$, $n = 5$, $p = 6.75\%$

$\$1,000,000 = R\ s_{\overline{5}|6.75\%}\ (1.0675)$

$R = \$163,710$

Payment interval number	Payment (at start)	Interest earned	Increase in the fund	Balance in fund (end of interval)
0	—	—	—	$0
1	$163,710	$11,050	$174,760	174,760
2	163,710	22,847	186,557	361,317
3	163,710	35,439	199,149	560,466
4	163,710	48,882	212,592	773,058
5	163,710	63,232	226,942	1,000,000
		Total: $181,450	$1,000,000	

Total Interest = $1,000,000 − 5 ($163,710) = $181,450

20. $S_n(due) = \$550,000$, $n = 8$, $p = 2.875\%$

$\$550,000 = R\ s_{\overline{8}|2.875\%}\ (1.02875)$

$R = \$60,390$

Exercise 15.6 *(continued)*

Payment interval number	Payment (at start)	Interest earned	Increase in the fund	Balance in fund (end of interval)
0	—	—	—	$0
1	$60,390	$1736	$62,126	62,126
2	60,390	3522	63,912	126,038
3	60,390	5360	65,750	191,788
4	60,390	7250	67,640	259,428
5	60,390	9195	69,585	329,013
6	60,390	11,195	71,585	400,598
7	60,390	13,253	73,643	474,241
8	60,390	15,371	75,761	550,002
	Total:	$66,882	$550,002	

Total interest = $550,002 − 8 ($60,390) = $66,882

21. From the solution to problem 2,

R = $302,720, n = 20, *p* = 1.5%

Payment interval number	Payment (at end)	Interest earned	Increase in the fund	Balance in fund (end of interval)
0	—	—	—	$0
1	$302,720	$0	$302,720	302,720
2	302,720	4541	307,261	609,981
3	302,720	9150	311,870	921,851
¦	¦	¦	¦	¦
10				3,239,928
11	302,720	48,559	351,319	3,591,247
12	302,720	53,869	356,589	3,947,836
¦	¦	¦	¦	¦
17				5,812,634
18	302,720	87,190	389,910	6,202,544
19	302,720	93,038	395,758	6,598,302
20	302,720	98,975	401,695	6,999,997

Exercise 15.6 (continued)

22. From the solution to problem 5,

R = $87,284, n = 60, p = 4.375%

Payment interval number	Payment (at start)	Interest earned	Increase in the fund	Balance in fund (end of interval)
0	—	—	—	$0
1	$87,284	$382	$87,666	87,666
2	87,284	765	88,049	175,715
3	87,284	1151	88,435	264,150
38				3,615,644
39	87,284	16,200	103,484	3,719,128
40	87,284	16,653	103,937	3,823,065
57				5,661,219
68	87,284	25,150	112,434	5,773,653
59	87,284	25,642	112,926	5,886,579
60	87,284	26,136	113,420	5,999,999

23. From the solution to problem 9,

R = $353,611, n = 20, p = 3.5%

Payment interval number	Payment	Interest earned	Increase in the fund	Balance in fund (end of interval)	Book value of the debt
0	—	—	—	$0	$10,000,000
1	$353,611	$0	$353,611	353,611	9,646,389
2	353,611	12,376	365,987	719,598	9,280,402
3	353,611	25,186	378,797	1,098,395	8,901,605
17				8,028,743	1,971,257
18	353,611	281,006	634,617	8,663,360	1,336,640
19	353,611	303,218	656,829	9,320,189	679,811
20	353,611	326,207	679,818	10,000,007	(7)

Exercise 15.6 *(continued)*

24. From the solution to problem 10,

$R = \$697,844$, $n = 10$, $p = 3\%$

Payment interval number	Payment	Interest earned	Increase in the fund	Balance in fund (end of interval)	Book value of the debt
0	—	—	—	$0	$8,000,000
1	$697,844	$0	$697,844	697,844	7,302,156
2	697,844	20,935	718,779	1,416,623	6,583,377
3	697,844	42,499	740,343	2,156,966	5,843,034
I	I	I	I	I	I
7				5,347,203	2,652,797
8	697,844	160,416	858,260	6,205,463	1,794,537
9	697,844	186,164	884,008	7,089,471	910,529
10	697,844	212,684	910,528	7,999,999	1

25. a. $S_n(\text{due}) = \$600,000$, $n = 60$, $p = 0.625\%$

$\$600,000 = R\, s_{\overline{60}|0.625\%}\, (1.00625)$

$R = \underline{\$8221}$

b. Interest earned in year 4

= Balance after year 4 – Balance after year 3 –12R

= $\$8221\, s_{\overline{48}|0.625\%}\, (1.00625) - \$8221\, s_{\overline{36}|0.625\%}\, (1.00625) - 12\,(\$8221)$

= $\$461,399 - \$332,809 - \$98,652$

= $\underline{\$29,938}$

c. Solve for n in

$\$300,000 = \$8221\, s_{\overline{n}|0.625\%}\, (1.00625)$

$n = 32.79$

Hence, the fund will pass the halfway point in the <u>33rd month</u>.

d. Interest earned in the 35th month

= $p \times$ (Balance after the 34th month + R)

= $0.00625\, [\$8221\, s_{\overline{34}|0.625\%}\, (1.00625) + \$8221]$

= $0.00625\, (\$312,297 + \$8221)$

= $\underline{\$2003}$

26. a. $S_n = \$600,000$, $n = 60$, $p = 0.625\%$

$\$600,000 = R\, s_{\overline{60}|0.625\%}$

$R = \underline{\$8273}$

Exercise 15.6 (continued)

b. Interest earned in year 4

   $=$ Balance after year 4 – Balance after year 3 –12R

   $= \$8273 \, s_{\overline{48}|0.625\%} - \$8273 \, s_{\overline{36}|0.625\%} - 12 \, (\$8273)$

   $= \$461,434 - \$332,834 - \$99,276$

   $= \underline{\underline{\$29,324}}$

c. Solve for n in

   $\$300,000 = \$8273 \, s_{\overline{n}|0.625\%}$

   $n = 32.79$

   Hence, the fund will pass the halfway point in the <u>33rd month</u>.

d. Interest earned in the 35th month

   $= p \times$ Balance after the 34th month

   $= 0.00625 \times \$8273 \, s_{\overline{34}|0.625\%}$

   $= \underline{\underline{\$1952}}$

27. a. $S_n = \$20,000,000$, $n = 40$, $p = 4.25\%$

   $\$20,000,000 = R \, s_{\overline{40}|4.25\%}$

   $R = \underline{\underline{\$198,368}}$

b. Interest earned in year 6

   $=$ Balance after year 6 – Balance after year 5 – 2R

   $= \$198,368 \, s_{\overline{12}|4.25\%} - \$198,368 \, s_{\overline{10}|4.25\%} - 2 \, (\$198,368)$

   $= \$3,023,741 - 2,409,422 - \$396,736$

   $= \underline{\underline{\$217,583}}$

c. Increase in the fund during interval 27

   $=$ Balance after interval 27 – Balance after interval 26

   $= \$198,368 \, s_{\overline{27}|4.25\%} - \$198,368 \, s_{\overline{26}|4.25\%}$

   $= \underline{\underline{\$585,395}}$

Exercise 15.6 (continued)

d.

Payment interval number	Payment	Interest earned	Increase in the fund	Balance in fund (end of interval)	Book value of the debt
0	—	—	—	$0	$20,000,000
1	$198,368	$0	$198,368	198,368	19,801,632
2	198,368	8431	206,799	405,167	19,594,833
3	198,368	17,220	215,588	620,755	19,379,245
I	I	I	I	I	I
37				17,104,453	2,895,547
38	198,368	726,939	925,307	18,029,760	1,970,240
39	198,368	766,265	964,633	18,994,393	1,005,607
40	198,368	807,262	1,005,630	20,000,023	(23)
	Total:	$12,065,303			

Total interest = $20,000,023 – 40 ($198,368) = $12,065,303

28. a. $S_n = \$4,500,000$, n = 34, $p = 3.75\%$

$$\$4,500,000 = R \, s_{\overline{34}|3.75\%}$$

$$R = \$67,603$$

b. Increase in the fund during interval 18

= Balance after interval 18 – Balance after interval 17

= $\$67,603 \, s_{\overline{18}|3.75\%} - \$67,603 \, s_{\overline{17}|3.75\%}$

= $\$126,405$

c. Interest earned in year 10

= Balance after year 10 – Balance after year 9 – 2R

= $\$67,603 \, s_{\overline{20}|3.75\%} - \$67,603 \, s_{\overline{18}|3.75\%} - 2 \, (\$67,603)$

= $\$1,961,662 - \$1,694,454 - \$135,206$

= $\$132,002$

Exercise 15.6 (continued)

d.

Payment interval number	Payment	Interest earned	Increase in the fund	Balance in fund (end of interval)	Book value of the debt
0	—	—	—	$0	$4,500,000
1	$67,603	$0	$67,603	67,603	4,432,397
2	67,603	2535	70,138	137,741	4,362,259
3	67,603	5165	72,768	210,509	4,289,491
I	I	I	I	I	I
8				617,388	3,882,612
9	67,603	23,152	90,755	708,143	3,791,857
10	67,603	26,555	94,158	802,301	3,697,699
I	I	I	I	I	I
31				3,840,980	659,020
32	67,603	144,037	211,640	4,052,620	447,380
33	67,603	151,973	219,576	4,272,196	227,804
34	67,603	160,207	227,810	4,500,006	(6)
	Total:	$2,201,504			

Total interest earned = $4,500,006 − 34 ($67,603) = $2,201,504

29. a. $S_n(\text{due}) = \$800,000$, $n = 40$, $p = 1.75\%$

$$\$800,000 = R\, s_{\overline{40}|1.75\%}\, (1.0175)$$

$$R = \$13,737$$

b.

Payment interval number	Payment	Interest earned	Increase in the fund	Balance in fund (end of interval)	Book value of the debt
0	—	—	—	$0	$800,000
1	$13,737	$240	$13,977	13,977	786,023
2	13,737	485	14,222	28,199	771,801
3	13,737	734	14,471	42,670	757,330
I	I	I	I	I	I
37				718,907	81,093
38	13,737	12,821	26,558	745,465	54,535
39	13,737	13,286	27,023	772,488	27,512
40	13,737	13,759	27,496	799,984	16
	Total:	$250,504			

Total interest = $799,984 − 40 ($13,737) = $250,504

Exercise 15.6 *(concluded)*

30. a. $S_n = \$800{,}000$, $n = 40$, $p = 1.75\%$

$$\$800{,}000 = R\ s_{\overline{40}|1.75\%}$$

$$R = \underline{\$13{,}978}$$

b.

Payment interval number	Payment	Interest earned	Increase in the fund	Balance in fund (end of interval)	Book value of the debt
0	—	—	—	$0	$800,000
1	$13,978	$0	$13,978	13,978	786,022
2	13,978	245	14,223	28,201	771,799
3	13,978	494	14,472	42,673	757,327
I	I	I	I	I	
37				718,938	81,062
38	13,978	12,581	26,559	745,497	54,503
39	13,978	13,046	27,024	772,521	27,479
40	13,978	13,519	27,497	800,018	(18)
	Total:	$240,898			

Total interest $= \$800{,}018 - 40\,(\$13{,}978) = \underline{\$240{,}898}$

Review Problems

1. Given: $F = \$1000$, $n = 39$, $b = 3.75\%$, $p = 4.3\%$

$$\text{Bond price} = \$37.50\left(\frac{1 - 1.043^{-39}}{0.043}\right) + \frac{\$1000}{1.043^{39}} = \$896.86$$

Bond discount $= \$1000 - \$896.86 = \underline{\$103.14}$

2. a. Given: $F = \$10{,}000$, $b = 4.75\%$, $n = 32$, $p = 3.9\%$

$$\text{Bond price} = \$475\left(\frac{1 - 1.039^{-32}}{0.039}\right) + \frac{\$10{,}000}{1.039^{32}} = \underline{\$11{,}538.78}$$

b. Capital gain $= \$11{,}538.78 - \$10{,}000 = \underline{\$1538.78}$

3. Given: For each bond, $F = \$1000$ and $b = 4.25\%$
At the time the bonds were purchased, $n = 36$ and $p = 4.9\%$

$$\text{Purchase price} = \$42.50\left(\frac{1 - 1.049^{-36}}{0.049}\right) + \frac{\$1000}{1.049^{36}} = \$891.05$$

Now, $n = 27$ and $p = 4.0\%$

$$\text{Current price} = \$42.50\left(\frac{1 - 1.04^{-27}}{0.04}\right) + \frac{\$1000}{1.04^{27}} = \$1040.82$$

Capital gain $= 15\,(\$1040.82 - \$891.05) = \underline{\$2246.55}$

Review Problems *(continued)*

4. Given: F = $1000, b = 4.75%, n = 20, price = $1082.50

   a. The bond's yield-to-maturity is 2p where

   $$\$1082.50 = \$47.50\left[\frac{1-(1+p)^{-20}}{p}\right] + \frac{\$1000}{(1+p)^{20}}$$
   $$p = 4.136\%$$

   Thus, YTM = 2p = 8.27% compounded semiannually

   b. If the bond's price rises abruptly to $1107.50, then

   $$\$1107.50 = \$47.50\left[\frac{1-(1+p)^{-20}}{p}\right] + \frac{\$1000}{(1+p)^{20}}$$
   $$p = 3.962\%$$

   YTM = 2p = 7.92% compounded semiannually

   The bond's yield to maturity declines by

   8.27% − 7.92% = 0.35% compounded semiannually

5. Given: F = $1000, b = 6.125%, p = 5.1%, maturity date = June 15, 2005
   (June 15, 2005) − (June 15, 1989) = 32 half-years
   (Dec. 10, 1989) − (June 15, 1989) = 178 days
   (Dec. 15, 1989) − (June 15, 1989) = 183 days

   $$\text{Price (June 15, 1989)} = \$61.25\left(\frac{1-1.051^{-32}}{0.051}\right) + \frac{\$1000}{1.051^{32}} = \$1160.07$$

   Price (Dec. 10, 1989) = $1160.07 (1.051)^{178/183} = $1217.58

6. Given: Quoted price on September 10 = 111.25% of face value
   F = $1000, b = 5.625% paid on May 15 and Nov. 15
   September 10 − May 15 = 118 days
   November 15 − May 15 = 184 days

   $$\text{Accrued interest to Sept. 10} = \$56.25\left(\frac{118}{184}\right) = \$36.07$$

   The client pays the flat price.
   Flat price = $1112.50 + $36.07 = $1148.57

7. Given: F = $1000, b = 5.25%, n = 22, p = 4.4%

   $$\text{Purchase price} = \$52.50\left(\frac{1-1.044^{-22}}{0.044}\right) + \frac{\$1000}{1.044^{22}} = \$1118.27$$

Review Problems *(continued)*

Coupon number	Coupon payment	Interest on book value	Premium amortized	Book value of bond	Unamortized premium
0	—	—	—	$1118.27	$118.27
1	$52.50	$49.20	$3.30	1114.97	114.97
2	52.50	49.06	3.44	1111.53	111.53
3	52.50	48.91	3.59	1107.94	107.94
I	I	I	I	I	I
				1023.41	23.41
20	52.50	45.03	7.47	1015.94	15.94
21	52.50	44.70	7.80	1008.14	8.14
22	52.50	44.36	8.14	1000.00	0.00
	$1155.00	$1036.73	$118.27		

8. Given: F = $1000, b = 4.125%, n = 14, p = 4.7%

$$\text{Purchase price} = \$41.25 \left(\frac{1 - 1.047^{-14}}{0.047} \right) + \frac{\$1000}{1.047^{14}} = \underline{\$941.98}$$

Coupon number	Coupon payment	Interest on book value	Discount amortized	Book value of bond	Unamortized discount
0	—	—	—	$941.98	$58.02
1	$41.25	$44.27	$3.02	945.00	55.00
2	41.25	44.42	3.17	948.17	51.83
3	41.25	44.56	3.31	951.48	48.52
I	I	I	I	I	I
				984.25	15.75
12	41.25	46.26	5.01	989.26	10.74
13	41.25	46.50	5.25	994.51	5.49
14	41.25	46.74	5.49	1000.00	0.00
	$577.50	$635.52	$58.02		

9. S_n(due) = $750,000, n = 6, p = 3%

$$\$750,000 = R \, s_{\overline{6}|3\%} \, (1.03)$$

$$R = \$112,571$$

Payment interval number	Payment (at start)	Interest earned	Increase in the fund	Balance in fund (end of interval)
0	—	—	—	$0
1	$112,571	$3377	$115,948	115,948
2	112,571	6856	119,427	235,375
3	112,571	10,438	123,009	358,384
4	112,571	14,129	126,700	485,084
5	112,571	17,930	130,501	615,585
6	112,571	21,845	134,416	750,001
	Total:	$74,575	$750,001	

Review Problems *(concluded)*

10. $S_n = \$18,000,000$, $p = 3.125\%$, $n = 30$, $b = 4.5\%$

    a. $\$18,000,000 = R\, s_{\overline{30}|3.125\%}$

          $R = \underline{\$370,747}$

    b. Annual cost of debt $= 2\,(R + b \times \$18,000,000)$

                        $= 2\,(\$370,747 + 0.045 \times \$18,000,000)$

                        $= \underline{\$2,361,494}$

c.

Payment interval number	Payment	Interest earned	Increase in the fund	Balance in fund (end of interval)	Book value of the debt
0	—	—	—	$0.00	$18,000,000
1	$370,747	$0	$370,747	370,747	17,629,253
2	370,747	11,586	382,333	753,080	17,246,920
3	370,747	23,534	394,281	1,147,361	16,852,639
I	I	I	I	I	I
27				15,366,531	2,633,469
28	370,747	480,204	850,951	16,217,482	1,782,518
29	370,747	506,796	877,543	17,095,025	904,975
30	370,747	534,220	904,967	17,999,992	8

Self-Test Exercise

1. Given: $F = \$1000$, $b = 4.9\%$, $n = 36$, $p = 4.75\%$

    $$\text{Bond price} = \$49\left(\frac{1 - 1.0475^{-36}}{0.0475}\right) + \frac{\$1000}{1.0475^{36}} = \$1025.64$$

    In order that YTM $= 2p = 10\%$ csa,

    $$\text{Price} = \$49\left(\frac{1 - 1.05^{-36}}{0.05}\right) + \frac{\$1000}{1.05^{36}} = \$983.45$$

    Therefore, the bond price will have to be
        $\$1025.64 - \$983.45 = \underline{\$42.19}$

    lower for the yield to maturity to be 0.5% higher.

2. The answer will be the same for any face value. Use $F = \$1000$. Currently, $n = 45$, $b = 6.25\%$, and $p = 5\%$.

    $$\text{Current price} = \$62.50\left(\frac{1 - 1.05^{-45}}{0.05}\right) + \frac{\$1000}{1.05^{45}} = \$1222.18$$

    $$\text{Percent capital gain} = \frac{\$1222.18 - \$1000}{\$1000} \times 100\% = \underline{22.22\%}$$

3. Given: F = $1000, b = 5.75%, n = 17, price = $1034.50
   The YTM is 2p where p is the solution to

   $$\$1034.50 = \$57.50\left[\frac{1-(1+p)^{-17}}{p}\right] + \frac{\$1000}{(1+p)^{17}}$$

   p = 5.434%
   YTM = 2p = <u>10.87% compounded semiannually</u>

4. Given: F = $1000, b = 6.625%, p = 4.65%, maturity date = Nov. 1, 2004
   (Nov. 1, 2004) – (May 1, 1992) = 25 half-years
   (June 10, 1992) – (May 1, 1992) = 40 days
   (Nov. 1, 1992) – (May 1, 1992) = 184 days

   $$\text{Price (May 1, 1992)} = \$66.25\left(\frac{1-1.0465^{-25}}{0.0465}\right) + \frac{\$1000}{1.0465^{25}} = \$1288.39$$

   Price (June 10, 1992) = $1288.39 (1.0465)$^{40/184}$ = <u>$1301.18</u>

5. Quoted price = Flat price – Accrued interest

   $$= \$1301.18 - \$66.25\left(\frac{40}{184}\right)$$

   $$= \underline{\$1286.78}$$

6. Given: F = $5000, b = 4.5%, n = 5, p = 5.25%

   $$\text{Purchase price} = \$225\left(\frac{1-1.0525^{-5}}{0.0525}\right) + \frac{\$5000}{1.0525^{5}} = \$4838.76$$

Coupon number	Coupon payment	Interest on book value	Discount amortized	Book value of bond	Unamortized discount
0	—	—	—	$4838.76	$161.24
1	$225.00	$254.03	$29.03	4867.79	132.21
2	225.00	255.56	30.56	4898.35	101.65
3	225.00	257.16	32.16	4930.51	69.49
4	225.00	258.85	33.85	4964.36	35.64
5	225.00	260.64	35.64	5000.00	0.00
	$1125.00	$1286.24	$161.24		

Self-Test Exercise *(concluded)*

7. $S_n = \$500,000$, $n = 14$, $p = 3.5\%$

   $\$500,000 = R \, s_{\overline{14}|3.5\%}$

   $R = \$28,285$

Payment interval number	Payment	Interest earned	Increase in the fund	Balance in fund (end of interval)	Book value of the debt
0	—	—	—	$0.00	$500,000
1	28,285	$0	$28,285	28,285	471,715
2	28,285	990	29,275	57,560	442,440
3	28,285	2015	30,300	87,860	412,140
⏐	⏐	⏐	⏐	⏐	⏐
11				371,721	128,279
12	28,285	13,010	41,295	413,016	86,984
13	28,285	14,456	42,741	455,757	44,243
14	28,285	15,951	44,236	499,993	7

16 Business Investment Decisions

Changes in the Second Edition:

No significant changes have been made in this chapter. Relatively few colleges cover this area in a business mathematics course — these topics are usually left to a later course in managerial finance. Please contact the author via email (JEROME@MALA.BC.CA) if you feel strongly that this chapter should be retained in a future edition of the text.

Exercise 16.1

1. a. The fair market value of the future cash flows (discounted at Vencap's cost of capital) is

   $$\frac{(-\$30,000)}{1.15} + \frac{(-\$10,000)}{1.15^2} + \frac{\$20,000}{1.15^3} + \frac{\$60,000}{1.15^4} + \frac{\$40,000}{1.15^5}$$

   $$= -\$26,087.0 - \$7561.4 + \$13,150.3 + \$34,305.2 + \$19,887.1$$

   $$= \$33,694$$

   Since the purchase price is less than the present value of the future cash flows, <u>the investment should be made.</u>

   b. The economic value, in current dollars, of Vencap will be increased by the amount which the present value of the expected cash flows exceeds the purchase price. <u>The increase in economic value is</u>

   $$\$33,694 - \$30,000 = \underline{\$3694}$$

2. a. If the cost of capital is 18%, the present value of the forecast cash flows is

   $$\frac{(-\$30,000)}{1.18} + \frac{(-\$10,000)}{1.18^2} + \frac{\$20,000}{1.18^3} + \frac{\$60,000}{1.18^4} + \frac{\$40,000}{1.18^5} = \$27,999$$

   In this case the required initial investment is greater than the present value of the expected cash flows. Therefore, <u>the investment should not be made.</u>

   b. If the investment is purchased for $30,000, the <u>economic value</u> of Vencap <u>would be decreased by</u>

   $$\$30,000 - \$27,999 = \underline{\$2001}$$

3. If Vencap requires a 20% rate of return on investment, it should offer an amount equal to the present value of the future cash flows discounted at 20%.

   $$Price = \frac{(-\$30,000)}{1.2} + \frac{(-\$10,000)}{1.2^2} + \frac{\$20,000}{1.2^3} + \frac{\$60,000}{1.2^4} + \frac{\$40,000}{1.2^5} = \underline{\underline{\$24,640}}$$

4. a. Arrowsmith Lumber should purchase the timber rights if the present value of the future net cash flows, discounted at 14%, is greater than or equal to $90,000.

   The present value of the net cash flows in years 1 to 6 is

   $$\frac{\$50,000}{1.14} + \frac{\$50,000}{1.14^2} + \frac{(-\$20,000)}{1.14^3} + \frac{\$50,000}{1.14^4} + \frac{\$50,000}{1.14^5} + \frac{(-\$20,000)}{1.14^6}$$

   $$= \$43,859.6 + \$38,473.4 - \$13,499.4 + \$29,604.0 + \$25,968.4 - \$9111.7$$

   $$= \$115,294$$

   Since the present value of the expected net cash flows exceeds the required investment, Arrowsmith <u>should buy the timber rights.</u>

   b. The investment would increase the current economic value of Arrowsmith Lumber by

   $$\$115,294 - \$90,000 = \underline{\$25,294}$$

Exercise 16.1 *(continued)*

5. a. If Arrowsmith's cost of capital is 18%, the present value of the forecast cash flows is

$$\frac{\$50,000}{1.18} + \frac{\$50,000}{1.18^2} + \frac{(-\$20,000)}{1.18^3} + \frac{\$50,000}{1.18^4} + \frac{\$50,000}{1.18^5} + \frac{(-\$20,000)}{1.18^6} = \$106,346$$

The present value of the expected cash flows is larger than the price of the timber rights. Arrowsmith should still buy the timber rights if its cost of capital is 18%.

b. The economic value of Arrowsmith Lumber would be increased by

$$\$106,346 - \$90,000 = \$16,346$$

6. If Arrowsmith requires a 20% rate of return on investment, it will be willing to purchase the timber rights at a price equal to the present value of the expected net cash flows discounted at 20%. That is, the maximum purchase price would be

$$\frac{\$50,000}{1.2} + \frac{\$50,000}{1.2^2} + \frac{(-\$20,000)}{1.2^3} + \frac{\$50,000}{1.2^4} + \frac{\$50,000}{1.2^5} + \frac{(-\$20,000)}{1.2^6} = \underline{\underline{\$102,323}}$$

7. The lower cost alternative should be selected. This will be the alternative having the lower present value of costs (net of any salvage or resale value).

a. The lease payments form a simple annuity due having
$R = \$1000$, $n = 48$, and $p = i = 1\%$. Then

$$PV\ (\text{lease}) = A_n\ (\text{due}) = \$1000\left(\frac{1 - 1.01^{-48}}{0.01}\right)1.01 = \$38,354$$

$$PV\ (\text{purchase}) = \$43,000 - \$5000\ (1.01)^{-48} = \$39,899$$

The machine should be leased since the current economic value of the lifetime costs is $1545 less than if the machine is purchased.

b. If the firm's cost of borrowing is only $p = 0.75\%$ per month,

$$PV\ (\text{lease}) = \$1000\left(\frac{1 - 1.0075^{-48}}{0.0075}\right)1.0075 = \$40,486$$

$$PV\ (\text{purchase}) = \$43,000 - \$5000\ (1.0075)^{-48} = \$39,507$$

The machine should be purchased since the current economic value of the lifetime costs is $979 less than if the machine is leased.

8. The alternative having the lower present value of costs (net of any trade-in value) should be chosen. The lease payments form a simple annuity due having $R = \$500$, $n = 60$, and $p = i = 0.8125\%$. Then

$$PV\ (\text{lease}) = A_n\ (\text{due}) = \$500\left(\frac{1 - 1.008125^{-60}}{0.008125}\right)1.008125 = \$23,862$$

a. $PV\ (\text{purchase}) = \$28,000 - \$5000\ (1.008125)^{-60} = \$24,923$

The car should be leased. Leasing will cost $1061 less (in current dollars).

b. $PV\ (\text{purchase}) = \$28,000 - \$8000\ (1.008125)^{-60} = \$23,077$

With the higher trade-in value, the car should be purchased. This would save $785 (in current dollars).

Exercise 16.1 *(concluded)*

9. a. The alternative having the lower present value of costs should be chosen. Since the college will continue to own the telephone system after 5 years, the fair comparison is between purchasing the system and leasing for 5 years followed by exercising the purchase option. For the lease, R = $1500, n = 20, and $p = i = 2.5\%$.

$$PV \text{ (lease)} = \$3000 + A_n \text{ (due)} + \$3000 \,(1.025)^{-20}$$

$$= \$3000 + \$1500 \left(\frac{1 - 1.025^{-20}}{0.025} \right) 1.025 + \$1830.81$$

$$= \$28,799$$

The college should choose to <u>lease the system</u>.

b. Leasing will save $30,000 – $28,799 = <u>$1201</u> in current dollars.

10. a. The alternative having the lower present value of costs should be chosen. The lease payments form a simple annuity due having R = $2100, n = 36, and $p = i = 1\%$.

$$PV \text{ (lease)} = A_n \text{ (due)} = \$2100 \left(\frac{1 - 1.01^{-36}}{0.01} \right) 1.01 = \$63,858$$

$$PV \text{ (purchase)} = \$120,000 - \$60,000 \,(1.01)^{-36} = \$78,065$$

Rocky Mountain Bus Tours should <u>lease the bus</u>.

b. Leasing will cost $78,065 – $63,858 = <u>$14,207</u> less in current dollars.

11. The alternative having the lower present value of costs should be chosen. The rental payments form a simple annuity due having R = $900 per month and n = 60.

a. If $p = i = 0.875\%$,

$$PV \text{ (rent)} = \$900 \left(\frac{1 - 1.00875^{-60}}{0.00875} \right) 1.00875 = \$42,239$$

$$PV \text{ (buy)} = \$120,000 + \$250 \left(\frac{1 - 1.00875^{-60}}{0.00875} \right) - \frac{\$145,000}{1.00875^{60}} = \$45,660$$

Mr. Harder <u>should rent, thereby saving $3421</u> in current dollars.

b. If $p = i = 0.75\%$,

$$PV \text{ (rent)} = \$900 \left(\frac{1 - 1.0075^{-60}}{0.0075} \right) 1.0075 = \$43,681$$

$$PV \text{ (buy)} = \$120,000 + \$250 \left(\frac{1 - 1.0075^{-60}}{0.0075} \right) - \frac{\$145,000}{1.0075^{60}} = \$39,432$$

Mr. Harder <u>should buy, thereby saving $4249</u>.

Exercise 16.2

1. a. $\text{NPV} = \$36,000\ a_{\overline{7}|12\%} + \dfrac{\$40,000}{1.12^7} - \$165,000$

    $= \$164,295.2 + \$18,094.0 - \$165,000$

    $= \$17,389$

    Since the investment has a positive NPV, St. Lawrence Bus Lines should <u>sign the contract.</u>

   b. $\text{NPV} = \$36,000\ a_{\overline{7}|15\%} + \dfrac{\$40,000}{1.15^7} - \$165,000 = -\$187$

    At a 15% cost of capital, the investment's NPV is a small negative amount. <u>The contract should not be signed.</u> (The small magnitude of the NPV in relation to the amounts involved means that the future profits and resale value would nearly be sufficient to pay back the $165,000 financing required along with a 15% rate of return to the providers of the financing.)

   c. As the discount rate (cost of capital) increases beyond 15%, the NPV will remain negative and grow in magnitude. At an 18% cost of capital, the NPV is – $15,228. The investment <u>should be rejected</u> at any cost of capital above 15%.

2.

Phase	Initial investment	Annual savings	Number of years	NPV
1	$100,000	$30,000	10	$56,483
2	100,000	27,000	9	33,552 ①
3	100,000	22,000	8	2055
4	100,000	22,000	7	−5657

   ① Sample calculation:

   $\text{NPV} = \$27,000\ a_{\overline{9}|14\%} - \$100,000 = \$33,552$

   <u>The first three phases</u> all have a positive NPV and should, therefore, <u>be accepted</u>. Phase 4 has a negative NPV and <u>should be rejected.</u>

3.

Time (years)	Cash flow	Present value
0	– $150,000	– $150,000
1	– 50,000	– 43,478
2	– 50,000	– 37,807
3	200,000	131,503
4	300,000	171.526
Total (NPV):		$ 71,744

   The economic value, at the time of planting, of the 20-hectare ginseng crop is $71,744.

Exercise 16.2 (continued)

4.

Time (years)	Capital cash flow	Operating profit	Net cash flow
0	− $1,000,000		− $1,000,000
1	− 1,500,000		− 1,500,000
2 to 10		$500,000	500,000
11	− 500,000	$500,000	0

$$NPV = \frac{\$500,000 \ a_{\overline{9}|18\%}}{1.18} - \frac{\$1,500,000}{1.18} - \$1,000,000$$

$$= \$1,823,314.3 - \$1,271,186.4 - \$1,000,000$$

$$= -\$447,872$$

Since the strip mine has a negative NPV when the cash flows are discounted at 18%, the rate of return on the investment would be less than 18%.

5.

Time (years)	Capital cash flow	Operating profit	Net cash flow
0	− $150,000		− $150,000
1	− 150,000		− 150,000
2	− 150,000		− 150,000
3	0	0	0
4 to 9		$90,000	90,000
10	100,000	90,000	190,000

$$NPV = \frac{\$90,000 \ a_{\overline{6}|14\%}}{1.14^3} + \frac{\$190,000}{1.14^{10}} - \$150,000 \ a_{\overline{3}|14\%} \ (1.14)$$

$$= \$236,226.6 + \$51,251.3 - \$396,999.1$$

$$= -\$109,521$$

Since the NPV of the new project is negative, it should be rejected.

6.

Time (years)	Capital cash flow	Operating profit	Net cash flow
0	− $45,000		− $45,000
1 to 3		$9000	9000
4 to 6		6000	6000
7 to 12		4000	4000

$$NPV = \$9000 \ a_{\overline{3}|15\%} + \frac{\$6000 \ a_{\overline{3}|15\%}}{1.15^3} + \frac{\$4000 \ a_{\overline{6}|15\%}}{1.15^6} - \$45,000$$

$$= \$20,549.0 + \$9007.5 + \$6544.5 - \$45,000$$

$$= -\$8899$$

Since the investment has a negative NPV, it should not be undertaken.

Exercise 16.2 *(continued)*

7.

Time (years)	Capital cash flow	Operating profit	Net cash flow
0	– $400,000		– $400,000
1	– 1,800,000		– 1,800,000
2 to 5		$300,000	300,000
6 to 12		500,000	500,000
13	400,000	500,000	900,000

$$NPV = \frac{\$300,000\ a_{\overline{4}|16\%}}{1.16} + \frac{\$500,000\ a_{\overline{7}|16\%}}{1.16^5} + \frac{\$900,000}{1.16^{13}} - \frac{\$1,800,000}{1.16} - \$400,000$$

$$= \$723,667.4 + \$961,406.8 + \$130,709.3 - \$1,551,724.1 - \$400,000$$

$$= -\$135,946$$

Since the project has a negative NPV at a discount rate of 16%, the rate of return on the investment will be below 16% and Jasper <u>should not proceed with the project.</u>

8.

Time (years)	Capital cash flow	Operating profit	Net cash flow
0	– $150,000		– $150,000
1		– $30,000	– 30,000
2		– 10,000	– 10,000
3		0	0
4	– 40,000	60,000	20,000
5 to 7		60,000	60,000
8 to 9		30,000	30,000
10	50,000	30,000	80,000

$$NPV = \frac{\$20,000}{1.17^4} + \frac{\$60,000\ a_{\overline{3}|17\%}}{1.17^4} + \frac{\$30,000\ a_{\overline{2}|17\%}}{1.17^7} + \frac{\$80,000}{1.17^{13}} - \frac{\$10,000}{1.17^2} - \frac{\$30,000}{1.17} - \$150,000$$

$$= \$10,673.0 + \$70,748.7 + \$15,845.6 + \$16,643.0 - \$7305.1 - \$25,641.0 - \$150,000$$

$$= -\$69,036$$

<u>The project is not acceptable</u> since it has a negative NPV when cash flows are discounted at 17%.

Exercise 16.2 *(concluded)*

9.
Time (years)	Capital cash flow	Operating profit	Net cash flow
0	– $275,000		– $275,000
1 to 2		$75,000	75,000
3	– 40,000	75,000	35,000
4		75,000	75,000
5	– 40,000	55,000	15,000
6		55,000	55,000
7	30,000	55,000	85,000

$$\text{NPV} = \$75,000\, a_{\overline{2}|14\%} + \frac{\$35,000}{1.14^3} + \frac{\$75,000}{1.14^4} + \frac{\$15,000}{1.14^5} + \frac{\$55,000}{1.14^6} + \frac{\$85,000}{1.14^7} - \$275,000$$

$= \$123,499.5 + \$23,624.0 + \$44,406.0 + \$7790.5 + \$25,057.3 + \$33,959.2 - \$275,000$

$= -\$16,653$

The product should not be manufactured since the investment has a negative NPV.

10.
Time (years)	Capital cash flow	Operating profit	Net cash flow
0	– $52,000		– $52,000
1 to 4		$13,500	13,500
5 to 7		12,500	12,500
8	5000	12,500	17,500

$$\text{NPV} = \$13,500\, a_{\overline{4}|15\%} + \frac{\$12,500\, a_{\overline{3}|15\%}}{1.15^4} + \frac{\$17,500}{1.15^8} - \$52,000$$

$= \$38,542.2 + \$16,318.0 + \$5720.8 - \$52,000$

$= \$8581$

The machine should be acquired because the investment has a positive NPV using a discount rate of 15%.

Exercise 16.3

1. Rank the projects in descending order of NPV per invested dollar.

Project	Initial investment	Project NPV	NPV per invested dollar	Cumulative investment
B	$60,000	$40,000	$0.67	$60,000
D	200,000	110,000	0.55	260,000
C	130,000	60,000	0.46	390,000
A	100,000	25,000	0.25	490,000

Now find the combination of projects having the largest aggregate NPV subject to the $300,000 constraint on total investment.

Exercise 16.3 (continued)

Combination of projects	Combined NPV	Total investment
B, D	$150,000	$260,000
B, C, A	125,000	290,000

<u>Projects B and D</u> have the highest NPV subject to the capital budgeting constraint.

2. Rank the projects in descending order of NPV per invested dollar.

Project	Initial investment	Project NPV	NPV per invested dollar	Cumulative investment
1	$1,000,000	$600,000	$0.60	$1,000,000
4	600,000	270,000	0.45	1,600,000
3	750,000	285,000	0.38	2,350,000
5	450,000	113,000	0.25	2,800,000
2	1,800,000	324,000	0.18	4,600,000
6	150,000	21,000	0.14	4,750,000
7	250,000	20,000	0.08	5,000,000

<u>Projects 1, 4, 3, 5, and 6 should be selected</u> (requiring a combined investment of $2,950,000).

3. Calculate each project's NPV and rank the projects in descending order of NPV per invested dollar.

Project	Initial investment	Project NPV	NPV per invested dollar	Cumulative investment
F	$20,000	$3375	$0.17	$20,000
E	28,000	4329	0.15	48,000
A	30,000	3935	0.13	78,000
C	18,000	2131	0.12	96,000
B	36,000	1188	0.03	132,000
D	22,000	−456	−0.02	154,000

<u>Projects F, E, and A should be selected</u> (requiring a combined investment of $78,000).

4. $\text{NPV(Eagle)} = \$75,000 \, a_{\overline{7}|15\%} + \dfrac{\$50,000}{1.15^7} - \$250,000$

$= \$312,031.5 + \$18,796.9 - \$250,000$

$= \$80,828$

$\text{NPV(Albatross)} = \$95,000 \, a_{\overline{7}|15\%} + \dfrac{\$150,000}{1.15^7} - \$325,000$

$= \$395,239.9 + \$56,390.6 - \$325,000$

$= \$126,630$

<u>The economic advantage</u>, in current dollars, of choosing the Albatross is <u>$126,630 − $80,828 = $45,802</u>

Exercise 16.3 *(continued)*

5. NPV(Massey) $= \$38,500\ a_{\overline{6}|11\%} + \dfrac{\$25,000}{1.11^6} - \$95,000 = \$81,242$

    NPV(Deere) $= \$35,000\ a_{\overline{6}|10\%} + \dfrac{\$20,000}{1.10^6} - \$78,000 = \$85,724$

    Carl should <u>purchase the Deere</u> combine, in current dollars, its economic value is

    $\$85,724 - \$81,242 = \underline{\$4482}$

    larger than the investment in a Massey combine.

6.

Time	Project A		Project B	
(years)	Capital cash flow	Operating profit	Capital cash flow	Operating profit
0	– $6000		– $5000	
1				$5200
2		$6000	– 8000	5200
3	– 8000			5200
4		18,000	– 5000	5200
5				5200
6				5200
7		12,000		5200

$$\text{NPV(A)} = \frac{\$6000}{1.16^2} + \frac{\$18,000}{1.16^4} + \frac{\$12,000}{1.16^7} - \frac{\$8000}{1.16^3} - \$6000 = \$7521$$

$$\text{NPV(B)} = \$5200\ a_{\overline{7}|16\%} - \frac{\$5000}{1.16^4} - \frac{\$8000}{1.16^2} - \$5000 = \$7294$$

<u>Project A should be selected</u> because is has a <u>$227 larger</u> economic value.

7.

Time (years)	Investment C		Time (years)	Investment D	
	Capital cash flow	Operating profit		Capital cash flow	Operating profit
0	– $50,000		0	– $25,000	
1		$16,000	1 to 3	– 25,000	
2	– 30,000	16,000	4 to 9		$35,000
3 to 9		16,000	10	20,000	35,000
10	30,000	16,000			

Exercise 16.3 *(continued)*

$$\text{NPV(C)} = \$16,000\ a_{\overline{10}|15\%} + \frac{\$30,000}{1.15^{10}} - \frac{\$30,000}{1.15^2} - \$50,000$$

$$= \$15,032$$

$$\text{NPV(D)} = \frac{\$35,000\ a_{\overline{7}|15\%}}{1.15^3} + \frac{\$20,000}{1.15^{10}} - \$25,000\ a_{\overline{3}|15\%} - \$25,000$$

$$= \$95,744.0 + \$4943.7 - \$57,080.6 - \$25,000$$

$$= \$18,607$$

The company should <u>choose investment D</u> whose current economic value is <u>$3575 more</u> than C's economic value.

8. We will use the Replacement Chain Method. By including one replacement cycle of Machine A, both mutually exclusive investments will have an 8-year time horizon.

$$\text{NPV(A, 4 years)} = \$15,000\ a_{\overline{4}|14\%} + \frac{\$10,000}{1.14^4} - \$40,000 = \$9626$$

$$\text{NPV(A, 8 years)} = \$9626 + \frac{\$9626}{1.14^4} = \$15,325$$

$$\text{NPV(B, 8 years)} = \$15,000\ a_{\overline{8}|14\%} + \frac{\$10,000}{1.14^8} - \$60,000 = \$13,089$$

<u>Machine A should be selected</u> since it has the larger NPV (with a common time horizon).

9. We will use the Equivalent Annual Cash Flow Method.

$$\text{NPV(H, 3 years)} = \$55,000\ a_{\overline{3}|16\%} - \$100,000 = \$23,524$$

$$\text{NPV(J, 4 years)} = \$58,000\ a_{\overline{4}|16\%} - \$140,000 = \$22,294$$

H's equivalent annual cash flow is the value of R in

$$\$23,524 = R\ a_{\overline{3}|16\%}$$

$$R = \$10,474$$

J's equivalent annual cash flow is the value of R in

$$\$22,294 = R\ a_{\overline{4}|16\%}$$

$$R = \$7967$$

<u>Model H should be purchased</u> because it has the larger equivalent annual cash flow.

10. Select the model having the largest equivalent annual cash flow.

$$\text{NPV(A, 2 years)} = \$700\ a_{\overline{2}|20\%} + \frac{\$200}{1.2^2} - \$1000 = \$208.33$$

$$\text{NPV(AA, 3 years)} = \$700\ a_{\overline{3}|20\%} + \frac{\$450}{1.2^3} - \$1400 = \$334.95$$

$$\text{NPV(AAA, 6 years)} = \$700\ a_{\overline{6}|20\%} + \frac{\$700}{1.2^6} - \$2100 = \$462.29$$

Exercise 16.3 *(continued)*

The equivalent annual cash flow in each case is the value of R satisfying

$$NPV = R\ a_{\overline{n}|20\%}$$

For model A,

$$\$208.33 = R\ a_{\overline{2}|20\%}$$
$$R = \$136.36$$

For model AA,

$$\$334.95 = R\ a_{\overline{3}|20\%}$$
$$R = \$159.01$$

For model AAA,

$$\$462.29 = R\ a_{\overline{6}|20\%}$$
$$R = \$139.01$$

Model AA should be chosen since it has the largest equivalent annual cash flow.

11. The truck that generates the larger equivalent annual cash flow (EACF) should be purchased.

$$NPV(\text{15-ton, 7 years}) = \$24{,}000\ a_{\overline{7}|12.5\%} + \frac{\$15{,}000}{1.125^7} - \$75{,}000 = \$39{,}392$$

This truck's EACF is the value of R in

$$\$39{,}392 = R\ a_{\overline{7}|12.5\%}$$
$$R = \$8769$$

$$NPV(\text{25-ton, 6 years}) = \$32{,}000\ a_{\overline{6}|12.5\%} + \frac{\$20{,}000}{1.125^6} - \$100{,}000 = \$39{,}588$$

The 25-ton truck's EACF is the value of R in

$$\$39{,}588 = R\ a_{\overline{6}|12.5\%}$$
$$R = \$9766$$

The 25-ton truck should be purchased. It will generate a

$$\$9766 - \$8769 = \underline{\$997}$$

larger annual economic benefit to the owner than the 15-ton truck.

12. The equivalent annual cost in each case is the value of R satisfying

$$\text{Purchase price} = R\ a_{\overline{\text{service life}}|10\%}$$

For battery X, $\$60 = R\ a_{\overline{3}|10\%}$ giving R = \$24.13

For battery Y, $\$75 = R\ a_{\overline{4}|10\%}$ giving R = \$23.66

For battery Z, $\$105 = R\ a_{\overline{6}|10\%}$ giving R = \$24.11

Battery Y has the lowest equivalent annual cost.

Exercise 16.3 (continued)

13. $\text{NPV(Hawk, 5 years)} = \dfrac{\$30,000}{1.09^5} - \$30,000\, a_{\overline{5}|9\%} - \$120,000$

$$= \$19,497.4 - \$116,689.5 - \$120,000$$

$$= -\$217,192$$

The equivalent annual cost (EAC) is the value of R in

$$-\$217,192 = R\, a_{\overline{5}|9\%}$$

$$R = -\$55,838$$

(The negative sign is interpreted as a cash outflow or cost.)

$\text{NPV(Falcon, 7 years)} = \dfrac{\$40,000}{1.09^7} - \$40,000\, a_{\overline{7}|9\%} - \$100,000$

$$= \$21,881.4 - \$201,318.1 - \$100,000$$

$$= -\$279,437$$

The Falcon's EAC is the value of R in

$$-\$279,437 = R\, a_{\overline{7}|9\%}$$

$$R = -\$55,521$$

The Falcon has a slightly lower ($317) equivalent annual cost.

14. $\text{NPV(used, 3 years)} = \dfrac{\$4000}{1.11^3} - \$1000\, a_{\overline{3}|11\%} - \$12,000 = -\$11,519$

The equivalent annual cost (EAC) is the value of R in

$$-\$11,519 = R\, a_{\overline{3}|11\%}$$

$$R = -\$4714$$

$\text{NPV(new, 5 years)} = \dfrac{\$4000}{1.11^5} - \$300\, a_{\overline{2}|11\%} - \dfrac{\$1000\, a_{\overline{3}|11\%}}{1.11^2} - \$20,000$

$$= \$2373.8 - \$513.8 - \$1983.4 - \$20,000$$

$$= -\$20,123$$

The EAC is the value of R in

$$-\$20,123 = R\, a_{\overline{5}|9\%}$$

$$R = -\$5445$$

The equivalent annual cost of buying 2-year-old used cars is $731 lower.

Exercise 16.3 *(concluded)*

15. The present value of the costs for 8 years with the Caterpillar is

$$\frac{\$10,000}{1.15^8} - \frac{\$15,000}{1.15^6} - \frac{\$15,000}{1.15^4} - \frac{\$15,000}{1.15^2} - \$80,000$$

$$= \$3269.0 - \$6484.9 - \$8576.3 - \$11,342.2 - \$80,000$$

$$= -\$103,134$$

The present value of the costs for 12 years with the International is

$$\frac{\$10,000}{1.15^{12}} - \frac{\$10,000}{1.15^9} - \frac{\$10,000}{1.15^6} - \frac{\$10,000}{1.15^3} - \$105,000$$

$$= \$1869.1 - \$2842.6 - \$4323.3 - \$6575.2 - \$105,000$$

$$= -\$116,872$$

The equivalent annual cost (EAC) of the Caterpillar is the value of R in

$$-\$103,134 = R \ a_{\overline{8}|15\%}$$

$$R = -\$22,983$$

The EAC of the International is the value of R in

$$-\$116,872 = R \ a_{\overline{12}|15\%}$$

$$R = -\$21,561$$

The International model should be purchased since its equivalent annual cost is $1422 lower.

Exercise 16.4

1. The NPV of the license at the discount rate p is

$$NPV = \$10,000 \ a_{\overline{10}|p} - \$50,000$$

The IRR is the value for p that makes the NPV = 0. The value is p = 15.1% (to the nearest 0.1%). The investment's IRR is 15.1%.

2. The IRR is the value for p that makes

$$NPV = \$400,000 \ a_{\overline{5}|p} - \$1,200,000 = 0$$

The solution is p = 19.9% (rounded to the nearest 0.1%). Burger Master will realize an IRR of 19.9%.

3. For the first stage, the IRR is the value of p satisfying

$$\$30,000 \ a_{\overline{10}|p} - \$100,000 = 0$$

$$p = 27.3\% = IRR \ for \ stage \ 1$$

Similarly, for stage 2, solve for p in

$$\$27,000 \ a_{\overline{9}|p} - \$100,000 = 0$$

$$p = 22.7\% = IRR \ for \ stage \ 2$$

Exercise 16.4 *(continued)*

For stage 3, solve for p in

$$\$22{,}000\ a_{\overline{8}|p} - \$100{,}000 = 0$$

$$p = \underline{14.6\%} = \text{IRR for stage 3}$$

For stage 4, solve for p in

$$\$22{,}000\ a_{\overline{7}|p} - \$100{,}000 = 0$$

$$p = \underline{12.1\%} = \text{IRR for stage 4}$$

<u>Stages 1, 2, and 3 should be approved</u> since their IRR's exceed the cost of capital (14%).

4. The project's IRR is the value of p satisfying

$$NPV = 0 = \$12{,}000\ a_{\overline{8}|p} + \frac{\$10{,}000}{(1 + p)^8} - \$60{,}000$$

$$p = \underline{\underline{13.6\%}} = \text{IRR of the project}$$

<u><u>The project should not be accepted</u></u> since its IRR (13.6%) is less than the cost of capital (15%).

5. The investment's IRR is the value of p satisfying

$$NPV = 0 = \$20{,}000\ a_{\overline{10}|p} + \frac{\$25{,}000}{(1 + p)^{10}} - \$100{,}000$$

$$p = \underline{16.6\%} = \text{IRR of the investment}$$

<u>The investment should be made</u> since the IRR (16.6%) exceeds the cost of capital (16%).

6. The investment's IRR is the value of p satisfying

$$NPV = 0 = \$36{,}000\ a_{\overline{7}|p} + \frac{\$40{,}000}{(1 + p)^7} - \$165{,}000$$

$$p = \underline{15.0\%} = \text{IRR of the investment}$$

<u>The contract would be acceptable</u> at any cost of capital below 15.0%. There is only one case <u>(12%)</u> where the cost of capital is less than 15.0%.

7. The investment's IRR is the value of p satisfying

$$NPV = 0 = \$25{,}000\ a_{\overline{5}|p} + \frac{\$15{,}000\ a_{\overline{5}|p}}{(1 + p)^5} - \$100{,}000$$

$$p = \underline{17.6\%} = \text{IRR of the investment}$$

The investment should be undertaken since its IRR exceeds the cost of capital (15%).

8. The project's IRR is the value of p satisfying

$$NPV = 0 = \frac{\$2{,}000{,}000\ a_{\overline{5}|p}}{(1 + p)^4} - \$1{,}000{,}000\ a_{\overline{5}|p}\ (1 + p)$$

$$p = \underline{14.9\%} = \text{IRR of the project}$$

<u>The project is not acceptable</u> because its IRR is less than the company's required rate of return on investment.

Exercise 16.4 (concluded)

9. The investment's IRR is the value of p satisfying

$$NPV = 0 = \frac{\$25,000}{1+p} + \frac{\$60,000}{(1+p)^2} + \frac{\$50,000}{(1+p)^3} + \frac{\$35,000}{(1+p)^4} - \$120,000$$

$p = 15.0\% = $ IRR of the investment

The investment just meets the minimum requirement for acceptance since its IRR equals the firm's cost of capital (15%). The product should, therefore, be introduced.

10. The investment's IRR is the value of p satisfying

$$NPV = 0 = \$150,000 \, a_{\overline{7}|p} - \frac{\$200,000}{(1+p)^3} - \$500,000$$

$p = 14.5\% = $ IRR of the investment

The investment should be undertaken since its IRR exceeds the cost of capital (13%).

11. Note that the year 11 operating profit will be exactly offset by the $500,000 expenditure for environmental restoration. The project's IRR is the value of p satisfying

$$NPV = 0 = \frac{\$500,000 \, a_{\overline{9}|p}}{1+p} - \frac{\$1,500,000}{1+p} - \$1,000,000$$

$p = 12.4\% = $ IRR of the project

The mine should be developed because the IRR is less than the company's cost of capital.

Exercise 16.5

1. a. The IRR on project C is the value p satisfying

    $$NPV = 0 = \$43,000 \, a_{\overline{6}|p} - \$150,000$$

    $p = 18.1\% = $ IRR of project C

    The IRR on project D is the value of p satisfying

    $$NPV = 0 = \$30,000 \, a_{\overline{6}|p} - \$100,000$$

    $p = 19.9\% = $ IRR of project D

    Project D should be selected on the basis of having the larger IRR.

   b. $NPV(C) = \$43,000 \, a_{\overline{6}|15\%} - \$150,000 = \$12,733$

     $NPV(D) = \$30,000 \, a_{\overline{6}|15\%} - \$100,000 = \$13,534$

     Project D has the larger NPV if the cost of capital is 15%.

   c. $NPV(C) = \$43,000 \, a_{\overline{6}|12\%} - \$150,000 = \$26,791$

     $NPV(D) = \$30,000 \, a_{\overline{6}|12} - \$100,000 = \$23,342$

     Project C has the higher NPV and should be selected if the firm's cost of capital is 12%.

Exercise 16.5 *(continued)*

2. a. The IRR on the larger book is the value of p satisfying

$$NPV = 0 = \$32,000\ a_{\overline{5}|p} - \$100,000$$

p = <u>18.0%</u> = IRR on the larger book

The IRR on the smaller book is the value of p satisfying

$$NPV = 0 = \$20,000\ a_{\overline{5}|p} - \$60,000$$

p = <u>19.9%</u> = IRR on the smaller book

On the basis of an IRR ranking, <u>the smaller book</u> should be published.

b. NPV(large book) = $\$32,000\ a_{\overline{5}|17\%} - \$100,000 = \$2379$

NPV(small book) = $\$20,000\ a_{\overline{5}|17\%} - \$60,000 = \$3987$

At a cost of capital of 17%, <u>the smaller book</u> has the higher NPV and it should be published.

c. NPV(large book) = $\$32,000\ a_{\overline{5}|14\%} - \$100,000 - \$9859$

NPV(small book) = $\$20,000\ a_{\overline{5}|14\%} - \$60,000 = \$8662$

<u>The larger book</u> has the higher NPV and should be published if the cost of capital is 14%.

3. a. The IRR on project XXX is the value of p satisfying

$$NPV = 0 = \frac{\$400,000}{1+p} + \frac{\$300,000}{(1+p)^2} + \frac{\$200,000}{(1+p)^3} - \$650,000$$

p = <u>20.8%</u> = IRR on project XXX

The IRR on project YYY is the value of p satisfying

$$NPV = 0 = \frac{\$1,050,000}{(1+p)^3} - \$650,000$$

p = <u>17.3%</u> = IRR on project YYY

Based on an IRR ranking, <u>project XXX</u> should be selected.

b. $$NPV(XXX) = \frac{\$400,000}{1.14} + \frac{\$300,000}{1.14^2} + \frac{\$200,000}{1.14^3} - \$650,000 = \$66,712$$

$$NPV(YYY) = \frac{\$1,050,000}{1.14^3} - \$650,000 = \$58,720$$

At a cost of capital of 14%, <u>project XXX</u> has the larger NPV and should be selected.

c. $$NPV(XXX) = \frac{\$400,000}{1.11} + \frac{\$300,000}{1.11^2} + \frac{\$200,000}{1.11^3} - \$650,000 = \$100,085$$

$$NPV(YYY) = \frac{\$1,050,000}{1.11^3} - \$650,000 = \$117,751$$

At a cost of capital of 11%, <u>project YYY</u> has the larger NPV and should be selected.

Exercise 16.5 (continued)

4. a. The IRR on project 1 is the value of p satisfying

$$NPV = 0 = \frac{\$10,000}{1+p} + \frac{\$15,000}{(1+p)^2} + \frac{\$60,000}{(1+p)^3} - \$50,000$$

$p = 23.3\% = $ IRR on project 1

The IRR on project 2 is the value of p satisfying

$$NPV = 0 = \frac{\$50,000}{1+p} + \frac{\$10,000}{(1+p)^2} + \frac{\$15,000}{(1+p)^3} - \$50,000$$

$p = 32.3\% = $ IRR on project 2

Project 2 has the higher IRR and should be selected on an IRR ranking.

b. $NPV(\text{project 1}) = \dfrac{\$10,000}{1.14} + \dfrac{\$15,000}{1.14^2} + \dfrac{\$60,000}{1.14^3} - \$50,000 = \$10,812$

$NPV(\text{project 2}) = \dfrac{\$50,000}{1.14} + \dfrac{\$10,000}{1.14^2} + \dfrac{\$15,000}{1.14^3} - \$50,000 = \$11,679$

At a cost of capital of 14%, project 2 has the larger NPV and should be selected.

c. Similarly, at a cost of capital of 12%,

NPV(project 1) = $13,593

NPV(project 2) = $13,291

Project 1 now has the higher NPV and should be selected.

5. a. The IRR on project X is the value of p satisfying

$$NPV = 0 = \frac{\$60,000 \, a_{\overline{3}|p}}{(1+p)^2} - \$100,000$$

$p = 16.0\% = $ IRR on project X

The IRR on project Y is the value of p satisfying

$$NPV = 0 = \frac{\$40,000 \, a_{\overline{4}|p}}{1+p} - \frac{\$50,000}{1+p} - \$50,000$$

$p = 17.5\% = $ IRR on Project Y.

Project Y is preferred on an IRR basis.

b. $NPV(\text{project X}) = \dfrac{\$60,000 \, a_{\overline{3}|15\%}}{1.15^2} - \$100,000 = \$3587$

$NPV(\text{project Y}) = \dfrac{\$40,000 \, a_{\overline{4}|15\%}}{1.15} - \dfrac{\$50,000}{1.15} - \$50,000 = \$5825$

At a cost of capital of 15%, project Y has the larger NPV and should be selected.

Exercise 16.5 *(concluded)*

c. Similarly, at a cost of capital of 12%,

NPV(project X) = $14,884

NPV(project Y) = $13,834

Project X now has the higher NPV and should be selected.

6. The IRR on project Alpha is the value of p satisfying

$$0 = \frac{\$140{,}000}{1+p} + \frac{\$80{,}000}{(1+p)^2} + \frac{\$60{,}000}{(1+p)^3} + \frac{\$20{,}000}{(1+p)^4} + \frac{\$20{,}000}{(1+p)^5} - \$240{,}000$$

p = 15.8% = IRR on project Alpha

The IRR on project Beta is the value of p satisfying

$$0 = \frac{\$20{,}000}{1+p} + \frac{\$40{,}000}{(1+p)^2} + \frac{\$60{,}000}{(1+p)^3} + \frac{\$100{,}000}{(1+p)^4} + \frac{\$180{,}000}{(1+p)^5} - \$240{,}000$$

p = 14.2% = IRR on project Beta

$$\text{NPV(Alpha)} = \frac{\$140{,}000}{1.12} + \frac{\$80{,}000}{1.12^2} + \frac{\$60{,}000}{1.12^3} + \frac{\$20{,}000}{1.12^4} + \frac{\$20{,}000}{1.12^5} - \$240{,}000$$

$$= \$15{,}541$$

$$\text{NPV(Beta)} = \frac{\$20{,}000}{1.12} + \frac{\$40{,}000}{1.12^2} + \frac{\$60{,}000}{1.12^3} + \frac{\$100{,}000}{1.12^4} + \frac{\$180{,}000}{1.12^5} - \$240{,}000$$

$$= \$18{,}140$$

Even though Alpha has the larger IRR, Beta should be chosen because it has the larger NPV. Since a project's NPV represents the economic value that it will add to the firm, Beta will add $2599 more value to the firm than project Alpha.

Exercise 16.6

1. a.

Year	Cumulative profit	
1	$8000	
2	20,000	Payback period = $4 + \dfrac{\$52{,}000 - \$44{,}000}{\$12{,}000}$
3	32,000	
4	44,000	
5	56,000	= 4.67 years

Exercise 16.6 *(continued)*

   b. Since it will take longer than 4 years to recover the initial investment from profits, the firm <u>would not make</u> <u>the investment.</u>

2. Cumulative profit after 5 years = $27,000

   Cumulative profit after 6 years = $33,000

   The machine's payback period is 5.5 years.

   a. <u>No</u> because the machine's payback period exceeds the required payback of 5 years.

   b. <u>Yes</u> because the machine's payback period is shorter than the required payback period.

3.

Year	Cumulative profit	
	Project X	Project Y
1	$25,000	0
2	50,000	$25,000
3	75,000	50,000
4	100,000	75,000
5	125,000	100,000
6	150,000	125,000
7		150,000
8		175,000

Payback period (project X) = 4 years

Payback period (project Y) = 5 years

NPV(project X) = $25,000 $a_{\overline{6}|10\%}$ – $100,000 = $8882

NPV(project Y) = $\dfrac{\$25,000\ a_{\overline{7}|10\%}}{1.10}$ – $100,000 = $10,646

<u>Project X</u> would be preferred on the basis of its shorter payback but <u>project Y</u> would be preferred on the basis of its larger <u>NPV.</u>

4. Since the investment's IRR is 17%, then the initial investment is the value of C satisfying

     NPV = 0 = $50,000 $a_{\overline{5}|17\%}$ – C

     C = $159,967

   Payback period = 3 + $\dfrac{\$9967}{\$50,000}$ = 3.2 years

Exercise 16.6 *(concluded)*

5.

	Proposal A		Proposal B	
Year	Profit	Cumulative profit	Profit	Cumulative profit
1	$16,250	$16,250	$12,500	$12,500
2	17,500	33,750	12,500	25,000
3	17,500	51,250	15,000	40,000
4	17,500	68,750	15,000	55,000

a. $NPV(A) = \dfrac{\$16,250}{1.14} + \dfrac{\$17,500\, a_{\overline{3}|14\%}}{1.14} - \$45,000 = \$4893$

$NPV(B) = \$12,500\, a_{\overline{2}|4\%} + \dfrac{\$15,000\, a_{\overline{2}|14\%}}{1.14^2} - \$35,000 = \$4589$

Proposal A is preferred on the basis of its larger NPV.

b. The IRR on proposal A is the value of p satisfying

$$NPV = 0 = \dfrac{\$16,250}{1+p} + \dfrac{\$17,500\, a_{\overline{3}|p}}{1+p} - \$45,000$$

p = 19.1% = IRR on proposal A

The IRR on proposal B is the value of p satisfying

$$NPV = 0 = \$12,500\, a_{\overline{2}|p} + \dfrac{\$15,000\, a_{\overline{2}|p}}{(1+p)^2} - \$35,000$$

p = 20.0% = IRR on proposal B

Proposal B is preferred on the basis of its larger IRR.

c. $Payback\ period(A) = 2 + \dfrac{\$45,000 - \$33,750}{\$17,500} = 2.64$ years

$Payback\ period(B) = 2 + \dfrac{\$35,000 - \$25,000}{\$15,000} = 2.67$ years

There is a weak preference for proposal A based on its slightly shorter payback period.

Review Problems

1. a. For the lease alternative,

   $R = \$385, n = 60, p = 0.75\%$

   $PV(lease) = A_n(due) = \$385\, a_{\overline{60}|0.75\%}\, (1.0075) = \$18,686$

   $PV(purchase) = \$22,500 - \dfrac{\$5000}{1.0075^{60}} = \$19,307$

   The car should be leased — the economic value of the net cash outflows is $621 lower.

b. If the trade-in value after 5 years is $7000,

$$PV(purchase) = \$22,500 - \frac{\$7000}{1.0075^{60}} = \$18,029$$

In this case, <u>purchasing</u> has a $657 advantage over leasing.

2. For the rent alternative,

$R = \$1150, n = 60, p = 0.6875\%$

$PV(rent) = A_n(due) = \$1150\ a_{\overline{60}|\ 0.6875\%}\ (1.006875) = \$56,771$

$$PV(purchase) = \$150,000 + \$300\ a_{\overline{60}|\ 0.6875\%} - \frac{\$175,000}{1.006875^{60}} = \$48,696$$

The <u>purchase</u> of the <u>house</u> has an economic advantage of $56,771 − $48,696 = $8075.

3.

Time (years)	Capital cash flow	Operating profit	Net cash flow
0	− $2,000,000		− $2,000,000
1	− 1,000,000		− 1,000,000
2 to 8		$750,000	750,000
9	− 1,000,000	750,000	− 250,000

$$NPV = \frac{\$750,000\ a_{\overline{7}|\ 16\%}}{1.16} - \$2,000,000 - \frac{\$1,000,000}{1.16} - \frac{\$250,000}{1.16^9}$$

$$= \$2,611,141.5 - \$2,000,000 - \$862,069.0 - \$65,738.2$$

$$= -\$316,666$$

Since the NPV is negative when the cash flows are discounted at 16%, <u>the project will not provide the company with a rate of return exceeding 16%.</u>

4.

Time (years)	Capital cash flow	Operating profit	Net cash flow
0	− $125,000		− $125,000
1	− 125,000		− 125,000
2	0	0	0
3 to 9		$50,000	50,000
10	75,000	50,000	125,000

$$NPV = \frac{\$50,000\ a_{\overline{7}|\ 14\%}}{1.14^2} + \frac{\$125,000}{1.14^{10}} - \$125,000 - \frac{\$125,000}{1.14}$$

$$= \$164,985.6 + \$33,718.0 - \$125,000 - \$109,649.1$$

$$= -\$35,946$$

<u>The firm should not proceed with the project</u> since it has a negative NPV.

Review Problems *(continued)*

5.

Time (years)	Capital cash flow	Operating profit	Net cash flow
0	– $60,000		– $60,000
1 to 4		$16,500	16,500
5 to 7		15,500	15,500
8	10,000	15,500	25,500

$$\text{NPV} = \$16,500 \, a_{\overline{4}|15\%} + \frac{\$15,500 \, a_{\overline{3}|15\%}}{1.15^4} + \frac{\$25,500}{1.15^8} - \$60,000$$

$$= \$47,107.1 + \$20,234.3 + \$8336.0 - \$60,000$$

$$= \$15,677$$

The machine should be acquired since the investment has a positive NPV.

6. Rank the projects in descending order of NPV per invested dollar.

Initial Project	Project investment	NPV	NPV per invested dollar	Cumulative investment
5	$1,500,000	$900,000	$0.60	$1,500,000
7	900,000	405,000	0.45	2,400,000
1	1,125,000	428,000	0.38	3,525,000
3	675,000	170,000	0.25	4,200,000
2	2,700,000	486,000	0.18	6,900,000
6	225,000	32,000	0.14	7,125,000
4	375,000	30,000	0.08	7,500,000

Select projects 5, 7, 1, 3, and 6 to obtain the highest aggregate NPV ($1,935,000) within the $4.5 million capital budget.

7. Choose the machine having the larger equivalent annual cash flow (EACF).

$$\text{NPV(X, 5 years)} = \$16,000 \, a_{\overline{5}|14\%} + \frac{\$10,000}{1.14^5} - \$50,000 = \$10,123$$

X's EACF is the value of R satisfying

$$\$10,123 = R \, a_{\overline{5}|14\%}$$

$$R = \$2949$$

$$\text{NPV(Y, 10 years)} = \$16,000 \, a_{\overline{10}|14\%} + \frac{\$10,000}{1.14^{10}} - \$72,000 = \$14,155$$

Y's EACF is the value of R satisfying

$$\$14,155 = R \, a_{\overline{10}|14\%}$$

$$R = \$2714$$

Machine X should be selected because its equivalent annual cash flow is $235 larger.

Review Problems (continued)

8. Choose the alternative that will produce the higher equivalent annual cash flow (EACF).

   NPV(Sonapanic, 4 years) = $14,000 $a_{\overline{4}|16\%}$ − $35,000 = $4175

   The Sonapanic's EACF is the value of R satisfying

   $4175 = R $a_{\overline{4}|16\%}$

   R = $1492

   NPV(Xorex, 5 years) = $17,000 $a_{\overline{5}|16\%}$ − $43,500 = $3715

   The Xorex's EACF is the value of R satisfying

   $3715 = R $a_{\overline{5}|16\%}$

   R = $3715

   <u>Choose the Xorex model</u> since it has the larger equivalent annual cash flow.

9. Choose the alternative having the lower equivalent annual cost. The present value of the net costs of a Songster for 5 years is

   $$\frac{\$10,000}{1.08^5} - \$5000 \, a_{\overline{5}|8\%} - \$45,000 = -\$58,158$$

   The equivalent annual cost (EAC) is the value of R in

   − $58,158 = R $a_{\overline{5}|8\%}$

   R = − $14,566

   The present value of the net costs of a Boston Wailer for 7 years is

   $$\frac{\$20,000}{1.08^7} - \$4000 \, a_{\overline{7}|8\%} - \$55,000 = -\$64,156$$

   The EAC is the value of R in

   − $64,156 = R $a_{\overline{7}|8\%}$

   R = − $12,323

   <u>The Boston Wailer's</u> equivalent annual cost is $2243 lower.

10. The license's IRR is the value of p satisfying

    NPV = 0 = $18,000 $a_{\overline{7}|p}$ − $70,000

    p = <u>17.3%</u> = IRR of the investment

11. The investment's IRR is the value of p satisfying

    $$NPV = 0 = \$55,000 \, a_{\overline{8}|p} + \frac{\$125,000}{(1+p)^8} - \$300,000$$

    p = <u>13.9%</u> = IRR of the investment

    <u>The investment should not be made</u> since its IRR is less than the cost of capital (15%).

Review Problems (concluded)

12. The investment's IRR is the value of p satisfying

$$NPV = 0 = \$100{,}000 \, a_{\overline{4}|p} + \frac{\$150{,}000 \, a_{\overline{4}|p}}{(1 + p)^4} - \$500{,}000$$

$p = \underline{16.65\%}$ = IRR of the investment

The investment should be undertaken since its IRR is greater than the cost of capital (15%).

13. a. The IRR on project P is the value of p satisfying

$$NPV = 0 = \frac{\$120{,}000 \, a_{\overline{4}|p}}{(1 + p)^3} - \$225{,}000$$

$p = \underline{15.0\%}$ = IRR on project P

The IRR on project Q is the value of p satisfying

$$NPV = 0 = \$55{,}000 \, a_{\overline{7}|p} - \$225{,}000$$

$p = \underline{15.6\%}$ = IRR on project Q

On the basis of their IRR ranking, project Q is preferred.

b. $NPV(\text{project P}) = \dfrac{\$120{,}000 \, a_{\overline{4}|16\%}}{1.16^3} - \$225{,}000 = -\$9879$

$NPV(\text{project Q}) = \$55{,}000 \, a_{\overline{7}|16\%} - \$225{,}000 = -\$2879$

Neither project should be selected because they both have a negative NPV.

c. $NPV(\text{project P}) = \dfrac{\$120{,}000 \, a_{\overline{4}|13\%}}{1.13^3} - \$225{,}000 = \$22{,}375$

$NPV(\text{project Q}) = \$55{,}000 \, a_{\overline{7}|13\%} - \$225{,}000 = \$18{,}244$

Project P has the larger NPV and should be selected.

Self–Test Exercises

1. If the plane is leased,

$R = \$2800, \, n = 60, \, p = 0.9375\%$

$PV(\text{lease}) = A_n(\text{due}) = \$2800 \, a_{\overline{60}|0.9375\%} (1.009375) = \$129{,}245$

If the plane is purchased,

$$PV(\text{purchase}) = \$180{,}000 - \frac{\$70{,}000}{1.009375^{60}} = \$140{,}011$$

Rainbow Aviation should lease the plane and thereby gain an economic advantage in current dollars of

$\$140{,}011 - \$129{,}245 = \underline{\$10{,}766}$

Self-Test Exercises *(continued)*

2.

Time (years)	Capital cash flow	Operating profit	Net cash flow
0	– $50,000		– $50,000
1	– 30,000	$12,000	– 18,000
2 to 4		12,000	12,000
5	– 8,000	12,000	4,000
6 to 9		15,000	15,000
10	30,000	15,000	45,000

$$NPV = \$12,000\, a_{\overline{5}|15\%} + \frac{\$15,000\, a_{\overline{5}|15\%}}{1.15^5} + \frac{\$30,000}{1.15^{10}} - \frac{\$8000}{1.15^5} - \frac{\$30,000}{1.15} - \$50,000$$

$$= \$40,225.9 + \$24,999.2 + \$7415.5 - \$3977.4 - \$26,087.0 - \$50,000$$

$$= -\$7424$$

<u>Huron should not purchase the boat</u> because the investment has a negative NPV.

3. Rank the projects in descending order of NPV per invested dollar.

Project	Initial investment	Project NPV	NPV per invested dollar	Cumulative investment
A	$200,000	$63,000	$0.32	$200,000
D	250,000	75,000	0.30	450,000
C	350,000	90,000	0.26	800,000
B	400,000	100,000	0.25	1,200,000
E	100,000	20,000	0.20	1,300,000

<u>Projects A, D, and C</u> give the highest aggregate NPV within the $800,000 capital budget constraint.

4. Choose the project having the larger NPV.

$$NPV(A) = \$6000\, a_{\overline{8}|18\%} + \frac{\$5000}{1.18^8} - \$25,000 = \$796$$

$$NPV(B) = \frac{\$15,000}{1.18} + \frac{\$19,000}{1.18^5} + \frac{\$24,000}{1.18^8} - \$25,000 = \$2402$$

<u>Choose project B</u> because its NPV is $1606 larger.

5. Choose the alternative possessing the larger equivalent annual cash flow (EACF).

$$NPV(C,\ 3\ years) = \$30,000\, a_{\overline{3}|16\%} + \frac{\$10,000}{1.16^3} - \$55,000 = \$18,783$$

C's EACF is the value of R satisfying

$$\$18,783 = R\, a_{\overline{3}|16\%}$$

$$R = \$8363$$

17 Depreciation and Depletion

Changes in the Second Edition

No significant changes have been made in this chapter. Relatively few colleges include depreciation and depletion in a business mathematics course — these topics are usually covered in a financial accounting course. Please contact the author via email (JEROME@MALA.BC.CA) if you feel strongly that this chapter should be retained in a future edition of the text.

Exercise 17.2

1. a. Annual depreciation expense = $\dfrac{\text{Acquisition cost} - \text{Scrap value}}{\text{Years in service life}}$

$$= \frac{\$48{,}000 - \$2000}{7}$$

$$= \underline{\$6571}$$

b.

Year	Depreciation expense	Accumulated depreciation	Book value
0	—	—	$48,000
1	$6571	$6571	41,429
2	6571	13,142	34,858
3	6571	19,713	28,287
4	6571	26,284	21,716
5	6571	32,855	15,145
6	6571	39,426	8574
7	6571	45,997	2003

2. a. Semiannual depreciation expense = $\dfrac{\text{Acquisition cost} - \text{Residual value}}{\text{Number of half-years in service life}}$

$$= \frac{\$19{,}700 - \$2000}{2(6)}$$

$$= \underline{\$1475}$$

b.

Period	Depreciation expense	Accumulated depreciation	Book value
0	—	—	$19,700
—	—	—	—
8	—	$11,800	7900
9	$1475	13,275	6425
10	1475	14,750	4950
11	1475	16,225	3475
12	1475	17,700	2000

3. a. Annual depreciation expense = $\dfrac{\$95{,}000 - \$17{,}000}{6} = \underline{\$13{,}000}$

The depreciation expense in the fourth year (and in every other year of the first 6 years) will be $13,000.

b. Book value after 4 years = Acquisition cost − Accumulated depreciation = $95,000 − 4 ($13,000) = $43,000

Exercise 17.2 *(concluded)*

4. a.   Quarterly depreciation expense $= \dfrac{\$386,000 - \$25,000}{4(20)} = \underline{\underline{\$4513}}$

    b.   Book value = Acquisition cost – Accumulated depreciation

    $$= \$385,000 - 4(12)(\$4513)$$

    $$= \underline{\underline{\$169,376}} \text{ after 12 years}$$

    c.   Book value after n quarters = $386,000 – n ($4513)

    Solve for the value of n that makes the book value $100,000.

    $$\$100,000 = \$386,000 - n\,(\$4513)$$

    $$n = \frac{\$286,000}{\$4513} = 63.37$$

    The book value will drop below $100,000 in the <u>64th quarter</u>.

Exercise 17.3

1. a.
    $$\text{Depreciation per 1000 air miles} = \frac{\text{Acquisition cost} - \text{Resale value}}{\text{Total lifetime 1000-mile units}}$$

    $$= \frac{\$1,350,000 - \$250,000}{\dfrac{2,000,000}{1000}}$$

    $$= \underline{\underline{\$550}}$$

    b.

Year	Units of use	Depreciation expense	Accumulated depreciation	Book value
0	—	—	—	$1,350,000
1	385	$211,750[①]	$211,750	1,138,250
2	463	254,650	466,400	883,600
3	342	188,100	654,500	695,500
4	417	229,350	883,850	466,150

    [①] Depreciation expense = 385 ($550) = $211,750

2. a.   Depreciation per air-hour $= \dfrac{\text{Acquisition cost} - \text{Resale value}}{\text{Total lifetime air-miles}}$

    $$= \frac{\$1,350,000 - \$250,000}{5000}$$

    $$= \underline{\underline{\$220}}$$

Exercise 17.3 *(concluded)*

b.

Year	Units of use	Depreciation expense	Accumulated depreciation	Book value
0	—	—	—	$1,350,000
1	962	$211,640[1]	$211,640	1,138,360
2	1134	249,480	461,120	888,880
3	855	188,100	649,220	700,780
4	1083	238,260	887,480	462,520

[1] Depreciation expense = 962 ($220) = $211,640

3. Depreciation per unit of output = $\dfrac{\text{Acquisition cost} - \text{Resale value}}{\text{Total lifetime units of output}}$

$$= \frac{\$73,000 - \$10,000}{3500}$$

$$= \$18.00$$

Year	Units of use	Depreciation expense	Accumulated depreciation	Book value
0	—	—	—	$73,000
1	637	$11,466[1]	$11,446	61,534
2	572	10,296	21,762	51,238
3	749	13,482	35,244	37,756
4	802	14,436	49,680	23,320

[1] Depreciation expense = 637 ($18.00) = $11,466

4. Depreciation per hour of use = $\dfrac{\text{Acquisition cost} - \text{Resale value}}{\text{Total lifetime hours of use}}$

$$= \frac{\$73,000 - \$10,000}{7500}$$

$$= \$8.40$$

Year	Units of use	Depreciation expense	Accumulated depreciation	Book value
0	—	—	—	$73,000
1	1265	$10,626[1]	$10,626	62,374
2	1046	8786	19,412	53,588
3	1621	13,616	33,028	39,972
4	1728	14,515	47,543	25,457

[1] Depreciation expense = 1265 ($8.40) = $10,626

Exercise 17.4

1. a. Using formula (17-3),

   Depreciation rate, $d = 2 \times \dfrac{100\%}{4} = 50\%$

Year	Depreciation expense	Accumulated depreciation	Book value
0	—	—	$12,400
1	$6200	$6200	6200
2	3100①	9300②	3100③
3	1550	10,850	1550
4	775	11,625	775

   ① Depreciation expense = d x Previous book value = 0.5 ($6200) = $3100

   ② Accumulated depreciation = $6200 + $3100 = $9300

   ③ Book value = Previous book value – Depreciation expense = $6200 – $3100 = $3100

   b. d = 30%

Year	Depreciation expense	Accumulated depreciation	Book value
0	—	—	$12,400
1	$1860①	$1860	10,540
2	3162⑤	5022	7378
3	2213	7235	5165
4	1549	8785	3615

   ④ Depreciation expense $= \dfrac{d}{2}$ ($12,400) = $1860

   ⑤ Depreciation expense = d ($10,540) = $3162

   c. Using formula (17-4),

   Depreciation rate, $d = \left[1 - \left(\dfrac{\$1500}{\$12,400} \right)^{0.25} \right] \times 100\% = 41.025\%$

Year	Depreciation expense	Accumulated depreciation	Book value
0	—	—	$12,400
1	$5087	$5087	7313
2	3000	8087	4313
3	1769	9857	2543
4	1043	10,900	1500

Exercise 17.4 (continued)

2. C = $160,000, residual value = $15,000, service life = 15 years

   a. Using formula (17-3),

   $$d = 2\left(\frac{100\%}{15}\right) = 13.\overline{3}\%$$

   for double-declining-balance depreciation.

   Using formulas (17–5),

Year, t	Depreciation expense		Book value (year-end)	
1	$0.1\overline{3}C(1 - 0.1\overline{3})^0 =$	$21,333	$C(1 - 0.1\overline{3})^1 =$	$138,667
8	$0.1\overline{3}C(1 - 0.1\overline{3})^7 =$	$7835	$C(1 - 0.1\overline{3})^8 =$	$50,926
15	$0.1\overline{3}C(1 - 0.1\overline{3})^{14} =$	$2877	$C(1 - 0.1\overline{3})^{15} =$	$18,703

   b. Using formulas (17-6) with d = 6%,

Year, t	Depreciation expense (CCA)		Book value (year–end)	
1	$0.0.3C =$	$4800	$C(1 - 0.03) =$	$155,200
8	$0.06C(1 - 0.03)(1 - 0.06)^6 =$	$6424	$C(1 - 0.03)(1 - 0.06)^7 =$	$100,644
15	$0.06C(1 - 0.03)(1 - 0.06)^{13} =$	$4166	$C(1 - 0.03)(1 - 0.06)^{14} =$	$65,265

   c. Using formula (17–4),

   $$d = \left[1 - \left(\frac{\$15,000}{\$160,000}\right)^{\frac{1}{15}}\right] \times 100\% = 14.5986\%$$

   for complex declining-balance depreciation.

   Using formulas (17-5),

Year, t	Depreciation expense		Book value (year-end)	
1	$dC(1 - d)^0 =$	$23,358	$C(1 - d)^1 =$	$136,642
8	$dC(1 - d)^7 =$	$7739	$C(1 - d)^8 =$	$45,273
15	$dC(1 - d)^{14} =$	$2564	$C(1 - d)^{15} =$	$15,000

Exercise 17.4 (continued)

3. C = $370,000, service life = 20 years, resale value = $150,000

   a. Using formula (17–3),

   $$d = 2 \left(\frac{100\%}{20} \right) = 10\%$$

   for double–declining–balance depreciation.

   Using formula (17–5),

Year, t	Book value (year–end)	
5	$370,000(1 – 0.10)t	= $218,481
10		= $129,011
15		= $76,180
20		= $44,983

Years	Total depreciation expense	
1–5	$370,000 – $218,481 =	$151,519
6–10	$218,481 – $129,011 =	$89,470
11–15	$129,011 – $76,180 =	$52,831
16–20	$76,180 – $44,983 =	$31,197

   b. Using formula (17–6) with d = 5%

Year, t	Book value (year–end)	
5	$370,000(1 – 0.025)	= $293,833
10	$370,000(1 – 0.025)(1 – 0.05)$^{t-1}$	= $227,362
15		= $175,929
20		= $136,130

Years	Total depreciation expense (CCA)	
1–5	$370,000 – $293,833 =	$76,167
6–10	$293,833 – $227,362 =	$66,471
11–15	$227,362 – $175,929 =	$51,433
16–20	$175,929 – $136,130 =	$39,799

Exercise 17.4 (continued)

3. c. Using formula (17-4),

$$d = \left[1 - \left(\frac{\$150,000}{\$370,000}\right)^{\frac{1}{20}}\right] \times 100\% = 4.413958\%$$

for complex declining-balance depreciation.

Using formulas (17-5),

Year, t	Book value (year-end)
5	$\$370,000(1 - 0.04413958)^t$ = $295,239
10	= $235,584
15	= $187,983
20	= $150,000

Years	Total depreciation expense
1–5	$370,000 − $295,239 = $74,761
6–10	$295,239 − $235,584 = $59,655
11–15	$235,584 − $187,983 = $47,601
16–20	$187,983 − $150,000 = $37,983

4. From the solution to problem 3,

d = 10% for double-declining-balance depreciation,

d = 5% for CCA, and

d = 4.413958% for complex declining–balance depreciation.

a. Using formula (17-5)

Year, t	Depreciation expense
10	$0.10(\$370,000)(1 - 0.10)^9$ = $14,335
20	$0.10(\$370,000)(1 - 0.10)^{19}$ = $4998

b. Using formula (17-6),

Year, t	CCA
10	$0.05(\$370,000)(1 - 0.025)(1 - 0.05)^8$ = $11,966
20	$0.05(\$370,000)(1 - 0.025)(1 - 0.05)^{18}$ = $7165

Exercise 17.4 *(concluded)*

5. C = $27,000, service life = 12 years, residual value = $5000

a. Using formula (17-3),

$$d = 2\left(\frac{100\%}{12}\right) = 16.\overline{6}\%$$

Year	Depreciation expense	Accumulated depreciation	Book value
0	—	—	$27,000
1	$4500	$4500	22,500
2	3750	8250	18,750
3	3125	11,375	15,625
I	I	I	I
6			9042
7	1507	19,465	7535
I	I	I	I
11			3634
12	606	23,972	3028

b. d = 10%

Year	Depreciation expense	Accumulated depreciation	Book value
0	—	—	$27,000
1	$1350	$1350	25,650
2	2565	3915	23,085
3	2309	6224	20,777
I	I	I	I
6			15,146
7	1515	13369	13,361
I	I	I	I
11			8944
12	894	18,950	8050

c. Using formula (17-4),

$$d = \left[1 - \left(\frac{\$5000}{\$27,000}\right)^{\frac{1}{12}}\right] \times 100\% = 13.11052\%$$

Year	Depreciation expense	Accumulated depreciation	Book value
0	—	—	$27,000
1	$3540	$3540	23,460
2	3076	6616	20,384
3	2672	9288	17,712
I	I	I	I
6			11,619
7	1523	16,904	10,096
I	I	I	I
11			5754
12	754	22,000	5000

Exercise 17.5

1. Using formula (17-7), the depreciation rate for year t is

$$\frac{7-t+1}{7(7+1)/2} \times 100\% = \frac{8-t}{28} \times 100\%$$

Year	Depreciation rate	Depreciation expense	Accumulated depreciation	Book value
0	—	—	—	$48,000
1	25.00%	$12,000	$12,000	36,000
2	21.43%	10,286①	22,286②	25,714③
3	17.86%	8571	30,857	17,143
4	14.29%	6857	37,714	10,286
5	10.71%	5143	42,857	5143
6	7.14%	3429	46,286	1714
7	3.57%	1714	48,000	0

① Depreciation expense = $\left(\dfrac{8-2}{28}\right)$ ($48,000 − 0) = $10,286

② Accumulated depreciation = $12,000 + $10,286 = $22,286

③ Book value = $36,000 − $10,286 = $25,714

2. Using formula (17-7), the depreciation rate for year t is

$$\frac{6-t+1}{6(6+1)/2} \times 100\% = \frac{7-t}{21} \times 100\%$$

Year	Depreciation rate	Depreciation expense	Accumulated depreciation	Book value
0	—	—	—	$19,700
1	28.57%	$5057	$5057	14,643
2	23.81%	4214	9271	10,429
3	19.05%	3371①	12,643②	7057③
4	14.29%	2529	15,171	4529
5	9.52%	1686	16,857	2843
6	4.76%	843	17,700	2000

① Depreciation expense = $\left(\dfrac{7-3}{21}\right)$ ($19,700 − $2000) = $3371

② Accumulated depreciation = $9271 + $3371 = $12,643 (including a rounding error of $1)

③ Book value = $10,429 − $3371 = $7057 (including a rounding error of $1)

Exercise 17.5 (concluded)

3. C = $12,400, resale value = $1500, useful life = 4 years

Depreciation rate for year t = $\dfrac{4-t+1}{4(5)/2}$ x 100% = $\dfrac{5-t}{10}$ x 100%

Year	Depreciation rate	Depreciation expense	Accumulated depreciation	Book value
0	—	—	—	$12,400
1	40.00%	$4360	$4360	8040
2	30.00%	3270	7630	4770
3	20.00%	2180	9810	2590
4	10.00%	1090	10,900	1500

4. C = $160,000, residual value = $15,000, useful life = 15 years

Depreciation rate for year t = $\dfrac{15-t+1}{15(16)/2}$ x 100% = $\dfrac{16-t}{120}$ x 100%

Year	Depreciation rate	Depreciation expense	Accumulated depreciation	Book value
0	—	—	—	$160,000
1	12.50%	$18,125	$18,125	141,875
2	11.67%	16,917	35,042	124,958
3	10.83%	15,708	50,750	109,250
4	10.00%	14,500	65,250	94,750

Exercise 17.6

1. Total capital investment = $24,000,000 + $18,000,000 = $42,000,000

Depletion charge per tonne = $\dfrac{\$42,000,000}{3,500,000}$ = $12.00

Year	Units produced	Depletion expense	Accumulated depletion	Book value
0	—	—	—	$42,000,000
1	55,300	$663,600	$663,600	41,336,400
2	63,200	758,400①	1,422,000②	40,578,000③
3	68,100	817,200	2,239,200	39,760,800
4	59,500	714,000	2,953,200	39,046,800

① Depletion expense = 63,200($12.00) = $758,400

② Accumulated depletion = $663,600 + $758,400 = $1,422,000

③ Book value = $41,336,400 − $758,400 = $40,578,000

Exercise 17.6 (concluded)

2. Total capital investment = $4,000,000 + $1,750,000 = $5,750,000

$$\text{Depletion charge per cubic metre} = \frac{\$5,750,000}{250,000} = \$23.00$$

Year	Units produced	Depletion expense	Accumulated depletion	Book value
0	—	—	—	$5,750,000
1	26,800	$616,400	$616,400	5,133,600
2	38,900	894,700	1,511,100	4,238,900
3	54,100	1,244,300	2,755,400	2,994,600
4	61,600	1,416,800	4,172,200	1,577,800

3. Acquisition and development costs = $400,000 + $775,000 + $1,800,000 = $2,975,000

$$\text{Depletion charge per barrel} = \frac{\$2,975,000 - \$200,000}{250,000} = \$11.10$$

Year	Units produced	Depletion expense	Accumulated depletion	Book value
0	—	—	—	$2,975,000
1	9550	$106,005	$106,005	2,868,995
2	14,420	160,062	266,067	2,708,933
3	13,780	152,958	419,025	2,555,975
4	15,130	167,943	586,968	2,388,032

4. Acquisition and development costs = $500,000 + $1,200,000 + $4,200,000 = $5,900,000

$$\text{Depletion charge per tonne} = \frac{\$5,900,000 - \$400,000}{1,250,000} = \$4.40$$

Year	Units produced	Depletion expense	Accumulated depletion	Book value
0	—	—	—	$5,900,000
1	31,400	$138,160	$138,160	5,761,840
2	45,600	200,640	338,800	5,561,200
3	42,900	188,760	527,560	5,372,440
4	39,500	173,800	701,360	5,198,640

Review Problems

1. a. Annual depreciation expense $= \dfrac{\$135,000 - \$30,000}{5} = \underline{\$21,000}$

 The depreciation expense in the fourth year (and in each of the 5 years) will be $21,000.

 b. Book value = Acquisition cost − Accumulated depreciation

 $= \$135,000 - 4(\$21,000)$

 $= \underline{\$51,000}$ after 4 years

2. Depreciation per unit of output $= \dfrac{\text{Acquisition cost} - \text{Resale value}}{\text{Total lifetime units of output}}$

 $= \dfrac{\$43,000 - \$5000}{5000}$

 $= \$7.60$

Year	Units of use	Depreciation expense	Accumulated depreciation	Book value
0	—	—	—	$43,000
1	850	$6460	$6460	36,540
2	610	4636	11,096	31,904
3	725	5510	16,606	26,394
4	685	5206	21,812	21,188

3. C = $80,000, residual value = $10,000, useful life = 10 years

 a. Using formula (17–3),

 $$d - 2\left(\frac{100\%}{10}\right) = 20\%$$

 for double-declining-balance depreciation.

 Using formulas (17-5),

Year, t	Depreciation expense	Book value (year-end)
1	$0.2C(1-0.2)^0 = \underline{\$16,000}$	$C(1-0.2)^1 = \underline{\$64,000}$
5	$0.2C(1-0.2)^4 = \underline{\$6554}$	$C(1-0.2)^5 = \underline{\$26,214}$
10	$0.2C(1-0.2)^9 = \underline{\$2147}$	$C(1-0.2)^{10} = \underline{\$8590}$

 b. Using formulas (17 6) with d − 20%

Year, t	Depreciation expense (CCA)	Book value (year-end)
1	$0.10C = \underline{\$8000}$	$C(1-0.1) = \underline{\$72,000}$
5	$0.2C(1-0.1)(1-0.2)^3 = \underline{\$7373}$	$C(1-0.1)(1-0.2)^4 = \underline{\$29,491}$
10	$0.2C(1-0.1)(1-0.2)^8 = \underline{\$2416}$	$C(1-0.1)(1-0.2)^9 = \underline{\$9664}$

Review Problems (continued)

3. c. Using formula (17-4) for complex declining-balance depreciation,

$$d = \left[1 - \left(\frac{\$10,000}{\$80,000}\right)^{\frac{1}{10}}\right] \times 100\% = 18.77476\%$$

Using formulas (17-5),

Year, t	Depreciation expense	Book value (year-end)
1	$dC(1-d)^0 = \underline{\$15,020}$	$C(1-d)^1 = \underline{\$64,980}$
5	$dC(1-d)^4 = \underline{\$6538}$	$C(1-d)^5 = \underline{\$28,284}$
10	$dC(1-d)^9 = \underline{\underline{\$2311}}$	$C(1-d)^{10} = \underline{\underline{\$10,000}}$

4. Using formula (17-7), the depreciation rate for year t is

$$\frac{5-t+1}{5(6)/2} \times 100\% = \frac{6-t}{15} \times 100\%$$

Year	Depreciation rate	Depreciation expense	Accumulated depreciation	Book value
0	—	—	—	$60,000
1	33.333%	$20,000	$20,000	40,000
2	26.667%	16,000	36,000	24,000
3	20.000%	12,000	48,000	12,000
4	13.333%	8000	56,000	4000
5	6.667%	4000	60,000	0

5. C = $800,000, service life = 4 years, salvage value = $50,000
Lifetime units of use = 2000 batches = 6000 hours

a. Annual depreciation expense = $\dfrac{\$800,000 - \$50,000}{4}$ = $187,500

Year	Depreciation expense	Accumulated depreciation	Book value
0	—	—	$800,000
1	$187,500	$187,500	612,500
2	187,500	375,000	425,000
3	187,500	562,500	237,500
4	187,500	750,000	50,000

b. Depreciation per batch = $\dfrac{\$800,000 - \$50,000}{2000}$ = $375.00

Year	Units of use	Depreciation expense	Accumulated depreciation	Book value
0	—	—	—	$800,000
1	438	$164,250	$164,250	635,750
2	527	197,625	361,875	438,125
3	489	183,375	545,250	254,750
4	390	146,250	691,500	108,500

Review Problems (continued)

c. $$\text{Depreciation per hour} = \frac{\$800,000 - \$50,000}{6000} = \$125.00$$

Year	Units of use	Depreciation expense	Accumulated depreciation	Book value
0	—	—	—	$800,000
1	1210	$151,250	$151,250	648,750
2	1545	193,125	344,375	455,625
3	1440	180,000	524,375	275,625
4	1160	145,000	669,375	130,625

d. $$\text{Depreciation rate} = 2\left(\frac{100\%}{4}\right) = 50\%$$

Year	Depreciation expense	Accumulated depreciation	Book value
0	—	—	$800,000
1	$400,000	$400,000	400,000
2	200,000	600,000	200,000
3	100,000	700,000	100,000
4	50,000	750,000	50,000

e. CCA rate = 25%

Year	Depreciation expense	Accumulated depreciation	Book value
0	—	—	$800,000
1	$100,000	$100,000	700,000
2	175,000	275,000	525,000
3	131,250	406,250	393,750
4	98,438	504,688	295,313

f. $$\text{Depreciation rate} = \left[1 - \left(\frac{\$50,000}{\$800,000}\right)^{\frac{1}{4}}\right] \times 100\% = 50.00\%$$

Year	Depreciation expense	Accumulated depreciation	Book value
0	—	—	$800,000
1	$400,000	$400,000	400,000
2	200,000	600,000	200,000
3	100,000	700,000	100,000
4	50,000	750,000	50,000

g. Depreciation rate (year t) $= \dfrac{4 - t + 1}{4(5)/2} \times 100\% = \dfrac{5 - t}{10} \times 100\%$

Year	Depreciation rate	Depreciation expense	Accumulated depletion	Book value
0	—	—	—	$800,000
1	40.00%	$300,000	$300,000	500,000
2	30.00%	225,000	525,000	275,000
3	20.00%	150,000	675,000	125,000
4	10.00%	75,000	750,000	60,000

6. Acquisition costs = $850,000

Depletion charge per tonne $= \dfrac{\$850,000}{100,000} = \$8.50$

Year	Depreciation rate	Depreciation expense	Accumulated depletion	Book value
0	—	—	—	$850,000
1	10,400	$88,400	$88,400	761,600
2	14,300	121,550	209,950	640,050
3	16,900	143,650	353,600	496,400
4	11,200	95,200	448,800	401,200

Self-Test Exercises

1. C = $90,000, service life = 4 years, trade-in value = $15,000

Lifetime units of use = 10,000 units (cars) = 5000 hours

a. Annual depreciation expense $= \dfrac{\$90,000 - \$15,000}{4} = \$18,750$

Year	Depreciation expense	Accumulated depreciation	Book value
0	—	—	$90,000
1	$18,750	$18,750	71,250
2	18,750	37,500	52,500
3	18,750	56,250	33,750
4	18,750	75,000	15,000

b. Depreciation per car produced $= \dfrac{\$90,000 - \$15,000}{10,000} = \$7.50$

Year	Depreciation rate	Depreciation expense	Accumulated depletion	Book value
0	—	—	—	$90,000
1	2153	$16,148	$16,148	73,852
2	2439	18,293	34,441	55,559
3	2645	19,838	54,279	35,721
4	2380	17,850	72,129	17,871

Self-Test Exercises (continued)

c. Depreciation per hour of use = $\dfrac{\$90,000 - \$15,000}{5000} = \$15.00$

Year	Hours of use	Depreciation expense	Accumulated depreciation	Book value
0	—	—	—	$90,000
1	1113	$16,695	$16,695	73,305
2	1278	19,170	35,865	54,135
3	1309	19,635	55,500	34,500
4	1247	18,705	74,205	15,795

d. Depreciation rate = $2\left(\dfrac{100\%}{4}\right) = 50\%$

Year	Depreciation expense	Accumulated depreciation	Book value
0	—	—	$90,000
1	$45,000	$45,000	45,000
2	22,500	67,500	22,500
3	11,250	78,750	11,250
4	5625	84,375	5625

e. CCA rate = 30%

Year	Depreciation expense	Accumulated depreciation	Book value
0	—	—	$90,000
1	$13,500	$13,500	76,500
2	22,950	36,450	53,550
3	16,065	52,515	37,485
4	11,246	63,761	26,240

f. Depreciation rate = $\left[1 - \left(\dfrac{\$15,000}{\$90,000}\right)^{\frac{1}{4}}\right] \times 100\% = 36.10569\%$

Year	Depreciation expense	Accumulated depreciation	Book value
0	—	—	$90,000
1	$32,495	$32,495	57,505
2	20,763	53,258	36,742
3	13,266	66,524	23,476
4	8476	75,000	15,000

g. Depreciation rate (year t) = $\dfrac{4 - t + 1}{4(5)/2}$ x 100% = $\dfrac{5 - t}{10}$ x 100%

Year	Depreciation rate	Depreciation expense	Accumulated depreciation	Book value
0	—	—	—	$90,000
1	40.00%	$30,000	$30,000	60,000
2	30.00%	22,500	52,500	37,500
3	20.00%	15,000	67,500	22,500
4	10.00%	7500	75,000	15,000

2. C = $330,000, service life = 15 years, salvage value = $30,000

a. Annual depreciation expense = $\dfrac{\$330{,}000 - \$30{,}000}{15}$ = $20,000

Depreciation expense in years 1 and 7 = $20,000

Book value (end of year 9) = $330,000 − 9($20,000) = $150,000

b. Using formula (17-3) for double-declining-balance depreciation,

$$d = 2\left(\dfrac{100\%}{15}\right) = 13.\overline{3}\%$$

Using formulas (17-5),

  Depreciation expense (year 1) = $dC(1 - d)^0$ = $44,000

  Depreciation expense (year 7) = $dC(1 - d)^6$ = $18,645

  Book value (end of year 9) = $C(1 - d)^9$ = $91,030

c. Using formulas (17-6) with d = 15%,

  Depreciation expense (year 1) = $dC/2$ = $24,750

  Depreciation expense (year 7) = $dC(1 - d/2)(1 - d)^5$ = $20,316

  Book value (end of year 9) = $C(1 - d/2)(1 - d)^8$ = $83,178

d. Using formula (17-4) for complex declining-balance depreciation,

$$d = \left[1 - \left(\dfrac{\$30{,}000}{\$330{,}000}\right)^{\frac{1}{15}}\right] \times 100\% = 14.773663\%$$

Using formulas (17-5),

  Depreciation expense (year 1) = $dC(1 - d)^0$ = $48,753

  Depreciation expense (year 7) = $dC(1 - d)^6$ = $18,683

  Book value (end of year 9) = $C(1 - d)^9$ = $78,285

Self-Test Exercises (concluded)

3. Acquisition and development costs = ($20 + $8 + $2) million = $30 million

Depletion charge per barrel = $\dfrac{\$30 \text{ million}}{2.4 \text{ million}}$ = $12.50

Year	Units produced	Depletion expense	Accumulated depletion	Book value
0	—	—	—	$30,000,000
1	76,500	$956,250	$956,250	29,043,750
2	135,200	1,690,000	2,646,250	27,353,750
3	158,700	1,983,750	4,630,000	25,370,000
4	150,900	1,886,250	6,516,250	23,483,750

18 Consumer Credit

Changes in the Second Edition:

Consumer Credit was the subject of Chapter 10 in the first edition. Consumer Credit has been moved out of the flow of core topics because it is an area that is not covered in a majority of business math courses.

1. The section on charge accounts has been rewritten, and new worksheet formats are presented for the calculation of interest charges and account balances. The calculation of interest charges on bank charge accounts is tricky because several rules operate simultaneously, and a couple of them are contingent or conditional in nature. A majority of instructors do not cover these topics in their business math courses because of the complexity of the rules and the absence of new concepts. Nevertheless, some are of the opinion that the topics should be retained as reference material since bank charge accounts are such an important (and growing) form of consumer credit.

2. "Personal Lines of Credit" and "Consumer Loans" (Sections 10.3 and 10.4 in the first edition) have been integrated with similar loans elsewhere in the text.

3. The "Student Loan" section has been revised to reflect changes to the rules and regulations governing Canada Student Loans and provincial student loans since the first edition was published.

Exercise 18.1

1. a. Service charge on September 14 statement

   $= \dfrac{0.18}{12} \times$ Previous balance $= 0.015(\$543.68) = \underline{\$8.16}$

   b. New balance $= \$543.68 + \$217.98 + \$8.16 - \$150 - \$48.33 = \underline{\$571.49}$

   c. Service charge on October 14 $= 0.015(\$571.49) = \underline{\$8.57}$

2. a. Credit charge on March 3 statement

   $= \dfrac{0.288}{12} \times$ Previous balance $= 0.024(\$832.79) = \underline{\$19.99}$

   b. New balance $= \$832.79 + \$113.62 + \$19.99 - \$250 - \$56.98 = \underline{\$659.42}$

   c. Since the \$400 payment exceeds 50% of the balance owed, the payment is deducted from the previous balance before the credit charge is calculated.

   Credit charge on April 3 $= 0.024(\$659.42 - \$400) = \underline{\$6.23}$

3. a.

Billing period	Purchases	Qualifying payments	Other payments	Adjusted previous balance	Interest	Ending balance
July 21-Aug 20	\$185.00				\$0.00	\$185.00
Aug 21-Sept 20	145.00		\$50.00		\$2.78 ①	\$282.78
Sept 21-Oct 20	65.00		100.00		\$4.24	\$252.02

   ① Interest $= \dfrac{0.18}{12} \times \$185 = \$2.78$

   b.

Date	Transaction	Amount	Balance earning interest in the current billing period	in the next billing period	Number of days interest	Statement balance
Aug 5	Purchase	\$75.00		\$75.00	13	
Aug 18	Purchase	110.00		185.00	3	
Aug 20	Interest charges	0.00	\$185.00		15	\$185.00
Sept 5	Payment	(50.00)	135.00		9	
Sept 14	Purchase	145.00	135.00	145.00	7	
Sept 20	Interest charges	3.19①	280.00		12	283.19
Oct 3	Payment	(100.00)	183.19		2	
Oct 5	Purchase	65.00	183.19	65.00	16	
Oct 20	Interest charge	3.78②	248.19			251.97

   ① Interest charges $= \left(\$75 \times 0.18 \times \dfrac{13}{365}\right) + \left(\$185 \times 0.18 \times \dfrac{13}{365}\right) + \left(\$185 \times 0.18 \times \dfrac{15}{365}\right) + \left(\$135 \times 0.18 \times \dfrac{9+6}{365}\right) = \$3.19$

   ② Interest charges $= \left(\$145 \times 0.18 \times \dfrac{7}{365}\right) + \left(\$280 \times 0.18 \times \dfrac{12}{365}\right) + \left(\$183.19 \times 0.18 \times \dfrac{2+16}{365}\right) = \$3.78$

Exercise 18.1 *(continued)*

4. a.

Billing period	Purchases	Qualifying payments	Other payments	Adjusted previous balance	Interest	Ending balance
Apr 6 - May 5	$700				$0.00	$700.00
May 6 - Jun 5		$400		$300	5.25①	305.25
Jun 6 - Jul 6		305.25		0.00	0.00	0.00

① Interest = $300 \times \dfrac{0.21}{12} = \$5.25$

b.

Billing period	Purchases	Qualifying payments	Other payments	Adjusted previous balance	Interest	Ending balance
April 6 - May 5	$700.00				$0.00	$700.00
May 6 - June 5			$400.00		12.25①	312.25
June 6 - July 6		$312.25		$0.00	0.00	0.00

① Interest = $700 \times \dfrac{0.21}{12} = \$12.25$

c.

Date	Transaction	Amount	Balance earning interest in the current billing period	Balance earning interest in the next billing period	Number of days interest	Statement balance
Apr. 10	Purchase	$ 500.00		$ 500.00	10	
Apr. 20	Purchase	200.00		700.00	16	
May 5	Interest charges	0.00	$700.00		20	$700.00
May 26	Payment	(400.00)	300.00		11	
June 5	Interest charges	19.27①	300.00		20	319.27
June 26	Payment	(319.27)	0.00			
July 5	Interest charges	3.45②				

① Interest charges $= \left(\$500 \times 0.21 \times \dfrac{10}{365}\right) + \left(\$700 \times 0.21 \times \dfrac{16+20}{365}\right) + \left(\$300 \times 0.21 \times \dfrac{11}{365}\right) = \$19.27$

② Interest charges $= \$300 \times 0.21 \times \dfrac{20}{365} = \$3.45$

Exercise 18.2 *(concluded)*

5.

Date	Transaction	Amount	Balance earning interest in the current billing period	in the next billing period	Number of days interest	Statement balance
Apr. 10	Purchase	$500.00		$500.00	6	
Apr. 16	Cash advance	200.00	200.00	500.00	4	
Apr. 20	Purchase	200.00	200.00	700.00	16	
May 5	Interest charges	2.30①	900.00		20	$902.30
May 26	Payment	(400.00)	502.30		11	
June 5	Interest charges	22.86②	502.30		20	525.16
June 26	Payment	(525.16)	0.00			
July 5	Interest charges	5.78③				5.78

① Interest charges $= \left(\$200 \times 0.21 \times \dfrac{4 + 16}{365} \right) = \$2.30$

② Interest charges $= \left(\$500 \times 0.21 \times \dfrac{6 + 4}{365} \right) + \left(\$700 \times 0.21 \times \dfrac{16}{365} \right)$

$\quad + \left(\$900 \times 0.21 \times \dfrac{20}{365} \right) + \left(\$502.30 \times 0.21 \times \dfrac{11}{365} \right) = \$22.86$

③ Interest charges $= \$502.30 \times 0.21 \times \dfrac{20}{365} = \$5.78$

Exercise 18.2

1. Interest accrued during the 6-month grace period

$= \$9400(0.0925)\dfrac{94}{365} + \$9400(0.09)\dfrac{89}{365} = \$430.21$

Date	Number of days	Interest rate	Interest	Accrued interest	Payment made	Principal portion	Balance
30-Nov	—	—	—	—	—	—	$9 830.21
31-Dec	31	9.00%	$75.14	~~$75.14~~	$135.00	59.86	9 770.35
16-Jan	16	9.00%	38.55	38.55		0.00	9 770.35
31-Jan	15	9.25%	37.14	~~75.69~~	135.00	59.31	9 711.04
28-Feb	28	9.25%	68.91	~~68.91~~	135.00	66.09	9 644.95

2. a. Interest accrued during the grace period

$= \$5800(0.105)\dfrac{87}{365} + \$5800(0.11)\dfrac{94}{365} = \underline{\underline{\$309.47}}$

Exercise 18.2 *(continued)*

b.

Date	Number of days	Interest rate	Interest	Accrued interest	Payment made	Principal portion	Balance
30-Jun	—	—	—	—	—	—	$5800.00
31-Jul	31	13.50%	$66.50	~~$66.50~~	$95.00	$28.50	5771.50
31-Aug	31	13.50%	66.17	~~66.17~~	95.00	28.83	5742.67
30-Sep	30	13.50%	63.72	~~63.72~~	95.00	31.28	5711.39
			$196.39				

3. Interest accrued during the grace period

$$= \$6800(0.115)\,\frac{83}{365} + \$6800(0.1125)\,\frac{101}{365} = \$389.50$$

Date	Number of days	Interest rate	Interest	Accrued interest	Payment made	Principal portion	Balance
31-Dec	—	—	—	—	—	—	$7189.50
31-Jan	31	11.25%	$68.69	~~$68.69~~	$200.00	$131.31	7058.19
28-Feb	28	11.25%	60.91	~~60.91~~	200.00	139.09	6919.10
1-Mar	1	11.25%	2.13	2.13			6919.10
25-Mar	24	10.75%	48.91	~~51.04~~	500.00	448.96	6470.14
31-Mar	6	10.75%	11.43	~~11.43~~	200.00	188.57	6281.57

4.

Date	Number of days	Interest rate	Interest	Accrued interest	Payment made	Principal portion	Balance
31-Oct	—	—	—	—	—	—	$4200.00
30-Nov	30	8.75%	$30.21	~~$30.21~~	$100.00	$69.79	4130.21
31-Dec	31	8.75%	30.69	~~30.69~~	100.00	69.31	4060.90
31-Jan	31	8.75%	30.18	~~30.18~~	100.00	69.82	3991.08
			$91.08				

5.

Date	Number of days	Interest rate	Interest	Accrued interest	Payment made	Principal portion	Balance
30-Nov	—	—	—	—	$500.00	$500.00	$5500.00
31-Dec	31	10.00%	$46.71	~~$46.71~~	150.00	103.29	5396.71
31-Jan	31	10.00%	45.84	~~45.84~~	150.00	104.16	5292.55
29-Feb	29	10.00%	42.05	~~42.05~~	150.00	107.95	5184.60
			$134.60				

Exercise 18.2 (concluded)

6.

Date	Number of days	Interest rate	Interest	Accrued interest	Payment made	Principal portion	Balance
30-June	—	—	—	—	—	—	$3800.00
31-Jul	31	9.50%	$30.66	$~~30.66~~	$60.00	$29.34	3770.66
31-Aug	31	9.75%	31.22	~~31.22~~	60.00	28.78	3741.88
27-Sep	27	9.75%	26.99	26.99			3741.88
30-Sep	3	10.00%	3.08	~~30.07~~	60.00	29.93	3711.95

7.

Date	Number of days	Interest rate	Interest	Accrued interest	Payment made	Principal portion	Balance
30-Nov	—	—	—	—	—	—	$5200.00
31-Dec	31	9.75%	$43.06	$~~43.06~~	$110.00	$66.94	5133.06
30-Jan	30	9.75%	41.13	41.13			5133.06
31-Jan	1	9.50%	1.34	~~42.47~~	110.00	67.53	5065.53
14-Feb	14	9.50%	18.46	~~18.46~~	300.00	281.54	4783.99
28-Feb	14	9.50%	17.43	~~17.43~~	110.00	92.57	4691.42

Exercise 18A

1. Total interest charges = 12($180.52) − $2000 = $166.24

   a. Payout amount = $10(\$180.52) - \dfrac{10(11)/2}{12(13)/2} \times \$166.24$

   $$= \$1805.20 - \$117.22$$
   $$= \underline{\underline{\$1687.98}}$$

   b. Payout amount = $2(\$180.52) - \dfrac{2(3)}{12(13)} \times \$166.24 = \underline{\underline{\$354.65}}$

2. Total interest charges = 36($208) − $6000 = $1488

   a. Payout figure = $34(\$208) - \dfrac{34(35)}{36(37)} \times \$1488 = \underline{\underline{\$5472.63}}$

   b. Payout figure = $26(\$208) - \dfrac{26(27)}{36(37)} \times \$1488 = \underline{\underline{\$4623.78}}$

3. Total interest charges = 120($242) − $15,000 = $14,040

   a. Payout amount = $118(\$242) - \dfrac{118(119)}{120(121)} \times \$14,040 = \underline{\underline{\$14,978.20}}$

   b. Payout amount = $110(\$242) - \dfrac{110(111)}{120(121)} \times \$14,040 = \underline{\underline{\$14,813.64}}$

Exercise 18A (continued)

4. Given: $A_n = \$10,000$, $p = i = 3\%$, $n = 20$

   a. Solve for R in

   $$\$10,000 = R\left(\frac{1-1.03^{-20}}{0.03}\right)$$

   $$R = \$672.16$$

   Total interest charges = 20($672.16) – $10,000 = $ 3443.20

   Payout amount = 18($672.16) – $\frac{18(19)}{20(21)}$ × $3443.20 = $9295.13

   b. The effective rate of interest on the loan for the 6 months is the discount rate that makes the combined present value of the two regular payments and the payout amount equal to the $10,000 borrowed. Solve for p in

   $$\$10,000 = \$672.16\left[\frac{1-(1+p)^{-2}}{p}\right] + \$10,000\,(1+p)^{-2}$$

   $$p = 3.2537\% \text{ per 3 months}$$

   The corresponding effective annual rate is

   $$f = (1+p)^m - 1 = 1.0325374 - 1 = 0.13664 = 13.66\%$$

5. Given: $A_n = \$15,000$, $n = 48$, $p = i = 1\%$
   Solve for R in

   $$\$15,000 = R\left(\frac{1-1.01^{-48}}{0.01}\right)$$
   $$R = \$395.01$$

   a. (i) Total interest charges = 48($395.01) – $15,000 = $3960.48

   Payout amount = 47($395.01) – $\frac{47(48)}{48(49)}$ × $3960.48 = $14,766.64

   Principal portion of first payment = $15,000 – $14,766.64 = $233.36

   Interest portion of first payment = $395.01 – $233.36 = $161.65

   (ii) Interest portion of first payment = 0.01 × $15,000 = $150.00

   b. Payout amount after 18 months

   = 30($395.01) – $\frac{30(31)}{48(49)}$ × $3960.48 = $10,284.29

   Total interest charged in the first 18 months
   = 18($395.01) – ($15,000 – $10,284.29) = $2394.47

Exercise 18A *(concluded)*

6. Given: $A_n = \$9000$, $n = 36$, $p = i = 0.875\%$
   Solve for R in

$$\$9000 = R\left(\frac{1 - 1.00875^{-36}}{0.00875}\right)$$

   $R = \$292.52$

   a. (i) Total interest charges = 36(\$292.52) − \$9000 = \$1530.72

   Payout amount = $35(\$292.52) - \frac{35(36)}{36(37)} \times \$1530.72 = \$8790.22$

   Principal portion of first payment = \$9000 − \$8790.22 = \$209.78

   Interest portion of first payment = \$292.52 − \$209.78 = \$82.74

   (ii) Interest portion of first payment = 0.00875(\$9000) = \$78.75

   b. Payout amount after 13 months

   $= 23(\$292.52) - \frac{23(24)}{36(37)} \times \$1530.72 = \$6093.61$

   Total interest charged in the first 13 months
   = 13(\$292.52) − (\$9000 − \$6093.61) = \$896.37

Self-Test Exercise

1. a. Credit charge $= \frac{0.204}{12}(\$834.65) = \$14.19$

   b. New balance = \$834.65 + \$345.79 + \$14.19 − \$300 − \$76.88 = \$817.75

   c. Credit charge (Feb 5) $= \frac{0.204}{12}(\$817.75) = \$13.90$

2. Interest accrued during the 6-month grace period
   $= \$7200(0.105)\frac{69}{365} + \$7200(0.1025)\frac{115}{365} = \$375.44$

Date	Number of days	Interest rate	Interest	Accrued interest	Payment made	Principal portion	Balance
31-Oct	—	—	—	—	—	—	\$7575.44
30-Nov	30	10.25%	\$63.82	~~\$63.82~~	\$120.00	\$56.18	7519.26
12-Dec	12	10.25%	25.34	25.34			7519.26
31-Dec	19	10.00%	39.14	~~64.48~~	120.00	55.52	7463.74
31-Jan	31	10.00%	63.39	~~63.39~~	120.00	56.61	7407.13

Case 1: Calculations for an Investment Portfolio

John is the trustee of a $100,000 trust established pursuant to the will of John's recently deceased mother. The beneficiaries are John's three young children. On her 21st birthday, the eldest child is to receive one-third of the value then in the trust. The second child will receive one-half of the value of the trust's assets when he turns 21. Finally, on the third child's 21st birthday, the trust will be liquidated and all proceeds paid to her. In the meantime, John is to manage the trust in the best interests of the children.

Since the eldest child is only 8 years old, John has decided to chose mainly growth-oriented investments for the next 5 years. He intends to allocate the $100,000 among four mutual funds—Monarch Canadian Equity Fund, Monarch Canadian Bond Fund, Excel North American Equity Fund, and Sentinel Asia-Pacific Fund—in the ratio 5 : 2 : 3 : 2. (Any purchase commission is to be included as part of the initial investment when calculating this ratio). The first two are "no-load" mutual funds available in Canada. The no-load feature means that shares (or units) can be purchased or redeemed with no commissions or other transaction costs. The other two investments are closed-end mutual funds trading on the New York Stock Exchange. Consequently, their share values are denominated in U.S. dollars, and a brokerage commission is charged on both the purchase and the sale of shares in these mutual funds. Through John's discount brokerage account, the commission rate will be 1%.

Over time, some investments will perform better than others. As a consequence, the actual *market* values of the four components of the portfolio will not remain in the original ratio. If a fund's rate of return is greater than the weighted average rate of return on the entire portfolio, the fund will represent an increased proportion of the portfolio's value. On the first anniversary of the original investment, John intends to rebalance the portfolio to the original ratio. The dividends that the mutual funds distribute on December 31 will be allocated to purchase additional shares of "underweight" components. If needed to complete the rebalancing, some shares of "overweight" mutual funds may have to be sold, and the proceeds used to purchase more shares of the "underweight" mutual funds. In the case of funds quoted in U.S. dollars, the rebalancing will be done in terms of the Canadian-dollar equivalent of their market values.

John made the investments on January 2. The purchase price per share was $24.47 for the Monarch Canadian Equity Fund, $13.55 for Monarch Canadian Bond Fund, US$9.76 for Excel North American Equity Fund, and US$18.50 for the Sentinel Asia-Pacific Fund. The exchange rate on the purchase of the U.S. mutual funds was US$1.00 = C$1.40.

On the following December 31, the various funds paid their annual dividends. The dividend per share was $1.36 for the Monarch Canadian Equity Fund, $0.97 for Monarch Canadian Bond Bund, US$0.51 for Excel North American Equity Fund, and US$0.33 for the Sentinel Asia-Pacific Fund. On the first anniversary of the original investment, the share price was $26.32 for the Monarch Canadian Equity Fund, $13.76 for Monarch Canadian Bond Fund, US$12.12 for Excel North American Equity Fund, and US$17.76 for the Sentinel Asia-Pacific Fund. The currency exchange rate was C$1.00 = US$.075.

Questions:

1. How much money did John allocate to each component of the portfolio?

2. How many shares did he purchase in each mutual fund? (If a commission was paid to purchase a particular mutual fund, the initial allocation in Question 1 should include the commission paid. Round the number of shares in each case to the nearest integer.)

3. For each of the four components of the portfolio, calculate the first year's rate of return on investment (*%ROI*). (For each U.S. mutual fund, the *%ROI* should be calculated using the Canadian dollar equivalents of the initial investment, the dividend received, and the market value on the first anniversary.)

4. Calculate the rate of return on investment for the entire portfolio.

5. What share transactions were needed on the first anniversary to rebalance the portfolio? State the number of shares of each fund bought or sold. (Again round the number to the nearest integer.)

6. Calculate the first year's *%ROI* for the Excel North American Equity Fund and the Sentinel Asia-Pacific Fund in terms of the U.S. dollar amounts of the initial investment, the dividend received, and the market value on the first anniversary. Explain why the *%ROIs* differ from the values obtained in question 3.

Comments to the Instructor:

This case <u>can be used after Section 3.5</u>. The case involves applications of weighted average (Section 1.5), rate of return on investment (Section 2.6), ratios and proportions (Sections 3.1 and 3.2), and currency conversion (Section 3.5). (Even if Section 3.5 is not covered in your curriculum, the case may still be utilized. The formalized notation of Section 3.5 is not employed. Students should be able to do the necessary currency conversions based on currency equivalents given in the form: US$1.00 = C$1.40.) To make the case shorter and less difficult, omit Question 5.

Responses to the Questions:

Question 1
Let E, B, N, and A represent the amount of money invested in the Monarch Canadian Equity Fund, the Monarch Canadian Bond Fund, the Excel North American Equity Fund, and the Sentinel Asia-Pacific Fund, respectively. The same symbols will also be used as a shorthand name for each fund. We require:

$$E : B : N : A : \$100,000 = 5 : 2 : 3 : 2 : 12$$

Hence,

$$E = \frac{5}{12} \times \$100,000 = \$41,666.67$$

Similarly, $B = \$16,666,67$, $N = \$25,000$,   and $A = \$16,666.67$.

Question 2

Fund	Share price (C$ including commission)	Number of shares purchased	Total investment
E	$24.47	$\frac{\$41,666.67}{\$24.47} = 1703$	$41,672
B	$13.55	$\frac{\$16,666.67}{\$13.55} = 1230$	$16,666
N	US$9.76 x 1.40 x 1.01 = C$13.80	$\frac{\$25,000.00}{\$13.80} = 1812$	$25,006
A	US$18.50 x 1.40 x 1.01 = C$26.16	$\frac{\$16,666.67}{\$26.16} = 637$	$16,664
		Total:	$100,008

Question 3
The calculation can be done on a per share basis.

Fund	V_i (C$)	Y(C$)	V_f (C$)	%ROI
E	$24.47	$1.36	$26.32	13.12%
B	$13.55	$0.97	$13.76	8.71%
N	$13.80	$\frac{US\$0.51}{0.75} = \$0.68$	$\frac{US\$12.12}{0.75} = \$16.16$	22.03%
A	$26.16	$\frac{US\$0.33}{0.75} = \$0.44$	$\frac{US\$17.76}{0.75} = \$23.68$	− 7.80%

Sample calculation:

$$\%ROI(E) = \frac{(V_f - V_i) + Y}{V_i} \times 100\% = \frac{(\$26.32 - \$24.47) + \$1.36}{\$24.47} \times 100\% = 13.12\%$$

Question 4

The *%ROI* for the entire portfolio is the weighted average of the rates of return on investment of the four components of the portfolio. That is,

$$\%ROI\text{(portfolio)} = \frac{5}{12}(13.12\%) + \frac{2}{12}(8.71\%) + \frac{3}{12}(22.03\%) + \frac{2}{12}(-7.80\%) = \underline{11.13\%}$$

Question 5

On the first anniversary, we have

Security name	Share price (C$)	Number of shares owned	Total market value	Dividend per share (C$)	Total cash received
E	$26.32	1703	$44,823	$1.36	$2316
B	$13.76	1230	$16,925	$0.97	$1193
N	$16.16	1812	$29,282	$0.68	$1232
A	$23.68	637	$15,084	$0.44	$280
			Total: $106,114		$5021

Total portfolio value on anniversary = $106,114 + $5021 = $111,135

Note: The increase in the value of the portfolio is $11,136. This verifies that the portfolio's *%ROI* was 11.13%.

Security name	Current market value	Proportion for balance	Amount for balance	Shortfall (surplus) for balance	Share price including commission	No. shares to buy (sell)
E	$44,823	41.67%	$46,306	$1483	$26.32	56
B	$16,925	16.67%	$18,523	$1598	$13.76	116
N	$29,282	25.00%	$27,784	($1498)	$16.32	(92)
A	$15,084	16.67%	$18,523	$3438	$23.92	144
Cash	$5,021	0.00%	$0	($5021)		
Total:	$111,135	100.00%	$111,135	$0		

To rebalance the portfolio, John needed to <u>purchase 56 shares of the Monarch Canadian Equity Fund, purchase 116 shares of the Monarch Canadian Bond Fund, sell 92 shares of the Excel North American Equity Fund, and purchase 144 shares of the Sentinel Asia-Pacific Fund</u>.

Question 6

Fund	V_i(US$)	Y(US$)	V_f(US$)	%ROI
N	$9.76	$0.51	$12.12	29.41%
A	$18.50	$0.33	$17.76	-2.22%

The *%ROI*s based on values expressed in C$ are not as high as the *%ROI*s based on US$ because the US$ weakened relative to the C$ during the year. At the beginning of the year, US$1.00 would buy C$1.40 but, at the end of the year, would buy only C1.3\overline{3}$.

Case 2: CVP Analysis with More Than One Selling Price per Unit

Peerless Cycles Ltd. has manufactured the Cyclone racing bike for several years at its Oshawa, Ontario factory. Peerless is now considering opening a facility in Burnaby, British Columbia to build its new Avalanche mountain bike. Peerless's Director of Marketing, Production Manager, and Controller have made the following estimates based on market research, engineering reports, and their experience at the Oshawa operation.

Unit labour cost	$280 per bike
Unit materials cost	$450 per bike
Factory and office rental	$6000 per month
Depreciation expense	$3000 per month
Other fixed administrative and overhead expenses	$8000 per month

Peerless expects that 10% of total unit sales will be from its factory outlet store in Burnaby, 60% of sales will be to its distributors in Canada and U.S., and 30% will be to its distributor for Japan. The factory outlet will sell bikes for 20% off the suggested retail price of $1495. The distributors in the U.S. and Canada will receive a further 10% discount, and the distributor in Japan will get a 7% discount as well as the 20% and 10% discounts.

Questions:

1. Determine the annual unit sales required for the proposed Burnaby factory to break even.

2. What minimum annual unit sales are required to pay expenses and to provide a 15% rate of return (before tax) on the $300,000 capital investment?

3. To match seasonal demand, temporary workers must be hired and trained during the November to March period in order to meet peak demand in the February to May period. The Production Manager estimates that unit labour costs can be reduced to $240 if production can be "smoothed out" during the year. Permanent experienced employees will be more productive than recently trained temporary workers. The Director of Marketing suggests offering an additional 5% early order discount to distributors for orders received in the August to October period (for shipment and payment in the October to December period). A poll of the distributors indicates that Peerless could expect half of the distributors' unit purchases to fall within the discount period.

    Again answer questions 1 and 2 assuming that the early order discount is in place.

4. Should Peerless "smooth" production and offer the 5% early order discount to the distributors? Give a brief justification for your recommendation.

Comments to the Instructor:

This case <u>should be used in conjunction with Section 5.2</u>. It involves applications of weighted average (Section 1.5), trade discount series (Section 4.2), and cost-volume-profit analysis (Section 5.2).

Responses to the Questions:

Question 1
The annual fixed costs are $FC = 12 (\$6000 + \$3000 + \$8000) = \$204,000$.

The total variable costs per unit are $VC = \$280 + \$450 = \$730$.

The factory outlet price is $L(1 - d) = \$1495(1 - 0.20) = \$1196.00$.

The price to distributors for Canada and the U.S. is $\$1196.00(1 - 0.10) = \$1076.40$.

The price to the distributor for Japan is $\$1076.40(1 - 0.07) = \$1001.05$.

The *weighted-average* selling price is

$$SP = 0.1(\$1196.00) + 0.6(\$1076.40) + 0.3(\$1001.05) = \$1065.76$$

The average contribution margin is $CM = SP - VC = \$1065.76 - \$730.00 = \$335.76$ and the

$$\text{Break-even point} = \frac{FC}{CM} = \frac{\$204,000}{\$335.76} = \underline{\underline{608 \text{ bikes per year}}}$$

Question 2
We now want the annual unit sales, X, required to generate a net income, NI, just sufficient to provide a 15% rate of return on $300,000. That is, $NI = 0.15(\$300,000) = \$45,000$.

$$X = \frac{FC + NI}{CM} = \frac{\$204,000 + \$45,000}{\$335.76} = \underline{\underline{742 \text{ bikes per year}}}$$

Question 3
With the new early order discount in place,

   10% of sales will be at $1196.00,
   30% of sales will be at $1076.40,
   30% of sales will be at $\$1076.40(1 - 0.05) = \$1022.58$,
   15% of sales will be at $1001.05 and
   15% of sales will be at $\$1001.05(1 - 0.05) = \$951.00$.

The *weighted-average* selling price will be

$$SP = 0.1(\$1196.00) + 0.30(\$1076.40) + 0.30(\$1022.58) + 0.15(\$1001.05) + 0.15(\$951.00) = \$1042.10$$

Then,

$$VC = \$240 + \$450 = \$690 \quad \text{and} \quad CM = \$1042.10 - \$690 = \$352.10$$

$$\text{Break-even point} = \frac{FC}{CM} = \frac{\$204,000}{\$352.10} = \underline{\underline{580 \text{ bikes per year}}}$$

and, to provide a 15% rate of return on investment,

$$X = \frac{FC + NI}{CM} = \frac{\$204,000 + \$45,000}{\$352.10} = \underline{\underline{708 \text{ bikes per year}}}$$

Question 4
Peerless should even out production during the year and offer the 5% early order discount to the distributors. The number of bikes that must be sold to break even, or to provide a 15% rate of return on investment, is reduced. Indeed, at any level of sales, the company's net income will be higher (or the loss will be smaller) with production smoothed and the extra discount in place.

Case 3: A Retirement Planning Worksheet for the Lay Person

The average person is unable to handle the mathematics of compound interest for long-term financial projections. Some financial institutions have prepared guides which lead the user through the steps required to estimate the monthly or annual savings required to provide a desired level of income in retirement. One way of avoiding the mathematics of compounding is to provide tables of compounding factors and discounting factors. The user can obtain the appropriate factor from the intersection of the row and column for the applicable values of interest rate and term.

The "Retirement Planner" presented in this case is typical of retirement planning worksheets prepared for the general public. It is intended to be used to <u>estimate the amount that must be saved each month in order to have a desired lifestyle in retirement</u>. It does not assume the user can perform compound interest calculations. Only addition, subtraction, multiplication, and division are required. Furthermore, the user is told what operation to do, when to do it, and what values to use.

The variables incorporated in the worksheet are:

- Time remaining until retirement.
- Savings already accumulated.
- Expected rate of inflation.
- Desired level of income in retirement.
- Retirement income from pensions.
- Expected duration of retirement.
- Average rate of return on savings/investments.

The main steps in the procedure are:

1. Determine the annual retirement income that must be provided by additional personal savings. This is income beyond that provided by government pensions and pensions resulting from employment.

2. Determine the amount of money needed at the beginning of retirement to provide the annual retirement income in step 1.

3. Determine the amount that must be saved each month so that savings already accumulated plus these further savings will reach the target amount in step 2.

To avoid compound interest calculations in their usual form, four tables are used in the Retirement Planner. The range of values for the two variables in each table is considerably reduced from what would appear in an actual case. The objectives here are to present the concepts and to illustrate the procedure.

Retirement Planner

<u>**Step 1**</u> : Determine the Annual Retirement Income Needed
   from Your Personal Savings

In current dollars, what annual income from all sources will you need to sustain your
desired lifestyle in retirement?   _____ (A)

In current dollars, what annual income do you expect from government and other
pensions?   _____ (B)

Subtract (B) from (A). This is the annual income (in current dollars) you will need
to supply from personal savings.   _____ (C)

The amount (C) must be adjusted for inflation between now and retirement to obtain
the nominal income that must come from personal savings. From the following
table, obtain the inflation factor for the expected annual rate of inflation and the
number of years remaining until retirement. Enter the factor on line (D).   _____ (D)

Inflation rate	Years until retirement				
	10	15	20	25	30
3%			1.806		
4%					

Multiply (C) by (D). This is the annual retirement income (in nominal dollars) to be
provided by personal savings.   _____ (E)

<u>**Step 2**</u>: Determine the amount of money needed at the beginning of retirement to
   provide the desired annual retirement income.

In the following table, select the factor at the intersection of the expected duration
of retirement and the expected rate of inflation during retirement. The inflation rate
built into these factors allows the nominal annual income calculated at (E) to grow
at the rate of inflation each year. (All factors assume that accumulated savings earn
6% compounded annually during retirement.) Enter the factor on line (F).   _____ (F)

Inflation rate	Years in retirement				
	10	15	20	25	30
3%		12.36		18.10	
4%					

Multiply (E) by (F). This is the amount of personal savings needed at the beginning   (G)
of retirement to provide the desired inflation-adjusted retirement income.   _____

Step 3: Determine the amount that must be saved each month.

Enter the amount of personal savings that have already been accumulated. ——————— (H)

In the following table, select the factor at the intersection of the number of years remaining until retirement and the average rate of return expected during these years on accumulated savings. Enter the factor on line (J). ——————— (J)

Inflation rate	Years until retirement				
	10	15	20	25	30
6%			3.207		
8%					

Multiply (H) by (J). This gives the amount your current savings will be worth at retirement. (The assumption here is that the funds are in an RRSP. Consequently, the investment returns are not taxed before retirement.) ——————— (K)

Subtract (K) from (G). This is the additional amount you must accumulate from additional savings during the years remaining until retirement. ——————— (L)

In the following table, select the factor at the intersection of the number of years remaining to retirement and the *annually compounded* rate of return expected on additional savings during these years. Enter the factor on line (M). ——————— (M)

Inflation rate	Years until retirement				
	10	15	20	25	30
6%			453.44		
8%		337.61			

Divide (L) by (M). This gives the amount you must save at the end of each month until the retirement date in order to meet your targets for savings and retirement income. ——————— (N)

Questions:

1. Most of the cells in the tables have been left blank because you already have the knowledge to calculate the factors in three of the four tables. Calculate and enter at least three of the missing values in each of the first and third tables. For each table, you will have to infer what the factor in the table represents from the way it is applied to a previous amount and from the interpretation placed on the calculated result. You can use the values provided in the tables to check your method.

2. Calculate and enter at least three of the missing values in the fourth table. The value in a particular cell is the future value of $1.00 invested at the end of each month for the number of years in the column heading. The investments earn the rate of return in the row heading.

   The final calculation for (N) can now be understood. Since (M) is the future value of an annuity of just $1.00 per month, the number of dollars that must actually be saved every month to have a future value equal to (L) is (L) divided by (M).

3. The values in the second table are for a situation not encountered in the text. The amount desired at (G) represents the present value, on the date of retirement, of all income received during retirement. Income during retirement is assumed to be received in a single payment at the beginning of each year, and to grow

each year at the rate of inflation. The formula for the present value of n periodic payments, starting at size R but increasing at the rate g per payment interval, is

$$\frac{R}{p-g}\left[1-\left(\frac{1+g}{1+p}\right)^n\right](1+p)$$

where the payments are made at the beginning of each payment interval and the time value of money is p per payment interval.

Determine the values for three cells in the second table.

4. Work through the Retirement Planner for Marco who is 30 years old and already has $23,000 in his RRSP. He wants to retire at age 60 on an income whose current purchasing power is $30,000 per year. One-third of this amount is expected to come from indexed government pensions. For planning purposes, assume an inflation rate of 3% per year, both before and after retirement. Assume that Marco's current and future savings will earn 6% compounded annually, both before and after retirement. Based on life expectancy tables, he is planning for 25 years in retirement.

Rounded to the nearest dollar, what amount must he save at the end of each month for the next 30 years?

Comments to the Instructor:

This case <u>can be used after completion of Section 10.3</u>. If you want a "real" example of a retirement planning worksheet for your students, try to obtain the Toronto-Dominion Bank's publication number 94362(11/96) entitled <u>TD's Retirement Planner</u>.

Responses to the Questions:

Question 1

The first and third tables contain compounding factors for the future value of a lump amount. The values can be obtained from $S = P(1 + i)^n$ with $P = \$1$, $n =$ Years to retirement, and $i =$ Inflation rate (for the first table) or $i =$ Rate of return (for the third table).

Inflation rate	Years until retirement				
	10	15	20	25	30
3%	1.344	1.558	1.806	2.094	2.427
4%	1.480	1.801	2.191	2.666	3.243

Rate of return	Years until retirement				
	10	15	20	25	30
6%	1.791	2.397	3.207	4.292	5.743
8%	2.159	3.172	4.661	6.848	10.063

Question 2

The fourth table contains compounding factors for the future value of ordinary general annuities. The values can be obtained from

$$S_n = R \left[\frac{(1 + p)^n - 1}{p} \right]$$

with $R = \$1$, $n =$ Number of months remaining until retirement, and $p =$ Interest rate per month (corresponding to the annually compounded nominal rates of return given in the row headings).

Rate of return	Years until retirement				
	10	15	20	25	30
6%	162.47	286.91	453.44	676.29	974.51
8%	180.12	337.61	569.00	908.99	1408.55

Question 3

The second table contains discount factors for the present value of payments whose size increases at the rate g between successive payments. Set $R = \$1$, $p =$ Time value of money $= 6\%$ per year, $g =$ Inflation rate, and $n =$ Years in retirement.

Inflation rate	Years in retirement				
	10	15	20	25	30
3%	8.82	12.36	15.44	18.10	20.40
4%	9.19	13.17	16.79	20.08	23.07

Question 4

Line	Amount
A	$30,000
B	$10,000
C	$20,000
D	2.427
E	$48,540
F	18.10
G	$878,574
H	$23,000
J	5.743
K	$132,089
L	$746,465
M	974.51
N	$766

Case 4: Is it wise to borrow money to make an RRSP contribution?

Contributing as much as possible to a Registered Retirement Savings Plan (RRSP) is considered to be one of the best strategies for accumulating retirement savings. Contributions to RRSPs are given favoured tax treatment. An eligible amount contributed to an RRSP can be deducted from an individual's total income when calculating *taxable* income on an income tax return. As a result, the amount of tax that must be paid is reduced. As a "rule-of-thumb" approximation, Canadians pay about $0.40 in combined federal and provincial income tax on each dollar of taxable income falling in the $30,000 to $60,000 bracket. (A lower rate is paid on the first $30,000 of income, and a higher rate is paid on any income in excess of $60,000.)

Consider Joyce who has $40,000 of taxable income. Because her last dollar of income falls in the $30,000 to $60,000 bracket, Joyce is said to have a **marginal tax rate** (MTR) of 40%. If she contributes $5000 to an RRSP, her taxable income will be reduced by $5000. Consequently, she will pay

$$40\% \text{ of } \$5000 = \$2000$$

less income tax for the year. With a net expenditure of $5000 - $2000 = $3000, Joyce can have an additional $5000 invested in her RRSP. Hence, the first advantage of using an RRSP to save for retirement is that the tax savings enable an individual to put substantially more investment capital "at work" than the net "out-of-pocket" expenditure.

A second way in which RRSPs receive favourable tax treatment is that investment income is not taxed until it is withdrawn from the plan. Consequently, investment earnings can compound over many years on a tax-exempt basis. In contrast, interest and dividends received outside an RRSP are subject to income tax in the year they are received. A capital gain is taxable in the year the investment is sold.

The tax advantages of using an RRSP to hold investments are so attractive that, if an individual does not have sufficient cash on hand, some financial advisors recommend borrowing money before the contribution deadline (usually March 1 following the taxation year). In this way, tax savings are "captured" for that taxation year.

In late 1996 and early 1997, the Bank of Nova Scotia ran a newspaper advertisement which, in a bold heading, asked:

Borrow money to save money? <u>Are you nuts?</u>

The advertisement described a dilemma faced by many Canadians.

> "Every year you start out with strong resolve. Good intentions. Promises. You know you ought to do it, but then March 1st rolls by and somehow the money's not there. Your unused RRSP contributions grow and grow, until they get way too big to handle. And you just give up. What to do! What to do!"

The advertisement went on to make a case for obtaining a "Scotia RRSP Catch-Up Loan" if the taxpayer does not have enough savings for a lump RRSP contribution. The following example was presented.

1. "Borrow $15,000" (at 4.75% compounded monthly).

2. "Pay back $157 per month" (based on a 10-year term).

3. "Get back $6000 on your tax return and pay down your loan." (The assumed MTR is 40%. The $6000 tax refund is assumed to be applied against the loan balance at the time of the fourth regular monthly payment.)

4. "Watch your RRSP grow to $19,361 in 5 years and 6 months, when your loan is paid out. In 25 years, you'll have $47,856. **So who's nuts?**" (The investments held in the RRSP are assumed to earn 4.75% compounded annually, which is essentially the same as the interest rate on the loan.)

The advertisement pointed out that, in addition to the $6000 tax refund, the borrower pays $10,348 on the loan ($9000 principal and $1348 interest). It concluded with the thoughts:

> "Of course, you'd rather not borrow. But this is borrowing to save. The idea is to do this once, so you can catch up and keep up ... The point is, you can do something. Because doing nothing is the worst idea of all."

The advertisement implies that the answer to the question in the heading ought to be evident from the given information. Furthermore, the implied conclusion is that borrowing funds to contribute to an RRSP makes financial sense even if the rate of return on investments held in the RRSP is no greater than the interest rate on the loan. The questions listed below address whether the implied conclusion can, in fact, be reached on the basis of the given data. Further questions lead to a more rigorous analysis of the proposition, and to an examination of alternatives not suggested in the advertisement.

Questions:

1. Verify the numbers presented in the advertisement. In other words, verify that:

    a. The monthly loan payment (rounded to the nearest dollar) is $127.
    b. The loan will be paid off in 5 years and 6 months if the $6000 tax saving is applied as a prepayment of principal along with the fourth regular payment. (Use $125 for the size of the 66th and final payment.)
    c. The total interest on the loan will be $1348 (rounded to the nearest dollar).
    d. The amount in the RRSP after 5 years and 6 months will be $19,361.

2. The reader is expected to answer the questions posed in the advertisement's heading by comparing the $10,348 paid on the loan with the $19,361 in the RRSP after 5 years and 6 months. Discuss the validity of this comparison. Of what use is the $47,856 figure for the amount projected to be in the RRSP after 25 years?

3. The way in which the Bank of Nova Scotia advertisement discusses the issue tends to close the reader's mind to alternatives. In the scenario presented, there is no cash on hand to make a lump contribution to an RRSP just prior to the March 1 contribution deadline (for the previous taxation year). However, if the reader can find the money in future years for the monthly payment on an "RRSP Catch-Up Loan", then presumably the reader can instead find the same monthly amount for regular contributions to an RRSP.

    Let us return to Joyce's situation. Determine which of the following two alternatives is better for her.

    (i)   Borrow $3000 enabling her to immediately invest a $5000 lump amount (including the $2000 tax savings) in an RRSP.
    (ii) Make RRSP contributions equal to the <u>equivalent</u> monthly amount she would pay on the loan under the first alternative. *Note:* Just as a net expenditure of $3000 allows Joyce to contribute $5000 (1.6̄ times as much) to her RRSP under alternative (i), the equivalent monthly RRSP contribution here is 1.6̄ times the monthly loan payment.

    The RRSP loan under the first alternative would be repaid by blended monthly payments over a 5-year term. Assume that the interest rate on the loan equals the rate of return on investments held within the RRSP. (This eliminates one factor that would contribute to differing outcomes.) Use 6% compounded monthly for both rates.

4. a. Does the outcome in question 3 depend on a taxpayer's marginal tax rate? Explain.
    b. How will the nature of the outcome in question 3 change if the investments in the RRSP earn a higher rate of return than the interest rate paid on the RRSP loan? Explain.

Business Math in Canada, 2/e

Comments to the Instructor:

This case <u>can be used after completion of Section 12.2</u>. The final blended loan payment in the bank's scenario is smaller than the others. We give the value of that payment to avoid a mathematical issue not covered until Section 14.2. To shorten and simplify the case, omit Question 4.

Responses to the Questions:

Question 1

a. With $A_n = \$15,000$, $p = i = 0.3958333\%$, and $n = 120$,

$$\$15,000 = R \left(\frac{1 - 1.003958333^{-120}}{0.003958333} \right)$$

Solving for R gives R = <u>$157.27</u>.

b. The balance after four regular payments will be $14,606.09. The balance after the $6000 prepayment will be $8606.09. Solving for the number of monthly payments of $157.27 required to pay off this balance gives n = 61.79458. In all, 4 + 62 = 66 payments are required to pay off the loan. (The precise amount of the last payment is $125.01.) The repayment of the loan will take 66 months or <u>5 years and 6 months</u>.

c. Total interest = 65 ($157.27) + $125.01 + $6000 - $15,000 = <u>$1347.56</u>

d. Amount in the RRSP after 5.5 years = $15,000 $(1.0475)^{5.5}$ = <u>$19,361.47</u>

Question 2

A comparison of the $10,348 *nominal* total of the out-of-pocket payments on the loan to the $19,361 in the RRSP when the loan is paid off has two serious flaws. The first is that the time value of money is ignored on the loan payment side of the comparison. The simple addition of nominal dollar amounts paid on different dates has the effect of placing the same economic value on the first dollar paid as on the last dollar paid. Since the $19,361 future value is at a focal date 5.5 years from now, it should be compared with the total economic value *on the*

same date of the relevant cash flows for the repayment of the loan. The latter *future* value is considerably greater than $10,348.

A second flaw is that comparing $1 within an RRSP to $1 outside an RRSP is somewhat of an "apples versus oranges" comparison. In order to spend money that has accumulated in an RRSP, the money must be withdrawn. It is then subject to income tax. Therefore, $1 within an RRSP has less economic value than $1 spent on the same date to repay the RRSP Catch-Up Loan.

The amount ($47,856) in the RRSP after 25 years is irrelevant to the economic evaluation of the proposition.

Question 3

Since both alternatives have the same timing and amounts of net "out-of-pocket" expenditures over the next 5 years, the preferred alternative is one that produces the larger future value in the RRSP after 5 years.

<u>Alternative (i)</u>

Amount in the RRSP after 5 years = 5000(1.005)^{60}$ = $6744.25

<u>Alternative (ii)</u>

The monthly payment on the RRSP loan in alternative (i) is the value of R in

$$\$3000 = R \left(\frac{1 - 1.005^{-60}}{0.005} \right)$$

The solution is $R = \$58.00$.

Monthly RRSP contribution $= 1.\overline{6}(\$58.00) = \$96.67$

Amount in the RRSP after 5 years $= \$96.67 \left(\frac{1.005^{60} - 1}{0.005} \right) = \$6744.67$

<u>The two alternatives produce identical results</u> after 5 years. (The $0.42 difference results from rounding both the loan payment and the monthly RRSP contribution to the nearest cent.) Joyce can make the choice on less tangible grounds. Alternative (i) is more likely to be carried through to completion—bank discipline is more compelling than self-discipline. On the other hand, alternative (ii) gives Joyce more flexibility to handle unforeseen expenditures or unexpected interruptions of her income.

Question 4

a. If Joyce's MTR is constant across all 5 years, the amounts in the RRSPs after 5 years under both alternatives will be equal. The effect of, say, a 50% MTR instead of a 40% MTR for all 5 years is to make the leverage factor (for converting the net expenditure to the corresponding RRSP contribution) 2.0 instead of 1.6. All contributions rise in the same proportion for both alternatives. The RRSP's future value also rises in the same proportion for both alternatives.

If Joyce's MTR should rise during the 5-year period, alternative (ii) will have a larger future value because the tax-savings component of Joyce's monthly contribution will be increased. For example, if her MTR increases to 50%, she can contribute $116 per month to the RRSP and still have a net "cost" of $58 per month. However, the future value under alternative (i) will be unchanged.

b. The most straightforward way for a student to answer this part is to repeat the calculations in question 3 for a situation in which the RRSP earns more than 6% compounded monthly. The loan payments are unchanged and the monthly RRSP contribution under alternative (ii) remains the same. In both cases, the future values of the RRSPs will be larger than before, but they will no longer be equal. The amount under alternative (i) will be greater than under alternative (ii). Alternative (i) gains an advantage from the "spread" or difference between the rate of return on investments and the interest rate paid on the borrowed funds.

Summary

In response to the questions asked in the title of this case and in the heading of the Bank of Nova Scotia advertisement, the following comments will apply to *most* individuals.

- It is wiser to borrow money to contribute to an RRSP than to not contribute to an RRSP at all.

- If the rate of return earned on investments held in an RRSP equals the interest rate on a loan, <u>there is no financial advantage or disadvantage</u> to borrowing funds for a lump RRSP contribution (compared to the alternative of making regular contributions equal to the amount that would otherwise be paid on the loan plus the resulting tax savings).

- If the rate of return earned on investments held in an RRSP exceeds the interest rate on a loan, <u>there is a financial advantage</u> to borrowing funds for a lump RRSP contribution (compared to the alternative making regular contributions equal to the amount that would otherwise be paid on the loan plus the resulting tax savings).

Case 5: BEWARE! Financial Quicksand!

Loans on which you can make payments for 10 years and still owe more money than you originally received are not restricted to desperate victims of organized crime syndicates. They can also be obtained from more respectable sources.

Some mortgage brokers (with the emphasis on *some*) charge exorbitant brokerage fees to arrange loans. The fees are charged to the borrower in the following way. Suppose you want to borrow $50,000. The broker lends you $50,000 + $X, but keeps $X for the brokerage charge. The net amount you receive is $50,000. However, the loan payments are calculated so that the full principal, ($50,000 + $X), is paid off over the life of the loan. In the sanitized language of the business, ($50,000 + $X) is called the *gross amount of the loan*, $50,000 is the *net amount of the loan*, and $X is the *brokerage fee* or *bonus*.

There is nothing wrong in principle with a broker earning a fee for arranging a deal between a borrower and a lender. What does seem questionable in some instances is the size of the fee in relation to the net amount of the loan. The following scenario is true; the broker's name is omitted.

In November, 1996, Joe approached a mortgage broker in Victoria, British Columbia. Joe wanted to borrow $20,000 which he would, in turn, lend to his son to help finance a new business. Joe's existing debt consisted of the $55,000 balance on a loan secured by a mortgage on his home (valued at $150,000) and the $10,000 balance on a car loan. Joe's income could comfortably handle both the new and the existing debt. The broker presented three alternatives to Joe. In each instance, the term of the loan is one year. Upon renewal, there would be a small "documentation fee" but no brokerage fee.

1. A net loan of $85,000 enabling Joe to consolidate all existing debt with the new debt. The $94,225 gross amount of the loan would be secured by a first mortgage on Joe's home. Monthly payments would be based on a 25-year amortization and an interest rate of 7.5% compounded monthly.

2. A net loan of $30,000 enabling Joe to consolidate the car loan with the new debt. The $34,525 gross amount of the loan would be secured by a second mortgage on Joe's home. Monthly payments would be based on a 25-year amortization and an interest rate of 11% compounded monthly.

3. A net loan of $20,000 loan (gross amount of $24,425) secured by a second mortgage on Joe's home. Monthly payments would be based on a 25-year amortization and an interest rate of 11% compounded monthly.

The quoted interest rates were similar to those offered by mainstream financial institutions. What is surprising (shocking?) is the amount of the brokerage fee, whether viewed in actual dollars or in relation to the net amount of the loan. The consequences of these large fees will be examined in the following questions.

Questions:
1. For each alternative, calculate the brokerage fee as a percentage of the net amount of the loan.

2. Calculate the monthly payment on each loan.

3. What will be the balance on each loan at the end of the 1-year term? How much more than the original net amount received does the borrower owe after one year?

4. Assuming that each loan is renewed after 1 year at the original interest rate, how long will it take the borrower to reduce the balance owed to the original net amount of the loan? (Now you understand the choice of title for this case!)

5. Suppose that, in "shopping around" for a loan, Joe found conventional lenders who would charge a higher rate of interest but no brokerage fee. A common method for comparing the overall cost of borrowing among such alternatives is to calculate an *equivalent interest rate* for the brokered loan. (In this method, the brokerage fees are treated as interest charges spread over the term of the loan.) This equivalent rate can then be directly compared to the interest rates available on loans having no brokerage fees (or to the equivalent interest rates on loans having different brokerage fees). To calculate the equivalent interest rate, answer the

question: If the same payments (as on the brokered loan) were made on a loan equal to the *net* amount of the brokered loan, what interest rate would result in the same end-of-term balance as the brokered loan? Using the balances obtained in question 3, calculate the equivalent monthly compounded interest rate for each of the three alternatives offered by the mortgage broker.

Comments to the Instructor:

<u>The most appropriate timing for this case is in conjunction with</u> the Effective Cost of Borrowing topic in <u>Section 14.3</u>. However, by omitting question 5 and supplementing the introduction by explaining the distinction between "the term" and "the amortization period" of a loan, a student could handle the case after Section 12.2.

Responses to the Questions:

Question 1

Net amount of loan	Gross amount of loan	Brokerage fee	Brokerage fee as a percentage of net loan
$85,000	$94,225	$9225	10.85%
30,000	34,525	4525	15.08%
20,000	24,425	4425	22.13%

Question 2

For the first loan, $A_n = \$94,225$, $n = 300$, and $p = i = \frac{7.5\%}{12} = 0.625\%$. Solving for R gives

$$R = \$696.31$$

For the second loan, $A_n = \$34,525$, $n = 300$, and $p = i = \frac{11\%}{12} = 0.91\overline{6}\%$. Solving for R gives

$$R = \$338.38$$

For the third loan, $A_n = \$24,425$, $n = 300$, and $p = i = \frac{11\%}{12} = 0.91\overline{6}\%$. Solving for R gives

$$R = \$239.39$$

Question 3

Loan number	Balance after 12 payments	Amount in excess of the original net loan
1	$92,891	$7891
2	$34,249	$4249
3	$24,229	$4229

Question 4

To answer this question, calculate the number of payments, n, such that the combined present value of these n payments and a remaining balance (equal to the original *net* amount of the loan) equals the original *gross* amount of the loan.

Loan number	n	Time
1	68.97 payments	5 years and 9 months
2	116.45 payments	9 years and 9 months
3	140.92 payments	11 years and 9 months

Remember, the "time" in the third column is the length of time it will take the borrower to reduce the loan balance to the original net amount of money actually received.

On the day the loan is made, the borrower's net worth declines by the amount of the brokerage fee. For example, in the third option presented by the broker, the borrower's net worth drops by $4425 because he receives $20,000 but would require $24,425 to pay off the loan on the next day. It will then take almost 12 years just to pay off the "dead-weight" loss represented by the brokerage fee! This is definitely not the route to financial independence!

Question 5
For the first alternative, we want the discount rate that makes the combined present value of 12 payments of $696.31 and a $92,891 balance after the 12th payment, equal to $85,000.

Solve for p in

$$\$85{,}000 = \$696.31 \left[\frac{1 - (1 + p)^{-12}}{p} \right] + \$92{,}891(1 + p)^{-12}$$

The solution is $p = 1.530\%$ per month. The corresponding nominal annual rate is $12p = \underline{18.36\% \text{ compounded monthly}}$. (The monthly payments at this interest rate cover only about half of each month's interest. Consequently, the ending balance is larger than the beginning balance.)

Similarly, the equivalent interest rate on the second option is $\underline{26.04\% \text{ compounded monthly}}$ and on the third option is $\underline{32.54\% \text{ compounded monthly.}}$ (Who said usury isn't alive and thriving?!)

Case 6: Which is a better investment — prepaying a mortgage or contributing to an RRSP?

Introduction Prepaying personal debt and contributing to a Registered Retirement Savings Plan (RRSP) are usually considered to be the two best investments an individual can make. There is considerable debate, however, about which of the two should be given priority. Consider the following opinion that appeared in the Winter 1997 issue of the *Trimark Investor* (published by Trimark Investment Management Inc., one of the largest mutual fund management companies in Canada).

> So, should you pay off your debts or contribute to your RRSP? The best solution is probably a mixture of both.
>
> If you make an RRSP contribution, you will be eligible for a tax refund of up to half the amount of your contribution) depending on your marginal tax rate and your province of residence). You could then use this refund to pay off debt. Plus, you'll have the advantage that any RRSP contributions you've made will start growing on a tax-deferred basis.

Trimark points to advantages of each alternative. Their suggested "solution" is typical of qualitative discussions of the alternatives. However, the vast majority of people are not able to save enough each year to make *both* their maximum eligible RRSP contribution and also a prepayment of mortgage principal. "A mixture of both" is not the best solution for most of these people. The outcome of an analysis of the alternatives is likely to be *either* that one alternative produces a larger financial benefit, *or* that the two alternatives are equally good. But the latter outcome does not imply that you should do a mixture of both; it implies that it doesn't matter whether you do one alternative *or* the other *or* any combination of both. (Doing both is the "feel good" solution for those who are unable to do a quantitative analysis — they gain comfort from the thought of capturing the advantages of both alternatives.)

Case Scenario Suppose that, 3 years ago, your older brother Zach and his partner Karen borrowed $100,000 on a mortgage loan to buy a house. The loan was for a 5-year term at an interest rate of 7.5% compounded *annually*. Monthly payments were based on a 20-year amortization. The mortgage contract permits a single prepayment each year of up to 10% of the original loan. Zach's annual salary is $55,000.

As an approximate rule of thumb, Canadians are subject to a (combined federal and provincial) income tax rate of close to 40% on the *portion* of employment and interest income falling in the $30,000 to $60,000 range. (The rate varies somewhat from province to province.) Zach's level of income puts his last several thousand dollars of income in this bracket. Assume that the tax rate in this bracket in Zach's province is exactly 40%. In tax jargon, Zach's **marginal tax rate** (MTR) is 40%. If he earns an additional $1 from employment or interest income, he will pay $0.40 additional tax and net only $0.60 after tax. If his taxable income decreases by $1, he will pay $0.40 less tax and the decline in after-tax income is only $0.60.

Now that their car loan is paid off, Zach and Karen expect to be able to save $4800 each year. However, they are unable to decide upon the best use of their annual savings during the next few years.

Zach's preference is to open an RRSP and use their savings for contributions to the plan. Zach argues that there are two advantages of investing using an RRSP. The first is that the total RRSP contribution for a year can be deducted from his total income when calculating *taxable* income on an income tax return. As a result, he would have tax savings that could also be invested. Zach tells Karen that "$4800 gets you $8000." By this slogan he means that, if he contributes $8000 to an RRSP (or to a spousal RRSP for Karen), he will pay

$$0.40(\$8000) = \$3200$$

less income tax. The net "cost" to them is therefore only

$$\$8000 - \$3200 = \$4800$$

which is the amount of their annual savings. In this way, they can "lever up" their savings by a factor of $8000 ÷ $4800 = 1.$\overline{6}$.

The second advantage Zach cites is that earnings on investments held within an RRSP are not taxed until withdrawn from the plan (usually many years later during retirement). Therefore, the funds in the plan compound at the *pre-tax* rate of return on investments held in the plan. Zach is confident that a diversified conservative portfolio can earn 7.5% compounded annually.

Karen thinks Zach's idea is a good one but she is not convinced that it is better than using their annual savings to make annual prepayments of mortgage principal. She points out that the rate of return effectively earned on funds used to reduce the principal amount of a loan is the rate of interest charged on the loan. Furthermore, the interest effectively "earned" is not subject to income tax — not now, not ever! On the other hand, the funds that accumulate in an RRSP are eventually taxed when they are withdrawn. Therefore, comparing $1 within an RRSP to a $1 reduction in the principal owed on a mortgage is, to some extent, an "apples versus oranges" comparison. Finally, Karen points out that, with their mortgage paid off sooner, they can then contribute *both* their $4800 annual savings *and* the monthly amount they had previously been paying on the mortgage, to an RRSP. (RRSP rules allow eligible but "unused" RRSP contributions to be carried forward and used in later years.) This might allow them to surpass the amount that would be accumulated in an RRSP under Zach's plan.

Zach and Karen are unable to compare the alternatives in a rigorous mathematical analysis. Aware that you are excelling in your business math course at college, they have approached you to determine which alternative is better. To avoid having to wrestle with the issue of comparing dollars inside an RRSP to dollars outside an RRSP, you suggest carrying the analysis 17 years into the future when the mortgage will be paid off under either alternative. A direct comparison can be made between the expected amounts in their RRSP's after 17 years under the two options.

After some discussion, all agree that the following assumptions are appropriate.

- The current interest rate on the mortgage loan will continue for the entire 17 years.
- RRSP contributions are made and the associated tax savings are realized at each year-end.
- Mortgage prepayments are made at each year-end.
- Zach's current marginal tax rate of 40% will apply to all RRSP contributions for the next 17 years.

Questions:

1. Which alternative is better for Zach and Karen? (When RRSP contributions begin under the mortgage prepayment alternative, don't forget to "lever up" *both* the $4800 annual savings *and* the former mortgage payments by the factor 1.$\overline{6}$.)

2. Which alternative has the greater increase in value if the RRSP earns a higher rate of return than the interest rate paid on the mortgage loan?

3. Which alternative will have the larger increase in value if income tax rates rise in future years, or if Zach's income rises enough to move him into a higher tax bracket?

Comments to the Instructor:

This case is best <u>used in conjunction with Section 14.3.</u>

In general, answering the question posed in the case's title can be quite complicated. Discussions of the question in the popular media are usually flawed in some respect — for example, the time value of money is often ignored when an "interest savings" approach is taken for the mortgage prepayment alternative. (See the Point of Interest in Chapter 14.) The scenario and assumptions described in this case make the analysis about as straightforward as it can get. Issues such as reaching RRSP contribution limits or the involvement of more than one tax bracket are avoided. In Zach's situation, he is not likely to reach his contribution limit during the next 17 years (assuming that he is not a member of a pension plan).

The scenario has also been created to be realistic and to give an outcome that is close to the indifference point. This makes it more apparent to the student that there is no single answer that applies to all situations. The interest rate on the mortgage has been set equal to the rate of return earned by investments held in the RRSP. This key variable is thereby eliminated as a cause of any difference between the alternative uses of Zach and Karen's savings. Questions 2 and 3 lead students to think about how the advantage could swing to one alternative or the other depending on the particular value of any one of a few key variables.

Responses to the Questions:

Question 1
<u>Zach's Plan</u> (Contribute annual savings to an RRSP.)

The amount in the RRSP after 17 annual contributions of $8000 earn 7.5% compounded annually will be

$$\$8000 \left[\frac{1.075^{17} - 1}{0.075} \right] = \underline{\$258,064}$$

<u>Karen's Plan</u> (First repay the mortgage loan; then contribute to an RRSP.)

The interest rate per payment interval on the mortgage is

$$p = (1.075)^{0.08\bar{3}} - 1 = 0.006044919 = 0.6044919\%$$

When $A_n = \$100,000$ and $n = 240$, the monthly payment on the mortgage is $790.61.

The length of time needed to pay off the loan must be determined next. The balance just before the first $4800 prepayment one year from now (4 years or 48 payments after the original mortgage loan) will be $89,671.18. The balance owed after the $4800 lump prepayment will be $84,871.18. This amount becomes the beginning balance for the second year. We must work through the calculation year by year—first calculate the balance after 12 additional monthly payments and then deduct another $4800 lump payment at the year-end. The following table summarizes the results. We see that the ninth prepayment (12 years after the date of the original loan) is $1247.14 in excess of the amount needed to extinguish the mortgage loan. The corresponding "levered-up" amount that Zach can contribute to an RRSP at the end of the 9th year (from now) is $1247.14 x 1.6 = $2078.57.

End of year	Balance before prepayment	Prepayment	Balance after prepayment
1	$89,671.18	$4800	$84,871.18
2	81,427.33	4800	76,627.33
3	72,565.19	4800	67,765.19
4	63,038.39	4800	58,238.39
5	52,797.08	4800	47,997.08
6	41,787.67	4800	36,987.67
7	29,952.56	4800	25,152.56
8	17,229.81	4800	12,429.81
9	3552.86	4800	(1247.14)

At the end of each of the subsequent 8 years, the contribution can be

$$1.\overline{6} \, [\$4800 + 12(\$790.61)] = \$23,812$$

The amount in the RRSP after the last contribution will be

$$\$2078.57(1.075)^8 + \$23,812 \left[\frac{1.075^8 - 1}{0.075} \right] = \$252,456$$

Discussion

The difference in the outcomes is in favour of Zach's plan (of contributing all annual savings to an RRSP). However, the difference between the RRSP amounts under the two alternatives is scarcely more than 2%. This is so small that the decision can be based on less tangible considerations. For example, accelerated prepayment of a mortgage loan may have more motivational appeal than contributing to an RRSP. Also prepayment of the mortgage reduced the family's financial risk. If the family runs into a tough financial "patch", money can be borrowed more readily on the security of the increased equity in their home than on the security of their RRSP portfolio. Furthermore, if money is withdrawn from an RRSP in a financial emergency, the funds will be taxed.

A consideration that may be too subtle a point on taxation to be raised with students is that the total of the *nominal* dollar contributions to the RRSP is $136,000 under the "RRSP-only" choice versus $192,575 under the mortgage prepayment alternative. Consequently, Zach will have $56,575 more contribution room still available under his plan. This is worth 0.4($56,575) = $22,630 in future (nominal) tax savings.

Question 2
If the RRSP earns a higher rate of return than is paid on the mortgage, the RRSP in both scenarios will be worth more at the end of the 17 years. However, the increase will be *proportionately* larger for Zach's plan because of the exponential dependence of future value on the number of payments.

Question 3
A higher marginal tax rate will not change the time required to pay off the mortgage under the prepayment option. It will increase the RRSP contributions in *both* cases by the *same* factor, and increase the RRSP amount after 17 years in *both* cases by the *same* factor. The *percentage* difference between the two future values will be the same. It will not, therefore, change the ranking of the alternatives. (An individual with a higher tax rate is more likely to run up against the RRSP contribution limit during the "catch-up" years under the mortgage prepayment scenario.)

Table 3.2
Cross Currency Rates (April 12, 1996)

Currency	Per C$	Per US$	Per DM	Per ¥	Per £	Per Fr. fr.
Canadian dollar (C$)	•	1.35645	0.90198	0.01249	2.05407	0.26574
U.S. dollar (US$)	0.73722	•	0.66496	0.00921	1.51430	0.19591
German mark (DM)	1.10867	1.50385	•	0.01385	2.27728	0.29461
Japanese yen (¥)	80.06	108.60	72.21	•	164.45	21.27
British pound (£)	0.48684	0.66037	0.43912	0.00608	•	0.12937
French franc (Fr. fr.)	3.76313	5.10450	3.39429	0.04700	7.72974	•

Figure 4.1
The Distribution Chain

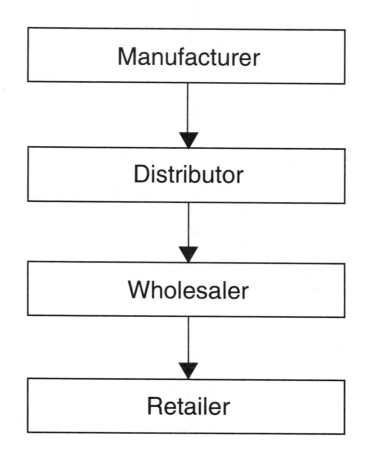

Figure 4.2
A Sample Sales Invoice

ATLANTIC ATHLETIC WHOLESALE LTD.
177 Main Avenue
Halifax, Nova Scotia B3M 1B4

Invoice No: 3498
Via: Beatty Trucking

Sold to:
McGarrigle Sports
725 Kings Road
Sydney, N.S. B1S 1C2

Date: July 17, 1997
Terms: 2/10, n30

Quantity	Product number	Description	Unit list price	Trade discount	Amount
5	W-32	Universal Gymnasium	$1150	30%	$4025.00
150	S-4	Soccer balls	$38.00	25%, 15%	3633.75
1000	H-8a	Hockey pucks	$2.10	35%, 10%, 7%	1142.51
				Invoice total:	$8,801.26
				GST:	616.09
				PST:	na
				Shipping charges:	346.00
				Total amount due:	$9,763.34

1.5% per month cn overdue accounts

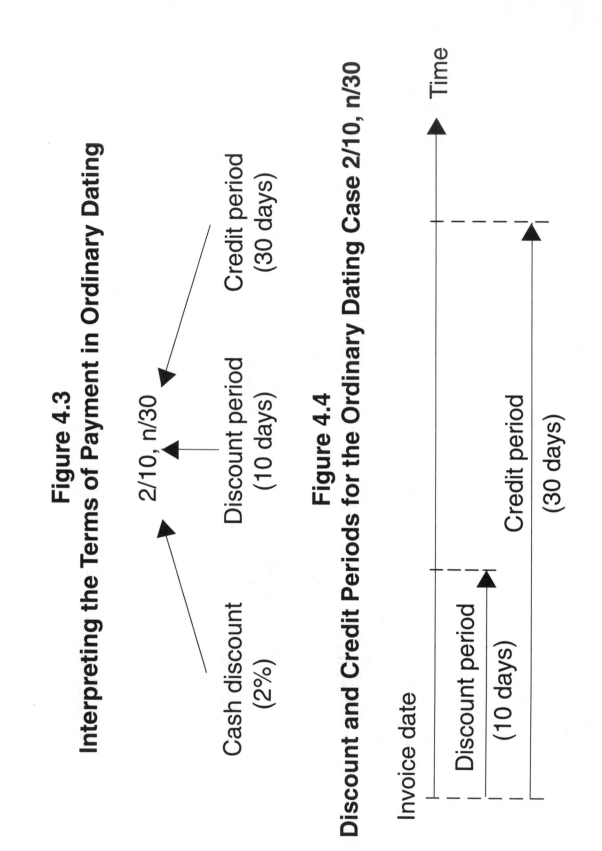

Figure 4.3
Interpreting the Terms of Payment in Ordinary Dating

2/10, n/30

Cash discount (2%)

Discount period (10 days)

Credit period (30 days)

Figure 4.4
Discount and Credit Periods for the Ordinary Dating Case 2/10, n/30

Invoice date

Discount period (10 days)

Credit period (30 days)

Time

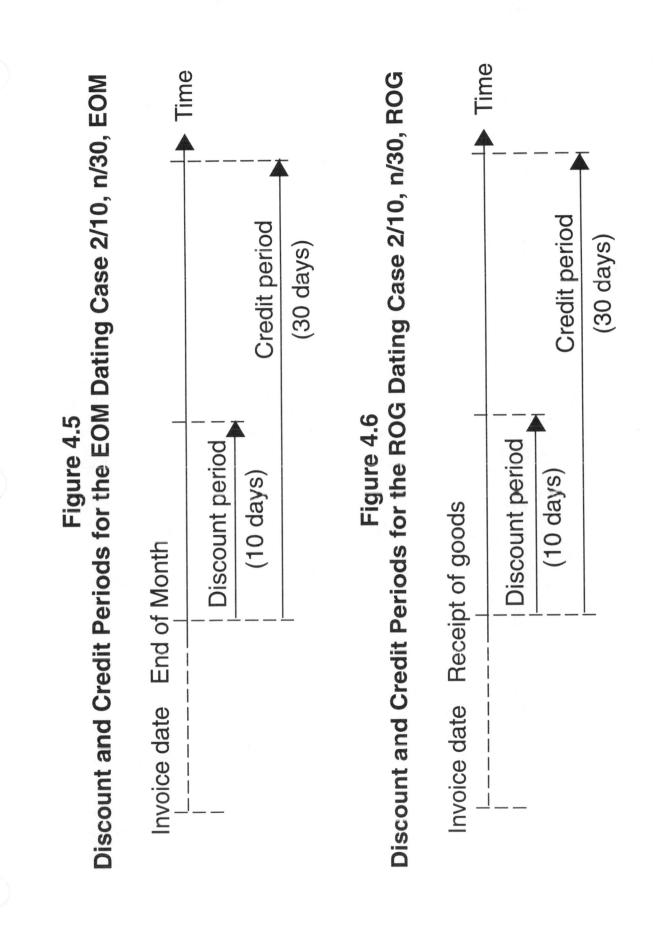

Figure 4.5

Discount and Credit Periods for the EOM Dating Case 2/10, n/30, EOM

Figure 4.6

Discount and Credit Periods for the ROG Dating Case 2/10, n/30, ROG

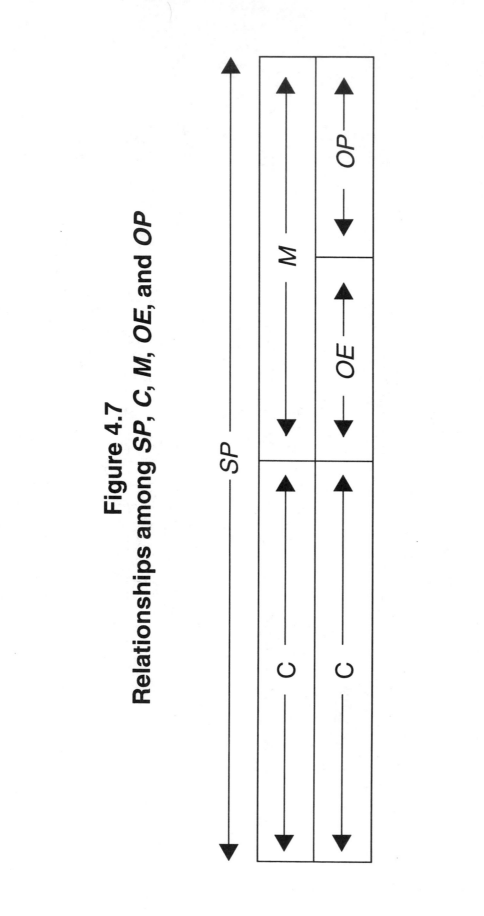

Figure 4.7
Relationships among *SP*, *C*, *M*, *OE*, and *OP*

Figure 4.8
Table Model for Solutions

	$	%
OE		
+ *OP*	+ ___	+ ___
M		
+ *C*	+ ___	+ ___
SP		100
– *D*	– ___	– ___
RSP		
– *C*	– ___	– ___
– *OE*	– ___	– ___
ROP		

Figure 5.1
Break-Even Chart

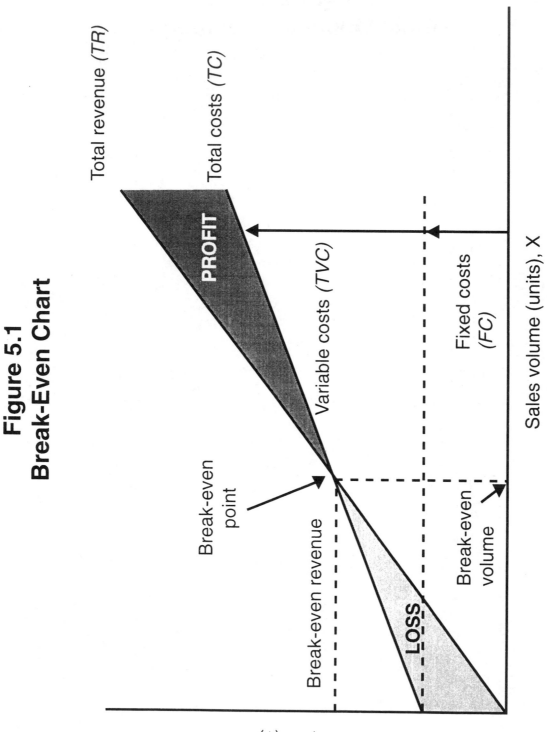

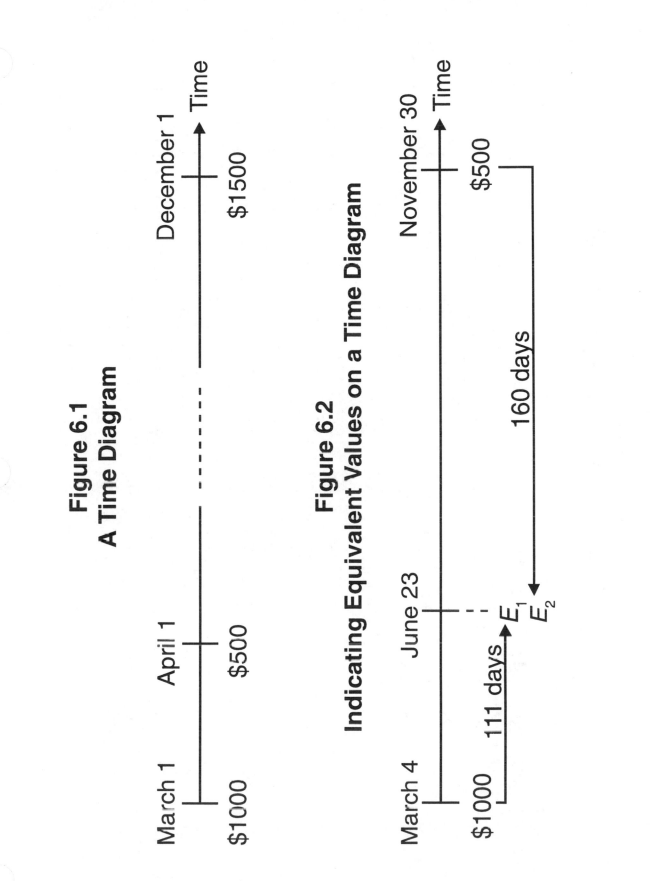

**Figure 6.1
A Time Diagram**

March 1   April 1   December 1 → Time

$1000 $500 $1500

**Figure 6.2
Indicating Equivalent Values on a Time Diagram**

March 4   June 23   November 30 → Time

$1000 $500

111 days   160 days

E_1
E_2

Table 6.2
The Serial Number of Each Day of the Year

Day of Month	Jan	Feb	Mar	Apr	May	Jun	Jul	Aug	Sep	Oct	Nov	Dec	Day of Month
1	1	32	60	91	121	152	182	213	244	274	305	335	1
2	2	33	61	92	122	153	183	214	245	275	306	336	2
3	3	34	62	93	123	154	184	215	246	276	307	337	3
4	4	35	63	94	124	155	185	216	247	277	308	338	4
5	5	36	64	95	125	156	186	217	248	278	309	339	5
6	6	37	65	96	126	157	187	218	249	279	310	340	6
7	7	38	66	97	127	158	188	219	250	280	311	341	7
8	8	39	67	98	128	159	189	220	251	281	312	342	8
9	9	40	68	99	129	160	190	221	252	282	313	343	9
10	10	41	69	100	130	161	191	222	253	283	314	344	10
11	11	42	70	101	131	162	192	223	254	284	315	345	11
12	12	43	71	102	132	163	193	224	255	285	316	346	12
13	13	44	72	103	133	164	194	225	256	286	317	347	13
14	14	45	73	104	134	165	195	226	257	287	318	348	14
15	15	46	74	105	135	166	196	227	258	288	319	349	15

(continued)

Table 6.2 (continued)
The Serial Number of Each Day of the Year

Day of Month	Jan	Feb	Mar	Apr	May	Jun	Jul	Aug	Sep	Oct	Nov	Dec	Day of Month
16	16	47	75	106	136	167	197	228	259	289	320	350	16
17	17	48	76	107	137	168	198	229	260	290	321	351	17
18	18	49	77	108	138	169	199	230	261	291	322	352	18
19	19	50	78	109	139	170	200	231	262	292	323	353	19
20	20	51	79	110	140	171	201	232	263	293	324	354	20
21	21	52	80	111	141	172	202	233	264	294	325	355	21
22	22	53	81	112	142	173	203	234	265	295	326	356	22
23	23	54	82	113	143	174	204	235	266	296	327	357	23
24	24	55	83	114	144	175	205	236	267	297	328	358	24
25	25	56	84	115	145	176	206	237	268	298	329	359	25
26	26	57	85	116	146	177	207	238	269	299	330	360	26
27	27	58	86	117	147	178	208	239	270	300	331	361	27
28	28	59	87	118	148	179	209	240	271	301	332	362	28
29	29	*	88	119	149	180	210	241	272	302	333	363	29
30	30		89	120	150	181	211	242	273	303	334	364	30
31	31		90		151		212	243		304		365	31

Note: For leap years February 29 becomes day number 60 and the serial number for each subsequent day in the table must be increased by 1.

Figure 6.3
Present and Future Values on a Time Diagram

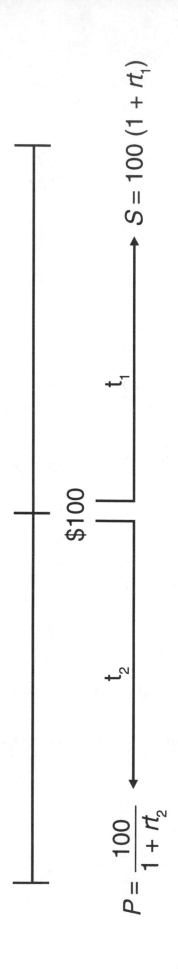

$100

$$S = 100\,(1 + rt_1)$$

t_1

t_2

$$P = \frac{100}{1 + rt_2}$$

Figure 6.4
Graph of Present and Future Values of $100

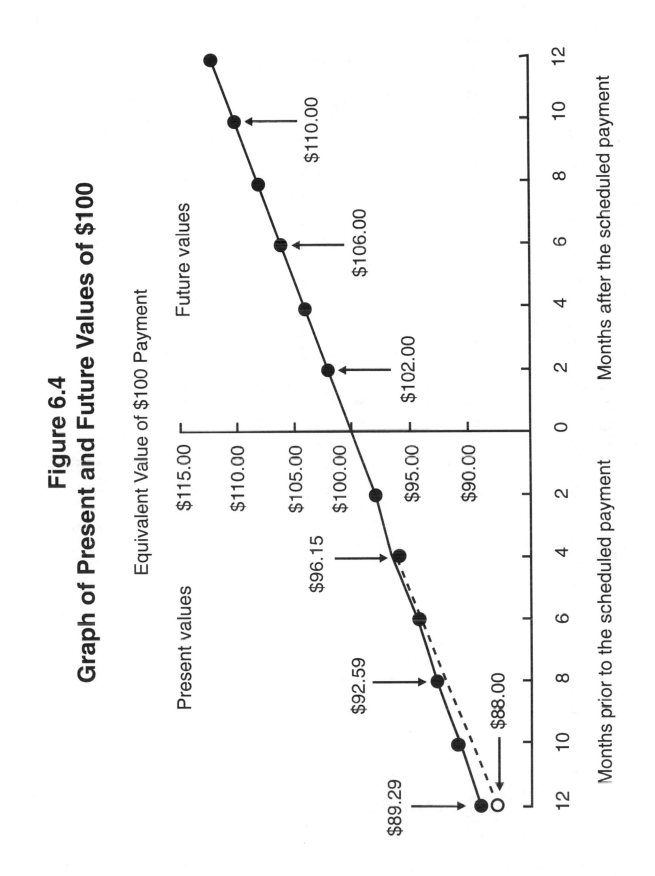

Figure 6.5
Time Diagram for the Equivalent Value of a Payment Stream

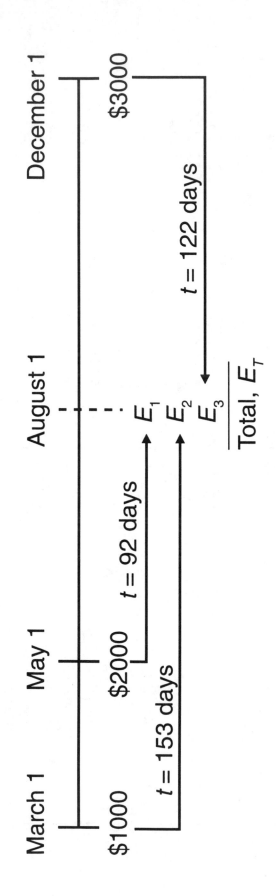

Figure 6.6
Partial Time Diagram for Equivalent Payment Streams

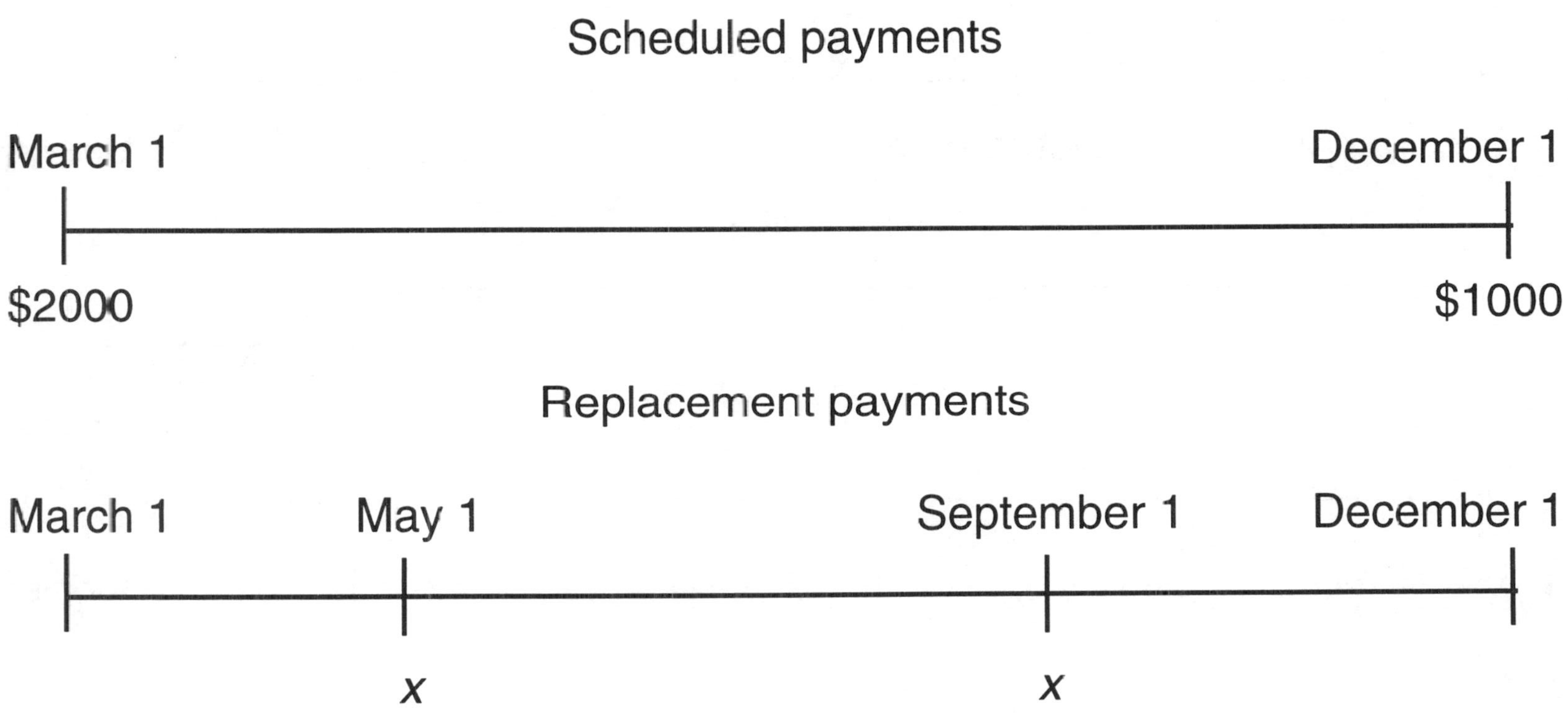

Scheduled payments

March 1 ——————————————————— December 1

$2000 $1000

Replacement payments

March 1 ——————— May 1 ——————— September 1 ——————— December 1

              x   x

Figure 6.7
Completed Time Diagram for Equivalent Payment Streams

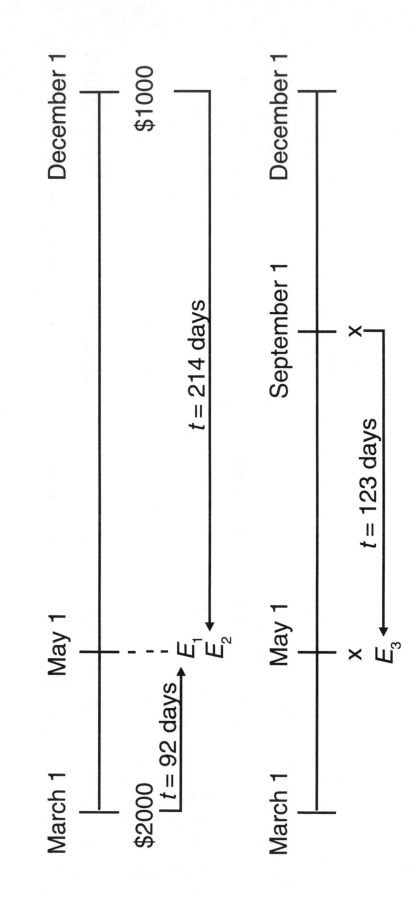

Figure 6.8
"Knuckle Months" Have 31 Days

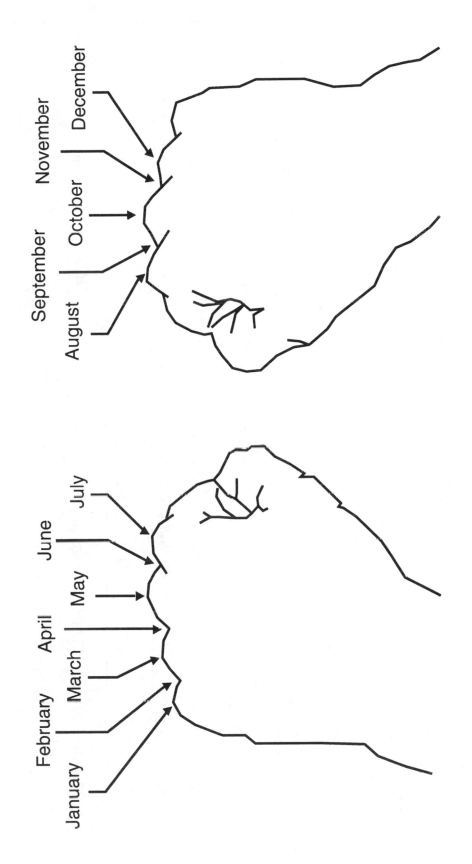

Figure 7.1
Term Promissory Note

PROMISSORY NOTE

(4)

_____Edmonton, Alberta_____ _____November 30, 1997_____

(3)

$7200.00

(5) _____Three months_____ after date _____I_____ promise to pay to the order of

(2) _____Western Builders Supply Ltd._____

the sum of _____seventy-two hundred and_____ - - - - - - - - - - - - - - - - _____00_/100 Dollars

at (8) _____Royal Bank, Terminal Plaza Branch_____

for value received, with interest at (7) _____12%_____ per annum.

Due: (6) _____March 3, 1998_____   Signed: (1) _____J. Anderson_____

Figure 7.2
Demand Promissory Note

(3)

$5000.00   _Hamilton, Ontario_   _April 30, 1997_

                                 (4)

ON DEMAND after date for value received, I promise to pay to the order of

(2)   _Acme Distributing Ltd._   at

(8)   _the Royal Bank of Canada, Limeridge Mall Branch_   the sum of

(3)   _five thousand_ - - - - - - - - - - - - - - - - - -00 /100 Dollars

(7) with interest thereon calculated and payable monthly at a rate equal to the Royal Bank of Canada's prime interest rate per annum in effect from time to time plus __2__ % per annum as well after as before maturity, default and judgement. At the date of this note, such prime interest rate is __8__ % per annum.

     Prime interest rate is the annual rate of interest announced from time to time by the Royal Bank of Canada as a reference rate then in effect for determining interest rates on Canadian dollar commercial loans in Canada.

Signed: (1)   _R.A. Matthews_

Figure 7.3
Calculating the Proceeds of a Promissory Note

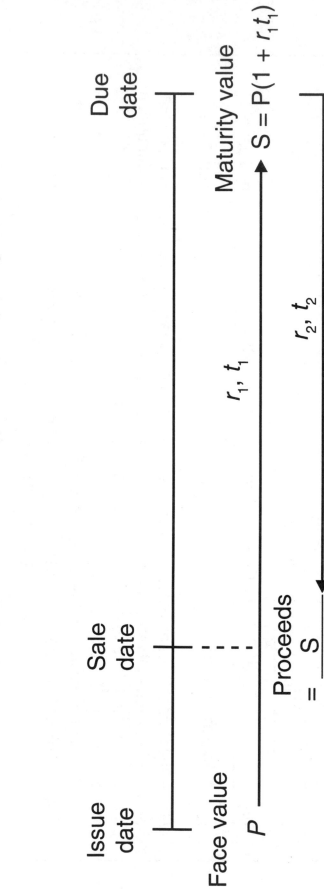

Figure 7.4
Revolving Loan Repayment Schedule

(1)	(2)	(3)	(4)	(5)	(6)	(7)	(8)
Date	Number of Days	Interest rate	Interest	Accrued interest	Interest charged to account	Principal repaid (advanced)	Balance

Figure 7.5
Blended-Payment Loan Repayment Schedule

(1)	(2)	(3)	(4)	(5)	(6)	(7)	(8)
Date	Number of days	Interest rate	Interest	Accrued interest	Payment made	Principal portion	Balance

Table 8.1
Compounding Frequencies and Periods

Compounding or conversion frequency	Number of compoundings or conversions per year	Compounding or conversion period
Annual	1	1 year
Semiannual	2	6 months
Quarterly	4	3 months
Monthly	12	1 month

Figure 8.1
Calculating the Maturity of a Loan or Investment

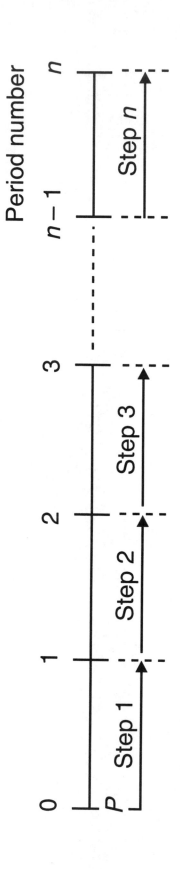

Figure 8.2
Comparison of Maturity Values at Compound and Simple Interest

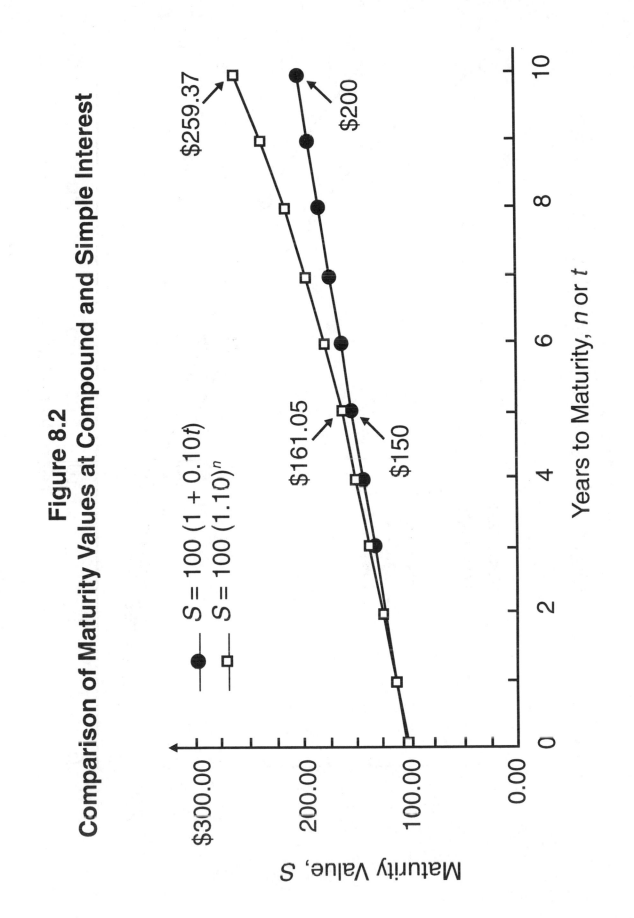

Figure 8.3
Maturity Values of $100 at Various Compound Rates of Interest

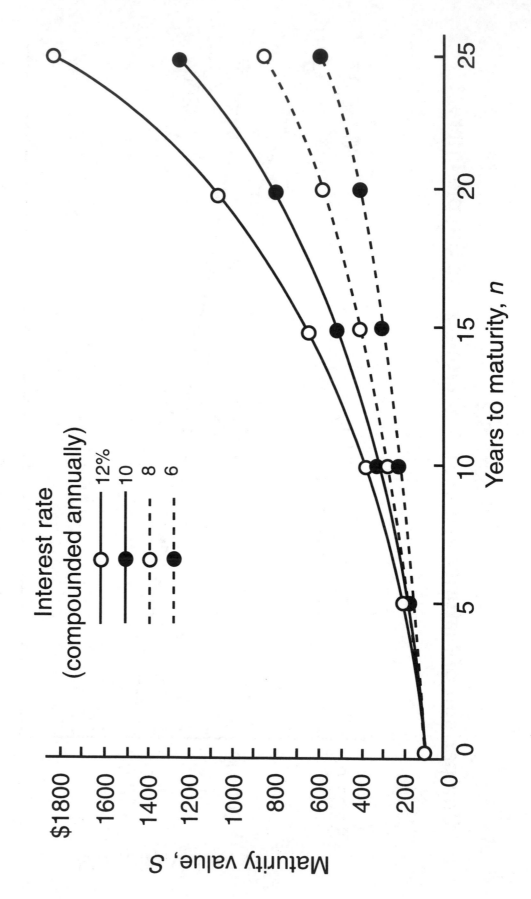

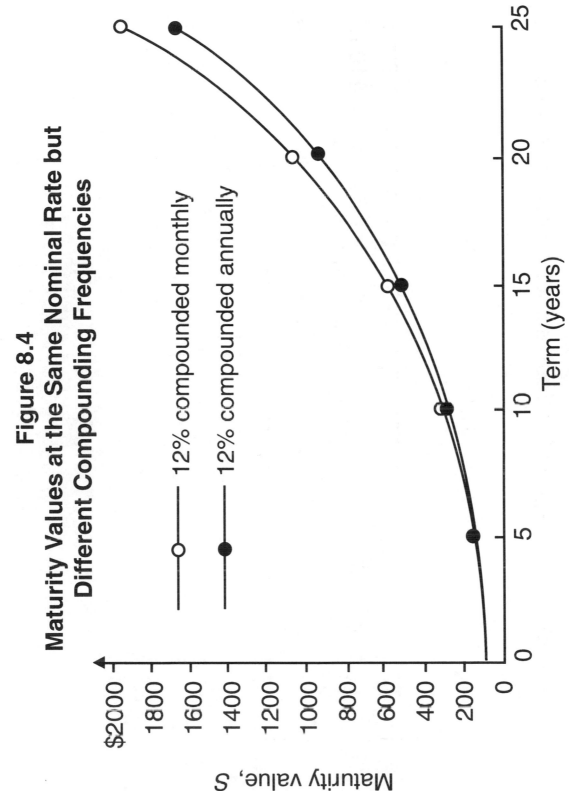

Figure 8.4
**Maturity Values at the Same Nominal Rate but
Different Compounding Frequencies**

12% compounded monthly

12% compounded annually

Term (years)

Maturity value, S

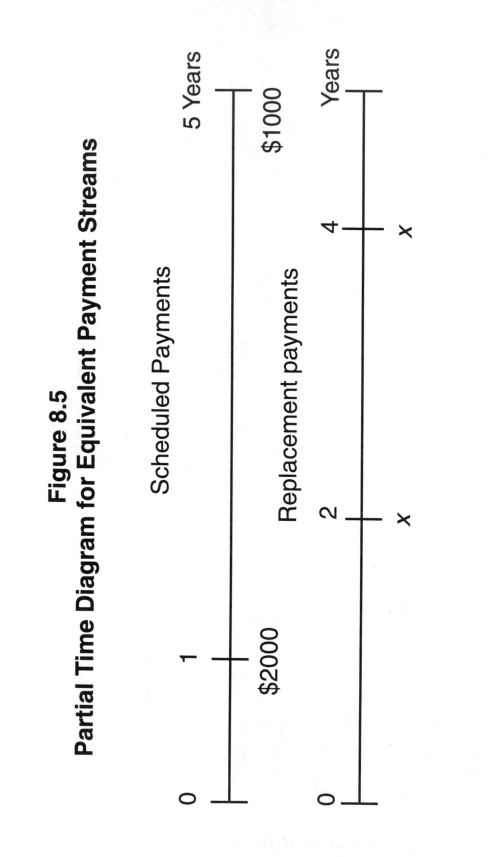

Figure 8.5
Partial Time Diagram for Equivalent Payment Streams

Figure 8.6
Completed Time Diagram for Equivalent Payment Streams

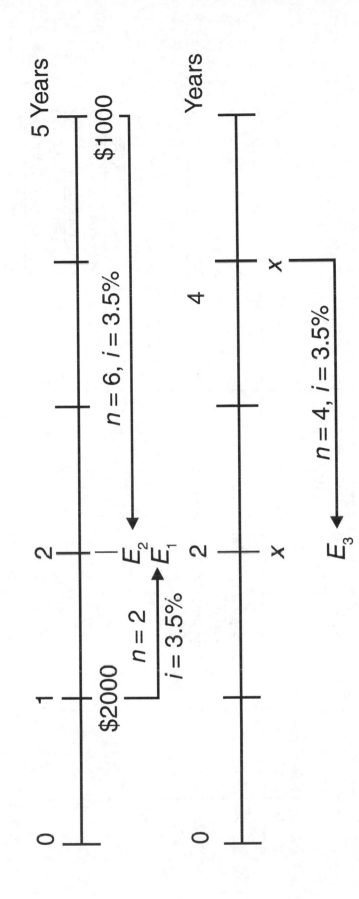

Figure 18.1
A Sample Bank Credit Card Monthly Statement

¢

Bank of Credit

	Last statement	This statement	Payment due by
Card number			
1234 2345 3456 4567	07 Mar 97	07 Apr 97	28 Apr 97

Trans. date M D	Posting date M D	Ref no.	Description	Amount
03/23	03/26	1	Shoppers Drug Mart Nanaimo BC	16.32
03/27	03/27	2	Payment Received-Thank you	109.07 CR

Previous balance	109.07
Purchases	16.32
Cash advances	
Interest	
Other	
Payments	109.07 CR
Credit adjustments	0.00 CR
New balance	$ 16.32
Amount past due	0.00
Minimum payment	0.00
Credit limit	7000.00
Credit available	7000.00
Paid $	0.00

Interest charges for current and past transactions:

	Current statement	Last month's statement	Previous statements	Total interest charge	Interest rate Annual %	Daily
Cash advances	0.00	0.00	0.00	0.00	16.75000	0.04589
Purchases and other	0.00	0.00	0.00	0.00	16.75000	0.04589

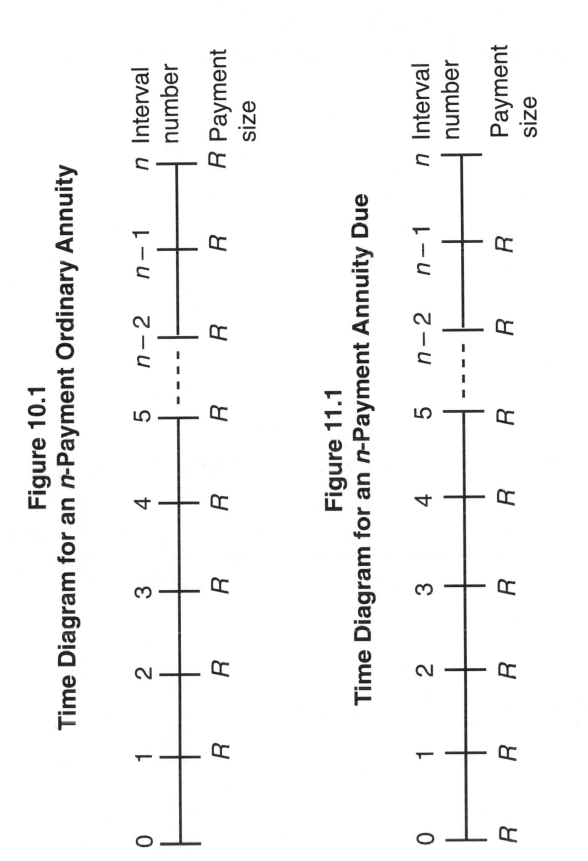

Figure 10.1
Time Diagram for an *n*-Payment Ordinary Annuity

Figure 11.1
Time Diagram for an *n*-Payment Annuity Due

Figure 10.2
The Future Value of a Four-Payment Annuity

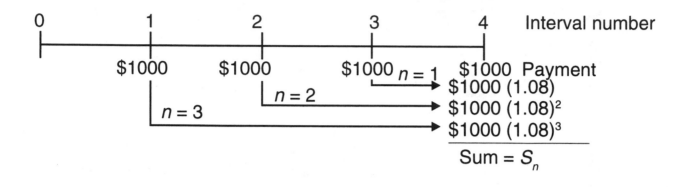

Figure 10.4
The Present Value of a Four-Payment Annuity

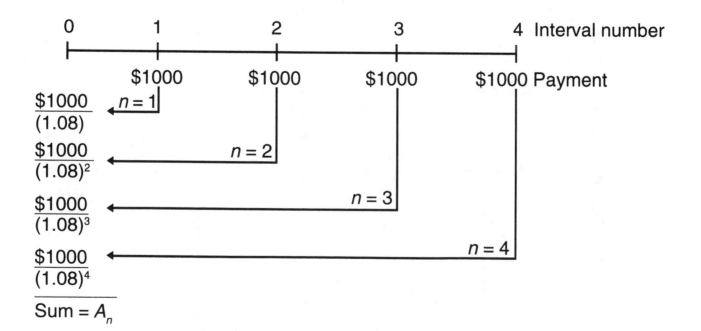

Figure 10.3

An n-Payment Ordinary General Annuity with Semiannual Payments and Interest Compounded Monthly

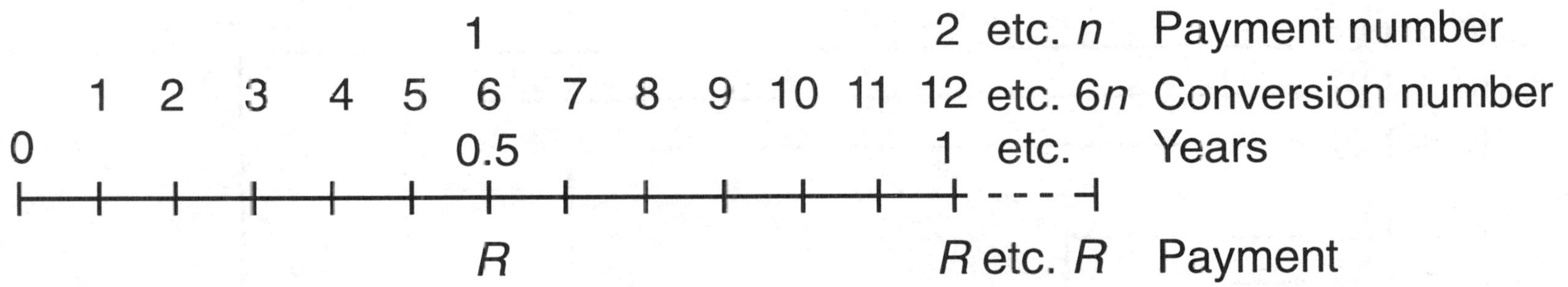

Figure 10.5
The Future Value of an Ordinary Annuity

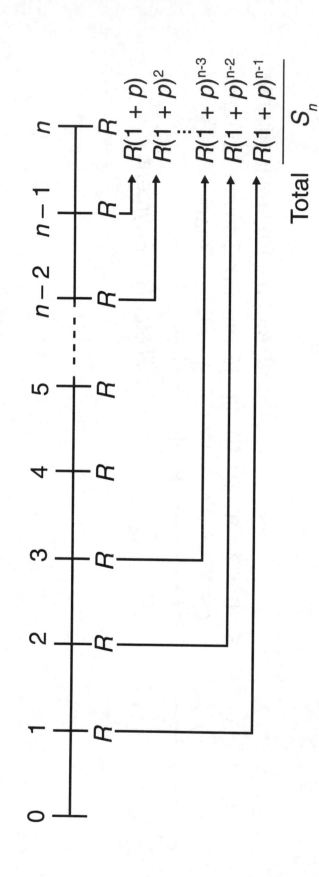

Table 11.1

Summary of the Formulas Applicable to Each Category of Annuity

	ORDINARY ANNUITIES (payment at the end of each payment interval)	ANNUITIES DUE (payment at the beginning of each payment interval)
SIMPLE ANNUITIES (Compounding interval = Payment interval)	$p = i$ Formulas $(10-1)$, $(10-4)$ for S_n, A_n	$p = i$ Formulas $(11-1)$, $(11-2)$ for S_n(due), A_n(due)
GENERAL ANNUITIES (Compounding interval ≠ Payment interval)	$p = (1+i)^c - 1$ Formulas $(10-1)$, $(10-4)$ for S_n, A_n	$p = (1+i)^c - 1$ Formulas $(11-1)$, $(11-2)$ for S_n(due), A_n(due)

Figure 11.2
The Relationship between $S_n(\text{due})$ and S_n

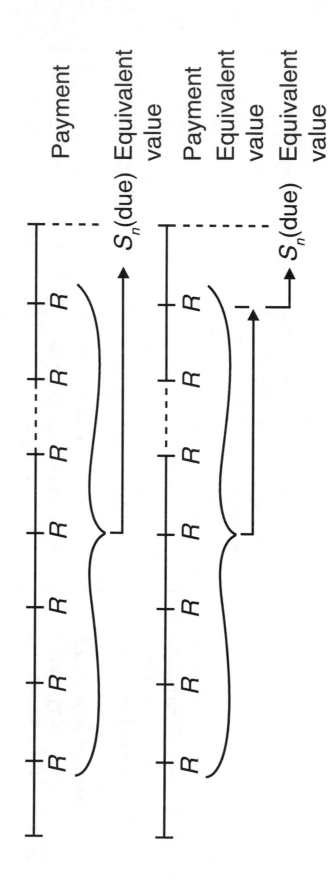

Figure 11.3
Annuity Classification Flowchart

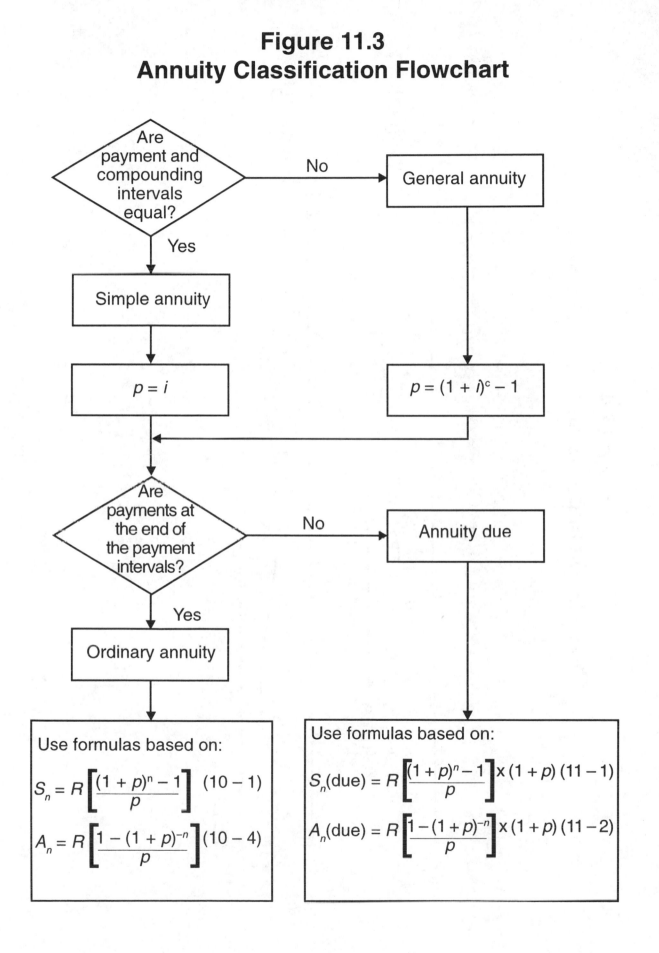

Figure 11.4
The Relationship between A_n(due) and A_n

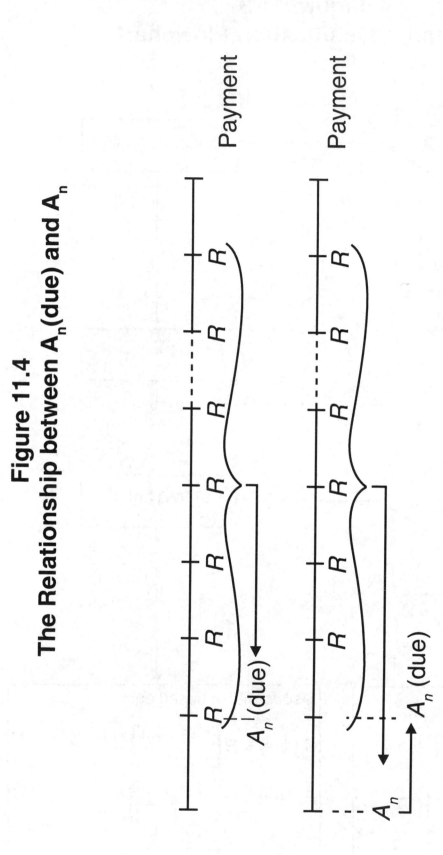

Table 12.1

Formulas for Calculating the Number of Payments in an Annuity

Known variables	Formula

Known variables

S_n, R, p

$$n = \dfrac{\ln\left(1 + \dfrac{pS_n}{R}\right)}{\ln(1 + p)} \qquad (10 - 1a)$$

A_n, R, p

$$n = -\dfrac{\ln\left(1 - \dfrac{pA_n}{R}\right)}{\ln(1 + p)} \qquad (10 - 4a)$$

$S_n(\text{due})$, R, p

$$n = \dfrac{\ln\left[1 + \dfrac{pS_n(\text{due})}{R(1 + p)}\right]}{\ln(1 + p)} \qquad (11 - 1a)$$

$A_n(\text{due})$, R, p

$$n = -\dfrac{\ln\left[1 - \dfrac{pA_n(\text{due})}{R(1 + p)}\right]}{\ln(1 + p)} \qquad (11 - 2a)$$

Figure 13.1
Time Diagram for the Payments of an Ordinary Perpetuity

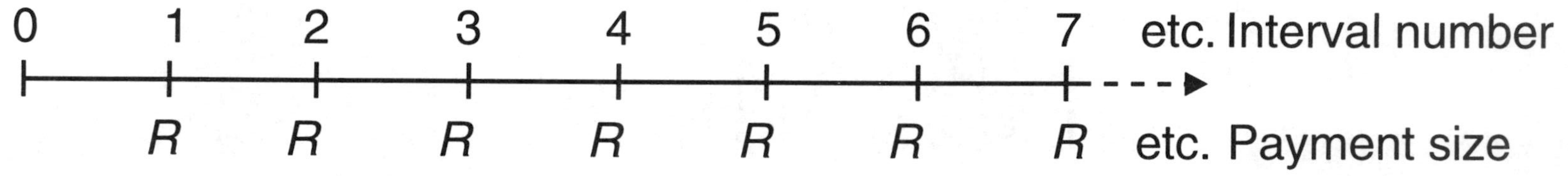

0	1	2	3	4	5	6	7	etc. Interval number
	R	R	R	R	R	R	R	etc. Payment size

Figure 13.2
Time Diagram for a Perpetuity Due

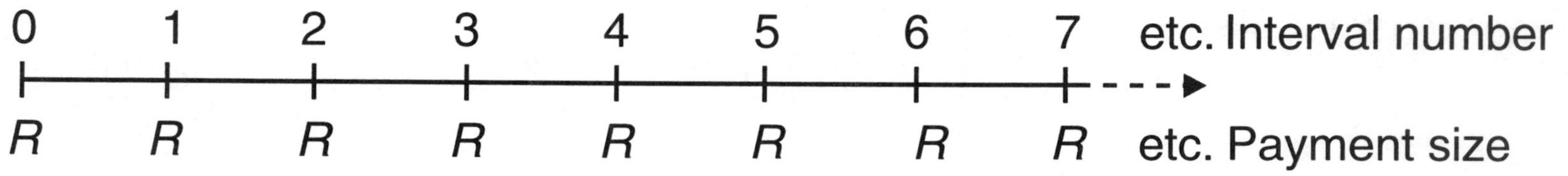

0	1	2	3	4	5	6	7	etc. Interval number
R	R	R	R	R	R	R	R	etc. Payment size

Figure 13.3
Time Diagram for a Deferred Annuity

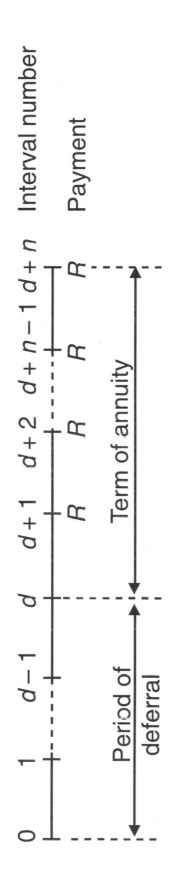

Figure 13.4
The Present Value of a Deferred Annuity

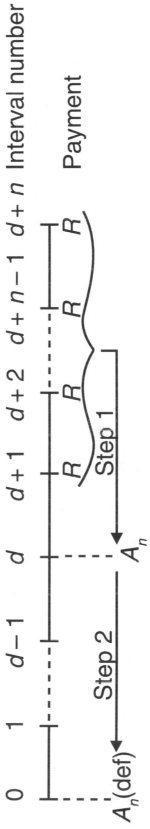

Figure 14.1
A Loan Is Equivalent to a Series of Payments and the Principal Balance at the End of the Payments

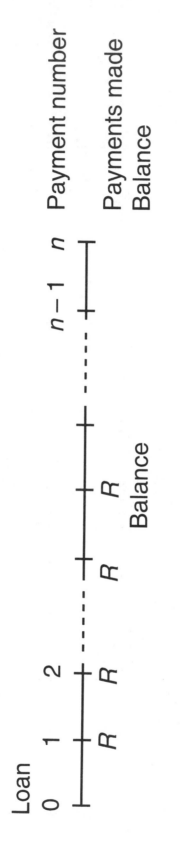

Loan

0   1   2   n − 1   n   Payment number

R   R   R   R   R   Payments made

Balance   Balance

Figure 14.2
Payments Taken to the Most Recent Payment Date as a Focal Date

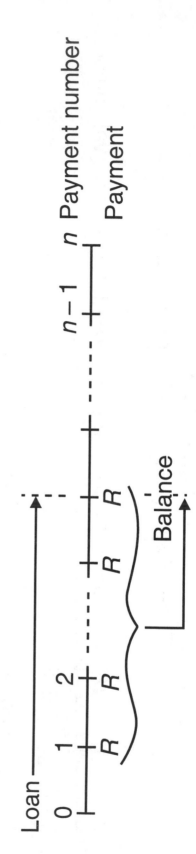

Loan

0   1   2   n − 1   n   Payment number

R   R   R   R   Payment

Balance

Table 14.1
Column Headings for an Amortization Schedule

Payment number	Payment	Interest portion	Principal portion	Principal balance
0	—	—	—	Loan
1	R			
etc.	etc.			

Figure 14.3
The Composition of Mortgage Payments during a 25-Year Amortization

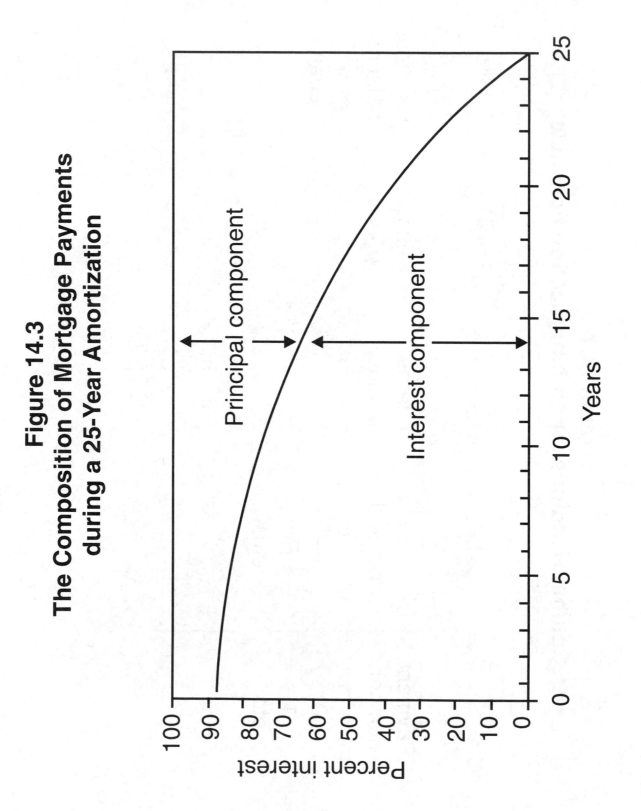

Figure 14.4

A Mortgage's Declining Balance during a 25-Year Amortization

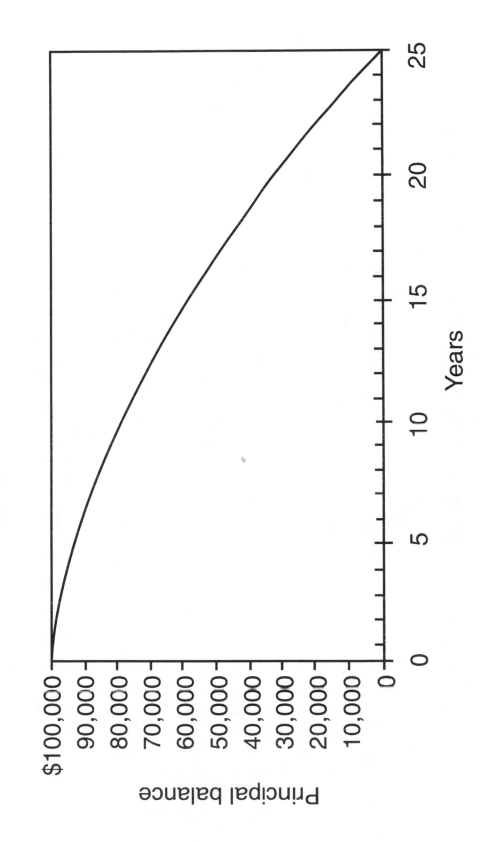

Figure 14.5
Mortgage Balance and Property Value versus Time

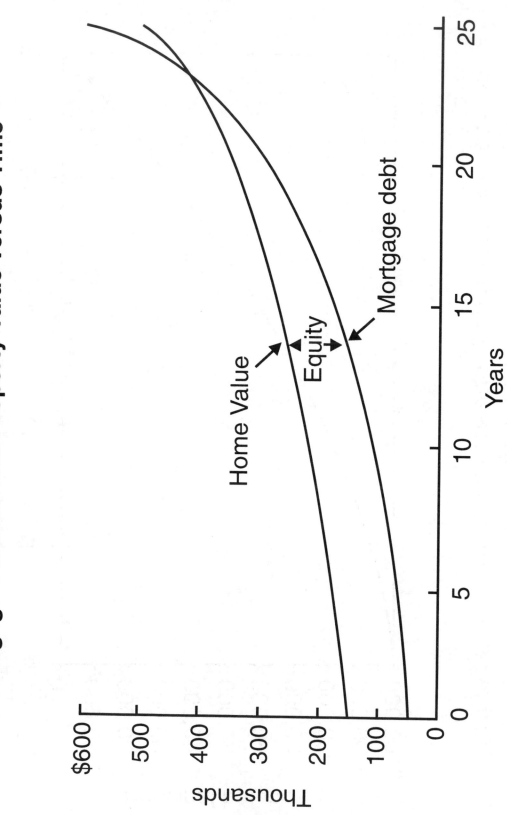